STREET ATLAS
Wiltshire
and Swindon

www.philips-maps.co.uk
First published in 2002 by
Philip's, a division of
Octopus Publishing Group Ltd
www.octopusbooks.co.uk
Carmelite House
50 Victoria Embankment
London EC4Y 0DZ
An Hachette UK Company
www.hachette.co.uk

Third edition with interim revision 2015
Third impression 2017
WILCA

ISBN 978-1-84907-365-3 (spiral)

© Philip's 2015

This product includes mapping data licensed from Ordnance Survey® with the permission of the Controller of Her Majesty's Stationery Office.
© Crown copyright 2015. All rights reserved. Licence number 100011710.

Contents

III	**Key to map symbols**
IV	**Key to map pages**
VI	**Route planning**
X	Major administrative and Postcode boundaries
1	**Street maps** at 3½ inches to 1 mile
163	**Street maps** at 1¾ inches to 1 mile
213	**Street maps** at 3½ inches to 1 mile
218	**Town maps** of Andover and Frome
219	**Index** of towns, villages, streets, hospitals, industrial estates, railway stations, schools, shopping centres, universities and places of interest

C000182164

Key to map symbols

Motorway with junction number (22)	
Primary route – dual/single carriageway	
A road – dual/single carriageway	
B road – dual/single carriageway	
Minor road – dual/single carriageway	
Other minor road – dual/single carriageway	
Road under construction	
Tunnel, covered road	
Rural track, private road or narrow road in urban area	
Gate or obstruction to traffic – may not apply at all times or to all vehicles	
Path, bridleway, byway open to all traffic, restricted byway	
Pedestrianised area	
BS22 Postcode boundaries	
County and unitary authority boundaries	
Railway with station	
Tunnel	
Railway under construction	
Metro station	
Private railway station	
Miniature railway	
Tramway, tramway under construction	
Tram stop, tram stop under construction	
Bus, coach station	

Abbreviations

Acad	Academy	Meml	Memorial
Allot Gdns	Allotments	Mon	Monument
Cemy	Cemetery	Mus	Museum
C Ctr	Civic centre	Obsy	Observatory
CH	Club house	Pal	Royal palace
Coll	College	PH	Public house
Crem	Crematorium	Recn Gd	Recreation ground
Ent	Enterprise		
Ex H	Exhibition hall	Resr	Reservoir
Ind Est	Industrial Estate	Ret Pk	Retail park
IRB Sta	Inshore rescue boat station	Sch	School
		Sh Ctr	Shopping centre
Inst	Institute	TH	Town hall / house
Ct	Law court	Trad Est	Trading estate
L Ctr	Leisure centre	Univ	University
LC	Level crossing	W Twr	Water tower
Liby	Library	Wks	Works
Mkt	Market	YH	Youth hostel

Ambulance station	
Coastguard station	
Fire station	
Police station	
Accident and Emergency entrance to hospital	
H Hospital	
Place of worship	
i Information centre – open all year	
Shopping centre	
P Parking	
P&R Park and Ride	
PO Post Office	
Camping site	
Caravan site	
Golf course	
Picnic site	
Church Non-Roman antiquity	
ROMAN FORT Roman antiquity	
Univ Important buildings, schools, colleges, universities and hospitals	
Built-up area	
Woods	
River Medway Water name	
River, weir	
Stream	
Canal, lock, tunnel	
Water	
Tidal water	

Adjoining page indicators

112 58 87

The small numbers around the edges of the maps identify the 1-kilometre National Grid lines

The dark grey border on the inside edge of some pages indicates that the mapping does not continue onto the adjacent page

The map scale on the pages numbered in green is 1¾ inches to 1 mile
2.76 cm to 1 km • 1 : 36 206

0	½ mile	1 mile	1½ miles	2 miles
0	500m	1 km	1½ km	2km

The map scale on the pages numbered in blue is 3½ inches to 1 mile
5.52 cm to 1 km • 1 : 18 103

0	¼ mile	½ mile	¾ mile	1 mile
0	250m	500m	750m	1km

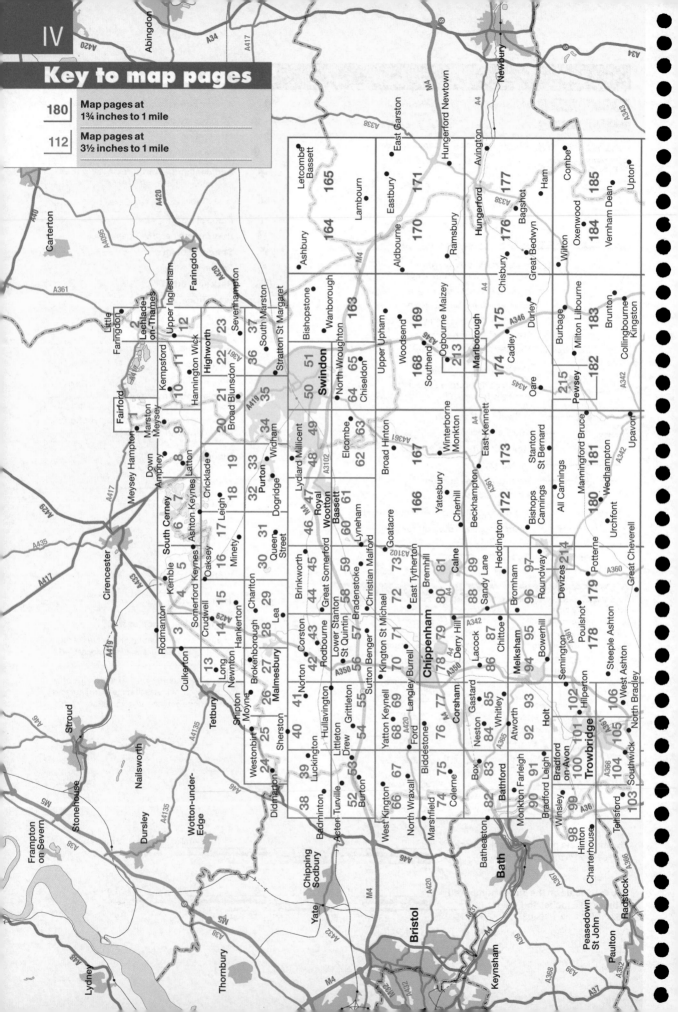

IV

Key to map pages

| 180 | Map pages at 1¾ inches to 1 mile |
| 112 | Map pages at 3½ inches to 1 mile |

Abingdon
Carterton
Newbury
East Garston
Hungerford Newtown
Avington
Letcombe Bassett
165
Combe
177
Upton
185
164 Ashbury
Lambourn 170 Eastbury
171
Hungerford
176 Ham
Vernham Dean
184 Oxenwood
Wilton
Little Faringdon
Faringdon
Lechlade-on-Thames
2 Upper Inglesham 12
Severnhampton
23
37 South Marston
Stratton St Margaret
Bishopstone 163 Wanborough
Chisbury 175
Durley
Burbage 182
Milton Lilbourne 183
Collingbourne Kingston
Brunton
Fairford
Kempsford
1 10 11 Hannington Wick
22 Highworth
36
Swindon 51
50 North Wroughton
Upper Upham 169 Woodsend
168 Southend
Ogbourne Maizey 213
Marlborough 174
Cadley
215
Pewsey
Oare
Meysey Hampton
Down Ampney
8 9 Latton
20 21 Broad Blunsdon
34 35
Elcombe
64 65 Chiseldon
62 63
Broad Hinton 167
Winterbourne Monkton
East Kennett 173
Stanton St Bernard
181 Wedhampton
Manningford Bruce 180
Upavon
South Cerney
6 7 Ashton Keynes
18 19 Leigh
32 33 Purton
Dogridge
Widham
48 49 Lydiard Millicent
47 Royal Wootton Bassett 61
60 Lyneham
166 Yatesbury
Cherhill
172 Beckhampton
Bishops Cannings
All Cannings
Urchfont
Great Cheverell
Kemble
Somerford Keynes
4 5 Oaksey
16 17 Minety
30 31 Queen Street
46 45 Brinkworth
Great Somerford 73 East Tytherton
Goatacre
81 Calne
89 Sandy Lane
96 97 Roundway
Devizes 214
179 Potterne
Crudwell
14 15 Charlton
28 29 Lea
Hankerton
42 43 Corston
Rodbourne 59
58 Bradenstoke
Christian Malford 72
80 Bremhill
88 Bromham
95 Poulshot
178 Steeple Ashton
West Ashton
106 North Bradley
Rodmanton
3 Crudwell
13 Long Newton
26 27 Brokenborough
41 Norton
Hullavington
54 55 Sutton Benger
Kington St Michael 71
78 79 Derry Hill
86 87 Chittoe
94 Melksham
Hilperton 102
Trowbridge 101
Culkerton
Shipton Moyne
40 Sherston
Littleton Drew 76 77 Ford
68 69 Yatton Keynell
Langley Burrell
Chippenham
85 Lacock
93 Whitley
Holt 92
Bradford Leigh 91
105 Southwick
Tetbury
25 Didmarton
39 Luckington
52 53 Burton
66 67 North Wraxall
75 Biddestone
84 Neston Gastard
Atworth
Bradford-on-Avon 100
104
Westonbirt
24
38 Badminton
Acton Turville
74 Marshfield
Colerne 82 Box
Bathford 90 Monkton Farleigh
99 Winsley 103
Stroud
Nailsworth
Wotton-under-Edge
Stonehouse
Dursley
Frampton on Severn
Lydney
Thornbury
Chipping Sodbury
Yate
Bristol
Bath
Batheaston
Keynsham
Hinton Charterhouse 98
Tellisford
Peasedown St John
Paulton
Radstock

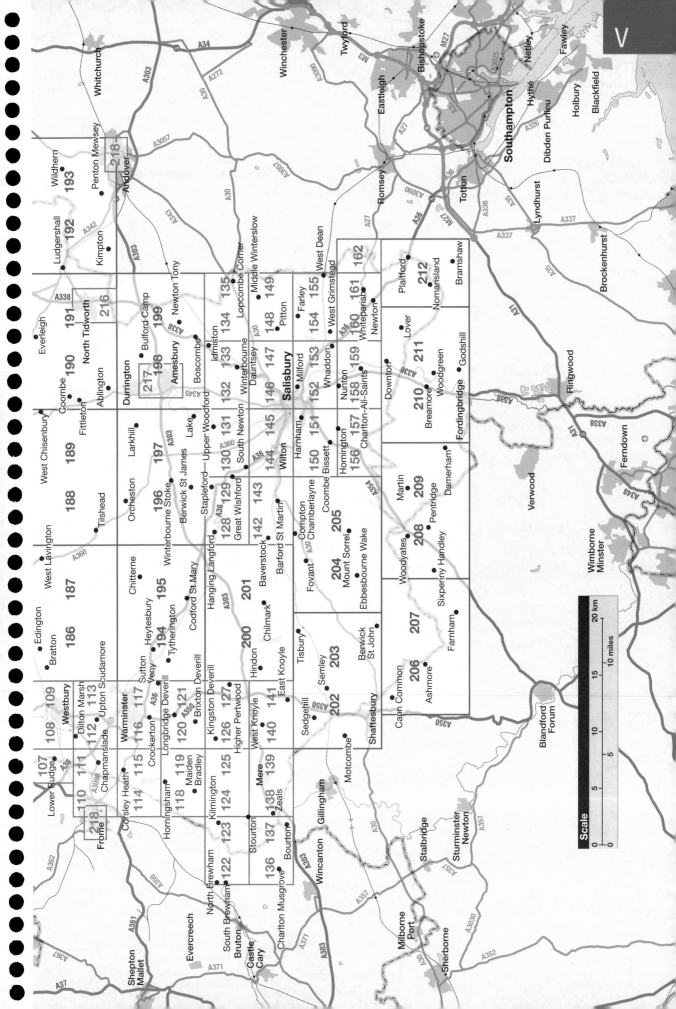

Scale

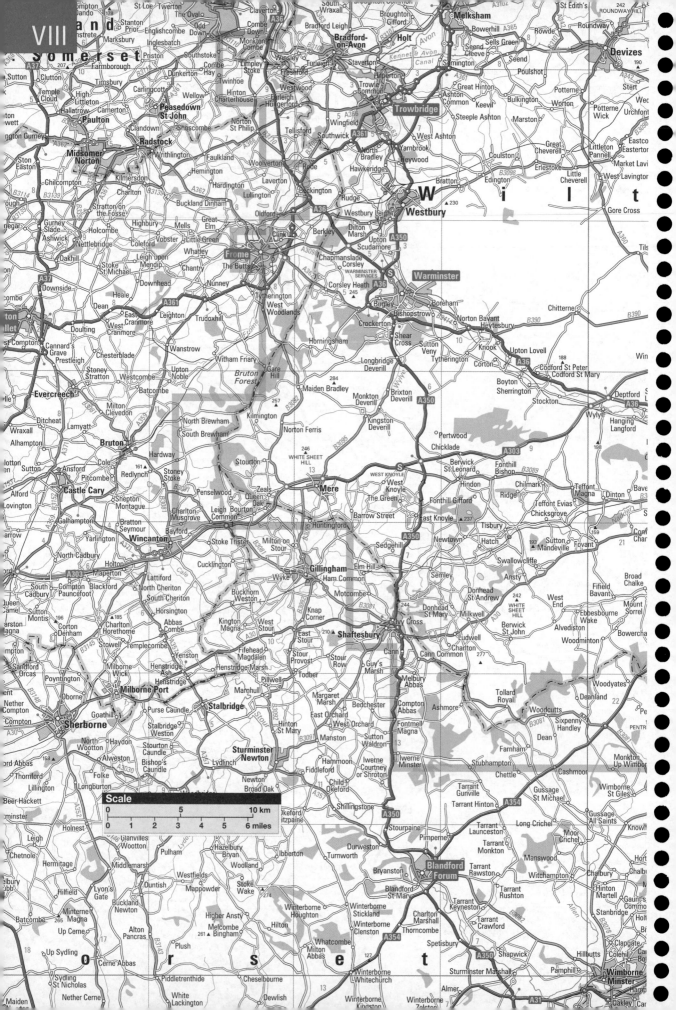

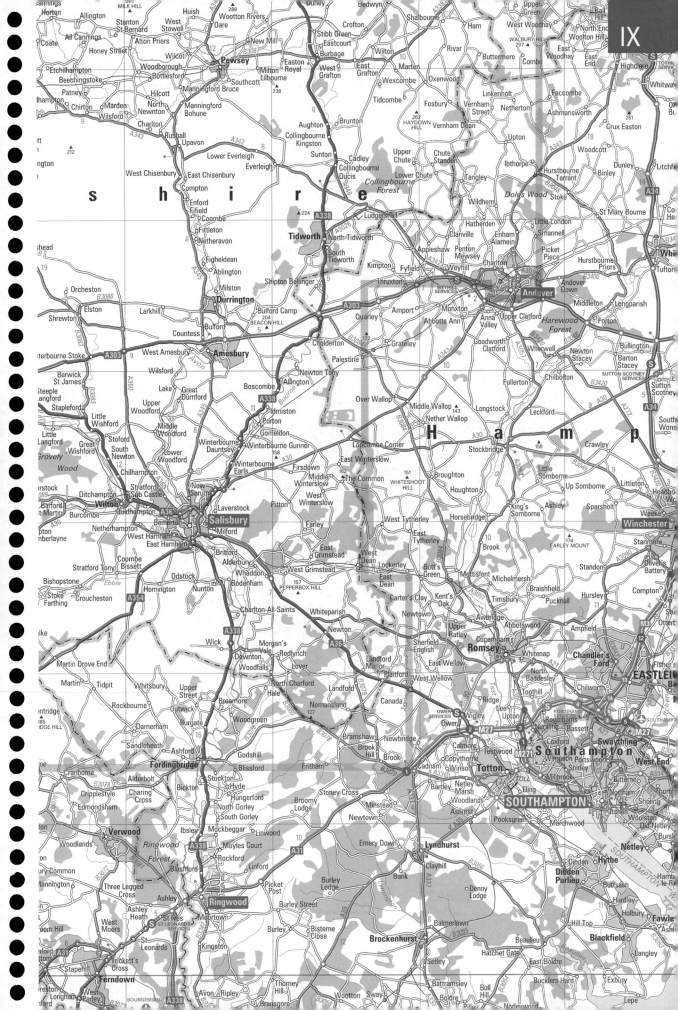

Major administrative and Postcode boundaries

County and unitary authority boundaries
District boundaries
Postcode boundaries
Area covered by this atlas

Gloucestershire

SO SP

Oxfordshire

South Gloucestershire

Swindon

West Berkshire

Bath & North East Somerset

Wiltshire

Somerset

Hampshire

Dorset

ST SU

Scale
0 5 10 15 20 25 km
0   5   10   15 miles

Kemble
South Cerney
Down Ampney
Lechlade-on-Thames
GL7
Kempsford
Culkerton
Ashton Keynes
SN6
Highworth
GL8
Crudwell
Crickdale
Broad Blunsdon
SN26
Shipton Moyne
Minety
SN16
SN25
Charlton
Haydon Wick
Stratton St Margaret
Didmarton
Purton
SN5
SN2
Letcombe
Malmesbury
Swindon
SN6
SN7
OX12
Sherston
Great Somerford
Coate
SN3
GL9
Royal Wootton Bassett
SN1
Bishopstone
Hullavington
Acton Turville
Lyneham
Broad Town
SN4
Chiseldon
Lambourn
Nettleton
Baydon
Eastbury
SN14
SN15
Broad Hinton
Aldbourne
Chippenham
Compton Bassett
Ogbourne St Andrew
Ramsbury
Colerne
Corsham.
SN11
Marlborough
RG17
Calne
Beckhampton
Froxfield
Hungerford
BA1
Box SN13
Lacock
SN8
Great Bedwyn
Inkpen
Bathford
Atworth
Bishops Cannings
Wootton Rivers
Shalbourne
SN12
Bromham
Alton Priors
BA15
Melksham
Devizes
Burbage
Oxenwood
Holt
Seend
Pewsey
Tidcombe
Vernham Dean
Bath & North East Somerset
BA2
Bradford-on-Avon
BA14
Potterne
Marden
SN9
Collingbourne Ducis
Ibthorpe
Hinton Charterhouse
Trowbridge
Keevil
SN10
Urchfont
Charlton
Upper Chute
BA13
Upavon
Everleigh
Ludgershall
Westbury
Edington
Market Lavington
Enford
SP9
Frome
Imber
Netheravon
North Tidworth
SP11
Enham Alamein
BA11
Tilshead
Durrington
Weyhill
SP10
Chapmanslade
Shipton Bellinger
Andover
BA12
Warminster
Chitterne
Shrewton
Larkhill
Cholderton
Somerset
Horningsham
Heytesbury
Amesbury
North Brewham
Maiden Bradley
Winterbourne Stoke
Upper Woodford
SP4
BA10
Kilmington
Stockton
Wylye
Stapleford
Porton
Lopcombe Corner
Mere
Great Wishford
The Common
BA9
Hindon
SP3
Wilton
SP1
Laverstock
Penselwood
Bourton
East Knoyle
Chilmark
SP2
Salisbury
Farley
SP8
Tisbury
Fovant
Harnham
SP5
Sedgehill
Coombe Bissett
Alderbury
SP7
Ludwell
Alvediston
Broad Chalke
Whiteparish
S051
Motcombe
Berwick St John
Wick
Downton
Shaftesbury
Redlynch
Ashmore
Sixpenny Handley
Martin
Whitsbury
Canada
Iwerne Minster
DT11
Farnham
BH21
SP6
Woodgreen
Nomansland
Dorset
Fordingbridge
S043
Brook

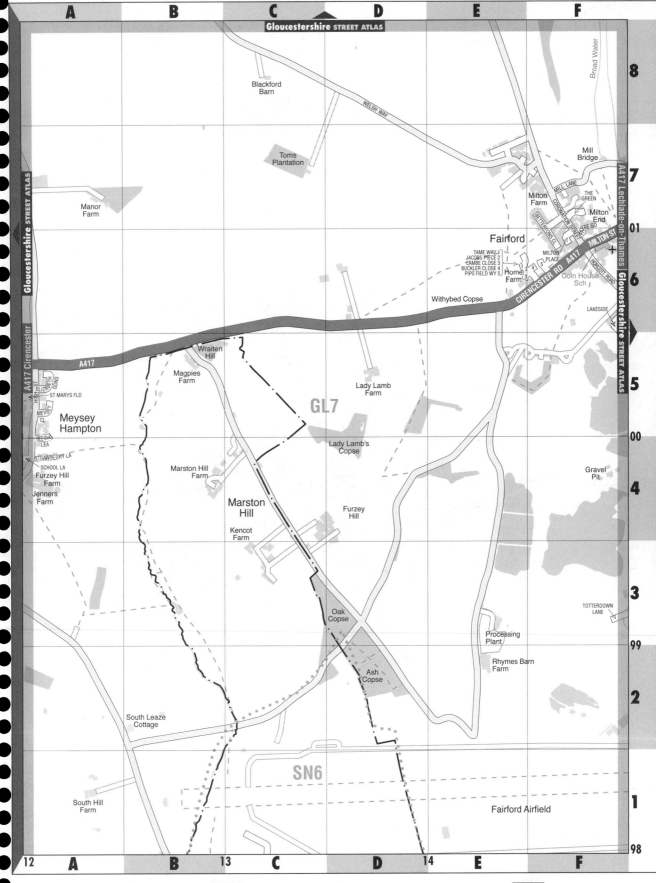

Gloucestershire STREET ATLAS

A B C D E F

8

Broad Water

Blackford Barn

WELSH WAY

Mill Bridge

Mill 7

Toms Plantation

Milton Farm

MILL LANE

THE GREEN

CORONATION STREET

Milton End

BETTERTONS CL

01

Manor Farm

Fairford

TAME WAY 1
JACOBS PIECE 2
LAMBE CLOSE 3
BUCKLER CLOSE 4
PIPS FIELD WY 5

MILTON PLACE

MILTON ST

CIRENCESTER RD

A417

Home Farm

Coln House Sch

6

Withybed Copse

LAKESIDE

A417 Cirencester

A417

Wraiten Hill

Magpies Farm

GL7

Lady Lamb Farm

5

ST ELIZ
HTH
GDNS

ST MARYS FLD

MEYS
CL

Meysey Hampton

00

BELOW
LEA

STRAWBERRY LA

Marston Hill Farm

Lady Lamb's Copse

Gravel Pit

SCHOOL LA

Furzey Hill Farm

Jenners Farm

Marston Hill

Furzey Hill

4

Kencot Farm

3

TOTTERDOWN LANE

Oak Copse

Processing Plant

99

Ash Copse

Rhymes Barn Farm

2

South Leaze Cottage

South Hill Farm

SN6

Fairford Airfield

1

98

12 A B 13 C D 14 E F

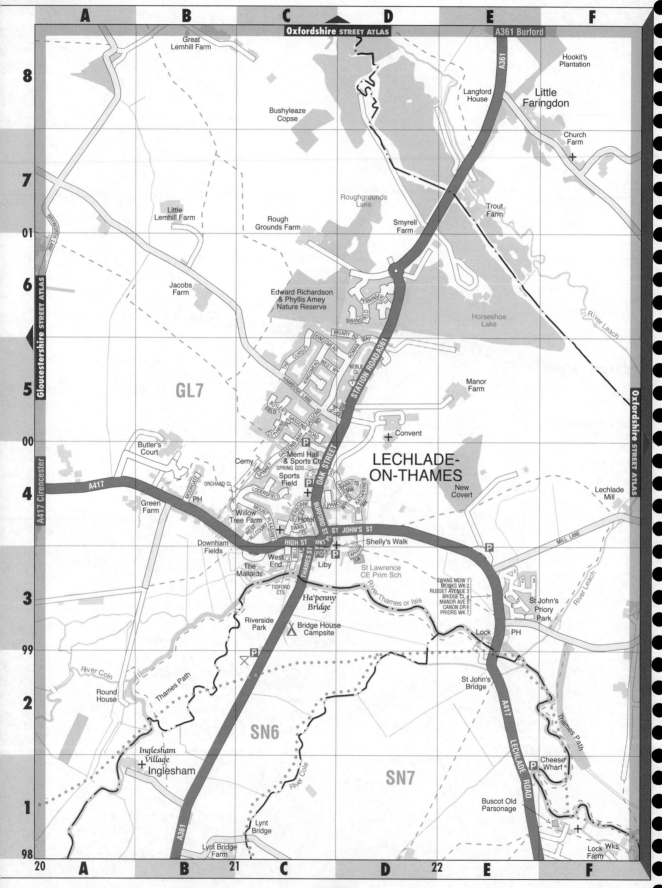

A361 Burford

Great
Lemhill Farm

Hookit's
Plantation

Little
Faringdon

Langford
House

Church
Farm

Bushyleaze
Copse

Roughgrounds
Lake

Little
Lemhill Farm

Rough
Grounds Farm

Smyrell
Farm

Trout
Farm

Jacobs
Farm

Edward Richardson
& Phyllis Amey
Nature Reserve

Horseshoe
Lake

River Leach

GL7

Manor
Farm

Butler's
Court

Convent

LECHLADE-
ON-THAMES

Lechlade
Mill

Cemy

Meml Hall
& Sports Ctr

Sports
Field

New
Covert

Green
Farm

Willow
Tree Farm

Hotel

St John's St

Shelly's Walk

MILL LANE

River Leach

Downham
Fields

High St

Liby

St Lawrence
CE Prim Sch

SWANS MDW 1
MONKS WK 2
RUSSET AVENUE 3
BRIDGE CL 4
MANOR AVE 5
CANON DR 6
PRIORS WK 7

St John's
Priory
Park

West
End

The
Mallards

Ha'penny
Bridge

River Thames or Isis

Lock

PH

Riverside
Park

Bridge House
Campsite

St John's
Bridge

River Coln

Round
House

Thames Path

SN6

St John's
Bridge

Thames Path

SN7

Cheese
Wharf

Inglesham
Village
Inglesham

River Cole

Buscot Old
Parsonage

Lynt
Bridge

Lynt Bridge
Farm

Lock Wks
Farm

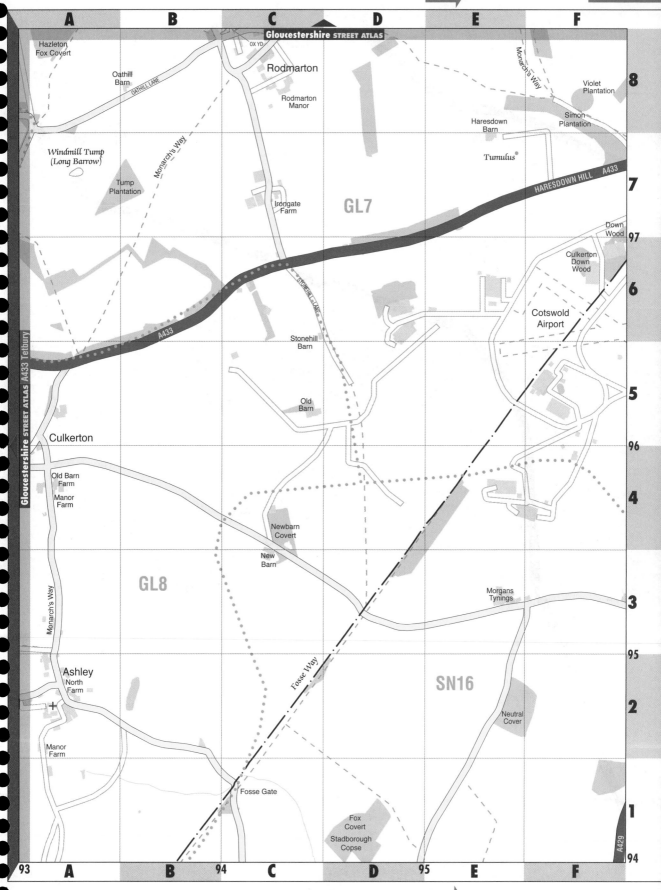

Gloucestershire STREET ATLAS

OX YD

Rodmarton

A B C D E F

Hazleton
Fox Covert

Oathill
Barn

OATHILL LANE

Rodmarton
Manor

Monarch's Way

Violet
Plantation

8

Monarch's Way

Windmill Tump
(Long Barrow)

Haresdown
Barn

Simon
Plantation

Tump
Plantation

Tumulus

HARESDOWN HILL A433

Irongate
Farm

GL7

Down
Wood

7

Gloucestershire STREET ATLAS A433 Tetbury

STONEHILL LANE

A433

Culkerton
Down
Wood

97

Cotswold
Airport

6

Stonehill
Barn

5

Old
Barn

Culkerton

96

Old Barn
Farm

Manor
Farm

4

Newbarn
Covert

New
Barn

GL8

Morgans
Tynings

3

Monarch's Way

Fosse Way

95

Ashley

North
Farm

SN16

2

Neutral
Cover

Manor
Farm

Fosse Gate

1

Fox
Covert

Stadborough
Copse

A429

94

93 A B 94 C D 95 E F 94

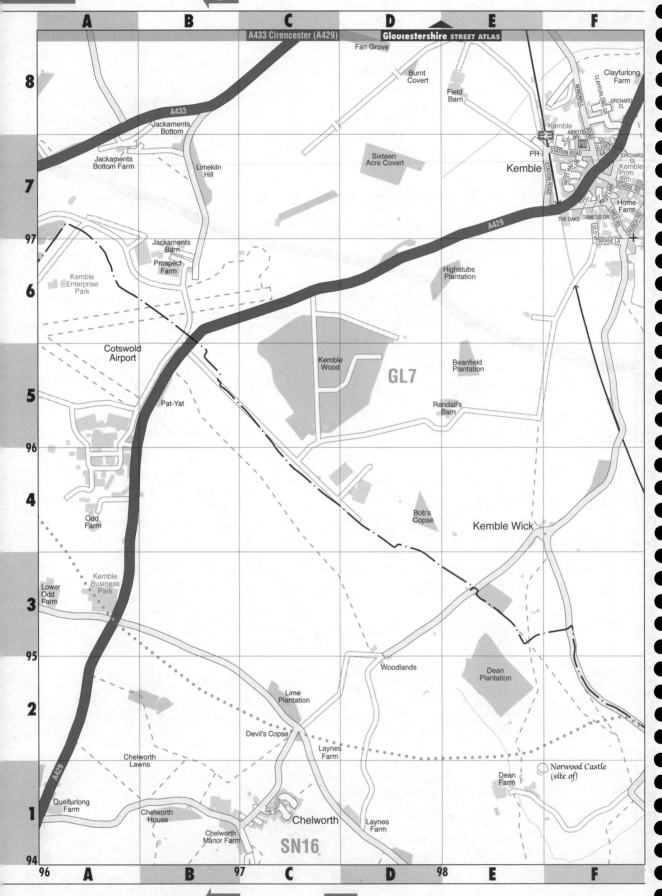

A433 Cirencester (A429)

Fan Grove

Burnt Covert

Field Barn

Clayfurlong Farm

WINDMILL

CLAYFURLONG GR

ORCHARD CL

A433

Jackaments Bottom

Kemble

ABBOTS WY

PO

STATION ROAD

GLEBE LA

ORCHARD CL

Kemble Prim Sch

Limekiln Hill

Jackaments Bottom Farm

Sixteen Acre Covert

PH

Kemble

WEST HILL OR

SCHOOL RD

WEST LANE

LIMES RD

CHURCH RD

Home Farm

Jackaments Barn

A429

THE OAKS

TAMESIS DR

Kemble Enterprise Park

Prospect Farm

Highstubs Plantation

OLD GARAGE LA

Kemble Wood

Beanfield Plantation

Cotswold Airport

GL7

Pat-Yat

Rendall's Barn

Odd Farm

Bob's Copse

Kemble Wick

Lower Odd Farm

Kemble Business Park

Woodlands

Dean Plantation

Lime Plantation

Devil's Copse

Laynes Farm

Chelworth Lawns

A429

Norwood Castle (site of)

Dean Farm

Quelfurlong Farm

Chelworth House

THE GROVE

Chelworth

Laynes Farm

Chelworth Manor Farm

SN16

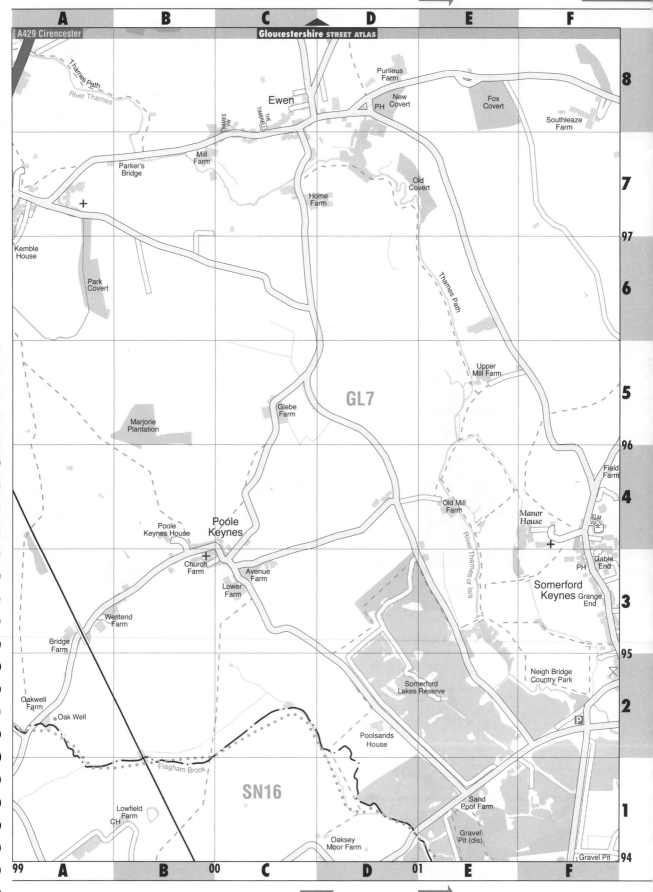

A429 Cirencester

Gloucestershire STREET ATLAS

Thames Path

River Thames

Ewen

Purlieus Farm

New Covert

PH

Fox Covert

Southleaze Farm

THAMES WY

THE TIMBRELLS

Parker's Bridge

Mill Farm

Home Farm

Old Covert

Kemble House

Thames Path

Park Covert

GL7

Upper Mill Farm

Glebe Farm

Marjorie Plantation

River Thames or Isis

Old Mill Farm

Field Farm

Poole Keynes House

Poole Keynes

Manor House

ELM VIEW

Church Farm

Avenue Farm

PH

Gable End

Lower Farm

Somerford Keynes

Grange End

Westend Farm

Bridge Farm

Neigh Bridge Country Park

Oakwell Farm

Oak Well

Somerford Lakes Reserve

P

Flagham Brook

Poolsands House

SN16

Sand Pool Farm

Lowfield Farm

CH

Gravel Pit (dis)

Oaksey Moor Farm

Gravel Pit

Hillview Farm

Camperdown *Castle*

Berry Farm

Dryleaze Covert

Ash Copse

Gravel Pit

Sewage Works

Cross Roads Farm

PH

RIVER WAY

MEADOW WAY

THE SECRET GDNS

LANGET

HIGH STREET

Upper Up

Langet End

Downs Farm

Shorncote

Manor Farm

Glebe Farm

Old Manor Farm

GL7

Ann Edwards CE Prim Sch

WINCHCOMBE GDNS

BEVERSTONE CL

Refuse/Slag Heap

Evergreen Ind Pk

Sewage Works

Keynes Country Park

Ashton Down

SPRATSGATE LANE

Millennium Visitor Centre

Cotswold Community

Cotswold Water Park

Works

Yacht Club

Bag End

Macks Farm

SPINE ROAD WEST

SPINE ROAD WEST

WHITEFRIARS LANE

North End Farm

North End

Clayhill Copse

SN6

Mill End

Furze Brake

Manor Farm

B4696

COX'S HILL

Old Manor Farm

Ring and Bailey

Bell Copse

Thames Path

Lower Mill Farm

Church Farm

Moat

Ashton Keynes

PH

CHURCH LA

CHURCH WK

HIGH ROAD

BACK STREET

RICHMOND

PO

PARK PL

FORE STREET

EASTFIELD

Manor House

Gravel Pit

Freeth's Wood

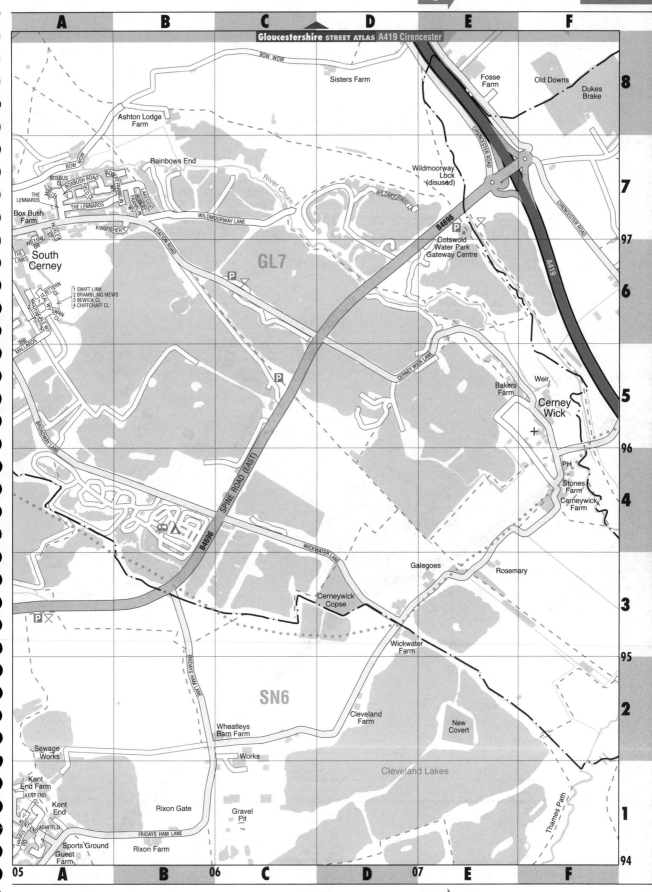

8

Gloucestershire STREET ATLAS A419 Cirencester

A B C D E F

8

BOW WOW

Sisters Farm

Fosse Farm

Old Downs

Dukes Brake

Ashton Lodge Farm

Rainbows End

River Churn

Wildmoorway Lock (disused)

7

BOW WOW

BOXBUSH CL

THE LENNARDS

BOXBUSH ROAD

FIELD CL

ROBERT FRANKLIN

LAKESIDE

KINGFISHER WY

FRANKLIN

WILDMOORWAY LA

97

Box Bush Farm

THE LENNARDS

KINGFISHER

WILDMOORWAY LANE

STATION ROAD

B4696

Cotswold Water Park Gateway Centre

CIRENCESTER ROAD

A419

THE LIMES

South Cerney

GL7

P

6

WILLOW GR

BITTERN CL

SWAN CL

NUTHATCH

1 SWIFT LINK
2 BRAMBLING MEWS
3 BEWICK CL
4 CHIFFCHAFF CL

P

CERNEY WICK LANE

Bakers Farm

Weir

Cerney Wick

5

THE MALLARDS

P

+

96

BROADWAY LANE

PH

Stones Farm

Cerneywick Farm

4

B4696

SPINE ROAD (EAST)

WICKWATER LANE

Galegoes

Rosemary

Cerneywick Copse

Wickwater Farm

3

95

FRIDAYS HAM LANE

SN6

Cleveland Farm

New Covert

2

Wheatleys Barn Farm

Sewage Works

Works

Cleveland Lakes

Kent End Farm

KENT END

Thames Path

1

KENT END CL

Kent End

ASHFIELD

HARRIS RD

Rixon Gate

Gravel Pit

94

Sports Ground

Guest Farm

FRIDAYS HAM LANE

Rixon Farm

05 A B 06 C D 07 E F

18

8

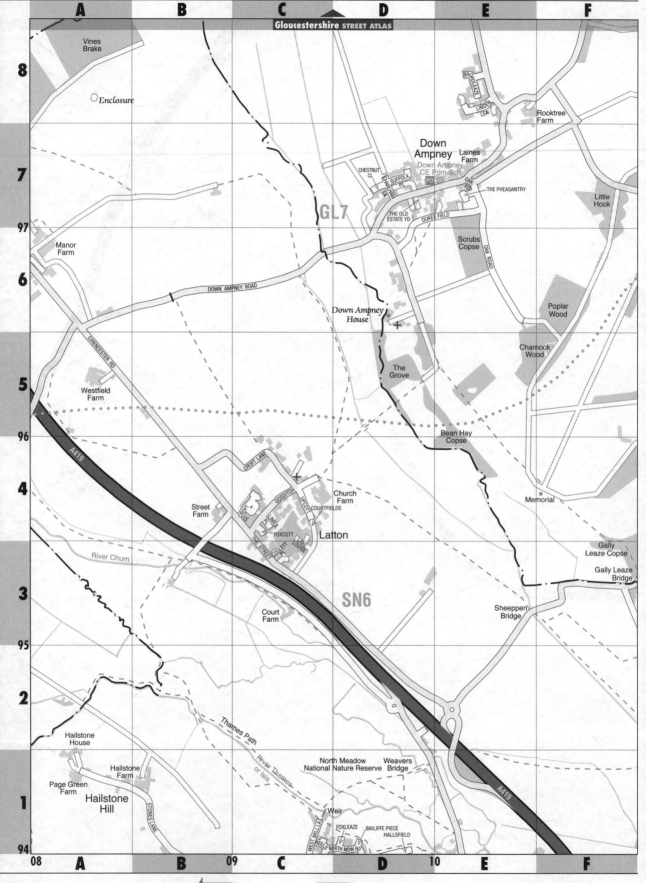

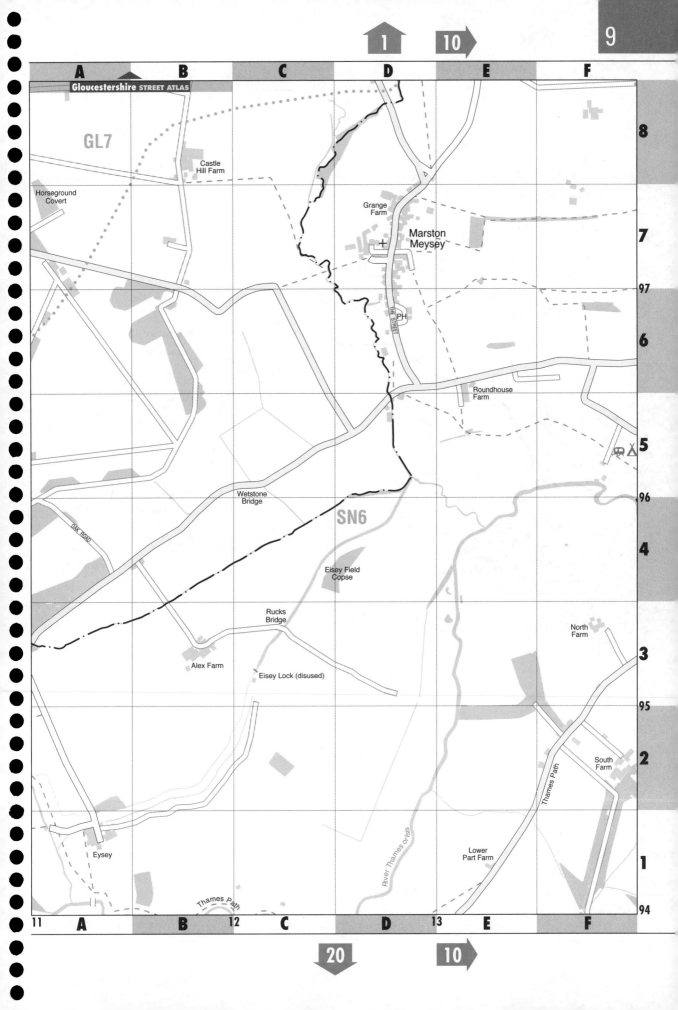

Gloucestershire STREET ATLAS

GL7

Horseground
Covert

Castle
Hill Farm

Grange
Farm

Marston
Meysey

THE STREET

PH

Roundhouse
Farm

Wetstone
Bridge

SN6

OAK ROAD

Eisey Field
Copse

Rucks
Bridge

North
Farm

Alex Farm

Eisey Lock (disused)

River Thames or Isis

Thames Path

South
Farm

Eysey

Lower
Part Farm

Thames Path

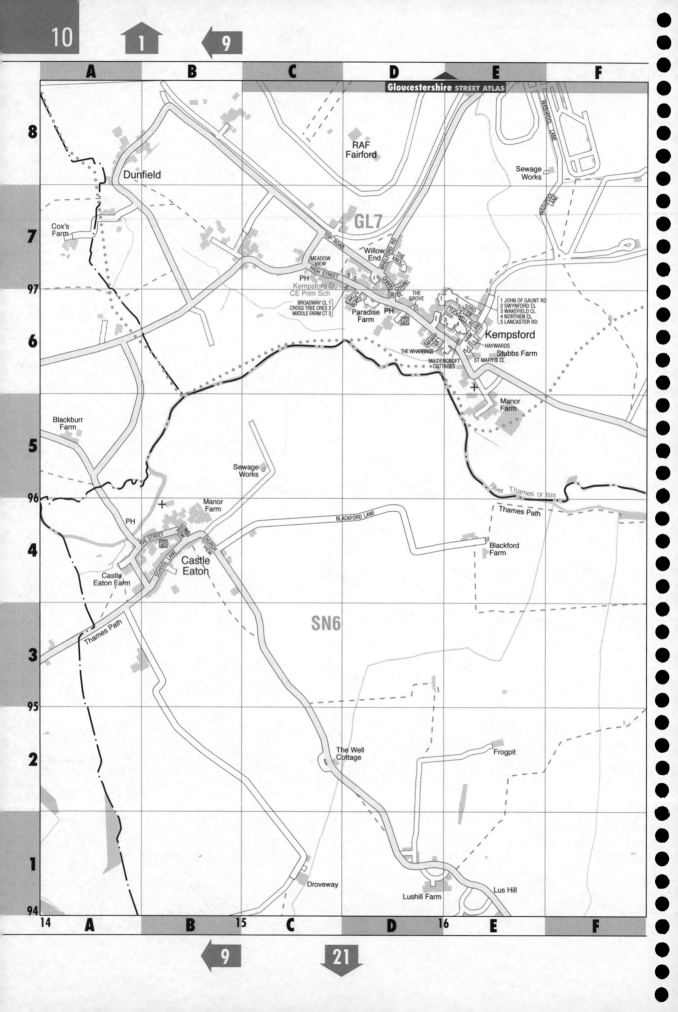

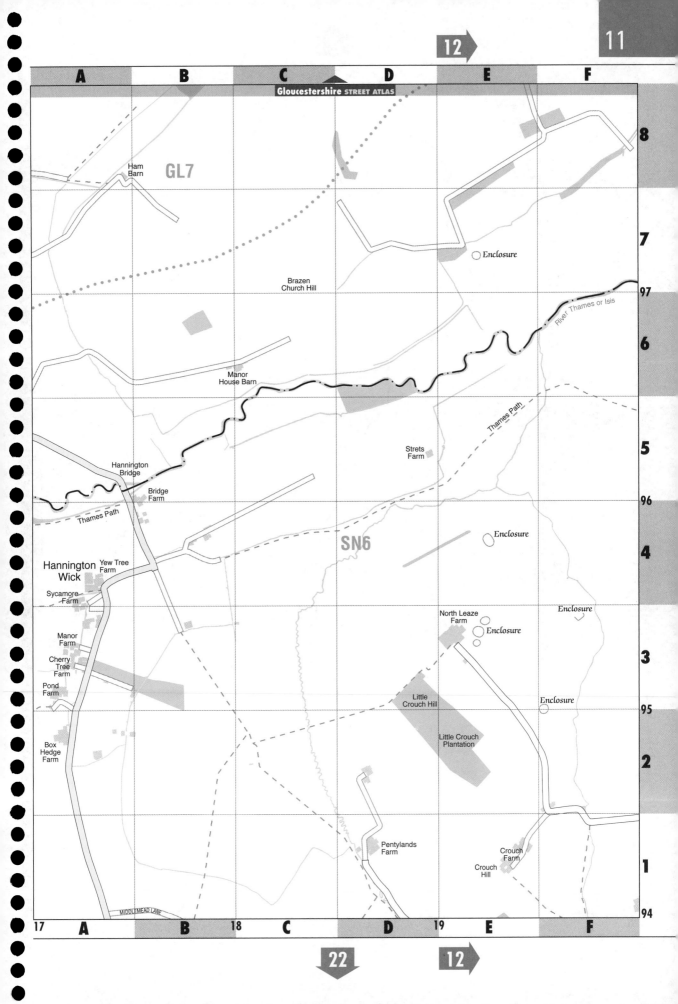

Gloucestershire STREET ATLAS

A   B   C   D   E   F

8

7

97

6

5

96

4

3

95

2

1

94

Ham
Barn

GL7

Brazen
Church Hill

Enclosure

River Thames or Isis

Manor
House Barn

Thames Path

Strets
Farm

Hannington
Bridge

Bridge
Farm

Thames Path

SN6

Enclosure

Hannington
Wick

Yew Tree
Farm

Sycamore
Farm

North Leaze
Farm

Enclosure

Enclosure

Manor
Farm

Cherry
Tree
Farm

Pond
Farm

Little
Crouch Hill

Enclosure

Box
Hedge
Farm

Little Crouch
Plantation

Pentylands
Farm

Crouch
Farm

Crouch
Hill

MIDDLEMEAD LANE

17   A   B   18   C   D   19   E   F

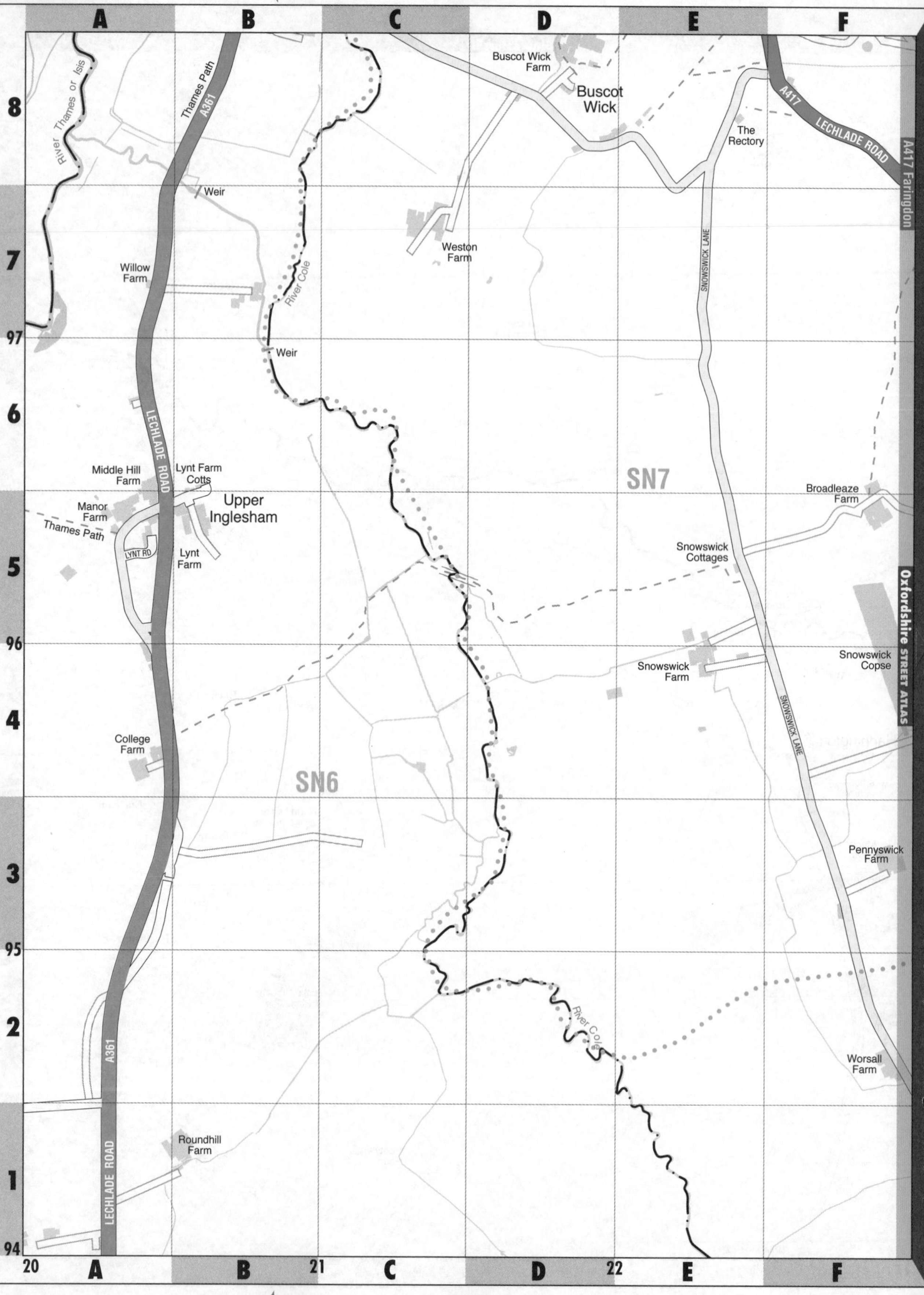

11
2

A B C D E F

8

River Thames or Isis

Thames Path

A361

Buscot Wick Farm

Buscot Wick

The Rectory

A417 LECHLADE ROAD

A417 Faringdon

Weir

7

Willow Farm

River Cole

Weston Farm

SNOWSWICK LANE

97

Weir

6

SN7

Broadleaze Farm

Middle Hill Farm

Lynt Farm Cotts

Upper Inglesham

LECHLADE ROAD

Manor Farm

Thames Path

LYNT RD

Lynt Farm

Snowswick Cottages

Oxfordshire STREET ATLAS

5

96

College Farm

Snowswick Farm

Snowswick Copse

4

SN6

SNOWSWICK LANE

Pennyswick Farm

3

95

River Cole

Worsall Farm

2

A361

LECHLADE ROAD

Roundhill Farm

1

94

20 A B 21 C D 22 E F

11
23

A　B　C　D　E　F

Gloucestershire STREET ATLAS

8

Newnton Gorse

Addy's Firs

Monarch's Way

7

Monarch's Way

Boldridge Farm

Ashley Marsh Covert

93

Church Farm

Wallgutters Covert

CRUDWELL LANE

6

GL8

Boldridge Brake

5

Long Newnton

92

B4014

SYCAMORE CL

Nursery Farm

The Priory

PUMP LA

Newnton Dairy Farm

4

Oak Covert

Orchard End

Newnton House

SN16

Gilboa Farm

3

River Avon (Tetbury Branch)

Weir　Weir

Shipton Mill

Merchants Farm

91

Shipton Wood

Coldharbour

2

Bell Farm

Hydes Brake

1

B4014

Quobwell Plantations

90

90　A　B　91　C　D　92　E　F

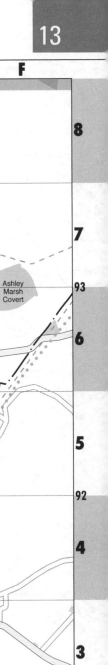

	A	B	C	D	E	F

8

GL8

Ashley Marsh

Ash Bed

Withy Bed

7

West Crudwell

Chedglow

Crudwell Court Farm

Hotel

Crudwell CE Prim Sch

93

CRUDWELL LANE

DAYS CT

BROOKSIDE

Manor Farm

6

Chedglow Barn

Gallops

TURERS LANE

THE RIDGEWAY

THE RIDGEWAY

PH

Crudwell

TETBURY LANE

THE DAWNEYS

Ravenhurst

THE BUTTS

THE STREET

5

GOOSELANDS

KINGS MD

PO

Hayleaze Farm

PH

Village End

92

SN16

Murcott

Murcott Park Farm

Meadow End

4

Murcott Farm

Upper Marsh Farm

Marsh Farm

3

Ashlands Court

Hankerton Field Farm

91

Bishoper Farm

2

Five Lanes Plantation

Messels Plantation

Bishoper Plantation

Five Lanes

The Wedge

The Cleaver

1

A429

Grandchild Plantation

90

93	A	B	94	C	D	95	E	F

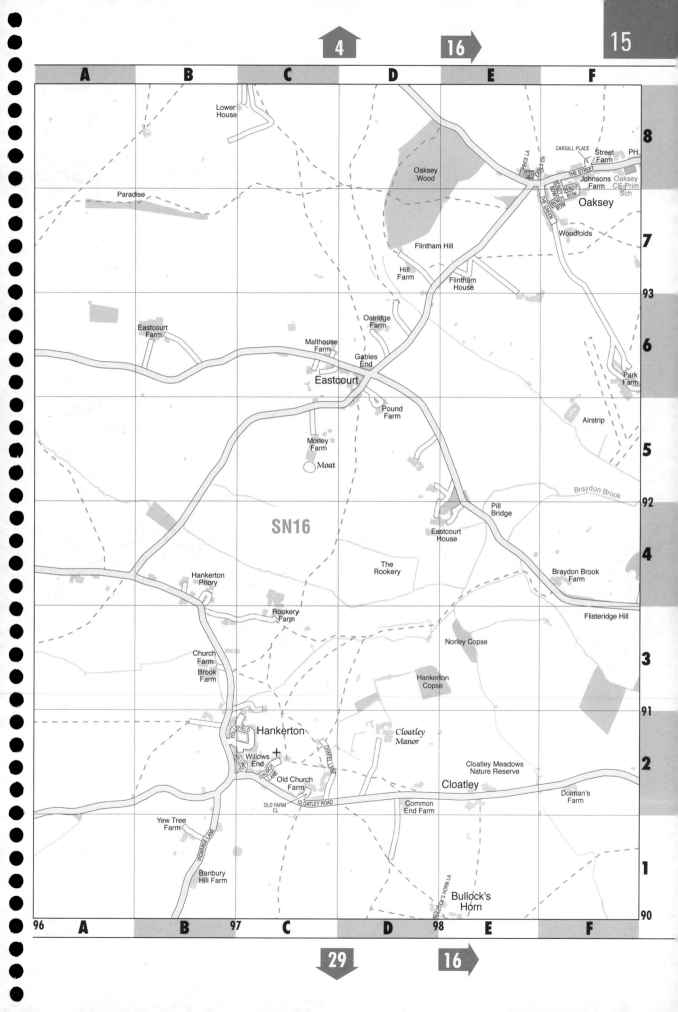

A B C D E F

8
7
93
6
5
92
4
3
91
2
1
90

Lower House

Paradise

Oaksey Wood

CARGILL PLACE
Street Farm
PH
COPPICE LA
PO
BENDY BOW
THE STREET
Johnsons Farm
Oaksey CE Prim Sch
THE GREEN
BENDY BOW
BENDY BOW
Oaksey

Woodfolds

Flintham Hill

Hill Farm

Flintham House

Oatridge Farm

Eastcourt Farm

Malthouse Farm

Gables End

Eastcourt

Pound Farm

Park Farm

Airstrip

Morley Farm

Moat

Braydon Brook

Pill Bridge

SN16

Eastcourt House

Hankerton Priory

The Rookery

Braydon Brook Farm

Rookery Farm

Flisteridge Hill

Norley Copse

Church Farm
Brook Farm

Hankerton Copse

FOLLYFIELD
Hankerton
MILL HILL
Willows End
CHURCH LANE
CHAPEL LANE
Old Church Farm
OLD FARM CL
CLOATLEY ROAD

Cloatley Manor

Cloatley Meadows Nature Reserve

Cloatley

Dolman's Farm

Common End Farm

Yew Tree Farm

VICARAGE LANE

Banbury Hill Farm

BULLOCK'S HORN LA

Bullock's Horn

96 A 97 B C 98 D E F

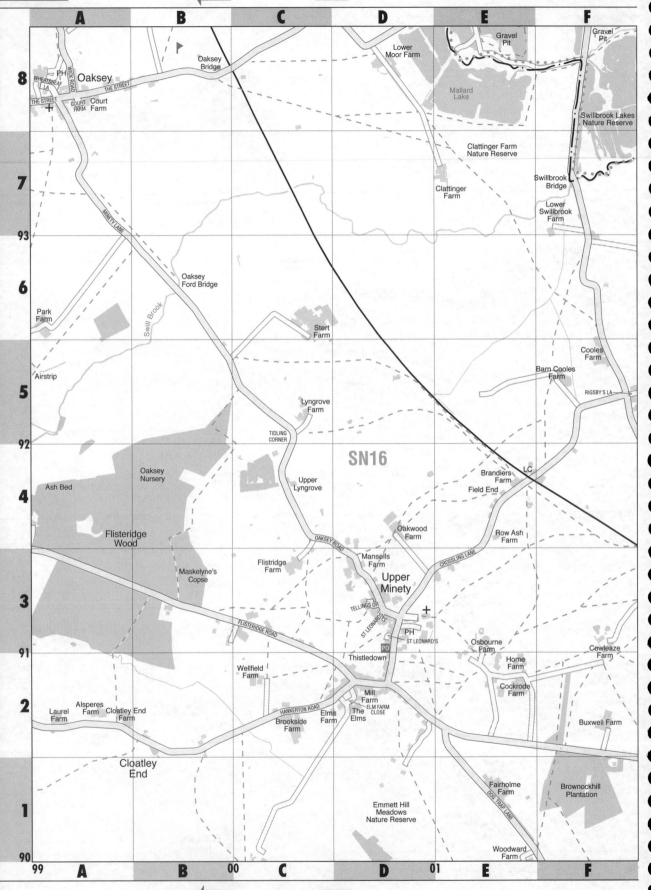

A B C D E F

8
PH Wheatsheaf LA
Oaksey
WICK ROAD
THE STREET
THE STREET
Court Farm
Court Farm
Oaksey Bridge
Lower Moor Farm
Gravel Pit
Mallard Lake
Gravel Pit
Swillbrook Lakes Nature Reserve

Clattinger Farm Nature Reserve

7
MINETY LANE
Oaksey Ford Bridge
Swill Brook
Clattinger Farm
Swillbrook Bridge
Lower Swillbrook Farm

93

6
Park Farm
Stert Farm

Airstrip
Lyngrove Farm
Cooles Farm
Barn Cooles Farm
RIGSBY'S LA

5
TIDLING CORNER

92
Oaksey Nursery
SN16
Brandiers Farm
LC

4
Ash Bed
Upper Lyngrove
Oakwood Farm
Field End
Row Ash Farm
Flisteridge Wood
OAKSEY ROAD
Mansells Farm
CROSSLING LANE

3
Maskelyne's Copse
Flistridge Farm
Upper Minety
TELLINGS OR
ST LEONARD'S CL
PH
ST LEONARD'S
Osbourne Farm
Cowleaze Farm
FLISTERIDGE ROAD
PO
Thistledown
Home Farm

91
Wellfield Farm
Cockrode Farm

2
Laurel Farm
Alsperes Farm
Cloatley End Farm
Mill Farm
ELM FARM CLOSE
Buxwell Farm
HANKERTON ROAD
Elms Farm
The Elms
Brookside Farm

Cloatley End
Fairholme Farm
DOG TRAP LANE
Brownockhill Plantation

1
Emmett Hill Meadows Nature Reserve

90
Woodward Farm

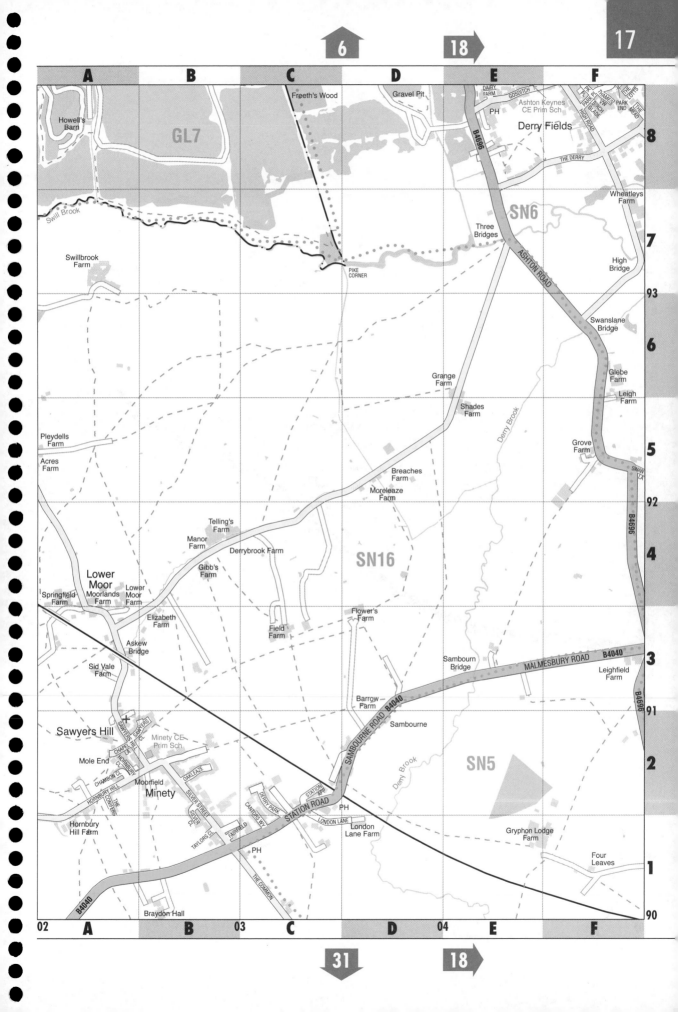

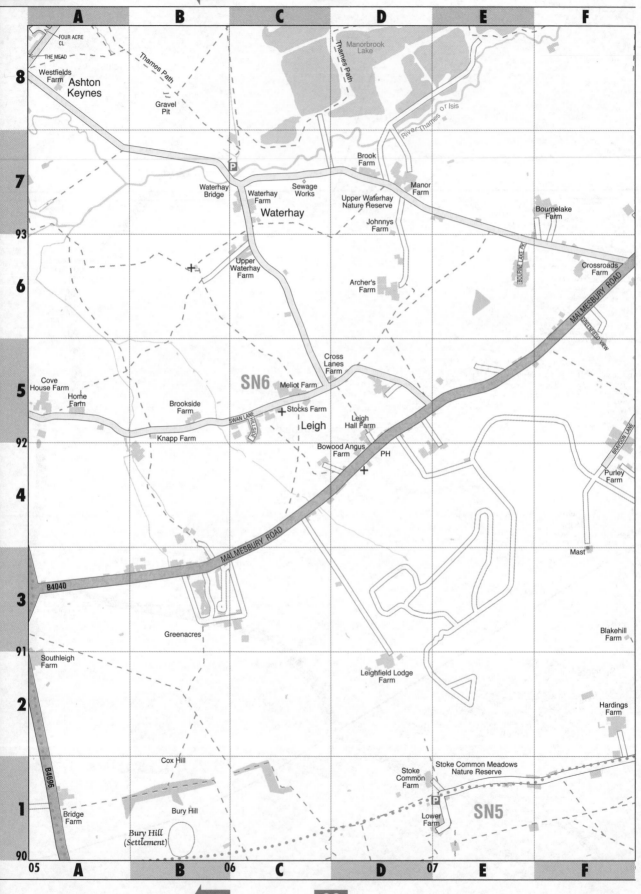

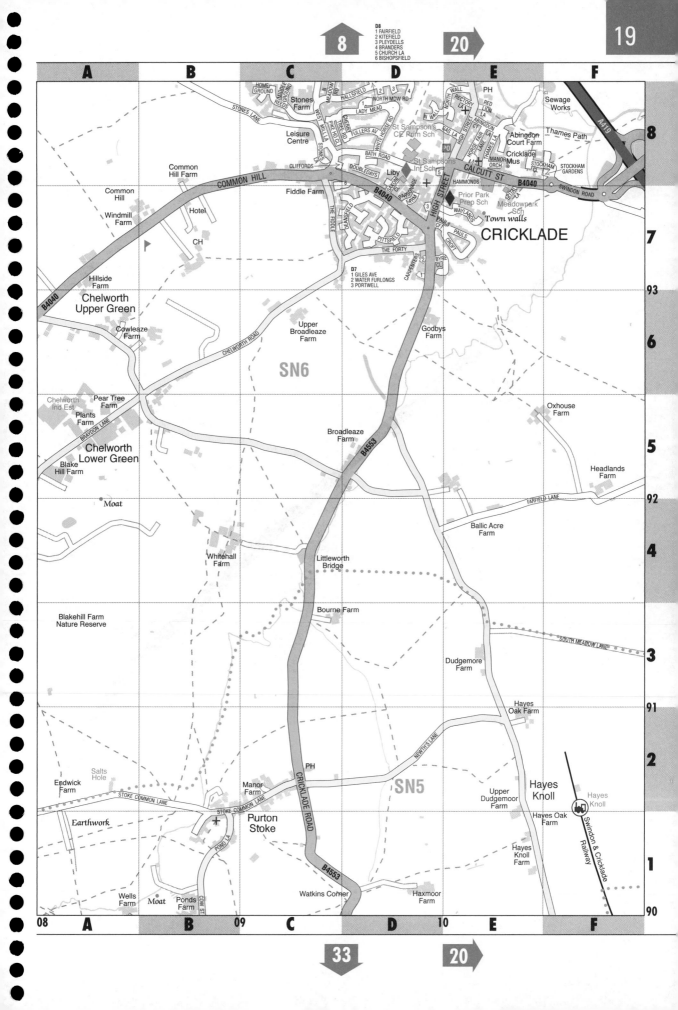

19

9

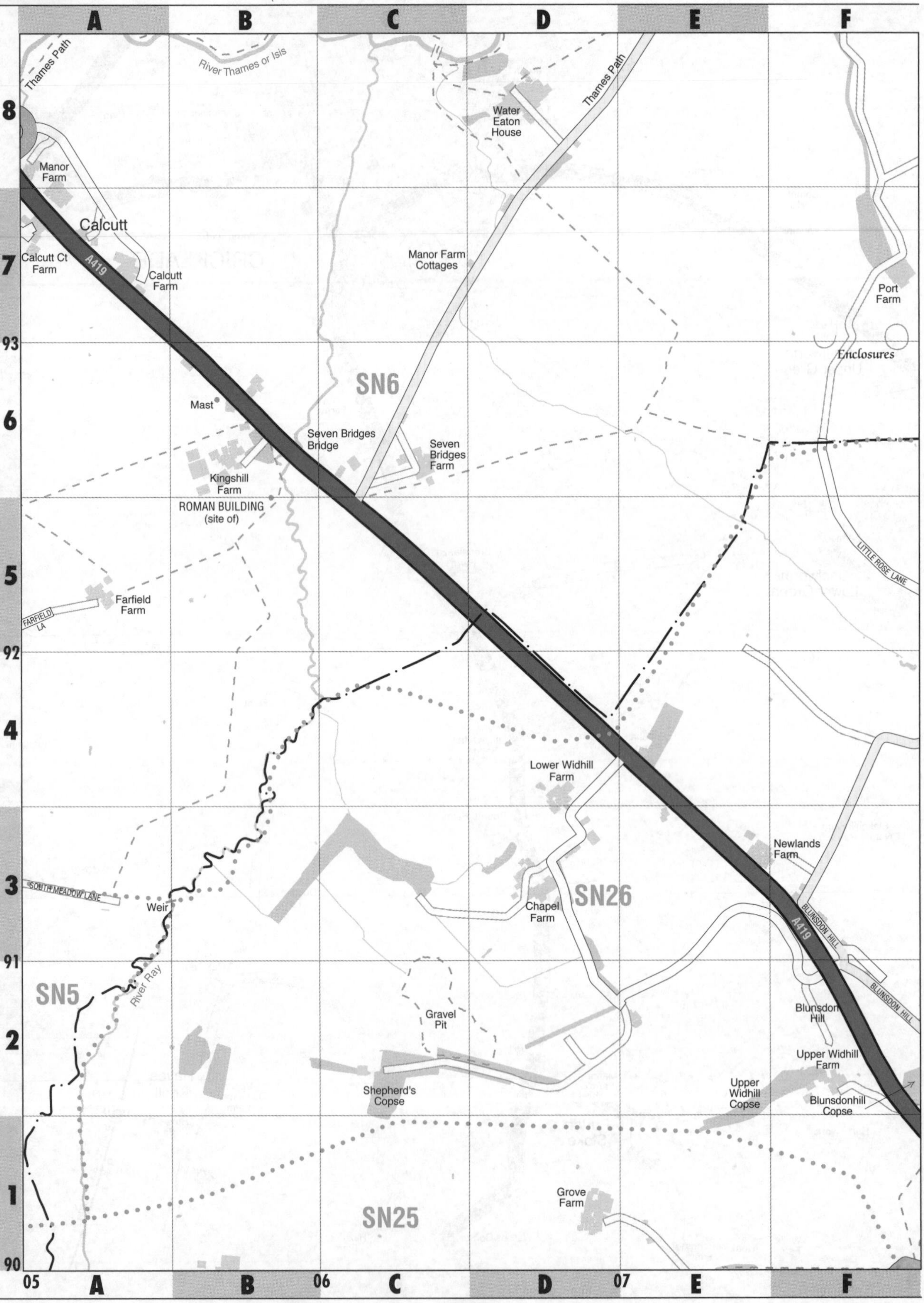

A B C D E F

Thames Path

River Thames or Isis

Water Eaton House

Thames Path

8

Manor Farm

Calcutt

Calcutt Ct Farm

7

A419

Calcutt Farm

Manor Farm Cottages

Port Farm

93

Enclosures

SN6

Mast

6

Kingshill Farm

Seven Bridges Bridge

Seven Bridges Farm

LITTLE ROSE LANE

ROMAN BUILDING (site of)

Farfield Farm

5

FARFIELD LA

92

4

Lower Widhill Farm

Newlands Farm

SOUTH MEADOW LANE

3

Weir

Chapel Farm

SN26

BLUNSDON HILL

A419

BLUNSDON HILL

91

River Ray

SN5

Blunsdon Hill

Gravel Pit

2

Upper Widhill Farm

Shepherd's Copse

Upper Widhill Copse

Blunsdonhill Copse

1

Grove Farm

SN25

90

05 A B 06 C D 07 E F

19

34

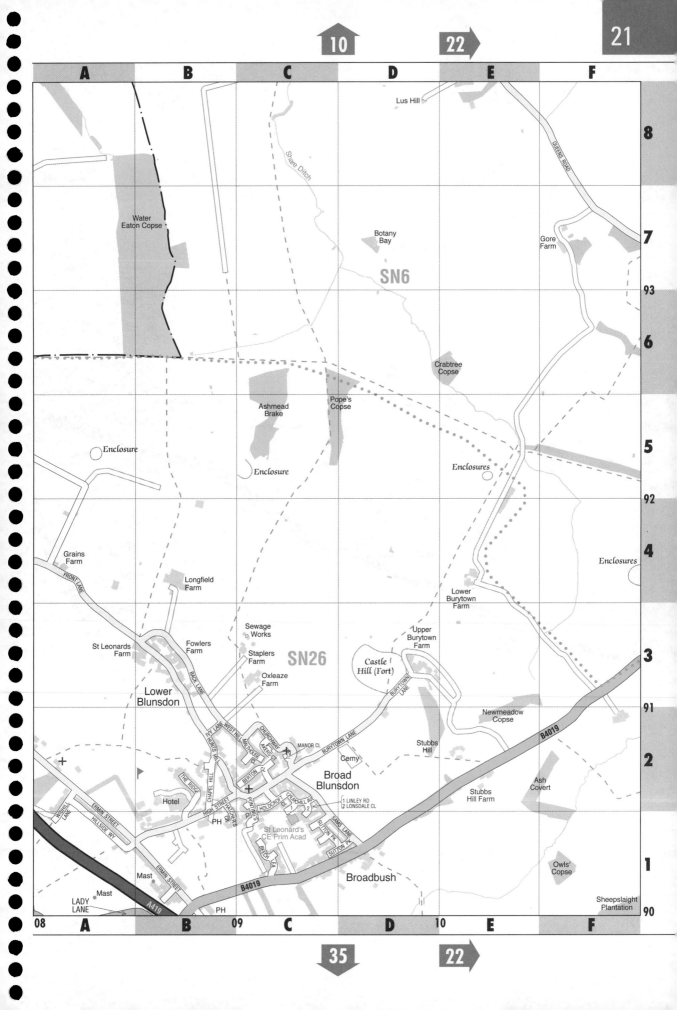

A   B   C   D   E   F

8

7

93

6

5

92

4

3

91

2

1

90

Lus Hill

Share Ditch

Water
Eaton Copse

Botany
Bay

SN6

Gore
Farm

QUEENS ROAD

Crabtree
Copse

Pope's
Copse

Ashmead
Brake

Enclosure

Enclosure

Enclosures

Enclosures

Enclosures

Grains
Farm

FRONT LANE

Longfield
Farm

Lower
Burytown
Farm

St Leonards
Farm

Fowlers
Farm

Sewage
Works

Staplers
Farm

SN26

Oxleaze
Farm

Upper
Burytown
Farm

Castle
Hill (Fort)

BURYTOWN LANE

Newmeadow
Copse

B4019

Lower
Blunsdon

BACK LANE

IVY LANE WEST HILL MALTHOUSE

HUNTS HILL

CHURCHWAL

AKERS CL

MANOR CL

BURYTOWN LANE

Cemy

Stubbs
Hill

THE RIDGE

CHAPEL HILL

HIGH STREET MATHER'S CR

PONTING'S CL

HOLDCROFT CL

BERTON CL

CHURCHILL AVE

1
2

Broad
Blunsdon

1 LINLEY RD
2 LONSDALE CL

Ash
Covert

Hotel

PH

St Leonard's
CE Prim Acad

SUTTON PK

SAMS LANE

SUTTON PK

BEECH LEA

Stubbs
Hill Farm

WIDHILL
LANE

ERMIN STREET

HILLSIDE WY

Mast

ERMIN STREET

Mast

A419

LADY
LANE

B4019

PH

Broadbush

Owls'
Copse

Sheepslaight
Plantation

08   A   B   09   C   D   10   E   F

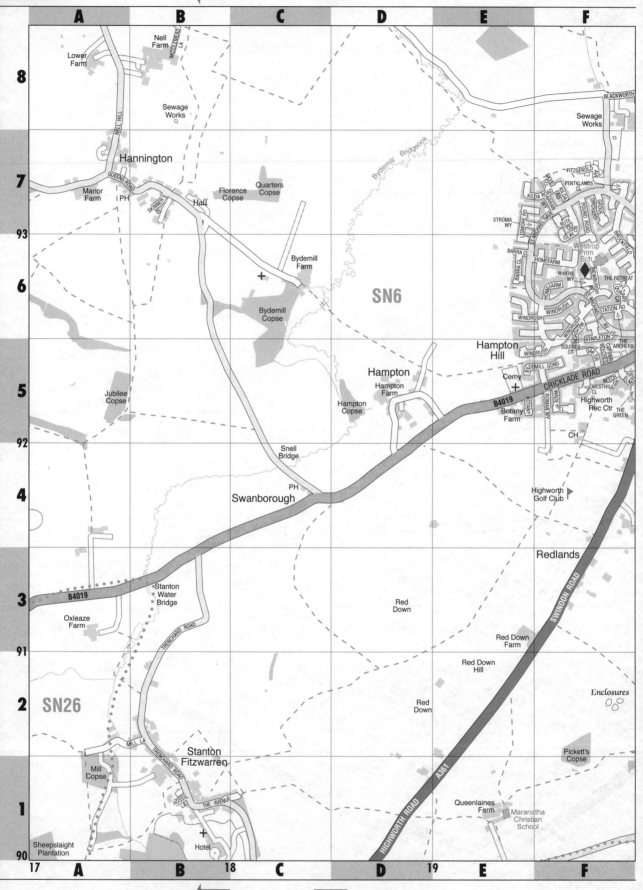

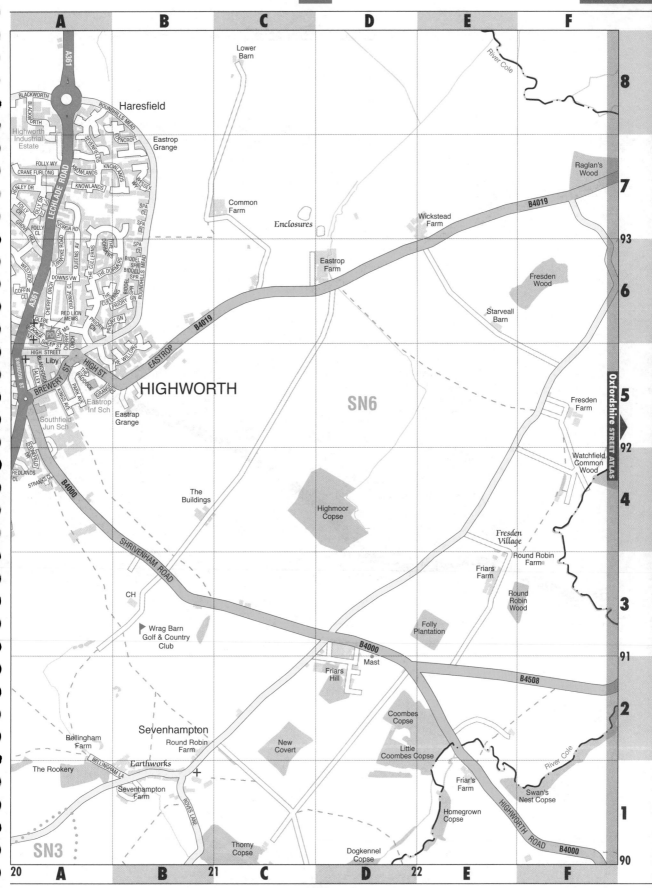

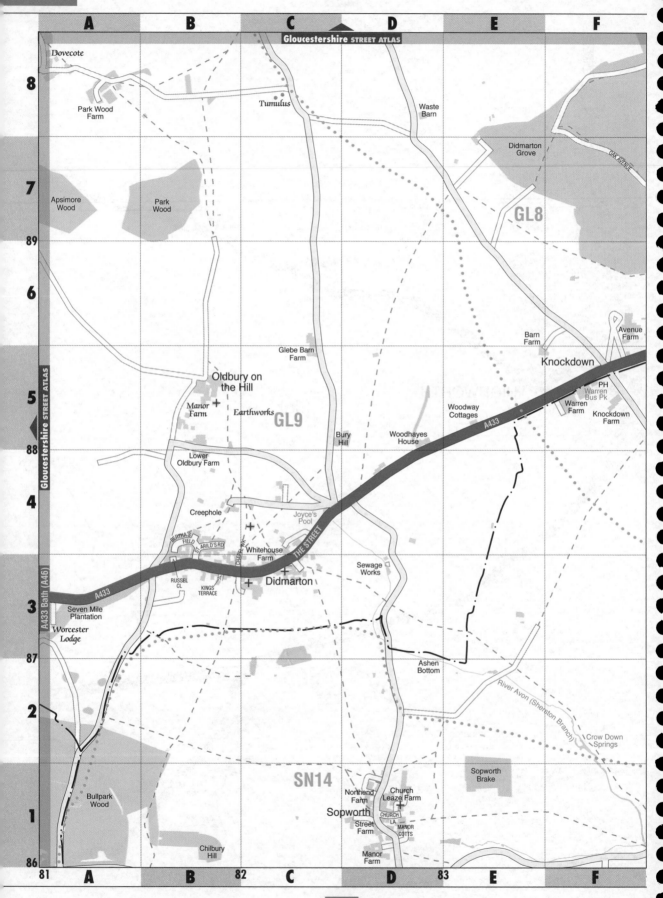

Dovecote

Park Wood Farm

Tumulus

Waste Barn

Didmarton Grove

OAK AVENUE

Apsimore Wood

Park Wood

GL8

Barn Farm

Avenue Farm

Knockdown

Glebe Barn Farm

PH
Warren Bus Pk

Warren Farm

Knockdown Farm

Oldbury on the Hill

Manor Farm

Earthworks

GL9

Bury Hill

Woodway Cottages

A433

Woodhayes House

Lower Oldbury Farm

Creephole

Joyce's Pool

BERTHA'S FIELD
ST ARILD'S RD

CHEPEL WAY

THE STREET

Whitehouse Farm

Sewage Works

RUSSEL CL

KINGS TERRACE

Didmarton

A433 Bath (A46)

A433

Seven Mile Plantation

Worcester Lodge

Ashen Bottom

River Avon (Sherston Branch)

Crow Down Springs

Bullpark Wood

SN14

Sopworth Brake

Nonhend Farm

Church Leaze Farm

Sopworth

CHURCH LA

Street Farm

MANOR COTTS

Chilbury Hill

Manor Farm

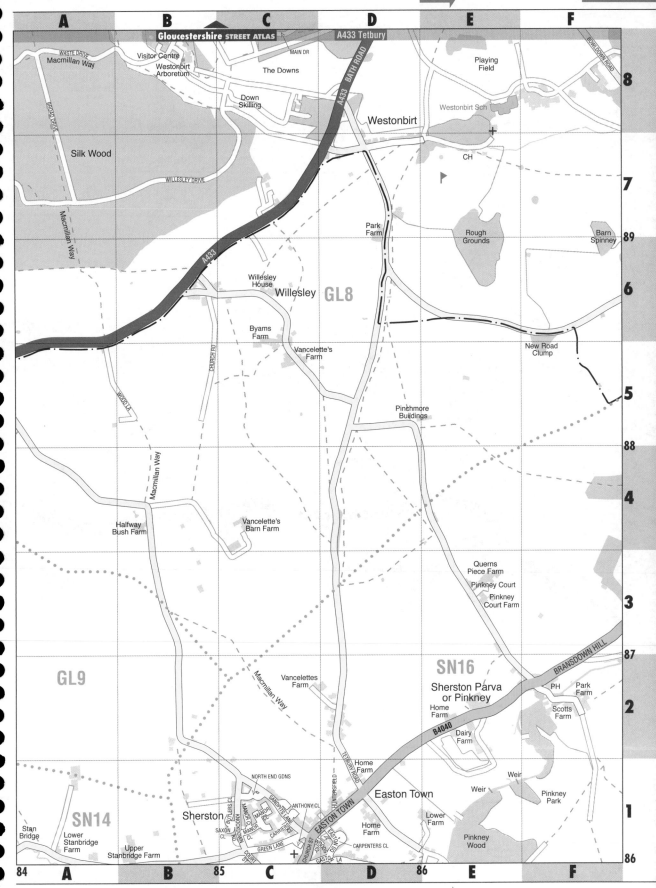

A | B | C | D | E | F

A433 Tetbury

WASTE DRIVE
Macmillan Way

Visitor Centre

Westonbirt
Arboretum

MAIN DR

The Downs

Down
Skilling

Playing
Field

BOWLDOWN ROAD

8

BROAD DRIVE

Westonbirt Sch

Westonbirt

Silk Wood

WILLESLEY DRIVE

Macmillan Way

A433 BATH ROAD

CH

7

Park
Farm

Rough
Grounds

Barn
Spinney

89

A433

CHURCH RD

Willesley
House

Willesley

GL8

6

Byams
Farm

Vancelette's
Farm

New Road
Clump

WOOD LA

Pinchmore
Buildings

5

Macmillan Way

88

Halfway
Bush Farm

Vancelette's
Barn Farm

4

Querns
Piece Farm

Pinkney Court

Pinkney
Court Farm

3

GL9

Macmillan Way

Vancelettes
Farm

SN16

BRANSDOWN HILL

87

Sherston Parva
or Pinkney

PH

Park
Farm

2

Home
Farm

Scotts
Farm

B4040

Dairy
Farm

TEBURY ROAD

Home
Farm

Weir

Weir

Pinkney
Park

Easton Town

NORTH END GDNS

BUTLERS CL

SANDPITS LANE

ANTHONY CL

Home
Farm

Lower
Farm

1

Stan
Bridge

SN14

Lower
Stanbridge
Farm

Sherston

SAXON
CL

MANOR CL

MANOR
CL

CARRIERS

GREEN LANE

CHURCH ST

EASTON TOWN

CARPENTERS CL

Pinkney
Wood

Upper
Stanbridge Farm

86

84 | A | 85 | B | C | 86 | D | E | F

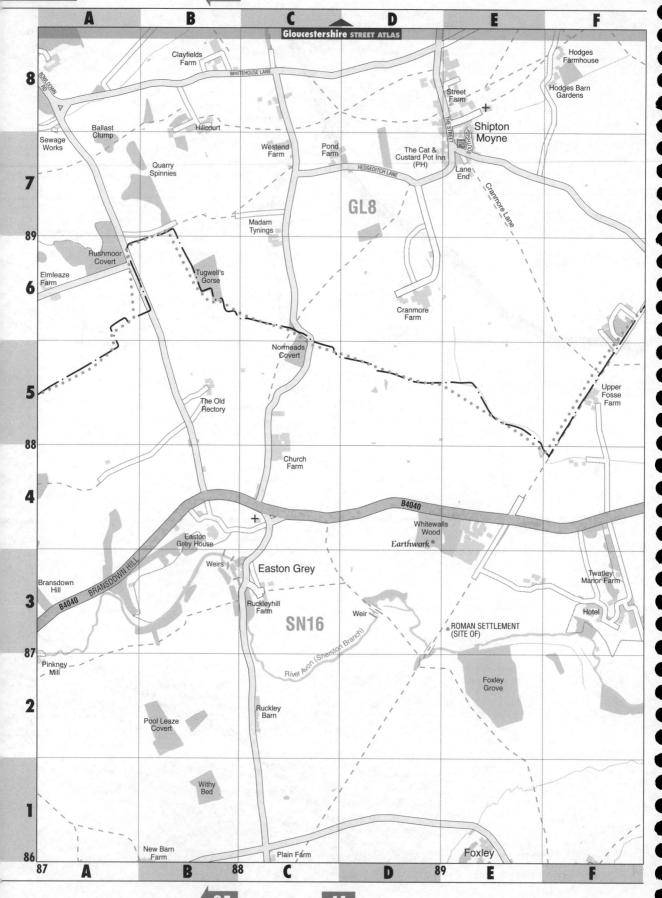

Gloucestershire STREET ATLAS

A B C D E F

8

Clayfields Farm
WHITEHOUSE LANE
Hodges Farmhouse
Hodges Barn Gardens
Street Farm
Hillcourt
Ballast Clump
Sewage Works
BOWLDOWN RD

7
Quarry Spinnies
Westend Farm
Pond Farm
The Cat & Custard Pot Inn (PH)
Shipton Moyne
Lane End
HEDGEDITCH LANE
THE STREET
SOUTHEND
GL8
Cranmore Lane

89
Madam Tynings
Rushmoor Covert
Elmleaze Farm

6
Tugwell's Gorse
Cranmore Farm

Normeads Covert

5
The Old Rectory
Upper Fosse Farm

88
Church Farm

4
B4040
Whitewalls Wood
Earthwork

Easton Grey House
Weirs
Twatley Manor Farm

3
Bransdown Hill
B4040
BRANSDOWN HILL
Easton Grey
Ruckleyhill Farm
SN16
Weir
ROMAN SETTLEMENT (SITE OF)
Hotel

87
Pinkney Mill
River Avon (Sherston Branch)
Foxley Grove

2
Pool Leaze Covert
Ruckley Barn

1
Withy Bed

86
New Barn Farm
Plain Farm
Foxley

87 A B 88 C D 89 E F

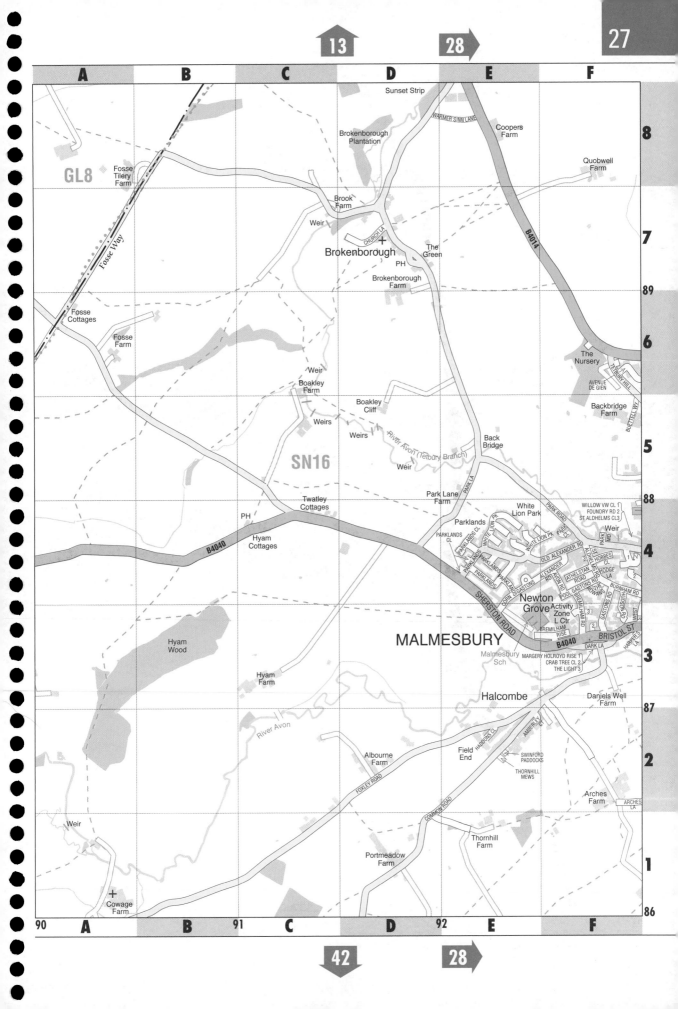

13
28
28

A   B   C   D   E   F

8
7
89
6
5
88
4
3
87
2
1
86

Sunset Strip
WARMER SINN LANE
Coopers Farm
Brokenborough Plantation
Quobwell Farm
GL8
Fosse Tilery Farm
B4014
Brook Farm
Weir
CHURCH LA
Brokenborough
The Green
PH
Brokenborough Farm
The Nursery
TETBURY HILL
AVENUE DE GIEN
Fosse Cottages
Fosse Farm
Fosse Way
BLUETELL WY
Backbridge Farm
Weir
Boakley Farm
Boakley Cliff
Back Bridge
Weirs
River Avon (Tetbury Branch)
Weirs
SN16
Weir
Park Lane Farm
PARK LA
PARK ROAD
WILLOW VW CL 1
FOUNDRY RD 2
ST ALDHELMS CL 3
Weir
White Lion Park
Parklands
Twatley Cottages
PARKLANDS CL
WHITE LION PK
PARK CL
PH
PARKLANDS CL
WHITE LION PK
ST HOBBES CL
B4040
Hyam Cottages
PARKLANDS
PARKLANDS
PARKLANDS
OLD ALEXANDER RD
ATHELSTAN RD
ST ALDHELMS RD
HODGE LA
BURNHAM RD
GASTONS
ALEXANDER RD
AVON RD
ATHELSTAN RD
POOL GASTONS RD
BREMILHAM RD
GASTONS RD
WEST
SHERSTON ROAD
Newton Grove
Activity Zone L Ctr
BREMILHAM RISE
HARPERS LA
Hyam Wood
MALMESBURY
Malmesbury Sch
B4040
BRISTOL ST
DARK LA
MARGERY HOLROYD RISE 1
CRAB TREE CL 2
THE LIGHT 3
Daniels Well Farm
Hyam Farm
Halcombe
AMBERLEY CT
HADDONS CL
Albourne Farm
Field End
SWINFORD PADDOCKS
THORNHILL MEWS
Arches Farm
ARCHES LA
River Avon
FOXLEY ROAD
COMMON ROAD
Thornhill Farm
Weir
Portmeadow Farm
Cowage Farm

90   91   92
A   B   C   D   E   F

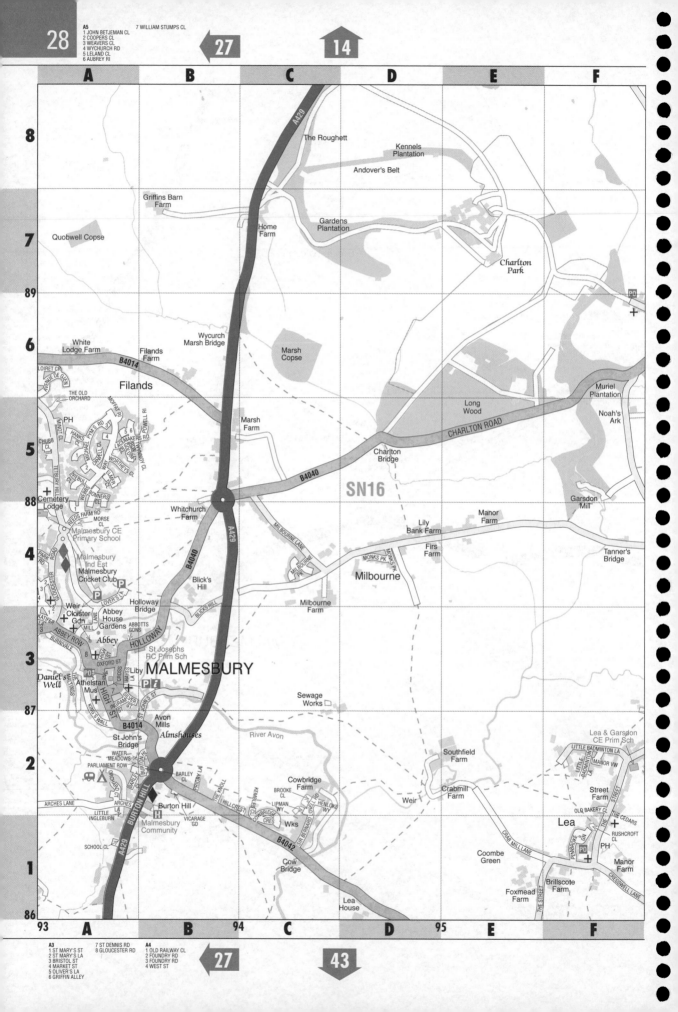

A5
1 JOHN BETJEMAN CL
2 COOPERS CL
3 WEAVERS CL
4 WYCHURCH RD
5 LELAND CL
6 AUBREY RI

7 WILLIAM STUMPS CL

27
14

A B C D E F

8

The Roughett

Kennels
Plantation

Andover's Belt

Griffins Barn
Farm

7
Quobwell Copse

Home
Farm

Gardens
Plantation

Charlton
Park

89

6
White
Lodge Farm

Filands
Farm

Wycurch
Marsh Bridge

Marsh
Copse

B4014

Muriel
Plantation

Filands

Long
Wood

Noah's
Ark

CHARLTON ROAD

Marsh
Farm

B4040

Charlton
Bridge

SN16

Garsdon
Mill

5
CHUBB CL

LOIRET CR
AVENUE DE GIEN
THE OLD
ORCHARD
PH
MINIOT CL
HANKS
CL
MICHAEL
CL
PYM'S RD
MOFFAT RI
ORWELL CL
WORTHEYS CL
LACEMAKERS CL
POWELL RI
HILL BULL
WAY
ELMER
PINNAY CL

Whitchurch
Farm

MILBOURNE LANE

Lily
Bank Farm

Manor
Farm

88
Cemetery
Lodge

WEBBS CL
BONNERS CL
REEDS FARM RD
MORSE
CL
TETBURY HILL

A429

MILBOURNE
PK

Firs
Farm

Tanner's
Bridge

Malmesbury CE
Primary School

MONKS PK

MONKS PK

4
PARK RD
GLOUCESTER RD

Malmesbury
Ind Est
Malmesbury
Cricket Club

B4040

Blick's
Hill

Milbourne
Farm

Milbourne

Weir
Cloister
Gdn

P
P
LOVER'S LA

Holloway
Bridge

BLICKS HILL

KATIFER LA

ABBEY ROW
MILL
LANE

Abbey
House
Gardens

ABBOTTS
GDNS

BURNIVALE

Abbey

HOLLOWAY

3
Daniel's
Well

St Josephs
RC Prim Sch

MALMESBURY

Sewage
Works

PO
HIGH
ST
OXFORD ST
CROSS
HAYES
ST MARY'S LA
Liby
INGRAM ST
Athelstan
Mus
P
i

ST JOHN'S ST

87
KING'S WALL
ST JOHN'S ST

Avon
Mills

River Avon

B4014
St John's
Bridge

Almshouses

Southfield
Farm

Lea & Garsdon
CE Prim Sch

LITTLE BADMINTON LA

2
WATER
MEADOWS
PARLIAMENT ROW

ORCHARD
BARLEY
BURTON HILL
BURTON HILL

BARLEY
CL

PRIORY LA

THE KNOLL

Cowbridge
Farm

BROOKE
CL

LIPMAN
WY

KENNET

HENLOKE
WY

Crabmill
Farm

Weir

MANOR VW

LITTLE
BADMINTON
LA

Street
Farm

THE STREET

ARCHES LANE
ARCHES
LA

LITTLE
INGLEBURN

Burton Hill
H

Malmesbury
Community

VICARAGE
GD

COWBRIDGE
CRES

Wks

ST BERNARD

OLD BAKERY CL

THE CEDARS

Lea

RUSHCROFT
CL

PH
THE

SCHOOL CL

A429

B4042

PENBROKE

CRAB MILL LANE

PO

Manor
Farm

CRESSWELL LANE

1
Cow
Bridge

Coombe
Green

Foxmead
Farm

Brillscote
Farm

THE STREET

86

A3
1 ST MARY'S ST
2 ST MARY'S LA
3 BRISTOL ST
4 MARKET ST
5 OLIVER'S LA
6 GRIFFIN ALLEY

7 ST DENNIS RD
8 GLOUCESTER RD

A4
1 OLD RAILWAY CL
2 FOUNDRY RD
3 FOUNDRY RD
4 WEST ST

27
43

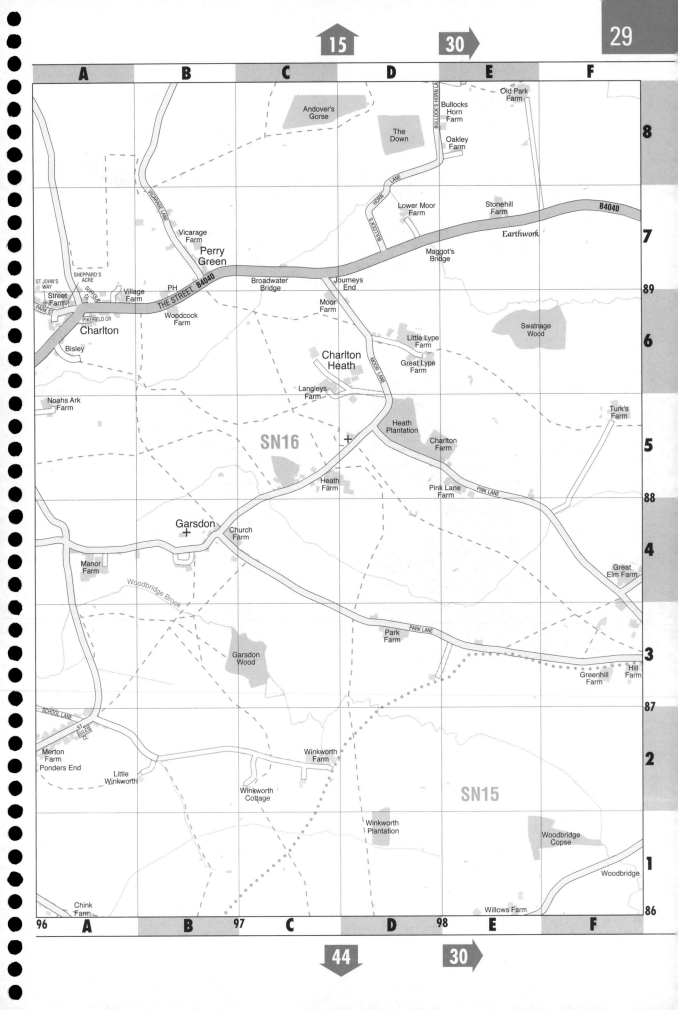

A **B** **C** **D** **E** **F**

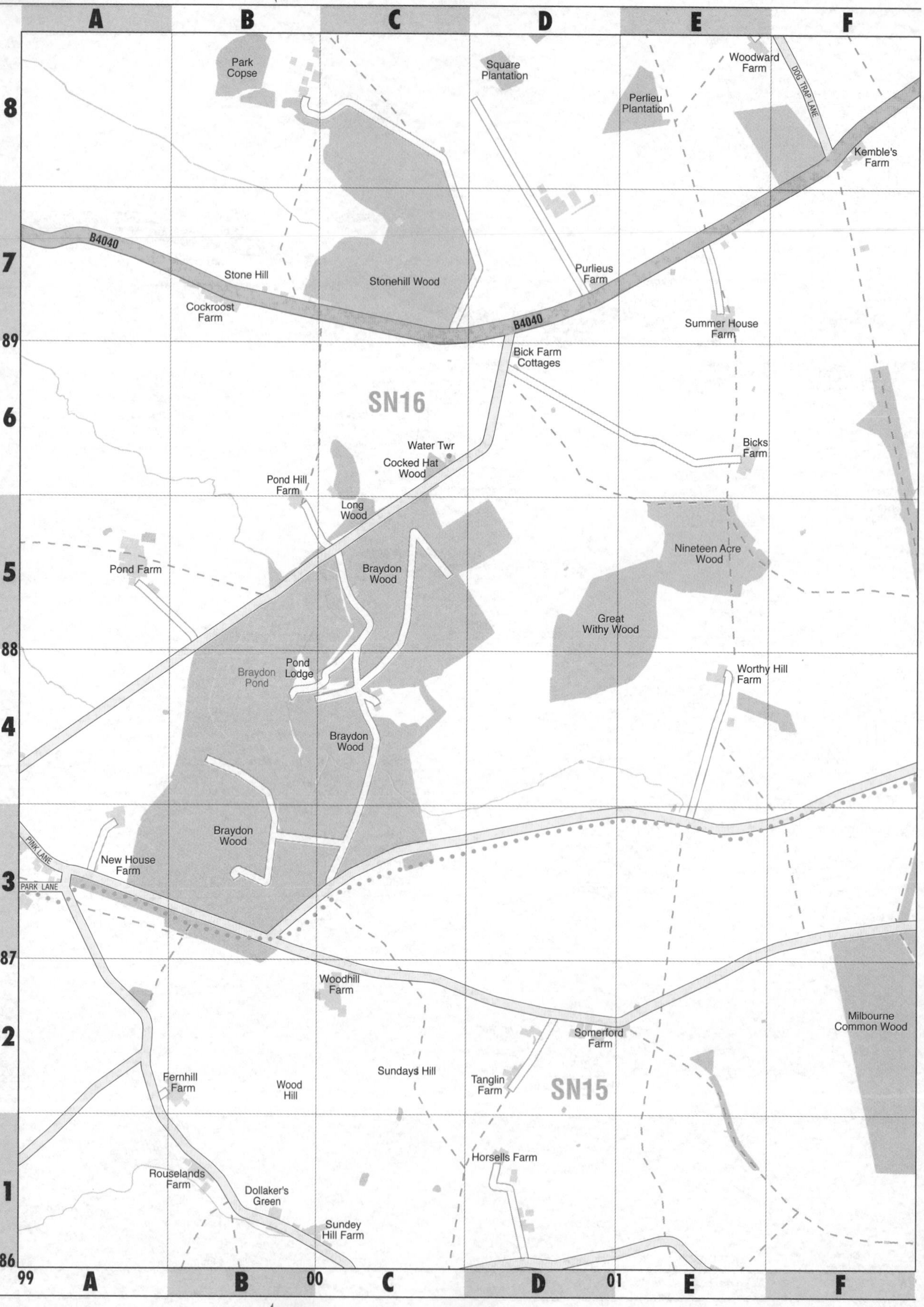

8

Park Copse

Square Plantation

Woodward Farm

DOG TRAP LANE

Perlieu Plantation

Kemble's Farm

7

B4040

Stone Hill

Stonehill Wood

Purlieus Farm

Cockroost Farm

B4040

Summer House Farm

89

Bick Farm Cottages

6

SN16

Water Twr

Cocked Hat Wood

Bicks Farm

Pond Hill Farm

Long Wood

Nineteen Acre Wood

5

Pond Farm

Braydon Wood

Great Withy Wood

88

Braydon Pond

Pond Lodge

Worthy Hill Farm

4

Braydon Wood

Braydon Wood

PARK LANE

New House Farm

3

PARK LANE

87

Woodhill Farm

Milbourne Common Wood

2

Somerford Farm

Fernhill Farm

Wood Hill

Sundays Hill

Tanglin Farm

SN15

Horsells Farm

1

Rouselands Farm

Dollaker's Green

Sundey Hill Farm

86

99 **A** **B** 00 **C** **D** 01 **E** **F**

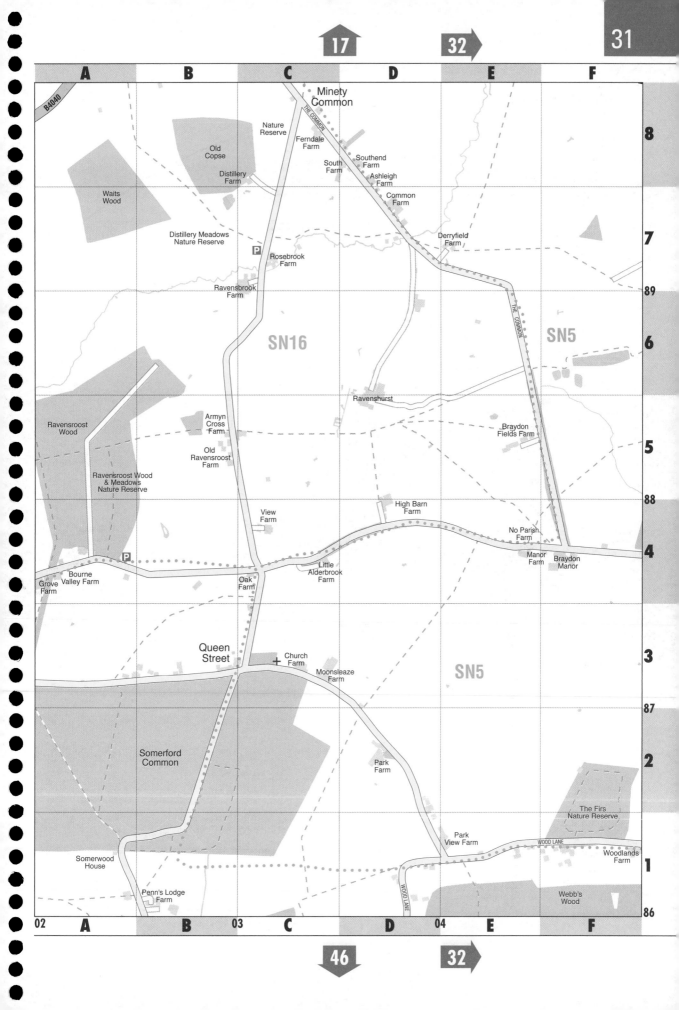

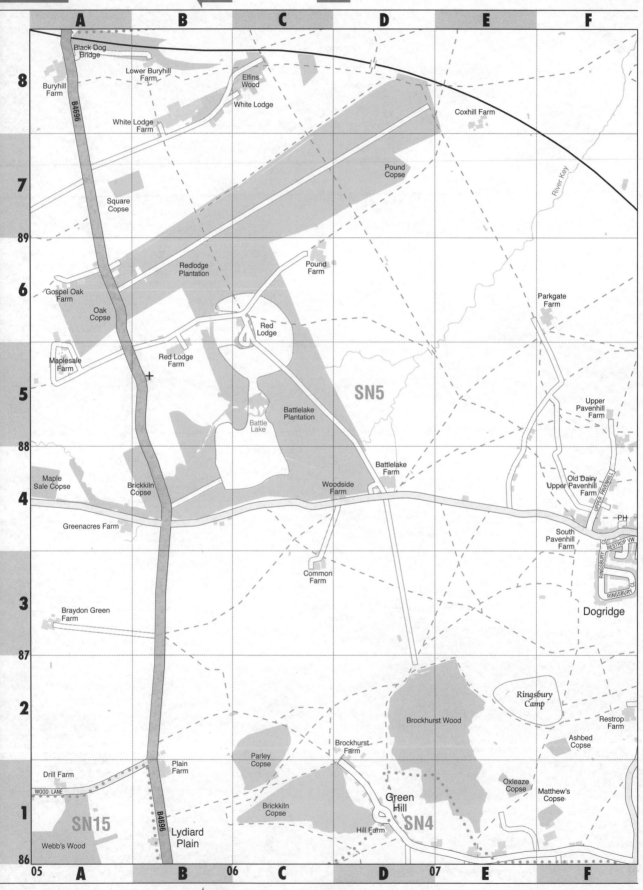

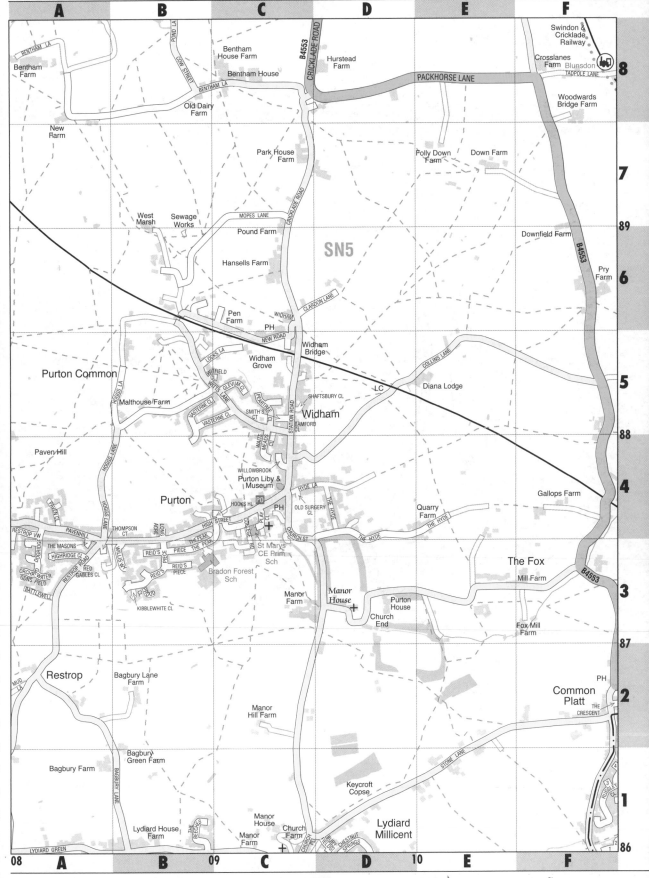

F1
1 MARDALE CL
2 DALEFOOT CL
3 BERRY COPSE
4 KEYCROFT COPSE

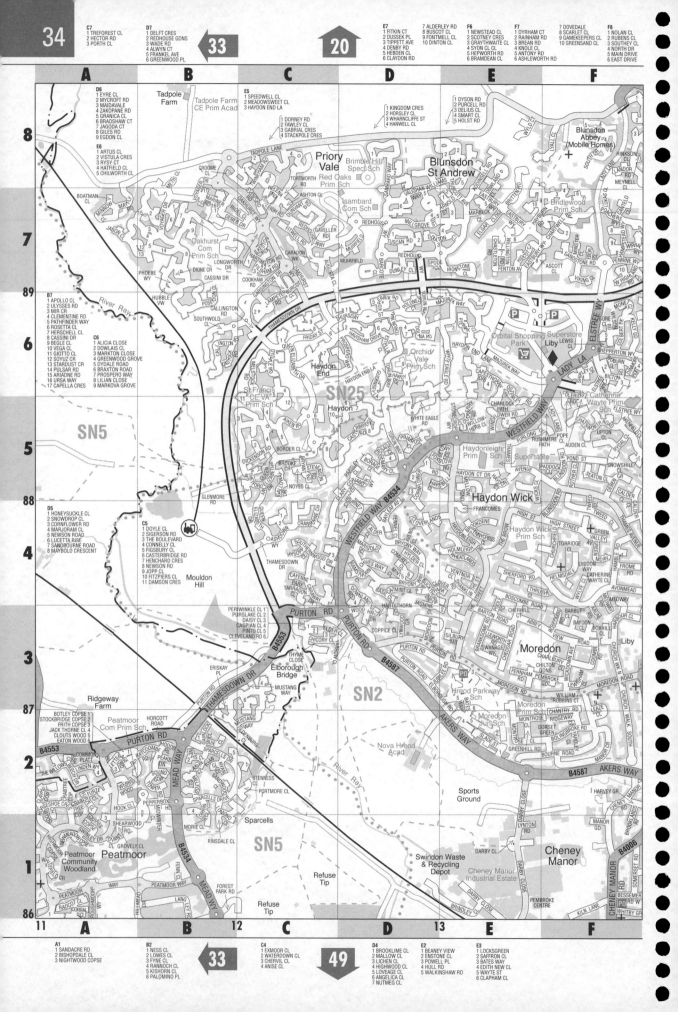

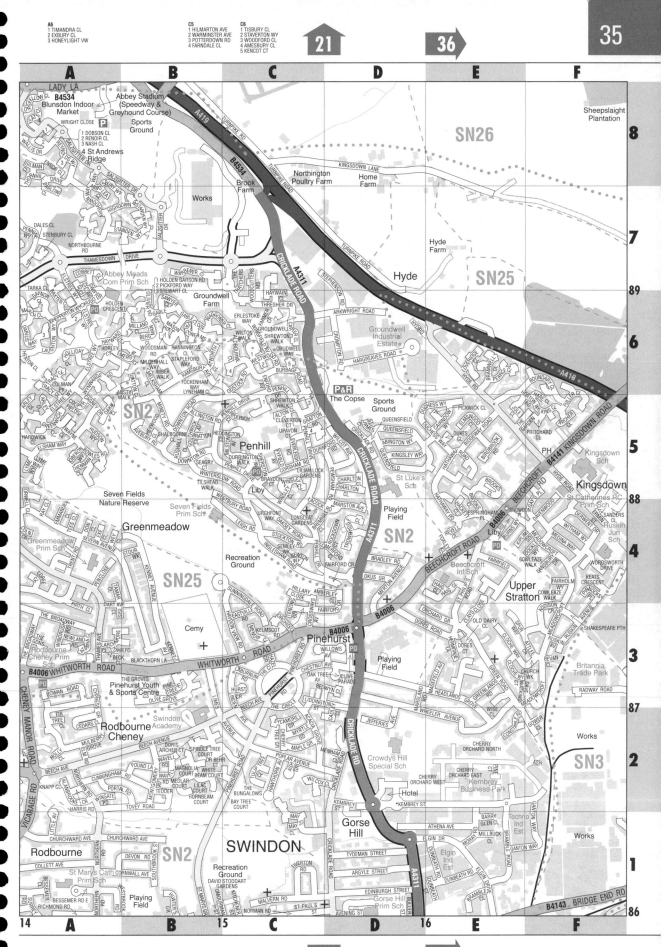

A6
1 TIMANDRA CL
2 EXBURY CL
3 HONEYLIGHT VW

C5
1 HILMARTON AVE
2 WARMINSTER AVE
3 POTTERDOWN RD
4 FARNDALE CL

C6
1 TISBURY CL
2 STAVERTON WY
3 WOODFORD CL
4 AMESBURY CL
5 KENCOT CT

21

36

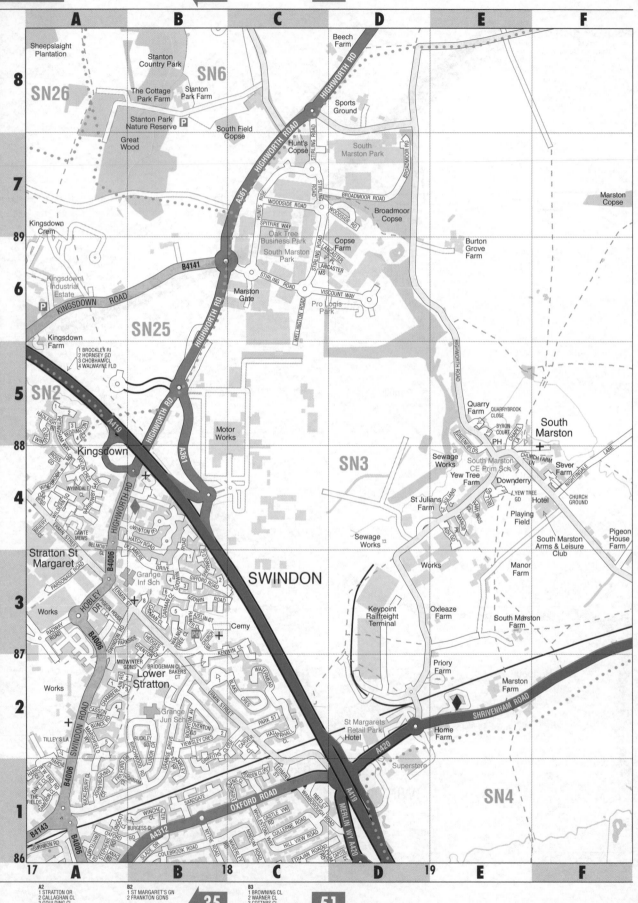

A2
1 STRATTON DR
2 CALLAGHAN CL
3 GOULDING CL
4 SHAPLANDS
5 THE PADDOCKS

B2
1 ST MARGARET'S GN
2 FRANKTON GDNS

B3
1 BROWNING CL
2 WARNER CL
3 COTTARS CL
4 BARON CL
5 BOWMAN CL
6 CRISPIN CL
7 CHURCH WAY
8 FRANK WARMAN CT

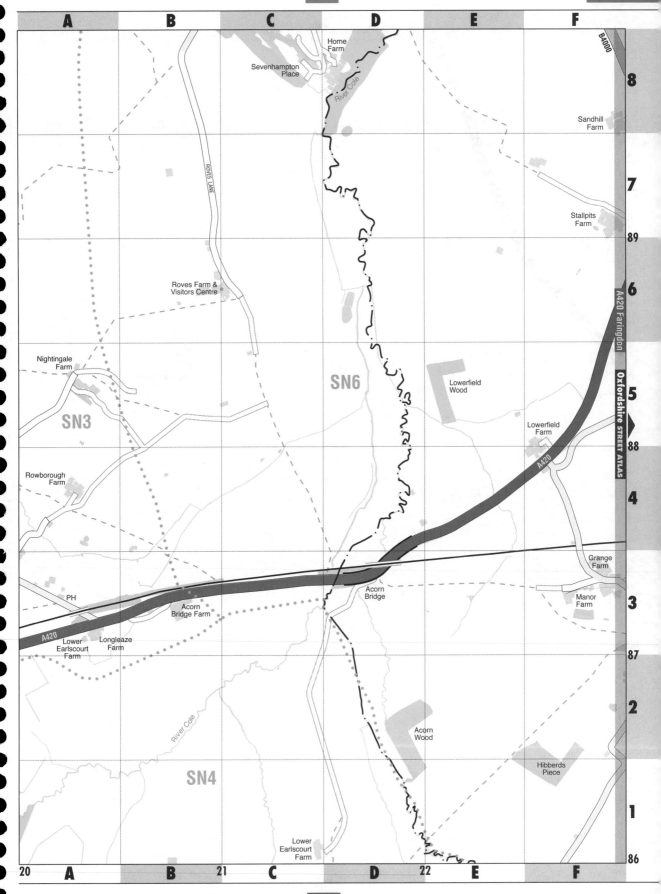

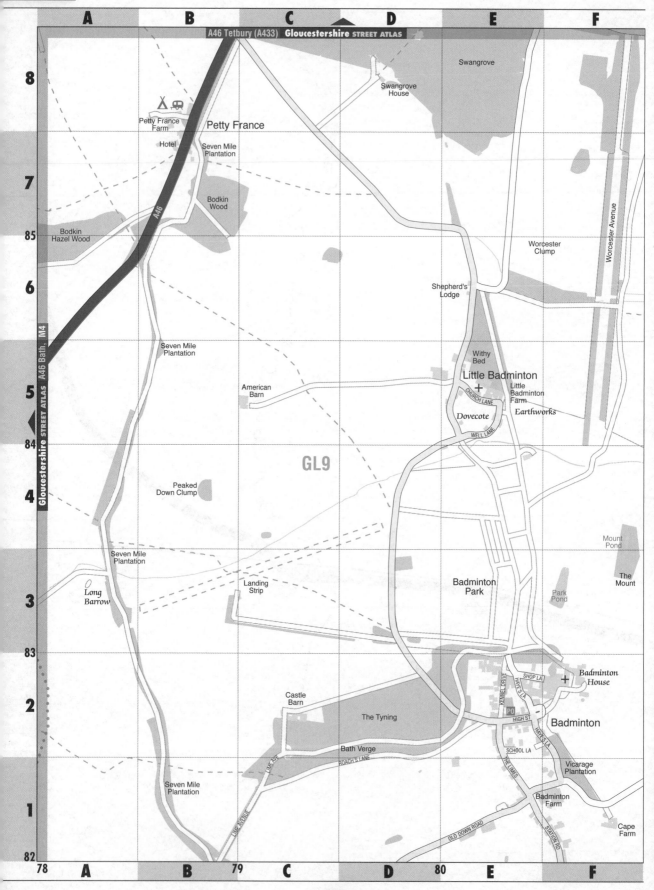

Petty France Farm

Petty France

Hotel

Seven Mile Plantation

Bodkin Wood

Bodkin Hazel Wood

Swangrove

Swangrove House

Worcester Clump

Worcester Avenue

Shepherd's Lodge

Seven Mile Plantation

Withy Bed

Little Badminton

Little Badminton Farm

CHURCH LANE

Earthworks

American Barn

Dovecote

WELL LANE

GL9

Peaked Down Clump

Mount Pond

The Mount

Seven Mile Plantation

Landing Strip

Badminton Park

Park Pond

Long Barrow

SHOP LA

Badminton House

KENNEL DRIVE

HAYES LA

PO

Castle Barn

The Tyning

HIGH ST

HAYES LA

Badminton

Bath Verge

SCHOOL LA

LIME AVE

ROACH'S LANE

THE LIMES

Vicarage Plantation

Seven Mile Plantation

LIME AVENUE

STATION RD

Badminton Farm

Cape Farm

OLD DOWN ROAD

Gloucestershire STREET ATLAS

A46 Bath, M4

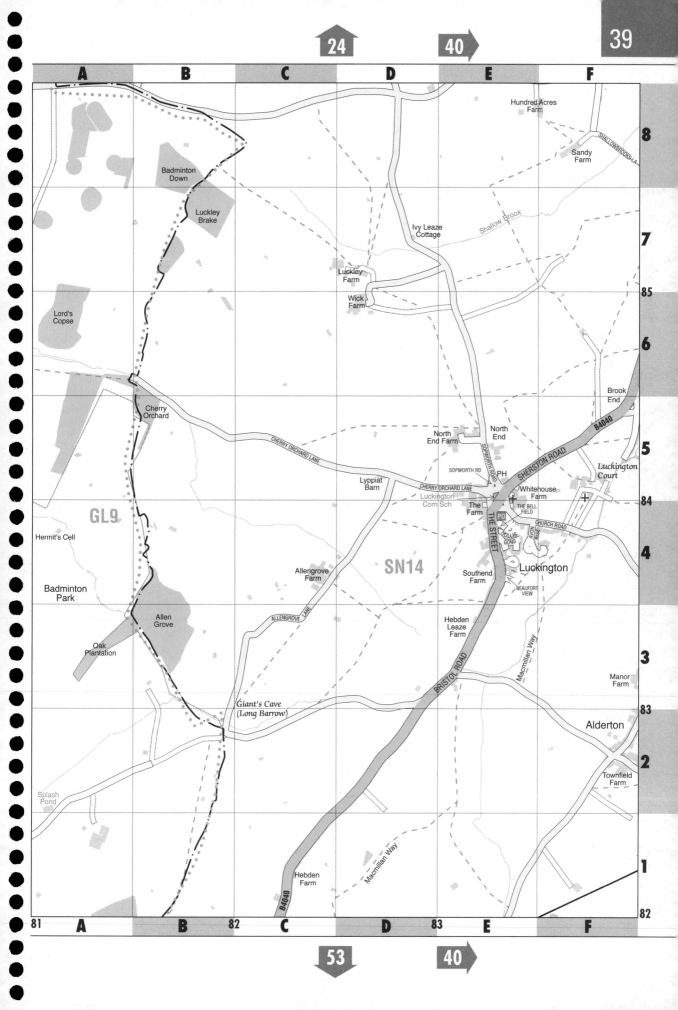

39
25

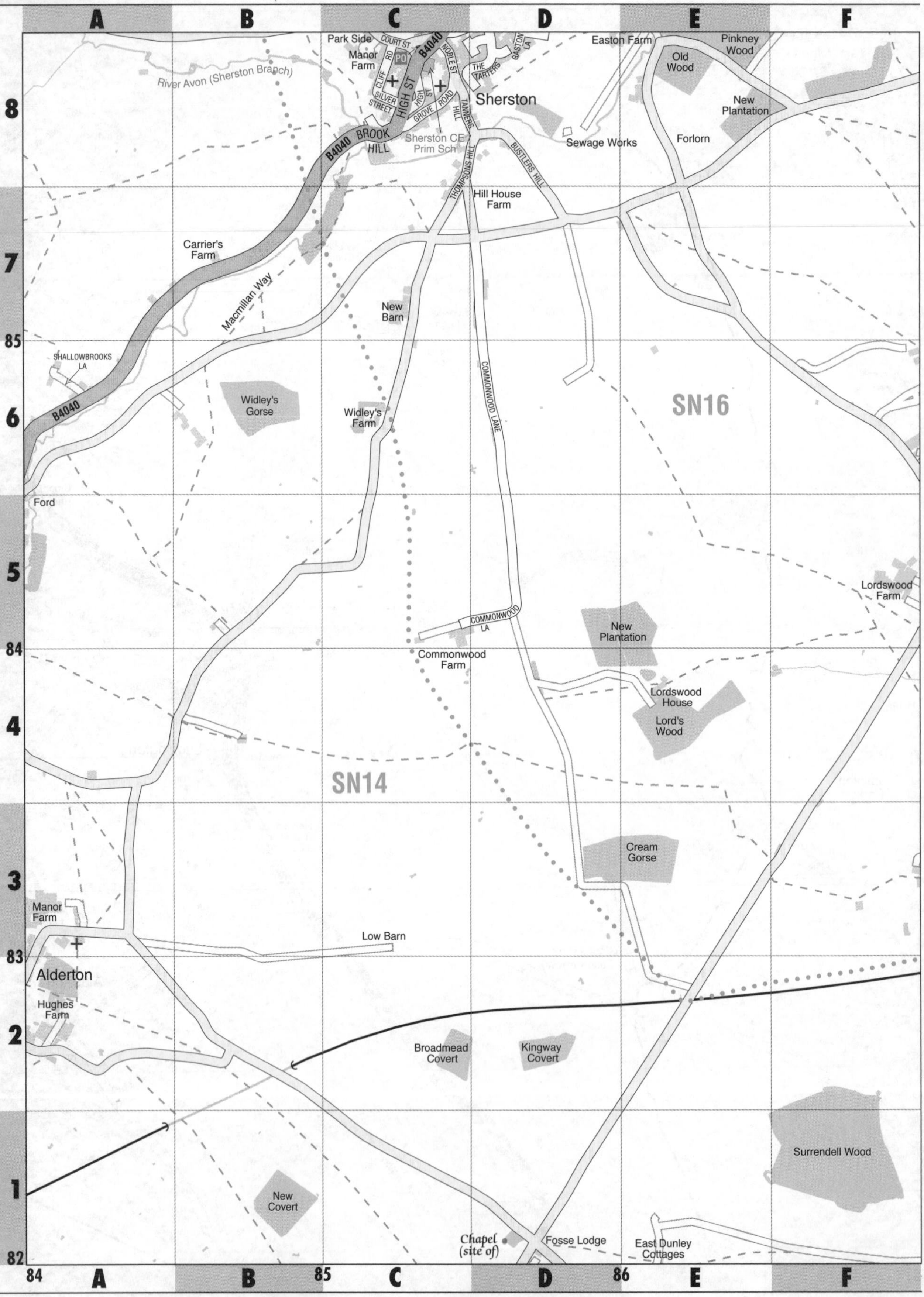

A B C D E F

8

River Avon (Sherston Branch)

Park Side
Manor Farm
COURT ST
CLIFF RD
PO
SILVER STREET
HIGH ST
B4040
GROVE ROAD
NOBLE ST
THE TARTERS
GASTON LA
Easton Farm
Old Wood
Pinkney Wood
New Plantation
Sherston
Sewage Works
Forlorn
B4040 BROOK HILL
Sherston CE Prim Sch
TANNERS
THOMPSON'S HILL
BUSTLERS HILL
Hill House Farm

7

Carrier's Farm
Macmillan Way
New Barn
COMMONWOOD LANE

85

SHALLOWBROOKS LA
6
B4040
Widley's Gorse
Widley's Farm
SN16

Ford

5
Lordswood Farm

84
Commonwood Farm
COMMONWOOD LA
New Plantation
Lordswood House

4
Lord's Wood

SN14

Cream Gorse

3

Manor Farm
Low Barn

83
Alderton
Hughes Farm
2
Broadmead Covert
Kingway Covert

Surrendell Wood

1
New Covert

82
Chapel (site of)
Fosse Lodge
East Dunley Cottages

84 A B 85 C D 86 E F

39
54

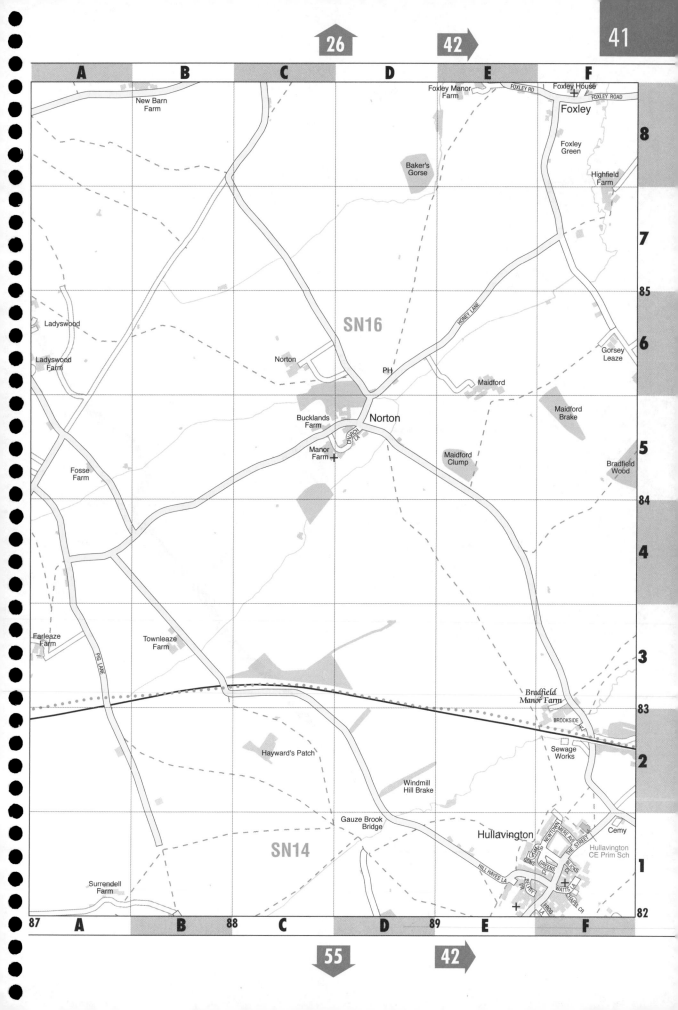

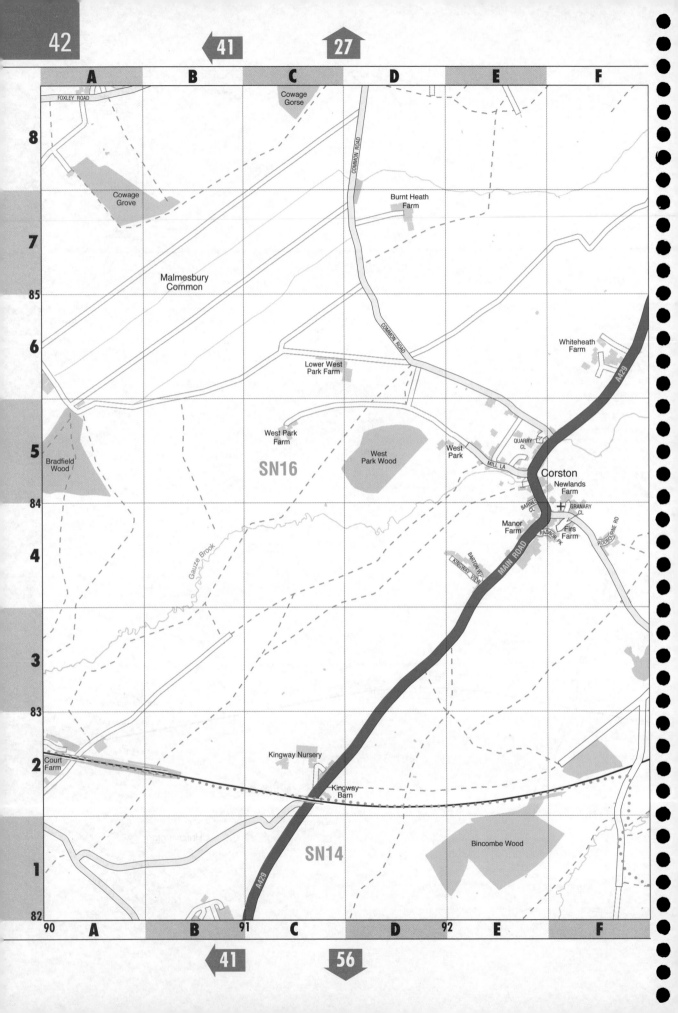

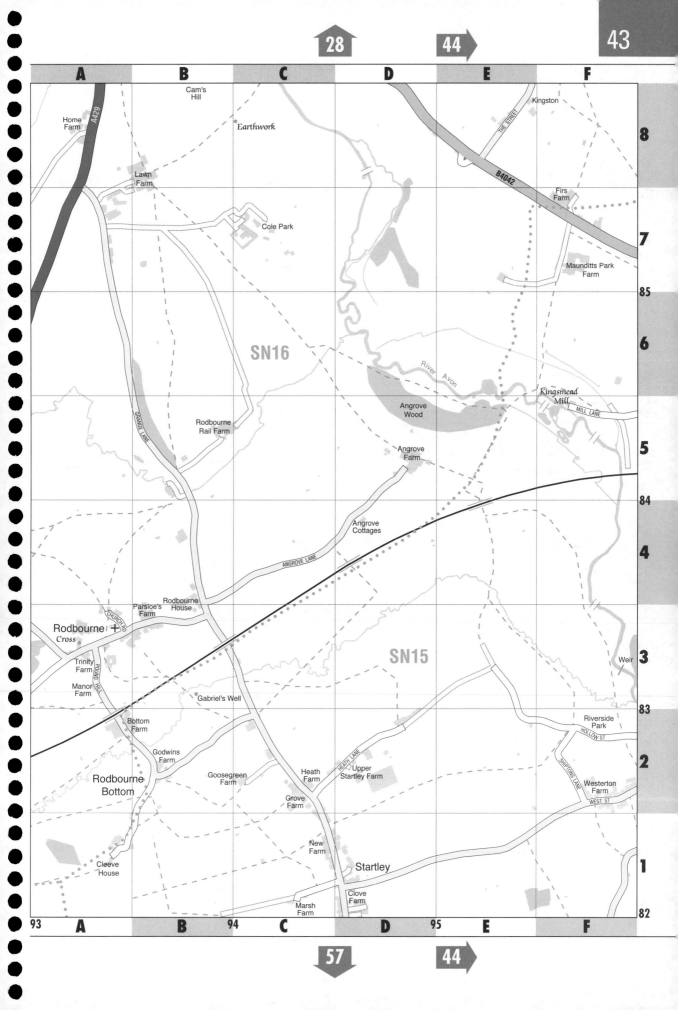

A   B   C   D   E   F

SN16

Chink Farm

Cleverton Farm

Manor Farm

Coles Farm

Cleverton

Lea Wood

CRESSWELL LANE

Street Farm

Crows Nest Farm

8

Malthouse Cottage Farm

7

B4042

Hillview Farm

Lovett Farm

B4042

Malthouse Farm

85

Coach House Farm

THE HILL

CLAY STREET

6

Field End

East End Farm

EAST END LANE

PH

Kingsmead House

Forge Mill Farm

THE STREET

MILL

Yew Tree Farm

5

Church Farm

Manor Farm

Little Somerford

MILL LANE

MEADOW LANE

Cemy

Brinkworth Brook

84

SN15

The Council Houses

Somerford Bridge

4

The Withy Bed

Idover Demesne Farm

3

Peter's Wood

Motte

River Avon

Home Idover Farm

Brook Farm

Nannies Belt

Church Farm

FROG LA

83

PARK LANE

THE FOLLY

WINKINS LA

Great Somerford

HOLLOW STREET

TOP STREET

WINKINS LA

PADDOCK CL

Somerfords Walter Powell VA CE Prim Sch

2

RIVERSIDE PK

MANOR PK

WEST STREET

The Lake Covert

Dauntsey Park

PH

PO

Dauntsey House

Dauntsey End

DAUNTSEY ROAD

CHURCH LANE

Broadfield Farm

Dauntsey Church Bridge

1

Downfield Farm

Idover House

Glebe Farm

RIDGEWAY LA

CHURCH LANE

82

MILE DR

Chestnut Farm

96   A   B   97   C   D   98   E   F

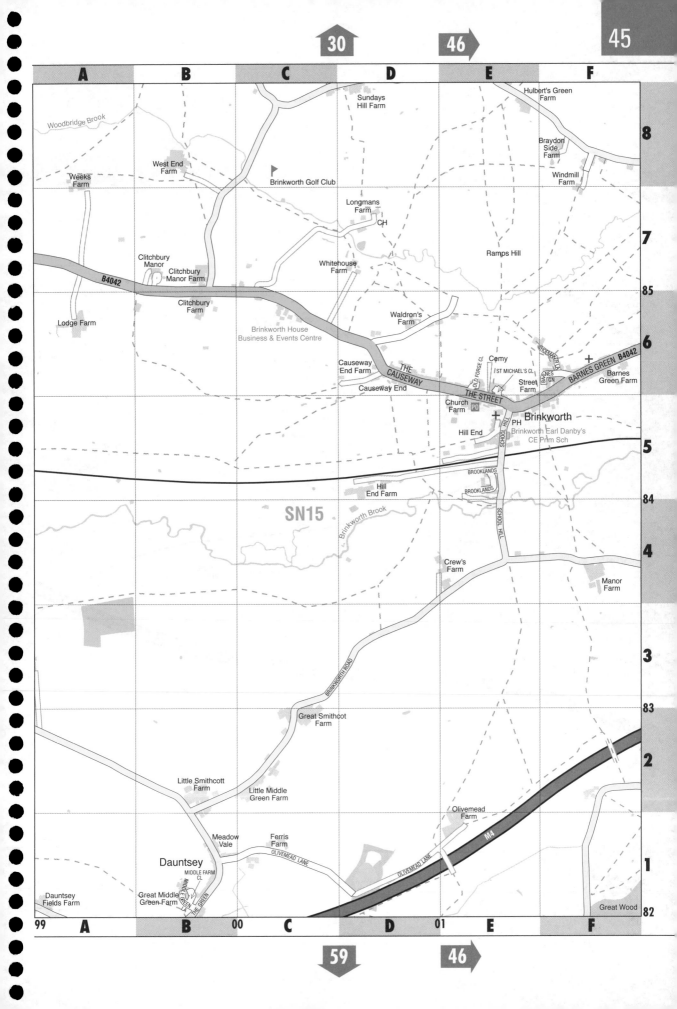

A B C D E F

8

Woodbridge Brook

Home Farm
Echo Lodge Farm
Webb's Wood

Woodside Farm

Wood Lane Farm

Echo Lodge Meadows Nature Reserve

WOOD LANE

P

Seven Island Pond

7

Stoppers Hill Farm
York La
Yorks Farm
YORK LANE
CUTS CL
Box Bush Farm
THE STREET
Lower Box Bush Farm
B4042
BARNES GREEN

Bellamys Farm

Mill House Farm

Fritterswell Farm
The Common
PH
SHEPPARDS RI

East End

85

East Side
East End Farm
Highgate Farm

6

CALLOWS CROSS
CROSSWAYS
Poplar Farm
Callow Hill
B4042

5

SN15

Pittsland Farm

Callow Hill Farm

Highgate Cottage

Withy Bed

84

Hillside Farm

4

Brinkworth Brook

Dovey's Farm
Dovey's Bridge

3

Whites Farm

M4

Hooker's Gate Farm

83

Lukers Farm
Vines Farm

2

Pinnells Farm
Grittenham
Ivy House Farm
Goddards Farm
SN4

Grove Farm
Old Park Farm

1

Great Wood

82

02 A 03 B C 04 D E F

F8		7 HARVESTER CL
1 KINGSCOTE CL		8 FENLAND CL
2 BRAYBROOKE CL		9 MALDWYN CL
3 SANDACRE RD		10 LUCERNE CL
4 GRANARY CL		11 ALBA CL
5 ASKERTON CL		12 LAMORA CL
6 STARING CL		13 CHEVALIER CL

A B C D E F

Godwins Farm
Lydiard Green
THE BUTTS
Cemy
Lydiard Millicent CE Prim Sch
Lydiard Farm
CHESTNUT SPRINGS
THE CLOSE
CHESTNUT SPRINGS
THE MEWS
CHESTNUT SPRINGS
CHERRY BRICK CL
THE MEWS
MEADOW SPRINGS
Lydiard Millicent
PH
THE ST
PARKWAY DR
FORGE FIELDS
WALNUT TREE GD
PARK LA
OLD SHAW LA
MAYLE
GARTONS RD
MIDDLELEZE DR
KITCHEN CL
CANTON CL
DANESTONE CL
TEWKESBURY WAY

Parkside Farm
Alder Plantation
TEWKESBURY WAY
SPENCER CLOSE
VILLIERS CL

Ash Plantation
Lydiard Tregoze
OLIVER CL
WHITGIFT CL 1
CHANCELLOR CL 2
TREGOZE WAY
WILMOT CL
WHITMORE CL

Park Copse
Lower Hook Farm
Cemy
Lydiard House
HAMPTON DR
HAY LANE
DARCY
Lydiard Park
BANCROFT CL

Hook Farm
Hook Street
SN5
Elm Plantation
Quarr Plantation
Lydiard Park Academy
GRANGE PK
HAMPTON DR
CAMPION CL

Letterage Copse
P
Park Farm
Grange Park
MULCASTER AVE
FOWINS
SIMBERSIDE WY
GRINDLE

M4
Midge Hall
KING HENRY DR
HOOK ST
LINGACRE CL

Church Hill Farm
Chiseldon Windmill
Windmill Hill Business Park
Lydiard Fields Business Park
CLINTON CL
VALE

Spittleborough Farm
Hotel
GREAT WESTERN WY
B4534
WHITEHILL WAY
STONEOVER LA
A3102
SWINDON ROAD
PH
SWINDON ROAD
A3102
SN4
16
Hagbourne Copse Nat Res
EURO CL
SN1
Hotel
Blagrove Employment Area
M4
FRANKLIN RD
RAMSDEN RD

Woodshaw
CHURCHILL CL
GARRAWAYS
MALGROUND
GARRAWAYS
BAILEY'S
HARRIS
RAVENS WK
HON GROVE
BINKNOLL LA
Wickfield Farm
Upper Studley Farm
B4005
HAY LA

Lower Woodshaw Farm
Harris Croft Farm
Butterfly World

08 A B 09 C D 10 E F

A2		F4	F5		10 BONNER CL
1 LINDISFARNE		1 LOUGHBOROUGH CL	1 GOWER CL		11 WARBECK GATE
2 WOOLFORD GRANGE		2 AUDLEY CL	2 JEWEL CL		12 MILDMAY CL
3 ORCHARD MEAD		3 HILLYARD CL	3 ASKEW CL		13 BYRD CL
4 BARDSEY CL		4 HEYTSBURY GDNS	4 SARLACDO CL		14 HADDON CL
5 ARRAN CL		5 CONYERS CL	5 TITCHFIELD CL		
6 ALDERNEY CL			6 BALE CL		
7 SQUIRES HL CL			7 PARHAM WK		
8 WOODSHAW MEAD			8 DEVEREUX CL		
9 SWALLOWS MEAD			9 BABINGTON PK		

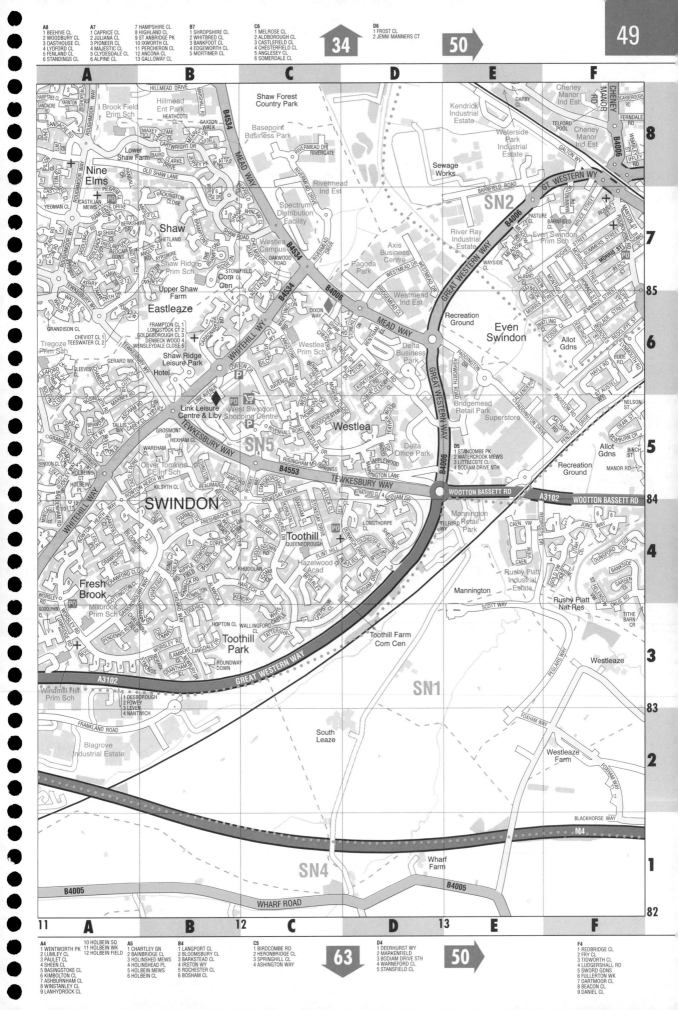

49

35

49

64

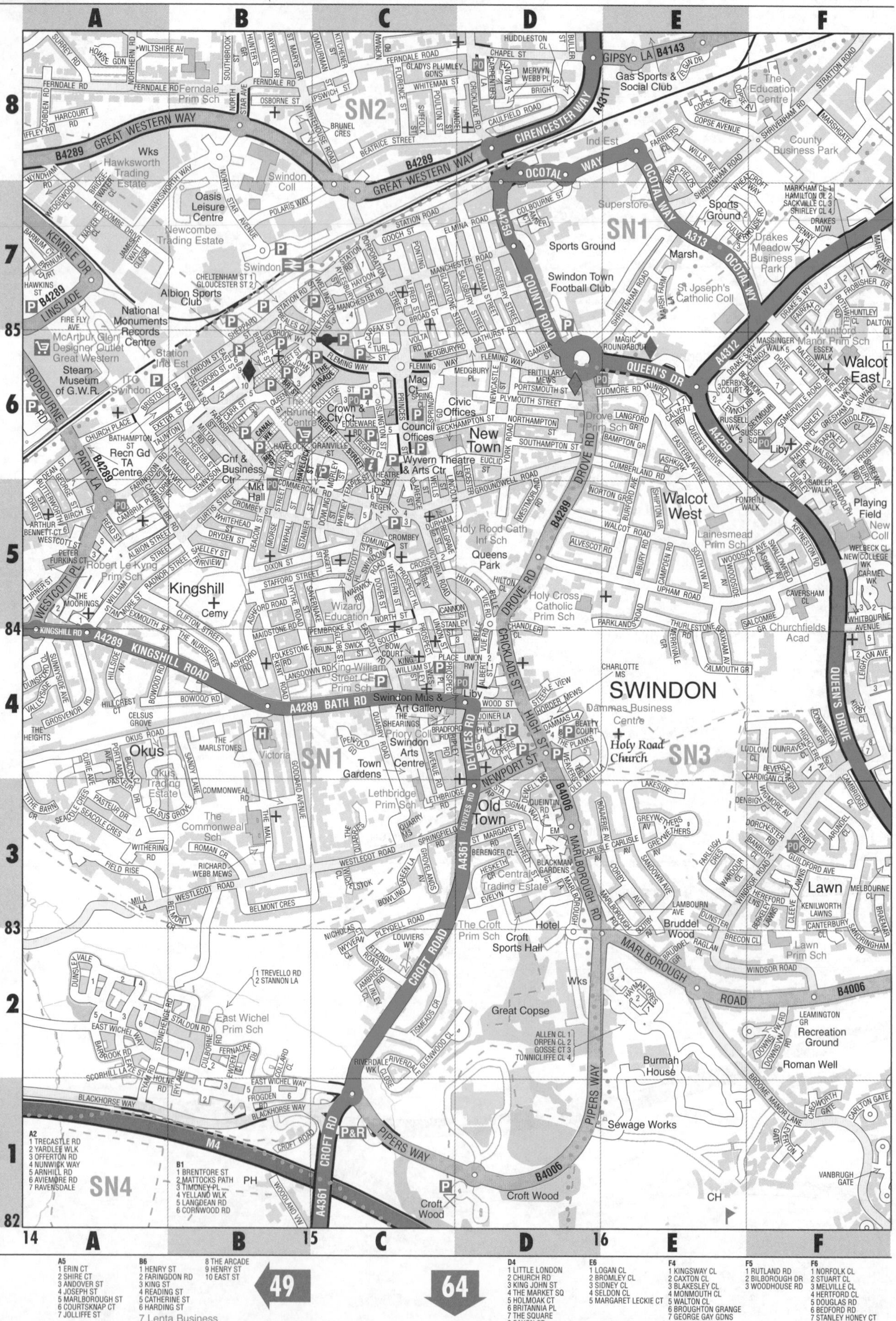

SWINDON

SN1 · SN2 · SN3 · SN4

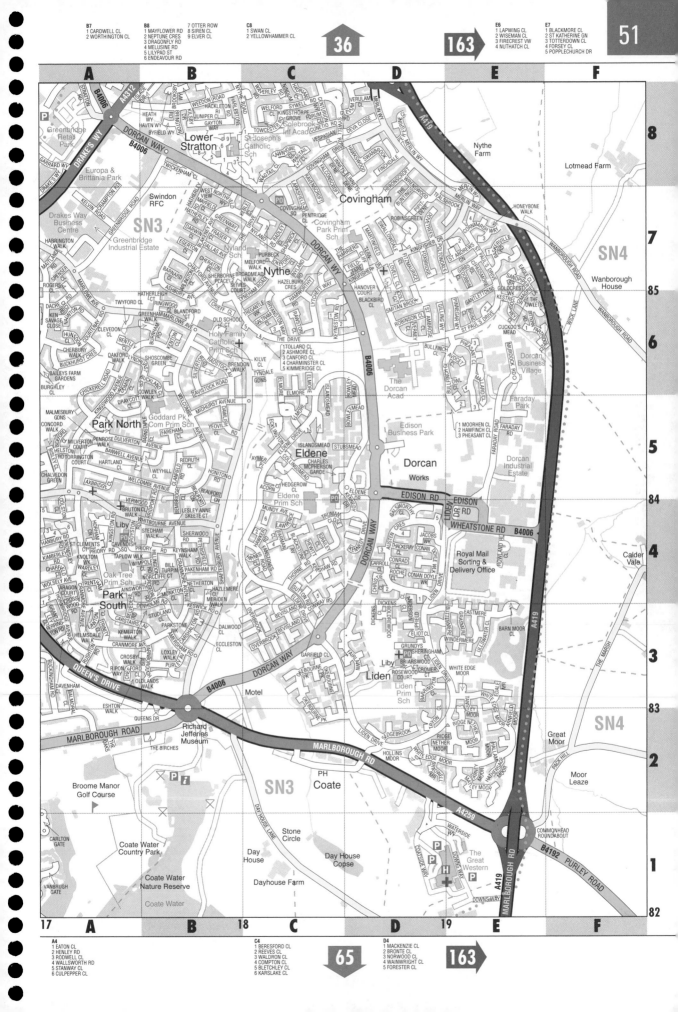

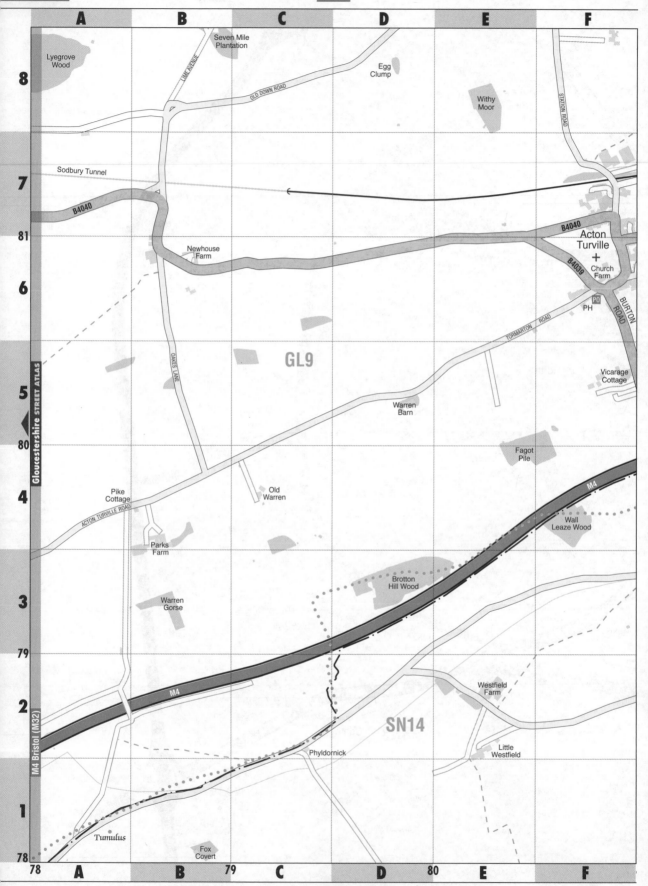

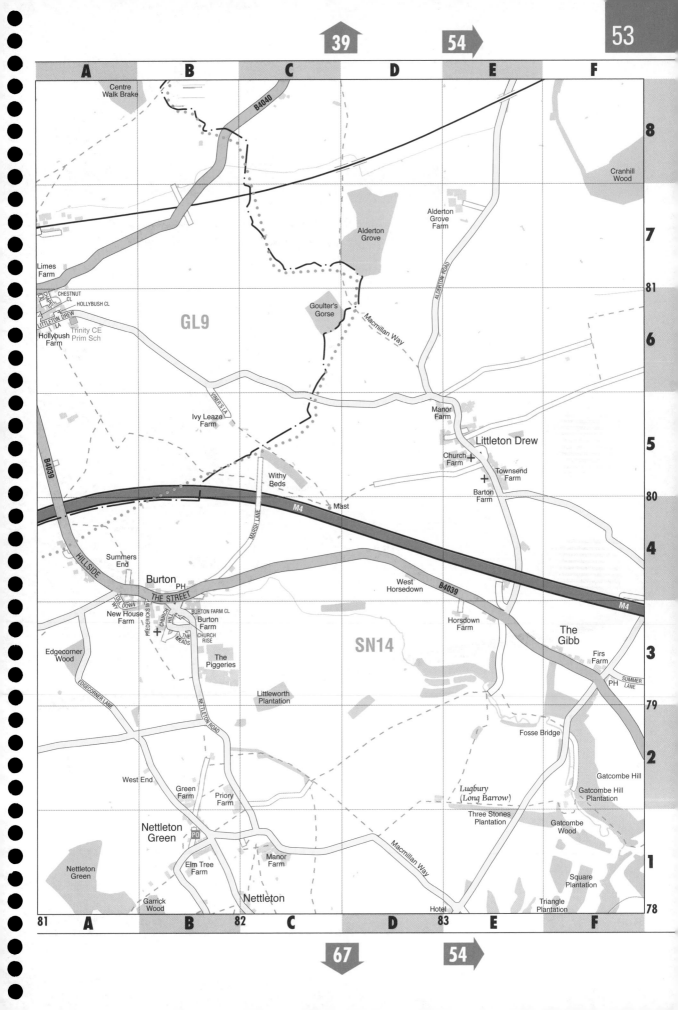

A   B   C   D   E   F

8

Centre
Walk Brake

B4040

Cranhill
Wood

7

Alderton
Grove
Farm

Alderton
Grove

81

Limes
Farm

CHESTNUT
CL
HOLLYBUSH CL

GL9

Goulter's
Gorse

Macmillan Way

ALDERTON ROAD

6

CHAPEL CL

LITTLETON DREW LA

Trinity CE
Prim Sch

Hollybush
Farm

VINER'S LA

Ivy Leaze
Farm

Manor
Farm

Littleton Drew

5

Church
Farm

Townsend
Farm

Withy
Beds

Barton
Farm

80

B4039

MARSH LANE

M4

Mast

4

HILLSIDE

Summers
End

Burton   PH

West
Horsedown

B4039

M4

THE STREET

TOLL DOWN WAY

FREDERICK'S WY

New House
Farm

CHURCH HILL

THE MEADS

BURTON FARM CL
Burton
Farm
CHURCH RISE

Horsdown
Farm

The
Gibb

3

Edgecorner
Wood

The
Piggeries

SN14

Firs
Farm

SUMMER LANE

PH

EDGECORNER LANE

NETTLETON ROAD

Littleworth
Plantation

79

Fosse Bridge

2

West End

Green
Farm

Priory
Farm

Lugbury
(Long Barrow)

Gatcombe Hill

Gatcombe Hill
Plantation

Nettleton
Green

Three Stones
Plantation

Gatcombe
Wood

PO

1

Nettleton
Green

Elm Tree
Farm

Manor
Farm

Macmillan Way

Square
Plantation

Garrick
Wood

Nettleton

Hotel

Triangle
Plantation

78

53

40

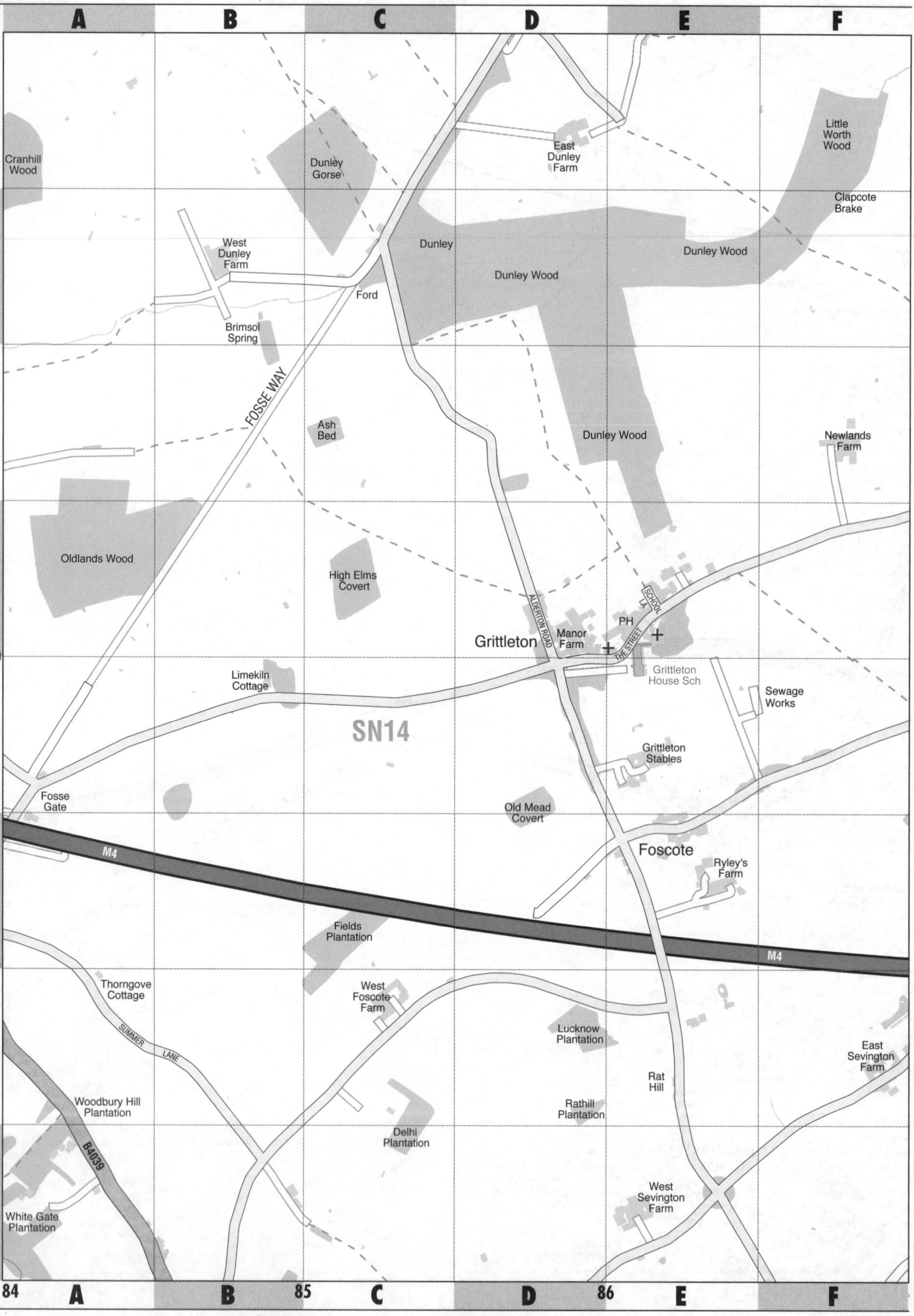

A B C D E F

8

Cranhill Wood

Dunley Gorse

East Dunley Farm

Little Worth Wood

Clapcote Brake

7

West Dunley Farm

Dunley

Dunley Wood

Dunley Wood

81

Brimsol Spring

Ford

FOSSE WAY

6

Ash Bed

Dunley Wood

Newlands Farm

Oldlands Wood

5

High Elms Covert

SCHOOL

ALDERTON ROAD

PH

THE STREET

Grittleton

Manor Farm

Grittleton House Sch

80

Limekiln Cottage

SN14

Sewage Works

4

Grittleton Stables

Fosse Gate

Old Mead Covert

M4

Foscote

Ryley's Farm

3

Fields Plantation

M4

79

Thorngove Cottage

West Foscote Farm

Lucknow Plantation

East Sevington Farm

2

SUMMER LANE

Rat Hill

Woodbury Hill Plantation

Delhi Plantation

Rathill Plantation

B4039

1

White Gate Plantation

West Sevington Farm

78

84 A B 85 C D 86 E F

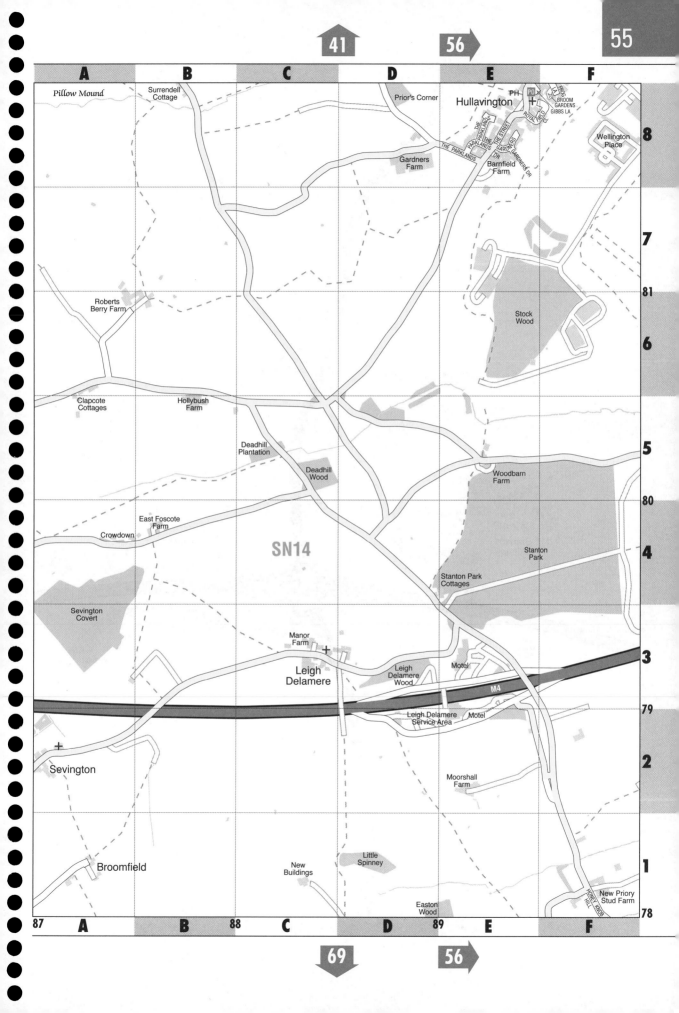

55
42

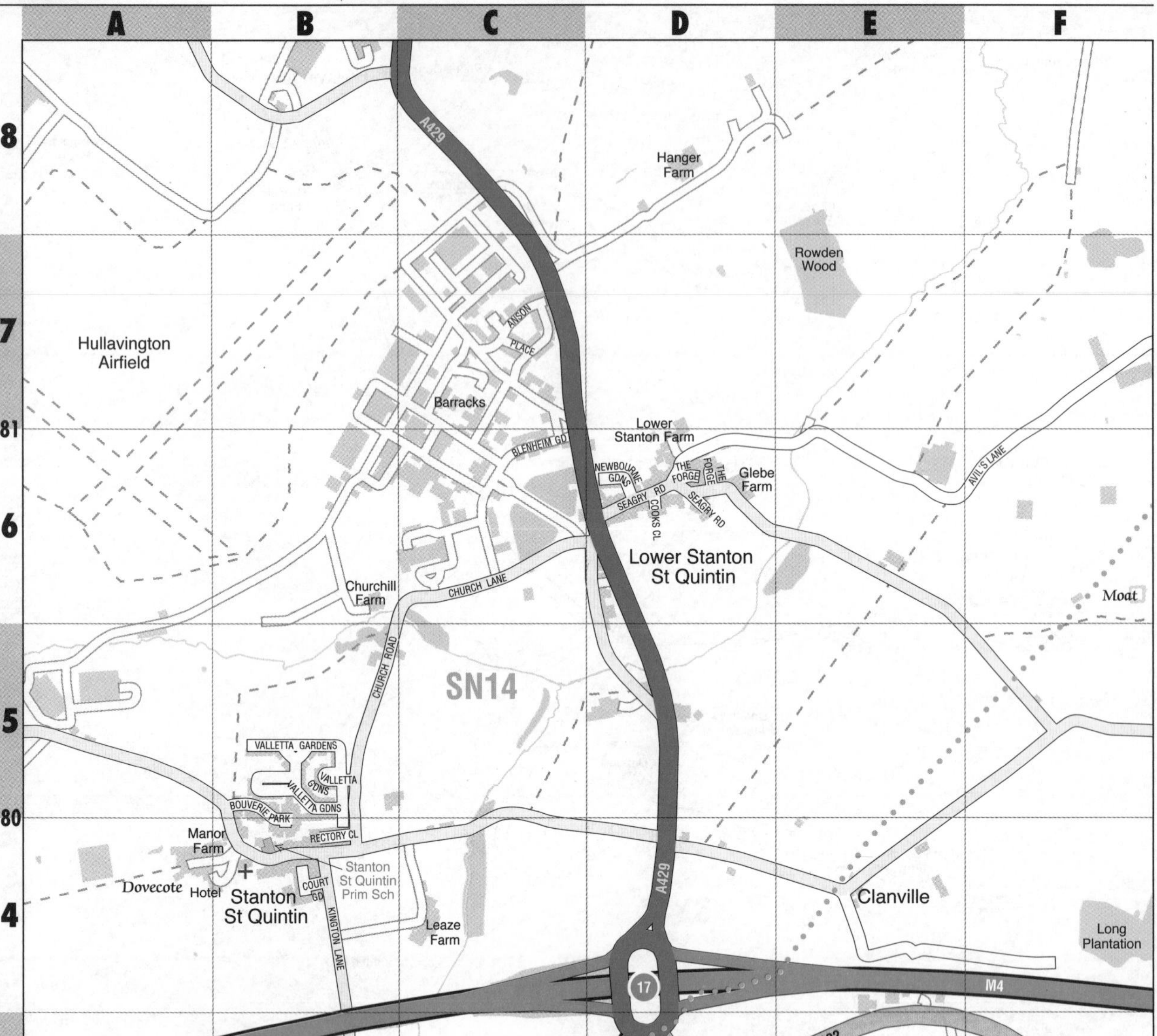

A   B   C   D   E   F

8

Hanger Farm

Rowden Wood

7

Hullavington Airfield

ANSON PLACE

81

Barracks

Lower Stanton Farm

BLENHEIM GD

NEWBOURNE GDNS

THE FORGE

Glebe Farm

SEAGRY RD

COONS CL

THE RIDGE

SEAGRY RD

AVIL'S LANE

6

Churchill Farm

CHURCH LANE

Lower Stanton St Quintin

Moat

CHURCH ROAD

SN14

5

VALLETTA GARDENS

VALLETTA GDNS

BOUVERIE PARK

VALLETTA GDNS

80

Manor Farm

RECTORY CL

Clanville

Dovecote

Hotel

Stanton St Quintin

COURT GD

Stanton St Quintin Prim Sch

A429

Long Plantation

4

KINGTON LANE

Leaze Farm

17

M4

Upper Swinley Farm

M4

B4122

Westbrook Farm

3

Mast

Springfield Farm

Lower Swinley Farm

79

SN15

2

A350

Whitelands Farm

DAY'S LANE

Ford

Southsea Farm

1

Draycot Cerne

STANTON LA

78

90   A   B   91   C   D   92   E   F

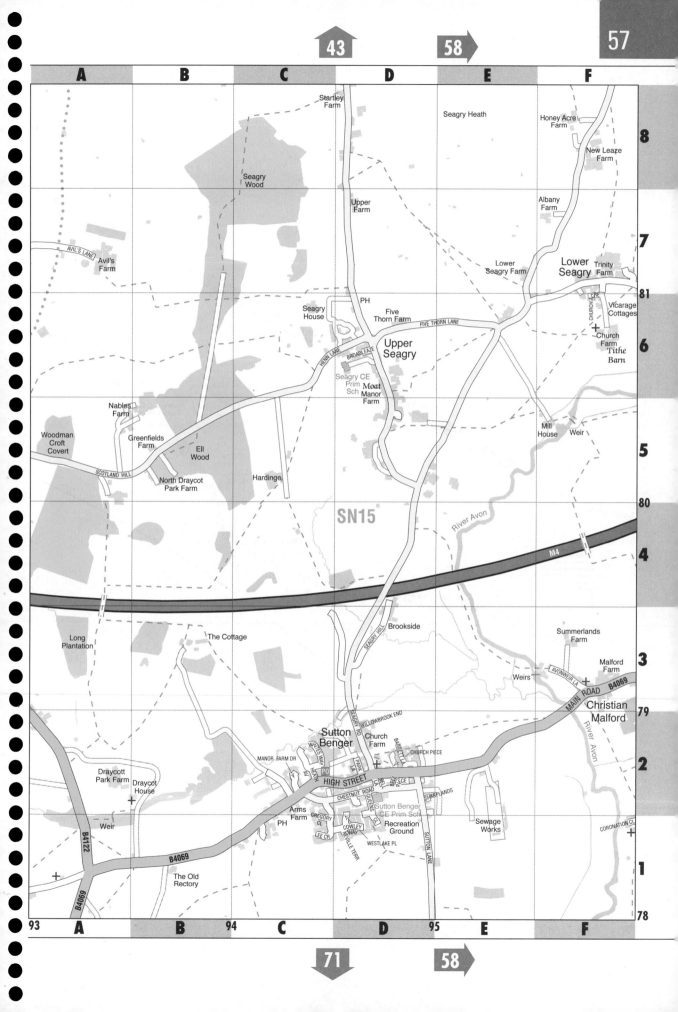

57
44

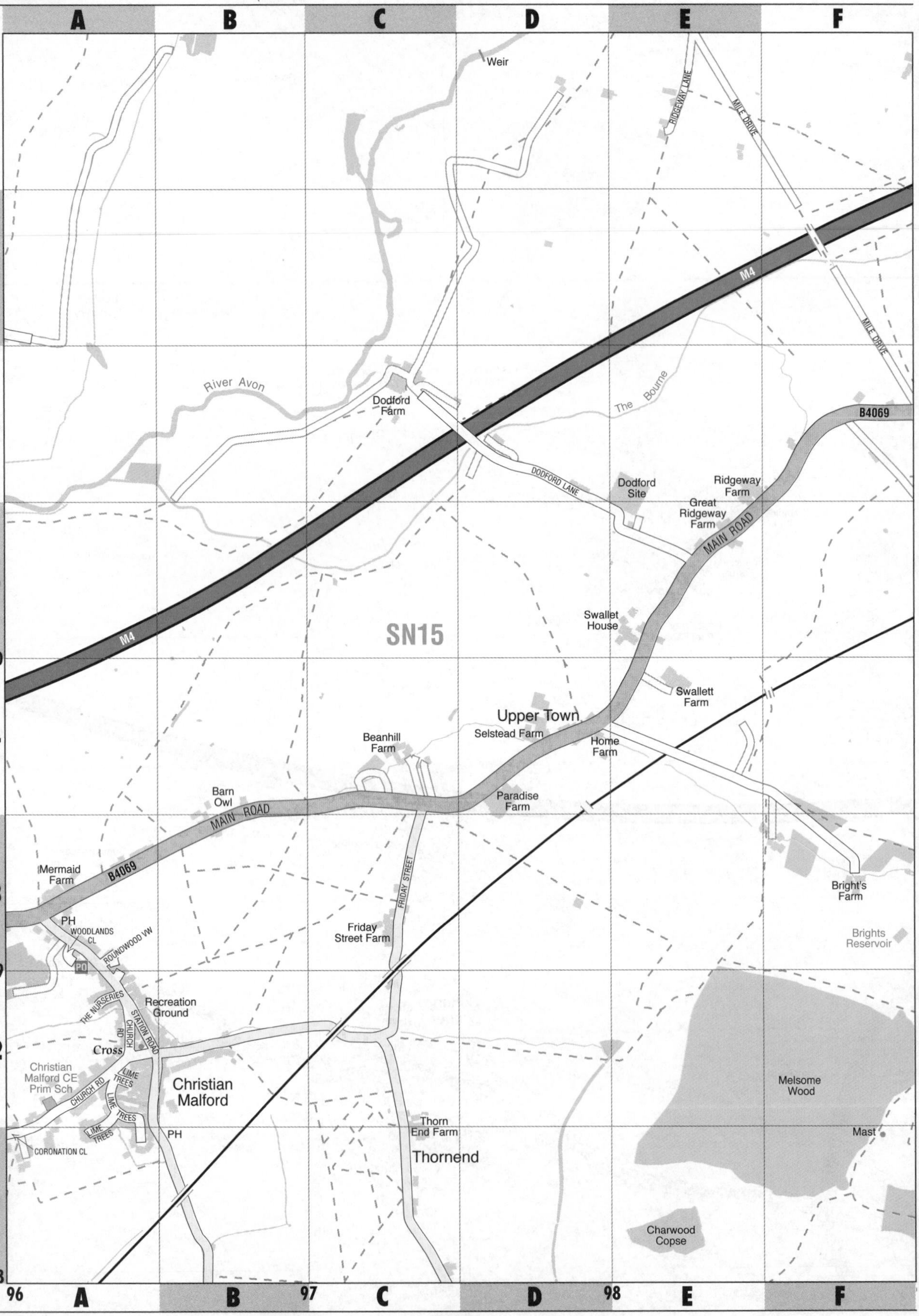

A B C D E F

8

7

81

6

5

80

4

3

79

2

1

78

Weir

RIDGEWAY LANE

MILE DRIVE

M4

River Avon

Dodford Farm

The Bourne

B4069

DODFORD LANE

Dodford Site

Ridgeway Farm

Great Ridgeway Farm

MAIN ROAD

MILE DRIVE

SN15

Swallet House

Swallett Farm

Upper Town

Selstead Farm

Home Farm

Beanhill Farm

Barn Owl

MAIN ROAD

Paradise Farm

Bright's Farm

Mermaid Farm

B4069

PH

WOODLANDS CL

ROUNDWOOD VW

FRIDAY STREET

Friday Street Farm

Brights Reservoir

PO

THE NURSERIES

Recreation Ground

STATION ROAD

CHURCH ROAD

Cross

CHURCH RD

LIME TREES

Christian Malford CE Prim Sch

Christian Malford

LIME TREES

LIME TREES

PH

Thorn End Farm

Melsome Wood

Mast

CORONATION CL

Thornend

Charwood Copse

96 A B 97 C D 98 E F

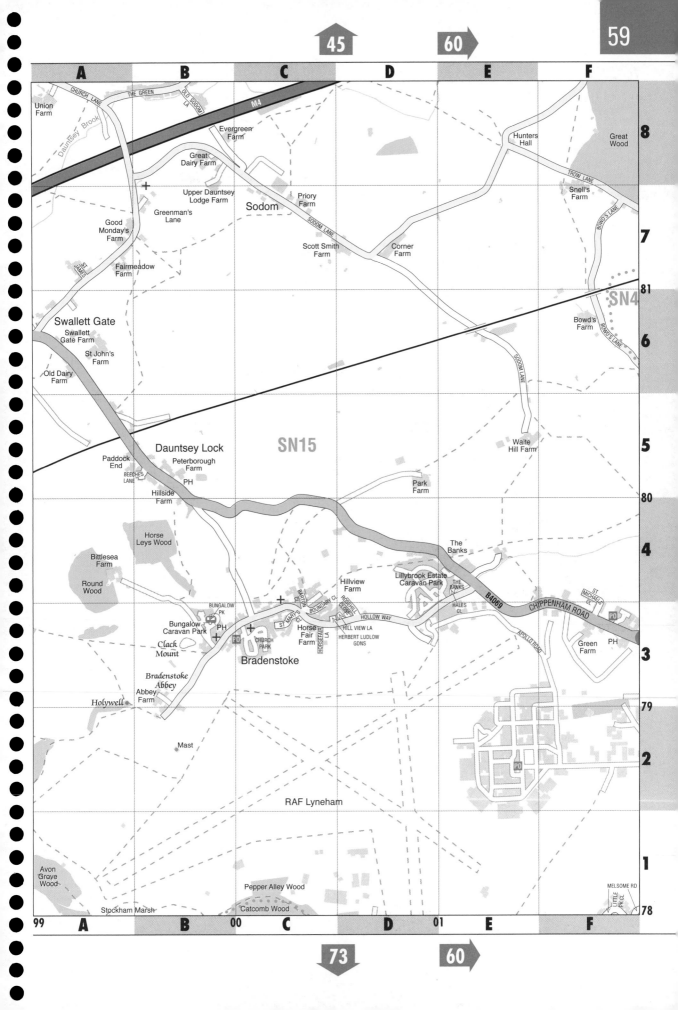

A   B   C   D   E   F

8

Great Wood

SN15

Manor House

Hart Farm

Vastern Wood

Vastern

Old Park Farm

Cheeseley Hill Farm

7

Great Wood Farm

Trow Lane Farm

TROW LANE

West Close Copse

Manor House

Tockenham Wick

A3102

Wiltshire Bassett Golf Club

81

BOWD'S LA

Hillocks Wood

Tockenham Reservoir

Teagles Copse

6

THE HILLOCKS

A3102

Tockenham Corner

PRIMROSE HILL

Tockenham Manor Farm

SN4

5

Shaw Farm

Rowley Copse

80

Brickkiln Copse

THE GREEN

4

FARTHING LA

SN15

Beckett's Copse

Shaw Farm

Court Farm

Queen Court Farm

Moat

Tockenham Farm

Cowleaze Copse

3

POUND CL

WEBBS CL

PH

Manorhouse Farm

✚ Tockenham

Greenway Farm

GREENWAY

A3102

HOCKEY'S LA

BAKERS FIELD

79

CHURCH FARM MEWS

Lancaster Square

Lyneham

HARROW GROVE

HASTINGS DRIVE

Tockenham Court Farm

Middlehill Farm

Church End

Liby

CHURCH LA

CALNE RD

Lyneham Prim Sch

BELFAST

MEAD

YORK RD

LIME CL

2

AF

Lyneham CHURCH END CL

ST JOSEPH'S

ARMSTRONG RD

COMET CL

CROSS

PO

BRITANNIA CL

ASH

SYCAMORE CL

VICTORIA DRIVE

A3102

ELDER AVE

TEAL AVENUE

SHIELD DR

MALLARD AVE

ALDER AV

PINTAIL

PINTAIL CT

ELM CL

ARGOSY RD

1

CALNE ROAD

SLESSOR RD

SLES TRENCHARD

DICKSON RD

PORTAL PL

PRESTON LANE

Preston End Farm

Preston

Preston East Farm

Thickthorn Farm

78

MELSOME RD

02   A   B   03   C   D   04   E   F

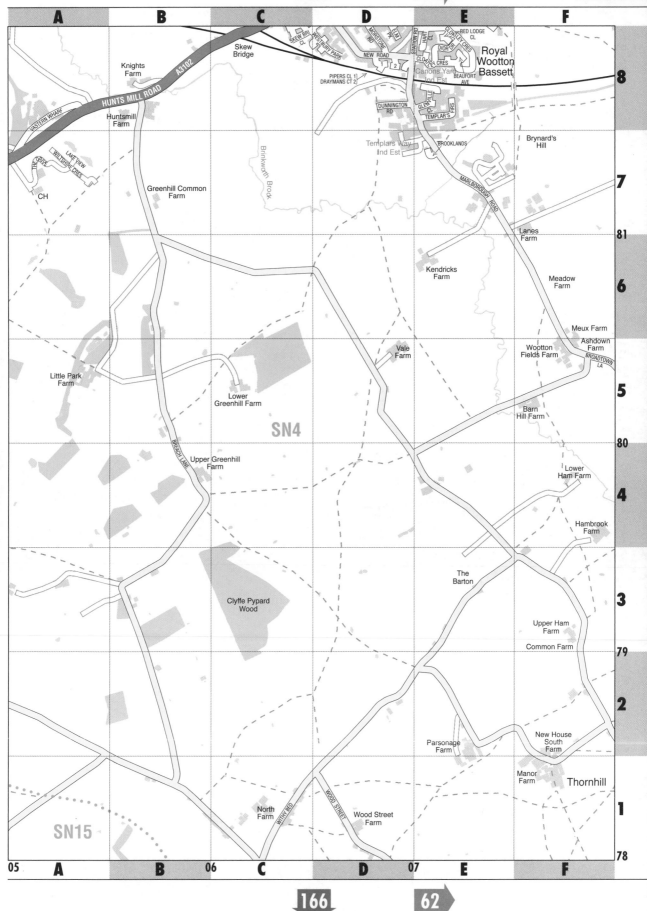

A B C D E F

A B C D E F

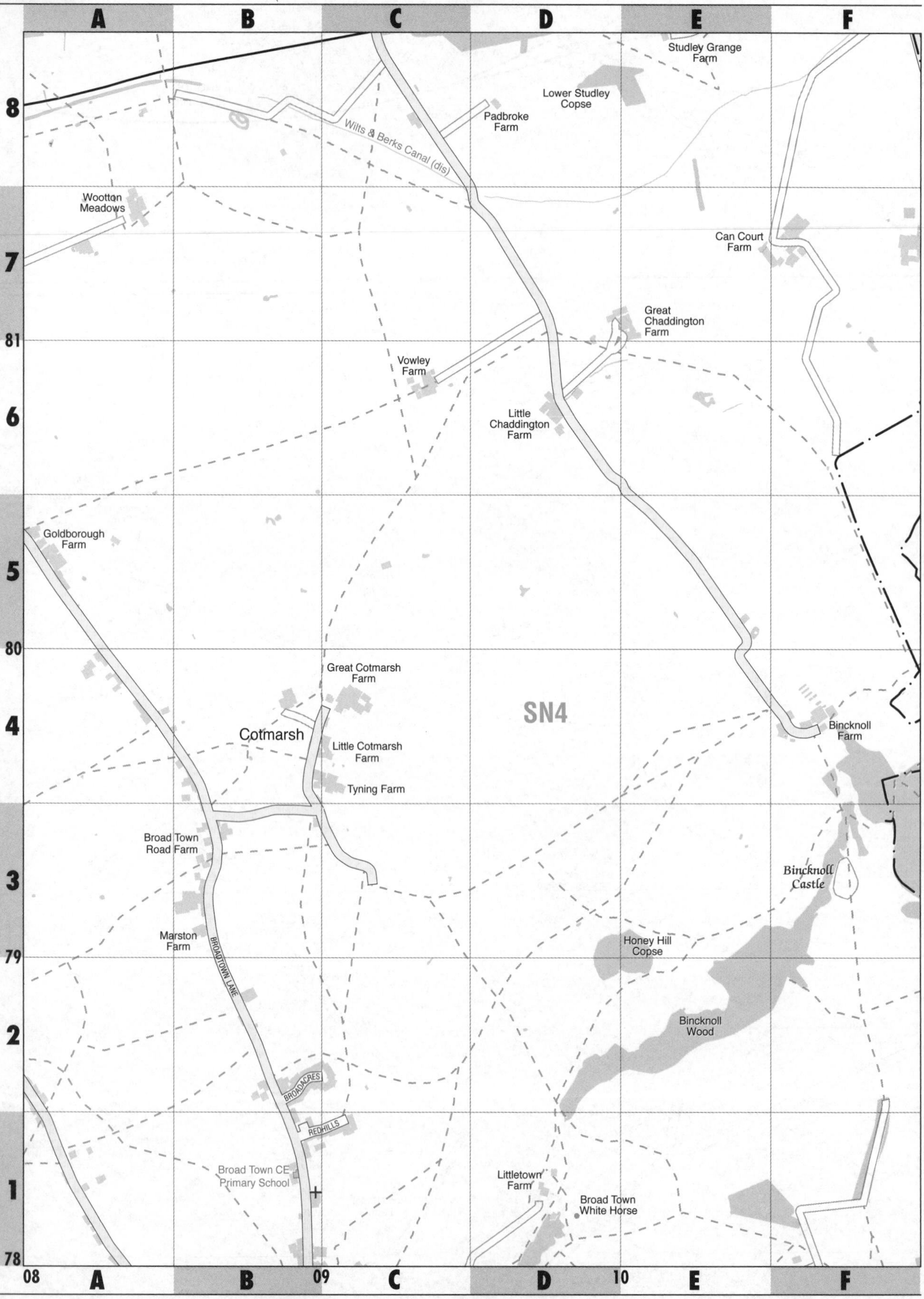

8

Wilts & Berks Canal (dis)

Studley Grange Farm

Lower Studley Copse

Padbroke Farm

Wootton Meadows

Can Court Farm

7

81

Great Chaddington Farm

Vowley Farm

6

Little Chaddington Farm

Goldborough Farm

5

80

SN4

Great Cotmarsh Farm

Bincknoll Farm

4

Cotmarsh

Little Cotmarsh Farm

Tyning Farm

Broad Town Road Farm

Bincknoll Castle

3

Marston Farm

Honey Hill Copse

BROADTOWN LANE

79

Bincknoll Wood

2

BROADACRES

REDHILLS

Littletown Farm

1

Broad Town CE Primary School

Broad Town White Horse

78

08 A 09 B C 10 D E F

A B C D E F

8

Whitehouse Farm
Common Farm

Glebe Farm

Costow Farm

Berrywood Farm

Nuttery Copse

B4005

SUMMERHOUSE RD

7

Elcombe House Farm

SAVILL CR
MANSELL WAY
VICTORIA CROSS
KELLSBOROUGH RD
ELLINGTON RD

WHARF ROAD

81

Hurst Copse

ASPEN COPSE RD
BALDEN CL

HAY LANE

Horseshoe Copse

MASKELEYNE WY 1
CHARTERHOUSE RD 2

WHARF LEY CT
ELCOMBE AV
COWLEAZE CR
PH

6

Lower Basset Down Farm

Cowleaze Farm

Elcombe

Wroughton House

5

Salthrop House

Chilton Farm

Elcombe Hall

CHURCH HILL

A4361

Salthrop Wood

SN4

80

Basset Down Farm

Basset Down Wood

Beech Copse

4

Clouts Wood Nature Reserve

Quidhampton Wood

Salthrop Farm

Markham Bottom

3

Red Barn

79

Wroughton Airfield

2

A4361

1

78

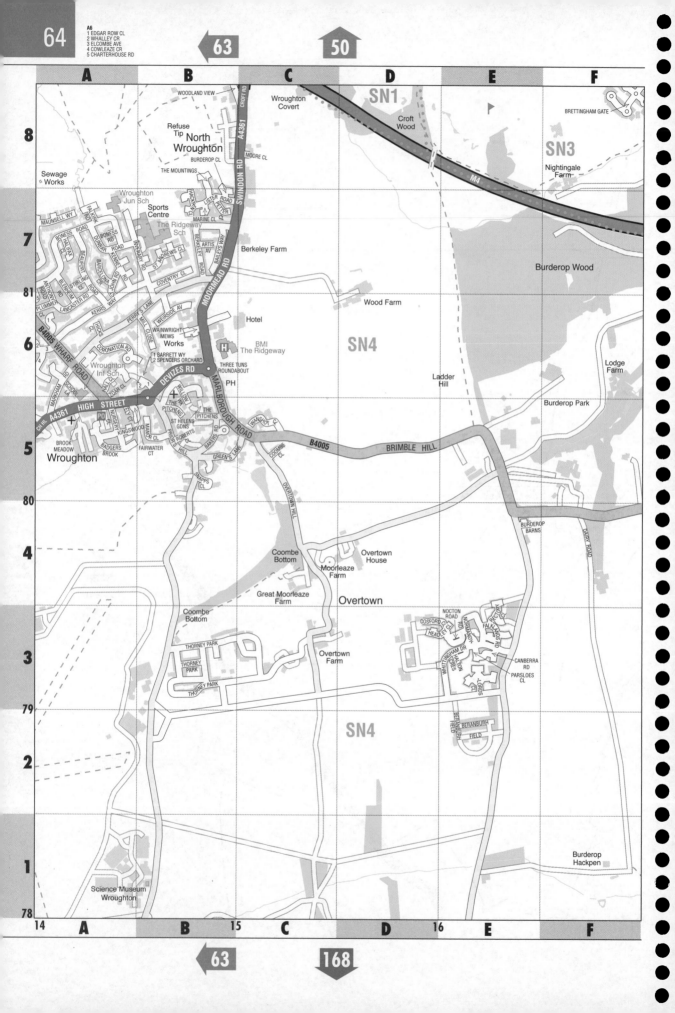

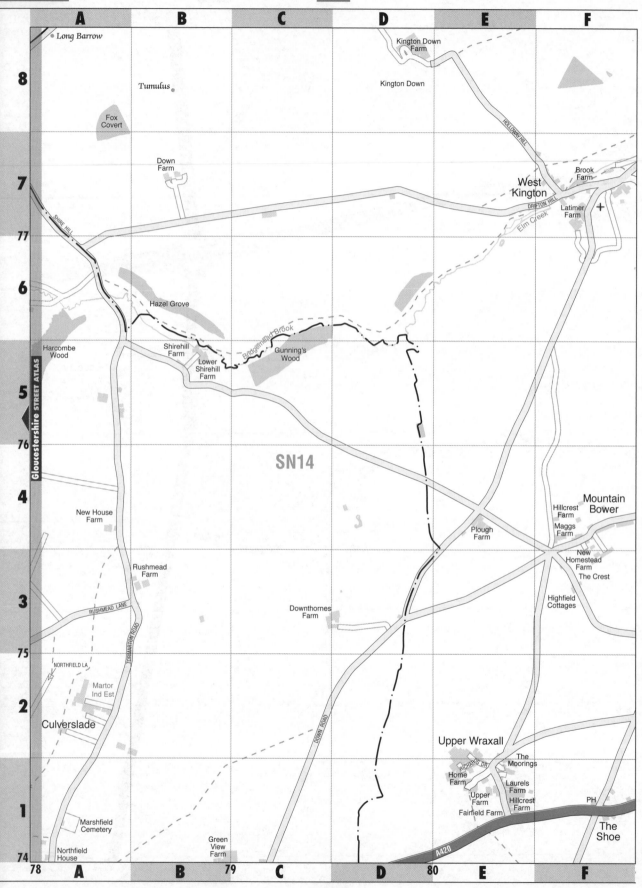

Gloucestershire STREET ATLAS

A   B   C   D   E   F

Long Barrow

8   Tumulus

Fox
Covert

Kington Down
Farm

Kington Down

HOLLOWAY HILL

7   Down
Farm

West
Kington

Brook
Farm

DRIFTON HILL

Elm Creek

Latimer
Farm

77

SHIRE HILL

6   Hazel Grove

Harcombe
Wood

Shirehill
Farm

Lower
Shirehill
Farm

Bridgemead Brook

Gunning's
Wood

5

76

SN14

4   New House
Farm

Hillcrest
Farm

Mountain
Bower

Maggs
Farm

Plough
Farm

New
Homestead
Farm
The Crest

Rushmead
Farm

Highfield
Cottages

3   RUSHMEAD LANE

Downthornes
Farm

TORMARTON ROAD

75

NORTHFIELD LA

DOWN ROAD

2   Martor
Ind Est

Culverslade

Upper Wraxall

The
Moorings

RICHARD'S DR

Home
Farm

Laurels
Farm

Hillcrest
Farm

PH

1   Marshfield
Cemetery

Upper
Farm
Fairfield Farm

The
Shoe

Northfield
House

Green
View
Farm

A420

74

78   A   B   79   C   D   80   E   F

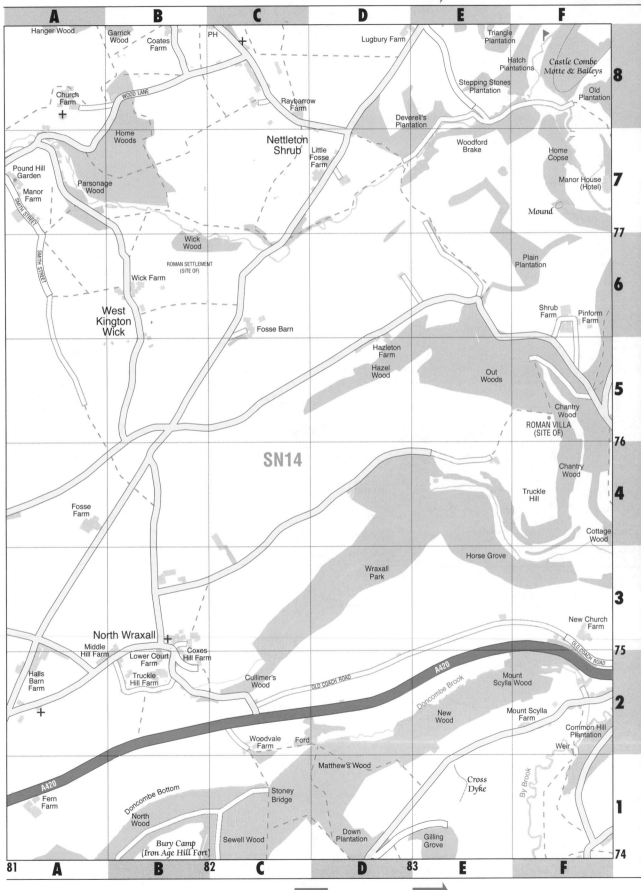

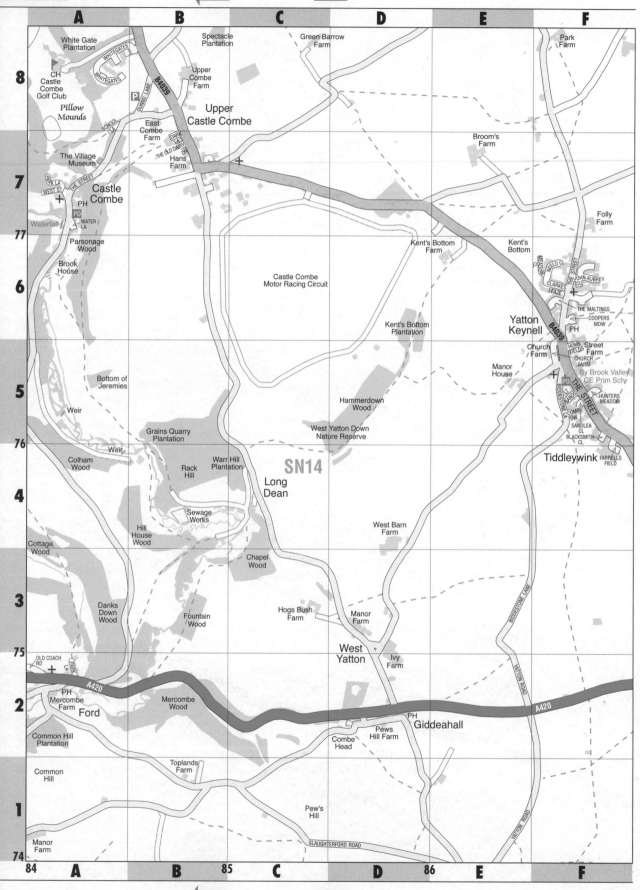

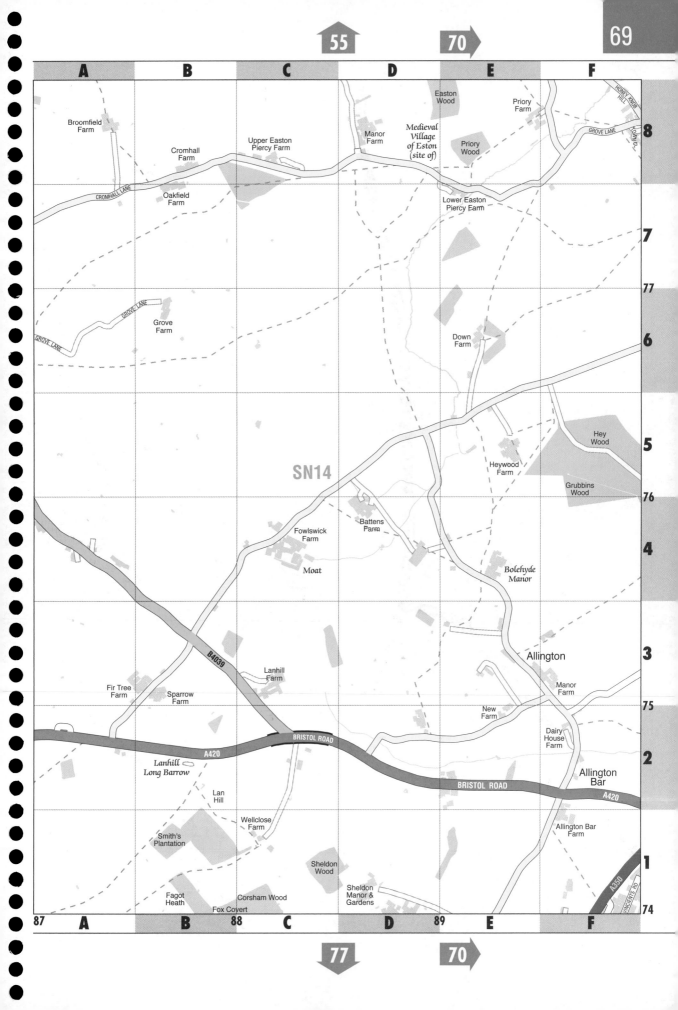

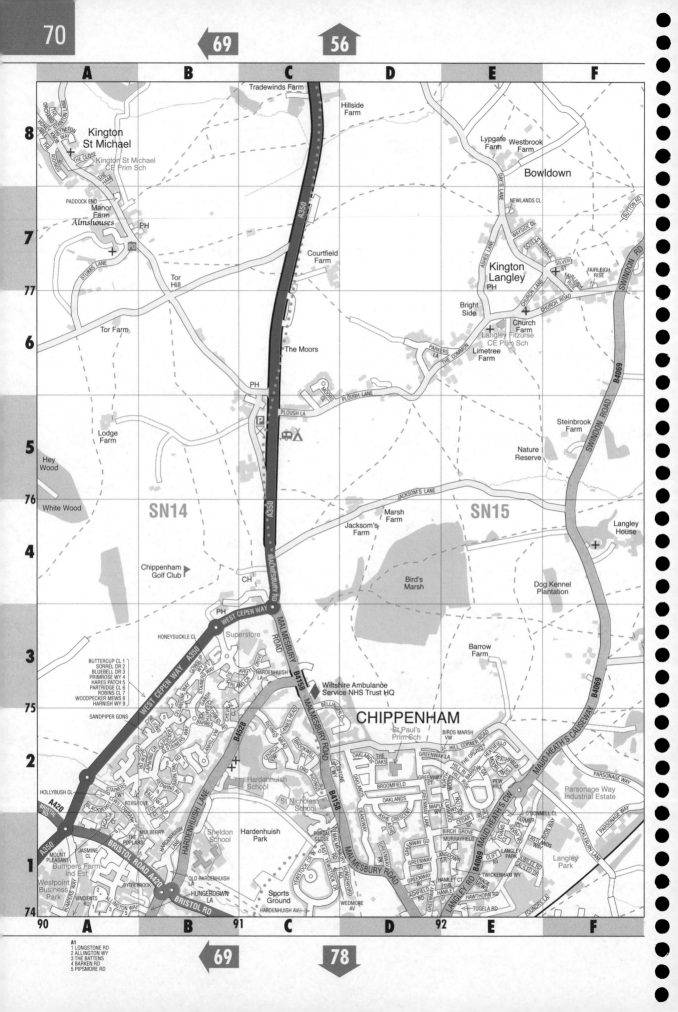

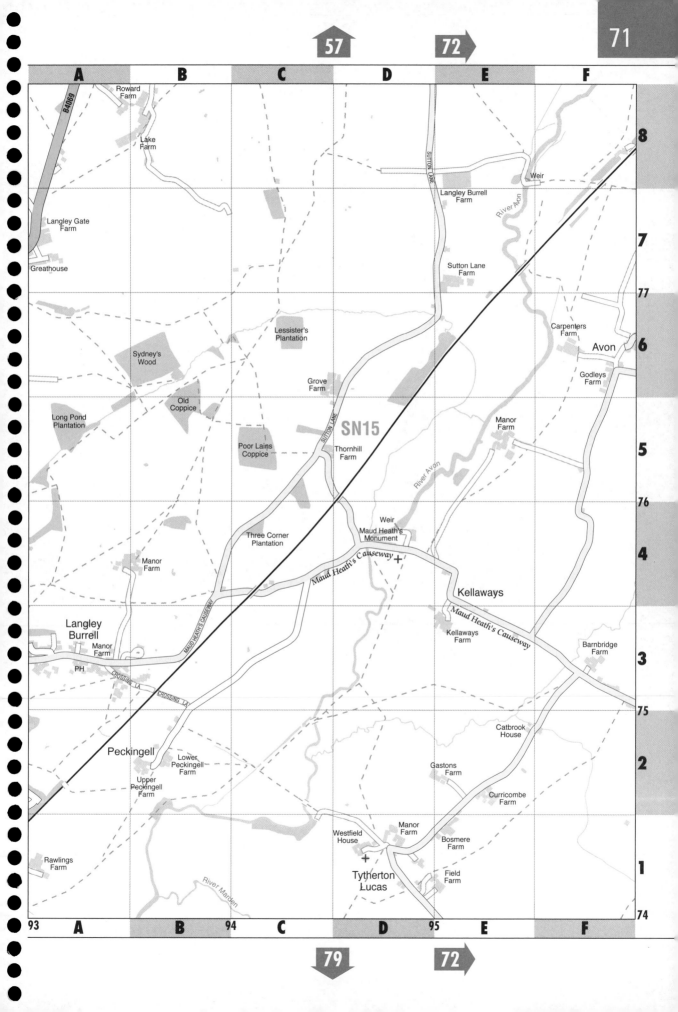

71
58

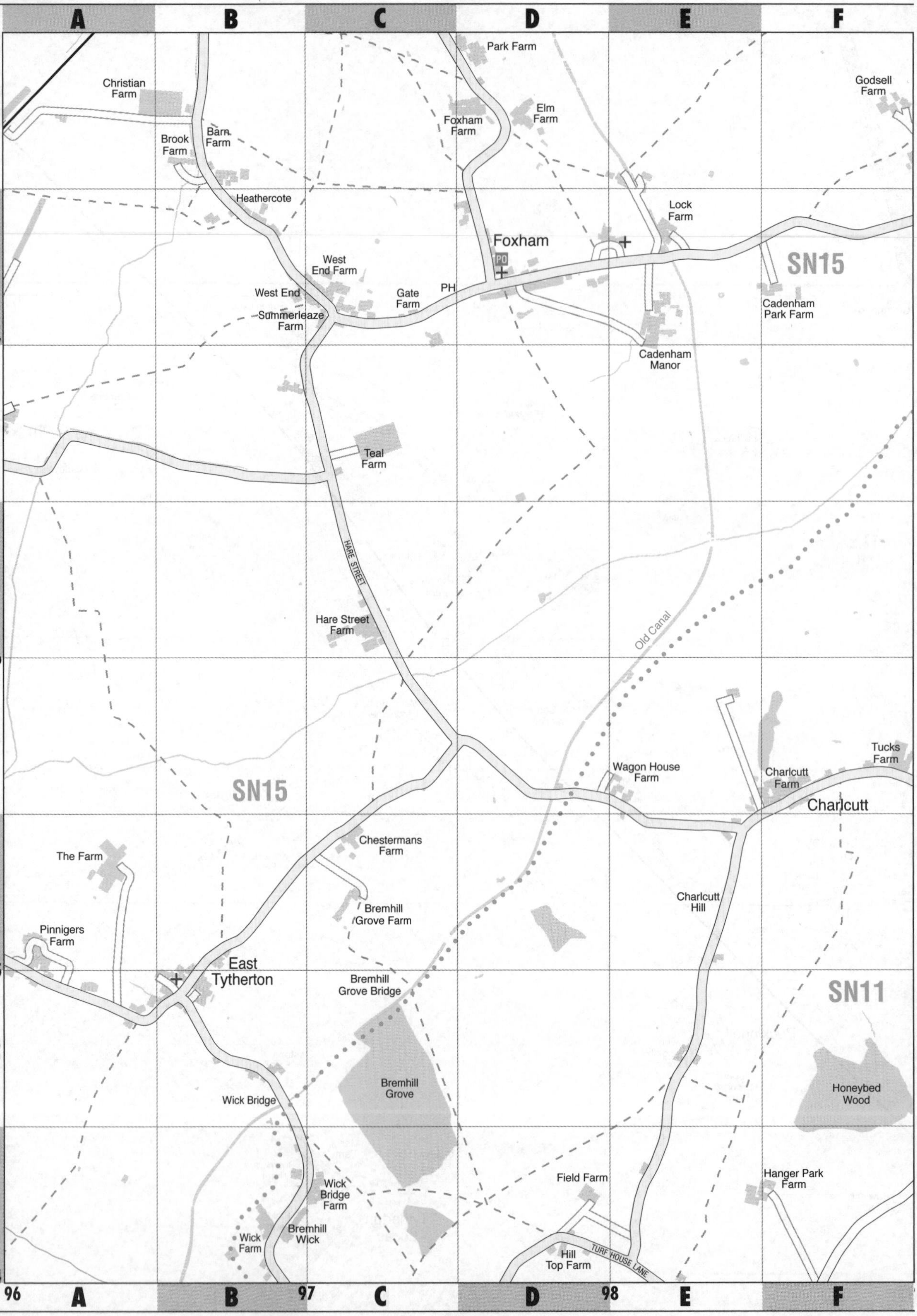

A **B** **C** **D** **E** **F**

8

Christian Farm

Brook Farm

Barn Farm

Park Farm

Foxham Farm

Elm Farm

Godsell Farm

Heathercote

7

West End Farm

West End

Summerleaze Farm

Gate Farm

PH

Foxham

PO

Lock Farm

SN15

Cadenham Park Farm

77

Cadenham Manor

6

Teal Farm

5

HARE STREET

Old Canal

76

Hare Street Farm

4

Wagon House Farm

Charlcutt Farm

Tucks Farm

SN15

Charlcutt

The Farm

Chestermans Farm

Charlcutt Hill

3

Pinnigers Farm

Bremhill Grove Farm

75

East Tytherton

Bremhill Grove Bridge

SN11

2

Wick Bridge

Bremhill Grove

Honeybed Wood

Wick Bridge Farm

1

Field Farm

Hanger Park Farm

Wick Farm

Bremhill Wick

Hill Top Farm

TURF HOUSE LANE

74

71
80

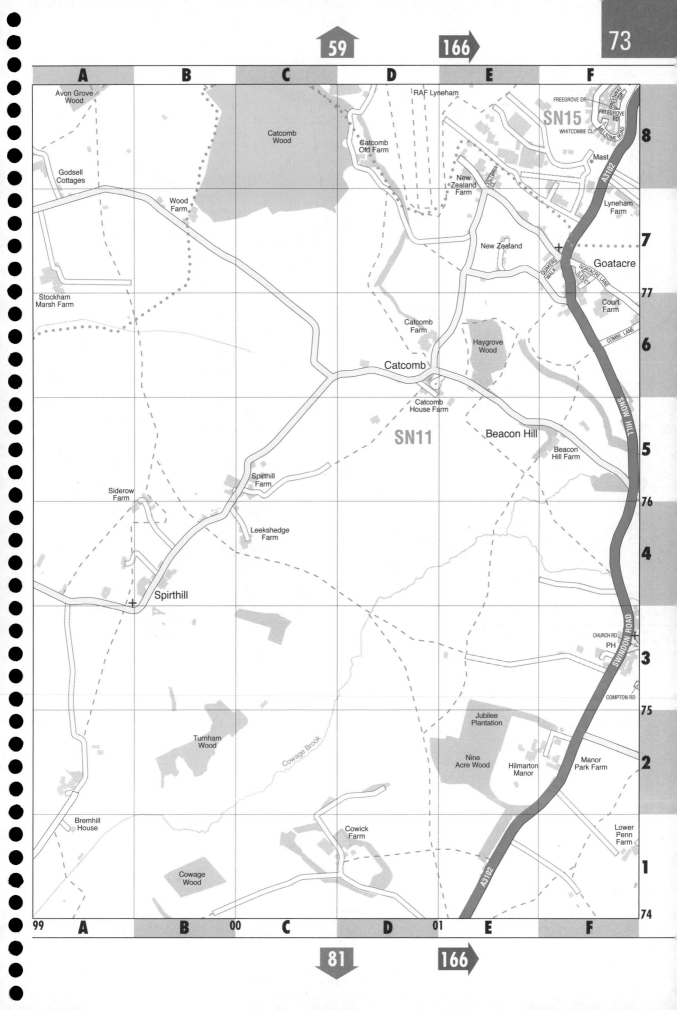

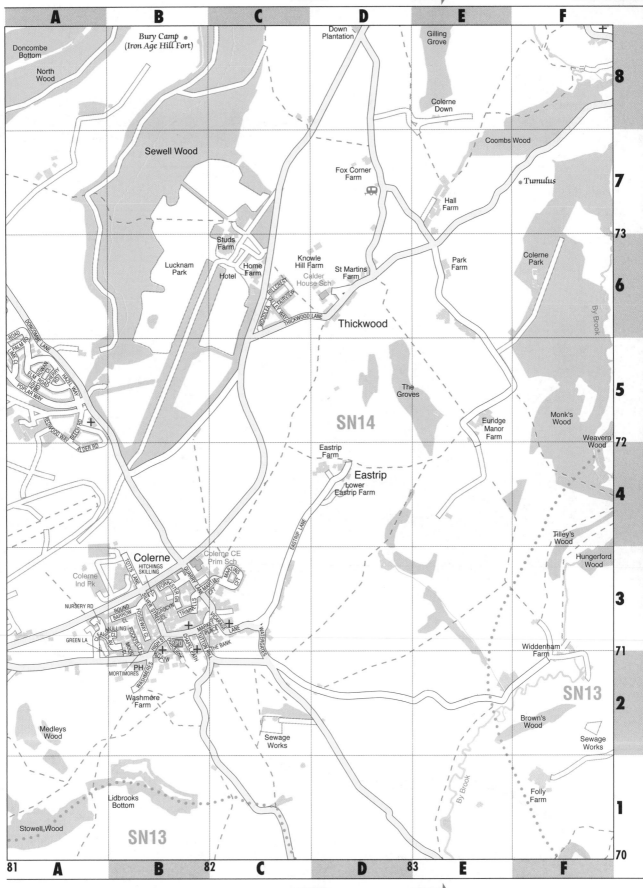

A B C D E F

Slaughterford
Backpath Wood
GERMAIN'S LANE
HAM LANE
Slaughterford RD
CUTTLE LANE
YATTON ROAD
Field Farm
Biddestone
Home Farm
Little Glebe
CHALLOWS LA
CHURCH ROAD
THE GREEN
Field Farm
Pool Farm PH
Biddestone Manor
Weir
By Brook
WEAVERN LANE
Honeybrook Farm
WEAVERN LA
White Cliff Wood
SN14
Cemy
TYNINGS
THE BUTTS
BUTTS CL
Mountjoy Farm

Macmillan Way
WEAVERN LANE
73

Field Barn Farm
WEAVERN LANE
Jubilee Wood

Husseyhill Wood
Mound
The Grove

Erkwell Wood
Home Farm
Hartham Farm
Leigh Wood

WEAVERN LANE
72
Square Covert
Tyning Wood
HARTHAM LANE
Hartham Park

Weavern Farm
Tyning Wood

Tyning Wood
Prestley Wood

Hungerford Wood
The Larches
MIDDLEWICK LANE
Church Farm
Long Plantation

Pickwick Lodge Farm
SN13 Middlewick
MIDDLEWICK LANE

Upper Pickwick
Broad Wood
CHURCHILL WAY
Pickwick

Rudloe Wood
71
Pickwick
DOVECOTE DR
METHUEN WAY
YORK CL
KINGS AVENUE
QUEENS AVENUE
WOODLANDS
The Corsham Regis Prim Acad
ARNOLDS MEAD

RAF Rudloe Manor
ACADEMY DR
ACADEMY DRIVE
CHARLES ST
MANOR RD
NEW RD
WELLER RD
CHAPMAN WAY
OLIVER
DICKENS CL
A4
PICKWICK ROAD
B3353

Bath Rd
BATH RD
BRUNEL CLOSE
BEECHFIELD RD
SPRING TINING
PURLEIGH
WEST PARK ROAD
ETHELRED
ELM GR
PAUL ST
PROVIDENCE LA
THE TYNINGS
ERNESTON CR

Lower Rudloe Farm
A4
BATH ROAD
Halfway Firs
Half Way Firs
BRADFORD ROAD
CHESTNUT GRANGE
STONE CL
NORTHLEAZE
SUTTAN LANE
PARK LANE
RANDALL
MASONS WY
SWAN RD
WEST PARK ROAD
BURN RD
BETHEL
SWAN CL
GLEBE
GREENWAY LANE
HATTON WAY
VALLEY ROAD
ROTHER RD
BRAMSTAR
Springfield Sports Centre
Sports Ground
The Corsham Sch

BOX HILL
LEAFY LANE
ASHWOOD RD
WOOD CLOSE
LONG CLOSE AV
LEYLANDS RD
TOGHILL CR
PINE CL
PINE CLOSE
Rudloe
B3109
TRAVELLERS REST
GUYERS LANE
PEEL CIRCUS
PICTOR CL
NINE ACRE
SHEPPARDS
Underground Quarry
Corsham
Hotel

84 A B 85 C D 86 E F

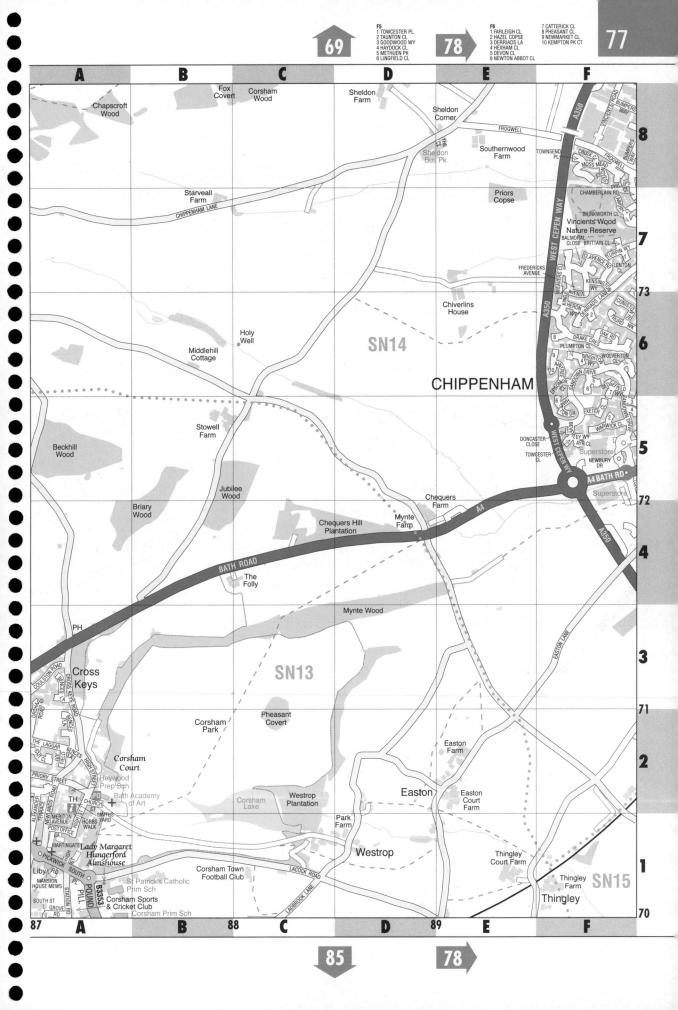

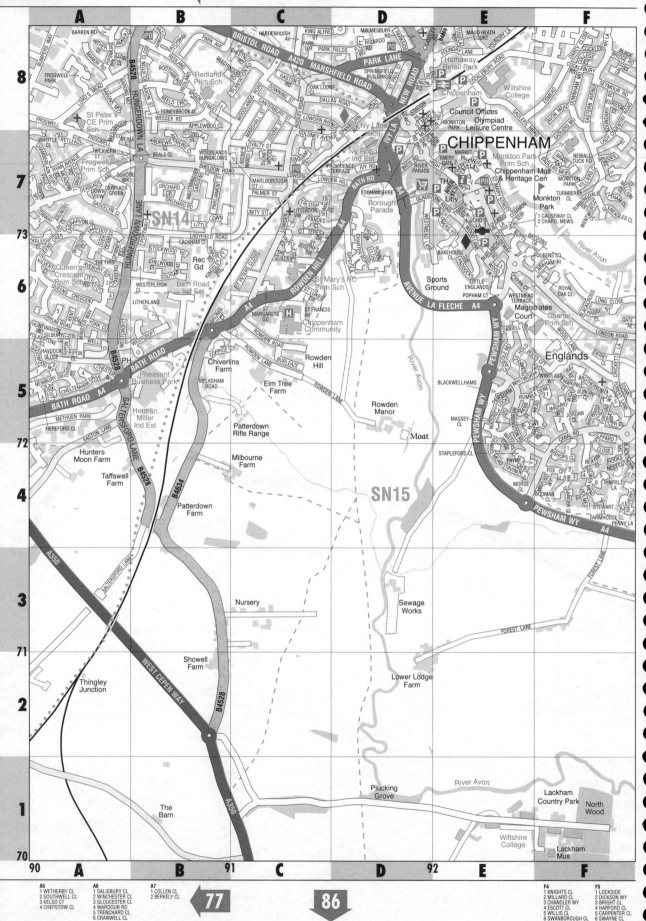

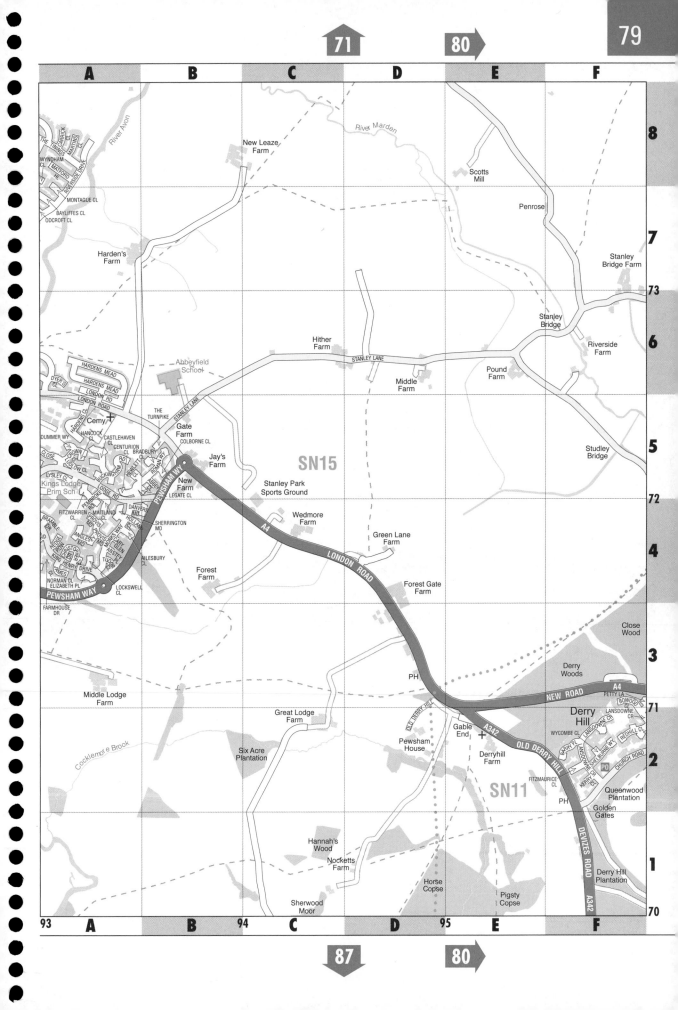

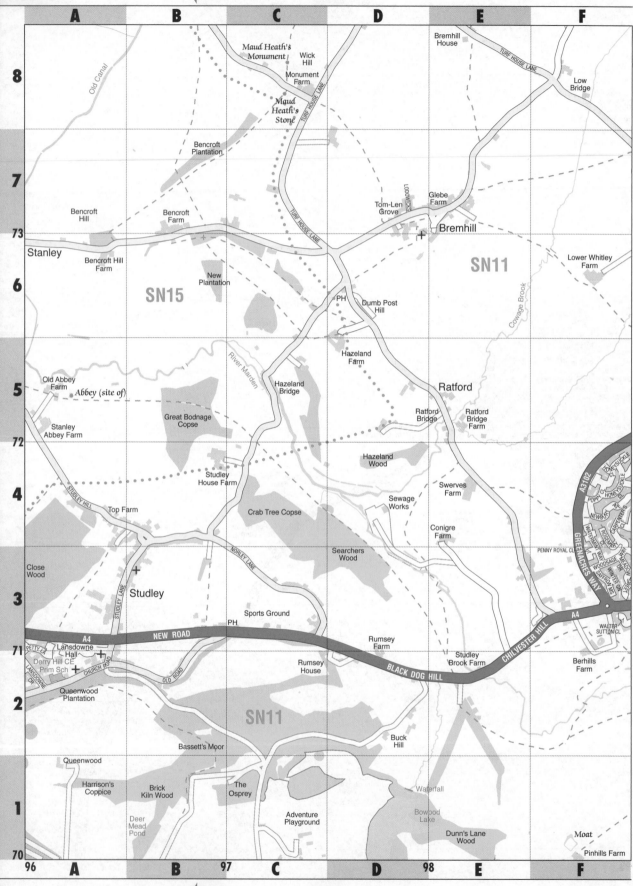

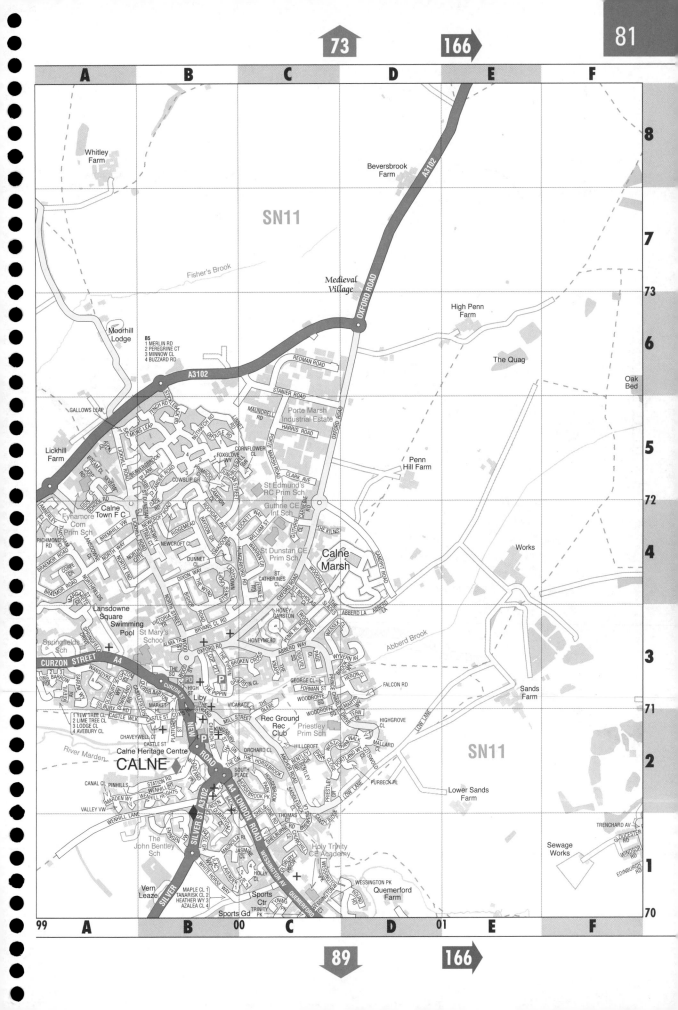

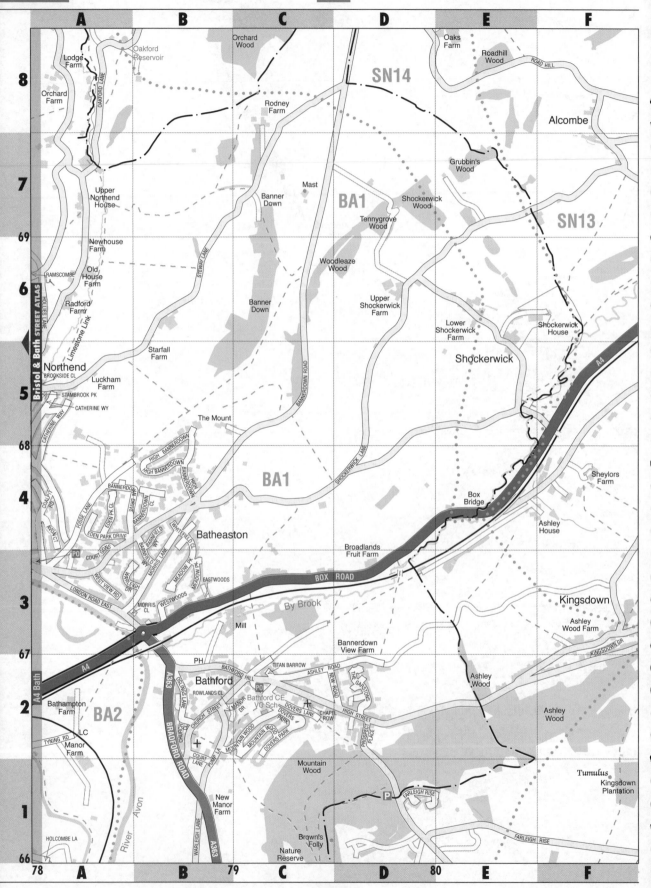

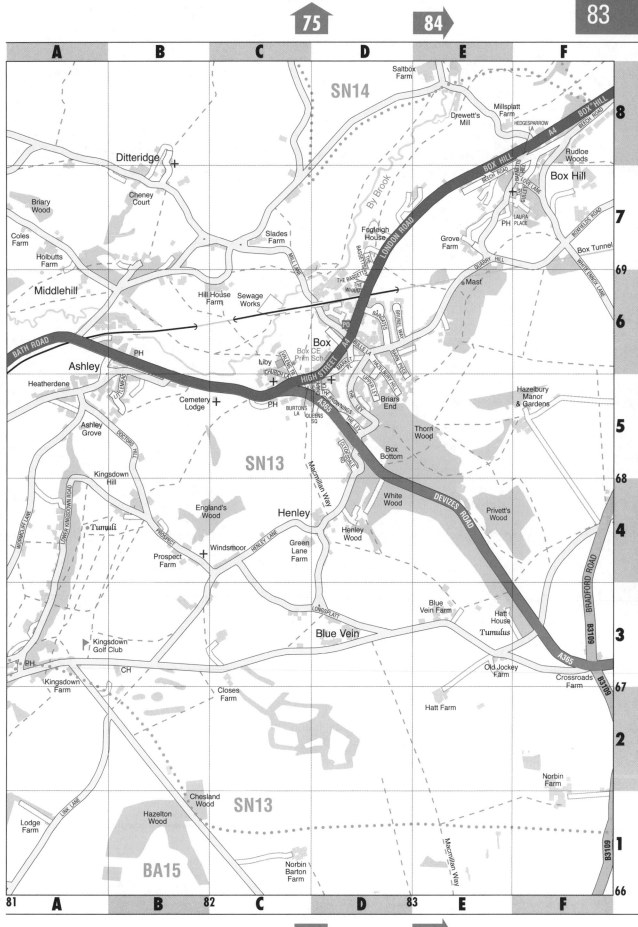

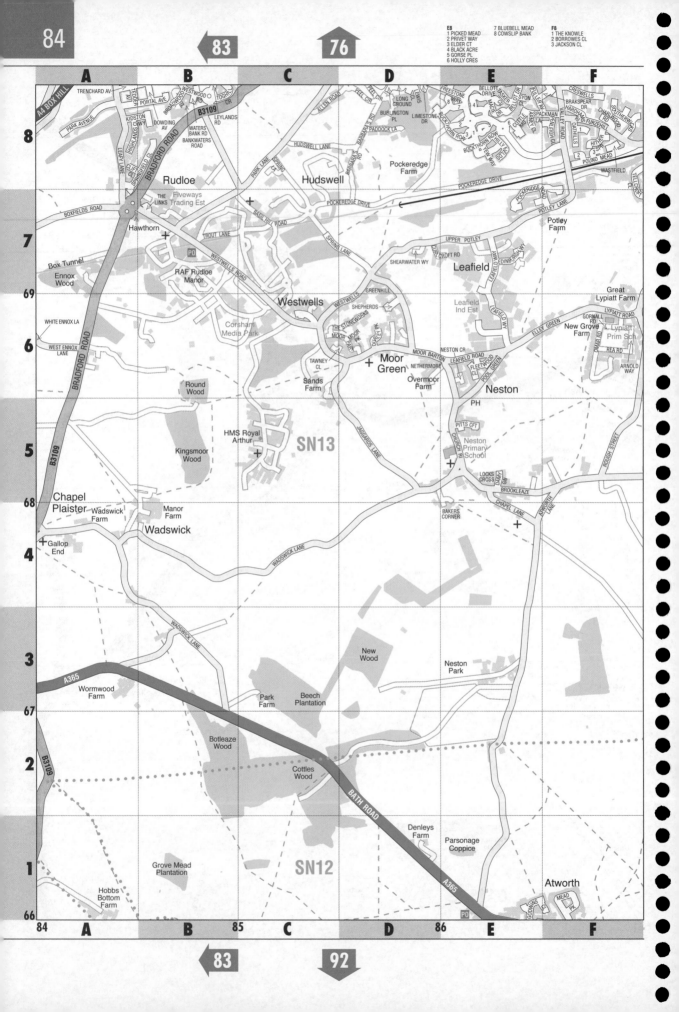

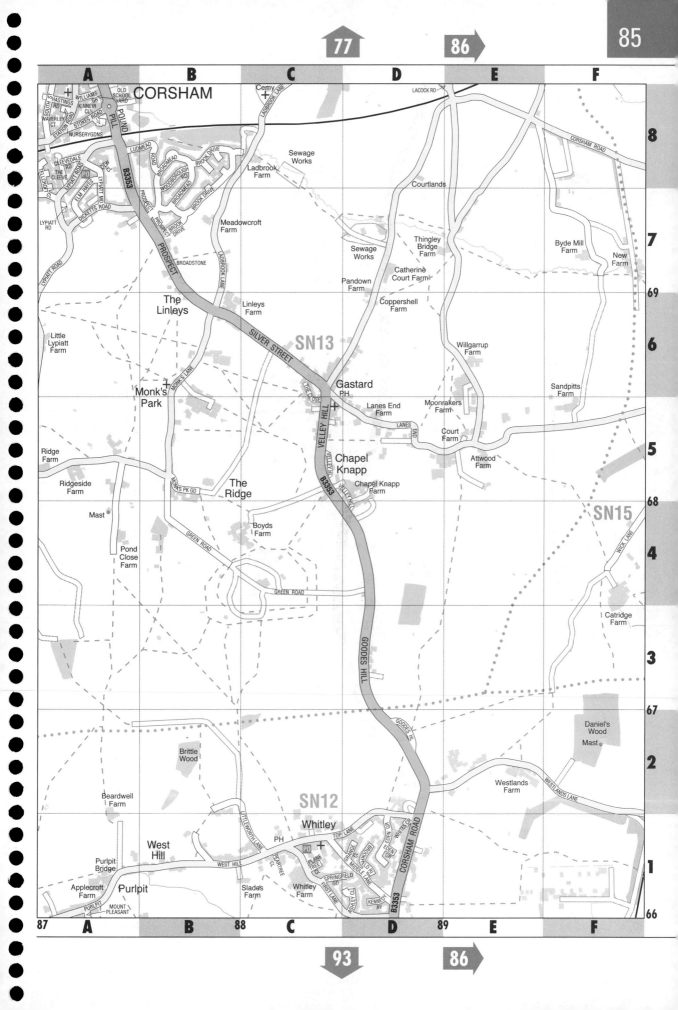

A B C D E F

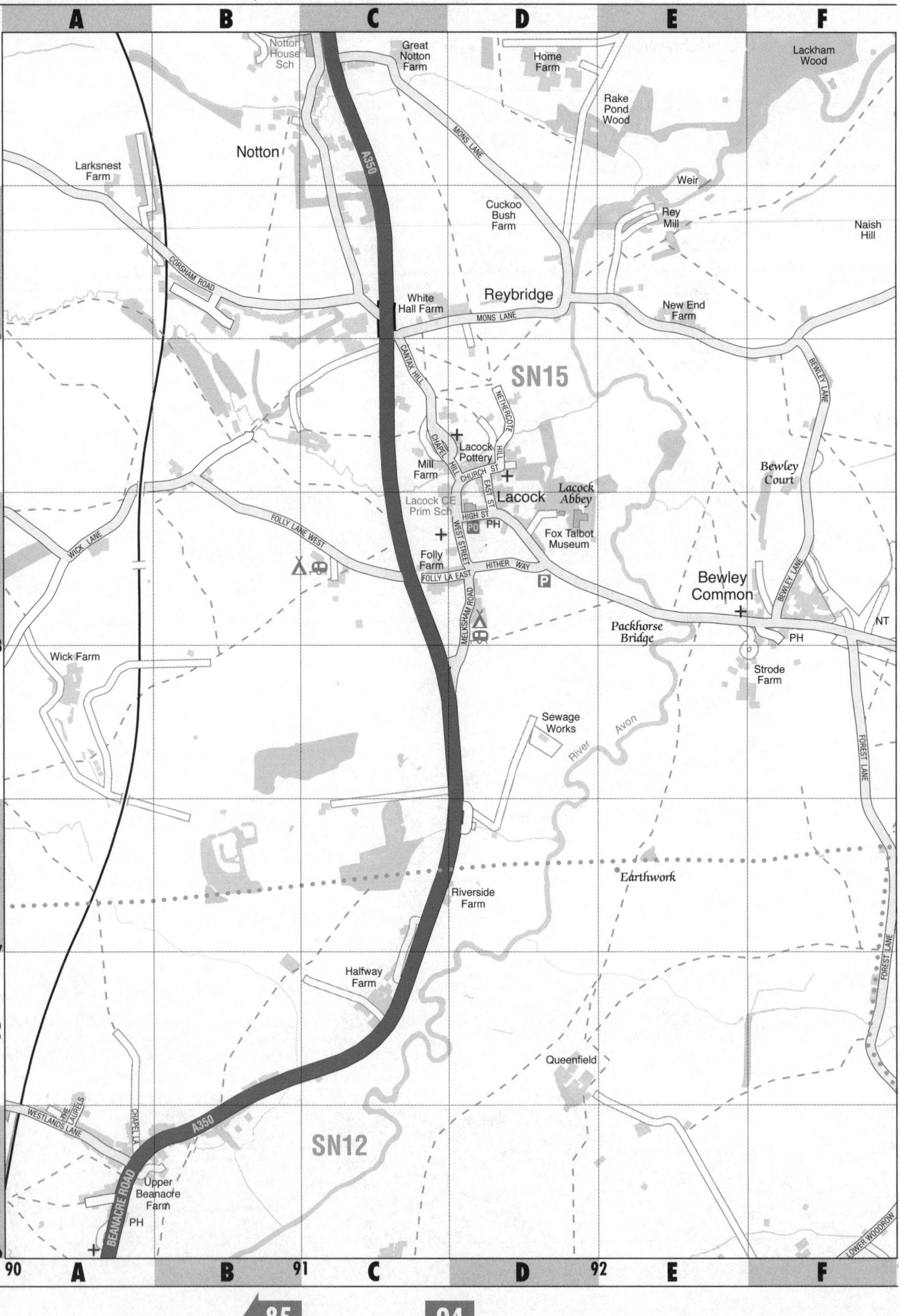

8

Notton House Sch
Great Notton Farm
Home Farm
Lackham Wood

Larksnest Farm
Notton
Rake Pond Wood

7

Weir

Corsham Road
Cuckoo Bush Farm
Rey Mill
Naish Hill

69
White Hall Farm
Mons Lane
Reybridge

A350
Mons Lane
New End Farm

6

SN15

Cantax Hill
Nethercote
Bewley Lane

Chapel Hill
Lacock Pottery

Mill Farm
Church Hill
Hill
East St
Bewley Court

Lacock CE Prim Sch
Lacock
Lacock Abbey

5

Wick Lane
Folly Lane West
High St
PO
PH
Fox Talbot Museum
Bewley Common

Folly Farm
West Street
Hither Way
NT

Folly La East
P

68

Wick Farm

Melksham Road
Packhorse Bridge
PH
Bewley Lane

Strode Farm

4

Sewage Works
River Avon
Forest Lane

3

Earthwork

67

Riverside Farm

Halfway Farm

2

Queenfield

Westlands Lane
The Laurels
Chapel La
A350

SN12

1

Beanacre Road
Upper Beanacre Farm
PH
Lower Woodrow

66

90 A 91 B C 92 D E F

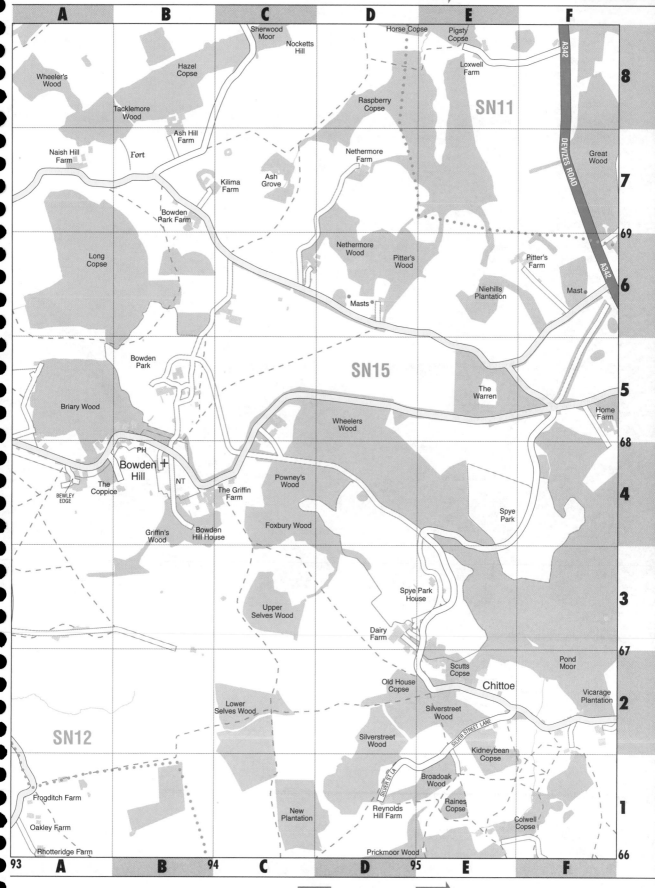

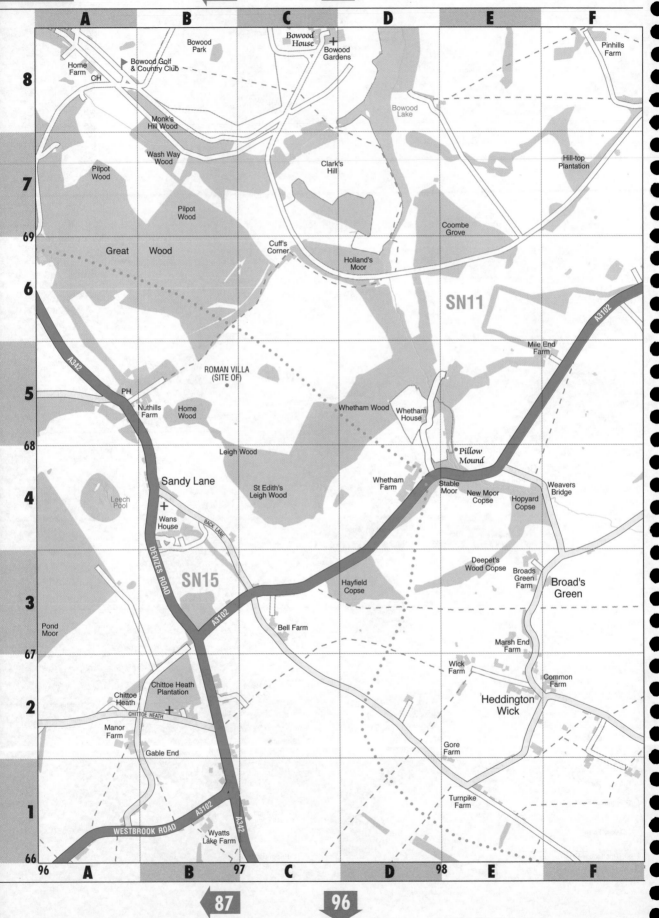

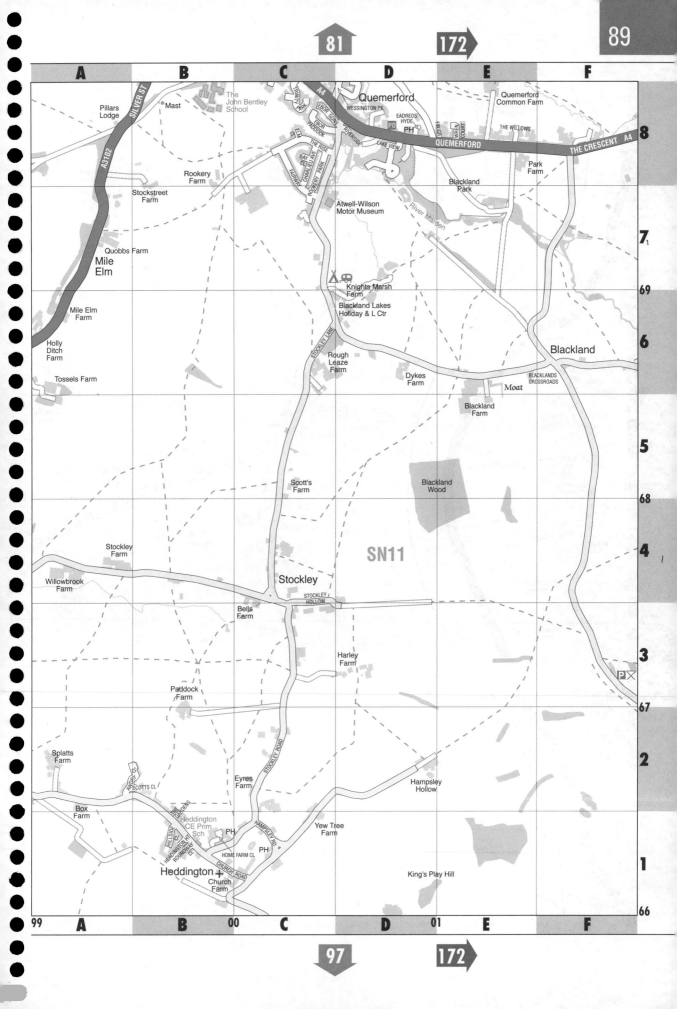

A B C D E F

Quemerford

Pillars Lodge

SILVER ST

Mast

The John Bentley School

Quemerford Common Farm

A3102

Rookery Farm

Stockstreet Farm

TRINITY PARK

EBOR GDNS

RIVERSIDE

A4

WESSINGTON PK

PO

EADREDS HYDE

PH

WREN COURT

THE WILLOWS

QUEMERFORD

THE CRESCENT A4

8

THE RISE

ELM CT

PADDOCK

BAY CT

CHARLIEU LANE

ROOKERY PARK

FAIRWAY

LAKE VIEW

Park Farm

Blackland Park

Quobbs Farm

Mile Elm

Atwell-Wilson Motor Museum

River Marden

7

Mile Elm Farm

Knights Marsh Farm

69

Holly Ditch Farm

Blackland Lakes Holiday & L Ctr

6

Tossels Farm

STOCKLEY LANE

Rough Leaze Farm

Dykes Farm

Moat

Blackland

BLACKLANDS CROSSROADS

Blackland Farm

5

Scott's Farm

Blackland Wood

68

Stockley Farm

SN11

4

Willowbrook Farm

Stockley

STOCKLEY HOLLOW

Bells Farm

Harley Farm

3

P

Paddock Farm

67

Splatts Farm

STOCKLEY ROAD

2

SCOTTS CL

IVY RD

Eyres Farm

Hampsley Hollow

Box Farm

Heddington CE Prim Sch

PH

HAMPSLEY RD

Yew Tree Farm

HILLSIDE CL

HEDDINGTON HT

ROUNDWAY CL

GARDENS

HOME FARM CL

PH

1 HEADINGTON HT

CHURCH ROAD

Heddington

Church Farm

King's Play Hill

1

66

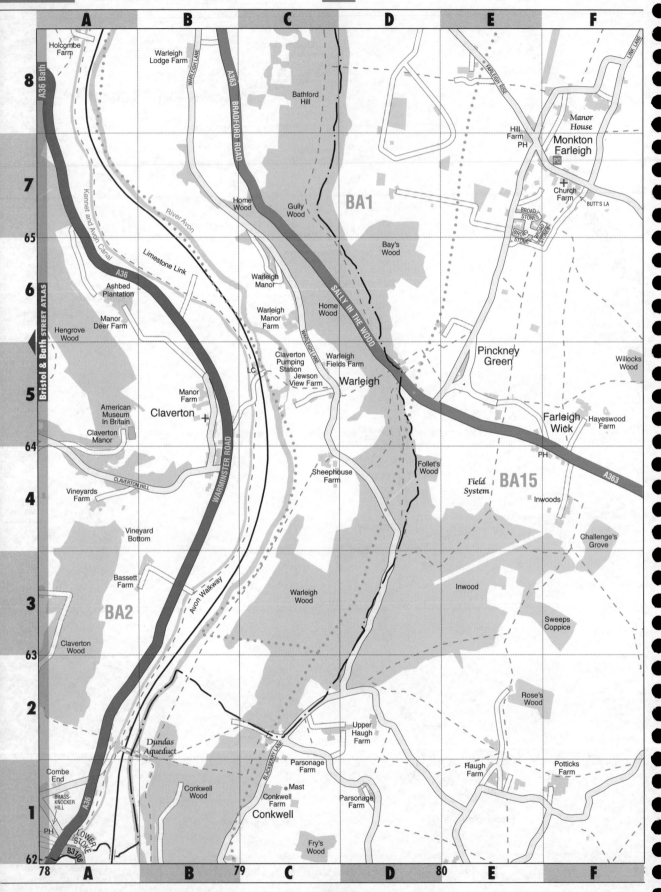

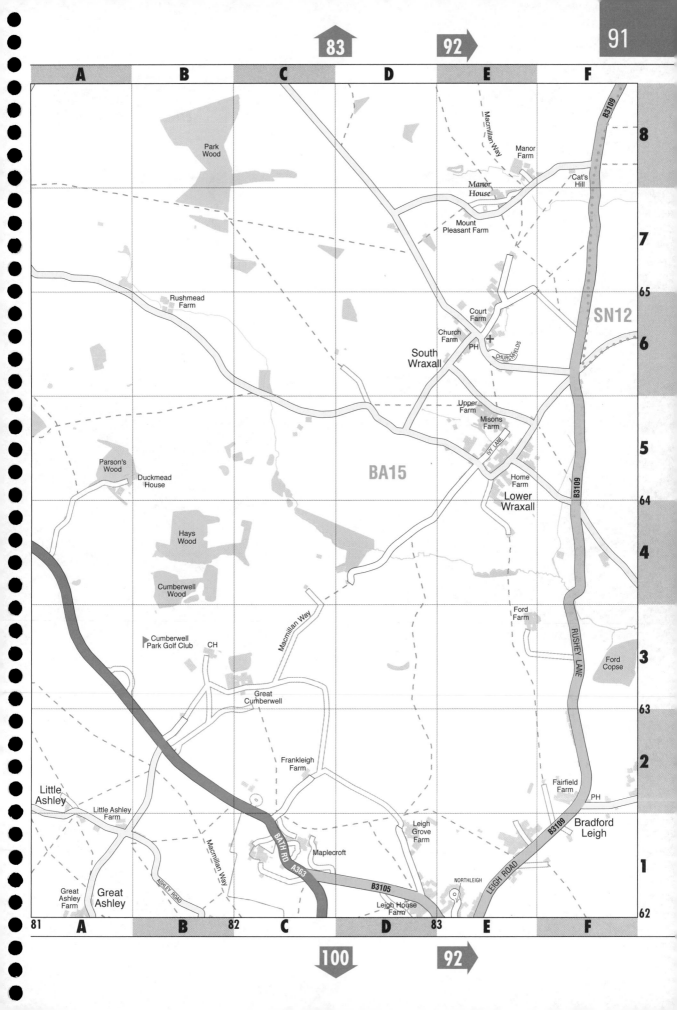

	A	B	C	D	E	F

8

Hobb's Bottom Farm

Cottles Farm

Stonar School

Withy Bed

PH
Poplar Farm
CHURCH ST
Church Farm

GREENLAND CL
NURSERY CL
CLOCK TOWER VIEW
CORONATION RD
CHAPEL RISE
Churchfields, The Village Sch

A365 PH
MEADOW PARK
ATWORTH CT
POST OFFICE LA
Atworth
PROSPECT FIELDS
Atworth Business Park

7

Cock Road Plantation

COOMBE LA

BRADFORD ROAD

Studley Farm

65

6

Lynch Bottom

Ganbrook Farm

SN12

COOMBE LANE

Newhouse Farm

5

64

BA15

Lenton Farm

4

3

Little Chalfield

Great Chalfield

Moat

Great Chalfield Manor House

63

BA14

Lady's Coppice

2

Mirkens Farm

Blackacre Farm

Holt Manor

LEIGH ROAD

GYPSY LANE

1

The Midlands Ind Est

THE SPA
HAWGROFT
STATION RD
B3107
THE GRAVEL
THE ELMS
THE MIDLANDS
PO
BECKGROVE LA
LITTLE PARKS
GREAT PARKS
CRANDON LEA
BRADLEY LA
Holt VC Prim Sch
THE COMMON
GT PARKS

Holt

62

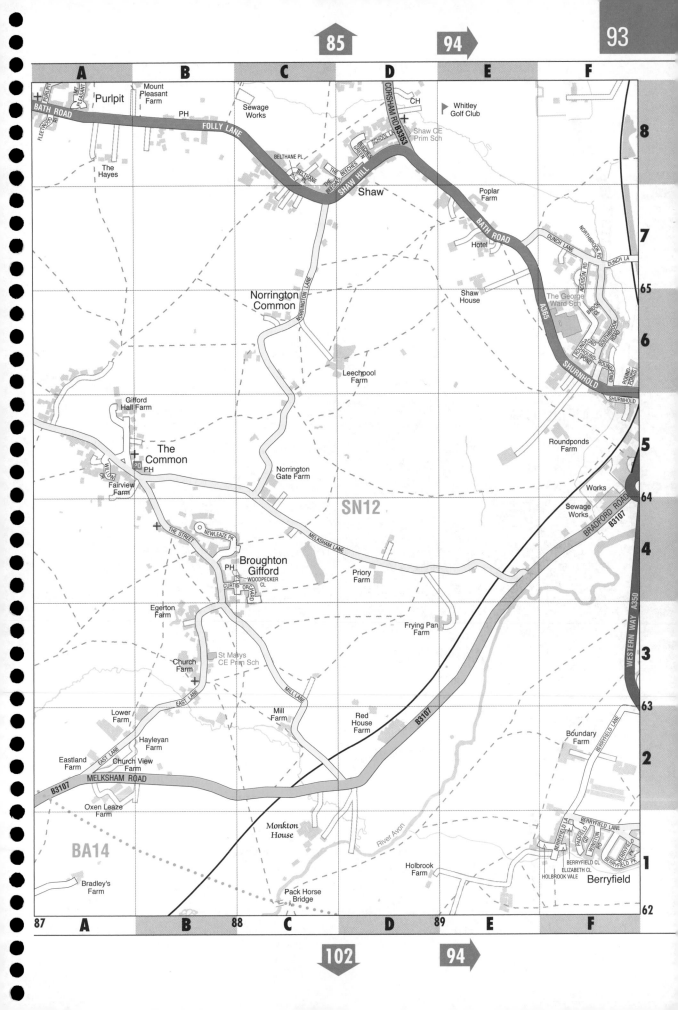

MELKSHAM

SN12

Melksham Forest

Beanacre

Bowerhill

WESTERN WAY A365

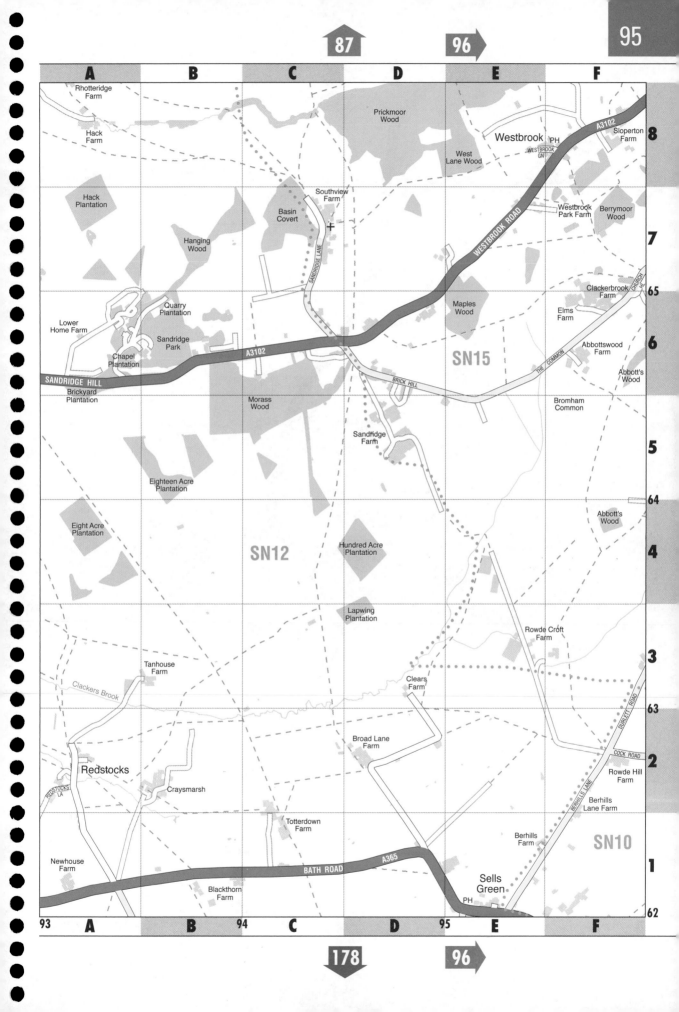

A3102

The Coppice

Wyatt's Wood

DEVIZES ROAD

Bromham House Farm

Netherstreet Farm

SN15

GREYSTONES

HORSEPOOL

MINTY'S CL

BRENCH CL

HIGHFIELD

THE CRESCENT

HIGHFIELD

THE POUND

A342

OLD SCHOOL CL

HIGHFIELD

YARD LANE

Bromham

PH

CHURCH HL RD

HUNTS MD

JOCKEY LANE

SCHOOL

LA

CHURCH HL

BANKLIN CL

HIGH ST

PO

St Nicholas CE VC Prim Sch

NETHERSTREET

ORCHARD GR

CHURCH PL

HAWKSTREET

Hobbs Farm

Moorhouse Farm

NEW ROAD

Abbott's Wood

HAWKSTREET

Stills Farm

The Fruit Farm

Homeleigh Farm

St Edith's

PH

Burbrook's Wood

NEW ROAD

Lower Hawk Street Farm

Caumans Coppice

ST EDITH'S MARSH

Nine Acre Wood

Long Pond Wood

SN15

Durlett Farm

Horse Lane Copse

Marsh Farm

Big Wood

DURLETT ROAD

Clinghill Wood

Horse Lane Farm

Rowdeford Sch

Withybed Wood

Durlett Wood

Ashen Wood

The Moors

Wick Farm

SN10

Tanis

COCK ROAD

West End Farm

CLOSE LA

CONSCIENCE LANE

Sewage Works

BUNNIES LA

MAUNDRELL CL

PH

Manor Farm

Rowde

COCK ROAD

HIGH STREET

A342

DEVIZES ROAD

TOWER VW

ST

MATTHEWS CL

SPRINGFIELD RD

Rowde CE Prim Acad

SANDS

ROWDE CT ROAD

CHESTNUT

FERRIS CL

Smithwick Farm

SANDS LANE

WALNUT CL

ELM CL

MARSH LANE

WHEELER PL

Vale Mead

FURLONG CL

B3101

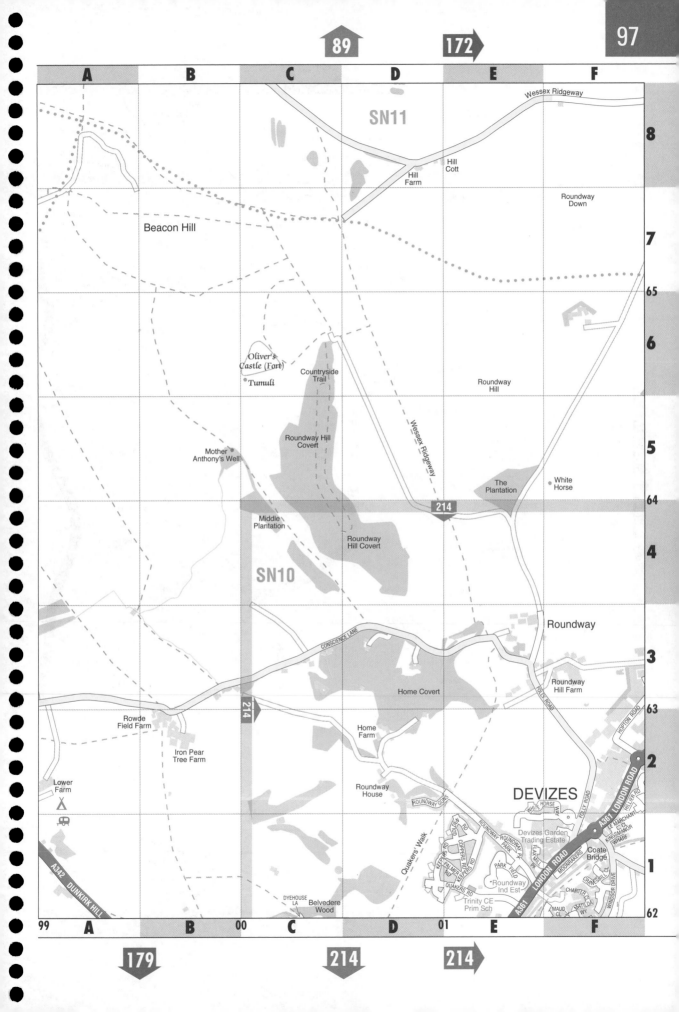

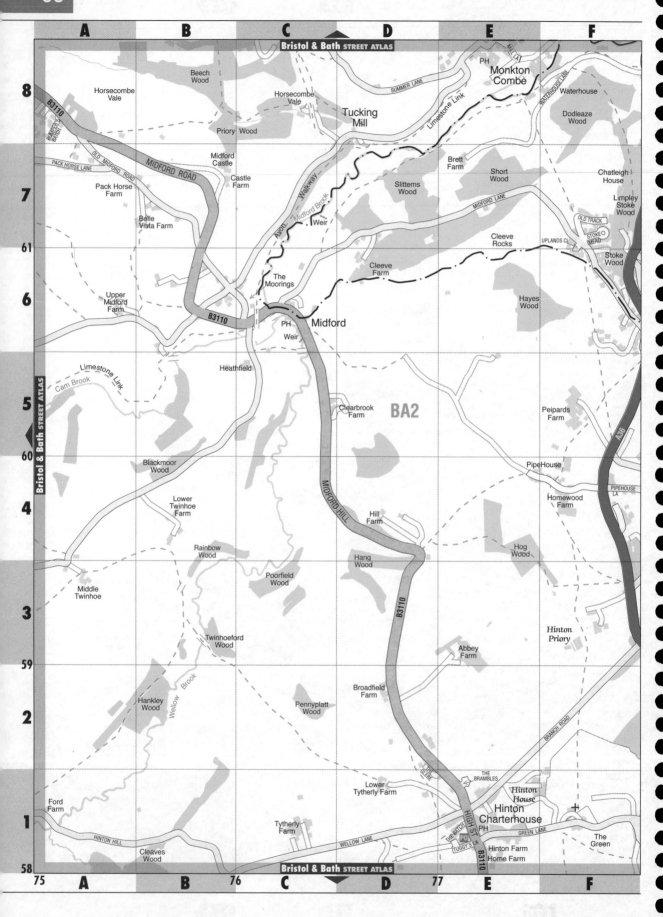

A B C D E F

8

B3110

Horsecombe Vale

Beech Wood

Horsecombe Vale

Tucking Mill

Monkton Combe

PH

Waterhouse

Dodleaze Wood

Priory Wood

Limestone Link

SUMMER LANE

PACK HORSE LANE

OLD MIDFORD ROAD

MIDFORD ROAD

Midford Castle

Castle Farm

Walkway

Midford Brook

Brett Farm

Short Wood

MIDFORD LANE

Chatleigh House

Limpley Stoke Wood

7

Pack Horse Farm

Belle Vista Farm

Avon

Weir

Slittems Wood

OLD TRACK

STOKE O MEAD

UPLANDS CL

Cleeve Rocks

Stoke Wood

61

Upper Midford Farm

B3110

The Moorings

Cleeve Farm

Hayes Wood

6

PH

Midford

Weir

Heathfield

Clearbrook Farm

BA2

Peipards Farm

A36

5

Limestone Link

Cam Brook

MIDFORD HILL

PipeHouse

PIPEHOUSE LA

60

Blackmoor Wood

Lower Twinhoe Farm

Hill Farm

Homewood Farm

4

Rainbow Wood

Hang Wood

Hog Wood

Middle Twinhoe

Poorfield Wood

B3110

Hinton Priory

3

Twinhoeford Wood

Abbey Farm

59

Hankley Wood

Wellow Brook

Pennyplatt Wood

Broadfield Farm

BRANCH ROAD

2

Ford Farm

THE GLEBE

THE BRAMBLES

Hinton House

Lower Tytherly Farm

Hinton Charterhouse

PH

The Green

1

HINTON HILL

Tytherly Farm

WELLOW LANE

HIGH ST

PO

TUGGY'S

THE HATCH

GREEN LANE

Cleaves Wood

Hinton Farm Home Farm

B3110

58

75 A B 76 C D 77 E F

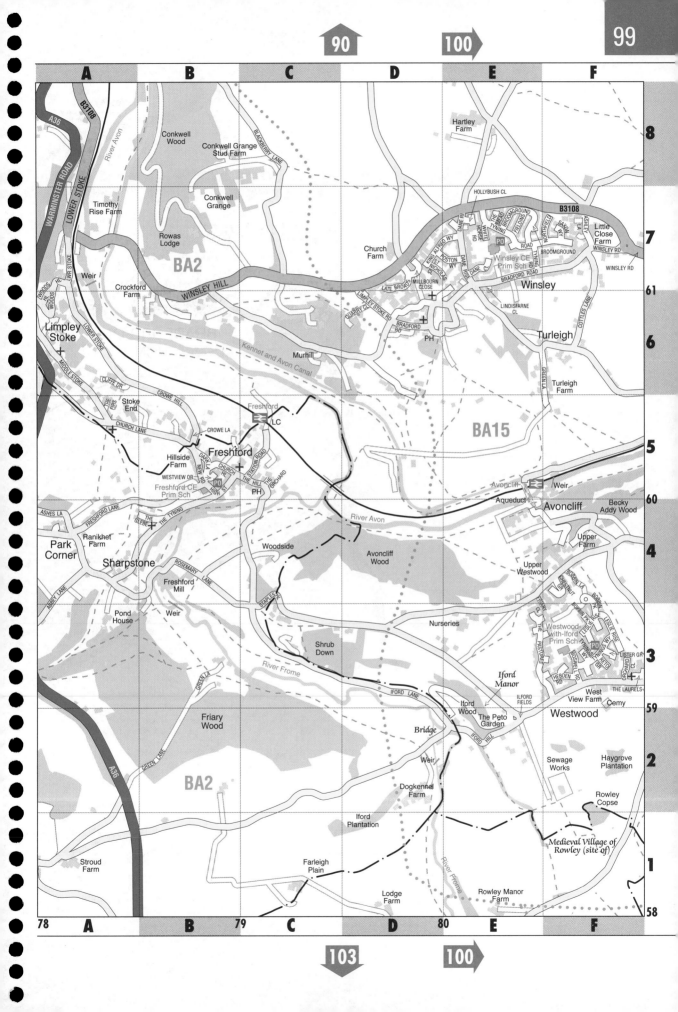

99
91

D6
1 ST MARGARET'S HILL
2 ST MARGARET'S PL
3 ST MARGARET'S VILLAS
4 KINGSTON RD
5 THE PADDOCK

	A	B	C	D	E	F

8

Lower Bearfield Farm

Wiltshire Music Centre

ASHLEY ROAD
Macmillan Way
BATH ROAD
Recreation Ground
NORTHLEIGH
Hotel
SLADESBROOK CL
B3109 SLADESBROOK
Christchurch CE Prim Sch
Woolley Green
Woolley Barn Farm
B3105
Woolley Grange Farm

7

St Laurence Sch
Bearfield Bldgs
Church Acre
MANOR GDNS
BERRYFIELD RD
CHRISTCHURCH RD
Winsley Rd
Ivy Terr
B3109 NEW ROAD
Coronation Ave
Woolley Street
Woolley

BEAR CL
MAGNON ROAD
CHURCHES
ELMFIELD
BUDBURY CL
PRIORY PK
THE WILDERNESS
HUNTINGDON
PRIORY
MASONS LANE
MOUNT PLEASANT
IVY TERR
KINGSFIELD ST
WOOLLEY TR
SPRINGFIELD

61

B3108
WINSLEY ROAD
DOWNS VW
WESTFIELD
NEWTOWN
SILVER STREET
MARKET ST
B3107
HOLT ROAD
KINGSFIELD GRANGE RD
CEMETERY LANE
Cemy

6

MEADOWFIELD
HARTLEAZE
RICKFIELD
COACH RD
Swimming Pool
BULL PIT
CHURCH ST
Liby & Mus
i
LC
UPR REGENTS
GREENLAND MILLS
Weir
River Avon
BRADFORD-ON-AVON

Belcombe Court

5

BELCOMBE ROAD
Bradford-on-Avon
FROME RD
A363
Barton Packhorse Bridge
Tithe Barn
Barton Farm
Grip Wood
Grip Wood Farm
SOUTHLEIGH
POUND LANE
FITZMAURICE PL
Fitzmaurice Prim Sch
FROME
KENNIE GDNS
POULTON
DOWNAVON
AVON
LAURENCE RD
KINGSTON AVE
CULVER RD
ST ALDHELM RD
SOUTHVILLE ROAD
MYTTERN MDW
CH
Bradford-on-Avon Golf Club
TROWBRIDGE RD
WIDBROOK VIEW
LODDON WAY

Sewage Works

BA15

60

Becky Addy Wood
Barton Farm Country Park
Lye Green Farm
JONES HILL
B3109
SPENCERS ORCHARD
ELMS CROSS DR
BAILEYS BARN
PIPLAR GROUND
POULTON
P LAUREL P LAUREL
SOUTHWAY RD
FOLLYFIELD
BASSETTS PASTURE
BEDDOE
METHUEN CL
MOULTON DRIVE
HORTON CL
DEVERELL
FITZMAURICE PL
JOHN RENNIE CL
TROWBRIDGE ROAD
PH

4

Lye Green
Mast

Rowden Farm
Widbrook
Old Farm

3

Vineyard
Hudds Farm
FROME ROAD
Hotel
A363

THE LAURELS
LINDA CR

59

Westwood Manor House

2

WESTWOOD ROAD
Midway Manor
Oxstall Farm
Trowle Common
Manor Farm
Manor Court Farm
BA14

1

B3109
Trowle Wood
SHERBOURNE
CHEPSTON PL
LEAFIELD
IVSON RD
KINGSLEY PL

58

81	A	B	82	C	D	83	E	F

99
104

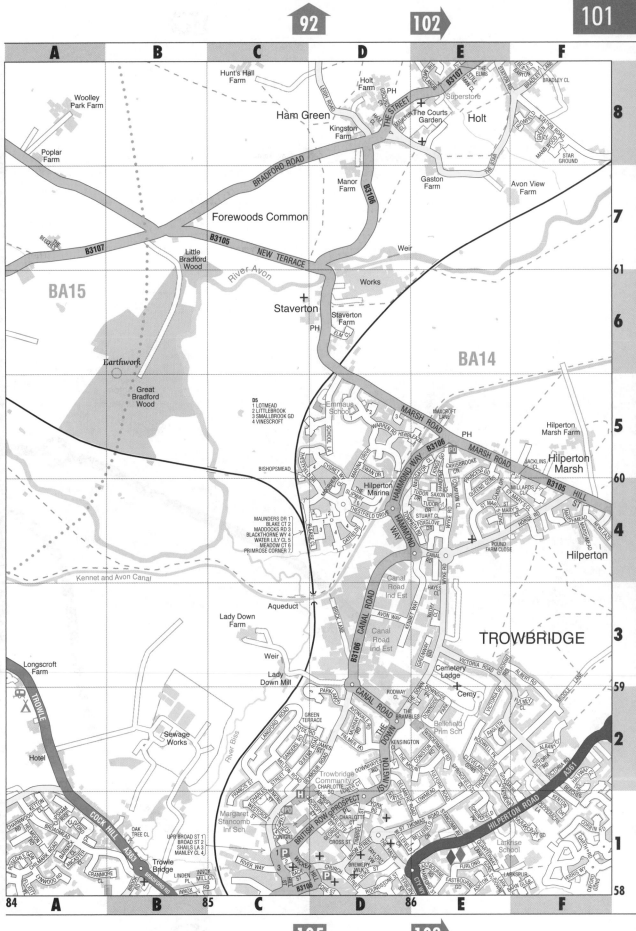

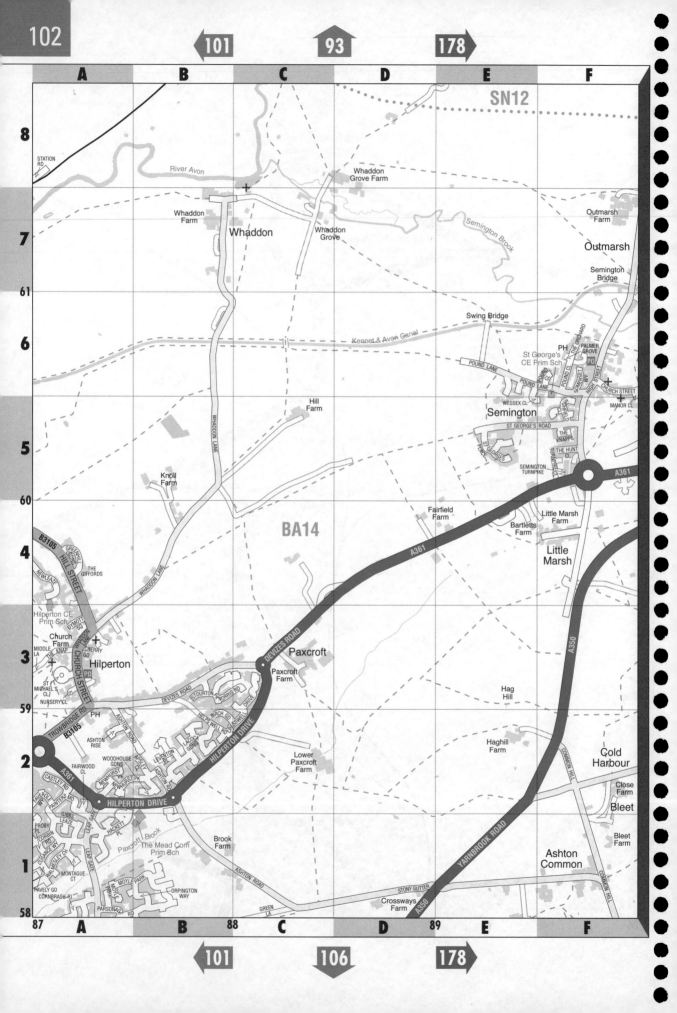

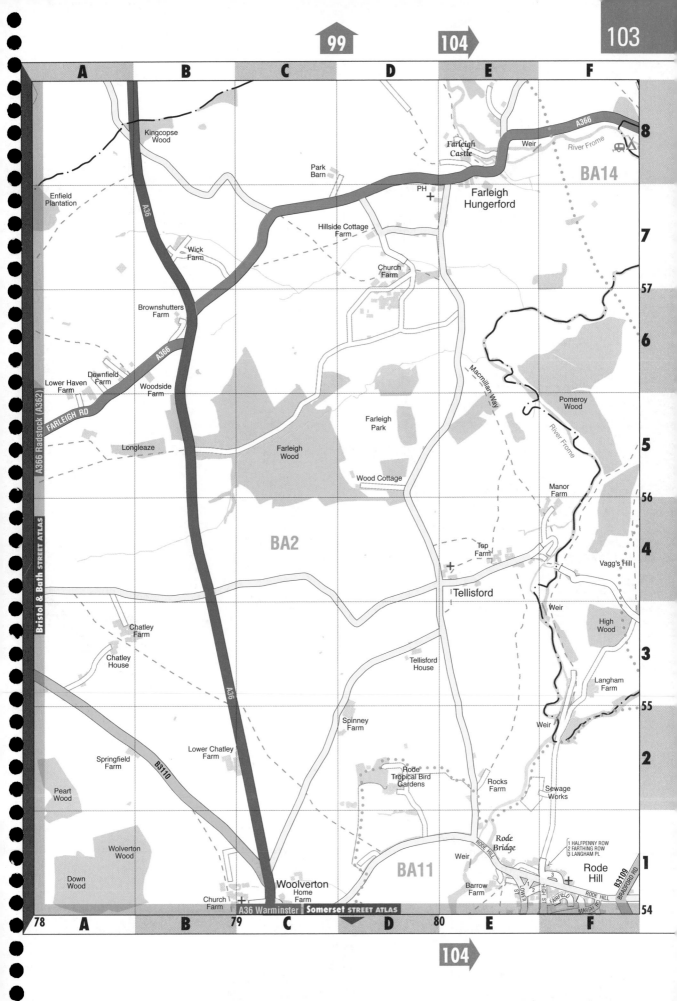

103 100

A B C D E F

8

Stowford Manor Farm

Trowle Farm

Wingfield House

B3109

Arnold's Hill

London Bridge Farm

7

Snarlton Farm

Stowford Farm

MAGDALEN LA

A366

London Bridge

Weir

Arnolds Hill Farm

SANDFORD PK

KENSINGTON FIELDS

57

Belle Coeur Farm

POMEROY LANE

FROME ROAD

Church Farm

Studley Green

WATERFORD BECK

KINGSWOOD CHASE

SHERIDAN

6

Pomeroy Farm

SHOP LANE

KIRK CLOS

Wingfield

PH

CHURCH LANE

MOORES YD

CHAPEL LA

PO

Wingfield CE Prim Sch

FIELDS WY

CAVENDISH DR

REGENTS PL

GREENBANK VIEW

LAMBROK CL

LAMBROK RD

OAK PARK

Birch Wood

5

BA2

Swansbrook Farm

BA14

Sleight Wood

Park Farm

Southwick Country Park

56

Romsey Oak Farm

HOGGINGTON LA

Hoggington Farm

4

Vagg's Hill Wood

Hoggington

HOGGINGTON LANE

Southwick

FROME ROAD

CHANTRY PL GD

3

Vaggs Hill Farm

BRADFORD ROAD

Dillybrook Farm

POPLAR TREE LANE

Newpool Farm

FAIRFIELD MS 1
CHANTRY CT 2
SWAN CT 3
THE MOWLEMS 4
CHAPEL CL 5

Pound Farm

ARNOLD RD

PH

Southwick CE Prim Sch

CHURCH

WYNSOME ST

HOLLIS WAY

HOLLIS WY

55

Frith Farm

Flaxfield Farm

ORCHARD DR

WESLEY LANE

SOUTHFIELD

SOUTHFIELD

BLIND LANE

2

Flexham Farm

Marshfield

GREEN LANE

Dunkirk Business Park

Dunkirk Farm

Lamberts Marsh

Blue Barn Farm

Poleshole Farm

Sparrows Rest Farm

B3109

MONKLEY LANE

A361

Whittakers Farm

Hoopers Pool

Marsh Mead

Pole's Hole

1

BA11

Rode Common

Rode Common Farm

Hoopers Pool Farm

Mutton Marsh Farm

RODE HILL

54

81 A B 82 C D 83 E F

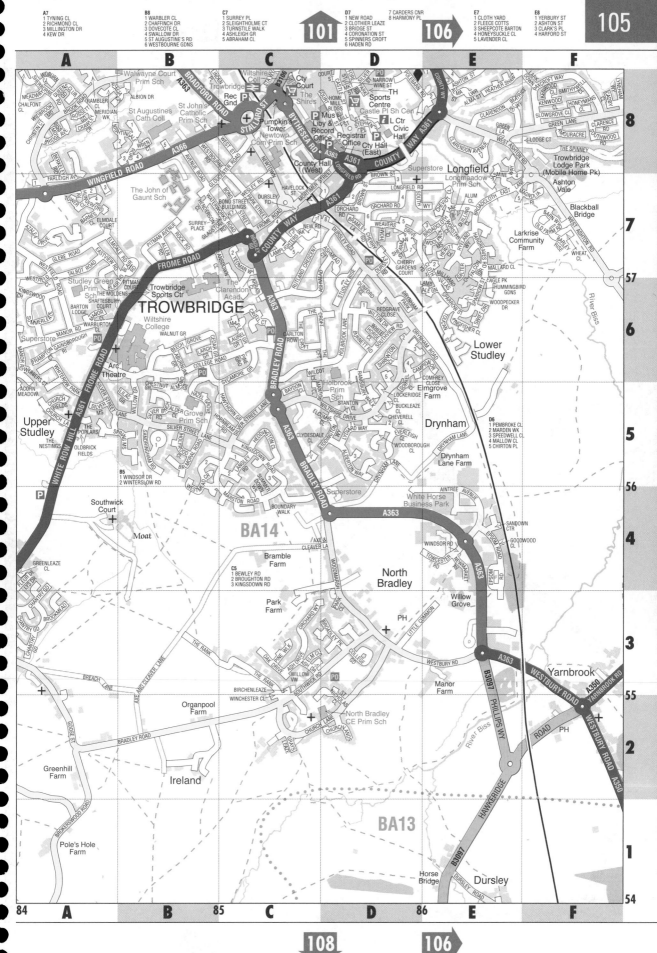

A7
1 TYNING CL
2 RICHMOND CL
3 MILLINGTON DR
4 KEW DR

B8
1 WARBLER CL
2 CHAFFINCH DR
3 DOVECOTE CL
4 SWALLOW DR
5 ST AUGUSTINE'S RD
6 WESTBOURNE GDNS

C7
1 SURREY PL
2 SLEIGHTHOLME CT
3 TURNSTILE WALK
4 ASHLEIGH CL
5 ABRAHAM CL

D7
1 NEW ROAD
2 CLOTHIER LEAZE
3 BRIDGE ST
4 CORONATION ST
5 SPINNERS CROFT
6 HADEN RD

7 CARDERS CNR
8 HARMONY PL

E7
1 CLOTH YARD
2 FLEECE COTTS
3 SHEEPCOTE BARTON
4 HONEYSUCKLE CL
5 LAVENDER CL

E8
1 YERBURY ST
2 ASHTON ST
3 CLARK'S PL
4 HARFORD ST

101

106

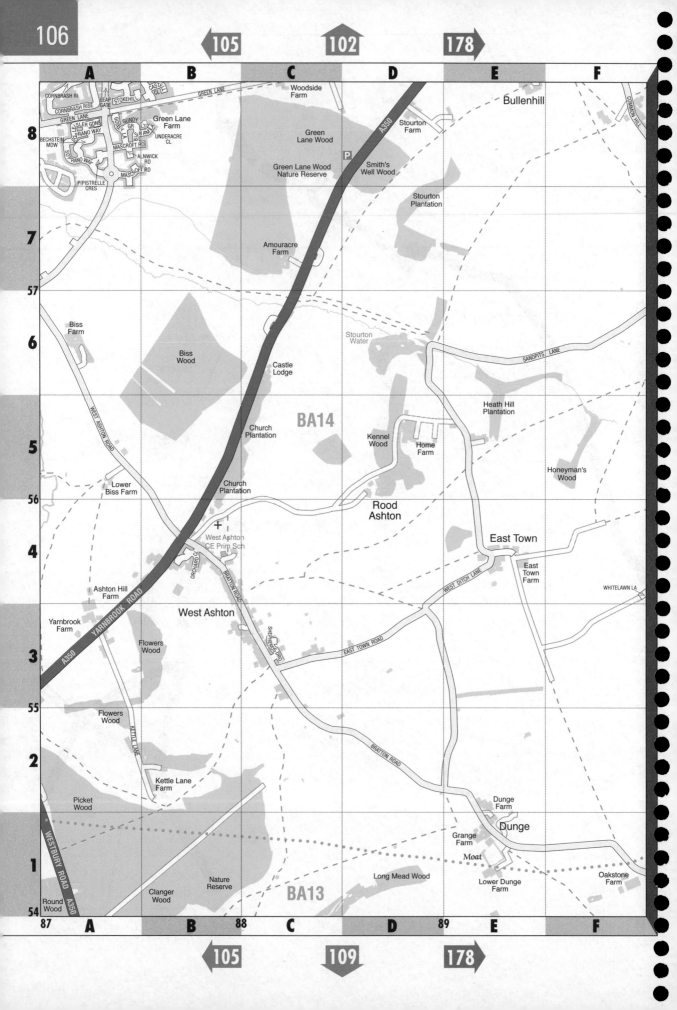

A B C D E F

Green Lane

Woodside Farm

Bullenhill

CORNBRASH RI
CORNBRASH RISE
GREEN LANE
LESLER GDNS
SOPRANO WAY
BECHSTEIN MDW
LEAP GATE
STOKEHILL
CASTLE CL
Green Lane Farm

8

Green Lane Wood

A350
Stourton Farm

GUNDY
GOSEY LA
GR
SHAW LA
UNDERACRE CL
MASCROFT RD
ALNWICK RD
MASCROFT RD

Green Lane Wood Nature Reserve

Smith's Well Wood

Stourton Plantation

PIPISTRELLE CRES

7

Amouracre Farm

57

Biss Farm

6

Biss Wood

Stourton Water

SANDPITS LANE

Castle Lodge

Heath Hill Plantation

BA14

Church Plantation

5

Kennel Wood

Home Farm

Honeyman's Wood

WEST ASHTON ROAD

Lower Biss Farm

56

Church Plantation

Rood Ashton

East Town

4

West Ashton CE Prim Sch

East Town Farm

WHITELAWN LA

ORCHARD CL

BRATTON ROAD

WEST DITCH LANE

Ashton Hill Farm

West Ashton

Yarnbrook Farm

YARNBROOK ROAD

Flowers Wood

SHEPHERDS DRO

3

A350

EAST TOWN ROAD

55

Flowers Wood

KETTLE LANE

BRATTON ROAD

2

Kettle Lane Farm

Picket Wood

Dunge Farm

Dunge

Grange Farm

Moat

1

WESTBURY ROAD

Nature Reserve

Long Mead Wood

Lower Dunge Farm

Oakstone Farm

Round Wood

A350

Clanger Wood

BA13

54

87 A B 88 C D 89 E F

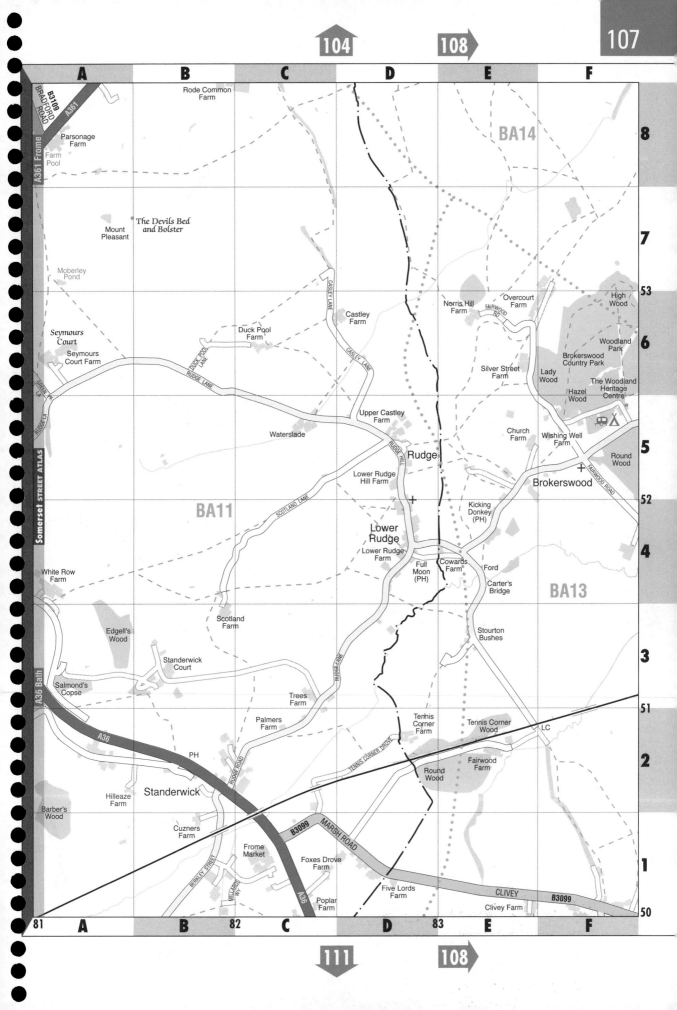

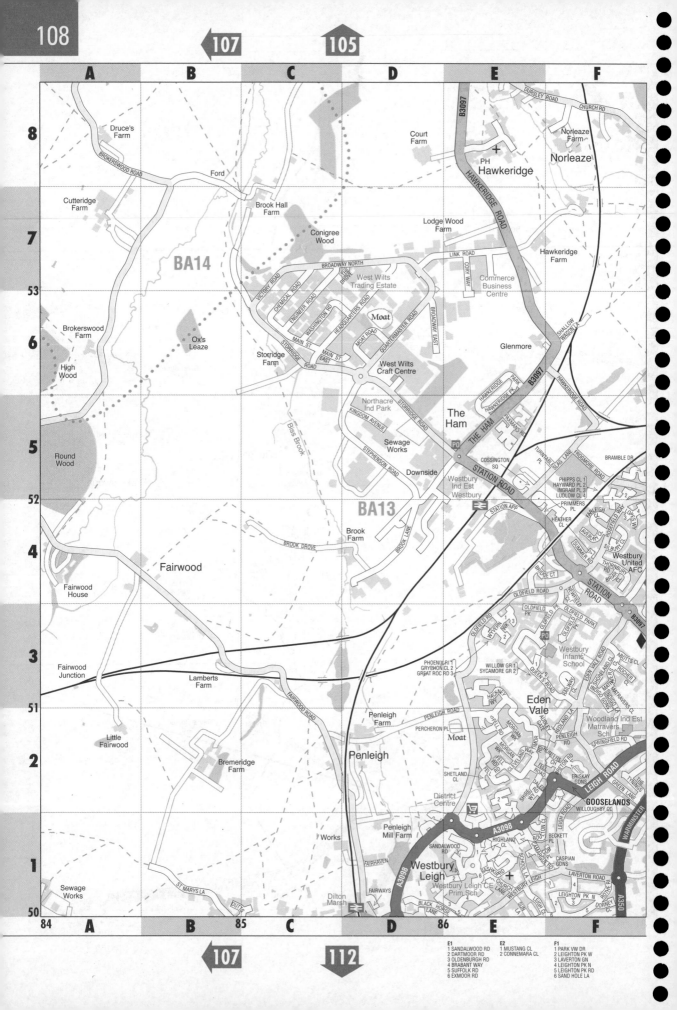

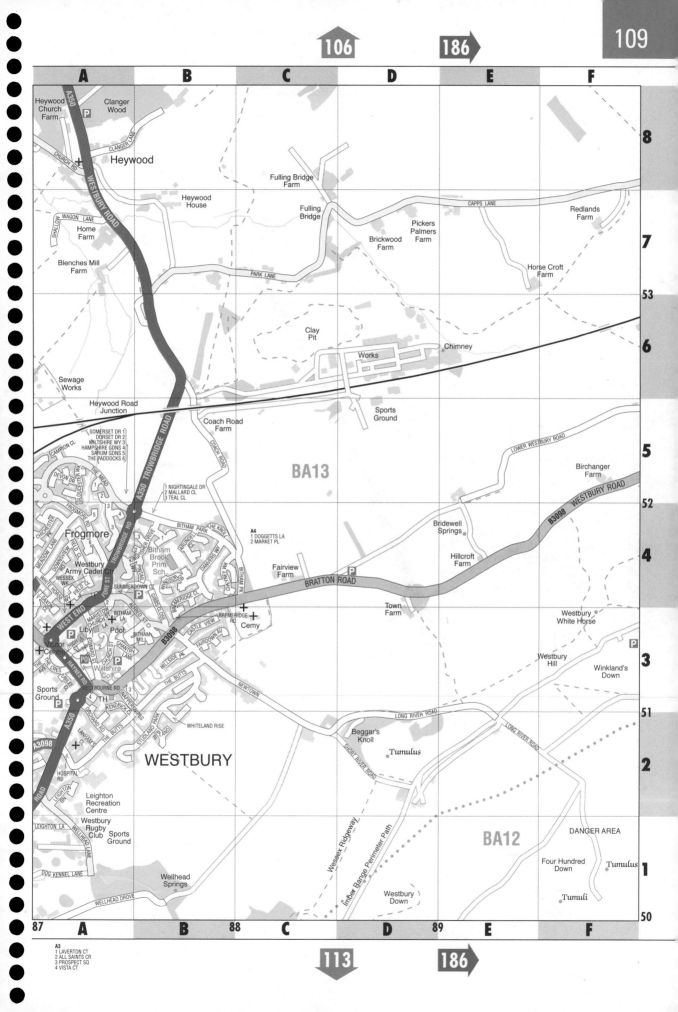

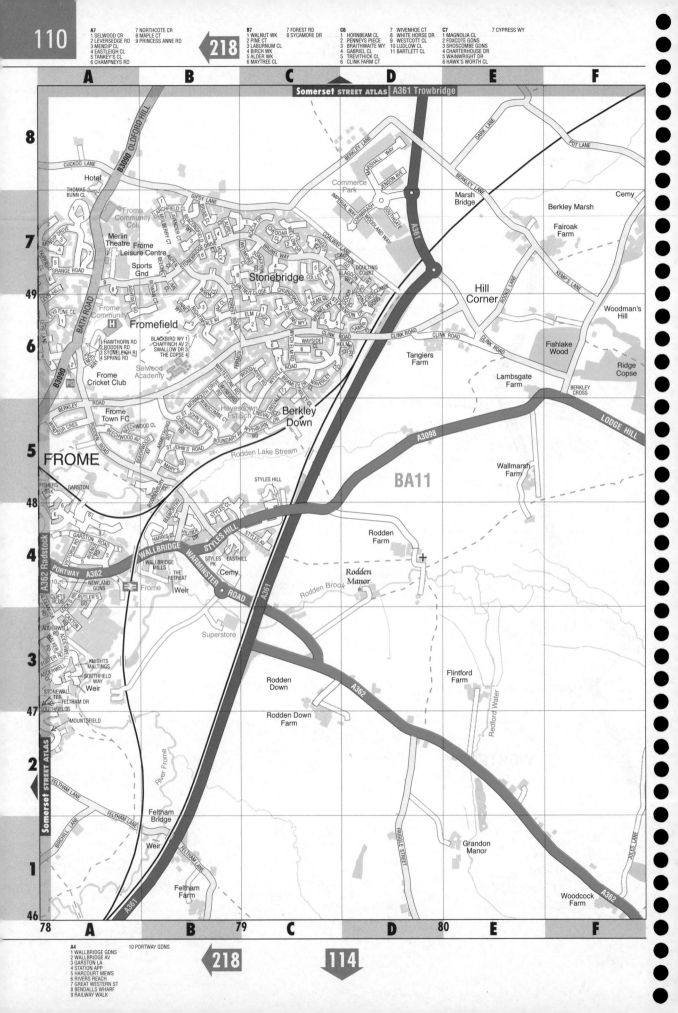

218

Somerset STREET ATLAS A361 Trowbridge

218

114

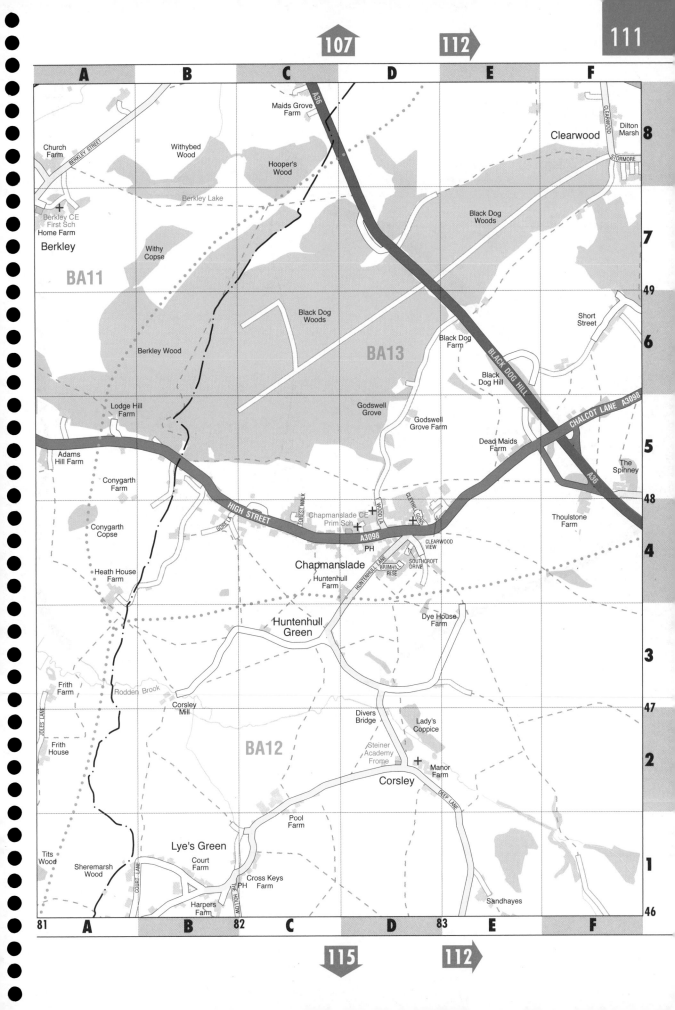

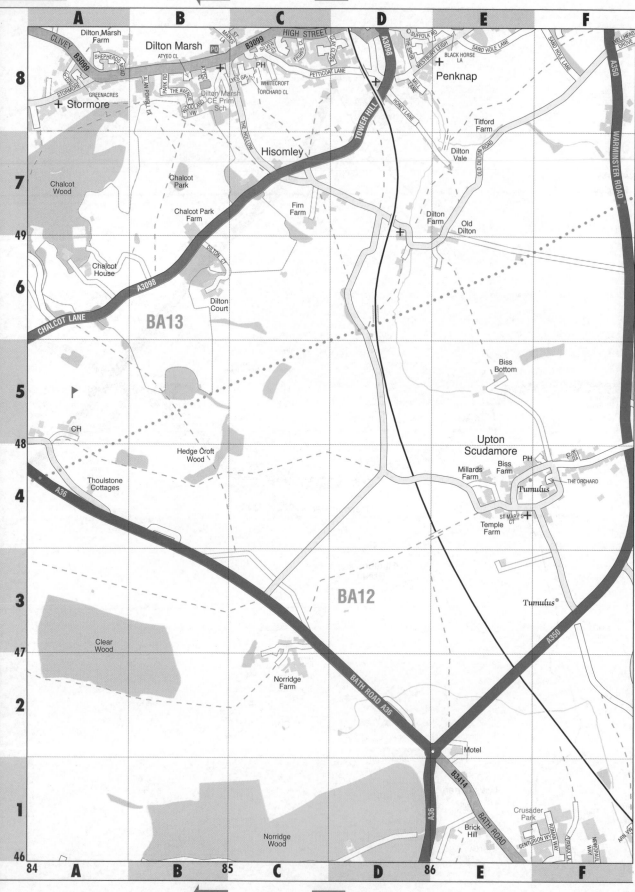

Chalford

BA13

Madbrook Farm

Earthworks

Tumulus

Upton Cow Down

DANGER AREA

Upton Cow Down

Field Barn

Wessex Ridgeway

Halfway Farm

Halfway

Fernicombe

Colloway Clump

Long Barrow

New Farm

Westbury Road

Arn Hill Down

Earthwork

Kidnapper's Hole

West Wilts Golf Club

Mast

CH

Mast

Wessex Ridgeway

Imber Range Perimeter Path

Cradle Hill

Parsonage Farm

Westbury Down

DANGER AREA

Dilton Middle Down

Ranscombe Bottom

Four Hundred Down

Tumuli

Tumuli

Thirteen Hundred Down

Tumuli

Tumulus

DANGER   AREA

Tumulus

Dirtley Wood

DANGER AREA

BA12

Earthwork

Warminster Down

Rifle Range

Mancombe Bottom

Mancombe Wood

Enclosure

Mancombe Down

Oxendean Bottom

Warminster Training Centre

Roberts of Kandahar Rd

Sack Hill

Sack Hill

Imber Rd

Imber Range Perimeter Path

8
7
49
6
5
48
4
3
47
2
1
46

A   B   C   D   E   F

87   88   89

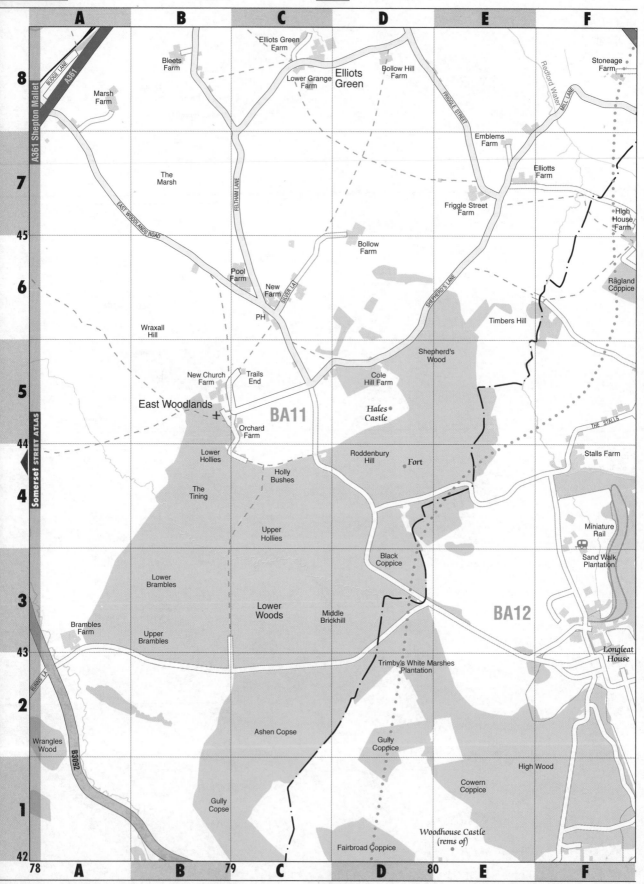

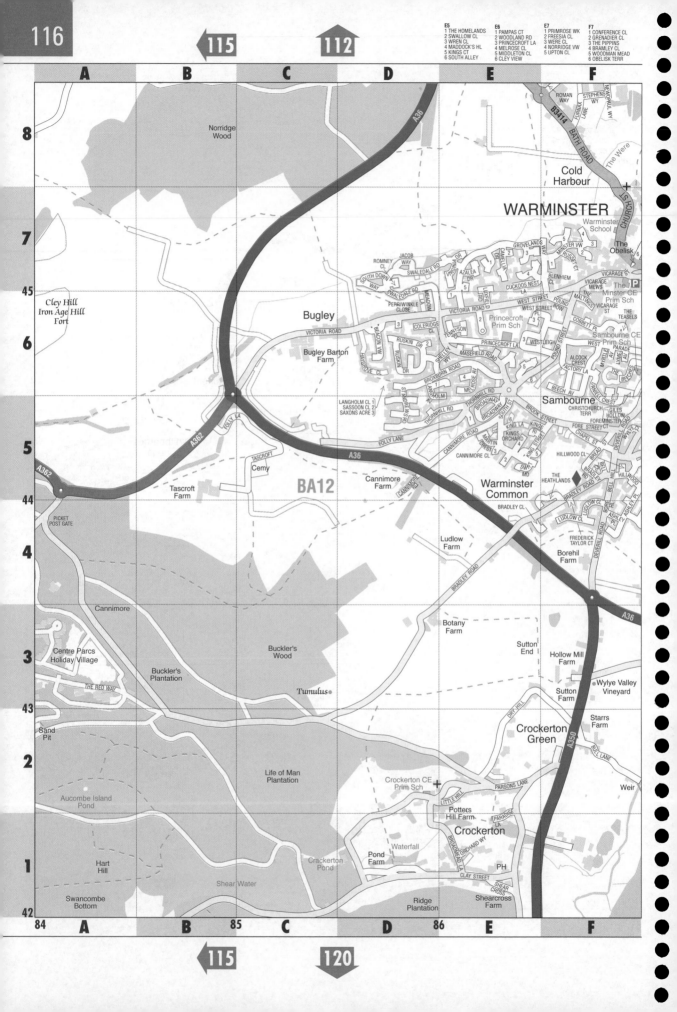

115
112

E5
1 THE HOMELANDS
2 SWALLOW CL
3 WREN CL
4 MADDOCK'S HL
5 KINGS CT
6 SOUTH ALLEY

E6
1 PAMPAS CT
2 WOODLAND RD
3 PRINCECROFT LA
4 MELROSE CL
5 MIDDLETON CL
6 CLEY VIEW

E7
1 PRIMROSE WK
2 FREESIA CL
3 WERE CL
4 NORRIDGE VW
5 UPTON CL

F7
1 CONFERENCE CL
2 GRENADIER CL
3 THE PIPPINS
4 BRAMLEY CL
5 WOODMAN MEAD
6 OBELISK TERR

Norridge Wood

Cold Harbour

WARMINSTER

Warminster School

The Obelisk

Cley Hill
Iron Age Hill
Fort

Bugley

Bugley Barton Farm

Princecroft Prim Sch

Sambourne CE Prim Sch

Sambourne

LANGHOLM CL 1
SASSOON CL 2
SAXONS ACRE 3

BA12

Cannimore Farm

Warminster Common

The Heathlands

Tascroft
Cemy

Tascroft Farm

Ludlow Farm

Borehil Farm

PICKET POST GATE

Cannimore

Buckler's Wood

Botany Farm

Sutton End

Hollow Mill Farm

Centre Parcs Holiday Village

Buckler's Plantation

THE RED WAY

Tumulus

Sutton Farm

Wylye Valley Vineyard

Sand Pit

Dry Hill

Crockerton Green

Starrs Farm

Life of Man Plantation

Aucombe Island Pond

Crockerton CE Prim Sch

Potters Hill Farm

Weir

Crockerton

Hart Hill

Waterfall

Pond Farm

Crackerton Pond

PH

Shear Water

Swancombe Bottom

Ridge Plantation

Shearcross Farm

115
120

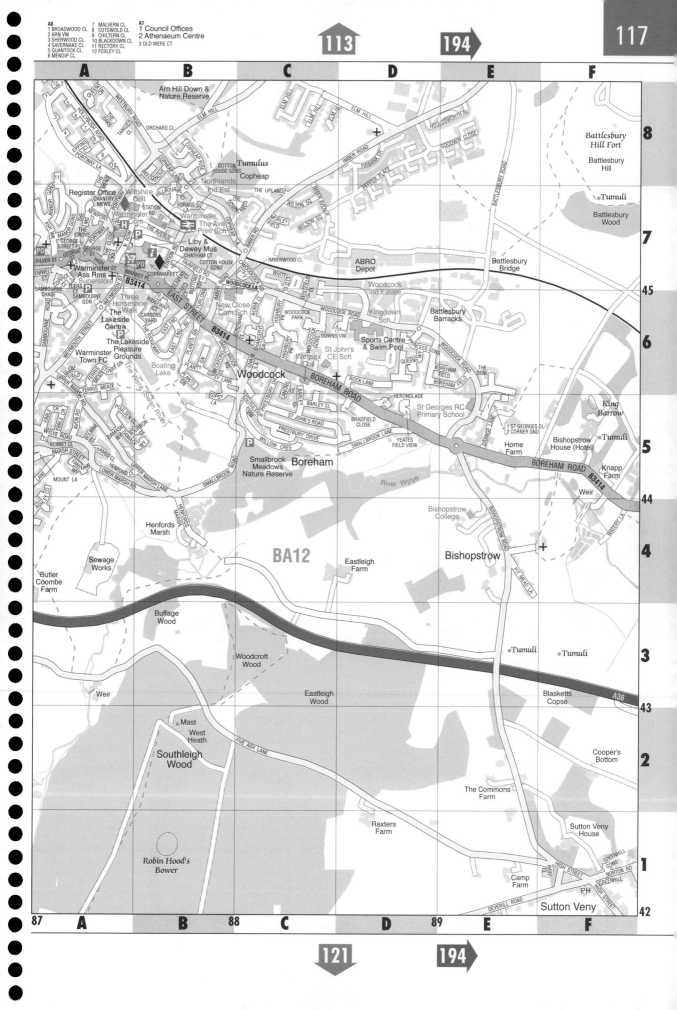

113
194
121
194

A8
1 BROADWOOD CL
2 ARN VW
3 SHERWOOD CL
4 SAVERNAKE CL
5 QUANTOCK CL
6 MENDIP CL
7 MALVERN CL
8 COTSWOLD CL
9 CHILTERN CL
10 BLACKDOWN CL
11 RECTORY CL
12 FOXLEY CL

A7
1 Council Offices
2 Athenaeum Centre
3 OLD WERE CT

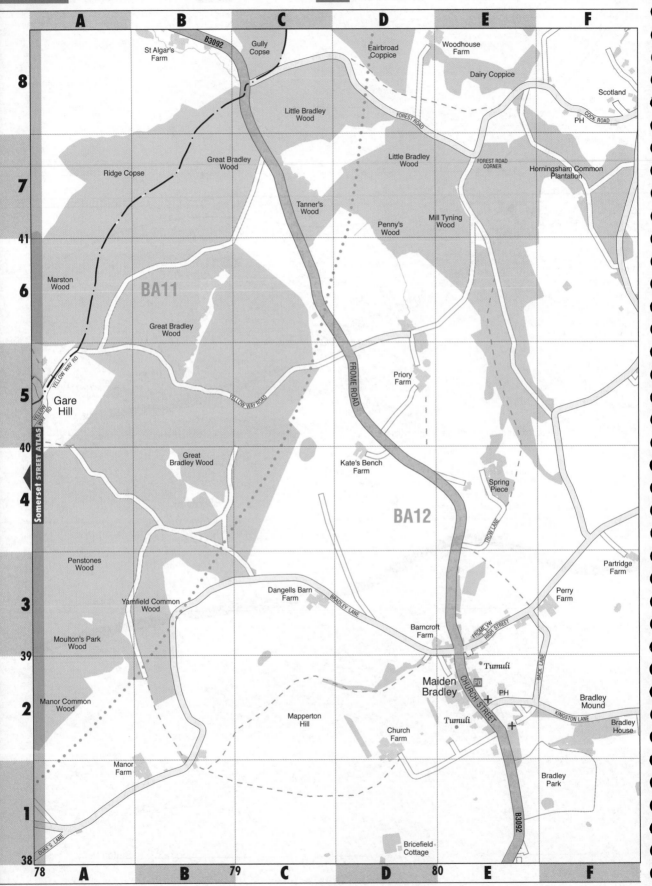

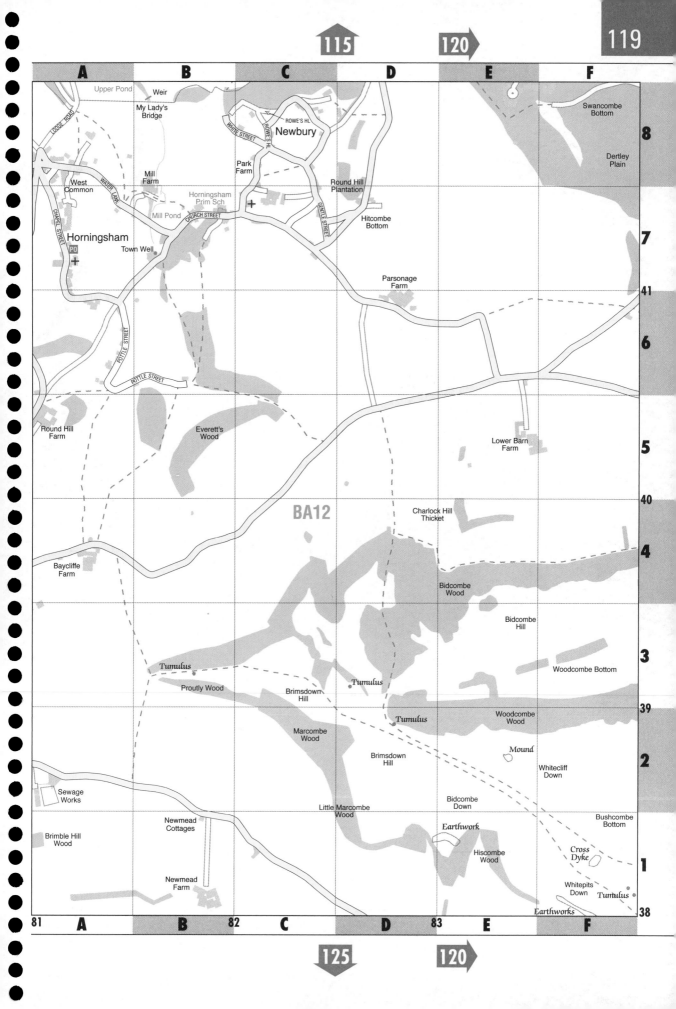

A B C D E F

Upper Pond
Weir
My Lady's Bridge
LODGE ROAD
WHITE STREET
ROWE'S HL
Newbury
ROWE'S HL
Mill Farm
Park Farm
Round Hill Plantation
Swancombe Bottom
Dertley Plain

8

West Common
WATER LANE
Horningsham Prim Sch
Mill Pond
CHURCH STREET
GENTLE STREET
Hitcombe Bottom

CHAPEL STREET
Horningsham
PO
Town Well

7

POTTLE STREET
Parsonage Farm

41

POTTLE STREET

6

Round Hill Farm
Everett's Wood
Lower Barn Farm

5

BA12

40

Baycliffe Farm

4

Charlock Hill Thicket
Bidcombe Wood
Bidcombe Hill
Woodcombe Bottom

3

Tumulus
Proutly Wood
Brimsdown Hill
Tumulus
Tumulus
Woodcombe Wood

39

Marcombe Wood
Brimsdown Hill
Mound
Whitecliff Down

2

Sewage Works
Little Marcombe Wood
Bidcombe Down
Bushcombe Bottom

Newmead Cottages
Earthwork
Cross Dyke

Brimble Hill Wood
Hiscombe Wood

1

Newmead Farm
Whitepits Down
Tumulus

Earthworks

38

81 A B 82 C D 83 E F

119 116

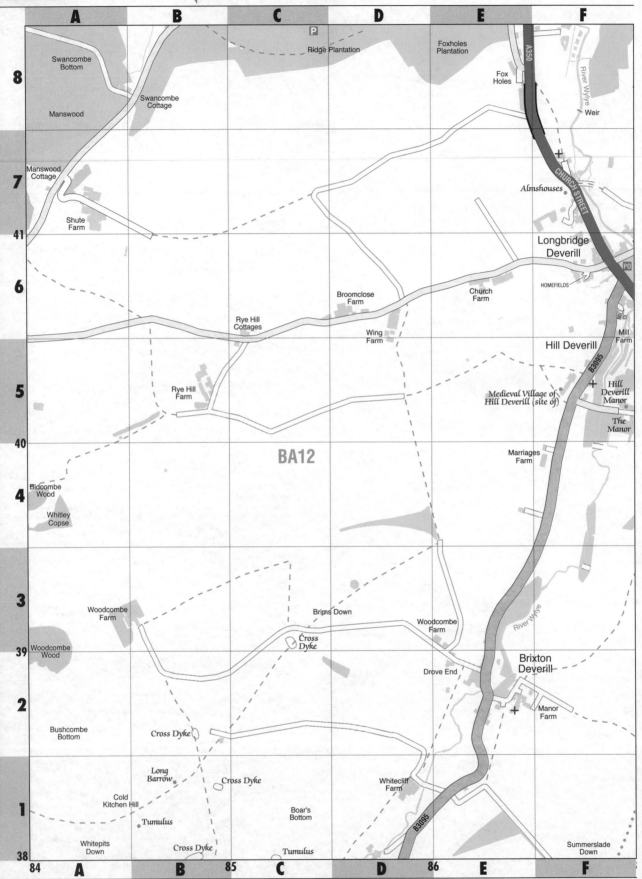

A B C D E F

Swancombe
Bottom

Ridge Plantation

Foxholes
Plantation

8

Manswood

Swancombe
Cottage

Fox
Holes

A350

River Wylye

Weir

Manswood
Cottage

Almshouses

CHURCH STREET

7

Shute
Farm

41

Longbridge
Deverill

PO

6

Broomclose
Farm

Church
Farm

HOMEFIELDS

Rye Hill
Cottages

Wing
Farm

Hill Deverill

B3095

Mill
Farm

5

Rye Hill
Farm

Medieval Village of
Hill Deverill (site of)

Hill
Deverill
Manor

40

Bidcombe
Wood

BA12

Marriages
Farm

The
Manor

4

Whitley
Copse

3

Woodcombe
Farm

Brims Down

Woodcombe
Farm

River Wylye

Woodcombe
Wood

39

Cross
Dyke

Brixton
Deverill

Drove End

2

Bushcombe
Bottom

Cross Dyke

Manor
Farm

Cross Dyke

Whitecliff
Farm

Long
Barrow

Cross Dyke

Cold
Kitchen Hill

Boar's
Bottom

1

Tumulus

B3095

Whitepits
Down

Cross Dyke

Tumulus

Summerslade
Down

38

84 A B 85 C D 86 E F

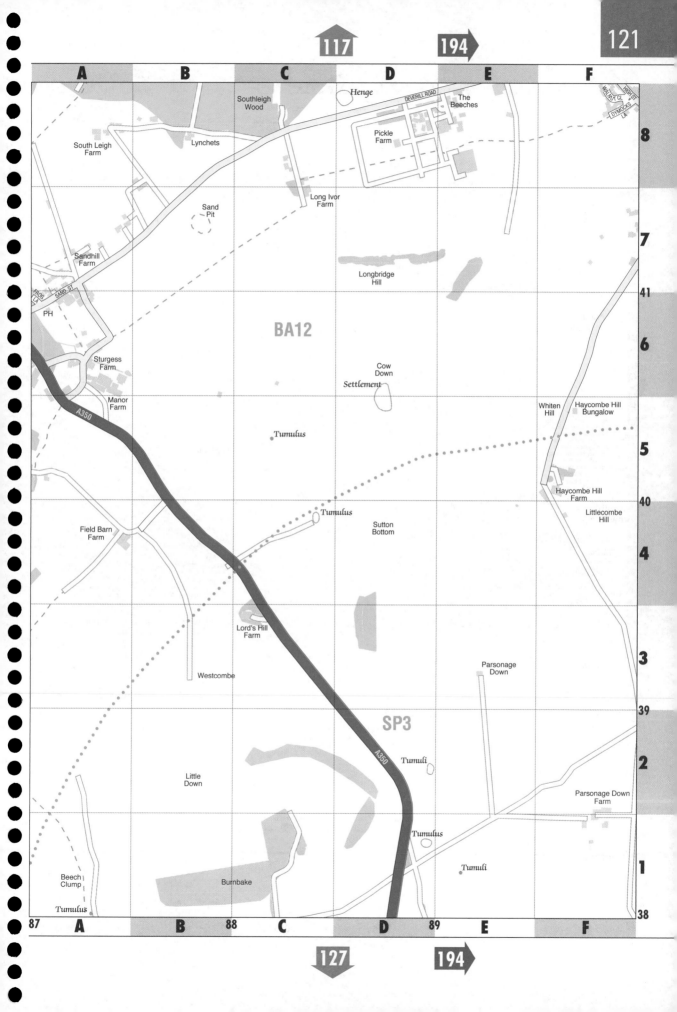

117
194

A B C D E F

8

Southleigh
Wood

Henge

DEVERILL ROAD

The
Beeches

WALNUT CL
HIGH ST
DYMOCKS LA

South Leigh
Farm

Lynchets

Pickle
Farm

Sand
Pit

Long Ivor
Farm

7

41

Sandhill
Farm

SAND ST

Longbridge
Hill

BA12

FROG LA

PH

6

Sturgess
Farm

Cow
Down

Settlement

Whiten
Hill

Haycombe Hill
Bungalow

Manor
Farm

A350

Tumulus

5

40

Field Barn
Farm

Tumulus

Sutton
Bottom

Haycombe Hill
Farm

Littlecombe
Hill

4

Lord's Hill
Farm

Westcombe

Parsonage
Down

3

39

SP3

A350

Tumuli

Little
Down

2

Parsonage Down
Farm

Tumulus

Beech
Clump

Burnbake

Tumuli

1

Tumulus

87 A B 88 C D 89 E F 38

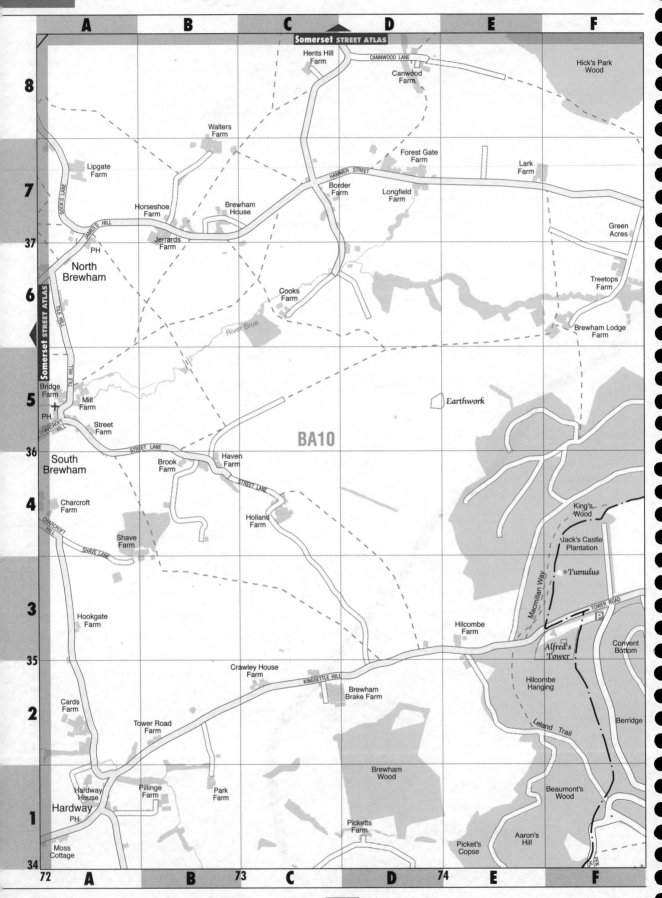

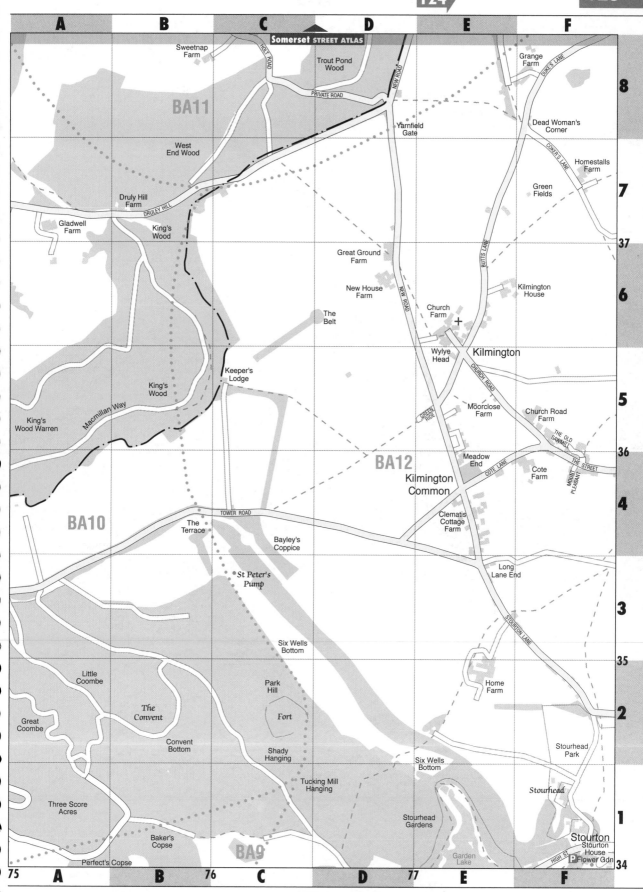

Somerset STREET ATLAS

A B C D E F

Sweetnap Farm

HOLT ROAD

Trout Pond Wood

NEW ROAD

PRIVATE ROAD

Grange Farm

DUKE'S LANE

8

BA11

Yarnfield Gate

Dead Woman's Corner

COKER'S LANE

West End Wood

Homestalls Farm

7

Druly Hill Farm

DRULEY HILL

Green Fields

King's Wood

Gladwell Farm

37

Great Ground Farm

BUTTS LANE

Kilmington House

6

New House Farm

NEW ROAD

Church Farm

The Belt

Keeper's Lodge

Wylye Head

Kilmington

King's Wood

CHURCH ROAD

5

King's Wood

Macmillan Way

Moorclose Farm

Church Road Farm

THE OLD SAWMILL

King's Wood Warren

GREEN RIDE

BA12

Meadow End

THE STREET

36

Kilmington Common

COTE LANE

Cote Farm

MOUNT PLEASANT

BA10

TOWER ROAD

Clematis Cottage Farm

4

The Terrace

Bayley's Coppice

Long Lane End

St Peter's Pump

STOURTON LANE

3

Six Wells Bottom

35

Little Coombe

Park Hill

Home Farm

2

The Convent

Fort

Great Coombe

Convent Bottom

Shady Hanging

Stourhead Park

Three Score Acres

Tucking Mill Hanging

Six Wells Bottom

Stourhead

1

Stourhead Gardens

Baker's Copse

Stourton

Stourton House Flower Gdn

BA9

Garden Lake

HIGH ST

34

Perfect's Copse

← 123
↑ 118

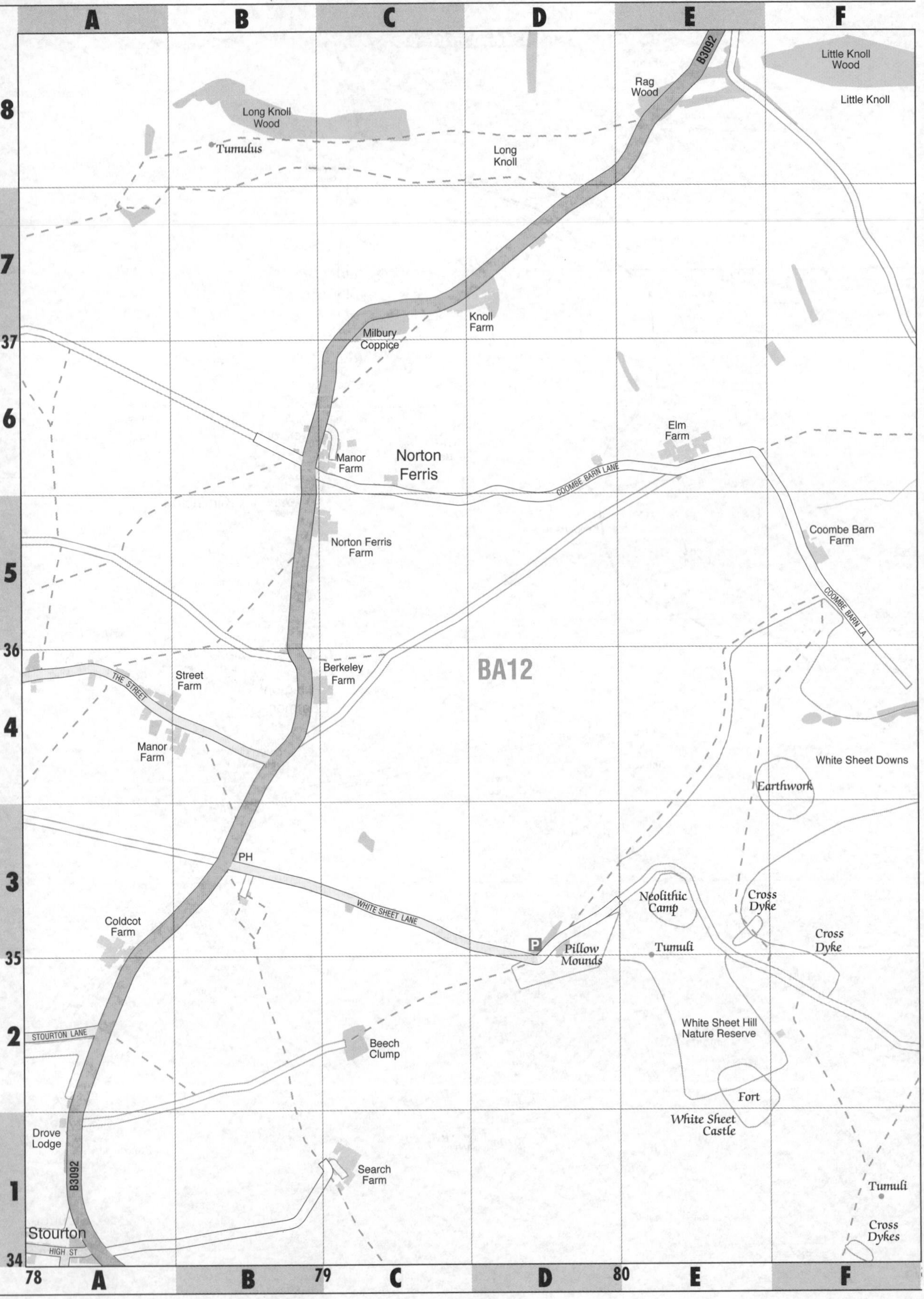

A **B** **C** **D** **E** **F**

8

Long Knoll Wood

Rag Wood

Little Knoll Wood

Little Knoll

Tumulus

Long Knoll

B3092

37

Milbury Coppice

Knoll Farm

6

Elm Farm

Manor Farm

Norton Ferris

COOMBE BARN LANE

Coombe Barn Farm

Norton Ferris Farm

COOMBE BARN LA

5

36

Street Farm

THE STREET

Berkeley Farm

BA12

4

Manor Farm

White Sheet Downs

Earthwork

3

PH

WHITE SHEET LANE

Neolithic Camp

Cross Dyke

Cross Dyke

Coldcot Farm

P

Pillow Mounds

Tumuli

35

White Sheet Hill Nature Reserve

2

STOURTON LANE

Beech Clump

Fort

1

Drove Lodge

B3092

Search Farm

White Sheet Castle

Tumuli

Cross Dykes

Stourton

HIGH ST

34

78 **A** **B** 79 **C** **D** 80 **E** **F**

← 123
⬡ 138

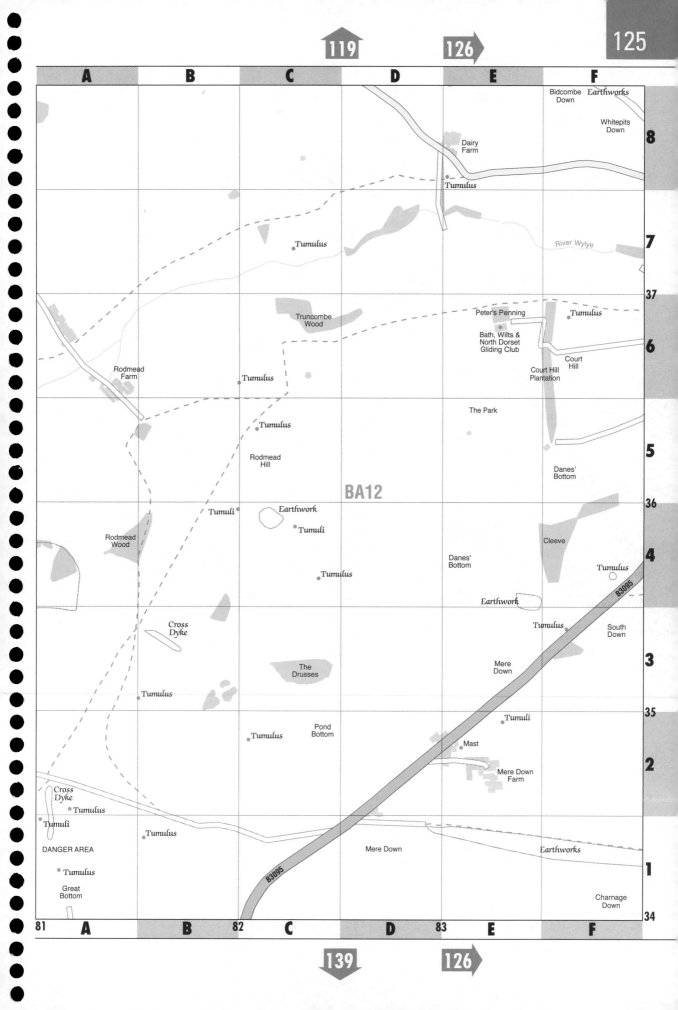

A | B | C | D | E | F

Bidcombe Earthworks
Down

Whitepits
Down

8

Dairy
Farm

Tumulus

Tumulus

River Wylye

7

37

Truncombe
Wood

Peter's Penning
Tumulus

Bath, Wilts &
North Dorset
Gliding Club

6

Court
Hill

Rodmead
Farm

Tumulus

Court Hill
Plantation

The Park

5

Tumulus

Danes'
Bottom

Rodmead
Hill

BA12

36

Tumuli

Earthwork

Cleeve

Tumuli

Rodmead
Wood

Tumulus

Danes'
Bottom

4

Tumulus

B3095

Tumulus

Earthwork

Cross
Dyke

Tumulus

South
Down

The
Drusses

Mere
Down

3

35

Tumulus

Tumuli

Tumulus

Pond
Bottom

Mast

2

Mere Down
Farm

Cross
Dyke

Tumulus

Tumulus

Tumulus

DANGER AREA

Mere Down

Earthworks

1

Tumulus

B3095

Great
Bottom

Charnage
Down

34

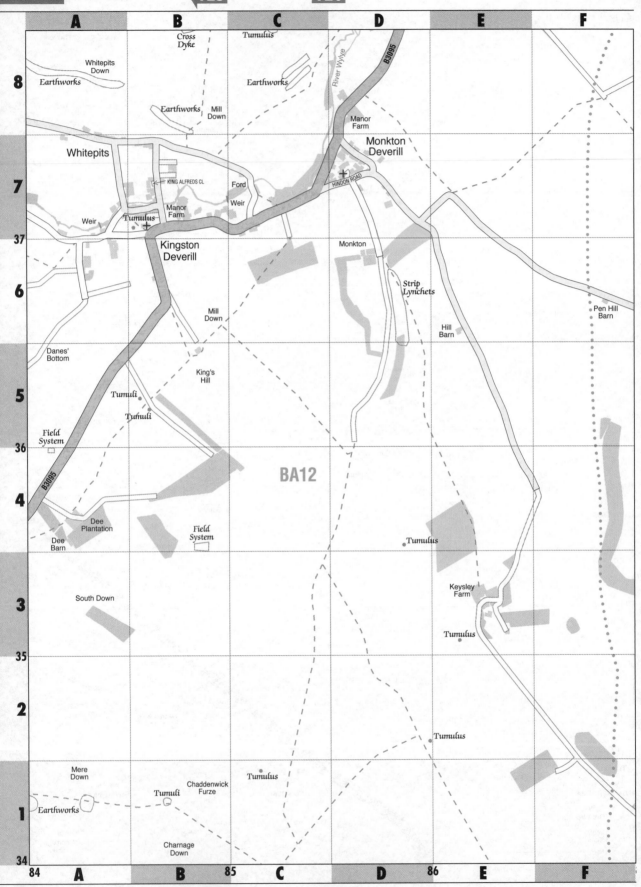

A   B   C   D   E   F

8

Earthworks

Whitepits
Down

Cross
Dyke

Tumulus

Earthworks

River Wylye

B3095

Earthworks

Mill
Down

Manor
Farm

Whitepits

Monkton
Deverill

7

KING ALFREDS CL

Ford

Weir

HINDON ROAD

37

Weir

Manor
Farm

Tumulus

Monkton

Kingston
Deverill

Strip
Lynchets

Pen Hill
Barn

6

Weir

Mill
Down

Hill
Barn

Danes'
Bottom

King's
Hill

5

Tumuli

Tumuli

Field
System

36

B3095

BA12

4

Dee
Plantation

Field
System

Tumulus

Dee
Barn

Keysley
Farm

3

South Down

Tumulus

35

2

Tumulus

Mere
Down

Chaddenwick
Furze

Tumulus

1

Tumuli

Earthworks

Charnage
Down

34

84   A   B   85   C   D   86   E   F

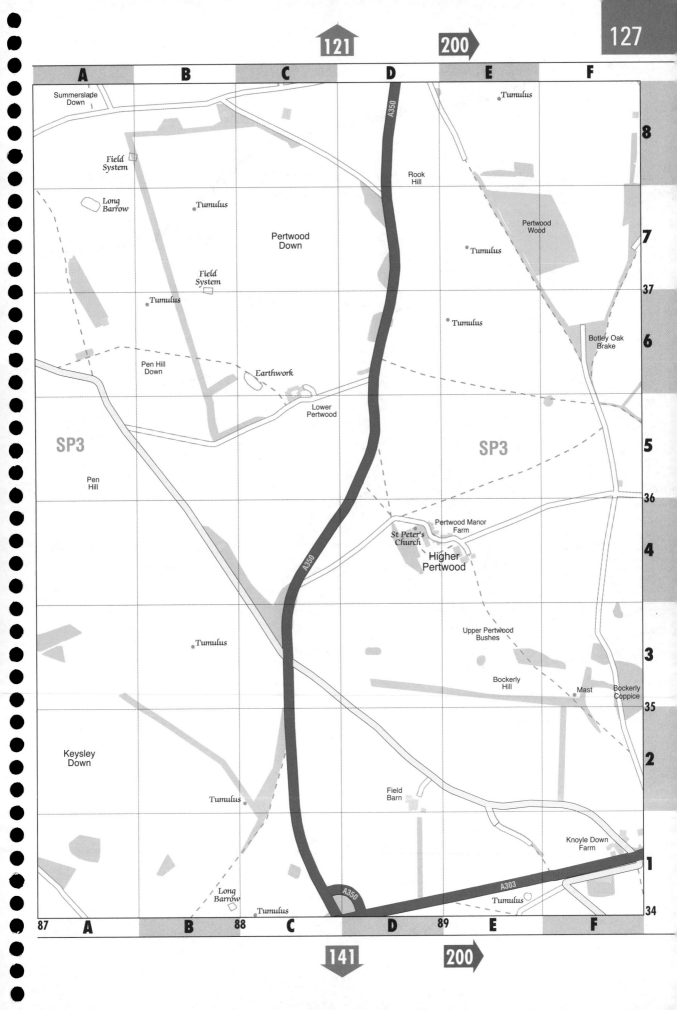

← 201
196 ↑

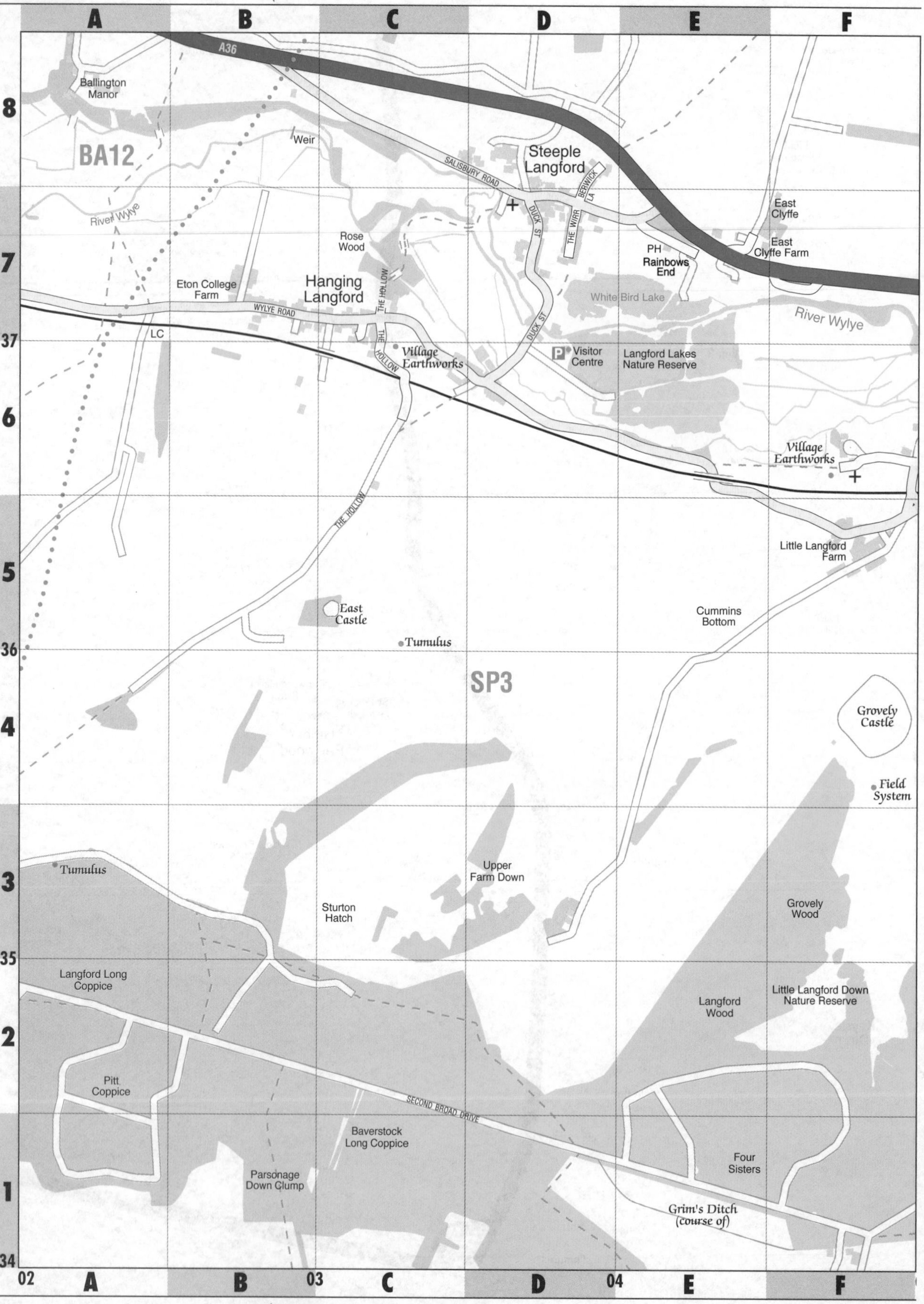

A B C D E F

A36

Ballington
Manor

BA12

Weir

Steeple
Langford

River Wylye

East
Clyffe

SALISBURY ROAD

BERWICK LA.

East
Clyffe Farm

Rose
Wood

DUCK ST.

THE WYR

Hanging
Langford

Eton College
Farm

WYLYE ROAD

THE HOLLOW

PH
Rainbows
End

White Bird Lake

River Wylye

LC

Village
Earthworks

P Visitor
Centre

Langford Lakes
Nature Reserve

THE HOLLOW

Village
Earthworks

Little Langford
Farm

East
Castle

Cummins
Bottom

Tumulus

Grovely
Castle

SP3

Field
System

Tumulus

Upper
Farm Down

Grovely
Wood

Sturton
Hatch

Langford Long
Coppice

Little Langford Down
Nature Reserve

Langford
Wood

Pitt
Coppice

SECOND BROAD DRIVE

Baverstock
Long Coppice

Four
Sisters

Parsonage
Down Clump

Grim's Ditch
(course of)

A B 03 C D 04 E F

02

34

← 201
142 ↓

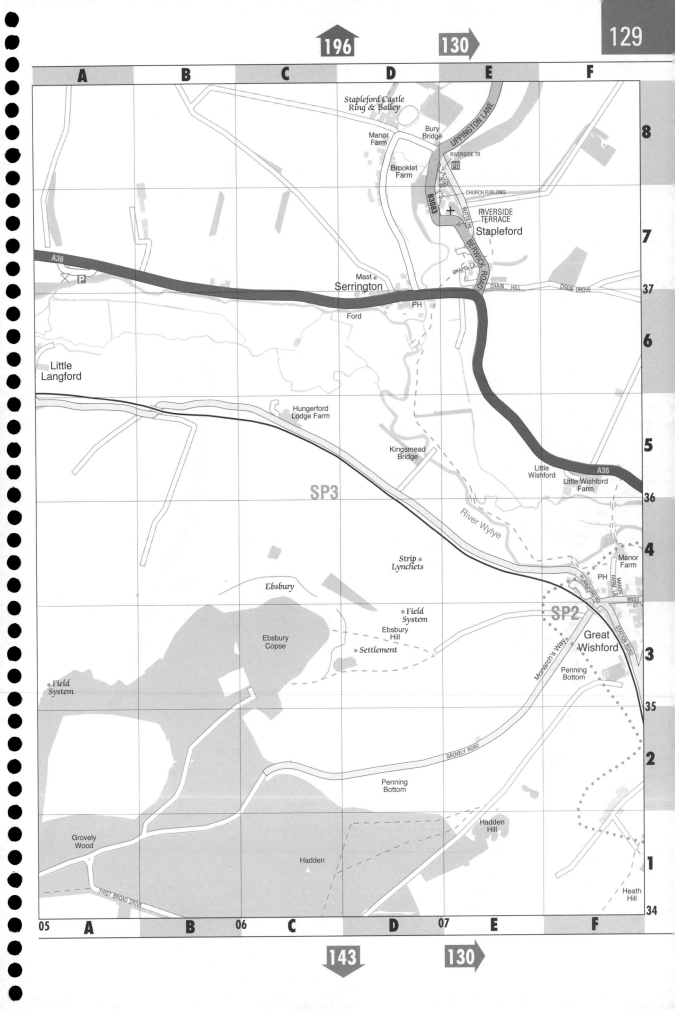

A B C D E F

8 7 37 6 5 36 4 35 2 1 34

Stapleford Castle Ring & Bailey

Manor Farm

Bury Bridge

UPPINGTON LANE

RIVERSIDE TR
PO

Brooklet Farm

HILL SIDE

B3083

CHURCH FURLONG

RIVERSIDE TERRACE

BUTTS TH

Stapleford

BERWICK ROAD

CHAPEL LA

A36

P

Mast

Serrington

CHAIN HILL

CHAIN DROVE

PH

Ford

Little Langford

Hungerford Lodge Farm

Kingsmead Bridge

Little Wishford

A36

Little Wishford Farm

River Wylye

SP3

Strip Lynchets

Manor Farm

PH

MANOR FARM LA

Ebsbury

Field System

LANGFORD RD

WEST ST

Ebsbury Copse

Ebsbury Hill

Settlement

SP2

Great Wishford

Field System

Monarch's Way

Penning Bottom

STATION ROAD

Grovely Road

Penning Bottom

Grovely Wood

Hadden

Hadden Hill

FIRST BROAD DRIVE

Heath Hill

A B C D E F

8

Eighteen Acre
Plantation

Stapleford
Down

Camp
Plantation

7

SP3

Chain
Hill

Camp
Cottages

Tumulus

37

Monarch's Way

6

CHAIN DROVE

Stoford Hill
Buildings

Tumulus

SP4

Monarch's Way

5

A360

Stoford
Bottom

36

A36

MOUNT PLEASANT

RIVERSIDE CL

Enclosure

4

Great
Wishford QE
First Sch

PH

Newton
Barrow

Charity
Farm

WEST ST

Stoford
Bridge

Stoford

3

PO

Wishford
Farm

Village
Earthworks

Masts

Town
End

SP2

SOUTH ST

Stoford
Farm

A360

KINGSMEAD

35

River Wylye

2

HIGHLAND
VALE VIEW RD
OAK CL
ASHLEIGH
CLOSE
ST. ANDREW'S RD
BRIDGE SIDE RD

South
Newton

PH

1

SP3

Manor
Farm

Mill
Farm

34

08 A B 09 C D 10 E F

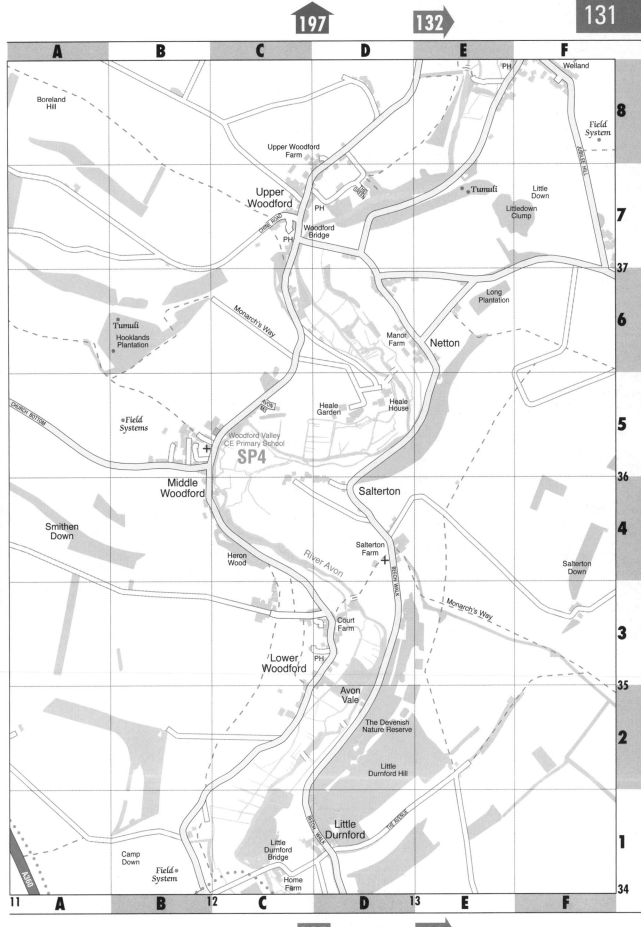

A B C D E F

8

7

37

6

Burnstack
Plantation

South
Farm

Factory

A345

High Post
Golf Club

Cusse's
Gorse

DOWN BARN ROAD

Enclosure

Hotel

High
Post

High Post
Bus Pk

CH

Coffee
Farm

SP4

Downbarn
West

5

36

4

Salterton
Down

FOURMILE HILL

Crabtree
Cottages

3

35

2

Monarch's Way

Hurdcott Farm

Monarch's Way

GREAT DROVE

1

34

Longhedge
Farm

A345

Longhedge
Cottages

SHERBOURNE DR
ROBIN RD
LAPWING DR
NORMAN DR
PORTWAY

Tumuli

14 A B 15 C D 16 E F

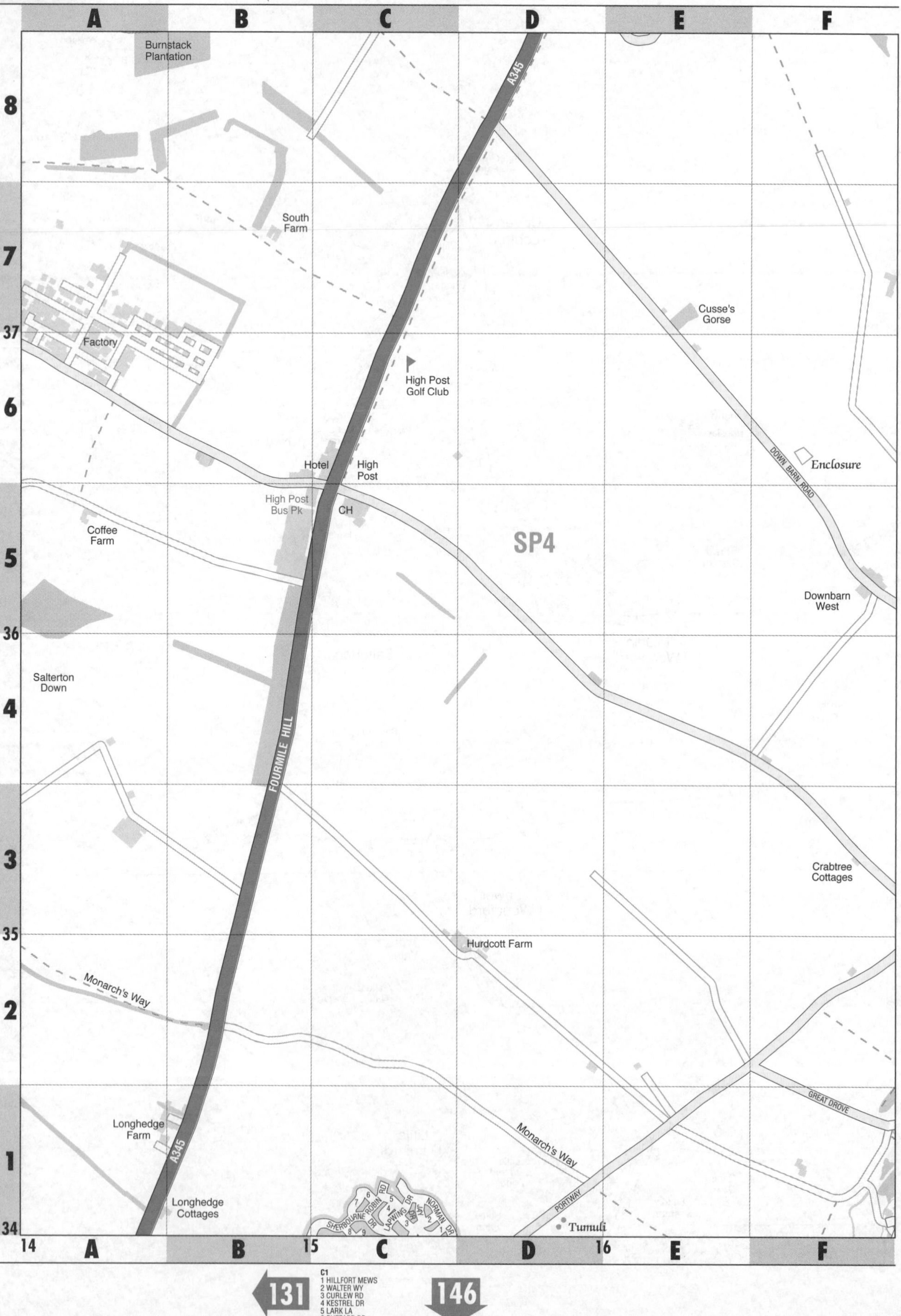

C1
1 HILLFORT MEWS
2 WALTER WY
3 CURLEW RD
4 KESTREL DR
5 LARK LA
6 BUZZARD RD
7 NORMAN DR
8 ROGER WY
9 BISSINGTON CL

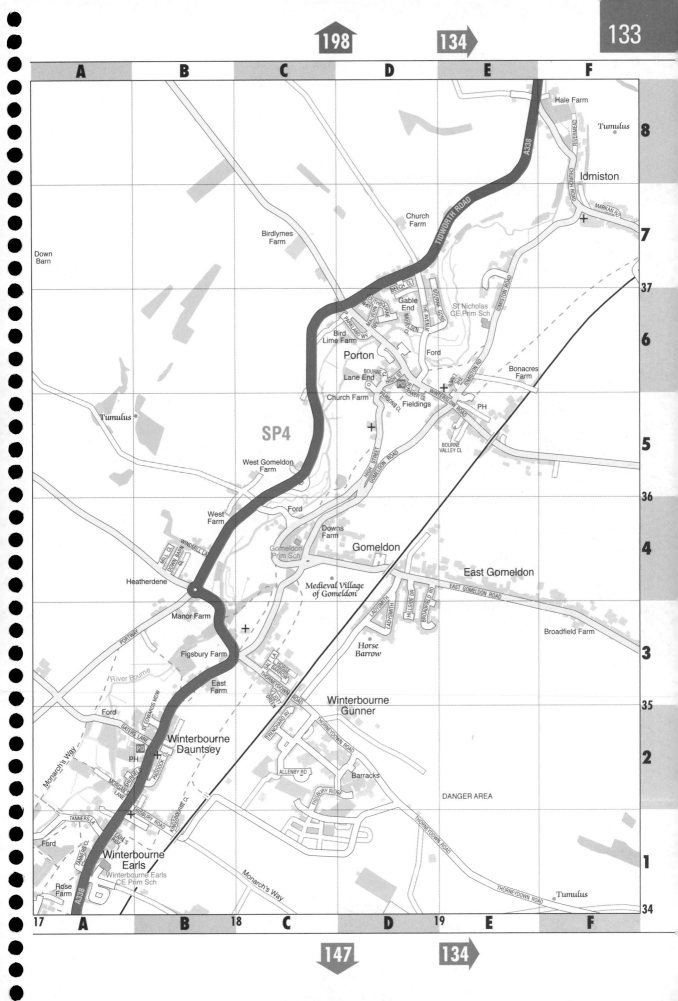

A　B　C　D　E　F

8

Hale Farm

Tumulus

Idmiston

7

Church Farm

37

Down Barn

Birdlymes Farm

Church Farm

St Nicholas CE Prim Sch

6

Gable End

Bird Lime Farm

Porton

Ford

Bonacres Farm

Lane End

Fieldings

PH

Tumulus

Church Farm

SP4

Bourne Valley Cl

5

West Gomeldon Farm

West Farm

Ford

Downs Farm

Gomeldon

East Gomeldon

36

Gomeldon Prim Sch

Medieval Village of Gomeldon

East Gomeldon Road

Heatherdene

4

Manor Farm

Broadfield Farm

Figsbury Farm

Horse Barrow

River Bourne

East Farm

Ford

Winterbourne Gunner

35

Winterbourne Dauntsey

PH

Barracks

2

Allenby Rd

DANGER AREA

Ford

Winterbourne Earls

1

Winterbourne Earls CE Prim Sch

Monarch's Way

Rose Farm

Ford

Tumulus

34

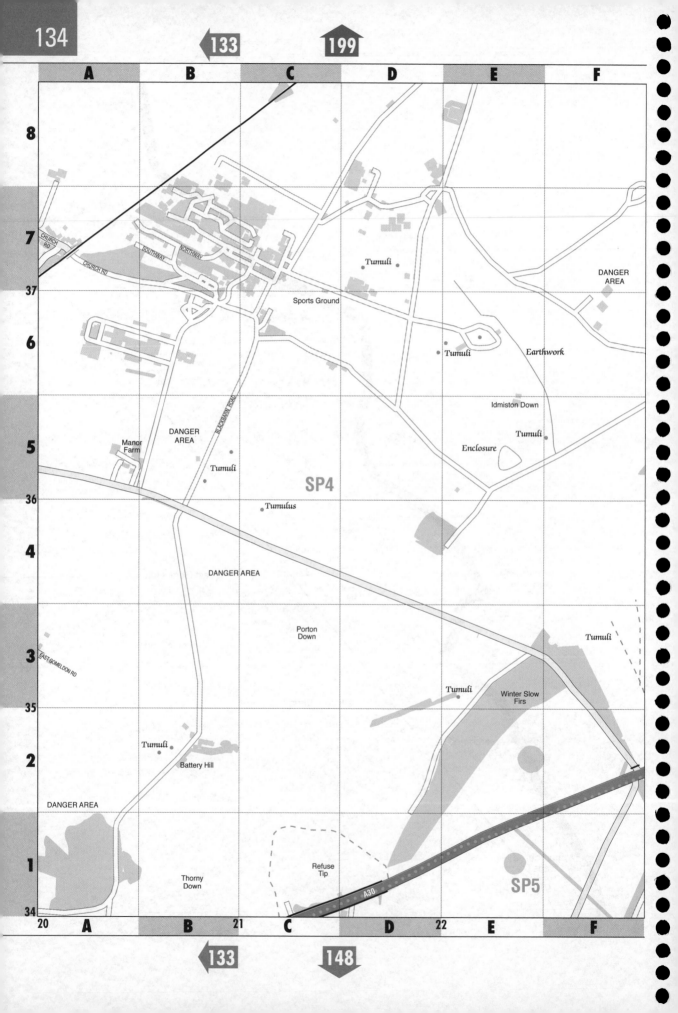

A B C D E F

8

7

CHURCH RD

CHURCH RD

SOUTHWAY

NORTHWAY

37

Sports Ground

Tumuli

DANGER
AREA

6

Tumuli

Earthwork

Idmiston Down

Tumuli

BLACKBARN ROAD

DANGER
AREA

Manor
Farm

Enclosure

5

Tumuli

SP4

36

Tumulus

4

DANGER AREA

Porton
Down

Tumuli

EAST GOMELDON RD

3

Tumuli

Winter Slow
Firs

35

Tumuli

Battery Hill

2

DANGER AREA

1

Thorny
Down

Refuse
Tip

A30

SP5

34

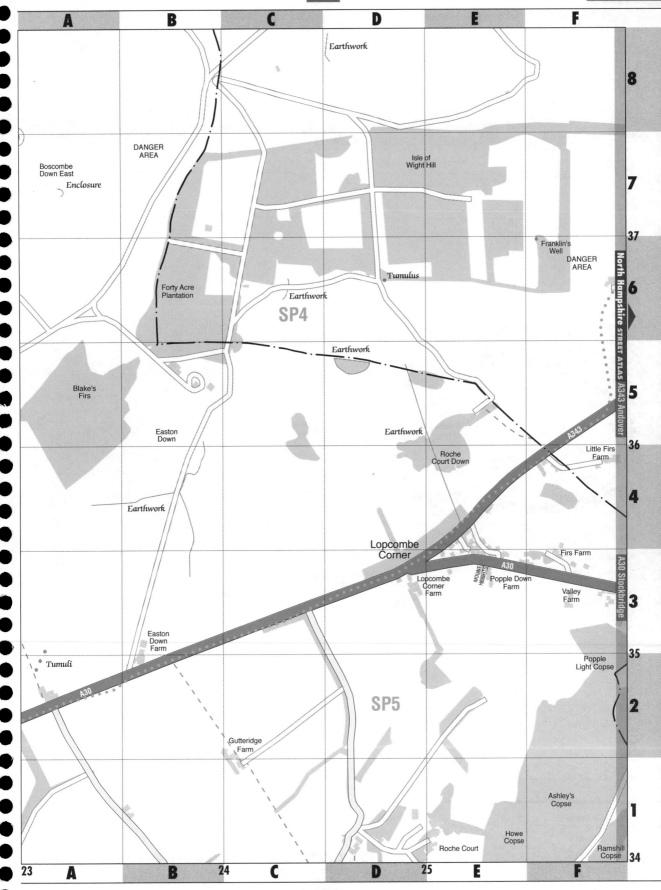

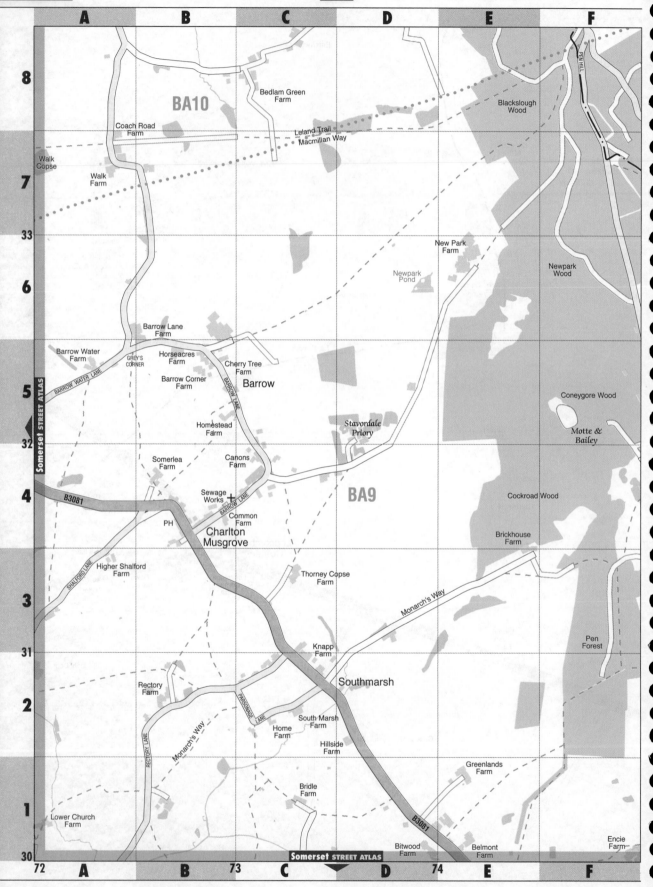

BA10

Bedlam Green
Farm

Coach Road
Farm

Leland Trail
Macmillan Way

Blackslough
Wood

Walk
Copse

Walk
Farm

New Park
Farm

Newpark
Pond

Newpark
Wood

Barrow Lane
Farm

Barrow Water
Farm

GREY'S
CORNER

Horseacres
Farm

Cherry Tree
Farm

Barrow Corner
Farm

Barrow

Coneygore Wood

BARROW WATER LANE

BARROW LANE

Homestead
Farm

Stavordale
Priory

Motte &
Bailey

Somerlea
Farm

Canons
Farm

BA9

Cockroad Wood

B3081

Sewage
Works

BARROW LANE

Common
Farm

Brickhouse
Farm

PH

Charlton
Musgrove

SHALFORD LANE

Higher Shalford
Farm

Thorney Copse
Farm

Monarch's Way

Pen
Forest

Knapp
Farm

Rectory
Farm

Southmarsh

RECTORY LANE

Monarch's Way

PASSAGE LANE

Home
Farm

South Marsh
Farm

Hillside
Farm

Greenlands
Farm

Lower Church
Farm

Bridle
Farm

B3081

Bitwood
Farm

Belmont
Farm

Encie
Farm

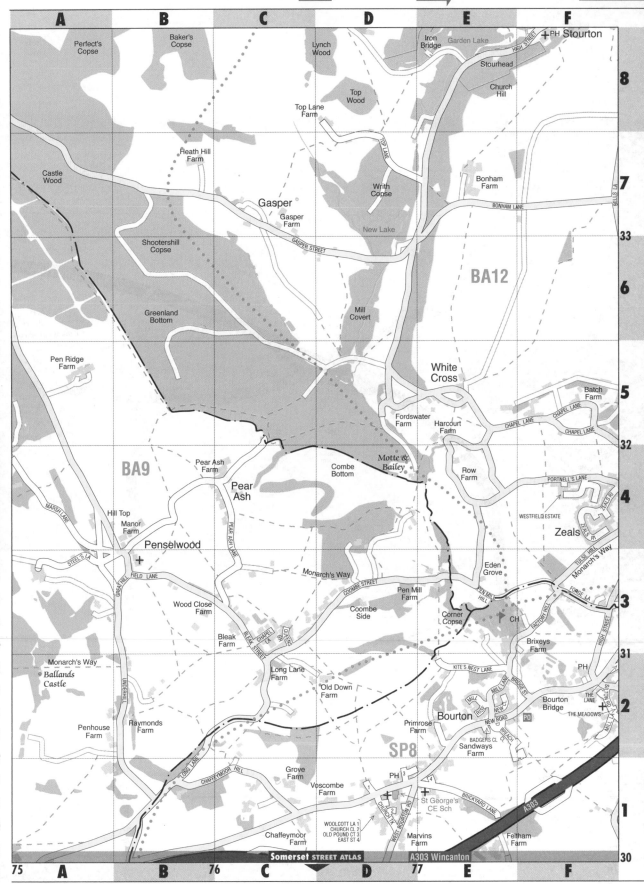

A B C D E F

8

Perfect's Copse
Baker's Copse
Lynch Wood
Iron Bridge
Garden Lake
+ PH Stourton
HIGH STREET
Stourhead
Church Hill
BELLS LA

Top Wood
Top Lane Farm
Heath Hill Farm
TOP LANE
Bonham Farm

7

Castle Wood
Gasper
Writh Copse
BONHAM LANE

Gasper Farm
Shootershill Copse
GASPER STREET
New Lake

33

BA12

6

Greenland Bottom
Mill Covert

Pen Ridge Farm
White Cross
Batch Farm

5

Fordswater Farm
Harcourt Farm
CHAPEL LANE
CHAPEL LANE
CHAPEL LANE

BA9
Pear Ash Farm
Combe Bottom
Motte & Bailey
Row Farm
PORTNELL'S LANE

32

Pear Ash
WESTFIELD ESTATE
ZEALS RD

4

Hill Top
Manor Farm
Monarch's Way
Eden Grove
Zeals
ZEALS RD
Monarch's Way
TULSE HILL

MARSH LANE
PEAR ASH LANE
Penselwood +
COOMBE STREET
Pen Mill Farm
PEN MILL HILL
FORGE LA

STEEL'S LA
Wood Close Farm
Coombe Side
Corner Copse
CH
FACTORY HILL
HIGH STREET

3

GREAT HILL
FIELD LANE
CHAPEL LA
Bleak Farm
BLEAK STREET
QUEENS GR
Brixeys Farm
PH

31

UNDERHILL
Long Lane Farm
Old Down Farm
KITE'S NEST LANE

Monarch's Way
Ballands Castle
MILL LANE
BRIDGE ST
Bourton Bridge
THE LANE
THE MEADOWS
MILL LA

2

Penhouse Farm
Raymonds Farm
LONG LANE
Bourton
NEW ROAD
PO
BREACH
MILL RISE

Grove Farm
Primrose Farm
Sandways Farm
BADGERS CL

SP8

1

CHAFFEYMOOR HILL
Voscombe Farm
PH 3
WOOLCOTT LA 1
CHURCH CL 2
OLD POUND CT 3
EAST ST 4
CHURCH TK
WEST BOURTON RD
St George's CE Sch
BRICKYARD LANE
A303
Feltham Farm

Chaffeymoor Farm
Marvins Farm

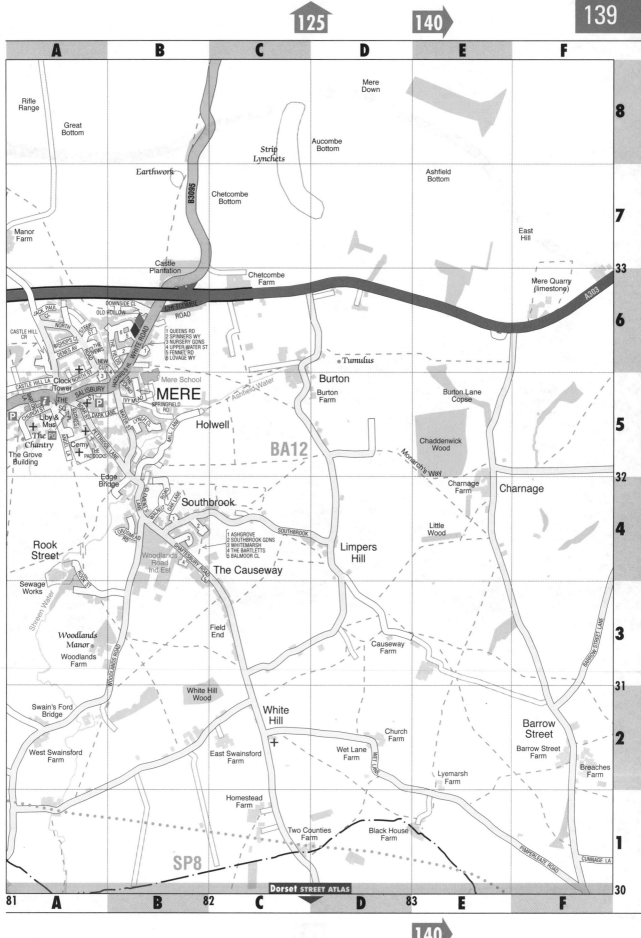

A B C D E F

8

Mere
Down

Rifle
Range

Great
Bottom

Strip
Lynchets

Aucombe
Bottom

Earthwork

Ashfield
Bottom

Chetcombe
Bottom

7

B3095

East
Hill

33

Manor
Farm

Mere Quarry
(limestone)

Castle
Plantation

A303

Chetcombe
Farm

6

JACK PAUL CL

DOWNSIDE CL

OLD HOLLOW

CHETCOMBE
ROAD

CASTLE HILL CR

NORTH

STEEP ST

THE YEWS

THE FIELDS

HAZZARD'S HL WHITE ROAD

NEW CUT

1 QUEENS RD
2 SPINNERS WY
3 NURSERY GDNS
4 UPPER WATER ST
5 FENNEL RD
6 LOVAGE WY

Tumulus

BISHOPS CL

DENES AV

Burton

CASTLE HILL LA

Clock
Tower

NORTH ST

THE END

SALISBURY
ST

Mere School

IVY MEAD

MERE

SPRINGFIELD
RD

Ashfield Water

Burton
Farm

Burton Lane
Copse

5

BURTON ST

THE
SQ

i

BOAR ST

BARNES'

P

WATER ST

DARK LANE

LYNCH CL

Chaddenwick
Wood

CHURCH ST

Liby &
Mus

P

PO

ANGEL LA

Holwell

MILL LANE

Monarch's Way

The
Chantry

Cemy

PETTRIDGE LANE

THE
PADDOCKS

BA12

The Grove
Building

32

Edge
Bridge

CLEMENTS LANE

WALNUT ROAD

OAK LANE

Charnage
Farm

Charnage

Southbrook

SOUTHBROOK

LORDSMEAD RD

Little
Wood

Limpers
Hill

1 ASHGROVE
2 SOUTHBROOK GDNS
3 WHITEMARSH
4 THE BARTLETTS
5 BALMOOR CL

4

Rook
Street

SHAFTESBURY ROAD

Woodlands
Road
Ind Est

The Causeway

ROOK ST

Sewage
Works

Field
End

Causeway
Farm

3

Shreen Water

Woodlands
Manor

Woodlands
Farm

WOODLANDS ROAD

31

White Hill
Wood

Swain's Ford
Bridge

White
Hill

Church
Farm

Barrow
Street

2

West Swainsford
Farm

East Swainsford
Farm

Wet Lane
Farm

WET LANE

Barrow Street
Farm

Breaches
Farm

Lyemarsh
Farm

BARROW STREET LANE

Homestead
Farm

1

Two Counties
Farm

Black House
Farm

PIMPERLEAZE ROAD

CUNNAGE LA

SP8

30

81 A B 82 C D 83 E F 30

A B C D E F

8

7

33

6

5

32

4

31

3

2

1

30

84 85 86

A B C D E F

Charnage Down

CHADDENWICK HILL

A303

A303

THE CLEEVE

West Hill Farm

Pinnock's Coppice

Tumulus

The Middles

BARROW STREET LANE

SIX ACRE LANE

SAWRIT HILL

Longmead Coppice

East Hill Farm

Atkin's Coppice

Hickmans Farm

Monarch's Way

BA12

THE STREET

STONEY BR

Parson's Coppice

West Knoyle

Manor Farm

The Warren

Tumulus

Broadoak Game Farm

Cleeve Hill

Cleeve Coppice

NEW CLOSE

P

Tumulus

Broadmead Farm

Puck Well Nature Reserve

Puckwell Coppice

Hang Wood

MARTHA'S LANE

Oxleaze Farm

Wood Farm

Mitchell's Coppice

Mackintosh Davidson Wood Nature Reserve

Skidmarsh Wood

Bush Farm Bison Centre

Common Wood

SP3

Great High Croft Wood

Windmill Hill

Convish Farm

Underhill

Underhill Farm

Park Corner Farm

Vernhill Farm

Windmill Farm

Park Pale

Brickyard Farm

Lugmarsh Farm

Knowl

CUNNAGE LANE

Lugmarsh Plantation

Moor's Farm

Park Pale

Park Pale

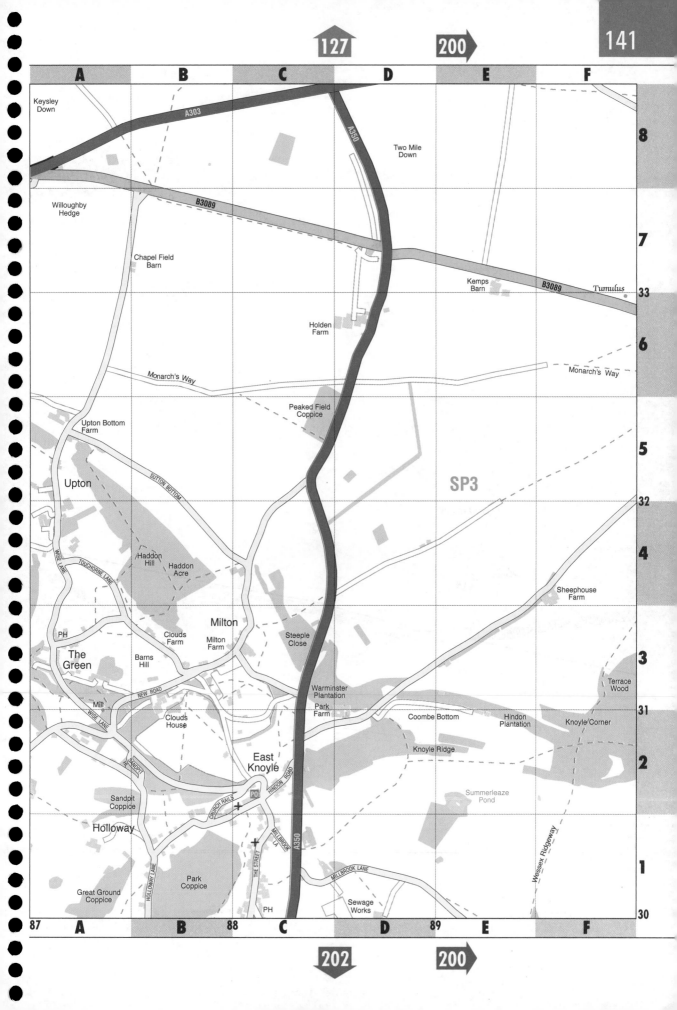

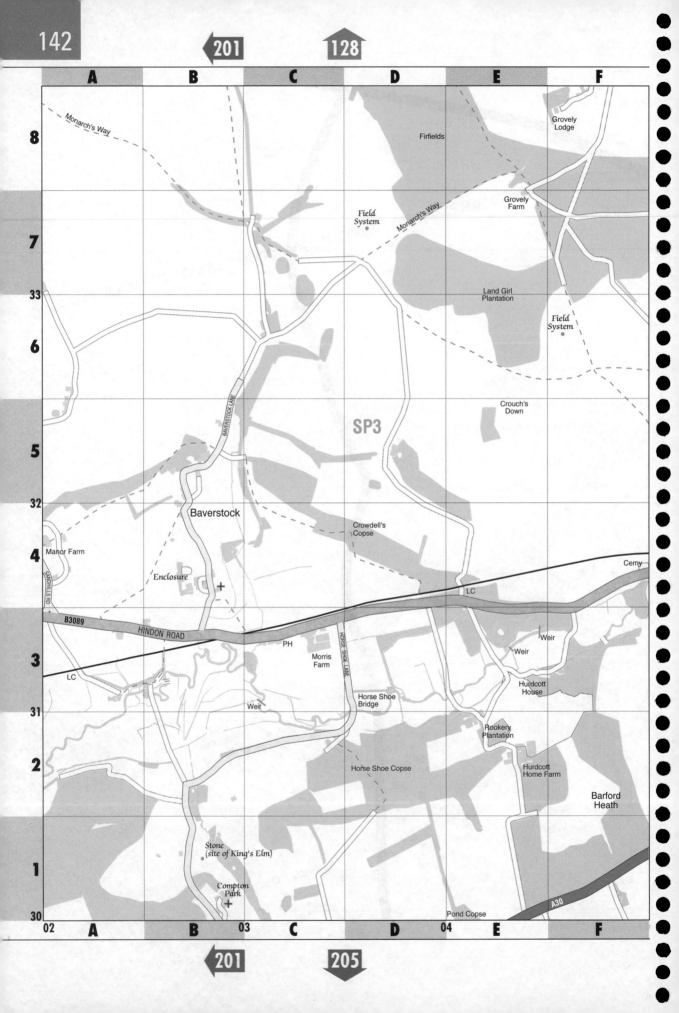

A B C D E F

8

Monarch's Way

Firfields

Grovely
Lodge

Field
System

Monarch's Way

Grovely
Farm

7

33

Land Girl
Plantation

6

Field
System

BAVERSTOCK LANE

SP3

Crouch's
Down

5

32

Baverstock

Crowdell's
Copse

4

Manor Farm

Enclosure

+

Cemy

SANDHILLS RD

LC

B3089

HINDON ROAD

PH

Weir

Weir

Weir

LC

HORSE SHOE LANE

Morris
Farm

Hurdcott
House

3

LC

Weir

Horse Shoe
Bridge

31

Rookery
Plantation

2

Horse Shoe Copse

Hurdcott
Home Farm

Barford
Heath

1

Stone
(site of King's Elm)

Compton
Park
+

A30

Pond Copse

30

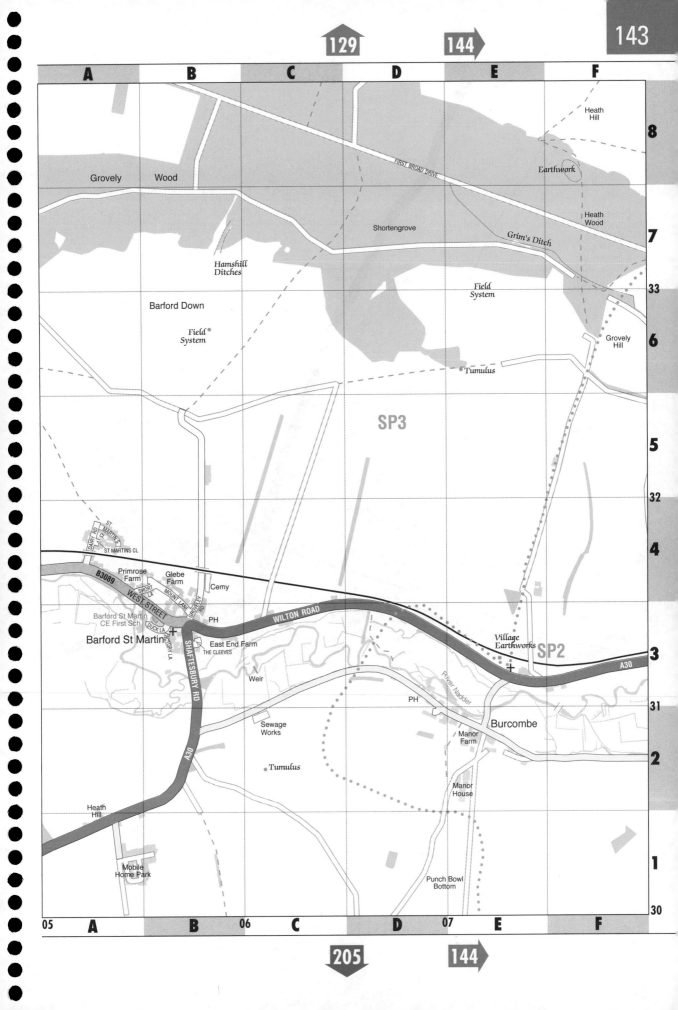

129
144

A B C D E F

8
7
33
6
5
32
4
3
31
2
1
30

Heath Hill

Earthwork

Heath Wood

FIRST BROAD DRIVE

Grovely Wood

Shortengrove

Grim's Ditch

Hamshill Ditches

Field System

Barford Down

Field System

Grovely Hill

Tumulus

SP3

St Martin's Rd
Dairy Cl
St Martins Cl

B3089
WEST STREET
Short La
Mount Lane
Grovely Rd

Primrose Farm
Glebe Farm
Cemy

PH

Barford St Martin CE First Sch

Barford St Martin

Duck La
Factory La
THE CLEEVES

East End Farm

Weir

WILTON ROAD

Village Earthworks

SP2

A30

River Nadder

PH

Burcombe

SHAFTESBURY RD

A30

Sewage Works

Tumulus

Manor Farm

Manor House

Heath Hill

Punch Bowl Bottom

Mobile Home Park

05 A B 06 C D 07 E F

205
144

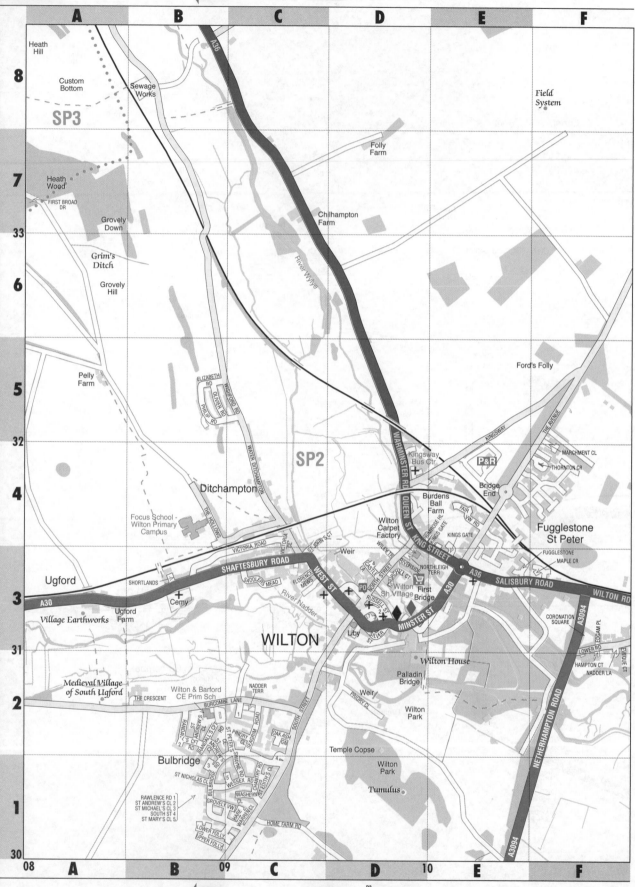

D3
1 GREYHOUND LA
2 PENNY'S LA
3 KINGSBURY SQ
4 CASTLE KEEP

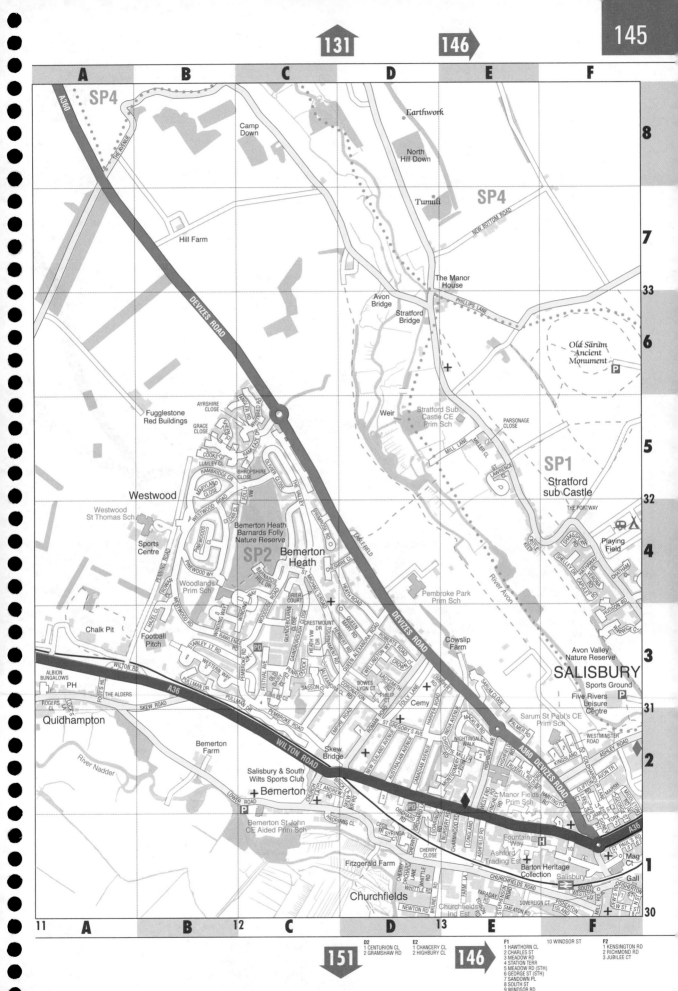

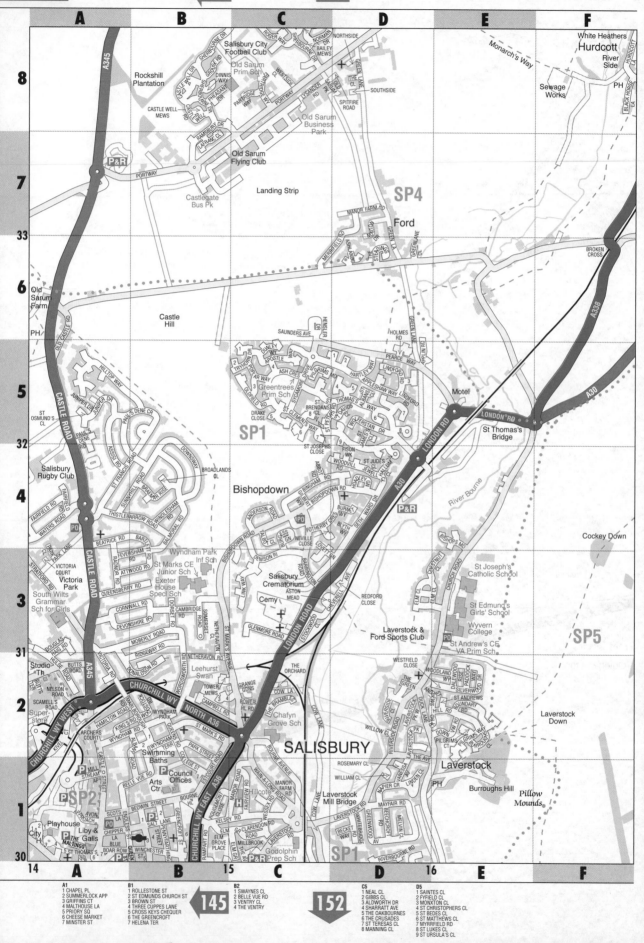

A1
1 CHAPEL PL
2 SUMMERLOCK APP
3 GRIFFINS CT
4 MALTHOUSE LA
5 PRIORY SQ
6 CHEESE MARKET
7 MINSTER ST

B1
1 ROLLESTONE ST
2 ST EDMUNDS CHURCH ST
3 BROWN ST
4 THREE CUPPES LANE
5 CROSS KEYS CHEQUER
6 THE GREENCROFT
7 HELENA TER

B2
1 SWAYNES CL
2 BELLE VUE RD
3 VENTRY CL
4 THE VENTRY

C5
1 NEAL CL
2 GIBBS CL
3 ALDWORTH DR
4 SHARRATT AVE
5 THE OAKBOURNES
6 THE CRUSADES
7 ST TERESAS CL
8 MANNING CL

D5
1 SAINTES CL
2 FYFIELD CL
3 MONXTON CL
4 ST CHRISTOPHERS CL
5 ST BEDES CL
6 ST MATTHEWS CL
7 MYRRFIELD RD
8 ST LUKES CL
9 ST URSULA'S CL

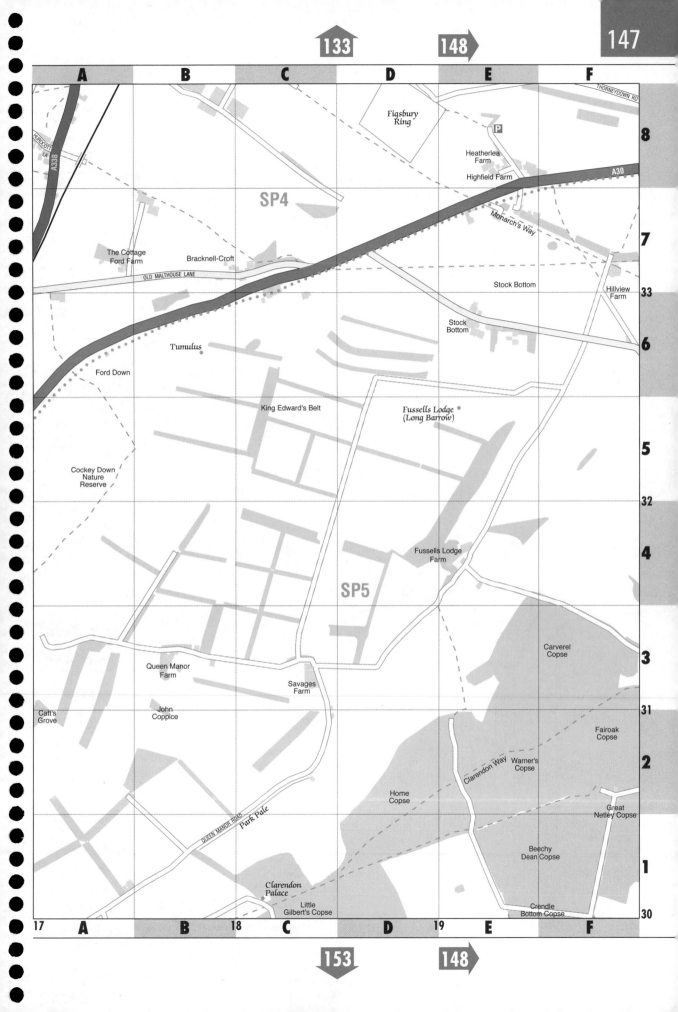

A B C D E F

THORNEYDOWN RD

Figsbury
Ring

8

Heatherlea
Farm

P

A30

Highfield Farm

Monarch's Way

SP4

7

The Cottage
Ford Farm

Bracknell-Croft

Stock Bottom

OLD MALTHOUSE LANE

Hillview
Farm

33

Stock
Bottom

Tumulus

6

Ford Down

King Edward's Belt

Fussells Lodge
(Long Barrow)

5

Cockey Down
Nature
Reserve

32

Fussells Lodge
Farm

4

SP5

Carverel
Copse

3

Queen Manor
Farm

Savages
Farm

Catt's
Grove

John
Coppice

31

Fairoak
Copse

Clarendon Way

Warner's
Copse

2

Home
Copse

Great
Netley Copse

QUEEN MANOR ROAD

Park Pale

Beechy
Dean Copse

1

Clarendon
Palace

Little
Gilbert's Copse

Crendle
Bottom Copse

30

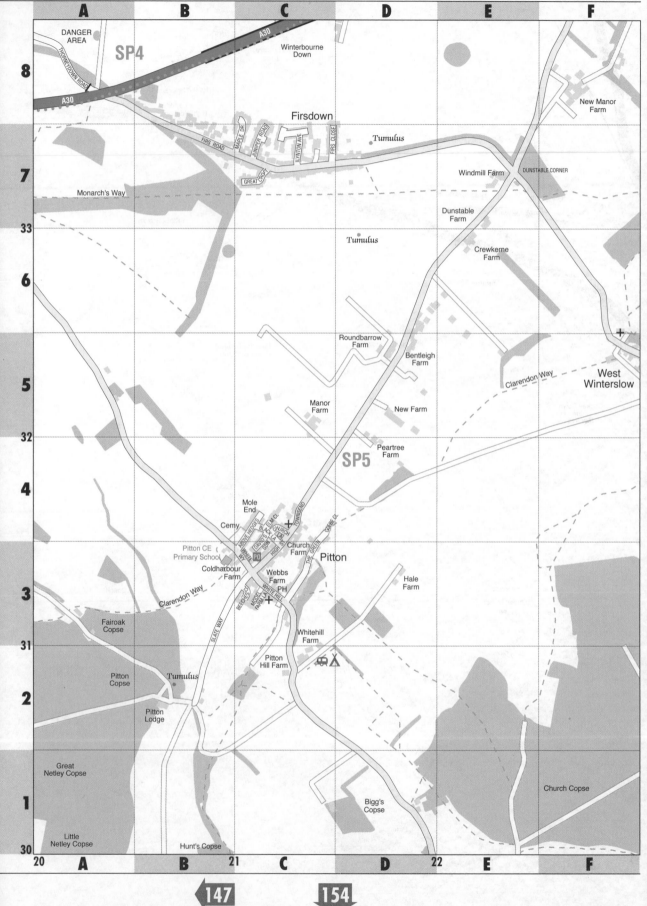

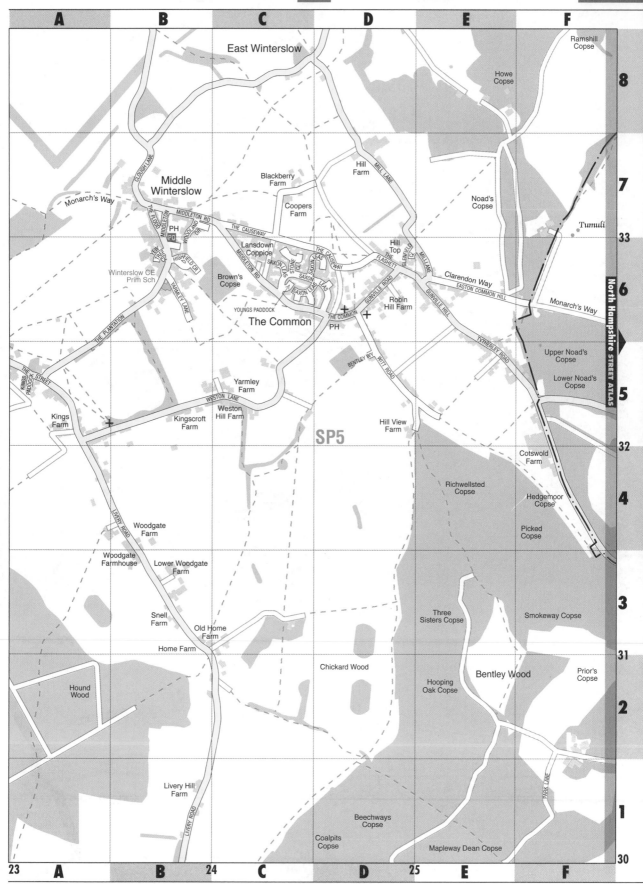

East Winterslow

Ramshill
Copse

Howe
Copse

Middle
Winterslow

Hill
Farm

Noad's
Copse

Blackberry
Farm

Monarch's Way

Tumuli

Coopers
Farm

Hill
Top

Clarendon Way

Lansdown
Coppice

Brown's
Copse

Winterslow CE
Prim Sch

Robin
Hill Farm

Monarch's Way

YOUNGS PADDOCK

The Common

Upper Noad's
Copse

Lower Noad's
Copse

Yarmley
Farm

Hill View
Farm

SP5

Kings
Farm

Weston
Hill Farm

Kingscroft
Farm

Cotswold
Farm

Richwellsted
Copse

Hedgemoor
Copse

Woodgate
Farm

Picked
Copse

Woodgate
Farmhouse

Lower Woodgate
Farm

Snell
Farm

Three
Sisters Copse

Smokeway Copse

Old Home
Farm

Home Farm

Chickard Wood

Bentley Wood

Prior's
Copse

Hound
Wood

Hooping
Oak Copse

Livery Hill
Farm

Beechways
Copse

Coalpits
Copse

Mapleway Dean Copse

North Hampshire STREET ATLAS

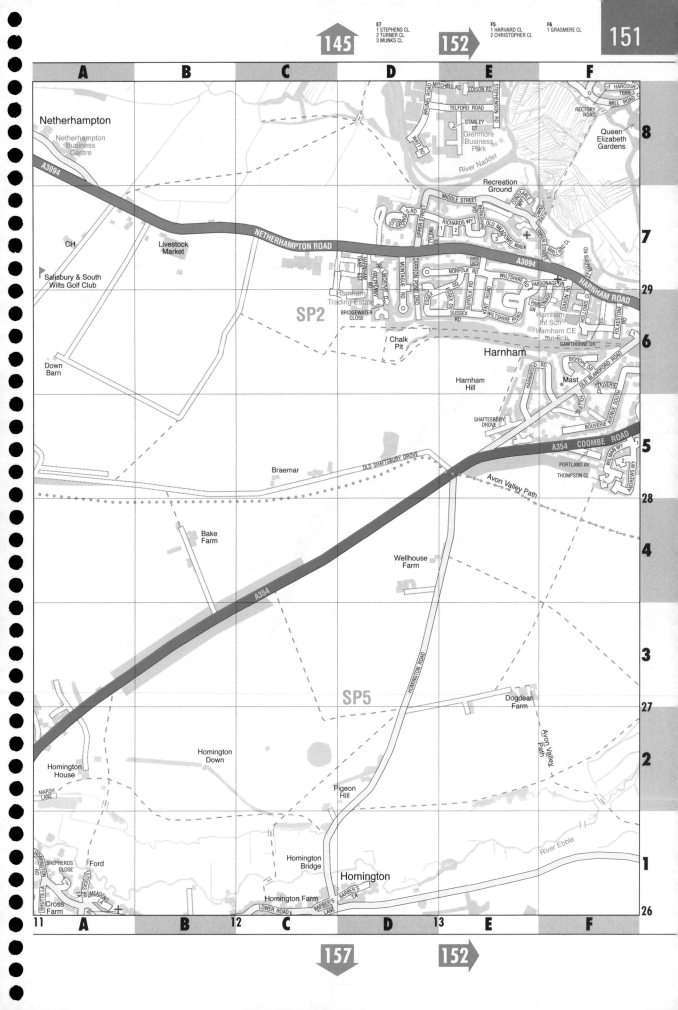

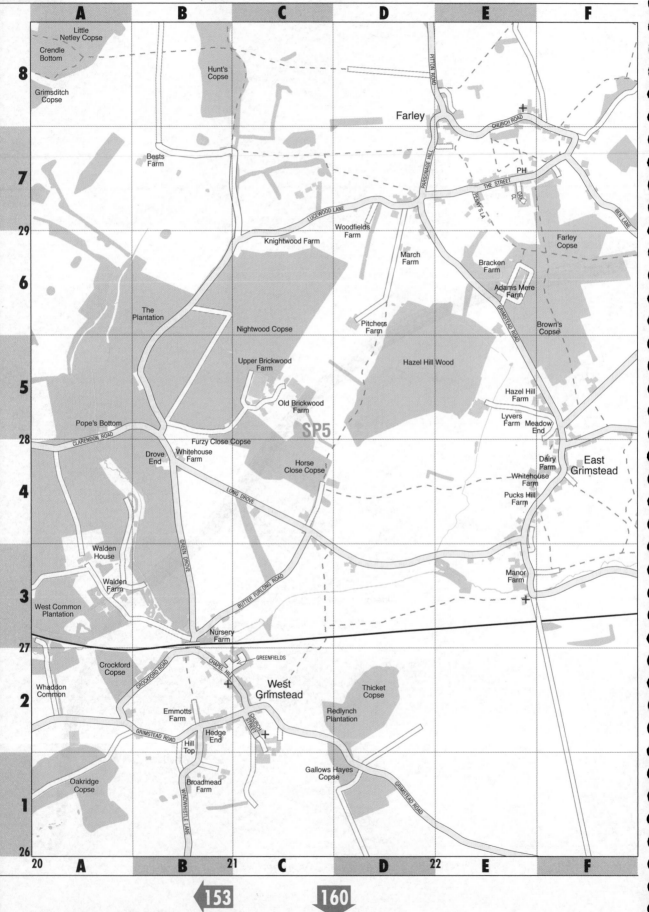

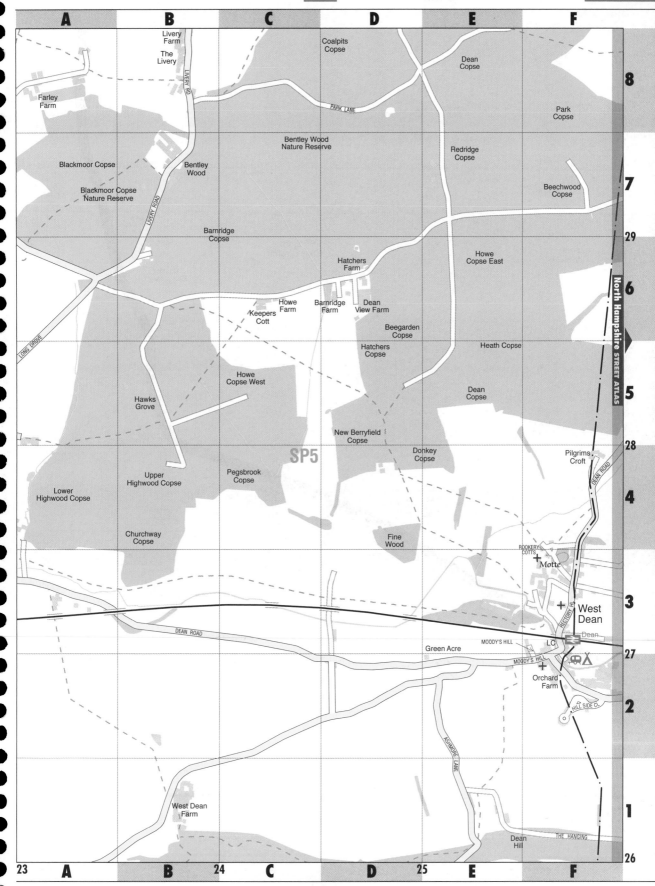

SP5

North Hampshire STREET ATLAS

Farley Farm

Livery Farm
The Livery
LIVERY RD

Coalpits Copse

Dean Copse

Park Copse

Blackmoor Copse

Bentley Wood

Blackmoor Copse Nature Reserve
LIVERY ROAD

PARK LANE

Bentley Wood Nature Reserve

Redridge Copse

Beechwood Copse

Barnridge Copse

Howe Copse East

Hatchers Farm

Keepers Cott
Howe Farm
Barnridge Farm
Dean View Farm

Beegarden Copse

Heath Copse

Hatchers Copse

LONG DRIVE

Howe Copse West

Hawks Grove

New Berryfield Copse

Dean Copse

Donkey Copse

Pilgrims Croft

DEAN ROAD

Upper Highwood Copse

Pegsbrook Copse

Lower Highwood Copse

Churchway Copse

Fine Wood

ROOKERY COTTS
Motte

West Dean

RECTORY HL

Dean
LC

DEAN ROAD

Green Acre

MOODY'S HILL

MOODY'S HILL

Orchard Farm

HILL SIDE CL

ASHMORE LANE

West Dean Farm

Dean Hill

THE HANGING

← 205
150

A B C D E F

8

7

25

6

5

24

4

3

23

2

1

22

Throope
Bottom

Throope
Hill

Throope
Down

Strip
Lynchets

Faulston

Eve
Hill

SP5

Faulston
Down

Stratford
Tony Down

Coombe
Bissett Down

Lower
Coombe
Farm

THE BEECHES

A354

BLANDFORD ROAD

OLD BLANDFORD ROAD

South
Down Farm

Southdown
Wood

Lower
Pennings
Farm

Jervoise
Farm

Sillens
Farm

Faulstone
Down Farm

New
Farm

Greenacres
Farm

Lower
Pennings Farm

College
Farm

A354

Toyd
Clump

Grims Lodge
Farm

Tumulus

Black
Hill

SP6

Long
Barrow

Long
Barrow

Croucheston
Down

08 A B 09 C D 10 E F

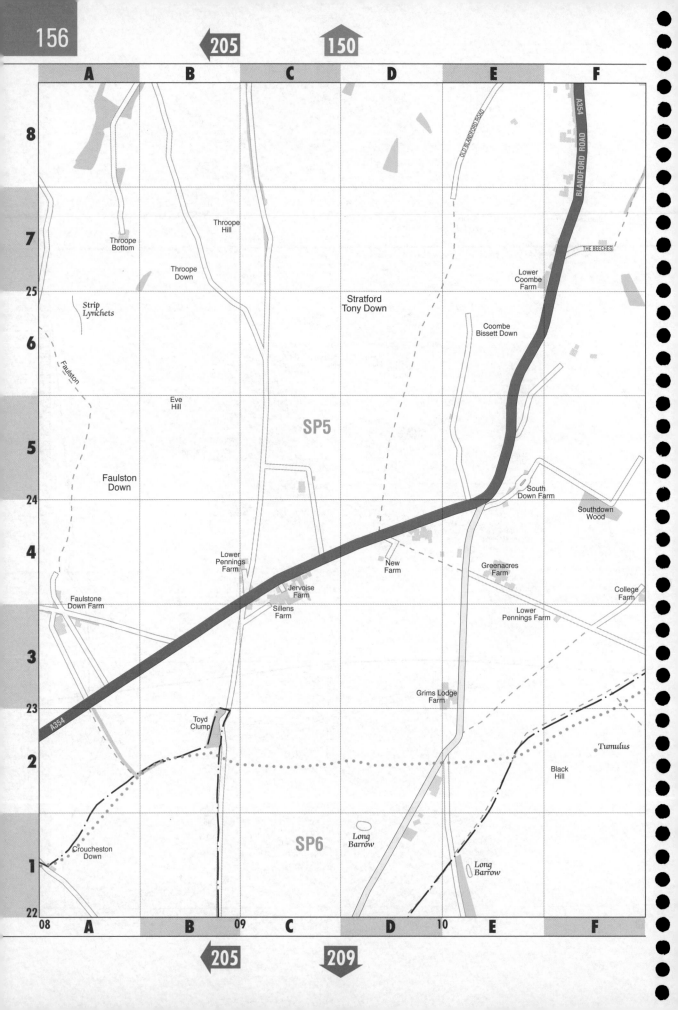

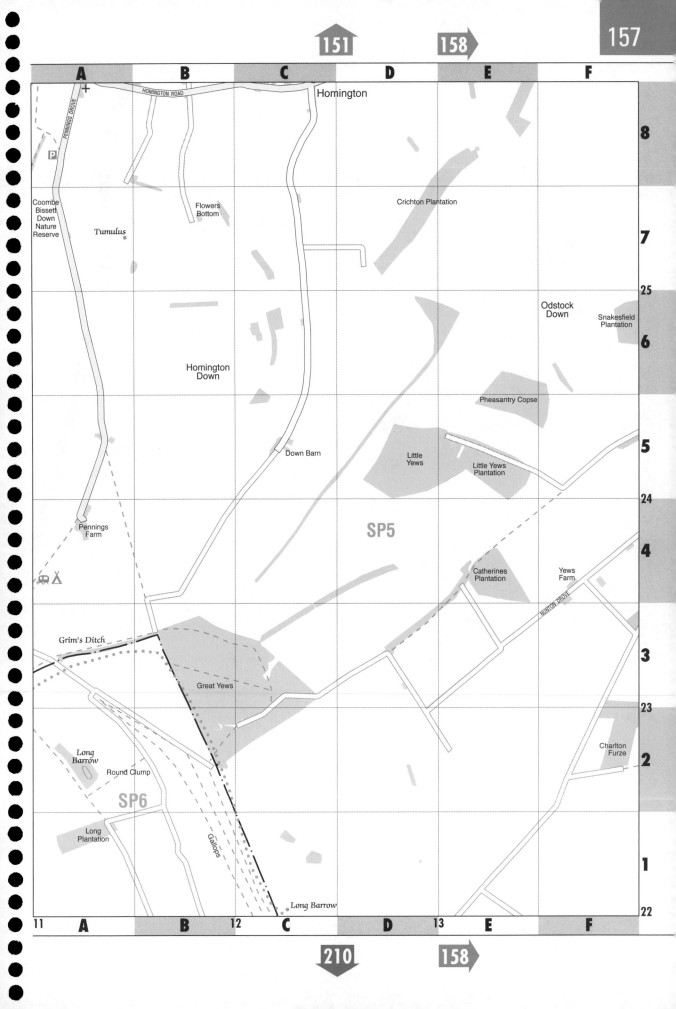

151
158

A B C D E F

8

Homington

HOMINGTON ROAD

Crichton Plantation

Flowers
Bottom

Coombe
Bissett
Down
Nature
Reserve

7

Tumulus

25

Odstock
Down

Snakesfield
Plantation

6

Homington
Down

Pheasantry Copse

5

Down Barn

Little
Yews

Little Yews
Plantation

24

SP5

4

Pennings
Farm

Catherines
Plantation

Yews
Farm

NUNTON DROVE

Grim's Ditch

3

Great Yews

23

Charlton
Furze

*Long
Barrow*

2

Round Clump

SP6

*Long
Plantation*

Gallops

1

Long Barrow

22

210
158

157
152

A B C D E F

8

Avon Valley Path

Nunton

New Hall

A338

7

Fir Plantation

Earthworks

Bodenham Hill Plantation

THE HIGHWAY

Matrimony Farm

25

Odstock Copse

Nunton Copse

Clearbury Plantation

Charlton Plantation

6

NUNTON DROVE

Clearbury Ring

SP5

Charlton Manor Farm

5

NUNTON DROVE

24

Clearbury Down

PH

4

3

Warren Plantation

North Field Copse

The Giant's Grave (Long Barrow)

23

Giant's Grave Plantation

2

The Giant's Chair (Tumulus)

New Court Down Barn

1

New Court Down

22

14 A B 15 C D 16 E F

Alderbury
Meadows

Hoyels
Copse

Bunckley's
Copse

A36

Rudghams
Copse

Treasurer's
Dean Wood

Nythefield
Copse

Little
Ridghams Copse

WITHERINGTON ROAD

Witherington Ring
(Field System)

Witherington Down

Ford

Witherington
Farm

Warren Field Plantation

SP5

River Avon

Avon Valley Path

CHAPEL LANE

Old
Standlynch
Farm

CHURCH LANE

Trafalgar
Park

LOWER ROAD

Charlton-
All-Saints

Trafalgar
House

Standlynch
Farm

WARRENS LANE

Barford Down
Farm

A338

Barford
Park

Barford Down

SALISBURY RD

Barford
Park Farm

Trafalgar
Fish Farm

Avon Valley Path

New Court
Farm

GRAVEL CL

Downton
Business Centre

BARFORD LANE

159
154

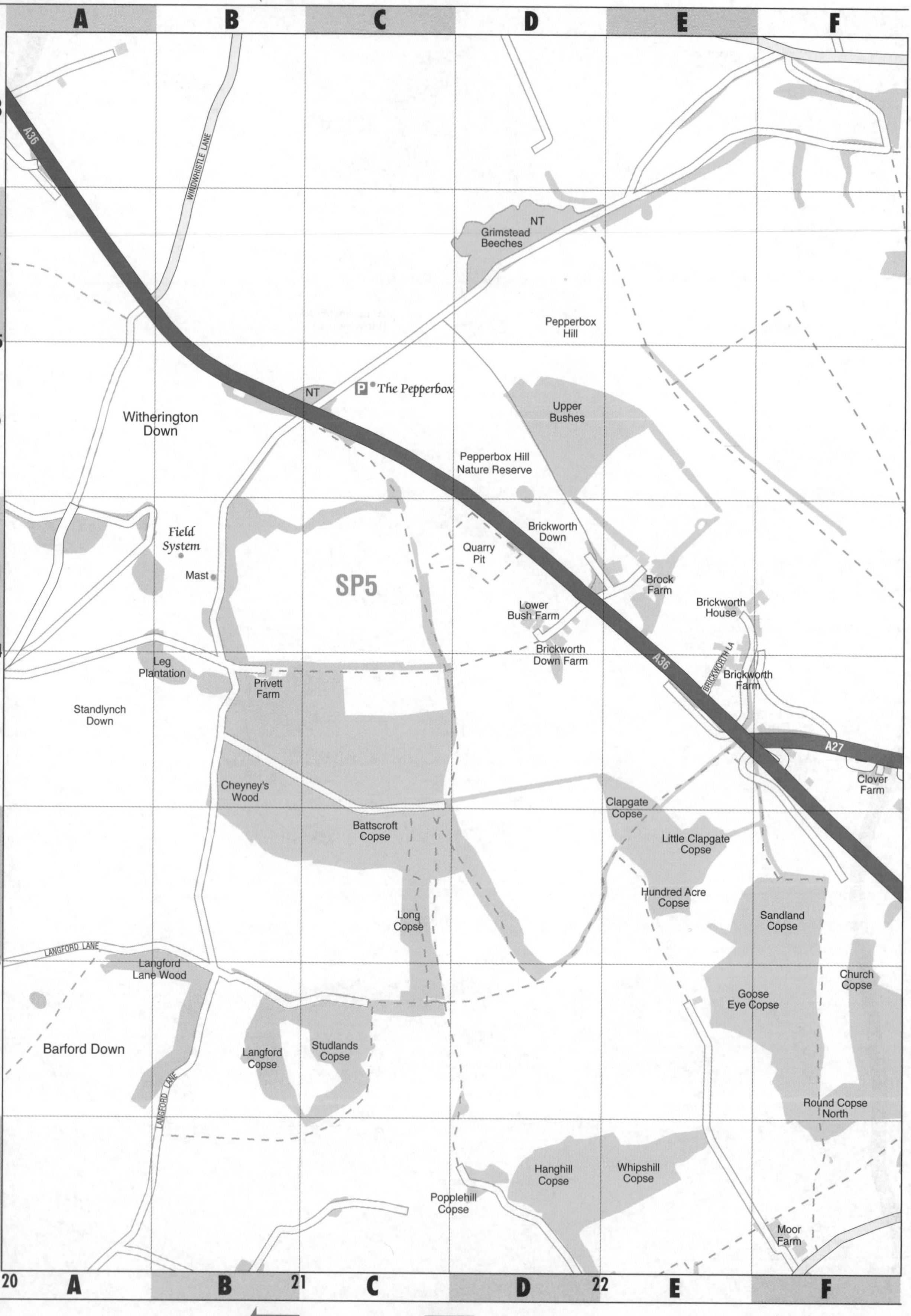

A B C D E F

8

7

25

6

5

24

4

3

23

2

1

22

A36

WINDWHISTLE LANE

NT
Grimstead
Beeches

Pepperbox
Hill

NT
P The Pepperbox

Witherington
Down

Upper
Bushes

Pepperbox Hill
Nature Reserve

Field
System

Brickworth
Down

Mast

SP5

Quarry
Pit

Brock
Farm

Brickworth
House

Lower
Bush Farm

Brickworth
Down Farm

A36

BRICKWORTH LA

Brickworth
Farm

Leg
Plantation

Privett
Farm

Standlynch
Down

A27

Clover
Farm

Cheyney's
Wood

Clapgate
Copse

Battscroft
Copse

Little Clapgate
Copse

Hundred Acre
Copse

Sandland
Copse

Long
Copse

Langford
Lane Wood

Church
Copse

LANGFORD LANE

Langford
Copse

Studlands
Copse

Goose
Eye Copse

Barford Down

LANGFORD LANE

Round Copse
North

Hanghill
Copse

Whipshill
Copse

Popplehill
Copse

Moor
Farm

20 A B 21 C D 22 E F

159
211

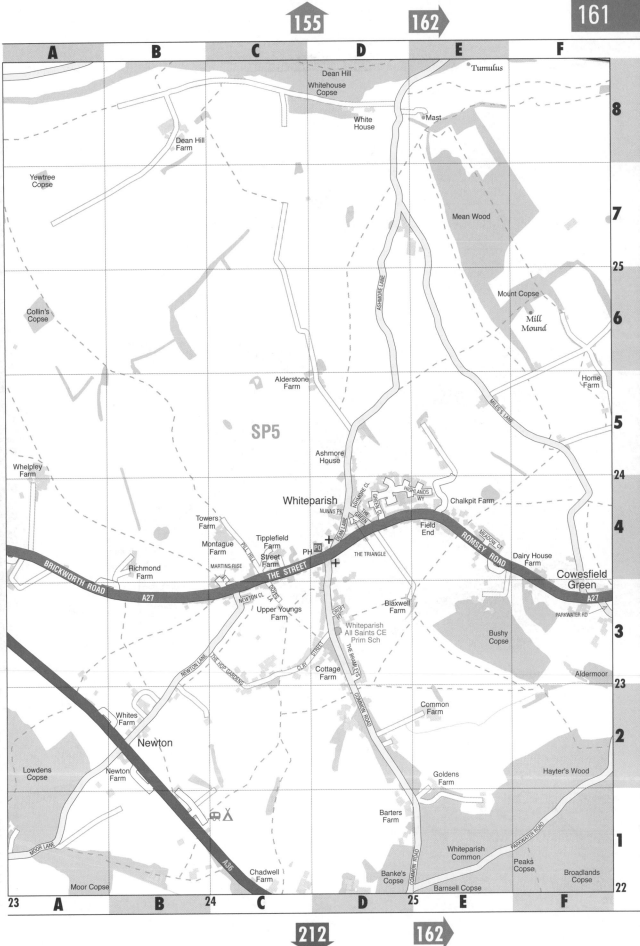

North Hampshire STREET ATLAS

South Hampshire STREET ATLAS

A   B   C   D   E   F

Deanhill Barn

Biddlesdown Row

Gatmore Copse

Deanwood Farm

Painshill Farm

Well Copse

Dean Copse

SP5

Brokes Copse

Bottom Row

Cowesfield House Farm

Worthy Hassock Copse

The Plantation

Rowdens Farm

Chapel Copse

Grantham's Copse

Lower Cowesfield Farm

Testwood Copse

Bryce's Farm

Morrisholt Farm

Cowesfield Gate

SO51

Frogmore End

Mill Mound

Great Plantation

ROMSEY ROAD

A27

Warren Copse

PARKWATER ROAD

Cowesfield Wood

Sandy Close Farm

CHURCH LANE

Yew Tree Farm

Watsons Farm

PARKWATER ROAD

The Heather

Warren Farm

Sole Hill Farm

Church Copse

Broxmore Farm

MELCHET VIEW

THE DRIVE

A27

GRAEMAR LANE

Woodfalls

Greenvale Farm

Hayter's Wood

THE DRIVE

Melchet Pond

EASTWOOD

Fir Copse

St Edwards Sch

THE DRIVE

MELCHET CL

Sack Hill Farm

GRAEMAR LANE

Broadlands Copse

Sack Copse

A27 Romsey

A   B   C   D   E   F

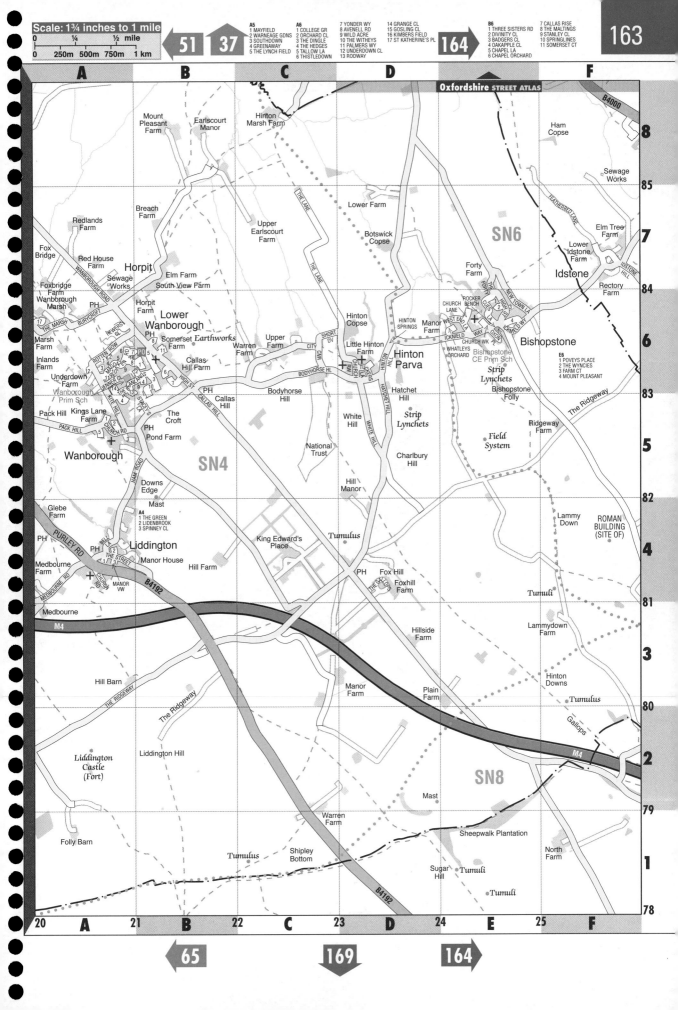

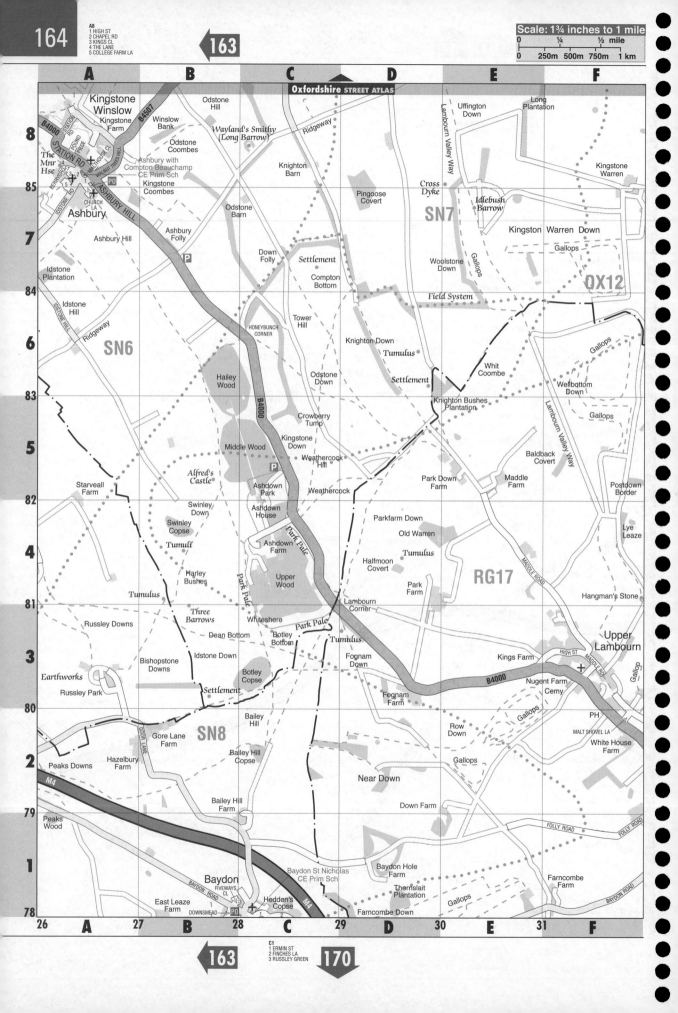

164

A8
1 HIGH ST
2 CHAPEL RD
3 KINGS CL
4 THE LANE
5 COLLEGE FARM LA

◄ 163

Scale: 1¾ inches to 1 mile
0   ¼   ½   mile
0   250m 500m 750m 1 km

Oxfordshire STREET ATLAS

A   B   C   D   E   F

8

Kingstone
Winslow
Kingstone
Farm
Winslow
Bank
Odstone
Coombes

Odstone
Hill

Wayland's Smithy
(Long Barrow)

Ridgeway

Uffington
Down

Long
Plantation

B4507

B4000

Ashbury with
Compton Beauchamp
CE Prim Sch

Knighton
Barn

Cross
Dyke

SN7

Idlebush
Barrow

Kingstone
Warren

85

The
Mnr
Hse

Kingstone
Coombes

Pingoose
Covert

Kingston Warren Down

Ashbury

CHURCH
LA

Odstone
Barn

Woolstone
Down

Gallops

Gallops

QX12

7

Ashbury Hill

Ashbury
Folly

P

Down
Folly

Settlement

Compton
Bottom

84

Idstone
Plantation

HONEYBUNCH
CORNER

Tower
Hill

Field System

SN6

6

Idstone
Hill

Ridgeway

Knighton Down

Tumulus

Whit
Coombe

Gallops

83

Hailey
Wood

B4000

Odstone
Down

Settlement

Knighton Bushes
Plantation

Wellbottom
Down

Gallops

5

Middle Wood

Crowberry
Tump

Kingstone
Down

Weathercock
Hill

Baldback
Covert

Alfred's
Castle

P

Park Down
Farm

Maddle
Farm

Postdown
Border

82

Starveall
Farm

Swinley
Down

Ashdown
Park

Ashdown
House

Weathercock

Parkfarm Down

Old Warren

Lye
Leaze

4

Swinley
Copse

Tumuli

Ashdown
Farm

Upper
Wood

Halfmoon
Covert

Tumulus

Park
Farm

RG17

MADDLE ROAD

81

Harley
Bushes

Tumulus

Three
Barrows

Whiteshere

Park Pale

Tumulus

Hangman's Stone

Russley Downs

Dean Bottom

Botley
Bottom

Park Pale

Fognam
Down

Kings Farm

HIGH ST

Upper
Lambourn

3

Earthworks

Bishopstone
Downs

Idstone Down

Botley
Copse

Settlement

Nugent Farm
Cemy

MADDLE RD

Gallop

Russley Park

B4000

PH

80

Gore Lane
Farm

SN8

Bailey
Hill

Fognam
Farm

Row
Down

Gallops

White House
Farm

MALT SHOVEL LA

2

Peaks Downs

Hazelbury
Farm

Bailey Hill
Copse

Near Down

Gallops

M4

79

Peaks
Wood

Bailey Hill
Farm

Down Farm

FOLLY ROAD

FOLLY ROAD

1

Baydon St Nicholas
CE Prim Sch

Baydon Hole
Farm

Farncombe
Farm

East Leaze
Farm

Baydon

FIVEWAYS
CL

Hedden's
Copse

Thornslait
Plantation

Farncombe Down

Gallops

BAYDON ROAD

78

26   A   27   B   28   C   29   D   30   E   31   F

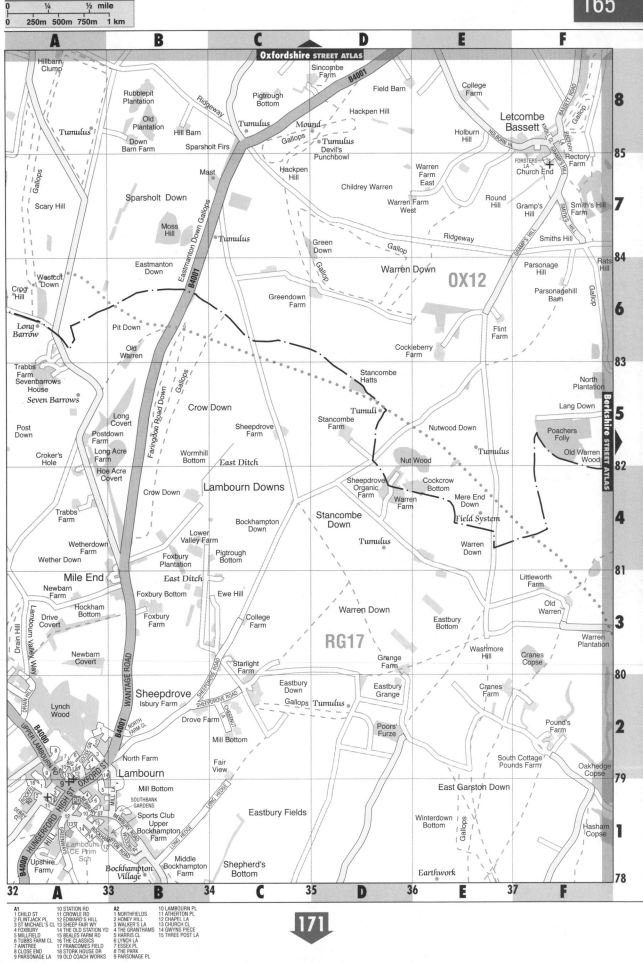

Scale: 1¾ inches to 1 mile

Berkshire STREET ATLAS

OX12

RG17

A1
1 CHILD ST
2 FLINTJACK PL
3 ST MICHAEL'S CL
4 FOXBURY
5 MILLFIELD
6 TUBBS FARM CL
7 AINTREE
8 CLOSE END
9 PARSONAGE LA
10 STATION RD
11 CROWLE RD
12 EDWARD'S HILL
13 SHEEP FAIR WY
14 THE OLD STATION YD
15 BEALES FARM RD
16 THE CLASSICS
17 FRANCOMES FIELD
18 STORK HOUSE DR
19 OLD COACH WORKS

A2
1 NORTHFIELDS
2 HONEY HILL
3 WALKER'S LA
4 THE GRANTHAMS
5 HARRIS CL
6 LYNCH LA
7 ESSEX PL
8 THE PARK
9 PARSONAGE PL
10 LAMBOURN PL
11 ATHERTON PL
12 CHAPEL LA
13 CHURCH CL
14 GWYNS PIECE
15 THREE POST LA

Scale: 1¾ inches to 1 mile

| 0 | ¼ | ½ mile |
| 0 | 250m | 500m | 750m | 1 km |

A **B** **C** **D** **E** **F**

A31N2

Sewage Works

Freegrove Farm

SLESSOR RD

Preston West Farm

PRESTON LA

Thickthorn Farm

Bishops Farm

PH

Bushton

Smiths Farm

The Strings

Ashen Copse

SN15

Upper Littlecote Farm

Mill Mead Wood

Bushton Manor Farm

Hollyhouse Farm

WOOD ST

8

77

COMBE LA

GRANGE LA

LWR GRANGE LA

Littlecott

Model Farm

Woodhill Village

Windmill Hill

Woodhill Park

Home Farm

PH

Clyffe Pypard

Lower End Farm

Bupton Farm

Windmill Hill Copse

SN4

Woodhill Park Farm

Manor Farm

Bellcroft Farm

Clyffe Hanging

7

Marsh Farm

Bushton Road Farm

Quentins Copse

Nonesuch

76

Corton Manor Farm

Bupton Village

Badgers' Copse

Nebo Farm

Spillmans Farm

Witcomb Farm

Bupton Copse

Stanmore Copse

6

CHURCH RD

Hilmarton

AMMAS CL

Hilmarton Prim Sch

Corton Wood

Bupton Hill Farm

POT DOOR PL

COMPTON ROAD

PO

Clevancy

Clevancy Hill

75

Sandy Furlong Farm

Cliffantsy Farm

HIGHWAY COMMON

SN11

Clevancy Farm

Clevancy Wood

Highway

5

Rodwell Farm

Highway Farm

Highway Hill

Lower End

74

Breach Farm

Theils End

Lower End Farm

4

Dugdales Farm

Roach Wood

Manor Farm

73

New Covert

Street Farm

White Horse Trail

Yatesbury Copse

Stert Pond

Freeth Farm

Blackwell Wood

SN11

3

BRIAR LEAZE

Compton Hill

Nolands Farm

Yatesbury

Compton Bassett

PH

Compton Farm

Croat Wood

West Nolands Farm

Manor Farm

THE STREET

THE LYMERS

Yatesbury House Farm

72

Home Farm

Whites Farm

Compton Bassett House

NOLANDS RD

BACK

Home Wood

JUGGLER'S LANE

THE AVENUE

Little London

2

Mount Wood

Old Camp Farm

Triangle Wood

Yatesbury Field

71

Cherhill Field

MARSH LANE

Cherhill

Mill Farm

Hunts Farm

MAIDEN LA

MILL LA

Upper Farm

1

1 2 3

4 5

WHITTLE RD

ATCHERLY RD

OLIVERS CL 1

OLIVERS HILL 2

Cherhill CE Sch

THE STREET

MIDDLE LANE

POTTOWS RD

PARK LA

MAIN ROAD

A4

70

02 **A** 03 **B** 04 **C** 05 **D** 06 **E** 07 **F**

A1
1 SPRECKLEY RD
2 BEAMISH CL
3 EMBRY CL
4 BOYLE AVE
5 DOWDING DR

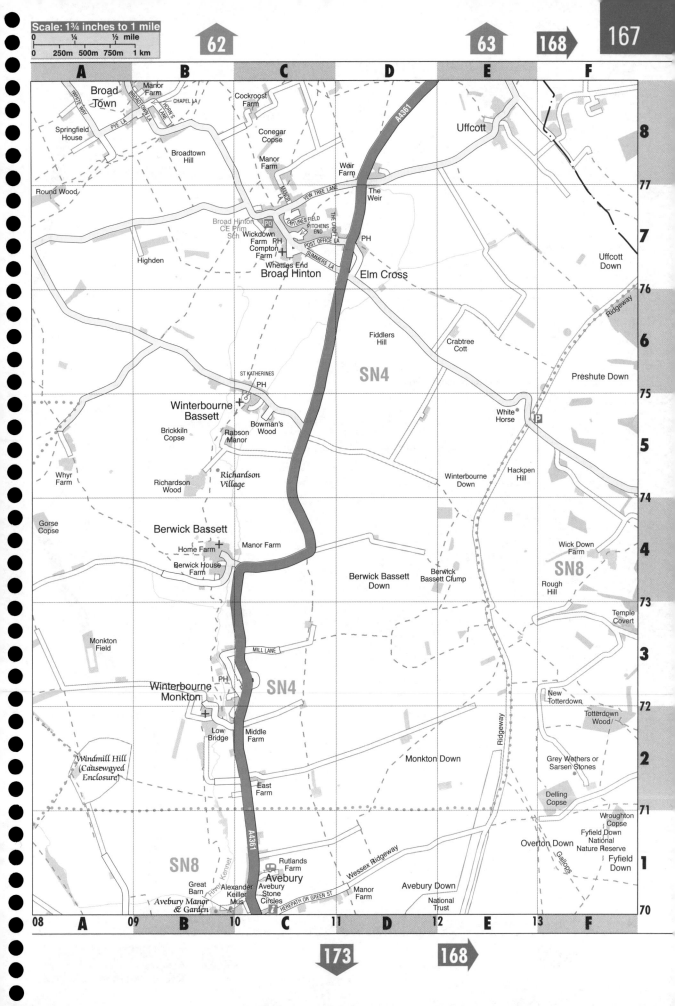

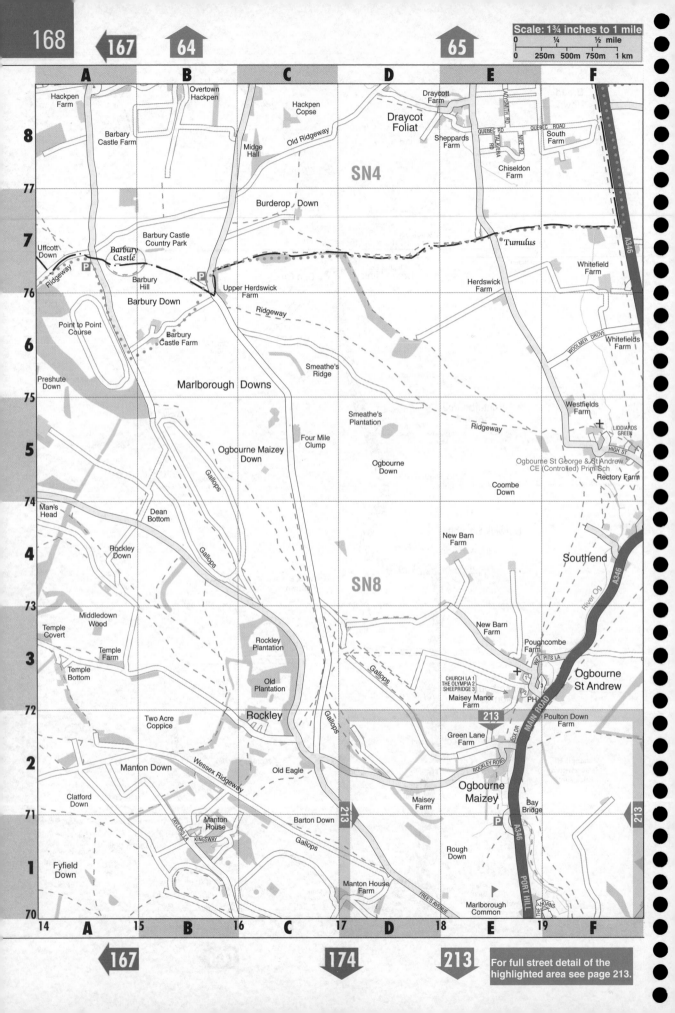

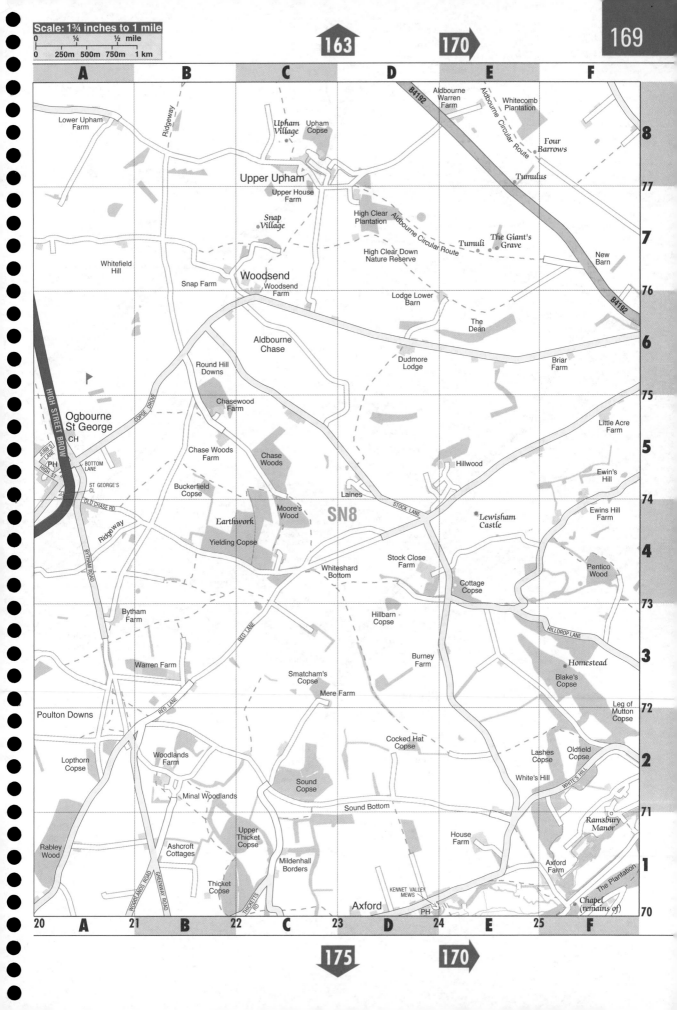

A6
1 RECTORY WOOD
2 SOUTHFIELD
3 CLARIDGE CL
4 TURNPIKE
5 MARLBOROUGH RD
6 THE GARLINGS

7 GLEBE CL
8 ST MICHAEL'S CL
9 BACK LA
10 THE PADDOCKS
11 GODDARDS LA
12 THE KNOLL
13 WESTFIELD CHASE

14 WHITELEY RD
15 HILLWOOD RD
16 HAWKINS RD
17 BARNES YD
18 VALLEY VIEW

Scale: 1¾ inches to 1 mile

0   ¼   ½ mile

0   250m   500m   750m   1 km

A7
1 CHANDLER'S LA
2 LOTTAGE WAY
3 WINDMILL CL
4 ALMA RD
5 COOK RD

Grid columns: A B C D E F
Grid rows: 8 77 7 76 6 75 5 74 4 73 3 72 2 71 1 70
Eastings: 26 A 27 B 28 C 29 D 30 E 31 F

North Field Barn · Downsmead · Newtons Wk · Barley Fields · Walronds Cl · Baydon · Sewage Works · Farncombe Down · Windmill Farm · Farn Combe

Greenhills · Midge Copse · Lodge Farm · Lodge Copse · Lodge Down · Coppington Down

Lottage Farm · Green Hill · Gore's Copse · Woodley's Copse · Coneygre Copse · Common Barn Copse · Hadley Farm · Kingwpod House · Great West Wood · Little West Wood · Holly Farm · Battens Farm

Baydon Hill Farm · St Michael's CE Aided Prim Sch · Aldbourne · West St · Castle St · B4192 · Liby · PO · Housedd's Hill · Pigs' Hill Wood · Baydon Wood · St Johns Wood · Membury Service Area · Hurst Farm · Dixon's Farm · Lyedown Copse

The Downs · Hawkins Rd · Stock Lane · Butts · South St · Southward Lane · Ford Farm · Woodcock Grove · Long Copse · Hillier's Copse · Paxlet Plantation · Membury Castle (site of) · Aerial Business Park · Aerial Farm · Cuckoo Copse

Hoddes Bridge · Southward Down · SN8 · Baydon Manor · Marridge Hill · Anchor Copse · Balak Farm · Membury Farm · Lyckweed Farm · Moon's Copse · Leigh Farm · RG17

Preston · Crowood Farm · Shell's Wood · Marridge Hill Wood · Witcha Copse · Ballard's Copse · Long Barrow · Tumulus · Witcha Farm · Ragnal

Love's Copse · Hunt's Copse · Hails Grove · Eastridge House · Raffin Stud · Wiltshire Bottom · Southern Copse · Pond Wood · Woodlands Farm · Bower Wood

Love's Farm · Crowood House · Little Wood · Whittonside Farm · Whittonditch · Balaam's Wood · Crooked Soley

Hilldrop Farm · Boltsridge Copse · Bolstridge Farm · Ramsbury Prim Sch · Ashley PC · Oaken Coppice · Foxbury Wood · Queen's Coppice · Princess Copse

Westfield Copse · Langfields · Ramsbury · Back La · Liby · PO · PH · New Town · Knighton · Fewley Coppice · Daffy Copse · King's Copse

Manor Farm · White's Hill · Ambrose Farm · Newtown Road · River Kennet · Weir · B4192 · Manor Farm · Chilton Foliat

Spring Hill · Bungalow Bridge Farm · Atherton Coppice · Whitehill Coppice · Park Coppice · ROMAN VILLA · Littlecote · Hotel · Weir

The Plantation · Bridge Farm · Darrell's Farm · Great Coppice

B2
1 HILLDROP CL
2 KNOWLEDGEHILL
3 LAWRENCE MD
4 BURDETT ST
5 ORCHARD CL
6 ISLES RD
7 SWAN'S BOTTOM
8 CHAPEL LA
9 SWAN'S CL

10 TOWNFIELD
11 WHITEHILL CL
12 ATHERTON CL
13 GREEN ACRES
14 THE PADDOCKS
15 TANKARD LANE
16 SCHOLAR'S LA

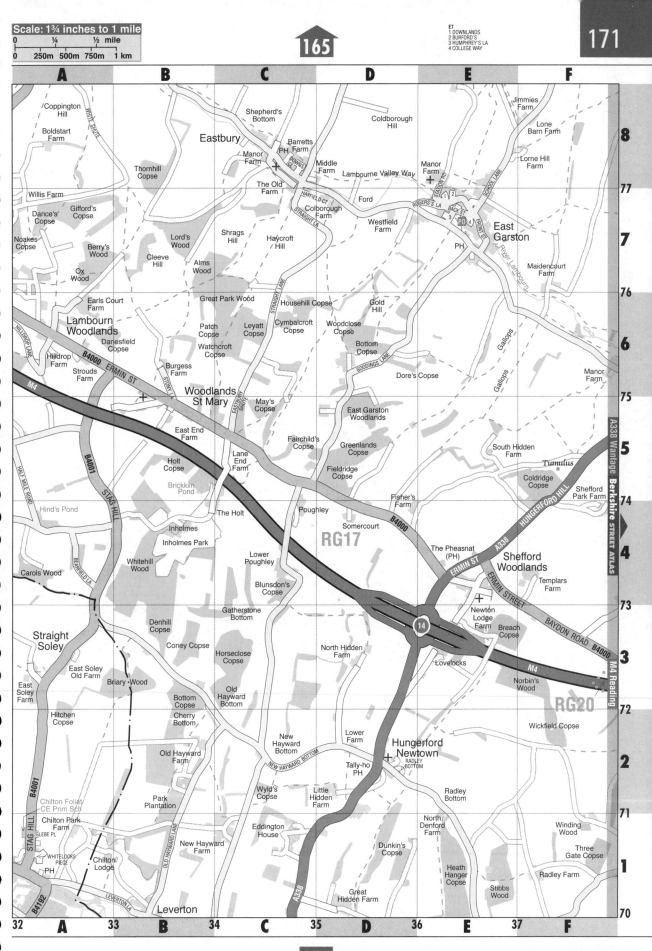

Scale: 1¾ inches to 1 mile

165

171

E7
1 DOWNLANDS
2 BURFORD'S
3 HUMPHREY'S LA
4 COLLEGE WAY

89
166

Scale: 1¾ inches to 1 mile

| 0 | ¼ | ½ mile |
| 0 | 250m 500m 750m | 1 km |

A **B** **C** **D** **E** **F**

A4
LABOUR-IN-VAIN HILL MAIN RD
OLIVERS HILL
PH
A4
SN8

8

Quemerford
Gate Farm
Wessex Ridgeway Tumulus
White Horse Plantation
Cherhill
White Horse
Knoll Down
P

Hayle
Farm
Cherhill Down

**Theobald's
Green**
Tumulus
Oldbury Castle
(Hillfort)

69
Sprays
Farm
Witch
Plantation
West Down

Harepit
Way
Tumuli

7
East
Farm
Ranscombe
Bottom
Calstone Down
Tumulus
Gallops

Manor Farm
South
Farm
SN11
Tumulus

**Calstone
Wellington**
North Down
The Firs

68
Wessex Ridgeway
Tumuli

Tumuli
Tumuli

6
Horsecombe
Bottom
North Down
Tumuli
Tumuli
A361

Morgan's Hill
Nature Reserve
Tumuli
Gallops

67
Tumuli
Masts
Enclosure
Hemp Knoll

CH
Baltic
Farm
**Bishop's
Canning Down**

Furze Knoll
Tumuli
Wansdyke
Tumuli
Gallops

5
Tumuli
Horton
Down

Long
Barrow
Shepherds'
Shore
Easton Down
Long
Barrow

66
Wansdyke Path

4
Roughridge
Hill

Easton
Hill
Tumulus

65
Strip Lynchets
Strip
Lynchets
Kitchen
Barrow

Roundway
Hill
Bourton
Tumuli
Tumuli
Earthwork

3
**Bishops
Cannings**
SN10
Tumuli

West End
Farm
West End
Easton
Farm

Bishops Cannings
CE Prim Sch
Bourton
Manor
Farm
Harepath Farm

Blackwell
Farm
THE
ESTATE YD
PH
Court
Farm

64
OAK CL

Kennet & Avon Canal
Horton Mill
Farm

2
Hopton Park
Ind Est
Swing-bridge
Townsend
Farm

Beechfield Rd
Horton
Chain Bridge

A361
Horton Road
PH
Horton
Bridge
Horton
Park Farm
Cannings Cross
Farm

63
HOPTON RD
WELLINGTON DR
214
Laywood
Bridge
Allington
Manor Farm
Home
Farm

LONDON RD
The
Knoll

**Little
Horton**
Lower Mill
Farm
Swing-bridge
Swing-bridge
Woodway
Bridge
All
Cannings
Bridge

1
Devizes
Marina
Calcote Farm
Manor
Farm

Sewage
Works
Allington
Bridge
MATTHEWS CL 1
WYCOMBE LA 2
GRANGEFIELD 3

62
COATE LANE

02 **A** **03** **B** **04** **C** **05** **D** **06** **E** **07** **F**

214

97
180

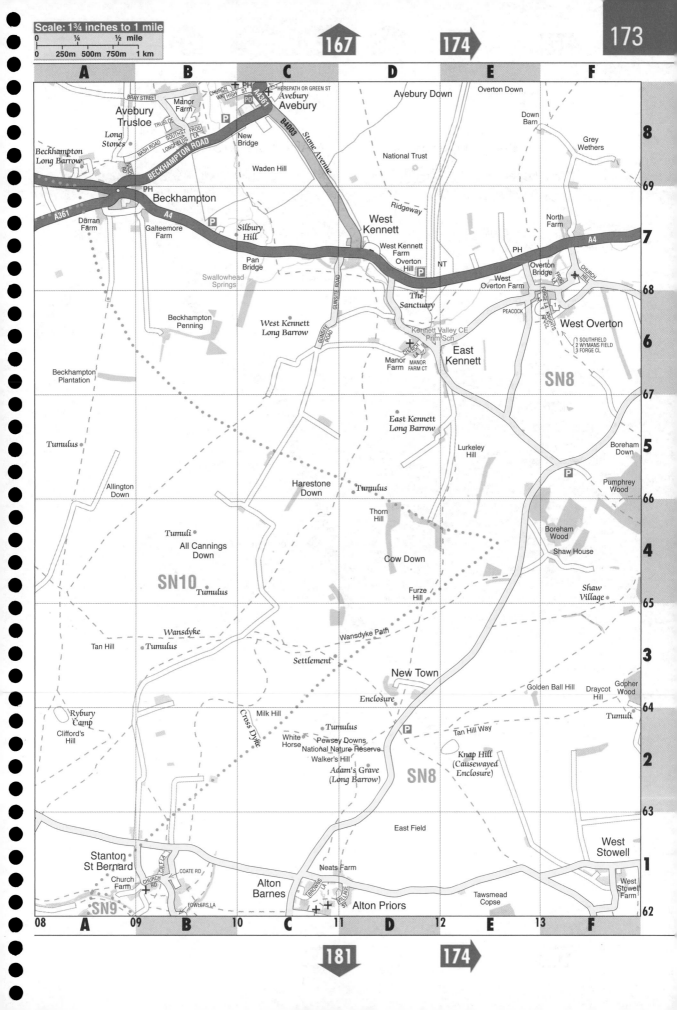

Scale: 1¾ inches to 1 mile

| 0 | ¼ | ½ mile |
| 0 | 250m | 500m | 750m | 1 km |

167
174

A **B** **C** **D** **E** **F**

BRAY STREET

Manor Farm

CHURCH WK HIGH ST
PO
PH

Avebury

HEREPATH OR GREEN ST

Avebury Down

Overton Down

Avebury Trusloe

TRUSLOE

SOUTH ST
MASH ROAD
LONGFIELDS
FROG LA

Long Stones

Stone Avenue

National Trust

Down Barn

Grey Wethers

8

Beckhampton Long Barrow

BECKHAMPTON ROAD

NASH RD

New Bridge

Waden Hill

69

A361

PH

Beckhampton

A4

Ridgeway

West Kennett

North Farm

PH

A4

7

Durran Farm

Galteemore Farm

P

Silbury Hill

Pan Bridge

West Kennett Farm
Overton Hill

NT

West Overton Farm

Overton Bridge

FROG LA

CHURCH HILL

KNIGHTS

68

Swallowhead Springs

The Sanctuary

West Overton

PEACOCK

1
2
3

Beckhampton Penning

GUNSITE ROAD

West Kennett Long Barrow

Kennett Valley CE Prim Sch

CHURCH LA

East Kennett

1 SOUTHFIELD
2 WYMANS FIELD
3 FORGE CL

6

Beckhampton Plantation

Manor Farm

MANOR FARM CT

SN8

67

Tumulus

East Kennett Long Barrow

Lurkeley Hill

Boreham Down

5

Allington Down

Harestone Down

Tumulus

Pumphrey Wood

66

Thorn Hill

Boreham Wood

Tumuli

All Cannings Down

Cow Down

Shaw House

4

SN10

Tumulus

Furze Hill

Shaw Village

65

Wansdyke

Wansdyke Path

Tan Hill

Tumulus

Settlement

New Town

Golden Ball Hill

Draycot Hill

Gopher Wood

3

Enclosure

64

Rybury Camp

Cross Dyke

Milk Hill

Tumulus

Tan Hill Way

Knap Hill (Causewayed Enclosure)

Tumuli

Clifford's Hill

White Horse

Pewsey Downs National Nature Reserve

Walker's Hill

P

SN8

2

Adam's Grave (Long Barrow)

63

East Field

West Stowell

1

Stanton St Bernard

CALE LA

COATE RD

Neats Farm

Tawsmead Copse

West Stowell Farm

Church Farm

CHURCH RD

BROWS LA

ST LA

Alton Barnes

Alton Priors

62

FOWLERS LA

SN9

A 09 **B** 10 **C** 11 **D** 12 **E** 13 **F**

08

181
174

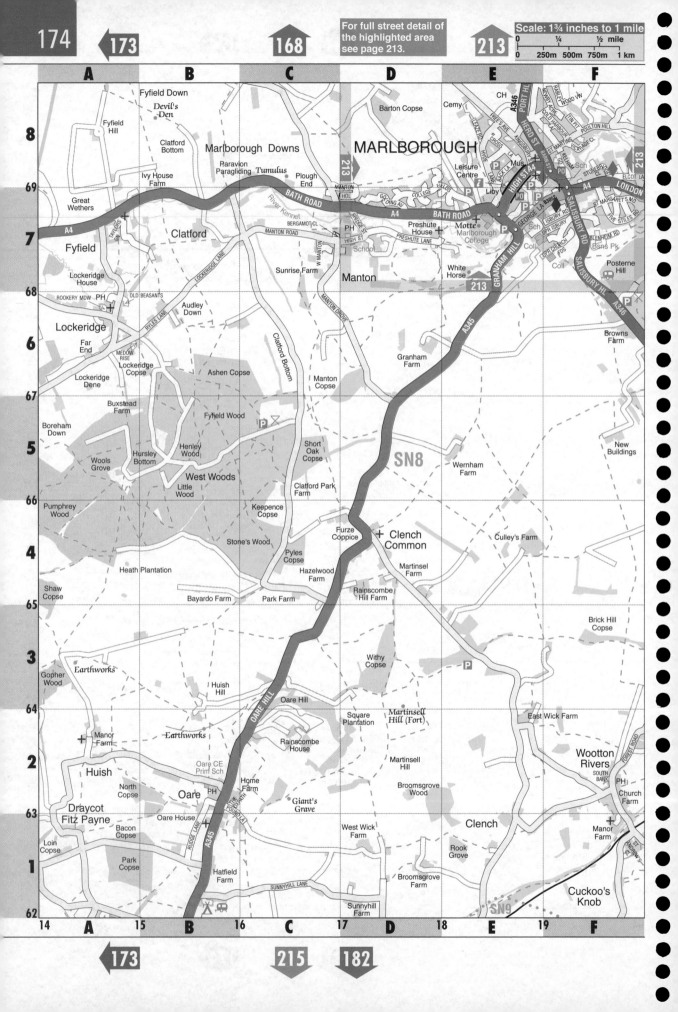

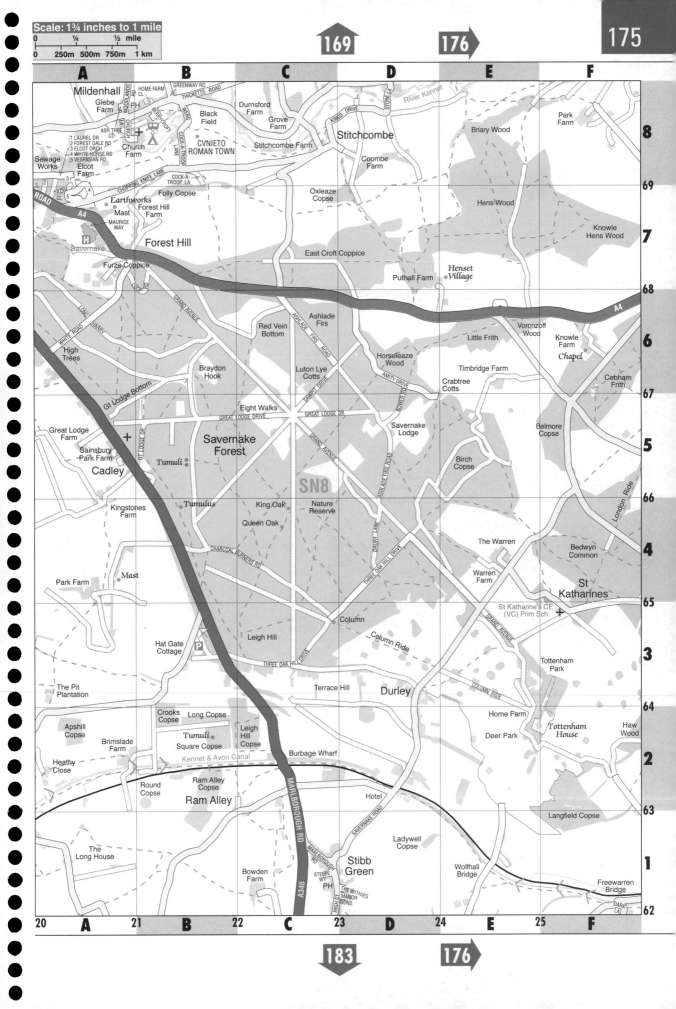

Scale: 1¾ inches to 1 mile
0   ¼   ½   mile
0   250m   500m   750m   1 km

A   B   C   D   E   F

8
Burnt Wood
Scrope Farm
Little Copse
Rudge
Rudge Coppice
Bottom Coppice
Lawn Coppice
The Plantation
Brickkiln Copse

69
Scrope's Wood
Rudge Manor Farm
Rudge Farm House
Littlecote Park Farm
Cake Wood

7
Froxfield
Highclose Farm
BATH ROAD

68
Harrow Farm
BATH ROAD   A4
Green Farm
MANOR PK
PH
Sewage Works
Lock
Stepping Stones Pre Prep Sch
RG17

6
Noke Wood
Almshouse Copse
Lock
Firth Copse
Oak Hill
North Standen House

67
Withy Copse
Round Copse
Bushelleys Copse
Upper Horsehall Hill Farm
Lower Farm
Trindledown Copse
Jugg's Wood
Long Walk
Lady's Wood

5
Chisbury Lane Farm
Oldhouse Wood
Strouds Farm
Chisbury
CHISBURY LANE
Chisbury Manor Farm
Church St
Fore Bridge
Stype Wood
Catmore Copse

66
Tumuli
Park Copse
St Martin's Chapel
SCHOOL LA
Lock
Little Bedwyn
PH
Stype Grange
Cowleaze Coppice

4
Faggotty Copse
Bewley Farm
Chisbury Wood
Chisbury Camp
SN8
Great Bedwyn CE Prim Sch
Parlow Bottom
Little Bonning's Copse
Barn Copse
Wentworth's Copse
Furze Copse
Bagshot

65
Brimley Copse
Horse Copse
WANSDYKE RD
Lock
Bonning's Copse
Burridge Heath
Burridgeheath Plantation
Gully Copse
Hillcroft Copse
Westcott Copse

3
Stokke Manor
Stock Common
Shawgrove Copse
ROSEMARY CL
PH
PH
PO
Great Bedwyn
WILLIS CL
Sewage Works
Bedwyn Dyke
Strockeridge Copse
Foxbury Wood
Foxwood Farm
Shalbourne Heath Plantation
Polesdon House
Baverstock's Copse
SIX ACRE LA
Eastcourt Farm

64
Haw Wood
Bloxham Copse
BOLLAND CL
Lock
Bedwyn Stone Museum
MILL CL
Mill Bridge
BROOK STREET
Round Copse
Birch Copse
Long Copse
A338

2
Bloxham Lodge
Kennet & Avon Canal
Brail Farm
Ivy's Copse
Castle Copse
Folly Farm
Newtown
Shalbourne CE Prim Sch
Shalbourne
Sewage Works

63
Crofton Farm
Lock
Weir
CROFTON ROAD
LC
Lock
Harding Copse
West Farm
Baverstock Farm
PH
PO
KINGSTON RD
Ropewind Farm

1
Crofton
LC
Wilton Brail
Bedwyn Brail
Harding Farm
CARVERS HILL
BURR LA
Westcourt Farm
LITTLE MEAD

62
Lock
Crofton Beam Engines
Wilton Water
Dodsdown Farm
Tumulus
Wilton Common
Wilton Down
Wilton Down
Marlmere Farm

26   A   27   B   28   C   29   D   30   E   31   F

B3
1 NAPIERS
2 COPYHOLD
3 CASTLE RD
4 FAIRFIELD
5 COSTER VIEW
6 GRANARY RD
7 MANOR RD

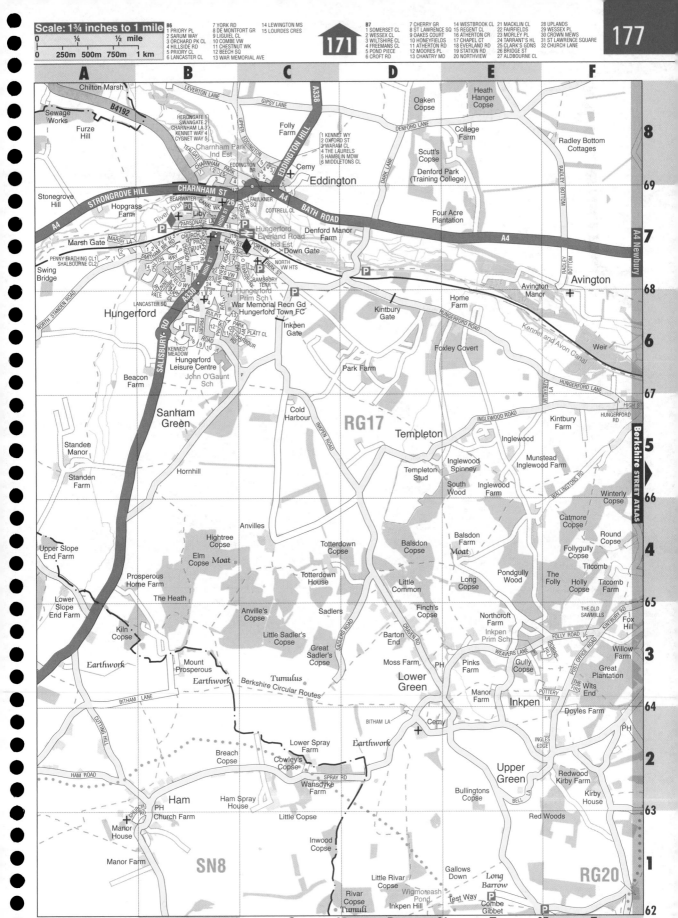

B8
1 HERCULES WY
2 CHESHIRE CL
3 STIRLING CL
4 DE HAVILLAND PL
5 BEAUFORT CL
6 HERONS CT
7 MALLARD CL
8 BRAMPTON CT
9 VALIANT CL
10 BADER PK
11 DUXFORD CL
12 BADER PK
13 TANGMERE CL
14 SUNDERLAND CL
15 BLENHEIM PK
16 HARVARD CL
17 CATALINA CT
18 WELLE SLEY CL
19 VALENTIA CT
20 HORNCHURCH RD
21 BLENHEIM PK
22 CHADWICK CLOSE

Scale: 1¾ inches to 1 mile
0   ¼   ½ mile
0   250m 500m 750m 1 km

A   B   C   D   E   F

8

Ashville Cen
Sports Gd
Shails La
Lancaster Rd
Halifax
Lysander Rd
Pegasus Wy
Mitchell Dr
Falcon Wy
Soho Farm
Barnes Cl
Wallis Cl
St Athan Cl
Bowerhill Lane
Little Bowerhill Farm
Carnation La
Little Mitchells Farm
Pile Farm
Totterdown Farm
Martinslade
Kennet and Avon Canal
Bath Road
A365
Bradley Rec Gd
Cooks Cl
Egypt Farm
Moat
Summerham Bridge
Seend Hill
A361
Seend Hl

61

Rly Farm
Newtown Farm
SN12
Park Farm
Perry's La
PH
Seend CE Prim Sch
High Street
Turner's Farm
Loiterton Farm

7

Manor Farm
Church St
Church Farm
Melksham Park Farm
Weir
Seend Park Farm
Weir
Littleton Mill Farm
Littleton Green Farm
Littleton
Littleton Wood Farm
Semington Brook
The Stocks
Row Lane Farm
Seend Head
Rew Farm
Whites Farm
Seend Cleeve
Trowbridge Road
New La
Cleeve House
Baldham Mill Farm
Home Farm
Bell Hill
Inmarsh
Turners Farm
Inmarsh Farm
Knightsmead Farm
Summerham Brook

60

Crem
A361
Brickfield Farm
Newhouse Farm
Strangers Corner Farm
The Strand
PH
Peppercorn Orch
Woodhouse Farm
Baldham Bridge
Sewage Works
Great Thornham Farm
Little Thornham Farm
Seend Bridge Farm
Seend Bridge

6

Great Hinton
Back La
Back St
Main St
PH

59

BA14
Hinton Lane
Seend Road Farm
Pantry Bridge
Bulkington
Westview Farm
Northfields
Home Farm
SN10

5

Manor House
School Cl
Hobbs Hl
Keevil CE Primary School
Southview Farm
Earthwork
Pinkney Farm
Chestnut
PH
The Close
Manor Farm
Lawn Farm
Ashatch Farm
Mill Lane
Lutsey Farm

58

Loppinger Farm
Talboys
Deans End
Main Street
Martins Vs
Strongs Cl
Martins Cl
Keevil
Wick Bridge
Brasspan Bridge
Gaston Green Farm
Mill Lane
Mill Farm

4

Newleaze
Common Hill La
Holmeleaze
Bartletts Mead
Church
Butts La
Wick Farms
New Hurst Park Farm
Wick Leaze Farm
Old Hurst Farm

57

The Manor
Sandpits La
St Marys Cl
High Street
Vicarage La
Dark La S
PH
Keevil Airfield
Oxenleaze Farm
Pudnell House Farm

3

Coach Barton
St Marys CE Prim Sch
The Butts
Silver St
Acres Cl
Home Mead
Edington Road
Steeple Ashton
Spiers Piece Farm
Ashton Mill Farm
New Hurst Farm
Stokes Marsh Farm

56

Elmsgate House
Raydown Leaze
Hill Farm
Spiers Piece
Southbrook Lane
BA13
Lower Rd
Lower Road
Brickfield Farm
Newtown Farm

2

Whitelawn La
Drove Lane
Dairyhouse Farm
Lambourn Lane

55

Newgrounds Farm
Cowleaze Lane
Lower Baynton Farm

1

Housecroft Farm
Cowleaze Lane
Brickfield Farm

54

Bratton Road
Cresswell Down Farm
Ivy Mill Farm
Coulston
North Close Wood

90   A   91   B   92   C   93   D   94   E   95   F

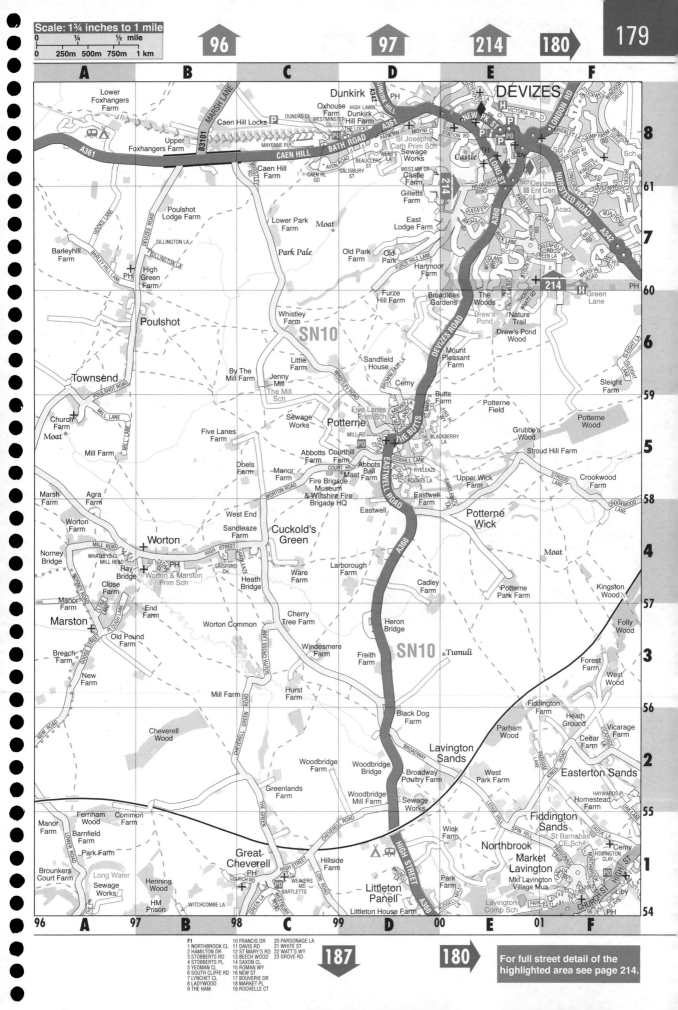

214   172

Scale: 1¾ inches to 1 mile

0   ¼   ½ mile
0   250m   500m   750m   1 km

214

A	B	C	D	E	F

Wessex Ridgeway

Lowerfields Farm

Coate

PH

All Cannings
PH
DREWITTS LA
THE STREET
CHANDLERS LA
UPRATE
SCHOOL LA

1 GREENHOUSE RD
2 PUB LA
3 THE GLEBE
4 TUMLINS
5 CHANDLERS CL

All Cannings CE Prim Sch

Manor Farm

BRICKLEY LANE

TEASEL CL
LONGLEYS CL

Nursteed Farm

Etchilhampton Water

SN10

Nursteed
BRICKLEY LA

Etchilhampton

Etchilhampton Hill

Wayside Farm

Heath Knapp

South Farm

South Farm

SLEIGHT RD
SLEIGHT LA
STERT VALLEY LA

MONUMENT HILL
A342

Manor Farm

Manor Farm
Stert

Westfield Farm

Etchilhampton Plantation

Patney Copse

Patney Bridge
WOODLAND ROAD
MANOR FARM LANE
PO

Field Head

Wabi Farm

Hatfield Farm

Byde Farm

Fullaway Farm

PH

Sunnyside Farm

PUCKLANDS

Patney

PATNEY ROAD

Marsh Farm

Crookwood Mill Farm

SN10

Bridge Farm

Stert Valley Farm

B4
1 PEPPERCOMBE LA
2 CHAPEL LA
3 THE ORCHARD
4 CHURCH VW
5 BOWDENS
6 PEPPERCOMBE CL

Franklins Farm

C4
1 CHURCH LA
2 THE HAM
3 FRIARS LA
4 ST MICHAEL'S CL
5 WALNUT CL

Sewage Works

CROOKWOOD LANE

Heron Nest Wood

Wickham Green Farm

Knightleaze Farm

Peppercombe Wood Nature Reserve

Manor Farm

G GATE RD
HIGH ST
CARTWAY
PLUM LA

Wedhampton

Chirton CE Prim Sch

CHERRINGTON FIELD
MILLER CL

Cuckoo's Corner

PO
PH

Urchfont

Foxley Fields

The Manor

Chirton

PARK VW
SMALL ST

Kingston Wood

Oakfrith Wood

Urchfont CE Prim Sch
BLACKBOARD LA

HIGH ST
CROOMS LA

Foxley Corner

B3098

A342

Manor Farm

Conock

THE ORCHARD
YEW TREE CL
THE HOLLOW

The Three Graves

Witchell La

Goosehole Farm

Townsend

THE CROFT
BULLDOG LA

Cemy

ANDOVER

B3
1 MANOR CL
2 THE PADDOCK
3 STONE PIT LA

Redhorn Plantation

BRACKLAND

Eastcott

EASTCOTT COMMON

Goosehole Plantation

Dogtail Plantation

Redhorn Hill

KINGS RD
B3098

Eastcott Manor

New Plantation
P

Chirton Bottom

Easterton
WHITE ST

PH
HIGH ST

Tumulus

Tumulus

Urchfont Hill

P

Chirton Maggot

Tumulus

STIRLING RD
MELROSE CL
PIDDINGTON HL
THE PADDOCK
SOUTH CLIFFE RD

THE CLAY

Penning Down

Westdown Artillery Range

DANGER AREA

Wessex Ridgeway

DANGER AREA

Tumuli

DANGER AREA

Tumulus

Old Plantation

Chirton Down

Great Fore Down

02	A	03	B	04	C	05	D	06	E	07	F

179   188

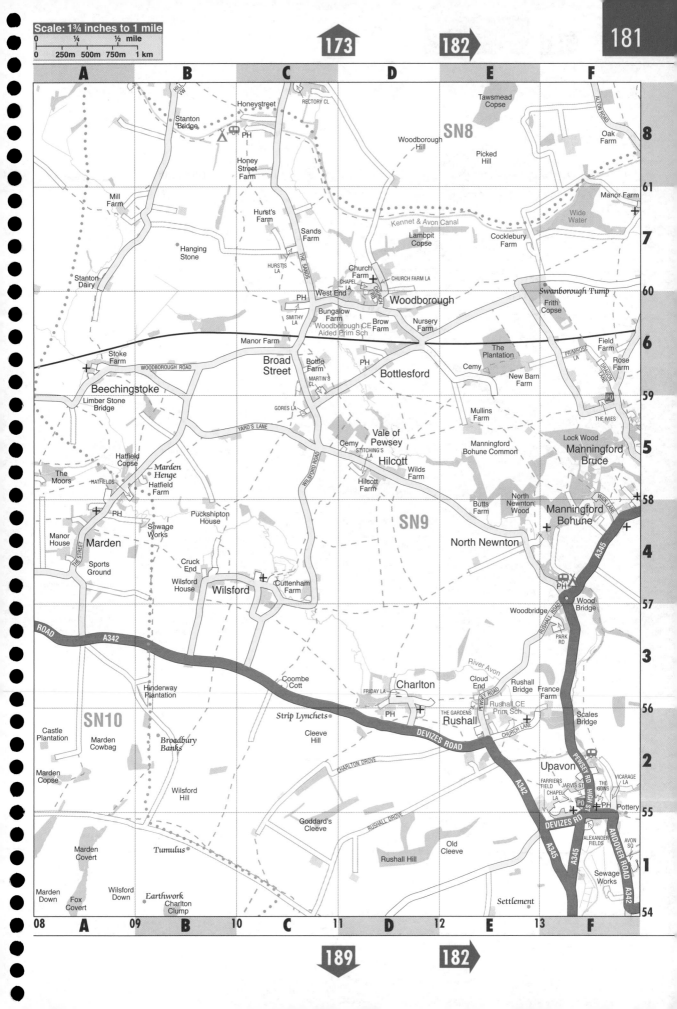

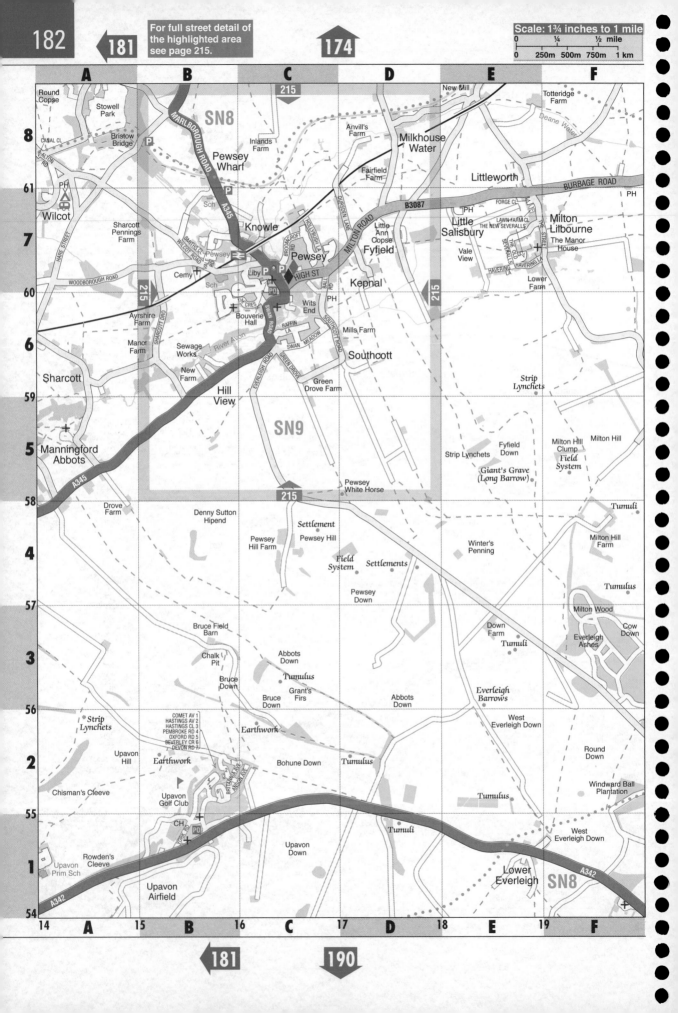

For full street detail of the highlighted area see page 215.

181

174

Scale: 1¾ inches to 1 mile

0 ¼ ½ mile
0 250m 500m 750m 1 km

Round Copse
Stowell Park
CANAL CL
Bristow Bridge
SN8
MARLBOROUGH ROAD
A345
SN8
Inlands Farm
Anvil's Farm
New Mill
Totteridge Farm
Deane Water

PH
HARE STREET
WALTON RD
Wilcot
Pewsey Wharf
Fairfield Farm
Milkhouse Water
Littleworth
BURBAGE ROAD
PH

Sharcott Pennings Farm
WOODBOROUGH ROAD
WILCOT ROAD
SMITH'S CL
Sch
A345
Knowle
Pewsey
BROADCROFT RD
HILLYBUSH LA
DURSDEN LANE
B3087
MILTON ROAD
Little Ann Copse
PH
FORGE CL
THE NEW SEVERALLS
Little Salisbury
Milton Lilbourne
THE STREET
THE OLD SEVERALLS
HAVERING LA
The Manor House

215
SHARCOTT DRO
Cemy
Liby
HIGH ST
Pewsey
PO
Fyfield
Kepnal
Vale View
HAVERING LA
Lower Farm

Ayrshire Farm
Manor Farm
TH CRES
Bouverie Hall
RAFFIN LA
SWAN MEADOW
BALL RD
SOUTHCOTT ROAD
PH
Wits End
Southcott
Mills Farm

Sharcott
New Farm
River Avon
Sewage Works
EVERLEIGH ROAD
GREEN DROVE
Green Drove Farm
Strip Lynchets

Manningford Abbots
A345
Hill View
SN9
Pewsey White Horse
Strip Lynchets
Fyfield Down
Milton Hill Clump
Milton Hill
Field System

Giant's Grave (Long Barrow)

215
Tumuli
Milton Hill Farm

Drove Farm
Denny Sutton Hipend
Pewsey Hill Farm
Settlement
Pewsey Hill
Field System
Settlements
Winter's Penning
Milton Wood
Cow Down

Pewsey Down

Pewsey Down
Tumulus

Bruce Field Barn
Chalk Pit
Bruce Down
Abbots Down
Tumulus
Bruce Down
Grant's Firs
Abbots Down
Everleigh Barrows
Down Farm
Tumuli
Everleigh Ashes

Strip Lynchets
COMET AV 1
HASTINGS AV 2
HASTINGS CL 3
PEMBROKE RD 4
OXFORD RD 5
BEVERLEY CR 6
DEVON RD 7
Earthwork
West Everleigh Down
Round Down

Upavon Hill
Earthwork
BRITANNIA AV
ARBOR AVE
Bohune Down
Tumulus
Windward Ball Plantation

Chisman's Cleeve
Upavon Golf Club
Tumulus

CH
YORK RD
PO
Tumuli
West Everleigh Down

Upavon Prim Sch
Rowden's Cleeve
Upavon Down
Tumuli
Lower Everleigh
SN8
A342

A342
Upavon Airfield

14 A 15 B 16 C 17 D 18 E 19 F

181

190

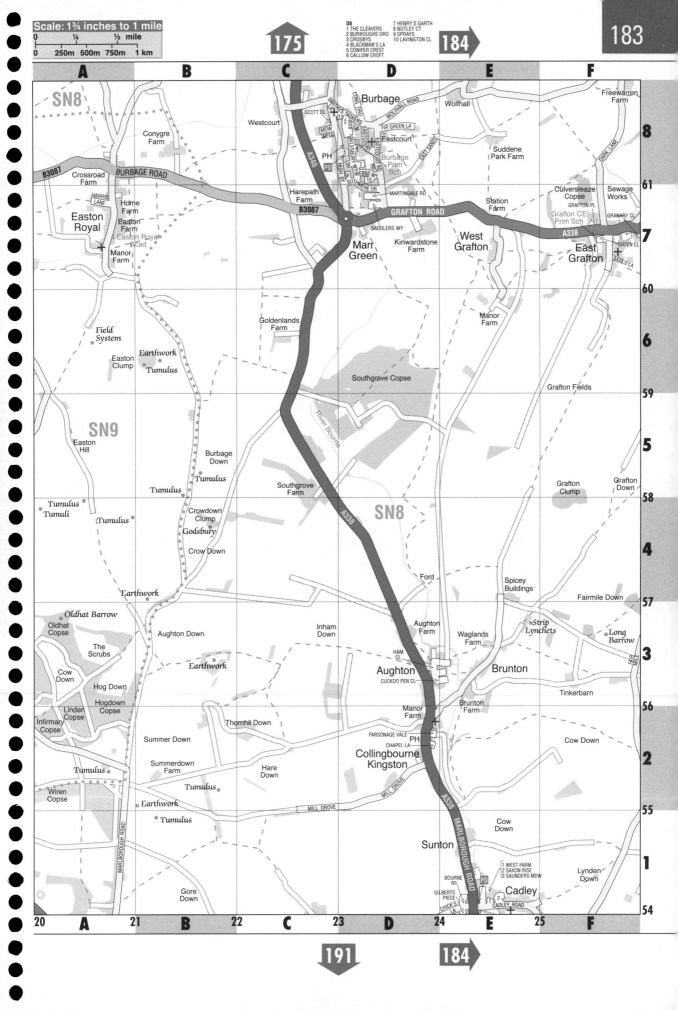

Scale: 1¾ inches to 1 mile

0   ¼   ½ mile

0   250m   500m   750m   1 km

D8
1 THE CLEAVERS
2 BURROUGHS DRO
3 CROSBYS
4 BLACKMAN'S LA
5 CONIFER CREST
6 CALLOW CROFT
7 HENRY'S GARTH
8 NUTLEY CT
9 SPRAYS
10 LAVINGTON CL

A   B   C   D   E   F

SN8

Burbage
Westcourt
Conygre Farm
SCOTT CL
LONG DRO
SMITH'S TASKERS
WOLFHALL ROAD
Wolfhall
Freewarren Farm

8

MDW WELL
FIR GREEN LA
Eastcourt
Eastcourt
Suddene Park Farm

61

Crossroad Farm
B3087
BURBAGE ROAD
HARRIS LANE
Home Farm
Harepath Farm
B3087
PH
PO
HIGH ST
AYLESBURY WY
WEBBS
SUTHMERE DR
Burbage Prim Sch
EAST SANDS
Culversleaze Copse
Sewage Works

DARK LANE
GRAFTON PL

Easton Royal
Easton Farm
Easton Royal Acad
MARTINGALE RD
GRAFTON ROAD
Station Farm
Grafton CE Prim Sch
GRANARY CL

7

A3J6
Manor Farm
SADDLERS WY
Marr Green
Kinwardstone Farm
West Grafton
A338
East Grafton
GREEN CL
BATE'S LA

60

Field System
Goldenlands Farm
Manor Farm
Grafton Fields

6

Easton Clump
Earthwork
Tumulus
Southgrove Copse

59

SN9
River Bourne
Grafton Clump
Grafton Down

5

Easton Hill
Burbage Down
Tumulus
Southgrove Farm

58

Tumulus
Tumulus
Tumulus
A338
SN8

Tumulus Tumuli
Crowdown Clump
Godsbury
Crow Down
Spicey Buildings
Fairmile Down

57

Earthwork
Ford
Strip Lynchets
Long Barrow

Oldhat Barrow
Oldhat Copse
Aughton Down
Inham Down
Aughton Farm
Waglands Farm

3

The Scrubs
Earthwork
HAM CL
Aughton
Brunton
Tinkerbarn

Cow Down
Hog Down
Hogdown Copse
CUCKOO PEN CL
Brunton Farm

56

Linden Copse
Thornhil Down
Manor Farm
Cow Down

Infirmary Copse
Summer Down
PARSONAGE VALE
PH
CHAPEL LA

2

Tumulus
Summerdown Farm
Hare Down
Collingbourne Kingston
MILL DROVE

Wiren Copse
Earthwork
Tumulus
MILL DROVE
A338

55

Tumulus
Cow Down
Sunton
MARLBOROUGH ROAD

Gore Down
Lynden Down

1

MARLBOROUGH ROAD
BOURNE RI
PO
1 WEST FARM
2 SAXON RISE
3 SAUNDERS MDW
Cadley
GILBERTS PIECE
CADLEY ROAD
CHICK'S LA

54

20   A   21   B   22   C   23   D   24   E   25   F

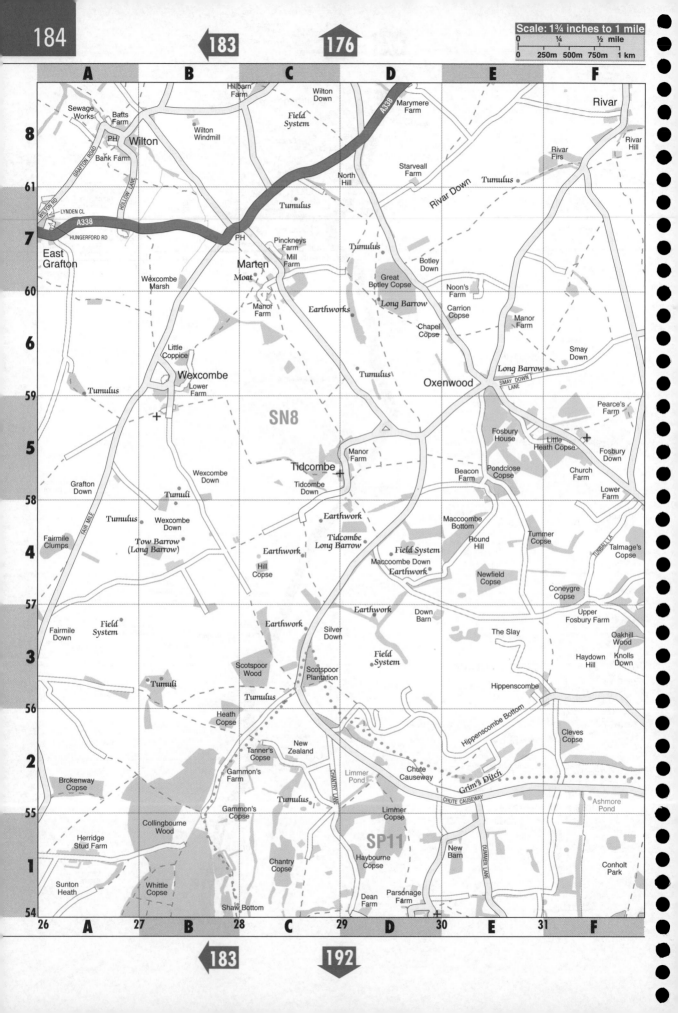

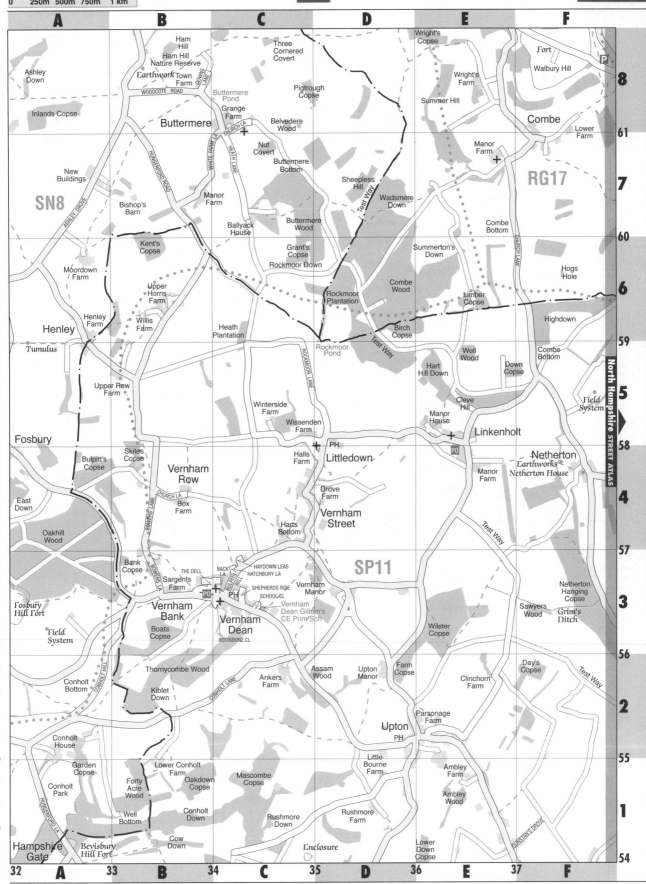

A   B   C   D   E   F

8

Ashley Down

Inlands Copse

Ham Hill
Ham Hill Nature Reserve
Earthwork Town Farm
WOODCOTE ROAD

Three Cornered Covert

Pigtrough Copse

Wright's Copse

Fort
Walbury Hill

Wright's Farm

Summer Hill

Combe

61

Buttermere Pond
Grange Farm
CHURCH LA

Nut Covert

Belvedere Wood

Manor Farm

Lower Farm

Buttermere

RG17

7

New Buildings

SN8

Bishop's Barn

ASHLEY DRIVE
HUNGERFORD ROAD
WHITE FARM LA
HEATH LANE
JENNIS LANE

Manor Farm

Ballyack House

Buttermere Bottom

Buttermere Wood

Sheepless Hill

Test Way

Wadsmere Down

Combe Bottom

60

Moordown Farm

Kent's Copse

Upper Horns Farm

Grant's Copse
Rockmoor Down

Summerton's Down

Combe Wood

Hogs Hole

6

Henley
Henley Farm

Willis Farm

Heath Plantation

Rockmoor Plantation

ROCKMOOR LANE

Birch Copse

Test Way

Limber Copse

Highdown

59

Tumulus

Upper Row Farm

Rockmoor Pond

Well Wood

Hart Hill Down

Down Copse

Combe Bottom

North Hampshire STREET ATLAS

5

Fosbury

Bulpitt's Copse

Skites Copse

BOWERS LANE
CHURCH LA

Winterside Farm

Wissenden Farm

Halls Farm

PH

Littledown

Manor House

Cleve Hill

Linkenholt

PO

Netherton
Earthworks
Netherton House

Field System

58

East Down

Oakhill Wood

Vernham Row

Box Farm

Drove Farm

Vernham Street

Manor Farm

4

Bank Copse

BOWERS LANE

Sargents Farm

THE DELL
BACK LA
BULPITS HILL
HATCHBURY LA
HAYDOWN LEAS
SHEPHERDS RISE
SCHOOL CL

Vernham Dean Gillum's CE Prim Sch

Vernham Manor

Wilster Copse

Sawyers Wood

Grim's Ditch

Netherton Hanging Copse

57

Fosbury Hill Fort

Field System

CONHOLT HILL

Vernham Bank

Boats Copse

PO

PH

Vernham Dean

BOTISDONE CL

SP11

3

Conholt Bottom

Thornycombe Wood

Kiblet Down

CONHOLT LANE

Ankers Farm

Assam Wood

Upton Manor

Farm Copse

Clinchorn Farm

Day's Copse

Test Way

56

Conholt House

Garden Copse

Conholt Park

HUNGERFORD LA

Lower Conholt Farm

Forty Acre Wood

Oakdown Copse

Conholt Down

Mascombe Copse

Little Bourne Farm

Parsonage Farm

Upton
PH

Ambley Farm

Ambley Wood

55

Well Bottom

Cow Down

Rushmore Down

Rushmore Farm

DUNSTAN'S DRIVE

Lower Down Copse

2

Hampshire Gate

Bevisbury Hill Fort

Enclosure

1

54

32   A   33   B   34   C   35   D   36   E   37   F

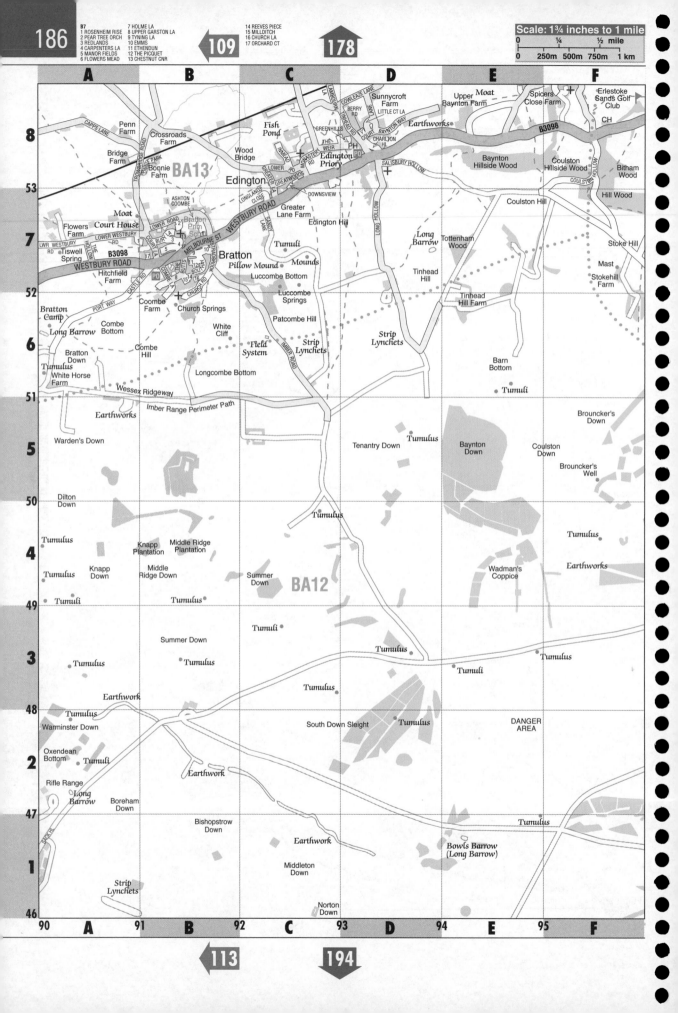

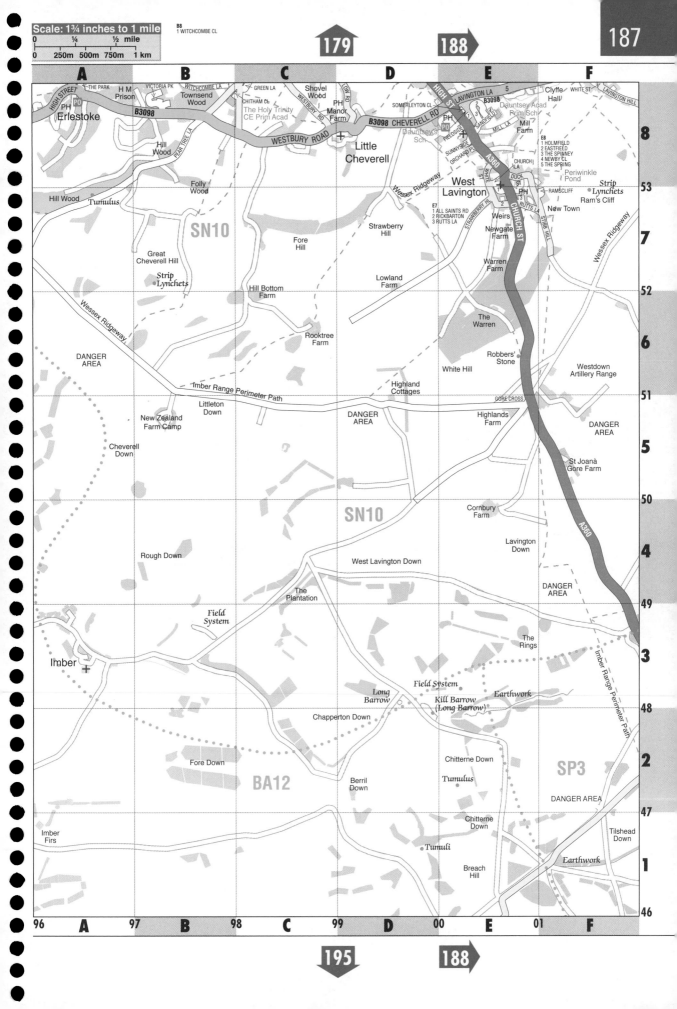

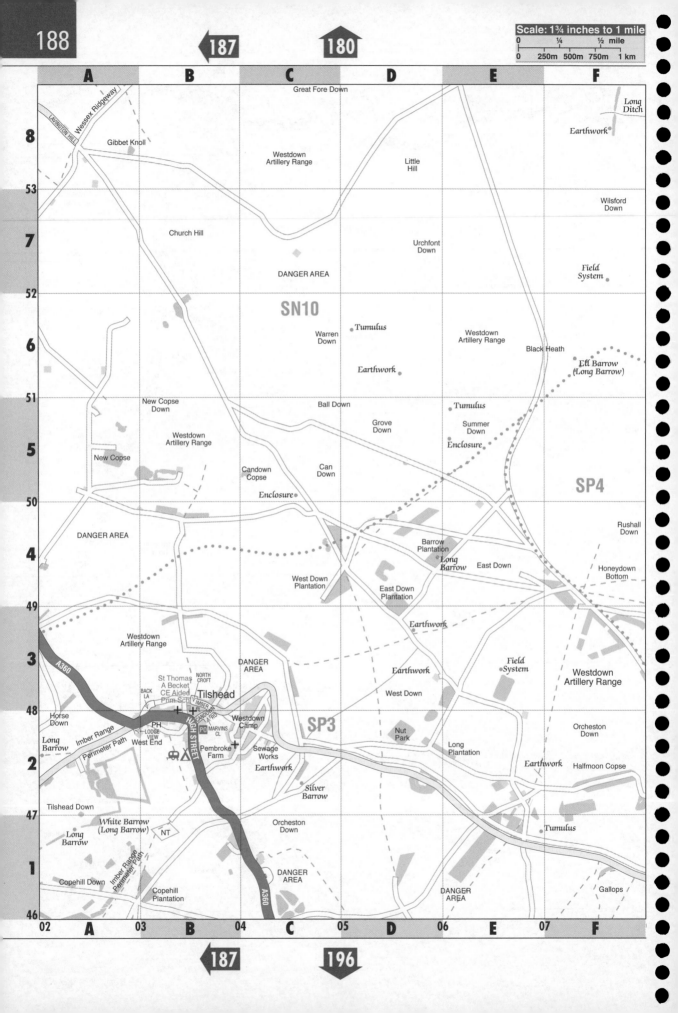

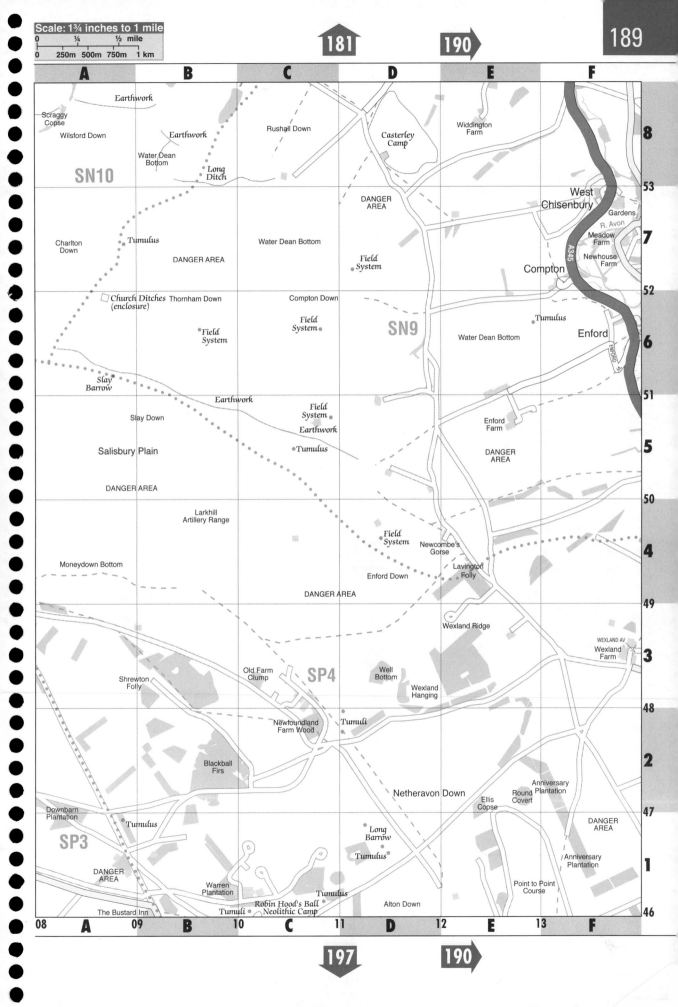

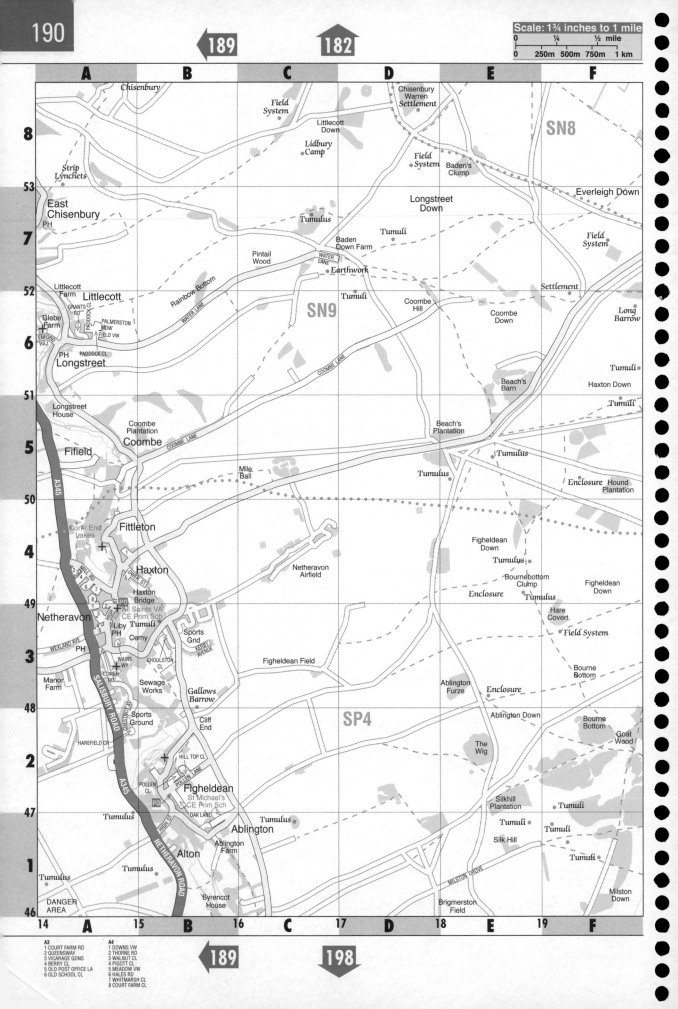

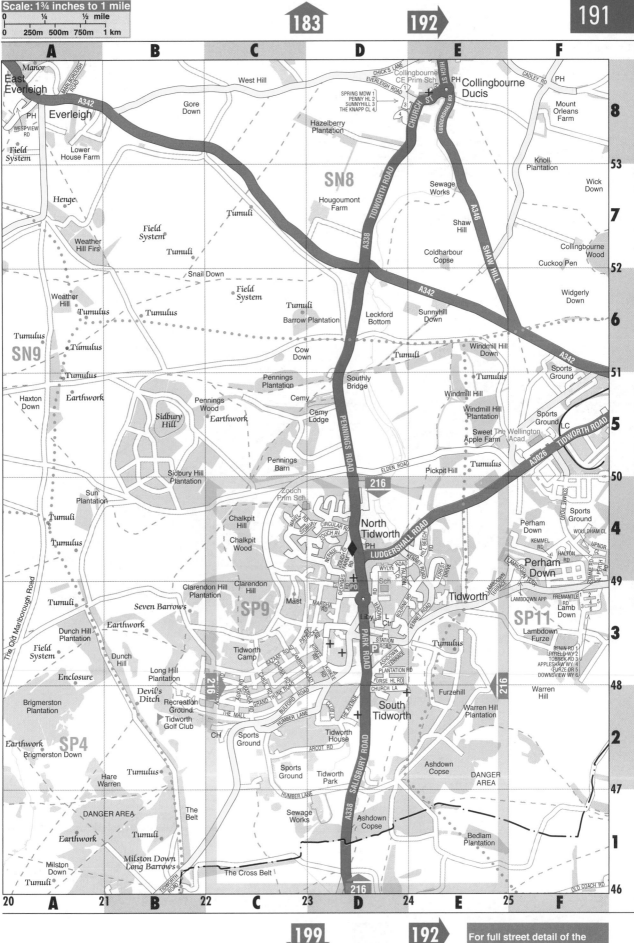

East Everleigh

Manor

PH
WEST VIEW RD
Field System

A342

Everleigh

Lower House Farm

Henge

Weather Hill Firs

Field System

Tumuli

Tumuli

Gore Down

West Hill

Hazelberry Plantation

Collingbourne CE Prim Sch
CHICK'S LANE
EVERLEIGH ROAD

SPRING MDW 1
PENNY HL 2
SUNNYHILL 3
THE KNAPP CL 4

CHURCH ST
HIGH ST

PH

Collingbourne Ducis

CADLEY RD

PH

Mount Orleans Farm

SN8

TIDWORTH ROAD
A338

Hougoumont Farm

Sewage Works

Shaw Hill

Coldharbour Copse

A346

SHAW HILL

Knoll Plantation

Wick Down

Collingbourne Wood

Cuckoo Pen

A342

Snail Down

Weather Hill

Tumulus

Tumulus

SN9

Tumulus

Tumulus

Tumulus

Haxton Down

Earthwork

Field System

Tumuli

Barrow Plantation

Cow Down

Leckford Bottom

Sunnyhill Down

Tumuli

Windmill Hill Down

Widgerly Down

Sports Ground

A342

Pennings Plantation

Cemy

Southly Bridge

Windmill Hill

Sports Ground

LC

Sidbury Hill

Pennings Wood

Earthwork

Cemy Lodge

PENNINGS ROAD

Windmill Hill Plantation

Sweet The Wellington
Apple Farm Acad

Sports Ground

TIDWORTH ROAD

Pennings Barn

Sidbury Hill Plantation

Sun Plantation

Tumuli

Tumulus

The Old Marlborough Road

ELDEN ROAD

Pickpit Hill

Tumulus

A3026

Zouch Prim Sch

216

North Tidworth

PH

Perham Down

SOMME RD
WOULDHAM CL

KEMMEL RD
HALTON CL
UPNOR CL
PERH

Chalkpit Hill

Chalkpit Wood

NEPAUL RD
ZOUCH AV
CIRCULAR RD
SIDBURY
HILL BEECH RD

LUDGERSHALL ROAD

Tidworth

SP11

LAMBDOWN TERR

Perham Down

FREMANTLE

Clarendon Hill Plantation

Clarendon Hill

Mast

SP9

MARGHA RD

WYLYE ROAD
KENNET ROAD
FOREST DRIVE
Sch

BOURNE RD
KENNET ROAD

LAMBDOWN APP

Lamb Down

LYFIELD WY 2
TOBRUK RD 3
APPLESHAW WY 4
FURZE DR 5
DOWNSVIEW WY 6

Seven Barrows

Earthwork

Tumuli

BAZAAR ROAD
PATROL RD
AMRITSAR RD
KHAJUR RD

Liby
L
Ctr
PO

STATION ROAD

Tumulus

Lambdown Furze

BENIN RD 1

Dunch Hill Plantation

Dunch Hill

Tidworth Camp

AGRA RD
BARODA RD
BULFORD ROAD
GRAND TRUNK ROAD

PARK ROAD

ASHDOWN TERRACE
PLANTATION RD
FURSE HL RD
CHURCH LA

South Tidworth

Furzehill

Warren Hill

Field System

Enclosure

Long Hill Plantation

Devil's Ditch
216

Recreation Ground
Tidworth Golf Club

THE MALL
HUMBER LANE

THE AVENUE

Warren Hill Plantation

216

Brigmerston Plantation

SP4

Earthwork
Brigmerston Down

Hare Warren

Tumulus

CH

Sports Ground

Sports Ground

ARCOT RD

Tidworth House

Tidworth Park

SALISBURY ROAD

Ashdown Copse

DANGER AREA

DANGER AREA

The Belt

HUMBER LANE

Sewage Works

A338

Ashdown Copse

Bedlam Plantation

Earthwork

Tumuli

Milston Down

Tumuli

Milston Down Long Barrows

TIDWORTH ROAD

The Cross Belt

216

OLD COACH RD

199 192

For full street detail of the highlighted area see page 216.

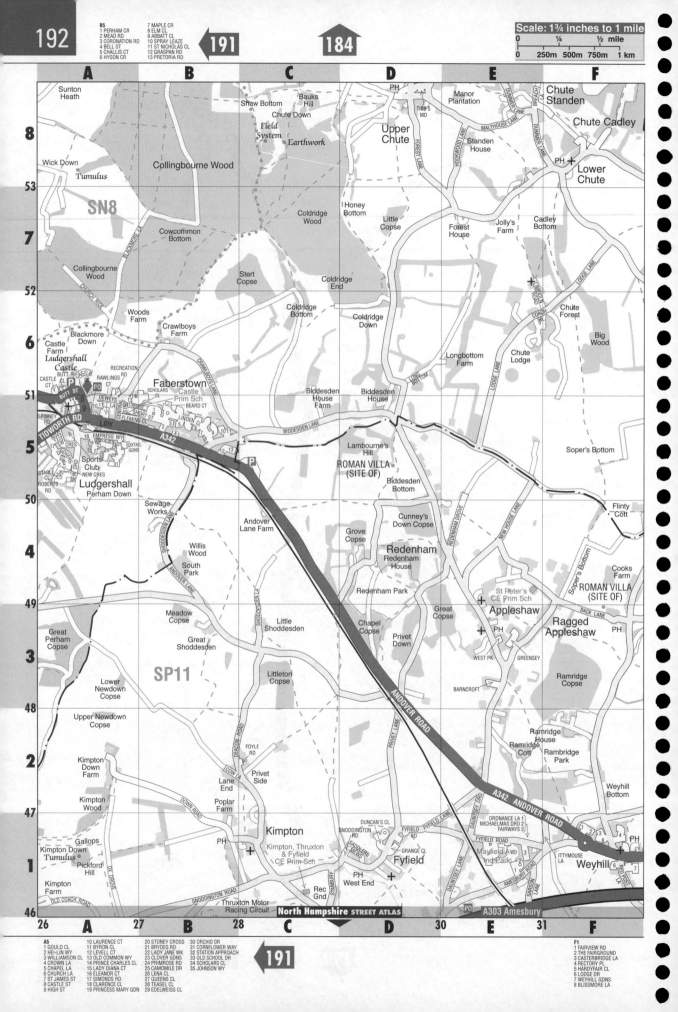

Scale: 1¾ inches to 1 mile

B5
1 PERHAM CR
2 MEAD RD
3 CORONATION RD
4 BELL ST
5 CHALLIS CT
6 HYSON CR

7 MAPLE CR
8 ELM CL
9 ABBATT CL
10 SPRAY LEAZE
11 ST NICHOLAS CL
12 GRASPAN RD
13 PRETORIA RD

A5
1 GOULD CL
2 HEI-LIN WY
3 WILLIAMSON CL
4 CROWN LA
5 CHAPEL LA
6 CHURCH LA
7 ST JAMES ST
8 CASTLE ST
9 HIGH ST

10 LAURENCE CT
11 BYRON CL
12 LEVELL CT
13 OLD COMMON WY
14 PRINCE CHARLES CL
15 LADY DIANA CT
16 ELEANOR CT
17 SIMONDS RD
18 CLARENCE CL
19 PRINCESS MARY GDN

20 STONEY CROSS
21 BRYDES RD
22 LADY JANE WK
23 CLOVER GDNS
24 PRIMROSE DR
25 CAMOMILE DR
26 LENA CL
27 QUEENS CL
28 TEASEL CL
29 EDELWEISS CL

30 ORCHID DR
31 CORNFLOWER WAY
32 STATION APPROACH
33 OLD SCHOOL DR
34 SCHOLARS CL
35 JOHNSON WY

F1
1 FAIRVIEW RD
2 THE FAIRGROUND
3 CASTERBRIDGE LA
4 RECTORY PL
5 HARDYFAIR CL
6 LODGE DR
7 WEYHILL GDNS
8 BLISSMORE LA

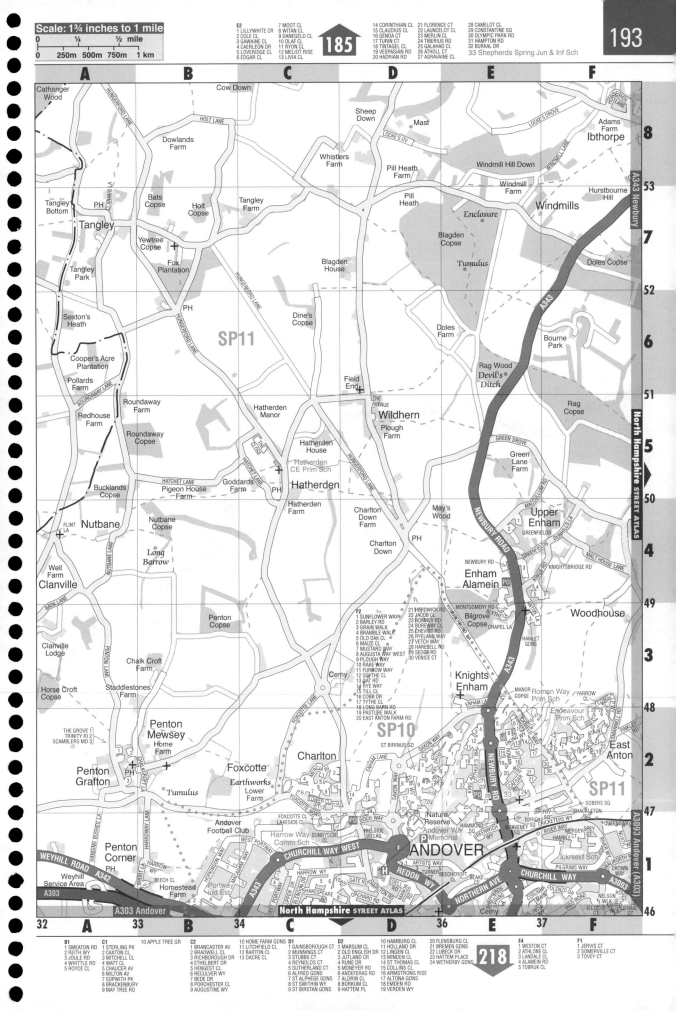

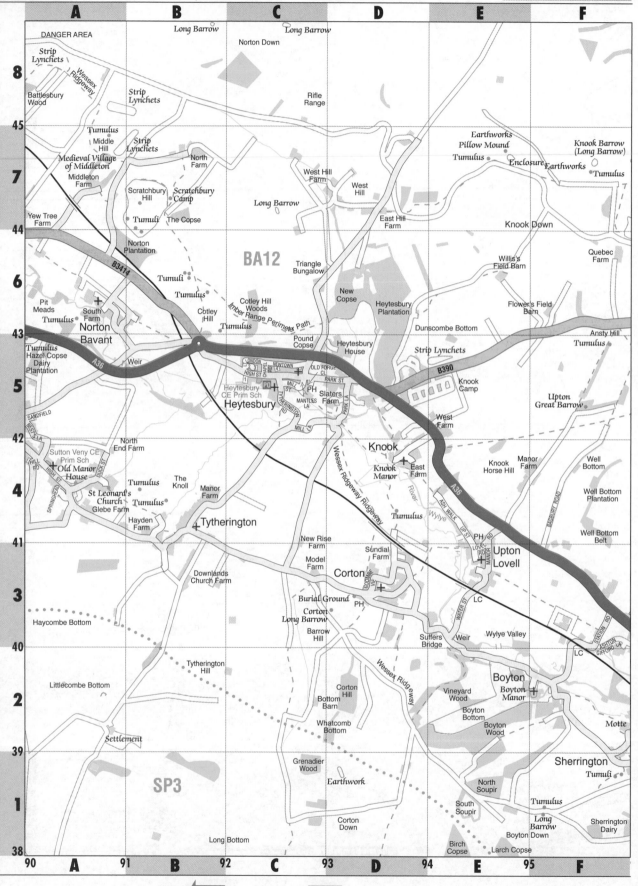

117 186

C5
1 GREENLANDS
2 WESTLANDS
3 GLEBELANDS
4 COTLEY PL

Scale: 1¾ inches to 1 mile
0   ¼   ½ mile
0   250m 500m 750m 1 km

A   B   C   D   E   F

DANGER AREA

Strip
Lynchets

Wessex Ridgeway

Battlesbury
Wood

Long Barrow

Long Barrow

Norton Down

Strip
Lynchets

Rifle
Range

Earthworks
Pillow Mound

Knook Barrow
(Long Barrow)

8

Tumulus

Middle
Hill

Strip
Lynchets

North
Farm

West Hill
Farm

West
Hill

Tumulus

Enclosure

Earthworks

Tumulus

45

Medieval Village
of Middleton

Middleton
Farm

Scratchbury
Hill

Scratchbury
Camp

Long Barrow

East Hill
Farm

Knook Down

7

Yew Tree
Farm

The Copse

Tumuli

Norton
Plantation

BA12

Triangle
Bungalow

Willis's
Field Barn

Quebec
Farm

44

Pit
Meads

South
Farm

Tumuli

Tumulus

Cotley
Hill

Cotley Hill
Woods

New
Copse

Heytesbury
Plantation

Flower's Field
Barn

6

Tumulus

Imber Range Perimeter Path

Tumulus

Dunscombe Bottom

Ansty Hill

43

Norton
Bavant

Hazel Copse

Tumulus

Dairy
Plantation

Weir

A36

B3414

Pound
Copse

Heytesbury
House

Heytesbury
Strip Lynchets

B390

Knook
Camp

Tumulus

5

LONDON
RD
CHAPEL RD
NEWTOWN
HIGH ST
OLD FORGE
CL
PARK ST

Upton
Great Barrow

Heytesbury
CE Prim Sch

PO
PH

MILL ST

Slaters
Farm

MANTLES
LA

PARK LA

West
Farm

42

Heytesbury

THYERINGTON
RD

MILL
RD

North
End Farm

North
Soupir

Wessex Ridgeway Ridgeway

Knook

Manor
Farm

Well
Bottom

Sutton Veny CE
Prim Sch

Old Manor
House

SANDFIELD

Knook
Manor

East
Farm

Knook
Horse Hill

Well Bottom
Plantation

4

HILL
RD

BEST LA

Tumulus

The Knoll

Manor
Farm

River

Wylye

Tumulus

A36

UP ST

Well Bottom
Belt

St Leonard's
Church

Glebe Farm

Tumulus

PH

41

SPRINGHEAD

DUCK ST

HIGH ST

Hayden
Farm

Tytherington

New Rise
Farm

Sundial
Farm

Upton
Lovell

LOVEL
ROW

3

Downlands
Church Farm

Model
Farm

Corton

Burial Ground

PH

WATER ST

LC

40

Haycombe Bottom

Corton
Long Barrow

Barrow
Hill

Suffers
Bridge

Weir

Wylye Valley

LC

STATION RD

ASHTON
GIFFORD LA

2

Tytherington
Hill

Corton
Hill

Boyton

Boyton
Manor

Littlecombe Bottom

Bottom
Barn

Vineyard
Wood

Boyton
Bottom

Motte

39

Settlement

Whatcomb
Bottom

Boyton
Wood

Sherrington

Tumuli

SP3

Grenadier
Wood

Earthwork

North
Soupir

Tumulus

1

South
Soupir

Tumulus

Long
Barrow

Sherrington
Dairy

Long Bottom

Corton
Down

Boyton Down

Birch
Copse

Larch
Copse

38

90   A   91   B   92   C   93   D   94   E   95   F

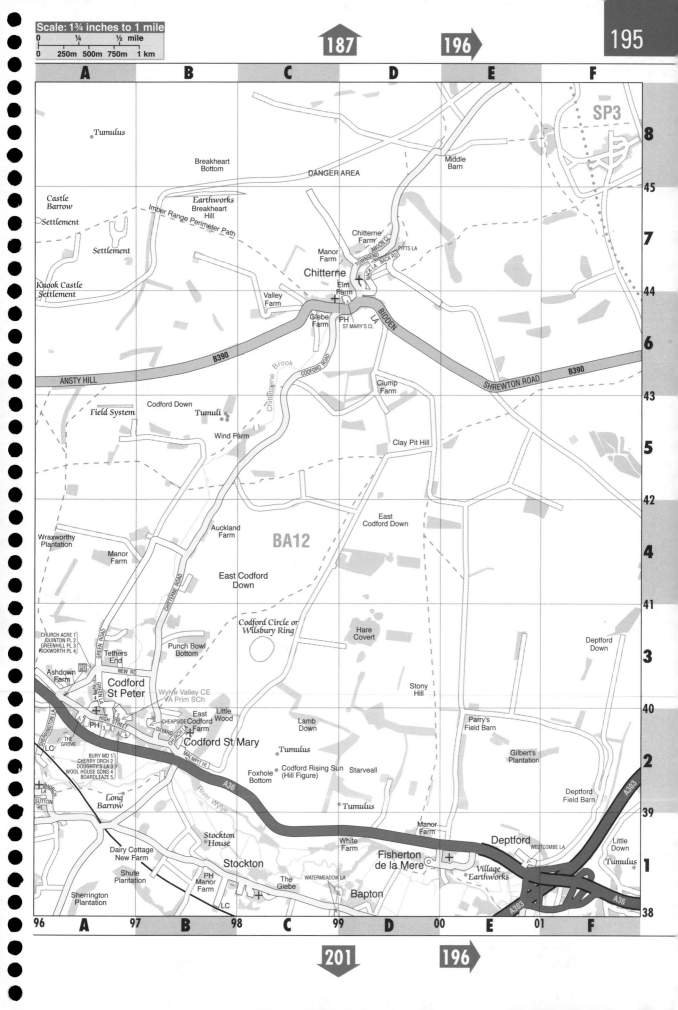

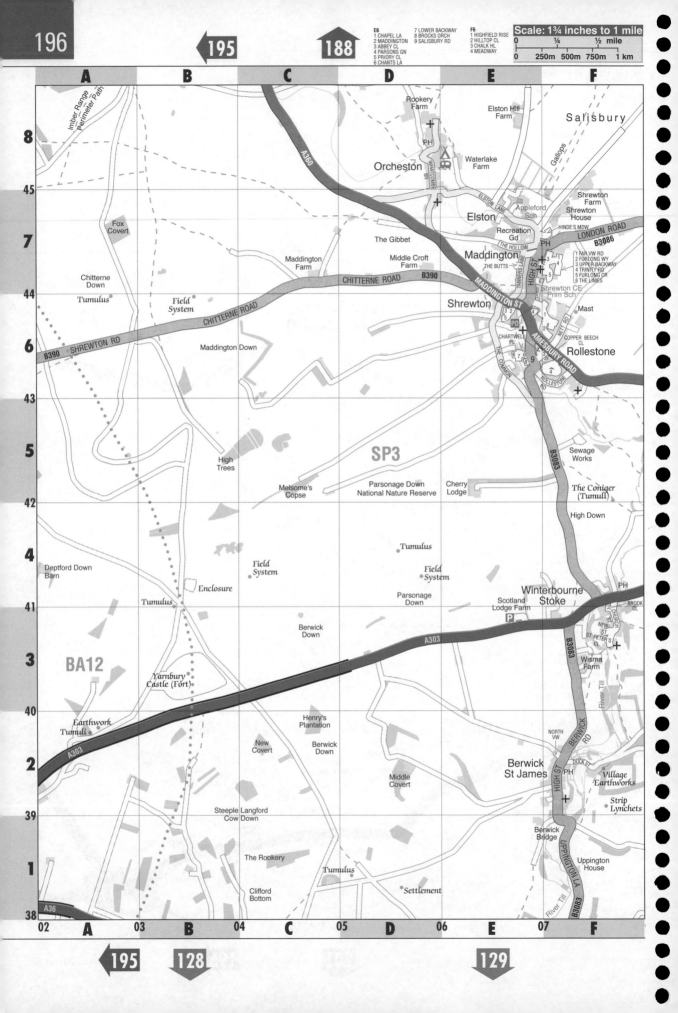

195
188

E6
1 CHAPEL LA
2 MADDINGTON
3 ABBEY CL
4 PARSONS GN
5 PRIORY CL
6 CHANTS LA

7 LOWER BACKWAY
8 BROCKS ORCH
9 SALISBURY RD

F6
1 HIGHFIELD RISE
2 HILLTOP CL
3 CHALK HL
4 MEADWAY

Scale: 1¾ inches to 1 mile

| 0 | ¼ | ½ mile |
| 0 | 250m | 500m | 750m | 1 km |

Imber Range Perimeter Path

A360

Rookery Farm

Elston Hill Farm

Salisbury

Orcheston

PH

WHATCOMBE BR

Waterlake Farm

Gallops

Elston

ELSTON LANE

Appleford Sch

Shrewton Farm

Shrewton House

HINDE'S MDW

LONDON ROAD

B3086

Fox Covert

The Gibbet

THE HOLLOW

PH

Maddington

1 FAR VW RD
2 FURLONG WY
3 UPPER BACKWAY
4 TRINITY RD
5 FURLONG CR
6 THE LIMES

Chitterne Down

Maddington Farm

Middle Croft Farm

THE BUTTS

TANNERS LANE

HIGH ST

Tumulus

CHITTERNE ROAD

B390

MADDINGTON ST

Shrewton

Shrewton CE Prim Sch

Mast

CHITTERNE ROAD

PO

Rollestone

B390 SHREWTON RD

Maddington Down

CHARTWELL PL

THE COMMON

AMESBURY ROAD

COPPER BEECH CL

KETT RD

ROLLESTONE RD

SP3

High Trees

Melsome's Copse

Parsonage Down National Nature Reserve

Cherry Lodge

Sewage Works

B3083

The Coniger (Tumuli)

High Down

Tumulus

Deptford Down Barn

Field System

Field System

Winterbourne Stoke

PH

Enclosure

Parsonage Down

Scotland Lodge Farm

BROOK CL

CHURCH ST

NEW ST

ST PETER'S CL

Tumulus

BA12

Berwick Down

A303

Wisma Farm

River Till

B3083

Yarnbury Castle (Fort)

Earthwork

Henry's Plantation

NORTH VW

BERWICK RD

A303

New Covert

Berwick Down

HIGH ST

Berwick St James

PH

DUCK'S

Village Earthworks

Strip Lynchets

Middle Covert

Tumuli

Steeple Langford Cow Down

Berwick Bridge

UPPINGTON LA

Uppington House

The Rookery

Tumulus

Settlement

Clifford Bottom

A36

River Till

B3083

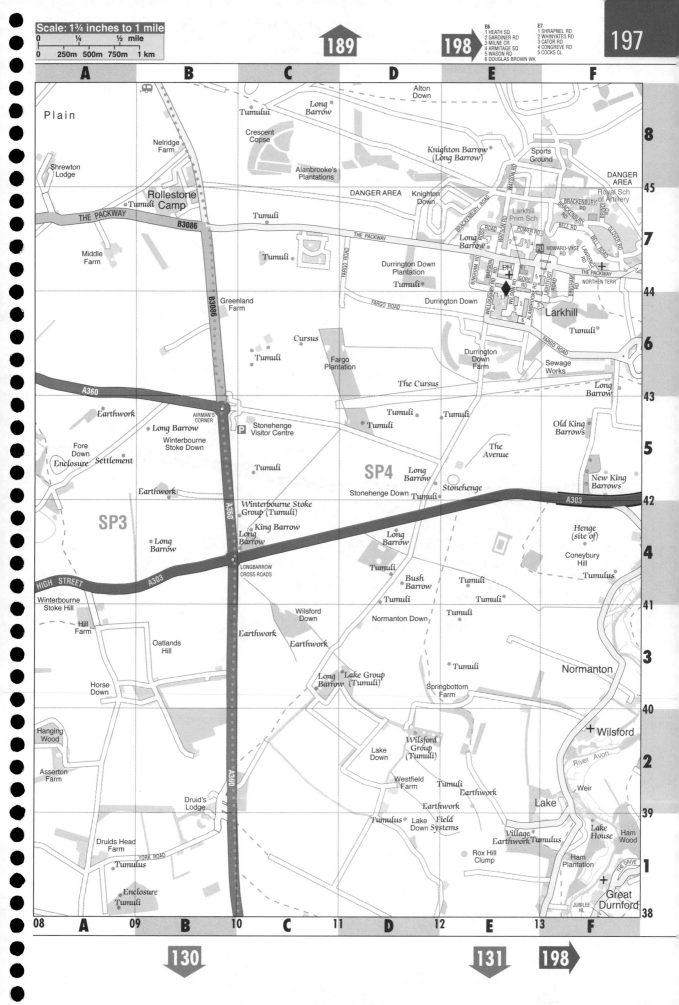

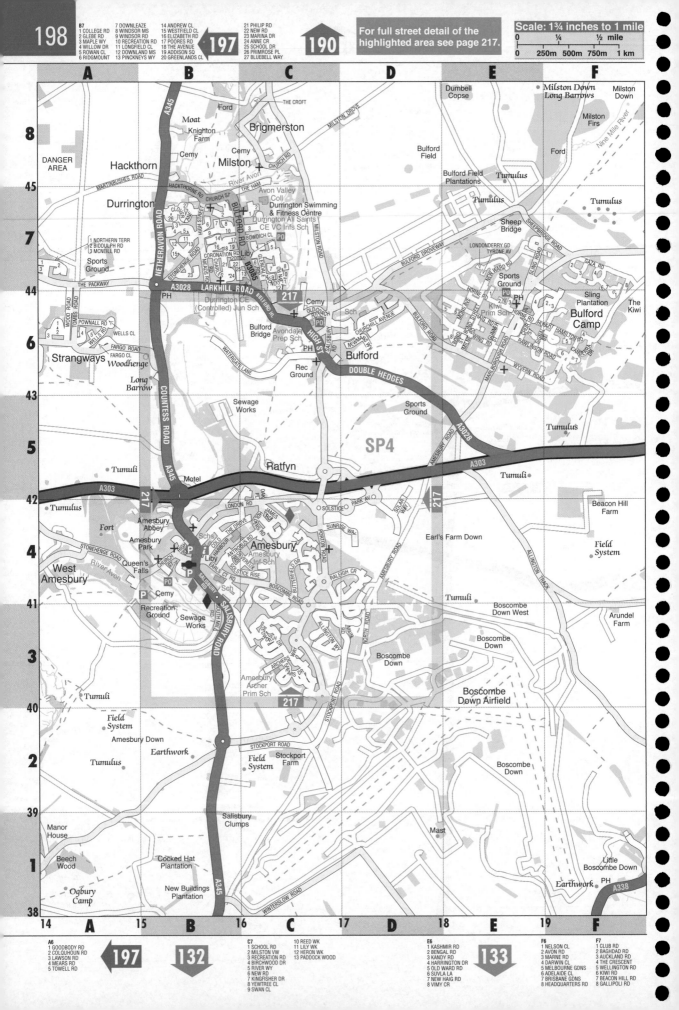

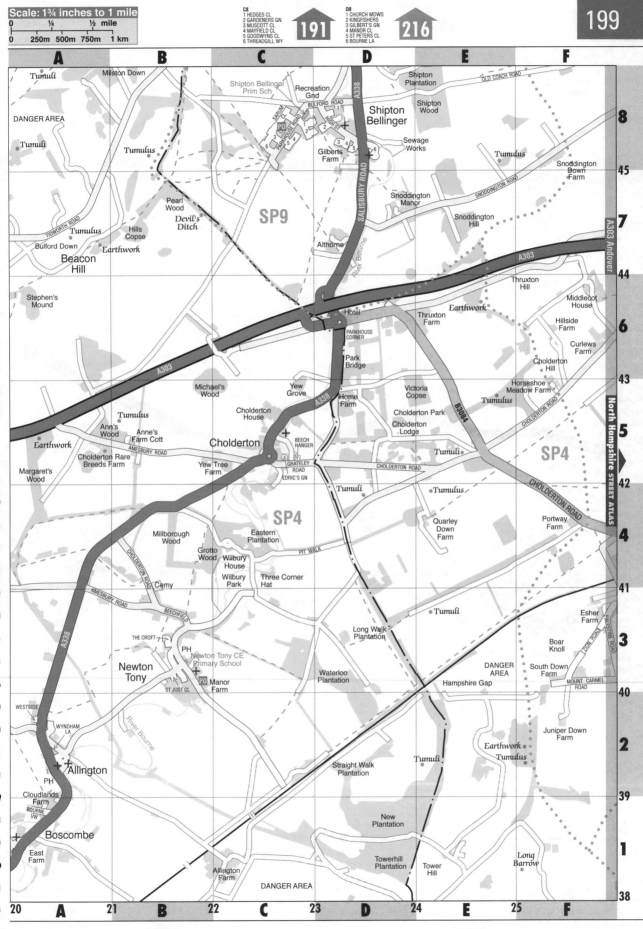

C8
1 HEDGES CL
2 GARDENERS GN
3 MUSCOTT CL
4 MAYFIELD CL
5 GOODWYNS CL
6 THREADGILL WY

D8
1 CHURCH MDWS
2 KINGFISHERS
3 GILBERT'S GN
4 MANOR CL
5 ST PETERS CL
6 BOURNE LA

191

216

A **B** **C** **D** **E** **F**

Tumuli
Milston Down
DANGER AREA
Tumuli
Tumulus
Hills Copse
Devil's Ditch
Pearl Wood
Earthwork
Tumulus
Bulford Down
Beacon Hill
Stephen's Mound

Shipton Bellinger Prim Sch
Recreation Gnd
BULFORD ROAD
SABIM
PARKHOUSE ROAD
PO
HIGH ST
Gilberts Farm
SP9

Shipton Plantation
Shipton Bellinger
Shipton Wood
Sewage Works
SALISBURY ROAD
A338
Althorne
River Bourne

Old Coach Road
Tumulus
Snoddington Down Farm
Snoddington Manor
SNODDINGTON ROAD
Snoddington Hill
A303
A303 Andover

8
45
7
44
6
43
5
42
4
41
3
40
2
39
1
38

Hotel
PARKHOUSE CORNER
Park Bridge
A303
Michael's Wood
Ann's Wood
Anne's Farm Cott
AMESBURY ROAD
Cholderton Rare Breeds Farm
Earthwork
Margaret's Wood
Tumulus
Cholderton House
Yew Grove
A338
Home Farm
Cholderton
Yew Tree Farm
BEECH HANGER
GRATELEY ROAD
EDRIC'S GN
Tumuli

Thruxton Hill
Thruxton Farm
Earthwork
Victoria Copse
Cholderton Park
Cholderton Lodge
CHOLDERTON ROAD
Tumulus
B3084
Middlecot House
Hillside Farm
Curlews Farm
Cholderton Hill
Horseshoe Meadow Farm
CHOLDERTON ROAD
SP4

North Hampshire STREET ATLAS

SP4
Millborough Wood
Grotto Wood
Wilbury House
Wilbury Park
Cemy
Eastern Plantation
Three Corner Hat
PIT WALK
Tumuli
Quarley Down Farm
Portway Farm
Tumuli

CHOLDERTON ROAD
AMESBURY ROAD
A338
BEECHFIELD
THE CROFT
PH
Newton Tony CE Primary School
Newton Tony
ST JUST CL
PO
Manor Farm
WESTSIDE
WYNDHAM LA
River Bourne
Allington
PH
Cloudlands Farm
BOURNE VW
Boscombe
East Farm
Allington Farm
DANGER AREA

Long Walk Plantation
Waterloo Plantation
Straight Walk Plantation
New Plantation
Towerhill Plantation
Tower Hill
DANGER AREA
Hampshire Gap
South Down Farm
MOUNT CARMEL ROAD
Tumuli
Esher Farm
Boar Knoll
PALESTINE ROAD
ZION ROAD
Juniper Down Farm
Earthwork
Tumulus
Long Barrow

A 20 **B** 21 **C** 22 23 **D** 24 **E** 25 **F**

134

135

Scale: 1¾ inches to 1 mile

0   ¼   ½   mile
0   250m   500m   750m   1 km

A   **B**   **C**   **D**   **E**   **F**

Long Bottom

Redding
Hanging

Tumulus

Well
Bottom

BA12

Well
Bottom

Nightingale
Wood

Larch Copse

Park
Bottom

8

Starveall

Picket
Grove

Rowdean
Hill

Tumulus

Sherrington Down

Stockton
Down

37

Musseldean
Copse

Stonehill
Copse

Corton
Wood

Great Ridge

Enclosure

Alsesetting
Copse

Longdean
Bottom

Stony
Hill

Great
Bottom

7

West
Wood

Pound Copse

Scrubbed Oak

Enclosure

Snail-creep Hanging

High Grove

36

Wessex
Ridgeway

Bernwick
Bushes

Enclosure
Penning
Wood

Point
Pond Wood

Enclosure

Grim's
Ditch

Sherrington
Wood

Gattrell's
Copse

Fonthill
Bushes

6

Cratt
Hill

Chilifinch
Hanging

Limekiln
Wood

High Park Wood

Tumulus

Tumulus

Hart
Coppice

35

Chilfinch Hill

Bake
Barn

Tumuli

Field
System

Fonthill
Down

Woodbine
Barn

Chicklade

Seymour Farm

Down
Place

Chicklade
Dairy

A303

Monarch's Way

5

A303

Wessex Ridgeway

Chicklade
Bottom

Cold
Berwick Hill

Chicklade
Bottom Farm

34

Berwick
Down

SP3

Berwick
Down Dairy

Berwick
St Leonard

Field Barn
Buildings

4

Two Mile
Down

Hawking
Down

Berwick
Glebe Farm

Berwick
Farm

Monarch's Way

Kingstead
Farm

B3089

Ridge
Farm

33

B3089

PH

Hindon CE VA
Prim Sch

ANGEL
LANE

HIGH ST

SCHOOL RD

THE DENE

STOP ST

Hindon

PO

PH
Fonthill
Bishop

Pinchpenny
Clump

Ridge
Hill

3

Crows Top

Wessex Ridgeway

THE DENE

Red House
Farm

THE DOWN

The Terraces

Greenwich

Little Ridge Wood

Knap
Farm

KNAP LA

KNAP LA

WOOD'S LANE

PADDOCK LA

MILL LANE

FRICKER'S LA

Ridge

Plowman's
Copse

32

Tumuli

Down
Dairy

Terrace
Farm

Fonthill
Gifford

STOP ST

Jerrards
Farm

Fonthill
Stables

Fonthill
Lake

Fonthill
House

Fonthill
Park

Grottos

Caves

Quarry Wood

Grottos

The
Bushes

Ashley
Wood

Field
System

Wollard
Copse

Farnell
Copse

2

New Close
Hanging

Copper
Close

Fonthill

Hinkley Hill

WOOD LA

PH

Fonthill
Abbey Wood

Ashley
Wood Farm

Paddock
Wood

Weir

Tumulus

Vicarage
Barn

Lady
Down

31

Oddways
Hanging

Ruddlemoor
Farm

GREAT WESTERN AVENUE

Fonthill
Abbey Wood

Bitham
Lake

Fonthill Abbey

BECKFORD CL

HINDON LANE

Hillground

Hillstreet
Farm

CHILMARK ROAD

1

Bottom
Copse

Clay Hill
Wood

Mockeny
Wood

Beacon
Hill

Lower Lawn House

30

90   **A**   91   **B**   92   **C**   93   **D**   94   **E**   95   **F**

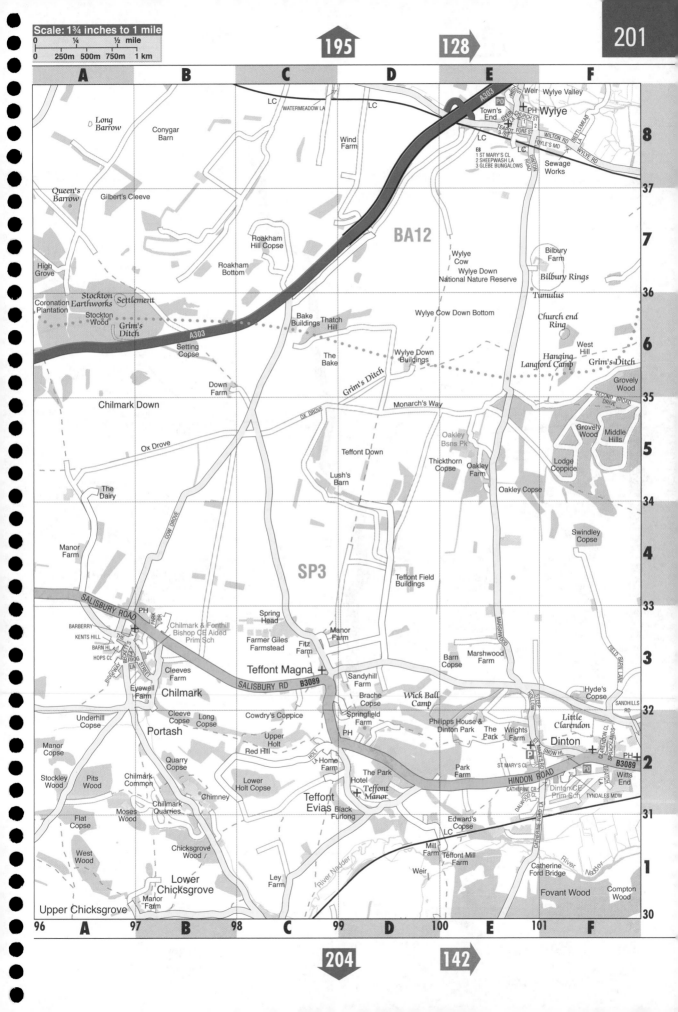

Scale: 1¾ inches to 1 mile

0   ¼   ½   mile
0   250m 500m 750m 1 km

195
128
204
142

A   B   C   D   E   F

8
37
7
36
6
35
5
34
4
33
3
32
2
31
1
30

Long Barrow
Conygar Barn
Watermeadow La
LC
LC
Wind Farm
A303
Town's End
Weir   Wylye Valley
High   PH   Wylye
Church St
Teapot St   Fore St
St Mary's Cl
1 ST MARY'S CL
2 SHEEPWASH LA
3 GLEBE BUNGALOWS
E8
Wilton Rd
Foyle's Md
Wylye Rd
Dinton Road
Sewage Works

Queen's Barrow
Gilbert's Cleeve
Roakham Hill Copse
Roakham Bottom
BA12
Wylye Cow
Wylye Down National Nature Reserve
Bilbury Farm
Bilbury Rings
Tumulus

High Grove
Stockton Earthworks   Settlement
Coronation Plantation
Stockton Wood
Grim's Ditch
A303
Setting Copse
Bake Buildings   Thatch Hill
The Bake
Wylye Cow Down Bottom
Wylye Down Buildings
Church end Ring
West Hill
Hanging Langford Camp   Grim's Ditch
Grovely Wood
Second Broad Drive

Chilmark Down
Down Farm
Ox Drove
Grim's Ditch
Monarch's Way
Grovely Wood   Middle Hills
Lodge Coppice

Ox Drove
Teffont Down
Lush's Barn
Oakley Bsns Pk
Thickthorn Copse   Oakley Farm
Oakley Copse

The Dairy
Cow Drove
SP3
Teffont Field Buildings
Swindley Copse

Manor Farm
Salisbury Road
PH
Park Dr
Barberry
Kents Hill
Barn Hl
Hops Cl
The   Bridge Pk
Frog La
Street
Chilmark & Fonthill Bishop CE Aided Prim Sch
Farmer Giles Farmstead
Spring Head
Fitz Farm
Manor Farm
Barn Copse   Marshwood Farm
Marshwood
Hyde's Copse
Sandhills Rd

Cleeves Farm
Teffont Magna
Salisbury Rd   B3089
Sandyhill Farm
Wick Ball Camp
Little Clarendon
Field Barn Lane

Eyewell Farm
Chilmark
Cleeve Copse   Long Copse
Cowdry's Coppice
Springfield Farm
Brache Copse
PH
Philipps House & Dinton Park
The Park
Wrights Farm
Dinton
PH
B3089
Spracklands Cl
Clarendon Cl

Underhill Copse
Portash
Quarry Copse
Upper Holt
Red Hill
HOLT
Home Farm
Park Farm
St Mary's Cl
P
Snow Hl
Steep Hollow
Marshwood
Catherine Cr
Dinton CE Prim Sch
Witts End
Tyndales Mdw

Manor Copse
Stockley Wood   Pits Wood
Chilmark Common
Chimney
Lower Holt Copse
The Park Hotel
Teffont Manor
Hindon Road
Catherine Crd Cl
Dalwood Cl
Catherine Ford La
PO

Flat Copse
Moses Wood
Chilmark Quarries
Teffont Evias
Black Furlong
Edward's Copse
LC
Catherine Ford Bridge
Fovant Wood
Compton Wood

West Wood
Chicksgrove Wood
Ley Farm
River Nadder
Weir
Mill Farm
Teffont Mill Farm
River Nadder

Lower Chicksgrove
Manor Farm
Upper Chicksgrove

96   97   98   99   100   101
A   B   C   D   E   F

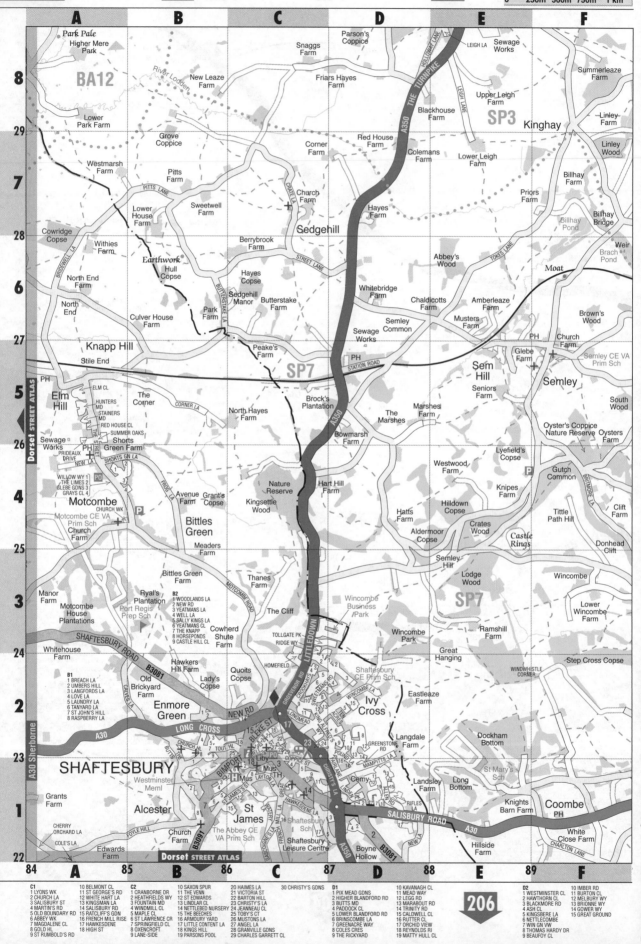

Scale: 1¾ inches to 1 mile

0   ¼   ½   mile
0   250m 500m 750m 1 km

C1
1 LYONS WK
2 CHURCH LA
3 SALISBURY ST
4 MARTIN'S RD
5 OLD BOUNDARY RD
6 ABBEY WK
7 MAGDALENE CL
8 GOLD HL
9 ST RUMBOLD'S RD

10 BELMONT CL
11 ST GEORGE'S RD
12 WHITE HART LA
13 KINGSMAN LA
14 SALISBURY RD
15 RATCLIFF'S GDN
16 FRENCH MILL RISE
17 HAWKESDENE
18 HIGH ST

C2
1 CRANBORNE DR
2 HEATHFIELDS WY
3 FOUNTAIN MD
4 WINDMILL CL
5 MAPLE CL
6 ST LAWRENCE CR
7 SPRINGFIELD CL
8 OXENCROFT
9 LANE-SIDE

10 SAXON SPUR
11 THE VENN
12 ST EDWARDS
13 LINDLAR CL
14 NETTLEBED NURSERY
15 THE BEECHES
16 ARMOURY YARD
17 LITTLE CONTENT LA
18 KINGS HILL
19 PARSONS POOL

20 HAIMES LA
21 VICTORIA ST
22 BARTON HILL
23 CHRISTY'S LA
24 JEANNEAU CL
25 TOBY'S CT
26 MUSTONS LA
27 ANGEL LA
28 GRANVILLE GDNS
29 CHARLES GARRETT CL

30 CHRISTY'S GDNS

D1
1 PIX MEAD GDNS
2 HIGHER BLANDFORD RD
3 BUTTS MD
4 PADDOCK CL
5 LOWER BLANDFORD RD
6 BRINSCOMBE LA
7 GREENACRE WAY
8 COLES CRES
9 THE RICKYARD

10 KAVANAGH CL
11 MEAD WAY
12 LEGG RD
13 MARABOUT RD
14 TRINITY RD
15 CALDWELL CL
16 RUTTER CL
17 ORCHID VIEW
18 REYNOLDS RI
19 MATTY HULL CL

D2
1 WESTMINSTER CL
2 HAWTHORN CL
3 BLACKMORE RD
4 ASH CL
5 KINGSBERE LA
6 NETTLECOMBE
7 WIN GN WE
8 THOMAS HARDY DR
9 BEAUFOY CL

10 IMBER RD
11 BURTON CL
12 MELBURY WY
13 BRIONNE WY
14 GOWER WY
15 GREAT GROUND

B2
1 WOODLANDS LA
2 NEW RD
3 YEATMANS LA
4 WELL LA
5 SALLY KINGS LA
6 YEATMANS CL
7 THE KNAPP
8 HORSEPONDS
9 CASTLE HILL CL

B1
1 BREACH LA
2 UMBERS HILL
3 LANGFORDS LA
4 LOVE LA
5 LAUNDRY LA
6 TANYARD LA
7 ST JOHN'S HILL
8 RASPBERRY LA

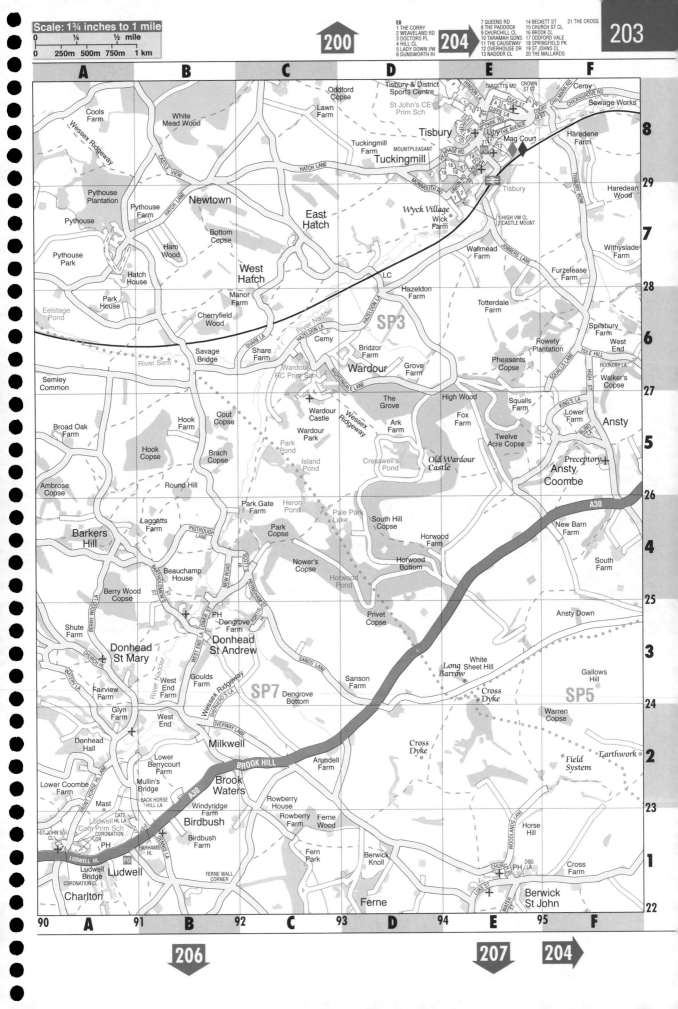

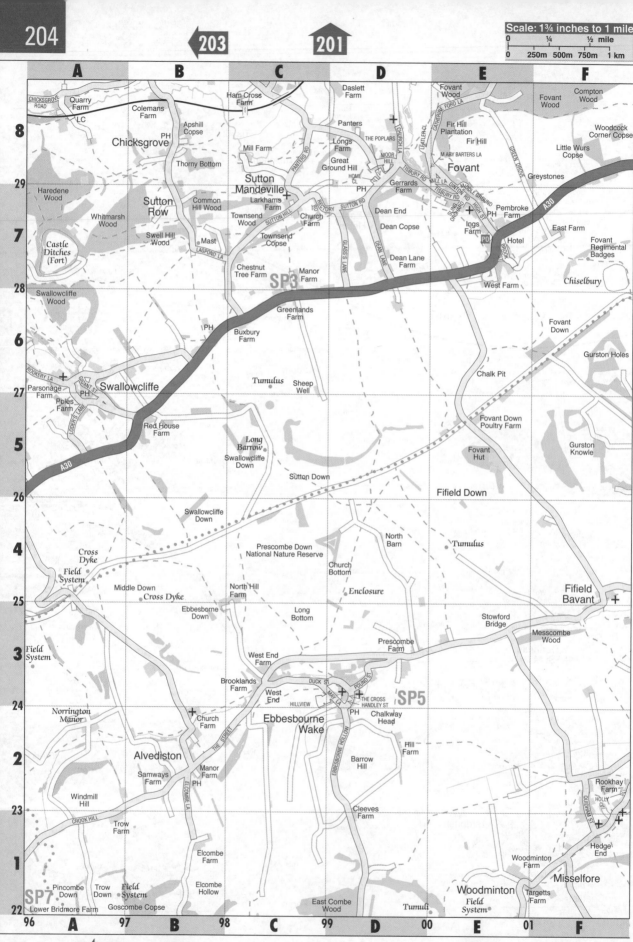

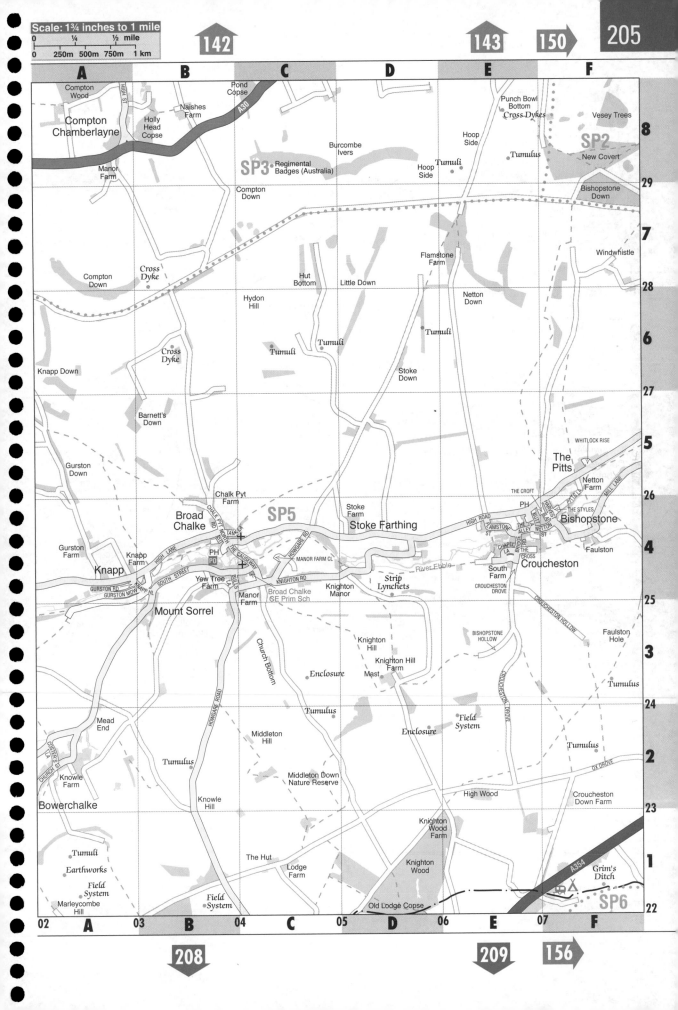

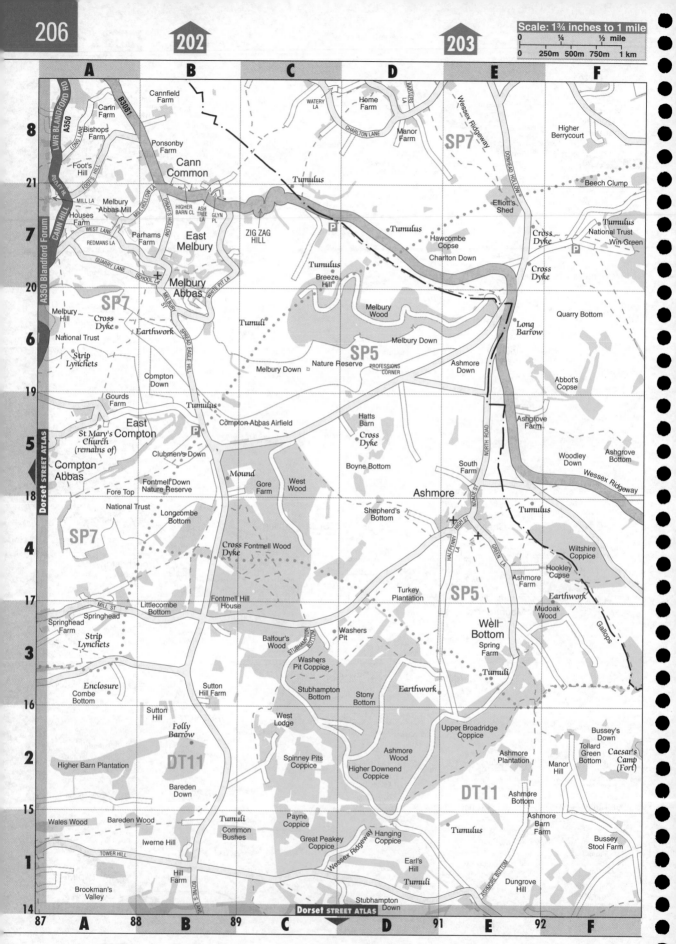

A   B   C   D   E   F

LWR BLANDFORD RD
A350
B3081
Cannfield Farm
Cann Farm
Bishops Farm
Ponsonby Farm
Foot's Hill
Cann Common
Watery La
Home Farm
Manor Farm
CHARLTON LANE
Wessex Ridgeway
SP7
Higher Berrycourt

8

21
Houses Farm
Melbury Abbas Mill
MILLHOLLOW LA
DINAH'S HOLLOW
HIGHER BARN CL
ASH TREE LA
GLYN PL
Tumulus
DONHEAD HOLLOW
Elliott's Shed
Beech Clump

7
MILL LA
WEST LANE
REDMANS LA
Parhams Farm
East Melbury
ZIG ZAG HILL
Cross Dyke
Tumulus
Hawcombe Copse
Charlton Down
Cross Dyke
Tumulus
National Trust
Win Green

20
QUARRY LANE
SCHOOL LA
MELBURY ST
WHITE PIT LA
Melbury Abbas
Tumulus
Breeze Hill
SP7
Cross Dyke
Melbury Wood
Cross Dyke
Long Barrow
Quarry Bottom

6
Melbury Hill
Cross Dyke
Earthwork
SPREAD EAGLE HILL
Tumuli
Melbury Down
Melbury Down
Nature Reserve
PROFESSIONS CORNER
SP5
Melbury Down
Ashmore Down
Abbot's Copse

19
National Trust
Strip Lynchets
Compton Down
Gourds Farm
Tumulus
Compton Abbas Airfield
Hatts Barn
Cross Dyke
Ashgrove Farm
Ashgrove Bottom

5
St Mary's Church (remains of)
East Compton
Clubmen's Down
Mound
Gore Farm
West Wood
Boyne Bottom
Ashmore
South Farm
NORTH ROAD
Woodley Down
Ashgrove Bottom
Wessex Ridgeway

18
Compton Abbas
Fontmell Down Nature Reserve
Fore Top
Longcombe Bottom
Shepherd's Bottom
HIGH ST
NODE ST
Tumulus

4
SP7
National Trust
Cross Dyke
Fontmell Wood
HALFPENNY LA
GREEN LA
SP5
Ashmore Farm
Wiltshire Coppice
Hookley Copse
Earthwork

17
MILL ST
Springhead
Littlecombe Bottom
Fontmell Hill House
Turkey Plantation
Well Bottom
Mudoak Wood
Earthwork
Gallops

3
Springhead Farm
Strip Lynchets
Balfour's Wood
STUBHAMPTON BOTTOM
Washers Pit
Washers Pit Coppice
Spring Farm
Tumuli

16
Enclosure Combe Bottom
Sutton Hill Farm
Stubhampton Bottom
Stony Bottom
Earthwork
Upper Broadridge Coppice

2
Higher Barn Plantation
Sutton Hill
Folly Barrow
DT11
West Lodge
Spinney Pits Coppice
Ashmore Wood
Higher Downend Coppice
Ashmore Plantation
Manor Hill
Bussey's Down
Tollard Green Bottom
Caesar's Camp (Fort)

15
Bareden Down
DT11
Ashmore Bottom
Ashmore Barn Farm

1
Wales Wood
Bareden Wood
Iwerne Hill
Tumuli
Common Bushes
Payne Coppice
Great Peakey Coppice
Wessex Ridgeway
Hanging Coppice
Earl's Hill
Tumulus
Bussey Stool Farm

TOWER HILL
Brookman's Valley
Hill Farm
BONE'S LANE
Tumuli
Stubhampton Down
ASHMORE BOTTOM
Dungrove Hill

14

87   A   88   B   89   C   D   91   E   92   F

A350 Blandford Forum
CANN HILL
FOOT'S HILL
LONG LANE
Dorset STREET ATLAS

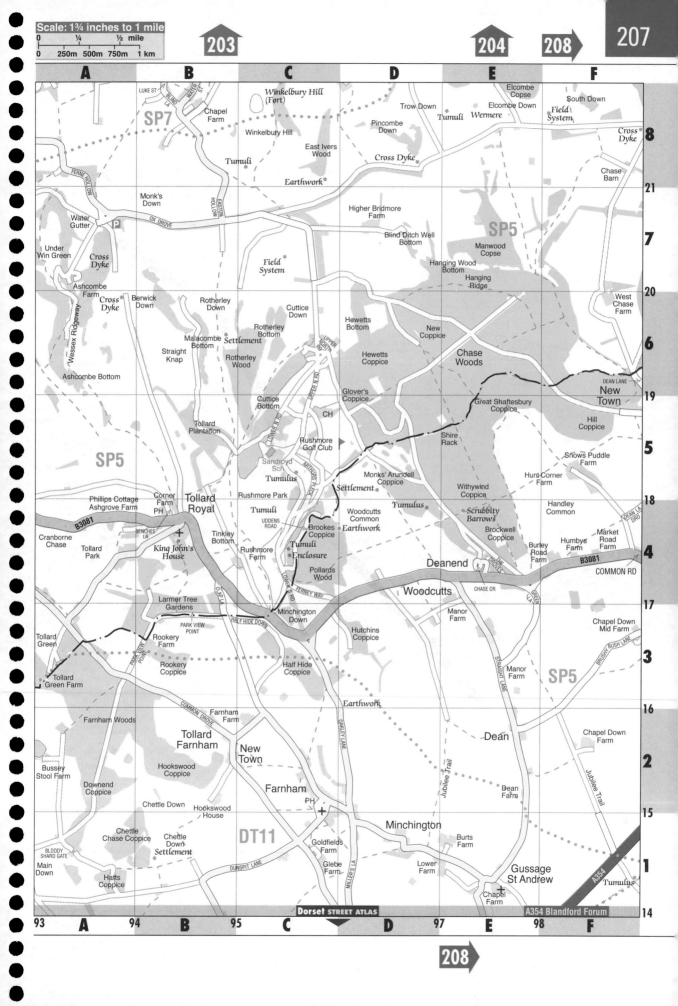

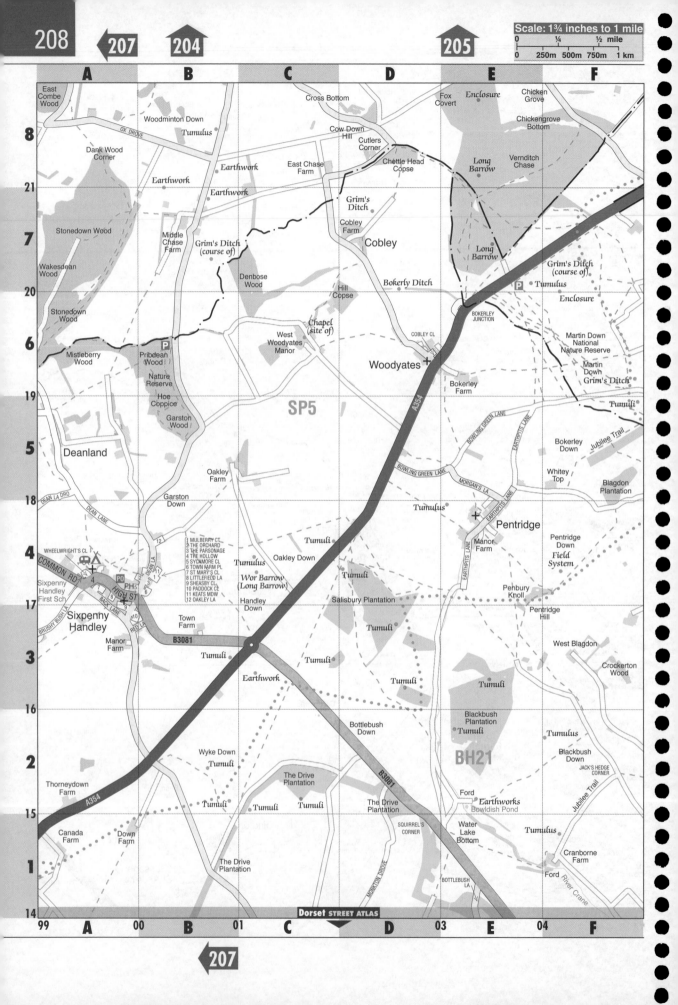

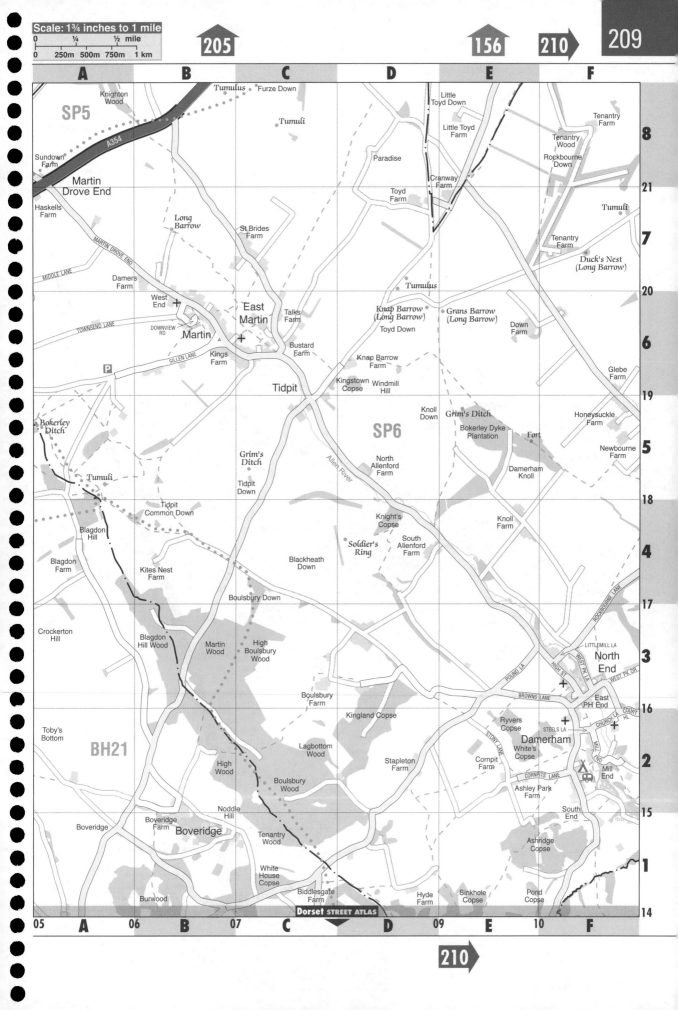

Scale: 1¾ inches to 1 mile

0   ¼   ½ mile
0 250m 500m 750m 1 km

A   B   C   D   E   F

SP5

Knighton Wood

Tumulus   • Furze Down

• Tumuli

Sundown Farm

A354

Little Toyd Down

Little Toyd Farm

Tenantry Farm

Tenantry Wood

Rockbourne Down

8

Martin Drove End

Paradise

Cranway Farm

21

Haskells Farm

Long Barrow

St Brides Farm

Toyd Farm

Tenantry Farm

Tumuli

7

Damers Farm

West End

MARTIN DROVE END

MIDDLE LANE

Tumulus

Duck's Nest (Long Barrow)

20

TOWNSEND LANE

DOWNVIEW RD

Martin

East Martin

Talks Farm

Tumulus

Knap Barrow (Long Barrow)

Grans Barrow (Long Barrow)

Down Farm

6

SILLEN LANE

Kings Farm

Bustard Farm

Toyd Down

Knap Barrow Farm

Glebe Farm

P

Tidpit

Kingstown Copse

Windmill Hill

19

Bokerley Ditch

Grim's Ditch

SP6

Knoll Down

Grim's Ditch

Bokerley Dyke Plantation

Fort

Honeysuckle Farm

5

Tumuli

Tidpit Down

North Allenford Farm

Damerham Knoll

Newbourne Farm

18

Blagdon Hill

Tidpit Common Down

Allen River

Knight's Copse

Knoll Farm

4

Blagdon Farm

Kites Nest Farm

Blackheath Down

Soldier's Ring

South Allenford Farm

Boulsbury Down

17

Crockerton Hill

Blagdon Hill Wood

Martin Wood

High Boulsbury Wood

ROCKBOURNE LANE

LITTLEMILL LA

North End

3

HIGH ST

WEST PK LA

WEST PK DR

Boulsbury Farm

POUND LA

BROWNS LANE

East End

PH

COURT HL

16

Toby's Bottom

BH21

Kingland Copse

Lagbottom Wood

Ryvers Copse

STEELS LA

STONY LANE

Damerham

White's Copse

CHURCH LA

MILL END

2

High Wood

Boulsbury Wood

Stapleton Farm

Cornpit Farm

CORNPITS LANE

Ashley Park Farm

Mill End

Noddle Hill

South End

15

Boveridge

Boveridge Farm

Boveridge

Tenantry Wood

Ashridge Copse

1

Burwood

White House Copse

Biddlesgate Farm

Hyde Farm

Sinkhole Copse

Pond Copse

14

05   A   06   B   07   C   08   D   09   E   10   F

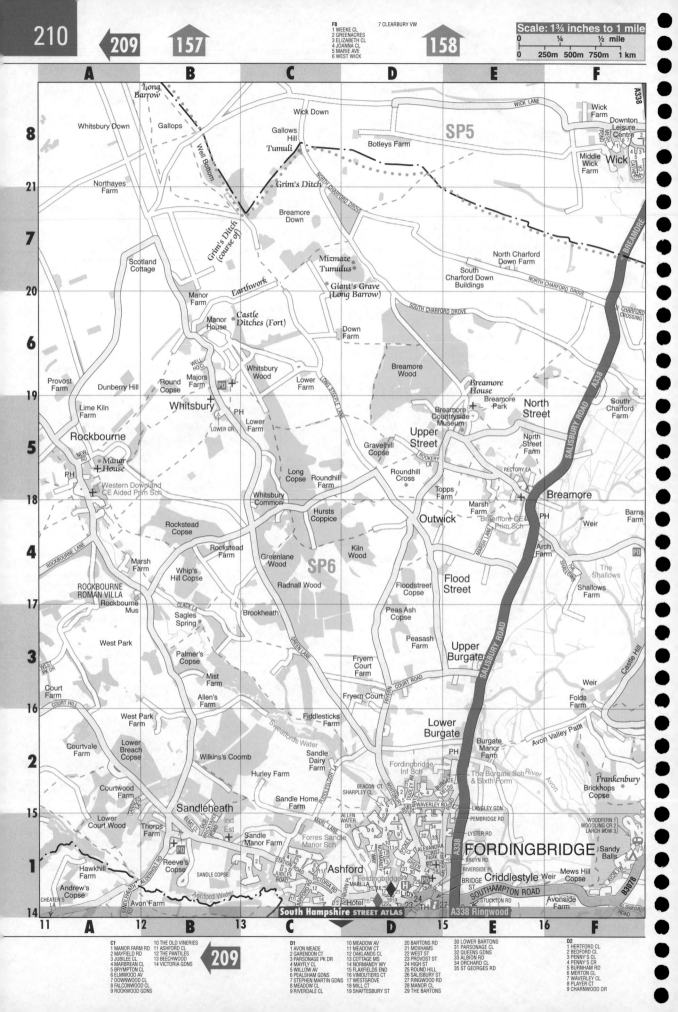

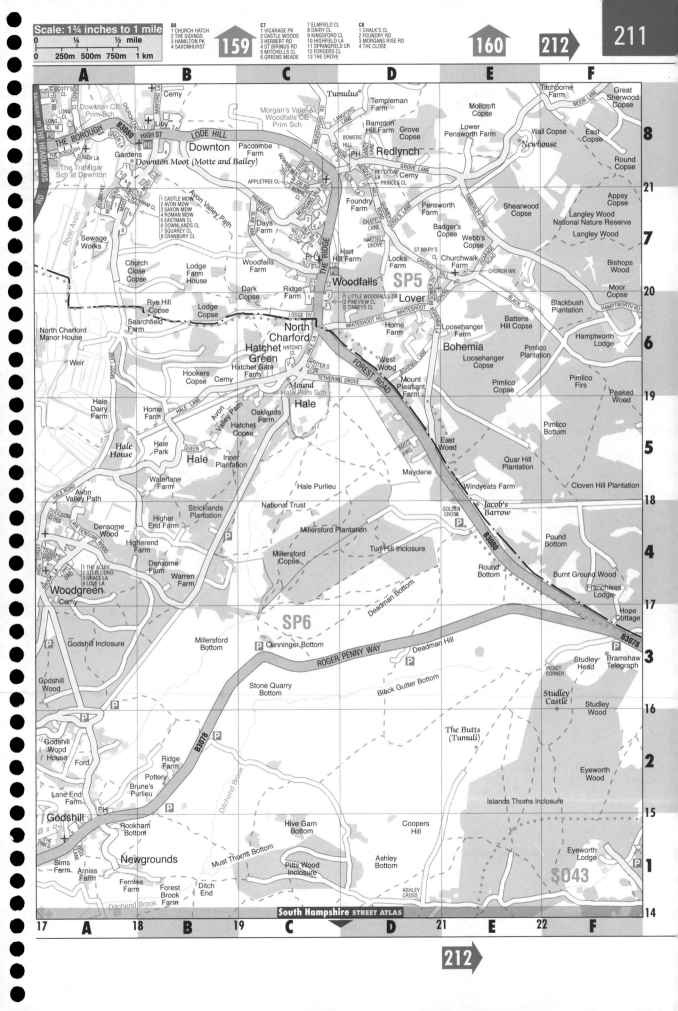

Scale: 1¾ inches to 1 mile

0   ¼   ½   mile
0   250m   500m   750m   1 km

B8
1 CHURCH HATCH
2 THE SIDINGS
3 HAMILTON PK
4 SAXONHURST

C7
1 VICARAGE PK
2 CASTLE WOODS
3 HERBERT RD
4 ST BIRINUS RD
5 MITCHELLS CL
6 GREENS MEADE

E7
1 ELMFIELD CL
8 DAIRY CL
9 KINGSFORD CL
10 HIGHFIELD LA
11 SPRINGFIELD CR
12 FORDERS CL
13 THE DROVE

C8
1 CHALK'S CL
2 FOUNDRY RD
3 MORGANS RISE RD
4 THE CLOSE

South Hampshire STREET ATLAS

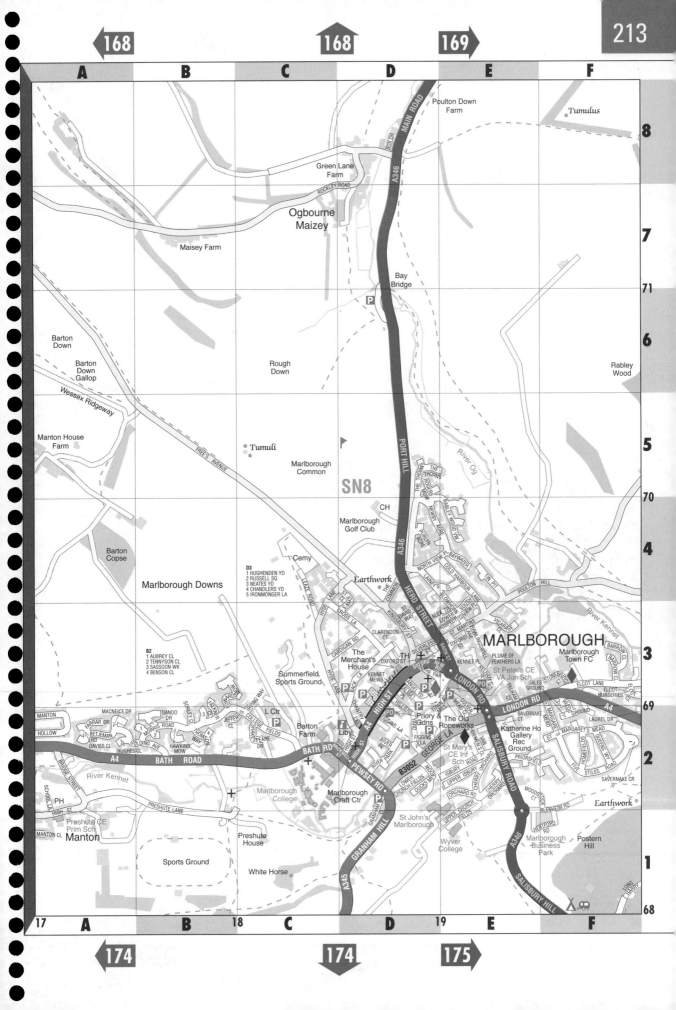

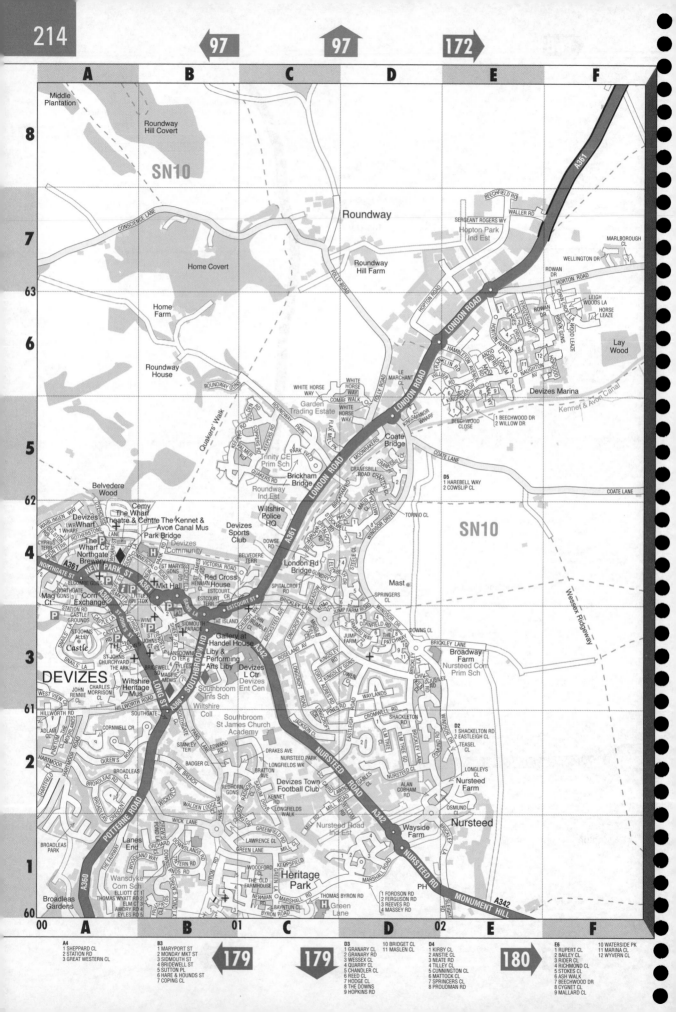

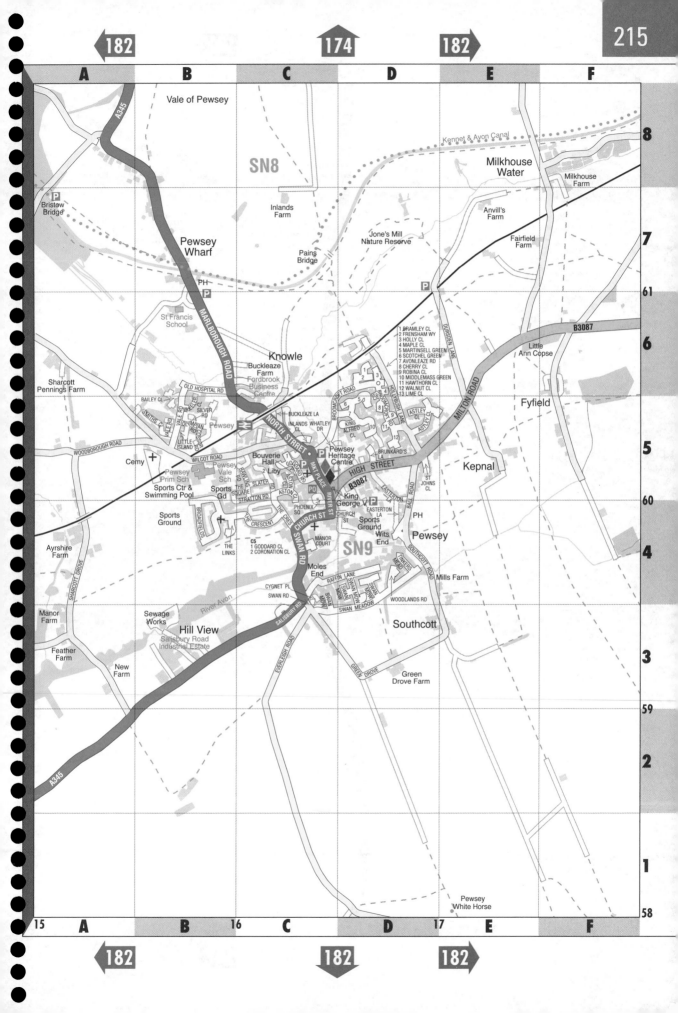

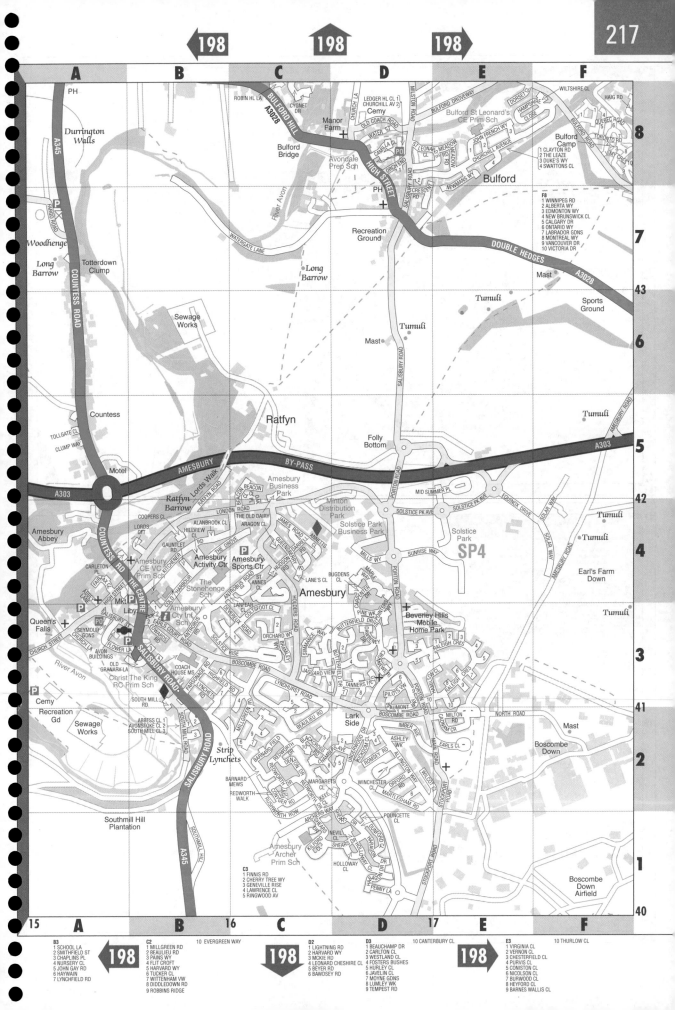

198 198 198

A B C D E F

8 / **7** / **43** / **6** / **5** / **42** / **4** / **3** / **41** / **2** / **1** / **40**

15 A B 16 C D 17 E F

Durrington Walls

PH

A345

Woodhenge

Long Barrow

Totterdown Clump

Countess Road

Sewage Works

Countess

Tollgate Cl
Clump Way

Amesbury Abbey

Motel

A303

COUNTESS RD

THE CENTRE

Queen's Falls

Church Street

River Avon

Cemy

Recreation Gd

Sewage Works

Southmill Hill Plantation

SALISBURY ROAD

SOUTHMILL HILL

A345

Strip Lynchets

ROBIN HL LA

CYGNET DR

BULFORD HILL

A3028

Bulford Bridge

River Avon

WATERGATE LANE

Long Barrow

Avondale Prep Sch

Manor Farm

Cemy

Water St

ORCHARD END

CANAL LA

HIGH STREET

PH

Recreation Ground

Ratfyn

Folly Bottom

AMESBURY BY-PASS

LEDGER HL CL 1
CHURCHILL AV 2

OLD COACH ROAD

CHURCH LA

MILSTON ROAD

SALISBURY ROAD

NEWMANS WY

ST LEONARD'S CL

PO

Bulford St Leonard's CE Prim Sch

BULFORD DROVEWAY

MEADOW RD

JOHN FRENCH WY

CHURCHILL AVENUE

HAMPSHIRE CLOSE

DORSET CL

Bulford

WILTSHIRE CL

HAIG RD

QUEBEC ROAD

TORONTO CL

VIMY CRES

Bulford Camp

1 CLAYTON RD
2 THE LEAZE
3 DUKE'S WY
4 SWATTONS CL

F8
1 WINNIPEG RD
2 ALBERTA WY
3 EDMONTON WY
4 NEW BRUNSWICK CL
5 CALGARY DR
6 ONTARIO WY
7 LABRADOR GDNS
8 MONTREAL WY
9 VANCOUVER DR
10 VICTORIA DR

DOUBLE HEDGES

A3028

Mast

Tumuli

Sports Ground

Tumuli

Mast

SALISBURY ROAD

AMESBURY ROAD

Tumuli

A303

PORTON ROAD

Amesbury Business Park

Minton Distribution Park

Solstice Park Business Park

MID SUMMER PL

SOLSTICE PK AVE SOLSTICE PK AVE

EQUINOX DRIVE

SOLAR WAY

Solstice Park

SP4

SUNRISE WY

Tumuli

Tumuli

Earl's Farm Down

Tumuli

Ratfyn Barrow

BATYN ROAD

Lords Walk

LONDON ROAD

COOPERS CL

LORDS GIFT

GAUNTLET RD

CARLETON PL

Amesbury CE VC Prim Sch

Amesbury Activity Ctr

Amesbury Sports Ctr

BEACON CL

THE OLD DAIRY

ALANBROOK CL

HILLVIEW

ARAGON CL

KITCHENER

THE DROVE

JAMES ROAD

ANNETTS

QUEENSWAY

HUDSON RD

Amesbury

LANE'S CL

BUGDENS CL

ST ANNES CL

MARIE

MILLS WY

CARPENTER

Beverley Hills Mobile Home Park

RALEIGH CRES

Tumuli

Mkt

Liby

PO

SEYMOUR GDNS

SALISBURY ST

FLOWER LA

Amesbury City Inf Sch

The Stonehenge Sch

OLD HARBOUR

AMPORIUS ROAD

LANFEAR

COLTSFOOT CL

DERECREEK ROAD

ORCHARD WY

PINE WK

DANE WY

PILOTS VW

PORTON

RALEIGH CRES

ABBEY LANE

TEASAR

HIGH STREET

EDWARDS RD

EARLS COURT ROAD

SOLSTICE RISE

BOSCOMBE ROAD

SIMMANCE WY

BUTTERFIELD DRIVE

JAGGARD VIEW

TANNERS FE

BEAUMONT

Lark Side

NORTH ROAD

Mast

Boscombe Down

AVON BUILDINGS

OLD GRANARY LA

Christ The King RC Prim Sch

SOUTH MILL RD

COACH HOUSE MS

PARSONAGE

HIGHFIELD RD

LYNCHETS

MILLGREEN RD

BEAULIEU RD

LYNDHURST ROAD

BEAULIEU RD

BOSCOMBE ROAD

IMBER AVE

MARIT CL

EARLS CL

MILTON RD

DUNHAM CR

ABBESS CL 1
AVONSTOKE CL 2
SOUTH MILL CL 3

BARNARD FIELD

BLACKFORD

REDWORTH DR

DENTON DR

CHAMBERS AVE

LARK DR

ASHLEY WK

UNDERWOOD DR

ALLINGTON WAY

WILCOX CL

STOCKPORT ROAD

Barnard Mews

REDWORTH WALK

BUSHWORTH ROW

CONGER WAY

MARGARETS CL

KEEP CL

WINCHESTER CL

ROMSEY RD

ORFORD RD

MARTLESHAM RD

POUNCETTE CL

Amesbury Archer Prim Sch

ARCHERS WAY

KILFORD CL

NEVIL CL

SHEARS DR

HOLLOWAY CL

HOLLOWAY CL

PENNY LA

PUKFORD CL

HARGON LA

DRO

Boscombe Down Airfield

C3
1 FINNIS RD
2 CHERRY TREE WY
3 GENEVILLE RISE
4 LAWRENCE CL
5 RINGWOOD AV

B3
1 SCHOOL LA
2 SMITHFIELD ST
3 CHAPLINS PL
4 NURSERY CL
5 JOHN GAY RD
6 HAYWAIN
7 LYNCHFIELD RD

C2
1 MILLGREEN RD
2 BEAULIEU RD
3 PAINS WY
4 FLIT CROFT
5 HARVARD WY
6 TUCKER CL
7 WITTENHAM VW
8 DIDDLEDOWN RD
9 ROBBINS RIDGE

10 EVERGREEN WAY

D2
1 LIGHTNING RD
2 HARVARD WY
3 MCKIE RD
4 LEONARD CHESHIRE CL
5 BEYER RD
6 BAWDSEY RD

D3
1 BEAUCHAMP DR
2 CARLTON CL
3 WESTLAND CL
4 FOSTERS BUSHES
5 HURLEY CL
6 JAVELIN CL
7 MOYNE GDNS
8 LUMLEY WK
9 TEMPEST RD

10 CANTERBURY CL

E3
1 VIRGINIA CL
2 VERNON CL
3 CHESTERFIELD CL
4 PURVIS CL
5 CONISTON CL
6 NICOLSON CL
7 BURWOOD CL
8 HEYFORD CL
9 BARNES WALLIS CL

10 THURLOW CL

198 198 198

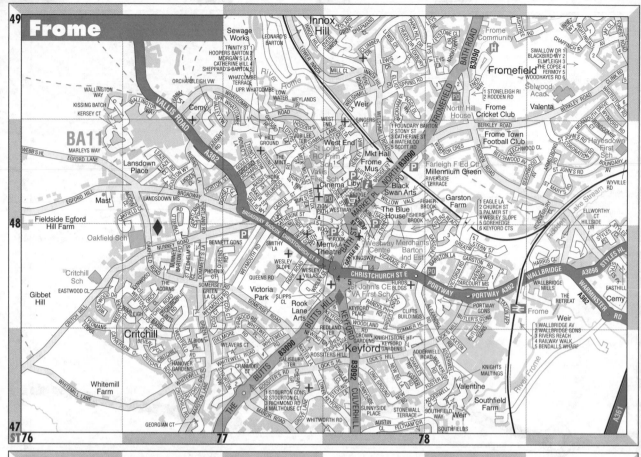

Frome

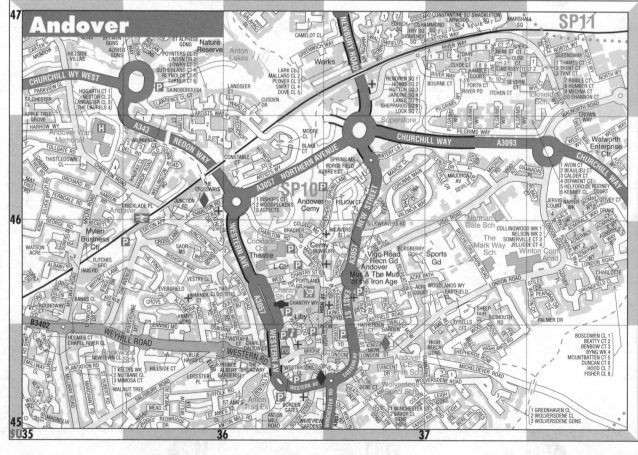

Andover

Index

Place name May be abbreviated on the map → Church Rd **6** Beckenham BR2..........**53** C6

Location number Present when a number indicates the place's position in a crowded area of mapping

Locality, town or village Shown when more than one place has the same name

Postcode district District for the indexed place

Page and grid square Page number and grid reference for the standard mapping

Cities, towns and villages are listed in CAPITAL LETTERS

Public and commercial buildings are highlighted in magenta **Places of interest** are highlighted in blue with a star★

Abbreviations used in the index

Acad	Academy	Comm	Common	Gd	Ground	L	Leisure	Prom	Promenade
App	Approach	Cott	Cottage	Gdn	Garden	La	Lane	Rd	Road
Arc	Arcade	Cres	Crescent	Gn	Green	Liby	Library	Recn	Recreation
Ave	Avenue	Cswy	Causeway	Gr	Grove	Mdw	Meadow	Ret	Retail
Bglw	Bungalow	Ct	Court	H	Hall	Meml	Memorial	Sh	Shopping
Bldg	Building	Ctr	Centre	Ho	House	Mkt	Market	Sq	Square
Bsns, Bus	Business	Ctry	Country	Hospl	Hospital	Mus	Museum	St	Street
Bvd	Boulevard	Cty	County	HQ	Headquarters	Orch	Orchard	Sta	Station
Cath	Cathedral	Dr	Drive	Hts	Heights	Pal	Palace	Terr	Terrace
Cir	Circus	Dro	Drove	Ind	Industrial	Par	Parade	TH	Town Hall
Cl	Close	Ed	Education	Inst	Institute	Pas	Passage	Univ	University
Cnr	Corner	Emb	Embankment	Int	International	Pk	Park	Wk, Wlk	Walk
Coll	College	Est	Estate	Intc	Interchange	Pl	Place	Wr	Water
Com	Community	Ex	Exhibition	Junc	Junction	Prec	Precinct	Yd	Yard

Index of towns, villages, streets, hospitals, industrial estates, railway stations, schools, shopping centres, universities and places of interest

A

Abberd La SN11 ....81 D3
Abberd Way SN11 ....81 C3
Abbess Cl SP4 ....217 B2
Abbey CE VA Prim Sch The SP3 ....202 B1
Abbey Cl
Chippenham SN15 ....79 B5
3 Shrewton SP3 ....196 E6
Abbeyfield Sch SN15 ....79 B6
Abbey House Gdns★ SN16 ....28 A3
Abbey La
Amesbury SP4 ....217 A4
Hinton Charterhouse BA2 ....99 A3
Swindon SN1 ....50 C5
Abbey Meads Com Prim Sch SN25 ....35 A7
Abbey Rw SN16 ....28 A3
Abbey Stadium SN25 ....35 A8
Abbey View Rd SN25 ....34 E3
Abbey Wlk 6 SP7 ....202 C1
Abbot Rd SP1 ....146 C4
Abbotsbury Way SN25 ....35 A8
Abbots Wlk GL7 ....2 D4
Abbots Wy GL7 ....4 F7
Abbotts Cl SP9 ....216 C7
Abbotts Gdn SN16 ....28 A3
Abbotts Rd SP9 ....216 C7
Abdon Cl BA12 ....195 D7
Abingdon Ct La SN6 ....19 E8
Abington Way SN2 ....35 D5
ABLINGTON 190 B1
Abney Moor SN3 ....51 E2
Abotts Cl BA13 ....108 F3
Above Hedges SP5 ....148 C3
Abraham Cl 5 BA14 ....105 C7
Acacia Cl SN14 ....70 A1
Acacia Cres BA14 ....105 A8
Acacia Dr BA11 ....110 C7
Acacia Gr SN2 ....35 C2
Academy Dr SN13 ....76 E2
Acorn Cl SN3 ....51 C5
Acorn Meadow BA14 ....105 A5
Acre Cl BA14 ....178 A3
Acreshort La BA14 ....178 A3
Acres Rd SN10 ....214 C3
Activity Zone Leisure Ctr SN16 ....27 F3
ACTON TURVILLE 52 F6
Acton Turville Rd GL9 ....52 A4
Adampur Rd SP9 ....216 A4
Adam's Grave (Long Barrow)★ SN8 ....173 D2
Adcroft Dr BA14 ....101 D1
Adcroft St BA14 ....101 C1
Adderwell BA11 ....110 A3
Adderwell Cl BA11 ....110 A3
Adderwell Rd BA11 ....110 A3
Addington Cl SN10 ....214 C2
Addinsell Rd SN25 ....34 E8
Addison Cres SN2 ....35 F3
Addison Rd SN12 ....93 F6
Addison Sq 19 SP4 ....198 B7
Adelaide Cl 6 SP4 ....198 F6
Adlam Cl SN10 ....214 A2
Adwalton Cl SN5 ....49 B4
Aerial Bsns Pk RG17 ....170 E6
Affleck Cl SN5 ....49 C5
Agra Rd SP9 ....216 A4
Agravaine Cl 27 SP10 ....193 E2
Aiken Rd SN25 ....34 C5
Ailesbury Cl SN15 ....79 A4
Ailesbury Way SN8 ....183 D8
Ainsworth Rd SN3 ....51 A4
Aintree 7 RG17 ....165 A1
Aintree Ave BA14 ....105 E4
Aintree Dr SN14 ....77 F6
Airman's Cnr SP3 ....197 B5
Aisne Rd SN4 ....65 D1
Akenfield Cl SN25 ....34 F5
Akers Ct SN26 ....21 C2
Akers Way SN2 ....34 E2
Alamein Rd 4 SP11 ....193 E4
Alanbrook Cl SP4 ....217 B4
Alanbrooke Cres SN2 ....35 A2
Alanbrooke Rd SP4 ....197 E6
Alan Cobham Rd SN10 ....214 D2
Alan Powell La BA13 ....112 B8
Alba Cl 11 SN5 ....48 F8
Albany Cl BA14 ....101 F2
Albany Rd SP1 ....146 B1
Alberta Wy 2 SP4 ....217 F8
Albert Rd BA14 ....101 F3
Albert St SN1 ....50 D4
Albion Bglws SP2 ....145 A3
Albion Dr BA14 ....105 B8
Albion Rd 33 SP6 ....210 D1
Albion St SN1 ....50 A5
ALCESTER 202 B1
Alcock Crest BA12 ....116 F6
ALCOMBE 82 F8
Aldborough Cl 2 SN5 ....49 C6
ALDBOURNE 170 A6
Aldbourne Cl
Blunsdon St Andrew SN2 ....35 C6
27 Hungerford RG17 ....177 B7
Aldbourne Four Barrows★ SN8 ....169 E8
Aldbourne Rd SN8 ....170 B7
Aldeburgh Pl BA14 ....104 F6
ALDERBURY 153 C3
Alderbury & West Grimstead CE Prim Sch SP5 ....153 E3
Alder Cl
Swindon SN2 ....34 D4
Trowbridge BA14 ....105 B5
Alderholt Rd SP6 ....210 B1
Alderley Rd 7 SN25 ....34 E7
Alderney Cl 6 SN4 ....48 A2
Alder Rd SN14 ....75 A4
Alders The SP2 ....145 A3
ALDERTON 39 F2
Alderton Rd
Grittleton SN14 ....54 D5
Luckington SN14 ....53 D6
Alderton Way BA14 ....105 D5
Alder Way SN12 ....94 A4
Alder Wlk 5 BA11 ....110 B7
Aldrin Cl 7 SP10 ....193 D2
Aldworth Dr 3 SP1 ....146 C5
Alexander Fields SN9 ....181 F1
Alexander Keiller Mus★ SN8 ....167 B1
Alexander Rd SN16 ....27 F4
Alexander Terr SN13 ....77 A1
Alexandra Cl SP2 ....145 C3
Alexandra Rd
Fordingbridge SP6 ....210 D1
Frome BA11 ....110 A4
1 Swindon SN1 ....50 C7
Alexandra Terr SN8 ....213 D3
Alfred Gdns 6 SP10 ....193 D1
Alfred's Castle★ RG17 ....164 B5
Alfred St
Swindon SN1 ....50 C7
Westbury BA13 ....109 A4
Alfred's Twr★ BA10 ....122 F3
Alicia Cl 1 SN25 ....34 C6
ALL CANNINGS 180 E8
All Cannings CE Prim Sch SN10 ....180 F8
Allenby Rd SP4 ....133 C2
Allen Cl SN3 ....50 E2
Allengrove La SN14 ....39 C3
Allen Rd
Corsham SN13 ....84 C8
Allen Rd *continued*
Shaftesbury SP7 ....202 D1
Trowbridge BA14 ....105 B7
Allen Wr Dr SP6 ....210 D2
Alley The
Bishopstone SP5 ....205 E4
Woodgreen SP6 ....211 A4
ALLINGTON
All Cannings 172 E2
Amesbury 199 A2
Chippenham Without 69 E3
ALLINGTON BAR 69 F2
Allington Rd SN2 ....35 B5
Allington Tk SP4 ....198 E4
Allington Way
Amesbury SP4 ....217 D2
2 Chippenham SN14 ....70 A1
All Saints Cres 2 BA13 ....109 A3
All Saints Rd 1 SN10 ....187 E7
All Saints VA CE Prim Sch SP4 ....190 A3
Alma Pl SN8 ....213 D3
Alma Rd
Aldbourne SN8 ....170 A7
4 Aldbourne SN8 ....170 A7
Alma St BA14 ....105 E8
Alma Terr SN11 ....81 B3
Almond Gr BA14 ....105 B5
Alnwick SN5 ....49 B4
Alnwick Rd BA14 ....106 A8
Aloeric Prim Sch SN12 ....94 A3
Alpine Cl 6 SN5 ....49 A7
ALTON 190 B1
Altona Gdns 17 SP10 ....193 D2
ALTON BARNES 173 C1
Alton Barnes White Horse★ SN8 ....173 C2
Alton Cl SN2 ....35 C5
ALTON PRIORS 173 D1
Alton Rd SN8 ....181 F8
Alum Cl BA14 ....105 E7
ALVEDISTON 204 B2
Alvescot Rd SN3 ....50 D5
Alveston Cl SN5 ....49 D6
Alwyn Ct 4 SN25 ....34 D7
Amber Ct SN1 ....50 D7
Amberley Cl
Calne SN11 ....81 A4
Swindon SN25 ....35 C4
Amberley Ct SN16 ....27 E2
Ambrose House Con & Management Ctr SN1 ....50 B6
Ambrose Rd SN1 ....50 C2

American Mus In Britain★ BA2 ....90 A5
Amersham Rd SN3 ....51 B3
AMESBURY 217 C4
Amesbury Archer Prim Sch SP4 ....217 C1
Amesbury Bsns Pk SP4 ....217 C5
Amesbury By-Pass SP4 ....217 B5
Amesbury CE VC Prim Sch SP4 ....217 B4
Amesbury Cl 4 SN2 ....35 C6
Amesbury Cty Inf Sch SP4 ....217 B3
Amesbury Rd
Amesbury SP4 ....217 F4
Amport SP11 ....192 E1
Newton Tony SP4 ....199 A3
Shrewton SP3 ....196 E6
Amesbury Sports Ctr SP4 ....217 C4
Amity Dr SN8 ....175 D6
Amouracre BA14 ....105 F8
Ancaster Cl BA14 ....101 A1
Anchor Rd SN11 ....81 C2
Ancona Cl 12 SN5 ....49 A7
Andeferas Rd 6 SP10 ....193 D2
Anderson Cl SN3 ....51 D3
Anderson Rd SP1 ....146 C4
Andover La SP11 ....192 B4
Andover Rd
Amport SP11 ....192 E2
Chirton SN10 ....180 F3
Fyfield SP11 ....192 D3
Upavon SN9 ....181 F1
Andover St 3 SN1 ....50 A5
Andrew Cl 14 SP4 ....198 B7
Andrews Cl SN14 ....78 B7
Andrews Way SP2 ....151 F5
Angelica Cl 6 SN2 ....34 D4
Angel La
Hindon SP3 ....200 A3
Mere BA12 ....139 A5
27 Shaftesbury SP7 ....202 C2
Angel Yd SN8 ....213 D3
Angler Rd
Salisbury SP2 ....145 C5
Swindon SN5 ....49 B7
Anglesey Cl 5 SN5 ....49 C6
Anglesey Mead SN15 ....79 A4
Angrove Cotts SN16 ....43 D4

Angrove La SN16 . . . . .43 C4
Angus Cl SN5 . . . . .49 B7
Anise Cl 4 SN2 . . . . .34 C4
Anne Cres 24 SP4 . . . . . . .198 F6
Annetts Cl SP4 . . . . .217 C4
Annett's La RG17 . . . . .176 F4
Anson Ave SN9 . . . . .182 B2
Anson Gr SN12 . . . . .94 C1
Anson Pl SN14 . . . . .56 C7
Anstey Pl SN15 . . . . .79 A4
ANSTY 203 F5
ANSTY COOMBE 203 F5
Ansty Hill BA12 . . . . .195 A6
Ansty Wlk SN2 . . . . .35 B6
Anthony Rd SN16 . . . . .25 C1
Anthony Rd SN4 . . . . .64 A7
Anton La SP11 . . . . .193 E4
Antony Rd 5 SP25 . . . . . . .34 F7
Antrobus Rd SP4 . . . . .217 B3
Anzio Rd SN10 . . . . .214 C6
Apollo Cl 1 SN25 . . . . .34 B7
Apollo Rd SN15 . . . . .59 E3
Apostle Way SP1 . . . . .146 C5
Appleford Sch SP3 . . . . . . .196 E7
APPLESHAW 192 E3
Appleshaw Way
  Perham Down SP11 . . . . . .191 E7
  Salisbury SP1 . . . . .146 D5
Appletree Cl SP5 . . . . .211 C8
Apple Tree Gr 10 SP10 . . .193 C1
Appletree Rd SP5 . . . . .211 C8
Applewood Cl SN14 . . . . . . .78 B8
Applewood Ct SN5 . . . . .49 D5
Applin Rd SP1 . . . . .146 D5
Apsley Cl BA14 . . . . .102 B2
Aragon Ct SP4 . . . . .217 C4
Aragon Cl SN3 . . . . .51 A4
Arcade The 8 SN1 . . . . . . .50 B6
Archer Cl SP2 . . . . .35 F5
Archers Ct SP2 . . . . .146 A2
Archers The SN6 . . . . .22 F5
Archers Wy SP4 . . . . .217 C1
Arches La SN16 . . . . .27 C2
Arcot Rd SP9 . . . . .216 B3
Arc Theatre BA14 . . . . . . .105 A6
Arden Cl SN12 . . . . .94 C5
Argosy Rd SN15 . . . . .60 B1
Argyle Dr SN14 . . . . .70 C3
Argyle St SN3 . . . . .35 D1
Ariadne Rd 15 SN25 . . . . . .34 B7
Ark The SN10 . . . . .214 A3
Arkwright Rd SN25 . . . . . . .35 D6
Arley Cl SN25 . . . . .35 A5
Arlington Cl SN3 . . . . .51 B7
Armitage Sq 4 SP4 . . . . . .197 E5
Armoury Yd 3 SP7 . . . . . .202 C2
Armstrong Rd BA11 . . . . . .110 B5
Armstrong Rise 16 SP10 . .193 D2
Armstrong St 2 SN1 . . . . . .50 C7
Arney Cl SN13 . . . . .84 E8
Arnfield Moor SN3 . . . . .51 E2
Arnhem Cross SN15 . . . . . .60 B2
Arn Hill Down & Nature
  Reserve★ BA12 . . . . .117 B8
Arnhill Rd 5 SN1 . . . . .50 A2
Arnold Rd BA14 . . . . .104 E3
Arnolds Mead SN13 . . . . . . .76 F2
Arnold St SN1 . . . . .34 E7
Arnold Wy SN13 . . . . .84 F6
Arn View
  Cold Harbour BA12 . . . . . .112 B5
  2 Warminster BA12 . . . . . .117 A8
Arran Cl 5 SN4 . . . . .48 A2
Arran Way SN6 . . . . .22 F7
Arras Cl BA14 . . . . .105 C6
Arthur Bennett Ct SN1 . . . .50 A5
Arthurs Pleck SP5 . . . . . . .207 C5
Artis Ave SN4 . . . . .64 B7
Artus Cl 1 SN25 . . . . .34 E6
Arundel Cl
  Chippenham SN14 . . . . .78 A7
  Swindon SN3 . . . . .50 F3
Arundell Cl BA13 . . . . .109 D4
Arun Rd SN25 . . . . .34 F3
Arun Way 6 SO51 . . . . . . .212 F6
Ascham Rd SN5 . . . . .49 A5
Ascot Cl SN14 . . . . .78 A5
Ascott Cl SN25 . . . . .34 F7
Ash SN2 . . . . .35 F2
Ashburnham Ct 7 SN5 . . . .49 A4
Ashburn Pl SP6 . . . . .210 D1
ASHBURY 164 A7
Ashbury Ave SN3 . . . . .51 B7
Ashbury Hill SN6 . . . . .164 A7
Ashbury with Compton
  Beauchamp CE Prim Sch
  SN6 . . . . .164 A8
Ash Cl
  Lyneham SN15 . . . . .60 C1
  4 Shaftesbury SP7 . . . . . .202 D2
  Swindon SN5 . . . . .34 A2
  Tidworth SP9 . . . . .216 E7
Ash Cres SP1 . . . . .146 C5
Ashcroft Cotts SN8 . . . . . .169 B1
Ashdown Dr SN12 . . . . .94 D6
Ashdown Pk★ RG17 . . . . .164 C5
Ashdown Terr SP9 . . . . . . .216 D5
Ashdown Way SN2 . . . . .34 C4
Ash Dr BA14 . . . . .105 C3
Ashe Cl SN15 . . . . .70 D1
Ashe Cres SN15 . . . . .70 D1
Ashen Copse Rd SN4 . . . . . .63 F7
Ashes La
  Freshford BA2 . . . . .99 A4
  Kington Langley SN15 . . . . .70 E7

Ashfield SN6 . . . . .7 A1
Ashfield Rd
  Chippenham SN15 . . . . .70 C1
  Salisbury SP2 . . . . .145 E1
ASHFORD 210 C1
Ashford Cl 11 SP6 . . . . . . .210 C1
Ashford Rd
  Fordingbridge SP6 . . . . . . .210 C1
  Swindon SN1 . . . . .50 B4
Ashford Trad Est SP2 . . . . .145 E1
Ash Gdns SN3 . . . . .36 E4
Ash Gr
  1 Melksham SN12 . . . . .94 A2
  Swindon SN2 . . . . .35 C2
Ashgrove BA12 . . . . .139 B4
Ashie Cl SN5 . . . . .34 B2
Ashington Wy 4 SN5 . . . . . .49 C5
Ashkirk Cl SN3 . . . . .50 E6
Ashlade Firs Rd SN8 . . . . .175 C6
Ashlands SP4 . . . . .146 D6
Ashleigh Cl SP2 . . . . .130 B2
Ashleigh Gr 4 BA14 . . . . .105 C7
Ashleworth Rd 6 SN25 . . . .34 F7
ASHLEY 3 A2
  Ashley 3 A2
  Box .83 A6
Ashley Cl
  Atworth/Whitley SN12 . . . . .85 D1
  Bradford-on-Avon BA15 . . .100 B8
  Swindon SN3 . . . . .50 F6
Ashley Coombe BA12 . . . . .117 A4
Ashleycross SP6 . . . . .211 D1
Ashley Dro SN8 . . . . .185 A4
Ashley La BA15 . . . . .99 F7
Ashley Piece SN8 . . . . .170 C2
Ashley Pl BA12 . . . . .116 F4
Ashley Rd
  Bath BA1 . . . . .82 C2
  Bradford-on-Avon BA15 . . . .91 B1
  Salisbury SP2 . . . . .145 F2
Ashley Wlk SP4 . . . . .217 D2
Ashley Wlk SP4 . . . . .217 D2
Ashmead BA14 . . . . .105 D6
Ashmead Ct BA14 . . . . . . .105 D7
ASHMORE 206 D5
Ashmore Bottom DT11 . . .206 E1
Ashmore Cl
  Swindon SN3 . . . . .51 C6
  Whiteparish SP5 . . . . .161 D4
Ashmore La
  West Dean SP5 . . . . .155 E2
  Whiteparish SP5 . . . . .161 D6
Ash Rd SN14 . . . . .75 A5
Ash Rd SN25 . . . . .34 C7
ASHTON COMMON 102 F1
Ashton Coombe BA13 . . . .186 B7
ASHTON KEYNES 6 F1
Ashton Keynes CE Prim Sch
  SN6 . . . . .17 E8
Ashton Rd
  Ashton Keynes SN16 . . . . . .17 E7
  Siddington GL7 . . . . .6 D8
  Trowbridge BA14 . . . . .102 A2
Ashton Rise BA14 . . . . .102 A2
Ashton St 2 BA14 . . . . . . .105 E8
Ash Tree SN8 . . . . .175 A8
Ash Tree La SP7 . . . . .206 B7
Ashtree Rd BA11 . . . . .110 A7
Ashville Ctr SN12 . . . . .178 A8
Ashwell Cl SN3 . . . . .50 F5
Ashwicke Rd SN14 . . . . .74 B3
Ash Wlk
  Upton Lovell BA12 . . . . . . .194 E4
  Warminster BA12 . . . . .117 A7
Ashwood Rd SN13 . . . . .76 A1
Ashworth Rd SN5 . . . . .49 E6
Askerton Cl 5 SN4 . . . . . . .48 F5
Askew Cl 3 SN5 . . . . .48 F5
Aspen Cl
  Colerne SN14 . . . . .74 F6
  Frome BA11 . . . . .110 B7
  Royal Wootton Bassett SN4 . .47 E3
Assheton Ct SP9 . . . . .216 D7
Assisi Rd SP1 . . . . .146 A4
Astley Cl SN9 . . . . .215 D5
Aston Cl SN9 . . . . .215 C5
Aston Mead SP1 . . . . .146 C3
Astor Cres SP11 . . . . .192 A5
Atbara Cl SN25 . . . . .35 A3
Atcherly Rd SN11 . . . . .166 A1
Athelstan Mus★ SN16 . . . . .28 A3
Athelstan Rd SN16 . . . . .27 F4
Athena Ave SN2 . . . . .35 E1
Atheneum Ctr 2 BA12 . . . .117 A7
Atherton Cl 12 SN8 . . . . . .170 B2
Atherton Cres 16 RG17 . . .177 B7
Atherton Pl 11 RG17 . . . . .165 A2
Atherton Rd 11 RG17 . . . . .177 B7
Athlone Cl 3 SP11 . . . . . . .193 E4
Atholl Ct 26 SP10 . . . . . . .193 E2
Attlee Cres SN2 . . . . .35 E3
Attwood Rd SP1 . . . . .146 A3
Atworth/Whitley SN12 . . . . .85 D1
ATWORTH 92 F8
Atworth Bsns Pk SN12 . . . .92 F8
Atworth Cl SN2 . . . . .35 B6
Atworth Ct SN12 . . . . .92 F8
Atworth La SN13 . . . . .84 E4
Atyec Cl BA13 . . . . .112 B8
Atyeo Cl BA13 . . . . .112 B8
Aubrey Rise 6 SN16 . . . . . .28 A5
Auckland Rd 3 SP4 . . . . . .198 F7
Auden Cl SN25 . . . . .34 F5
Audley Cl 2 SN5 . . . . .48 F4
Audley Gate BA13 . . . . .108 E2
Audley Rd SN14 . . . . .78 C8
AUGHTON 183 D3
Augusta Cl SN25 . . . . .34 C7

Augusta Wy W 8 SP11 . . .193 F2
Augustine Way 9 SP10 . . .193 C2
Austen Cres SP4 . . . . .51 D4
Australian Ave SP2 . . . . . . .145 D2
AVEBURY 173 C8
Avebury Cl
  Calne SN11 . . . . .81 A3
  Westbury BA13 . . . . .108 F4
Avebury Manor & Gdns★
  SN8 . . . . .167 B1
Avebury Mus★ SN8 . . . . . .167 B1
Avebury Rd
  Chippenham SN14 . . . . .78 A6
  Swindon SN2 . . . . .35 B5
Avebury Stone Circles★
  SN8 . . . . .167 C1
AVEBURY TRUSLOE 173 B8
Avenell Rd 8 SN4 . . . . .163 A6
Avening St SN2 . . . . .35 D1
Avens Cl SN2 . . . . .34 D4
Avenue De Gien
  Malmesbury SN16 . . . . .27 F6
  Malmesbury SN16 . . . . .28 A6
Avenue La Fleche SN15 . . . .78 D6
Avenue Prim Sch The
  BA12 . . . . .117 B7
Avenue Rd
  Frome BA11 . . . . .110 A4
  Swindon SN1 . . . . .50 C4
  Trowbridge BA14 . . . . .105 B8
Avenue The★ SN4 . . . . . . .197 E5
Avenue The
  Cherhill SN11 . . . . .166 E2
  Claverton BA2 . . . . .90 A4
  Durnford SP4 . . . . .131 D1
  18 Durrington/Bulford SP4 198 B7
  Porton SP4 . . . . .133 D6
  Salisbury SP1 . . . . .146 C1
  South Tedworth SP9 . . . . . .216 C4
  Stanton Fitzwarren SN6 . . . .22 B1
  Tangley SP11 . . . . .193 D5
  Tisbury SP3 . . . . .203 E8
  Warminster BA12 . . . . .117 A7
  Westbury BA13 . . . . .109 A3
  Wilton SP2 . . . . .144 F5
  Woodford SP2 . . . . .145 A8
Aviemore Rd 6 SN1 . . . . . . .50 A2
Avil's La SN14 . . . . .56 F6
AVINGTON 177 F7
Avocet Cl SN3 . . . . .51 E6
AVON 71 F6
Avon App SP2 . . . . .146 A1
Avon Bldgs SP4 . . . . .217 A3
Avon Cl
  Bradford-on-Avon BA15 . . .100 E5
  Calne SN11 . . . . .81 A5
AVONCLIFF 99 F4
Avoncliff Sta BA15 . . . . .99 E5
Avon Ct BA1 . . . . .82 A4
Avondale Prep Sch SP4 . . .217 D8
Avondown Rd SP4 . . . . . . .198 C7
Avon Dr SP5 . . . . .153 E2
Avondyke SP5 . . . . .211 A7
Avonfield BA14 . . . . .101 F8
Avonfield Ave BA15 . . . . . .100 E5
Avonleaze Rd SN9 . . . . . . .215 D5
Avonmead SN25 . . . . .34 F4
Avon Mead SN15 . . . . .78 F8
Avon Meade 1 SP6 . . . . . .210 D1
Avon Meadow SP5 . . . . . . .211 A8
Avon Meadows SP4 . . . . . .131 C5
Avon Mills SN16 . . . . .28 B2
Avon Pl SP1 . . . . .152 C8
Avon Rd
  Devizes SN10 . . . . .179 C8
  2 Durrington/Bulford SP4 198 F6
  Malmesbury SN16 . . . . .27 F4
  Melksham SN12 . . . . .94 A6
  Tidworth SP9 . . . . .216 C5
  Warminster BA12 . . . . .117 A5
Avon Reach SN15 . . . . .78 D7
Avon Rise SN14 . . . . .39 E4
Avonside Enterprise Pk
  SN12 . . . . .94 A5
Avon Sq SN9 . . . . .181 F1
Avonstoke Cl SP4 . . . . .217 B2
Avon Terr
  Devizes SN10 . . . . .214 A4
  Salisbury SP2 . . . . .145 F2
Avonvale Rd BA14 . . . . .101 D2
Avon Valley Coll SP4 . . . . .198 C7
Avon Valley Nature Reserve★
  SP1 . . . . .145 F3
Avon View SP6 . . . . .210 D1
Avon Way BA14 . . . . .101 D3
Avonweir La SN15 . . . . .57 F3
Avon Wy SN15 . . . . .70 F1
Avro Way SN12 . . . . .94 C1
Awdry Ave SN12 . . . . .94 C6
Awdry Cl
  Chippenham SN14 . . . . .77 F7
  Heddington SN11 . . . . .89 A2
Awdry Rd SN10 . . . . .214 B1
Axbridge Cl SN3 . . . . .51 A5
Axe & Cleaver La BA14 . . .105 C4
AXFORD 169 D1
Axis Bsns Ctr SN5 . . . . .49 D7
Aylesbury St SN1 . . . . .50 C7
Ayleswade Rd SP2 . . . . . . .152 A6
Aymer Pl SN3 . . . . .51 C5
Ayr Cl SN14 . . . . .77 F5
Ayrshire Cl
  Salisbury SP2 . . . . .145 B5
  Swindon SN5 . . . . .49 B7
Azalea Cl SN11 . . . . .81 C1
Azalea Dr
  Trowbridge BA14 . . . . .105 A7

Azalea Dr continued
  Warminster BA12 . . . . .116 E7
Azelin Ct SN3 . . . . .36 B3

B

Babington Pk 9 SN5 . . . . . .48 F5
Back Horse Hill La SP7 . . .203 A6
Back La
  9 Aldbourne SN8 . . . . .170 A6
  Blunsdon St Andrew SN26 . .21 B3
  Calne Without SN15 . . . . . . .88 A4
  Cherhill SN11 . . . . .166 E2
  Chitterne BA12 . . . . .195 D7
  Great Bedwyn SN8 . . . . . . .176 B3
  Great Hinton BA14 . . . . . . .178 A5
  Maiden Bradley with Yarnfield
    BA12 . . . . .118 F2
  Marlborough SN8 . . . . .213 D3
  Penton Grafton SP11 . . . . .193 A3
  Ramsbury SN8 . . . . .170 B2
  Sixpenny Handley SP5 . . . .208 A4
  Tilshead SP3 . . . . .188 B3
  Vernhams Dean SP11 . . . . .185 C3
Back Rd
  Calne SN11 . . . . .81 B2
  Chitterne BA12 . . . . .195 D7
Back St
  Ashton Keynes SN6 . . . . .6 F1
  East Garston RG17 . . . . . . .171 E7
  Great Hinton BA14 . . . . . . .178 A6
  Trowbridge BA14 . . . . .101 C1
Bacon Cl SN1 . . . . .50 A4
BADBURY 65 F5
BADBURY WICK 65 D8
Bader Pk 10 SN12 . . . . . . .178 B8
Badger Cl
  Devizes SN10 . . . . .214 D3
  2 Royal Wootton Bassett
    SN4 . . . . .47 F2
Badgers Brook SN4 . . . . . . .64 A5
Badgers Cl
  Bourton SP8 . . . . .137 E2
  3 Wanborough SN4 . . . . . .163 B6
BADMINTON 38 F2
Badminton House★ GL9 . . .38 F2
Badminton Pk★ GL9 . . . . . .38 F3
Bagbury La SN5 . . . . .33 B1
Bagbury Rd BA12 . . . . .194 F4
Baghdad Rd 2 SP4 . . . . . .198 F7
BAGSHOT 176 F4
Bailey Cl SN9 . . . . .215 B5
Bailey Mews SP4 . . . . .146 C8
Baileys Barn BA15 . . . . . . .100 D5
Baileys Farm Gdns SN3 . . . .51 A6
Bailey's Mead SN4 . . . . .48 A2
Baileys Way SN4 . . . . .64 B7
Bailiffe Piece SN6 . . . . .8 D1
Bainbridge Cl 2 SN5 . . . . . .49 A5
Bainton Cl BA15 . . . . .100 D7
Baird Cl SN5 . . . . .49 B8
Bakehouse Cl SN15 . . . . . . .78 E6
Bakers Cnr SN13 . . . . .84 E4
Bakers Cl SN3 . . . . .36 B2
Bakers Field SN3 . . . . .60 A3
Bakers Rd SN4 . . . . .64 B5
Balden Cl SN4 . . . . .63 F6
Baldwin Cl SN4 . . . . .65 D4
Bale Cl 6 SN5 . . . . .48 F5
Ballands Castle★ BA9 . . . .137 A2
BALLARD'S ASH 47 F5
Ball Rd SN9 . . . . .215 D4
Balmoor Cl BA12 . . . . .139 B3
Balmoral Cl
  Chippenham SN14 . . . . .77 F7
  Swindon SN3 . . . . .51 A3
Balmoral Rd
  Salisbury SP1 . . . . .146 B4
  Trowbridge BA14 . . . . .105 B5
Bamford Cl SN5 . . . . .33 C5
Bampton Gr SN3 . . . . .50 E6
Banbury Cl SN3 . . . . .50 F3
Bancroft BA15 . . . . .100 D7
Bancroft Cl SN5 . . . . .48 F6
Bankfoot Cl 3 SN5 . . . . . . .49 B7
Bankside SN1 . . . . .49 F4
Bank St SN12 . . . . .94 A4
Banks The SN15 . . . . .59 E4
Bank The SN14 . . . . .75 C3
Bankwaters Rd SN13 . . . . . .84 B8
Bannerdown Cl BA1 . . . . . . .82 B4
Bannerdown Dr BA1 . . . . . . .82 A4
Bannerdown Rd BA1 . . . . . .82 C5
Banwell Ave SN3 . . . . .51 A5
BAPTON 195 D1
Barbara's Rd SN13 . . . . .84 D8
Barbel Cl SN11 . . . . .81 B5
Barberry SP3 . . . . .201 A3
Barber's La SP5 . . . . .151 C1
Barbrook Rd SN1 . . . . .50 A2
Barbury Castle★ SN4 . . . . .168 A7
Barbury Castle Ctry Pk★
  SN4 . . . . .168 B7
Barbury Cl SN25 . . . . .34 F3
Barcelona Cres SN4 . . . . . . .64 A7
Barcete SN25 . . . . .34 D7
Bardsey Cl 5 SN4 . . . . .47 F2
Barford La SP5 . . . . .159 C1
BARFORD ST MARTIN 143 A3
Barford St Martin CE Fst Sch
  SP3 . . . . .143 A3
Bargates SN13 . . . . .83 D6
Barken Rd
  4 Chippenham SN14 . . . . . .70 A1
  Chippenham SN14 . . . . .78 A4
BARKERS HILL 203 A4
Barkstead Cl 3 SN5 . . . . . .49 B4

Barley Cl
  Malmesbury SN16 . . . . .28 A2
  Warminster BA12 . . . . .117 C5
Barley Fields SN8 . . . . .170 B8
Barley Hill La SN10 . . . . . .179 A7
Barley Rd 2 SP11 . . . . . . .193 F2
Barley Rise BA14 . . . . .105 F7
Barlow Cl SN25 . . . . .35 A8
Barnard Cl SN3 . . . . .51 B7
Barnard Ct SN3 . . . . .51 B7
Barnard Field SP4 . . . . .217 C2
Barnard Mews SP4 . . . . . . .217 C2
Barnards Hill Dr SP2 . . . . .145 C2
Barnard St 1 SP1 . . . . .152 B8
Barn Cl
  Chippenham SN14 . . . . .78 A8
  Corsham SN13 . . . . .76 E1
Barncroft SP11 . . . . .192 E3
Barn End SN14 . . . . .74 A8
Barnes Cl
  Corston SN16 . . . . .42 E4
  Trowbridge BA14 . . . . .105 A7
Barnes Gn SN15 . . . . .45 C4
Barnes Pl BA12 . . . . .139 A5
Barnes Rd SN14 . . . . .70 B2
Barnes Wallis Cl
  9 Amesbury SP4 . . . . .217 E3
  Melksham Without BA14 . . .178 B8
Barnes Yd 17 SN8 . . . . . . .170 A6
Barnetts Hill SN13 . . . . .83 F3
Barnfield Cl SN2 . . . . .49 F7
Barnfield Rd SN2 . . . . .49 F7
Barnfield Way BA1 . . . . .82 B4
Barn Glebe BA14 . . . . .101 E1
Barn Hill SP3 . . . . .201 A3
Barn Moor Cl SN3 . . . . .51 E3
Barn Owl Rd SN14 . . . . .70 B2
Barn Piece
  Box SN13 . . . . .83 D6
  Bradford-on-Avon BA15 . . .100 D4
Barn St SN8 . . . . .213 D3
Barnstaple Cl SN3 . . . . .51 B5
Barnum Ct SN2 . . . . .50 A7
Barn Wy BA14 . . . . .105 F7
Baroda Rd SP9 . . . . .216 A4
Baron Cl
  Lyneham SN15 . . . . .59 C4
  4 Swindon SN3 . . . . .36 B3
Barons Mead SN14 . . . . .78 A8
Barracks SN14 . . . . .74 F4
Barra Cl SN6 . . . . .22 E6
Barrett La SN15 . . . . .57 D2
Barrett Way SN4 . . . . .64 B6
Barrington Cl SN3 . . . . .51 D3
Barrington Rd SP1 . . . . .146 C1
BARROW 136 C5
Barrowby Gate SN3 . . . . . . .36 A4
Barrow Cl
  Marlborough SN8 . . . . .213 F3
  Royal Wootton Bassett SN4 . .47 E1
  Salisbury SP5 . . . . .152 C5
Barrow Gn SN15 . . . . .70 E2
Barrow La BA9 . . . . .136 B5
Barrow St La
  Mere BA12 . . . . .139 F3
  West Knoyle BA12 . . . . . . .140 A4
Barrows La SP5 . . . . .212 B7
BARROW STREET 139 F2
Barrow Water La BA9 . . . . .136 A5
Barry Glen Cl SN2 . . . . .35 E1
Barry Pl SN11 . . . . .79 F2
Barters La SP7 . . . . .206 D8
Bartlett Cl 11 BA11 . . . . . .110 C6
Bartlett Rd SP1 . . . . .146 B4
Bartletts SN10 . . . . .179 C1
Bartletts Mead BA14 . . . . .178 A4
Bartletts The BA12 . . . . . . .139 B4
Barton Cl 12 SP10 . . . . . . .193 C2
Barton Farm Ctry Pk★
  BA15 . . . . .100 A5
Barton Hill 22 SP7 . . . . . . .202 C2
Barton La BA12 . . . . .139 A5
Barton Lodge BA14 . . . . . . .105 A6
Barton Orch BA15 . . . . .100 C6
Barton Rd SN25 . . . . .34 E3
Bartons Rd 20 SP6 . . . . . .210 D1
Bartons The 29 SP6 . . . . . .210 D1
Barton Way SN16 . . . . .42 E4
Basepoint Bsns Ctr SN5 . . .49 C8
Bashkir Rd BA13 . . . . .108 E1
Basil Cl SN2 . . . . .34 D4
Basil Hill Rd SN13 . . . . .84 C7
Basingstoke Cl 5 SN5 . . . . .49 A4
Baskerville Rd SN3 . . . . .51 E7
Bassett Rd OX12 . . . . .165 F8
Bassetts Pasture BA15 . . . .100 D4
Bassetts The SN13 . . . . .83 D6
Batch The BA2 . . . . .98 E1
Bates Wy
  Swindon SN25 . . . . .34 E3
  3 Swindon SN25 . . . . .34 E3
Bath Acad of Art SN13 . . . .77 A2
Bathampton St SN1 . . . . . . .50 A6
BATHEASTON 82 B4
BATHFORD 82 B2
Bathford CE VC Sch BA1 . .82 C2
Bathford Hill BA1 . . . . .82 B2
Bath Rd
  Atworth SN12 . . . . .84 D2
  Atworth/Whitley SN12 . . . . .93 A3
  Box SN13 . . . . .83 A6
  Bradford-on-Avon BA15 . . . .91 C1
  Chippenham Without SN14 . .77 F5
  Colerne SN14 . . . . .74 F3
  Corsham SN13 . . . . .77 B4
  Cricklade SN6 . . . . .19 D8
  Devizes SN10 . . . . .179 C8
  Frome BA11 . . . . .110 A6

Bath Rd continued
Hungerford RG17 . . . . .176 F7
Marlborough SN8 . . . . .213 B2
Melksham SN12 . . . . .94 A5
Melksham Without SN12 . . . .93 E7
Preshute SN8 . . . . .174 C7
Royal Wootton Bassett SN4 .47 C1
Seend SN12 . . . . .95 C1
Swindon SN1 . . . . .50 C4
Upton Scudamore BA12 . .112 D2
Warminster BA12 . . . . .112 E1
Westonbirt with Lasborough
GL8 . . . . .25 D8
Bath Rd Ind Est SN14 . . . . .78 B6
Bath Stone Cres 1 SN13 . .76 D1
Bathurst Rd SN1 . . . . .50 D6
Batten Rd SP4 . . . . .211 A4
Battens The 3 SN14 . . . . . .70 A1
Battlesbury Barracks
BA12 . . . . .117 E6
Battlesbury Hill Fort★
BA12 . . . . .117 F8
Battlesbury Rd BA12 . . . . .117 E7
Battlewell SN5 . . . . .33 A3
Batt's La SN8 . . . . .183 F7
BAVERSTOCK 142 B4
Baverstock La SP3 . . . . . . .142 B5
Bawdsey Rd 6 SP4 . . . . . .217 D2
Baxter Cl SN25 . . . . .35 A7
Bay Cl SN11 . . . . .89 C8
BAYDON 170 C8
Baydon Cl
Swindon SN25 . . . . .34 F3
Trowbridge BA14 . . . . .105 C5
Baydon Gr SN11 . . . . .81 B4
Baydon Rd
Aldbourne SN8 . . . . .164 B1
Great Shefford RG17 . . . . . .171 F3
Baydon St Nicholas CE Prim
Sch SN8 . . . . .164 C1
Baydons La SN15 . . . . .78 E6
Bayleaf Ave SN2 . . . . .34 D4
Bayliffes Cl SN15 . . . . .79 A7
Baynton Way BA13 . . . . . .186 D8
Bayntun Cl
Bromham SN15 . . . . .96 A7
Devizes SN10 . . . . .214 C1
Baytree Cl BA12 . . . . .115 C7
Bay Tree Cl SN2 . . . . .35 C2
Baywater SN8 . . . . .213 E4
Bazaar Rd SP9 . . . . .216 B5
Beacon Cl
Amesbury SP4 . . . . .217 C4
8 Swindon SN1 . . . . .49 F4
Beacon Ct SP6 . . . . .210 D2
BEACON HILL
Bromham 97 B7
Bulford 199 A7
Hilmarton 73 E5
Beacon Hill Rd 7 SP4 . . . .198 F7
Beaconsfield Way BA11 . .110 B7
Beacon View BA12 . . . . . . .116 D6
Beale Cl SN14 . . . . .78 B7
Beale Ct SN14 . . . . .78 A7
Beale's Barton BA14 . . . . .101 F8
Beales Cl SN1 . . . . .50 B7
Beales Farm Rd 15 RG17 .165 A1
Beamish Cl 2 SN11 . . . . . .166 A1
BEANACRE 94 A8
Beanacre Old Manor★
SN12 . . . . .94 A8
Beanacre Rd
Melksham SN12 . . . . .94 A7
Melksham Without SN12 . . .86 A1
Beaney Vw 1 SN2 . . . . .34 E2
Beanlands The SN4 . . . . . .163 A6
Bear Cl BA15 . . . . .100 B7
Beard Ct SP11 . . . . .192 B5
Bearfield Bldgs BA15 . . . .100 C8
Bearfield La RG17 . . . . . . .171 A4
Bearwater RG17 . . . . .177 B7
Beatrice Rd SP1 . . . . .146 A4
Beatrice St SN2 . . . . .50 C8
Beatrice Way BA14 . . . . . .105 E8
Beatty Ct SN3 . . . . .50 D4
Beauchamp Dr 1 SP4 . . . .217 D3
Beauclerc St SN10 . . . . . . .179 D8
Beaufort Ave SN4 . . . . .61 E8
Beaufort Cl 5 SN12 . . . . .178 B8
Beaufort Gn SN3 . . . . .51 B5
Beaufort Rd SN4 . . . . .64 A7
Beaufort Vw SN14 . . . . .39 E4
Beaufoy Cl 9 SP7 . . . . . . .202 D2
Beaulieu Cl SN5 . . . . .49 C4
Beaulieu Rd 2 SP4 . . . . . .217 C2
Beaumaris Rd SN5 . . . . . . .49 B5
Beaumont Rd SN3 . . . . .50 E6
Beaumont Way SP4 . . . . . .217 D2
Beaven Cl SN15 . . . . .78 F4
Bechstein Mdw BA14 . . . . .106 A8
Beck Cl SN25 . . . . .35 A3
Beckerley La SN4 . . . . .92 F1
Beckett Pl BA13 . . . . .108 F1
Beckett's La SP3 . . . . .201 A3
Beckett St 14 SP3 . . . . . . .203 E8
Becket Way SP1 . . . . .146 D1
Beckford Cl
Tisbury SP3 . . . . .200 D1
Warminster BA12 . . . . .117 B6
BECKHAMPTON 173 D7
Beckhampton (Long
Barrow)★ SN8 . . . . .173 A8
Beckhampton Rd SN8 . . . . .173 B8
Beckhampton St SN1 . . . . . .50 C6
Beddington Ct SN2 . . . . . . .36 A5
Beddoe Cl BA15 . . . . .100 E4
Bede Dr 7 SP10 . . . . .193 C2

Bedford Cl 1 SP6 . . . . . . .210 D2
Bedford Rd
Salisbury SP2 . . . . .145 E2
6 Swindon SN3 . . . . .50 F6
Bedwin St SP1 . . . . .146 B1
Bedwyn Cl SN2 . . . . .35 C3
Bedwyn Dyke★ SN8 . . . . .176 C3
Bedwyn Sta SN8 . . . . .176 B3
Bedwyn Stone Mus★
SN8 . . . . .176 B2
Beech Ave
Melksham SN12 . . . . .94 A3
Swindon SN2 . . . . .35 A2
Warminster BA12 . . . . .116 F6
Beech Cl
Andover SP11 . . . . .193 B1
Porton SP4 . . . . .133 D6
Beechcroft Inf Sch SN25 . .35 E4
Beechcroft Rd
Salisbury SP1 . . . . .146 D1
Swindon SN2 . . . . .35 A2
Beech Ct BA11 . . . . .110 B7
Beech Dr SN5 . . . . .34 A2
Beeches Cl SP5 . . . . .148 C3
Beeches Gn SN12 . . . . .93 D8
Beeches La SN15 . . . . .59 A5
Beeches The
Bradford-on-Avon BA15 . . . .101 A7
Coombe Bissett SP5 . . . . . .156 F7
Lydiard Millicent SN5 . . . . . .33 B1
Melksham Without SN12 . . .93 C7
5 Salisbury SP1 . . . . .152 C8
15 Shaftesbury SP7 . . . . .202 C1
Trowbridge BA14 . . . . .101 F2
Warminster BA12 . . . . .116 F6
4 West Wellow SO51 . . . .212 F6
Beechfield SP4 . . . . .199 B3
Beechfield Dr SN10 . . . . . .214 E5
Beechfield Rd
Corsham SN13 . . . . .76 E1
Roundway SN10 . . . . .214 E7
Beech Gr
Highworth SN6 . . . . .22 F5
Trowbridge BA14 . . . . .105 B6
Beech Grange SP5 . . . . . . .212 C5
Beechgrove BA12 . . . . .117 B8
Beech Hanger SP4 . . . . . . .199 C5
Beech Hill Rd SP9 . . . . . . .216 E7
BEECHINGSTOKE 181 A6
Beech Lea
Broad Blunsdon SN26 . . . . .21 C1
Meysey Hampton GL7 . . . . . .1 A4
Beech Rd
Colerne SN14 . . . . .75 A5
Corsham SN13 . . . . .83 E7
Beech Sq 12 RG17 . . . . . .177 B6
Beech Wlk SP4 . . . . .131 C1
Beechwood 13 SP6 . . . . . .210 C1
Beech Wood 13 SN10 . . . .179 F1
Beechwood Ave BA11 . . . .110 A5
Beechwood Cl
Frome BA11 . . . . .110 A5
Roundway SN10 . . . . .214 E6
Beechwood Rd SN14 . . . . . .78 B8
Beehive Cl 1 SN5 . . . . .49 A8
Begle Cl 9 SN25 . . . . .34 B7
Belcombe Ct★ BA15 . . . . .100 B6
Belcombe Pl BA15 . . . . . . .100 C6
Belcombe Rd BA15 . . . . . . .100 B6
Belfast Mead SN15 . . . . . . .60 C2
Belfry Dr SN14 . . . . .41 E1
Belgrave Cres SP9 . . . . . . .216 E6
Belgrave St SN1 . . . . .50 C5
Bellamy La SP1 . . . . .152 B8
Bell Cl BA12 . . . . .116 F5
Bellefield Cres BA14 . . . . .101 D1
Bellefield Prim Sch
BA14 . . . . .101 E2
Belle Vue Rd
Salisbury SP1 . . . . .146 A1
Swindon SN1 . . . . .50 D4
Bell Field The SN14 . . . . . .39 E4
Bell Gdns SN3 . . . . .36 E4
Bell Hill
Seend SN12 . . . . .178 E7
Warminster BA12 . . . . .116 F5
Bellinger Cl SN15 . . . . .70 C2
Bellingham La SN6 . . . . . . .23 A2
Bell La
Inkpen RG17 . . . . .177 E2
Lechlade GL7 . . . . .2 C3
Liddington SN4 . . . . .163 A4
Sutton Benger SN15 . . . . . .57 D2
Bellot Dr
3 Corsham SN13 . . . . . . .76 E1
Corsham SN13 . . . . .84 E8
Bellott Dr SN13 . . . . .84 E8
Bell Piece SN15 . . . . .57 D2
Bell Rd SP4 . . . . .197 F7
Bells La BA12 . . . . .137 F7
Bell St
4 Ludgershall SP11 . . . . .192 B5
Shaftesbury SP7 . . . . .202 C1
Bellver SN5 . . . . .49 B5
Belmont Cl
10 Shaftesbury SP7 . . . . .202 C1
Swindon SN3 . . . . .36 A4
Belmont Cres SN1 . . . . .50 A3
Belsay SN5 . . . . .49 C4
Belthane Pl SN12 . . . . .93 C8
Belvedere Rd
Bowerhill SN12 . . . . .94 D1
Swindon SN3 . . . . .51 A3
Belvedere Terr SN10 . . . . .214 C4
Bembridge Cl SN3 . . . . .51 B4
BEMERTON 145 C2
BEMERTON HEATH 145 C4

Bemerton St John CE Aided
Prim Sch SP2 . . . . .145 C2
Bences La SN13 . . . . .77 A2
Benches La SP5 . . . . .207 B4
Bendalls Wharf 8 BA11 . .110 A4
Bendy Bow SN16 . . . . .15 F7
Benin Rd SP11 . . . . .191 F3
Ben La SP5 . . . . .154 F7
Bennett Cl SP5 . . . . .211 C7
Bennett Hill Cl 3 SN4 . . . . .47 F2
Bentham Cl SN5 . . . . .49 D6
Bentham La SN5 . . . . .33 A8
Bentley Cl SN3 . . . . .51 A6
Bentley Dr SN1 . . . . .81 C2
Bentley Way SP5 . . . . .149 D5
Benwell Cl SN5 . . . . .49 C6
Beranburh Field SN4 . . . . . .64 E2
Berenger Cl SN1 . . . . .50 D3
Beresford Cl 1 SN3 . . . . . . .51 C4
Bergamot Cl SN8 . . . . .174 C7
Bergman Cl SN25 . . . . .35 B6
Berhills La SN10 . . . . .95 F2
Berkeley Cl
Melksham SN12 . . . . .94 A2
South Cerney GL7 . . . . .6 F6
Berkeley Lawns SN3 . . . . . .50 F3
Berkeley Rd
Trowbridge BA14 . . . . .105 A8
Wroughton SN4 . . . . .64 B7
Berkely Cl 2 SN4 . . . . .78 A7
BERKLEY 111 A7
Berkley CE Fst Sch BA11 .111 A7
Berkley Cross BA11 . . . . . .110 F6
BERKLEY DOWN 110 C5
Berkley La BA11 . . . . .110 F6
Berkley Rd BA11 . . . . .110 A5
Berkley St BA11 . . . . .107 B1
Berkshire Dr SN5 . . . . .49 A7
Bermerton Heath & Barnards
Folly Nature Reserve★
SP2 . . . . .145 C4
Berrington Rd SN3 . . . . .51 A3
Berry Cl SP4 . . . . .190 A3
Berrycroft
Ashbury SN6 . . . . .164 A7
Mildenhall SN8 . . . . .175 B8
BERRYFIELD 93 F1
Berryfield Cl SN12 . . . . .93 F1
Berryfield La SN12 . . . . .93 F1
Berryfield Pk SN12 . . . . .93 F1
Berryfield Rd BA15 . . . . . . .100 D8
Berry Rd BA13 . . . . .186 D8
Berry Wood La SP7 . . . . . . .203 A3
Bertha's Field GL9 . . . . .24 B4
Berton Cl SN26 . . . . .21 C2
BERWICK BASSETT 167 B4
Berwick La SP3 . . . . .128 D7
Berwick Rd
Berwick St James SP3 . . . .196 F2
Stapleford SP3 . . . . .129 E7
BERWICK ST JAMES 196 E2
BERWICK ST JOHN 203 E1
BERWICK ST LEONARD . . .200 C4
Besomer Dro SP5 . . . . .211 D6
Bessemer Cl SN2 . . . . .35 A1
Bessemer Rd E SN2 . . . . . .35 A1
Bessemer Rd W SN2 . . . . . .34 F1
Bess Rd SN5 . . . . .48 F4
Best's La BA12 . . . . .194 A5
Bethel Rd SN13 . . . . .76 E1
Betjeman Ave SN4 . . . . .47 E3
Betjeman Rd SN8 . . . . .213 A2
Betony Cl SN25 . . . . .35 E5
Bettertons Cl GL7 . . . . .1 F7
Bettorns Cl GL7 . . . . .1 F7
Bevan Cl SN2 . . . . .35 F3
Beverley SN5 . . . . .49 C4
Beverley Cl SN12 . . . . .94 C1
Beverley Cres SN9 . . . . . . .182 B2
Beverley Hills Mobile Home
Pk SP4 . . . . .217 D3
Beverley Way SN14 . . . . . . .77 F5
Beversbrook La SN11 . . . . . .81 B5
Beverstone Cl GL7 . . . . .6 F6
Beverstone Gr SN3 . . . . . . .50 F4
Beverstone Rd★ SN6 . . . . . .6 F5
Bevil SN5 . . . . .49 A3
Bevisbury Hill Fort★
SP11 . . . . .185 A1
Bevisland SN3 . . . . .51 C3
Bewick Cl GL7 . . . . .7 A6
BEWLEY COMMON 86 E5
Bewley Ct★ SN15 . . . . .86 F6
Bewley Edge SN15 . . . . .87 A4
Bewley La SN15 . . . . .86 F5
Bewley Rd 1 BA14 . . . . . . .105 C5
Beyer Rd 5 SP4 . . . . .217 D2
Bibury Rd SN3 . . . . .50 E5
Bicton Rd SN25 . . . . .34 F6
Biddel Springs SN6 . . . . . . .23 B6
Bidden La SP4 . . . . .195 D6
Biddesden La SP11 . . . . . .192 C5
BIDDESTONE 76 F8
Biddestone La SN14 . . . . . .68 C3
Biddestone Manor★ SN14 .76 F7
Biddulph Rd SP4 . . . . .198 A7
Bideford Cl SN3 . . . . .51 A5
Big La RG17 . . . . .165 A2
Bilborough Dr 2 SN3 . . . . . .50 F5
Bilbury Rings★ BA12 . . . . .201 D4
Bill Turpin Ct SN3 . . . . .51 B4
Bimport SP7 . . . . .202 B1
Bincknoll Castle★ SN4 . . . . .62 F3
Bindon Cl SN5 . . . . .49 A5
Bingham Rd
Durrington SP4 . . . . .197 E7
Salisbury SP1 . . . . .146 C4

Binknoll La SN4 . . . . .47 F1
Birchenleaze BA14 . . . . . . .105 C3
Birches The SN3 . . . . .51 B2
Birch Gdns BA14 . . . . .102 B2
Birch Glade SN6 . . . . .17 F8
Birch Gr
Bower Hill SN12 . . . . .94 C1
Chippenham SN15 . . . . .70 E1
Whaddon SP5 . . . . .153 E2
Birchill La BA11 . . . . .110 A1
Birch St SN1 . . . . .49 F5
Birch Wlk 4 BA11 . . . . . . .110 B7
Birchwood Cl BA12 . . . . . .115 C7
Birchwood Dr 4 SP4 . . . . .198 C2
Birchwood Rd SN3 . . . . .36 B2
Birdbrook Rd SN2 . . . . .35 E5
BIRDBUSH 203 B1
Birdcombe Rd 1 SN5 . . . . . .49 C5
Birds Marsh View SN15 . . . .70 C2
Bisham BA14 . . . . .106 A8
Bishopdale Cl 2 SN5 . . . . . .34 A1
BISHOPDOWN 146 C4
Bishopdown Rd SP1 . . . . . .146 B3
Bishop Rd SN11 . . . . .81 B4
BISHOPS CANNINGS 172 B3
Bishops Cannings CE Pri Sch
SN10 . . . . .172 B3
Bishops Cl
Chippenham SN15 . . . . .78 F4
Mere BA12 . . . . .139 A6
Tidworth SP9 . . . . .216 D4
Bishops Dr SP2 . . . . .151 E4
Bishopsfield 6 SN6 . . . . . . .19 D8
Bishopsmead BA14 . . . . . .101 C5
Bishops Mead SP1 . . . . . . .152 A6
Bishop's Palace★ SP1 . . . .152 A7
BISHOPSTONE
Shaftesbury 205 F4
Swindon 163 E6
Bishopstone CE Prim Sch
SN6 . . . . .163 E6
Bishopstone Hollow SP5 . .205 E3
BISHOPSTROW 117 E4
Bishopstrow Coll BA12 . . . .117 E4
Bishopstrow Rd BA12 . . . . .117 E4
Bishop's Wlk SP1 . . . . .152 A8
Bishop Wordsworth's Gram
Sch SP1 . . . . .152 A8
Bisley SN16 . . . . .29 A6
Bisley Cl SN3 . . . . .51 A5
Biss Cl BA12 . . . . .112 F4
Bissington Cl 9 SN4 . . . . .132 C1
Biss Meadow BA14 . . . . . .105 A8
Bitham Brook Prim Sch
BA13 . . . . .109 B4
Bitham La
Ham RG17 . . . . .177 A3
Westbury BA13 . . . . .109 A3
Bitham Mill BA13 . . . . .109 B3
Bitham Pk BA13 . . . . .109 B4
Bittern Cl GL7 . . . . .7 A6
Bittern Rd SN3 . . . . .51 E6
BITTLES GREEN 202 B4
Black Acre 4 SN13 . . . . . . .84 E8
Blackbarn Rd SP4 . . . . . . .134 B5
Blackberry Cl SN14 . . . . . . .70 A2
Blackberry La
Potterne SN10 . . . . .179 D5
Winsley BA15 . . . . .90 C1
Blackbird Cl
7 Melksham SN12 . . . . . .94 D5
Swindon SN3 . . . . .51 D7
Blackbird Way BA11 . . . . . .110 B6
Blackford La SN6 . . . . .10 C4
Blackfriars Way SP1 . . . . . .152 B8
Blackhill Rd SO51 . . . . .212 F1
Black Horse La
Westbury BA13 . . . . .108 D1
Westbury BA13 . . . . .112 E8
Winterbourne SP4 . . . . . . .146 F8
Blackhorse Wy
Swindon SN5 . . . . .49 F1
Swindon SN1 . . . . .50 A1
Black La
Pitton & Farley SP5 . . . . . .148 C4
Redlynch SP5 . . . . .211 E6
BLACKLAND 89 F6
Blacklands Crossroads
SN11 . . . . .89 E6
Blackman Gdns SN1 . . . . . . .50 D3
Blackman's La 4 SN8 . . . . .183 D8
Blackmoor Copse Nature
Reserve★ SP5 . . . . .155 A7
Blackmore Cl 1 SN3 . . . . . . .51 E7
Blackmore La SN8 . . . . . . .192 A7
Blackmore Rd
Melksham SN12 . . . . .94 C4
3 Shaftesbury SP7 . . . . .202 D2
Blacksmith Cl SN14 . . . . . . .68 F5
Blackstone Ave SN3 . . . . . . .51 C4
Blackthorn Cl SN4 . . . . .47 E4
Blackthorn La SN25 . . . . . . .35 B3
Blackthorn Mews SN15 . . . .78 F5
Blackthorn Way BA14 . . . . .101 D4
Blackworth SN6 . . . . .22 F8
Blagdon Wlk BA11 . . . . . . .110 C7
Blagrove Ind Est SN1 . . . . . .49 A2
Blain Pl
Royal Wootton Bassett
SN4 . . . . .47 F1

Blain Pl continued
Royal Wootton Bassett SN4 .47 F2
Blair Rd BA14 . . . . .105 B7
Blake Cres SN3 . . . . .36 C2
Blake Ct BA14 . . . . .101 D4
Blakehill Farm Nature
Reserve★ SN6 . . . . .19 A3
Blakeney Ave SN3 . . . . .51 B7
Blakesley Cl 3 SN3 . . . . . . .50 F4
Blakey Rd SP1 . . . . .152 C8
Blandford Alley SN6 . . . . . . .23 A5
Blandford Ct SN3 . . . . .51 B6
Blandford Rd SP5 . . . . .150 F1
Blaygrove Ind Est SN1 . . . . .49 A2
Bleak St BA9 . . . . .137 C3
Blease Cl BA14 . . . . .101 D4
BLEET 102 F2
Bleke St SP7 . . . . .202 C2
Blendon Dr SP10 . . . . .193 C1
Blenheim Pk
21 Bowerhill SN12 . . . . . .178 B8
15 Bowerhill SN12 . . . . . .178 B8
Blenheim Rd
Marlborough SN8 . . . . .213 F2
Wroughton SN4 . . . . .64 A7
Blenhiem Cl BA12 . . . . .116 F7
Bletchley Cl 5 SN3 . . . . . . .51 C4
Blicks Cl SN14 . . . . .41 F1
Blicks Hill SN16 . . . . .28 B3
Blick's Hill SN16 . . . . .28 B4
Blind La
Ansty SP3 . . . . .203 F5
Berwick St John SP7 . . . . .207 B8
Southwick BA14 . . . . .104 F2
Blissford Rd SP6 . . . . .210 F1
Blissmore La 8 SP11 . . . . .192 F1
Bloody Shard Gate DT11 . .207 A1
Bloomsbury Cl 2 SN5 . . . . . .49 B4
Blounts Ct SN10 . . . . .179 D5
Blowhorn St SN8 . . . . .213 D4
Bluebell Dr SN14 . . . . .70 B3
Bluebell Gr SN11 . . . . .81 B5
Bluebell Mead 7 SN13 . . . .84 E8
Bluebell Wy 27 SN4 . . . . . .198 B7
Blueberry Rd SN12 . . . . .94 D3
Blue Boar Row SP1 . . . . . .146 A1
BLUE VEIN 83 D3
Blunsdon Abbey SN25 . . . . .34 F8
Blunsdon Hill SN26 . . . . . . .20 F3
Blunsdon Rd SN25 . . . . .34 F4
BLUNSDON ST ANDREW . . .34 E8
Blunsdon Sta SN5 . . . . .33 F8
Blythe Cl SP11 . . . . .193 E3
Blyth Way SP1 . . . . .146 D4
BMI The Ridgeway Hospl
SN4 . . . . .64 C6
Boardleaze BA12 . . . . .195 A2
Boar St BA12 . . . . .139 A5
Boatman Cl SN25 . . . . .34 A7
Bobbin La BA15 . . . . .99 F4
Bobbin Pk
Westwood BA15 . . . . .99 F3
Westwood BA15 . . . . .99 F3
Bockhampton Rd RG17 . . . .165 A1
Bockhampton Village★
RG17 . . . . .165 B1
BODENHAM 152 F2
Bodiam Dr SN5 . . . . .49 D4
Bodiam Dr N 4 SN5 . . . . . . .49 D5
Bodiam Dr S 3 SN5 . . . . . . .49 D4
Bodman Cl SN15 . . . . .78 F4
Bodmin Cl SN3 . . . . .51 A6
Bodyhorse Hill SN4 . . . . . . .163 C6
BOHEMIA 211 E6
Bohemia La SP5 . . . . .211 D6
Bokerley Ditch★ SP6 . . . . .209 A5
Bokerley Junc SP5 . . . . . . .208 E6
Boldrewood SN3 . . . . .51 D3
Bolehyde Manor★ SN14 . . .69 E4
Boleyn Cl SN5 . . . . .49 A6
Bolingbroke Cl SN5 . . . . . . .47 F6
Bolingbroke Rd SN2 . . . . . . .34 F2
Bolland Cl SN5 . . . . .176 B2
Bolland's Hill SN12 . . . . . . .178 D8
Bonaker Cl SN4 . . . . .133 D6
Bond St Bldgs BA14 . . . . . .105 C7
Bond St
Durrington/Bulford SP4 . . . .198 E6
Trowbridge BA14 . . . . .105 C7
Boness Rd SN4 . . . . .64 A7
Bonham La BA12 . . . . .137 E7
Bonner Cl 10 SN5 . . . . .48 F5
Bonners Cl SN16 . . . . .28 A5
Bonnewe Rise SP4 . . . . . . .217 D3
Bonnie Pk BA13 . . . . .186 B8
Boothmead SN14 . . . . .78 B8
Borage Cl SN2 . . . . .34 D5
Border Cl SN25 . . . . .34 C5
BOREHAM 117 C5
Boreham Cl BA12 . . . . .117 C6
Boreham Field BA12 . . . . . .117 D6
Boreham Rd BA12 . . . . .117 C5
Bore Hill BA12 . . . . .116 F4
Boreway Cl 7 SP4 . . . . . . .193 F2
Borkum Cl 8 SP10 . . . . . . .193 D2
Borough Fields SN4 . . . . . . .47 D2
Borough Parade Sh Ctr
SN15 . . . . .78 D7
Borough The SP5 . . . . .211 A8
Borrowes Cl 2 SN13 . . . . . .84 F4
BOSCOMBE 199 A1
Boscombe Down Airfield
SP4 . . . . .198 E3

Boscombe Rd
Amesbury SP4 . . . . .217 C3
Swindon SN25 . . . . .34 E4
Bosham Cl 6 SN5 . . . . .49 B4
Boswell Rd SN5 . . . . .99 F3
Bosworth Rd SN5 . . . . .49 A4
Botany SN6 . . . . .22 E5
Bothwell Rd SN3 . . . . .50 F7
Botisdone Cl SP11 . . . . . . .185 C3
Botley Copse SN5 . . . . .34 A2
Bottlebush La BH21 . . . . . .208 E1
BOTTLESFORD 181 D6
Bottom La
Ogbourne St George SN8 . .169 A1
1 West Wellow SO51 . . . . .212 F6
Bouchers Way SP2 . . . . . . .152 A5
Boulevard The 3 SN25 . . . .34 C5
Boulton Cl BA13 . . . . .108 E1
Boundary Ave BA11 . . . . . .110 B5
Boundary Cl
Lyneham SN15 . . . . .59 C3
Swindon SN2 . . . . .35 F6
Boundary Rd
Chippenham SN15 . . . . .78 F8
Salisbury SP1 . . . . .146 E2
Boundary Wlk BA14 . . . . . .105 C4
Bourbon Cl BA12 . . . . .117 B5
Bourne Ave SP1 . . . . .146 C2
Bourne Cl
Porton SP4 . . . . .133 D6
1 Salisbury SP1 . . . . .152 B8
Warminster BA12 . . . . .117 A5
3 West Wellow SO51 . . . . .212 F6
Bourne Gdns SP4 . . . . .133 D6
Bourne Hill SP1 . . . . .146 B1
Bourne La 6 SP9 . . . . .199 D8
Bourne Lake Pk SN6 . . . . . .18 E6
Bourne Pk★ SP11 . . . . . . .193 F6
Bourne Rd
Swindon SN2 . . . . .34 F2
Tidworth SP9 . . . . .216 D6
Bourne Ret Pk SP1 . . . . . . .152 D7
Bourne Rise SN8 . . . . .183 E1
Bourne Vale RG17 . . . . . . .177 B7
Bourne Valley Cl SP4 . . . . .133 C5
Bourne View SP4 . . . . .199 A1
Bourne Way SP1 . . . . .152 D7
BOURTON
Bishops Cannings 172 C3
Bourton 137 E2
Bourton Ave SN3 . . . . .36 B2
Bourton La SN10 . . . . .172 C3
Bouverie Ave
Salisbury SP2 . . . . .152 A6
Swindon SN3 . . . . .50 D3
Bouverie Ave S SP2 . . . . . .151 F5
Bouverie Cl SP2 . . . . .151 F6
Bouverie Dr 17 SN10 . . . . .179 F1
Bouverie Pk SN14 . . . . .56 B5
BOVERIDGE 209 B1
Bow Ct SN1 . . . . .50 C4
Bowden Cres SN12 . . . . .94 C6
BOWDEN HILL 87 B4
Bowden Pk★ SN15 . . . . . . .87 B5
Bowdich Cl SP4 . . . . .198 C2
Bowd's La SN15 . . . . .60 A6
BOWERCHALKE 205 A2
Bower Gdns SP1 . . . . .152 C8
BOWERHILL 94 D1
Bowerhill Ind Est SN12 . . . .94 C1
Bowerhill La SN12 . . . . .94 E1
Bowerhill Prim Sch SN12 . .94 C1
Bower Hill Rd SP1 . . . . . . .146 C2
Bower Rd SN8 . . . . .175 D5
Bowers Hill SP5 . . . . .211 D8
Bowers La SP11 . . . . .185 B4
Bowes Lyon Ct SP2 . . . . . . .145 D3
BOWLDOWN 70 E8
Bowldown Rd GL8 . . . . .25 F8
Bowles Rd SN25 . . . . .35 A5
Bowleymead SN3 . . . . .51 D5
Bowling Gn La
Pentridge SP5 . . . . .208 D5
Swindon SN1 . . . . .50 C3
Bowls Barrow (Long Barrow)★ BA12 . . . . .186 E1
Bowman Cl 5 SN3 . . . . .36 B3
Bowman Ct SN4 . . . . .47 C1
Bowmans Ct SN12 . . . . .94 C6
Bowood Cl SN11 . . . . .79 F3
Bowood House & Gdns★ SN11 . . . . .88 C8
Bowood Rd SN1 . . . . .50 B4
Bow Wow GL7 . . . . .7 A7
BOX 83 D6
Boxbush Cl GL7 . . . . .7 A7
Boxbush Rd GL7 . . . . .7 A7
Box CE Prim Sch SN13 . . . .83 C6
Box Dr SN8 . . . . .213 D8
Boxfields Rd SN13 . . . . .83 F7
BOX HILL 83 F7
Box Hill
Box SN13 . . . . .76 A1
Corsham SN13 . . . . .83 E7
Box Rd BA1 . . . . .82 C3
Box View SN14 . . . . .75 B2
Boydell Cl SN5 . . . . .49 B8
Boyle Ave 4 SN11 . . . . . . .166 A1
Boyne's La DT11 . . . . .206 B1
BOYTON 194 E2
Boyton Manor★ BA12 . . . .194 E2
Bozley Rd SP7 . . . . .206 A8
Brabant Way 4 BA13 . . . . .108 E1
Brackenbury 8 SP10 . . . . .193 C1
Brackenbury Rd SP4 . . . . . .197 E7

Bracken Cl SP5 . . . . .153 D3
Brackland SN10 . . . . .180 A2
Bradbury Cl SN15 . . . . .79 A5
Bradene Cl 3 SN4 . . . . .47 E2
Bradenham Rd SN5 . . . . . . .49 A5
BRADENSTOKE 59 C3
Bradenstoke Abbey★ SN15 . . . . .59 B3
Bradfield Cl BA12 . . . . .117 D5
BRADFORD LEIGH 91 F1
BRADFORD-ON-AVON 100 E6
Bradford-on-Avon Mus★ BA15 . . . . .100 D6
Bradford-on-Avon Sta BA15 . . . . .100 C6
Bradford-on-Avon Swimming Pool BA15 . . . .100 C6
Bradford Rd
Atworth SN12 . . . . .92 E7
Bathford BA1 . . . . .82 B2
Box SN13 . . . . .83 F3
Broughton Gifford SN12 . . . .93 F4
Corsham SN13 . . . . .76 C1
Melksham SN12 . . . . .94 A5
Rode BA11 . . . . .103 F1
Swindon SN1 . . . . .50 C4
Winsley BA15 . . . . .99 D6
Bradley Cl
Holt BA14 . . . . .101 F8
Warminster BA12 . . . . .116 E4
Bradley La
Holt BA14 . . . . .92 F1
Maiden Bradley with Yarnfield BA12 . . . . .118 C3
Bradley Mound★ BA12 . . . .118 F2
Bradley Pk★ BA12 . . . . . . .118 F1
Bradley Rd
Southwick BA14 . . . . .105 B2
Swindon SN2 . . . . .35 D4
Trowbridge BA14 . . . . .105 C5
Warminster BA12 . . . . .116 E4
Bradon Forest Sch SN5 . . . .33 B3
Bradshaw Cl 6 SN25 . . . . . .34 D6
Bradwell Cl 2 SP10 . . . . . .193 C2
Bradwell Moor SN3 . . . . . . .51 D2
Braemar Cl SN3 . . . . .50 F3
Braemar Rise SP1 . . . . . . .146 B4
Braemore CE Prim Sch SP6 . . . . .210 E4
Braemor Rd SN11 . . . . .81 A4
Braithwaite Way 3 BA11 . . . . .110 C6
Brake Mead SN15 . . . . .78 F7
Brakspear Dr SN13 . . . . . . .76 E1
Bramble Cl SN2 . . . . .35 E1
Bramble Dr
Chippenham SN15 . . . . .79 A4
Westbury BA13 . . . . .108 F5
Bramble Rd SN2 . . . . .35 E1
Brambles The
Hinton Charterhouse BA2 . . .98 E1
Salisbury SP1 . . . . .146 C2
Trowbridge BA14 . . . . .101 D2
Bramble Wlk 4 SP11 . . . . .193 F2
Brambling Mews GL7 . . . . . .7 A6
Bramblings The 1 SN12 . . .94 D5
Bramdean Cl 6 SN25 . . . . . .34 F6
Bramley Cl
Pewsey SN9 . . . . .215 D6
4 Warminster BA12 . . . . . .116 F7
Bramley Dr BA11 . . . . .110 C6
Bramley Hill BA12 . . . . .138 F5
Bramley La BA14 . . . . .105 D7
Bramleys The SP5 . . . . . . .161 D3
Bramley Way SP4 . . . . .217 C3
Brampton Ct 8 SN12 . . . . .178 B8
Bramptons The SN5 . . . . . . .49 B7
BRAMSHAW 212 E3
Bramshaw Telegraph★ SP6 . . . . .211 F3
Bramwell Cl SN2 . . . . .35 E6
Brancaster Ave 1 SP10 . . .193 C2
Branch Rd BA2 . . . . .98 F2
Branders 4 SN6 . . . . .19 D8
Brandon Cl SN5 . . . . .49 A5
Branksome Rd SN25 . . . . . . .34 E3
Branscombe Dr SN4 . . . . . . .47 E1
Bransdown Hill
Easton Grey SN16 . . . . .26 A3
Sherston SN16 . . . . .25 F2
Brassknocker Hill BA2 . . . . .90 A1
Bratch La SP3 . . . . .201 F2
BRATTON 186 B7
Bratton Ave SN10 . . . . .214 C2
Bratton Cl SN2 . . . . .35 B5
Bratton Prim Sch BA13 . . .186 B7
Bratton Rd
West Ashton BA14 . . . . . . .106 B4
Westbury BA13 . . . . .109 C4
Braxton Rd 6 SN25 . . . . . . .34 C6
Braybrooke Cl 2 SN5 . . . . . .48 F8
Braydon Ct SN2 . . . . .35 C5
Braydon La SN6 . . . . .18 F4
Bray St SN8 . . . . .173 A8
Breach Cl
Bourton SP8 . . . . .137 E2
Bromham SN15 . . . . .96 A7
Breach La
Chute SP11 . . . . .192 E8
Royal Wootton Bassett SN4 .61 B5
1 Shaftesbury SP7 . . . . . . .202 B1
Southwick BA14 . . . . .105 A3
Breach The SN10 . . . . .214 B2
Bread St BA12 . . . . .116 F5
Bream Cl
Calne SN11 . . . . .81 A5
Melksham SN12 . . . . .94 D6

BREAMORE 210 F5
Breamore Countryside Mus★ SP6 . . . . .210 E5
Breamore House★ SP6 . . . .210 E6
Breamore Rd SP5 . . . . .210 F7
Brean Rd 3 SN25 . . . . .34 F7
Brecon Cl
Melksham SN12 . . . . .94 D4
Swindon SN3 . . . . .50 E2
Bremen Gdns 21 SP10 . . . .193 D2
Bremeridge Cl BA13 . . . . . .109 B3
Bremeridge Rd BA13 . . . . . .109 B3
BREMHILL 80 E2
Bremhill Cl SN2 . . . . .35 C4
Bremhill View SN11 . . . . . . .81 A4
Bremilham Rd SN16 . . . . . . .27 C4
Bremilham Rise SN16 . . . . . .27 C3
Brendon Wlk SN3 . . . . .51 B6
Brentfore St 1 SN1 . . . . . . .50 B1
Breton Rd BA13 . . . . .108 F2
Brettingham Gate SN3 . . . . .64 F8
Brewer Mead SN15 . . . . .78 F4
Brewers La SN11 . . . . .81 C1
Brewery Rd 8 SP1 . . . . . . .152 B8
Brewery St SN6 . . . . .23 A5
Brewery Wlk BA14 . . . . . . .101 D1
Brewhouse Hill SN8 . . . . . .176 D6
Briar Cl
Frome BA11 . . . . .110 B7
Westbury BA13 . . . . .108 F4
Briar Fields SN1 . . . . .50 E7
Briar Leaze SN11 . . . . .166 B3
Briars SN1 . . . . .47 E3
Briarswood Ct SN3 . . . . .51 D3
Briary Rd GL7 . . . . .2 C6
Brickham Rd 1 SN10 . . . . .214 D5
Brick Hill SN15 . . . . .95 D6
Brick La
Salisbury SP2 . . . . .145 C2
Trowbridge BA14 . . . . .101 D3
Brickley La SN10 . . . . .214 D2
Brickstead Ave SN10 . . . . .214 C3
Brickworth La SP5 . . . . . . .160 E4
Brickyard La SP8 . . . . .137 E1
Bridewell La SP7 . . . . .202 A6
Bridewell Sq SN10 . . . . . . .214 B3
Bridewell St SN8 . . . . .213 C2
Bridge Ave BA14 . . . . .105 A4
Bridge Cl GL7 . . . . .2 E3
Bridge Ct BA13 . . . . .108 E4
Bridge End Rd SN3 . . . . .35 F1
Bridgeman Cl SN3 . . . . .36 B2
Bridgemead Cl SN5 . . . . . . .49 D7
Bridgemead Ret Pk Sch SN5 .49 E5
Bridge Rd SP5 . . . . .205 E4
Bridge St
Bourton SP8 . . . . .137 E2
Fordingbridge SP6 . . . . . . .210 D1
26 Hungerford RG17 . . . . .177 B7
Marlborough SN8 . . . . .213 A2
Salisbury SP2 . . . . .152 A8
Swindon SN1 . . . . .50 B6
3 Trowbridge BA14 . . . . . .105 D7
Bridge The SN15 . . . . .78 D7
Bridgewater Cl
Harnham SP2 . . . . .151 D6
Swindon SN2 . . . . .50 A7
Bridlewood Prim Sch SN25 . . . . .34 F7
Bridport Rd SN3 . . . . .51 B4
Brier Ct SP2 . . . . .145 C4
Briery Cl SN3 . . . . .36 A4
Bright Cl 3 SN15 . . . . .78 F5
Brighton Way SN14 . . . . . . .77 F6
Bright St SN2 . . . . .50 D8
BRIGMERSTON 198 E4
Brimble Hill SN4 . . . . .64 D5
Brimble Hill Specl Sch SN25 . . . . .34 D8
Brimhill Rise BA13 . . . . . . .111 D4
Brind Cl SN3 . . . . .51 E6
Brindley Cl SN2 . . . . .34 E1
Brind Rd SP4 . . . . .197 F7
Brington Rd SN3 . . . . .51 B8
BRINKWORTH 45 E5
Brinkworth Cl SN14 . . . . . . .77 F7
Brinkworth Earl Danby's CE Prim Sch SN15 . . . . .45 E5
Brinkworth House Bsns & Events Ctr SN15 . . . . .45 C6
Brinkworth Rd SN15 . . . . . . .45 C3
Brinscombe La 6 SP7 . . . . .202 D1
Brionne Way 13 SP7 . . . . .202 D2
Brisbane Gdns 7 SP4 . . . . .198 F6
Bristol Rd
Chippenham SN14 . . . . .78 C8
Chippenham Without SN14 . .69 C2
Luckington SN14 . . . . .39 D3
Bristol St
3 Malmesbury SN16 . . . . . .28 A3
Swindon SN1 . . . . .50 A6
Britannia Ave SN9 . . . . .182 B2
Britannia Cres SN15 . . . . . . .60 B2
Britannia Pl 6 SN1 . . . . . . .50 D4
Britannia Trade Pk SN3 . . . .35 F3
BRITFORD 152 E5
Britford La SP2 . . . . .152 B6
Britford La W 1 SP2 . . . . . .152 A6
British Row BA14 . . . . .101 C1
Britmore La SP7 . . . . .202 F4
Brittain Cl SN14 . . . . .77 F7
Britten Rd SN25 . . . . .34 E7
Brittox The SN10 . . . . .214 B3
Brixham Ave SN3 . . . . .50 E5
BRIXTON DEVERILL 120 C2
Broadacres SN4 . . . . .62 B2
BROAD BLUNSDON 21 C2
Broadbury Banks★ SN9 . .181 B2

BROADBUSH 21 D1
BROAD CHALKE 205 B4
Broad Chalke CE Prim Sch SP5 . . . . .205 B4
Broadcloth E La BA14 . . . . .105 E7
Broadcloth La BA14 . . . . . . .105 E7
Broad Dr GL8 . . . . .25 A8
Broadfield Rd SN4 . . . . .133 C3
Broadfields SN9 . . . . .215 B4
BROAD HINTON 167 C7
Broad Hinton CE Prim Sch SN4 . . . . .167 C7
Broad Hinton (Hackpen) White Horse★ SN4 . . . . .167 E5
Broadlands Cl SP1 . . . . .146 B4
Broadleas Cl SN10 . . . . .214 A2
Broadleas Cres SN10 . . . . . .214 A2
Broadleas Gdns★ SN10 . . . .214 A1
Broadleas Pk SN10 . . . . . . .214 A1
Broadleas Rd SN10 . . . . . . .214 A2
Broadleaze
Down Ampney GL7 . . . . .8 E8
Seagry SN15 . . . . .57 D6
Broadleaze Pk BA14 . . . . . .105 D3
Broadmead
Corsham SN13 . . . . .85 B7
Trowbridge BA14 . . . . .101 A1
Broadmead La BA12 . . . . . .116 E1
Broadmead Wlk SN3 . . . . . . .51 B7
Broadmoor Rd SN3 . . . . .36 D7
BROAD'S GREEN 88 F3
Broad St
Swindon SN1 . . . . .50 C7
Trowbridge BA14 . . . . .101 C1
Broadstone SN13 . . . . .85 B7
Broad Stones BA15 . . . . . . .90 E7
BROAD STREET 181 C6
BROAD TOWN 167 A8
Broad Town CE Prim Sch SN4 . . . . .62 B1
Broadtown La
Broad Town SN4 . . . . .62 B3
Royal Wootton Bassett SN4 .61 F5
Broad Town White Horse★ SN4 . . . . .62 D1
Broadway
Market Lavington SN10 . . .179 D2
Warminster BA12 . . . . .116 E5
Broadway Cl GL7 . . . . .10 D7
Broadway E BA13 . . . . .108 D6
Broadway La GL7 . . . . .7 A5
Broadway N BA13 . . . . .108 C7
Broadway The SN25 . . . . . . .35 A3
Broadwood Ave SN13 . . . . . .84 B8
Broadwood Cl 1 BA12 . . . . .117 A8
Brockley Rise SN2 . . . . .36 A5
Brocks Orch 8 SP3 . . . . . . .196 E6
BROKENBOROUGH 27 D7
Broken Cross
Calne SN11 . . . . .81 B3
Laverstock SP4 . . . . .146 F6
BROKERSWOOD 107 F5
Brokerswood Ctry Pk★ BA13 . . . . .107 F6
Brokerswood Rd BA14 . . . . .105 A1
BROMHAM 96 A7
Bromley Cl 2 SN3 . . . . .50 E6
Bronte Cl 2 SN3 . . . . .51 D4
BROOK 212 E1
Brook Cl
Melksham SN12 . . . . .93 F6
16 Tisbury SP3 . . . . .203 E8
Winterbourne Stoke SP3 . .196 F3
Brookdene SN25 . . . . .34 E4
Brook Dr SN13 . . . . .85 B7
Brook Dro BA13 . . . . .108 C4
Brooke Cl SN16 . . . . .28 C2
Brooke Cres SN2 . . . . .34 C5
Brookfield SN6 . . . . .22 F7
Brook Field Prim Sch SN5 .49 A8
Brookfield Rise SN12 . . . . . .85 D1
Brookfields SO51 . . . . .212 F6
Brook Gdns SN10 . . . . .214 F6
BROOK HILL 212 D1
Brook Hill
Donhead St Andrew SP7 . .203 B2
Sherston SN16 . . . . .40 C8
Brook La
Westbury BA13 . . . . .108 D4
Woodgreen SP6 . . . . .211 A4
Brooklands
Brinkworth SN15 . . . . .45 E5
Royal Wootton Bassett SN4 .61 E7
Brooklands Ave SN2 . . . . . . .34 F1
Brookleaze SN13 . . . . .84 E5
Brooklime Cl 1 SN2 . . . . . . .34 D4
Brook Mdw SN4 . . . . .64 A5
Brookmead BA14 . . . . .105 A3
Brook Rd BA14 . . . . .101 B1
Brooksby Way SN3 . . . . .51 B8
Brooks Cl SN2 . . . . .35 E5
Brookside
Crudwell SN16 . . . . .14 E6
Hullavington SN14 . . . . .41 F2
Brookside Cl BA1 . . . . .82 A5
Brook St
Chippenham SN14 . . . . .78 B8
Fovant SP3 . . . . .204 E7
Great Bedwyn SN8 . . . . . . .176 C3
Warminster BA12 . . . . .116 E5
BROOK WATERS 203 B2
Brook Way SN1 . . . . .81 C3
Brookwell Cl SN14 . . . . .70 C2
Broomcroft Rd SN9 . . . . . . .215 C5
Broome Manor La SN3 . . . . .50 F2
BROOMFIELD 55 A1
Broomfield SN15 . . . . .70 D2
Broom Gdns SN14 . . . . .55 F8

Broomground BA15 . . . . . . .99 E2
Broomhill SP5 . . . . .212 C5
Brotherton Cl SN15 . . . . .78 F5
BROUGHTON GIFFORD 93 C4
Broughton Grange 6 SN3 . .50 F4
Broughton Rd 2 BA14 . . . . .105 C5
Brouncker's Well★ BA12 . .186 F5
Browning Cl 1 SN3 . . . . . . .36 B3
Brownings The SN13 . . . . . .83 D5
Brownleaze La SN10 . . . . . .179 D6
Brown's Folly★ BA1 . . . . . . .82 C1
Browns La
Alton SN8 . . . . .173 C1
Damerham SP6 . . . . .209 E3
Brown's La SN8 . . . . .176 B3
Brown St
3 Salisbury SP1 . . . . .146 B1
Salisbury SP1 . . . . .152 B8
Trowbridge BA14 . . . . .105 D7
Brow The SN25 . . . . .34 E4
Broxburn Rd BA12 . . . . .116 D6
Bruce St SN2 . . . . .49 F7
Bruddel Gr SN3 . . . . .50 E2
Bruges Cl SN15 . . . . .78 F7
Brunel Cl SN13 . . . . .76 F1
Brunel Cres SN2 . . . . .50 B8
Brunel Cl SN15 . . . . .78 B6
Brunel Ctr The SN1 . . . . . . .50 B6
Brunel Rd SP2 . . . . .145 D1
Brunel Way
Box SN13 . . . . .83 D6
Frome BA11 . . . . .110 C7
Brunkard's La SN9 . . . . .215 D5
Brunswick St SN1 . . . . .50 C4
BRUNTON 183 E3
Brushy Bush La SP5 . . . . . .207 F3
Bruton Wlk SN3 . . . . .51 A4
Bruyn Rd SP6 . . . . .210 E1
Bryans Cl Rd SN11 . . . . .81 B3
Bryanston Way SN3 . . . . . . .51 C6
Bryant Rd SN25 . . . . .34 C5
Brydes Rd 21 SP11 . . . . . . .192 A5
Brympton Cl 5 SP6 . . . . . . .210 C1
Brynards Hill SN4 . . . . .47 E1
Bryony Way SN2 . . . . .34 D4
Bryworth La GL7 . . . . .2 A6
Buckhurst Cres SN3 . . . . . . .51 A6
Buckingham Rd
Chippenham SN15 . . . . .79 A5
Swindon SN3 . . . . .51 A3
Buckland Cl SN3 . . . . .51 A6
Buckleaze Cl BA14 . . . . . . .105 D5
Buckleaze La SN9 . . . . .215 C5
Bucklebury Cl SN3 . . . . .36 A1
Buckler Cl GL7 . . . . .1 F6
Buckthorn Dr SN2 . . . . .34 D4
Buckthorn Row SN13 . . . . . .84 E8
Budbury Circ BA15 . . . . . . .100 C7
Budbury Cl BA15 . . . . .100 C7
Budbury Pl BA15 . . . . .100 C7
Budbury Ridge BA15 . . . . . .100 C7
Budbury Tyning BA15 . . . . .100 C7
Bude Rd SN5 . . . . .49 F6
Budge La BA11 . . . . .114 A8
Buettell Way SN16 . . . . .27 F5
Bugdens Cl SP4 . . . . .217 D4
BUGLEY 116 C6
Buie Cl SN5 . . . . .34 B2
BULBRIDGE 144 B1
Bulbridge Rd SP2 . . . . .144 B1
BULFORD 217 E8
BULFORD CAMP 198 F6
Bulford Droveway SP4 . . . .198 D7
Bulford Hill SP4 . . . . .217 C8
Bulford Rd
Bulford SP4 . . . . .217 F8
Durrington/Bulford SP4 . . .198 B7
Shipton Bellinger SP9 . . . .199 C8
South Tedworth SP9 . . . . .216 A4
Bulford St Leonard's CE Prim Sch SP4 . . . . .217 E8
BULKINGTON 178 E5
Bulldog La SN10 . . . . .180 C3
BULLENHILL 106 E8
Buller St SN2 . . . . .35 D1
Bullfinch Cl SN3 . . . . .51 D6
Bull La BA12 . . . . .116 F2
BULLOCK'S HORN 15 E1
Bullock's Horn La
Charlton SN16 . . . . .29 D7
Hankerton SN16 . . . . .15 D1
Bull Pit BA15 . . . . .100 C6
Bulls La
Box SN13 . . . . .83 D6
Broad Chalke SP5 . . . . .205 B4
Bulpit La RG17 . . . . .177 B6
Bulpits Hill SP11 . . . . .185 C3
Bumper's Batch BA2 . . . . . . .98 A8
Bumpers Fram Ind Est SN14 . . . . .70 A1
Bumpers Way SN14 . . . . .70 A1
Bunce Rd SN3 . . . . .36 A2
Bungalow Pk SN15 . . . . .59 B3
Bungalows The SN2 . . . . . . .35 C2
Bunnies La SN10 . . . . .96 D2
Bunns La BA11 . . . . .114 A2
Bunny La SP5 . . . . .162 C4
Buntings The SN3 . . . . .51 D7
Bupton Village★ SN11 . . . .166 D7
BURBAGE 183 D8
Burbage Prim Sch SN8 . . .183 D8
Burbage Rd
Easton SN9 . . . . .183 A8
Milton Lilbourne SN9 . . . . .182 F7
Swindon SN2 . . . . .35 C6
Burbage Wharf★ SN8 . . . .175 C2
BURCOMBE 143 E2
Burcombe La SP2 . . . . .144 B2

Burcot Cl SN25 . . . . .34 C7
Burden Cl SN3 . . . . .36 C1
Burderop Barns SN4 . . . . . .64 E4
Burderop Cl
　[1] Trowbridge BA14 . . . .105 D5
　Wroughton SN4 . . . . .64 B8
Burderop Pk★ SN4 . . . . . . .64 F5
Burdett St [4] SN8 . . . . .170 B2
Burford Ave
　Salisbury SP2 . . . . .152 A6
　Swindon SN3 . . . . .50 E5
Burford La SP2 . . . . .152 B6
Burford Rd SP2 . . . . .152 B6
Burford's [2] RG17 . . . . .171 E7
Burford St GL7 . . . . .2 C4
Burgate Fields SP6 . . . . . . .210 D2
Burgate Sch & Sixth Form
　The SP6 . . . . .210 E2
Burgess Cl SN3 . . . . .36 A1
Burgess Gn SP1 . . . . .146 A4
Burghley Cl SN3 . . . . .51 A6
Burkal Dr [32] SP10 . . . . .193 C2
Burlands Rd SN15 . . . . .78 E6
Burleaze SN15 . . . . .78 C5
Burlington Pl SN13 . . . . .84 D8
Burnet Cl
　Melksham SN12 . . . . .94 B2
　Swindon SN2 . . . . .34 D5
Burnett Rd BA14 . . . . .105 D6
Burnet Way SP1 . . . . .146 D4
Burnham Rd
　[5] Fordingbridge SP6 . . . .210 D2
　Swindon SN3 . . . . .51 B6
Burnhams Cl [1] SP10 . . . . . .193 C2
Burnivale SN16 . . . . .28 A3
Burn Rd SN13 . . . . .76 E1
Burnston Cl SN12 . . . . .94 D5
Burns Way SN2 . . . . .35 E4
Burr La SN8 . . . . .176 F1
Burroughs Cl SP1 . . . . .146 E2
Burroughs Dro [2] SN8 . . . . .183 D8
BURTON
　Mere 139 D5
　Nettleton 53 B4
Burton Cl [1] SP7 . . . . .202 D2
Burton Farm Cl SN14 . . . . . .53 B3
Burton Hill SN16 . . . . .28 B2
Burton Rd GL9 . . . . .52 F6
Burtons La SN13 . . . . .83 C5
Burwood Cl [7] SP4 . . . . . . .217 D3
Bury Camp (Hill Fort)★
　SN14 . . . . .67 B1
Burycroft SN4 . . . . .163 A6
Bury Fields SN5 . . . . .33 D1
Bury Hill (Settlement)★
　SN6 . . . . .18 B1
Bury La BA13 . . . . .186 B7
Bury Mead BA12 . . . . .195 A2
Burytown La SN26 . . . . .21 C2
Buscot Cl
　Swindon SN25 . . . . .34 E7
　[8] Swindon SN25 . . . . . . .34 E7
Buscot Old Parsonage★
　SN7 . . . . .2 E1
BUSCOT WICK 12 D8
Bush Barrow★ SP4 . . . .197 D4
Bush Farm Bison Ctr★
　BA12 . . . . .140 B3
BUSHTON 166 E8
Bustlers Hill SN16 . . . . .40 D8
Bute Cl SN6 . . . . .22 F7
Butleigh Rd SN25 . . . . .34 C7
Butler Cl SP2 . . . . .152 B6
Butlers Cl SN16 . . . . .25 C1
Butler's Field★ 2 C5
Butler's Gdns BA11 . . . . . . .110 A4
Butt Cl SN11 . . . . .192 A6
Buttercup Cl SN14 . . . . .70 B3
Butterfield Dr SP4 . . . . .217 D3
Butterfly World★ SN1 . . . . .48 F1
Butter Furlong Rd SP5 . . . . .154 C3
BUTTERMERE 185 B8
Buttermere SN3 . . . . .51 B3
Butterstake La SP7 . . . . . . .202 B6
Butterworth St SN1 . . . . .50 A5
Butt La SP5 . . . . .205 E4
Buttons Yd BA12 . . . . .117 B7
Butts Cl SN14 . . . . .76 E1
Butts Hill SP3 . . . . .129 E7
Butts La
　Kilmington BA12 . . . . .123 E6
　Steeple Ashton BA14 . . . .178 A3
Butt's La BA15 . . . . .90 F7
Butts Mead [3] SP7 . . . . . . .202 D1
Butts Rd
　Chiseldown SN4 . . . . .65 D5
　Salisbury SP1 . . . . .146 A2
Butt St SP11 . . . . .192 A5
Butts Terr SP2 . . . . .146 A2
Butts The
　Aldbourne SN8 . . . . .170 A6
　Biddestone SN14 . . . . .76 D7
　Bratton BA13 . . . . .186 B7
　Chippenham SN15 . . . . . . .78 B4
　Crudwell SN16 . . . . .14 E6
　Lydiard Millicent SN5 . . . . .48 C8
　Potterne SN10 . . . . .179 D5
　Shaftesbury SP7 . . . . .202 B2
　Shrewton SP3 . . . . .196 E4
　Steeple Ashton BA14 . . . .178 A3
　Westbury BA13 . . . . .109 A4
Butts (Tumuli) The★
　SP6 . . . . .211 E2
Buzzard Cl [2] SN12 . . . . . . .94 D5
Buzzard Rd
　[4] Calne SN11 . . . . .81 B5
　[6] Winterbourne SP4 . . . .132 C1

By Brook Valley CE Prim Sch
　SN14 . . . . .68 F5
Bydemill Gdns SN6 . . . . .22 E5
Byfield Way SN3 . . . . .51 B8
Byrd [13] SN5 . . . . .48 F5
Byre Cl SN6 . . . . .19 D7
Byron Ave SN4 . . . . .47 F2
Byron Cl
　[11] Ludgershall SP11 . . . .192 A5
　[5] Melksham SN12 . . . . . .94 B4
Byron Ct SN3 . . . . .36 C5
Byron Rd SN10 . . . . .214 B1
Byron St [3] SN1 . . . . .50 C5
Bytham Rd SN8 . . . . .169 A4
Bythebrook SN14 . . . . .70 B1
Bythesea Rd BA14 . . . . .105 C8
Byways Cl [4] SP1 . . . . .152 C8

C

Cabot Dr SN5 . . . . .48 F6
Cabul Rd SP9 . . . . .216 B5
Cadby Cl BA14 . . . . .105 F8
Caddy La BA12 . . . . .138 F5
CADLEY 175 A5
Cadley Cl SN2 . . . . .35 D2
Cadley Clay Shooting Gd
　SN8 . . . . .175 A5
Cadley Rd SN8 . . . . .183 E1
Cadnam Cres SP4 . . . . .217 E2
Caen Hill SN10 . . . . .179 C8
Caen Hill Gdns SN10 . . . . . .179 C8
Caen Hill Locks★ SN10 . . . .179 C8
Caen View SN1 . . . . .49 E4
Caerleon Dr [4] SP10 . . . . . .193 E2
Caesar Rd SP10 . . . . .193 E2
Caesar's Camp (Fort)★
　DT11 . . . . .206 F2
Cagney Dr SN25 . . . . .35 A5
Caird Lawns SN10 . . . . .214 C2
Cairndow Way SN2 . . . . .35 E5
CALCUTT 20 A7
Calcutt St SN6 . . . . .19 E8
Calder Cl SN25 . . . . .34 F5
Calder House Sch SN14 . . . .75 D6
Caldwell Cl [15] SP7 . . . . . .202 D1
Calf La SN8 . . . . .173 B1
Calgary Dr [5] SP4 . . . . .217 F8
Callaghan Cl [2] SN3 . . . . . .36 B2
Callas Hill SN4 . . . . .163 B5
Callas Rise [3] SN4 . . . . . . .163 B6
Callenders SN5 . . . . .49 E5
Callington Rd SN25 . . . . .34 B6
Callow Croft [6] SN8 . . . . . .183 D8
CALLOW HILL 46 D6
Callows Cross SN15 . . . . . . .46 C6
CALNE 81 B2
Calne Heritage Ctr★ SN11 .81 B2
CALNE MARSH 81 C4
Calne Rd SN15 . . . . .60 A1
Calstock Rd SN25 . . . . .34 B6
CALSTONE
　WELLINGTON 172 A7
Calvert Rd SN3 . . . . .50 E6
Calves La SP7 . . . . .202 A2
Camargue Rd BA13 . . . . . . .108 E1
Cambrai Rd SN4 . . . . .50 A5
Cambria Bridge Rd SN1 . . . .50 A5
Cambria Pl SN1 . . . . .50 A5
Cambridge Cl SN3 . . . . .50 F4
Cambridge Rd SP1 . . . . .146 B3
Camden Cl SN5 . . . . .49 A5
Camellia Dr BA12 . . . . .116 E7
Camelot Cl [28] SP10 . . . . . .193 E2
Cameron Cl SN3 . . . . .36 A1
Camilla Cl SP4 . . . . .217 D8
Camomile Dr [25] SP11 . . . .192 A5
Campbell Rd SP1 . . . . .146 B2
Campden Rd SN3 . . . . .50 E5
Campion Cl
　Calne SN11 . . . . .81 B5
　Westbury BA13 . . . . .109 A5
Campion Dr
　Melksham SN12 . . . . .94 C2
　Trowbridge BA14 . . . . . . .105 D6
Campion Gate SN5 . . . . .48 F5
Camton Cl SN5 . . . . .48 F7
CANADA 212 F4
Canada Rd S051 . . . . .212 F5
Canada Rise SN10 . . . . .179 F1
Canadian Ave SP2 . . . . .145 D2
Canal Cl
　Calne SN11 . . . . .81 A2
　Wilcot SN8 . . . . .182 A8
Canal La SP5 . . . . .153 C2
Canal Rd
　Chippenham SN15 . . . . . . .78 F5
　Trowbridge BA14 . . . . . . .101 D3
Canal Rd Ind Est BA14 . . . .101 D3
Canalside SN5 . . . . .153 E2
Canal Way SN10 . . . . .214 E6
Canal Wlk
　Hungerford RG17 . . . . . . .177 B7
　Swindon SN1 . . . . .50 B6
Canberra Dr SP4 . . . . .198 F6
Canberra Rd SN4 . . . . .64 E3
Candown Rd SP3 . . . . .188 B2
Canford Cl SN3 . . . . .51 C6
CANN COMMON 206 B8
Canney Cl SN4 . . . . .65 D4
Canney The SN4 . . . . .65 D4
Cann Hill SP7 . . . . .206 A7
Cannimore Cl BA12 . . . . . . .116 E5
Cannimore Rd BA12 . . . . . . .116 D5
Cannon Sq SN12 . . . . .94 A4
Cannon St SN1 . . . . .50 C5
Cannwood La BA10 . . . . . . .122 D8

Canon Dr GL7 . . . . .2 E3
Canons Cl
　Tidworth SP9 . . . . .216 D4
　Warminster BA12 . . . . . . .117 C5
Canons Ct SN12 . . . . .94 A4
Canons Yard Ind Est SN4 . . .61 E8
Cantax Hill SN15 . . . . .86 C6
Cantelo Cl SN25 . . . . .34 F7
Canterbury Cl
　[10] Amesbury SP4 . . . . .217 D3
　Swindon SN3 . . . . .50 F3
Canterbury St SN14 . . . . . . .78 C8
Cantors Way SN16 . . . . .17 C2
Capella Cres [17] SN25 . . . . .34 B7
Capesthorne Dr SN25 . . . . . .34 E6
Capitol Cl SN3 . . . . .36 D1
Capps La BA13 . . . . .109 E7
Caprice Cl [1] SN5 . . . . .49 A7
Capulet Rd SP1 . . . . .145 F4
Caradon Wlk SN25 . . . . .34 C7
Caraway Dr SN4 . . . . .34 C4
Carders Cnr [7] BA14 . . . . . .105 D7
Cardigan Cl SN3 . . . . .50 E4
Cardigan Rd SN8 . . . . .213 C3
Cardwell Cl [1] SN3 . . . . . . .51 B7
Carey Cl SN5 . . . . .49 A5
Carfax Cl [1] SN1 . . . . .50 C6
Carfax St SN1 . . . . .50 C6
Cargill Pl SN16 . . . . .15 F8
Carisbrooke Cres BA14 . . . .101 E5
Carisbrook Rd SN12 . . . . . . .94 B2
Carisbrook Terr SN4 . . . . . . .65 C3
Carleton Pl SP4 . . . . .217 A4
Carlisle Ave SN3 . . . . .50 D3
Carlton Cl [2] SP4 . . . . .217 D3
Carlton Gate SN3 . . . . .50 F1
Carlton Row BA14 . . . . .105 C6
Carman Cl SN3 . . . . .36 B3
Carmelite Way SP1 . . . . . . .152 B7
Carmel Wlk SN3 . . . . .50 F5
Carnarvon Cl SN14 . . . . .78 A7
Carnation La SN12 . . . . .178 C8
Carnegie Rd SN11 . . . . .81 C4
Carpenter Cl [5] SN15 . . . . .78 F5
Carpenter Dr SP4 . . . . .217 D4
Carpenters Cl SN16 . . . . . . .25 D1
Carpenter's Cl SN11 . . . . . . .80 F1
Carpenters La
　[4] Bratton BA13 . . . . . . .186 B7
　Swindon SN2 . . . . .50 D8
Carp Cl SN11 . . . . .81 A5
Carrick Cl SN15 . . . . .79 A8
Carriers Cl SN16 . . . . .25 C1
Carrion Pond Dro SP2 . . . . .151 D7
Carroll Cl SN3 . . . . .51 D4
Carronbridge Rd SN5 . . . . . .49 B6
Carr St SN1 . . . . .50 B6
Carshalton Rd SN3 . . . . .51 B3
Carsons Yd BA12 . . . . .117 B6
Carstairs Ave SN3 . . . . .51 A3
Carter Cl SN25 . . . . .35 C6
Carter's Cl SP6 . . . . .211 C6
Cartway SN10 . . . . .180 E4
Cartwright Dr SN5 . . . . .49 B8
Carver Cl SN3 . . . . .36 C2
Carvers Hill SN8 . . . . .176 E1
Cary Glen SN15 . . . . .79 A4
Casley La BA11 . . . . .107 C7
Caspian Cl SN2 . . . . .34 C3
Caspian Gdns BA13 . . . . . . .108 F1
Cassini Dr [8] SN25 . . . . . . .34 B7
Casson Rd SN3 . . . . .36 A2
Castell Cl BA14 . . . . .106 B8
Casterbridge La [3] SP11 . .192 F1
Casterbridge Rd
　Swindon SN2 . . . . .34 D5
　[6] Swindon SN25 . . . . . . .34 C5
Casterley Camp★ SN9 . . . .189 D8
Castilian Mews SN5 . . . . . . .49 A7
Castle Barrow★ BA12 . . . .195 A7
CASTLE COMBE 68 A7
Castle Combe Motor Racing
　Circuit★ SN14 . . . . .68 C6
Castle Combe Motte &
　Baileys★ SN14 . . . . .67 F8
Castle Ct SP11 . . . . .192 A6
Castle Ditches Hill Fort★
　SP3 . . . . .204 A7
Castle Dore SN5 . . . . .49 A5
CASTLE EATON 10 B4
Castlefield Cl [3] SN5 . . . . . .49 C6
Castlefields SN11 . . . . .81 A3
Castlegate Bsns Pk SP4 . . .146 B7
Castle Grounds SN10 . . . . . .214 A3
Castlehaven Cl SN15 . . . . . .79 A5
Castle Hill Cl [9] SP7 . . . . . .202 B2
Castle Hill (Fort)★ SN26 . . .21 D3
Castle Hill La BA12 . . . . . . .139 A5
Castle Keep
　Salisbury SP1 . . . . .145 E4
　[4] Wilton SP2 . . . . .144 D3
Castle La
　Alderbury SP5 . . . . .153 E1
　Devizes SN10 . . . . .214 A3
　Wilton SP2 . . . . .144 D3
Castle Meadow SP5 . . . . . . .211 A8
Castle Pl Sh Ctr BA14 . . . . .105 D8
Castle Prim Sch SP11 . . . . .192 B5
Castle Rd
　Bratton BA13 . . . . .186 A6
　Devizes SN10 . . . . .214 A3
　[3] Great Bedwyn SN8 . . .176 B3
　Salisbury SP1 . . . . .146 A3
Castle St
　Aldbourne SN8 . . . . .170 A6
　Calne SN11 . . . . .81 B2

Castle St continued
　[8] Ludgershall SP11 . . . .192 A5
　Mere BA12 . . . . .138 C4
　Salisbury SP2 . . . . .146 A2
　Trowbridge BA14 . . . . . . .105 D8
Castleton Rd SN5 . . . . .49 A7
Castle View
　Westbury BA13 . . . . .109 B3
　West Tisbury SP3 . . . . . . .203 B8
Castle View Rd
　Chiseldown SN4 . . . . .65 E4
　Swindon SN3 . . . . .36 C1
Castle Well Dr SP4 . . . . .146 B8
Castle Well Mews SP4 . . . . .146 B8
Castle Wlk SN11 . . . . .81 A2
Castle Woods [2] SP5 . . . . .211 C7
Castley Rd SP4 . . . . .102 A2
Catalina Ct [17] SN12 . . . . .178 B8
CATCOMB 73 D6
Cathedral Ct SP1 . . . . .152 B8
Catherine Cres
　Dinton SP3 . . . . .201 E2
　Downton SP5 . . . . .210 F8
Catherine Ct SP1 . . . . .152 A8
Catherine Ford La
　Dinton SP3 . . . . .201 E1
　Fovant SP3 . . . . .204 E8
Catherine St
　Salisbury SP1 . . . . .152 B8
　[5] Swindon SN1 . . . . .50 B6
Catherine Way BA1 . . . . . . .82 A5
Catherine Wayte Cl SN25 . . .34 F4
Catherine Wayte Prim Sch
　SN25 . . . . .34 F5
Catmint Cl SN2 . . . . .34 D4
Cator Rd [3] SP4 . . . . .197 E7
Cats Hill La SP7 . . . . .203 A1
Catterick Cl [7] SN14 . . . . . .77 F6
Caulfield Rd SN2 . . . . .50 D8
Causeway Cl SN15 . . . . .78 E7
CAUSEWAY THE. 139 C4
Causeway The
　Brinkworth SN15 . . . . .45 D6
　Broad Chalke SP5 . . . . . . .205 B4
　Chippenham SN15 . . . . . . .78 E7
　The Common SP5 . . . . . . .149 C7
　[11] Tisbury SP3 . . . . .203 E8
Cavell Ct BA14 . . . . .105 C6
Cavendish Ct BA14 . . . . .104 F6
Cavendish Sq SN3 . . . . .51 A4
Caversham Cl SN3 . . . . .50 F5
Cavie Cl SN5 . . . . .49 A8
Cawte Mews SN3 . . . . .36 A4
Caxton Cl
　[1] Andover SP10 . . . . . . .193 C1
　[2] Swindon SN3 . . . . .50 F4
Caxton Rd BA11 . . . . .110 A3
Cayenne Pk SN2 . . . . .34 C4
Cecil Ave SP2 . . . . .152 A5
Cecil Rd SN3 . . . . .51 A6
Cecil Terr SP2 . . . . .145 D1
Cedar Cl
　Melksham SN12 . . . . .94 A3
　Salisbury SP2 . . . . .145 A3
　Worton SN10 . . . . .179 B4
Cedar Gr
　Chippenham SN15 . . . . . . .70 E1
　Trowbridge BA14 . . . . . . .105 B6
Cedars Cl SN2 . . . . .35 A2
Cedars The SN6 . . . . .28 F2
Celandine Way SN14 . . . . . .70 B2
Celsus Gr SN1 . . . . .50 A3
Cemetery La BA15 . . . . .100 F7
Central St SP11 . . . . .192 A5
Central Trad Est SN3 . . . . . .50 D3
Centre The SP4 . . . . .217 A4
Centurion Cl
　Chippenham SN15 . . . . . . .79 A5
　[1] Salisbury SP2 . . . . . . .145 D2
Centurion Way SN3 . . . . .51 C8
Centurion Wy BA12 . . . . . . .112 E1
CERNEY WICK 7 F5
Cerney Wick La GL7 . . . . . . .7 D5
Chaddenwick Hill SP4 . . . . .140 B7
Chadwick Cl [22] SN12 . . . .178 B8
Chaffeymoor Hill SP8 . . . . . .137 B1
Chaffinch Ave BA11 . . . . . . .110 B6
Chaffinch Dr [2] BA14 . . . . .105 B8
Chafyn Gr Sch SP1 . . . . .146 C2
Chain Dro
　South Newton SP3 . . . . . .130 B6
　Stapleford SP3 . . . . .129 F7
Chain Hill SP3 . . . . .129 E7
Chain La BA12 . . . . .117 C6
Chalcot La
　Chapmanslade BA13 . . . .111 F5
　Upton Scudamore BA13 . .112 A6
Chalfield Cres SN12 . . . . . . .94 C5
Chalfont Cl BA14 . . . . .105 A8
CHALFORD 113 A8
Chalford Ave SN3 . . . . .51 B7
Chalgrove Field SN5 . . . . . . .49 A3
Chalkcroft La SP11 . . . . . . .193 A2
Chalk Down SP9 . . . . .216 E5
Chalk Hill [3] SP3 . . . . .196 F6
Chalk Pyt Rd SP5 . . . . .205 B4
Chalk's Cl SP5 . . . . .211 C8
Challis Ct [5] SP11 . . . . .192 B5
Challows La SN14 . . . . .76 D8
Chalvedon Gn SN3 . . . . .51 A5
Chamberlain Rd
　Chippenham Without SN14 .77 F7
　Swindon SN3 . . . . .36 A2
Chambers Ave SP4 . . . . .217 C2
Chambon Cl SN16 . . . . .17 A2
Champneys Rd [6] BA11 . . . .110 A7
Chancellor Cl SN5 . . . . .48 F6
Chancel Way GL7 . . . . .2 C4

Bur–Cha 223

Chancery Cl [1] SP2 . . . . . . .145 E2
Chancery La BA12 . . . . .117 C6
Chandler Cl SN3 . . . . .50 D5
Chandlers Cl SN10 . . . . .180 F8
Chandlers Ct SP9 . . . . .216 C7
Chandlers La
　All Cannings SN10 . . . . . . .180 F8
　Bishops Cannings SN10 . . .172 B2
Chandler's La [1] SN8 . . . . .170 A7
Chandler Way [3] SN15 . . . . .78 F4
Chandos Cl SN5 . . . . .49 A6
Chanterelle Pk BA15 . . . . . .100 D5
Chantry Ct BA14 . . . . .104 F3
Chantry Gdns BA14 . . . . . . .104 F3
Chantry La
　Chute SP11 . . . . .184 C2
　Marlborough SN8 . . . . . . .213 D2
　Westbury BA13 . . . . .109 A3
Chantry Mead [13] RG17 . . .177 B7
Chantry Mews BA12 . . . . . . .117 A7
Chantry Rd
　Swindon SN2 . . . . .34 F2
　Wilton SP2 . . . . .144 C1
Chantry The★ BA12 . . . . . .139 A5
Chants La [6] SP3 . . . . .196 E6
CHAPEL BARTON 115 D6
Chapel Cl
　Kempsford GL7 . . . . .10 D6
　Southwick BA14 . . . . .104 F3
Chapel Cnr SN14 . . . . .41 F1
Chapel Ct [17] RG17 . . . . . .177 B7
Chapel Hill
　Broad Blunsdon SN26 . . . .21 B2
　Grimstead SP5 . . . . .154 B2
　Lacock SN15 . . . . .86 C6
CHAPEL KNAPP 85 D5
Chapel La
　Acton Turville GL9 . . . . . . .53 A6
　Andover SP11 . . . . .193 C2
　Bishopstone SP5 . . . . .205 E4
　Box SN13 . . . . .83 D5
　Broad Town SN4 . . . . .167 B8
　Chippenham SN15 . . . . . . .78 E7
　Collingbourne Kingston
　SN8 . . . . .183 D2
　Corsham SN13 . . . . .84 E4
　Downton SP5 . . . . .159 B5
　Hankerton SN16 . . . . .15 C2
　[12] Lambourn RG17 . . . .165 A2
　[5] Ludgershall SP11 . . . .192 A5
　Melksham Without SN12 . .86 A1
　Minety SN16 . . . . .17 A2
　Nomansland SP5 . . . . .212 C4
　Pen Selwood BA9 . . . . . . .137 C3
　[8] Ramsbury SN8 . . . . . .170 B2
　Redlynch SP5 . . . . .211 D7
　[1] Shrewton SP3 . . . . . . .196 E6
　South Marston SN3 . . . . . .36 E5
　Stapleford SP3 . . . . .129 E7
　Upavon SN9 . . . . .181 F2
　[5] Wanborough SN4 . . . .163 B6
　Wingfield BA14 . . . . .104 C6
　Woodborough SN9 . . . . . .181 D7
　Zennor BA12 . . . . .137 E5
Chapel Mews SN15 . . . . .78 E7
Chapel Orch [6] SN4 . . . . . .163 B6
Chapel Path SN14 . . . . .75 B3
Chapel Pl [1] SP2 . . . . .146 A1
CHAPEL PLAISTER 84 C4
Chapel Rd
　[2] Ashbury SN6 . . . . .164 A8
　Heytesbury BA12 . . . . . . .194 C5
　Kempsford GL7 . . . . .10 D7
Chapel Rise SN12 . . . . .92 E8
Chapel Row BA1 . . . . .82 C2
Chapel St
　Horningsham BA12 . . . . . .119 A7
　Swindon SN2 . . . . .50 D8
　Warminster BA12 . . . . . . .116 F5
Chapel Wlk GL9 . . . . .24 B3
Chaplins Pl [3] SP4 . . . . .217 B3
CHAPMANSLADE 111 C4
Chapmanslade CE Prim Sch
　BA13 . . . . .111 C4
Charcoal Burners Rd
　SN8 . . . . .175 B4
Charcroft Hill BA10 . . . . . . .122 A5
Charfield Cl SN3 . . . . .51 A4
Charlbury Cl SN25 . . . . .34 E3
CHARLCUTT 72 F4
Charles Garrett Cl [39]
　SP7 . . . . .202 C2
Charles McPherson Gdns
　SN3 . . . . .51 C5
Charles Morrison Cl
　SN10 . . . . .214 A3
Charles Rd SP4 . . . . .198 B7
Charles St
　Corsham SN13 . . . . .76 F2
　[2] Salisbury SP2 . . . . . . .145 F1
　Trowbridge BA14 . . . . . . .101 C1
Charles Vesey Rd SP9 . . . . .216 C7
Charlham La GL7 . . . . .8 D7
Charlieu Ave SN11 . . . . .89 C8
Charlock Path SN25 . . . . .34 E5
Charlotte Ct BA14 . . . . .101 D1
Charlotte Mews SN3 . . . . . . .50 D4
Charlotte Sq BA14 . . . . .101 D1
Charlotte St BA14 . . . . .101 D1
CHARLTON
　Andover 193 C2
　Donhead St Mary 203 A1
　Malmesbury 29 A6
　Pewsey 181 D3

CHARLTON-ALL-SAINTS...........159 A4
Charlton Cl SN2.............35 D5
Charlton Dro SN9.........181 D2
CHARLTON HEATH.........29 D6
Charlton Hill BA13.......186 D8
Charlton La SP7...........202 F1
CHARLTON MUSGROVE....136 B4
Charlton Pl★ SN16........28 E7
Charlton Rd SN16..........28 E5
Charlwood Rd SN15........84 F8
Charminster Cl SN3.......51 C6
CHARNAGE.................139 E4
Charnham La RG17.........177 B8
Charnham Pk RG17.........177 B8
Charnham Pk Ind Est
  RG17....................177 B8
Charnwood Dr 9 SP6.....210 D2
Charnwood Rd
  Salisbury SP2...........145 E1
  Trowbridge BA14........101 A1
Charter Cl 3 SN10.......214 D5
Charterhouse Dr 4
  BA11....................110 C7
Charterhouse Rd
  Wroughton SN4...........63 F6
  5 Wroughton SN4.........64 A6
Charter Prim Sch SN15...78 F6
Charter Rd SN15...........78 D7
Chartley Gn 1 SN5.........49 A5
Chartwell Pl SP3.........196 E6
Chartwell Rd SN25........34 F7
Chase Cres SP5...........207 E4
Chase Wood SN5...........34 A2
Chastleton Rd SN25.......34 F7
Chatham Cl SP1...........145 F4
Chatham Ct BA12..........117 B7
Chatsworth Rd SN25.......34 F5
Chaucer Ave 5 SP10......193 C1
Chaucer Cl SN1...........47 E3
Chaveywell Ct SN11........81 B2
Cheapside BA12...........195 A2
Cheater's La SP6.........210 A1
Cheddar Cl BA11..........110 C7
Cheddar Rd SN25..........34 E3
CHEDGLOW..................14 C7
Chedworth Gate SN3.......50 F1
Cheese Mkt 6 SP1........146 A1
Cheese Wharf★ SN7........2 F1
Chelmsford Rd SN5........49 C7
Cheltenham Rd SN14.......78 A5
Cheltenham St SN1........50 B7
Chelwood Cl SN14.........78 B6
CHELWORTH..................4 C1
Chelworth House SN5......4 B1
Chelworth Ind Est SN6...19 A5
CHELWORTH LOWER
  GREEN....................19 A5
Chelworth Rd SN6.........19 B6
CHELWORTH UPPER
  GREEN....................19 A6
Chemical Rd BA13........108 C6
CHENEY MANOR.............34 F1
Cheney Manor Ind Est
  SN2......................34 E1
Cheney Manor Rd SN2.....34 F2
Chepston Pl BA14........100 F1
Chepstow Cl
  4 Chippenham SN14......78 A5
  Swindon SN5.............49 C3
Cheraton Cl SN3..........51 B7
Cherbury Wlk SN3.........51 A6
CHERHILL.................166 B1
Cherhill CE Sch SN11....166 B1
Cherhill Ct SN25.........34 E3
Cherhill White Horse★
  SN11....................172 C8
Cherrington Field SN10..180 F4
Cherry Cl
  Pewsey SN9.............215 D5
  Salisbury SP2..........145 D1
Cherry Gdns BA14........102 A3
Cherry Gdns Ct SN15.....105 D7
Cherry Gr 7 RG17........177 B7
Cherry Orch
  Codford St Peter BA12..195 A2
  Highworth SN6...........23 A5
  Marlborough SN8........213 E2
Cherry Orch E SN2........35 E2
Cherry Orch La
  Cann SP7...............202 A1
  Luckington SN14.........39 C5
  Salisbury SP2..........145 D1
Cherry Orch N SN2........35 E2
Cherry Orch W SN2........35 D2
Cherry Rd SN14...........75 A5
Cherry Tree Ave SP9.....216 C2
Cherry Tree Ct SN11......81 B4
Cherry Tree Gr SN2.......35 C2
Cherry Tree Rd SN6......119 B8
Cherry Tree Way 2 SP4..217 C3
Chervil Cl 3 SN2.........34 C4
Chesford Cl SN3..........51 A3
Cheshire Cl
  2 Bower Hill SN12.....178 B8
  Salisbury SP2..........145 C4
Chesterfield Cl
  3 Amesbury SP4.........217 E3
  4 Swindon SN5..........49 C6
Chester St SN1...........50 B6
Chesters The SN5.........49 C6
Chester Way SN14.........78 A5
Chestnut Ave
  Netheravon SP4.........190 A4
  Swindon SN2.............35 C3

Chestnut Ave continued
  Tidworth SP9...........216 D7
Chestnut Cl
  Acton Turville GL9.......53 A6
  Down Ampney GL7.........8 D7
  Frome BA11.............110 B7
  Rowde SN10..............96 D2
  Salisbury SP1..........146 D3
Chestnut Cnr 13 BA13....186 B7
Chestnut Dr SN10........178 E5
Chestnut Gr
  Trowbridge BA14........105 B5
  Westwood BA15..........99 F4
Chestnut Grange SN13....76 D1
Chestnut La RG17........165 C2
Chestnut Mews SN12......94 A3
Chestnut Rd
  Chippenham SN14.........78 B8
  Sutton Benger SN15.....57 D2
Chestnut Springs SN5.....33 D1
Chestnut Wlk 11 RG17....177 B6
Chetcombe Rd BA12......139 B6
Chevalier Cl 19 SN5.....48 F8
Cheverell Ave SP1.......146 C3
Cheverell Cl BA14.......105 D5
Cheverell Gn Rd SN10...179 C2
Cheverell Rd
  Cheverell Parva SN10..179 C1
  West Lavington SN10...187 D8
Cheviot Cl
  Swindon SN5.............49 A6
  Trowbridge BA14........105 E7
Cheviot Rd 25 SP11......193 F2
Chevral Cl SN14..........70 B2
Cheyney Wlk BA13........109 B4
Chichester Cl SP2.......152 B6
Chichester Pk BA13......109 A4
Chickerell Rd SN3........51 A6
CHICKLADE...............200 A5
CHICKSGROVE.............204 B8
Chicksgrove Rd SP3......203 F8
Chick's La SN8...........183 E1
Chicory Cl SN2...........34 C3
Chiffchaff Cl GL7.........7 A6
Child St 1 RG17.........165 A1
CHILMARK................201 B3
Chilmark & Fonthill Bishop
  CE Aided Prim Sch
  SP3....................201 B3
Chilmark Rd
  Tisbury SP3............200 F1
  Trowbridge BA14........101 A1
Chiltern Cl
  Melksham SN12...........94 C4
  9 Warminster BA12......117 A8
CHILTON FOLIAT..........170 F1
Chilton Foliat CE Prim Sch
  RG17....................171 A2
Chilton Gdns SN25........34 F3
Chilton Way RG17........177 B7
Chilvester Hill SN11.....80 E2
Chilworth Cl
  Swindon SN25............34 E6
  5 Swindon SN25.........34 E6
Chine Rd SP4............131 C7
CHIPPENHAM...............78 E7
Chippenham Com Hospl
  SN15....................78 C6
Chippenham La SN14......77 B7
Chippenham Mus & Heritage
  Ctr★ SN15...............78 E7
Chippenham Rd
  Lyneham & Bradenstoke
  SN15....................59 E3
  Marshfield SN14.........74 A8
Chippenham Sta SN15.....78 E8
Chipper La SP1..........146 A1
CHIRTON.................180 F4
Chirton CE Prim Sch
  SN10....................180 F4
Chirton Pl 5 BA14......105 D6
CHISBURY................176 B5
Chisbury Camp★ SN8.....176 C4
Chisbury La SN8.........176 C5
Chiselbury Gr SP2.......152 A6
CHISELDON................65 D3
Chiseldon Ct SN4.........65 D4
Chiseldon Prim Sch SN4..65 D4
Chitham Cl SN10.........187 C8
CHITTERNE...............195 C7
Chitterne Rd
  Codford BA12...........195 B3
  Shrewton SP3...........196 B6
CHITTOE...................87 E2
Chittoe Heath SN15.......88 A2
Chivers Rd
  Chippenham SN15........78 C8
  Devizes SN10...........214 D3
Chives Way SN2...........34 D4
Chobham Cl SN2...........36 A5
CHOLDERTON..............199 C5
Cholderton Rare Breeds
  Farm★ SP4..............199 A5
Cholderton Rd
  Amport SP4.............199 D5
  Quarley SP4............199 F5
Chopping Knife La SN8...175 A7
Choristers Sq 1 SP1.....152 A8
Choulston Cl SP4........190 B3
Christchurch CE Prim Sch
  BA15....................100 C8
Christchurch Rd BA15...100 D8
Christchurch Terr BA12..116 F5
CHRISTIAN MALFORD......58 B2
Christian Malford CE Prim
  Sch SN15................58 A2
Christie Cl SN3..........51 D4
Christie Miller Rd SP2..145 E2

Christie Miller Sports Ctr
  SN12....................94 B1
Christin Ct SP4.........105 A8
Christopher Cl 2 SP2...151 F5
Christopher Dr SN15......79 A4
Christ the King RC Prim Sch
  SP4....................217 B3
Christy's Gdns 30 SP7..202 C2
Christy's La 23 SP7.....202 C2
Chubb Cl SN16............28 A5
Chudleigh SN5............49 B4
Church Acre
  Bradford-on-Avon BA15..100 C7
  Codford BA12...........195 A3
  Seagry BA15.............57 F6
Church Bottom SP4......131 A5
Church Cl
  Bath BA1................82 B2
  Bourton SP8............137 D1
  13 Lambourn RG17......165 A2
  Church End Cl SN15......60 A2
Church Farm SN14.........68 F5
Church Farm La
  South Marston SN3.......36 E4
  Woodborough SN9........181 D7
Church Farm Mews SN15..60 A2
Churchfield SN25.........34 F4
CHURCHFIELDS...........145 D1
Churchfields BA15........91 E6
Church Fields BA14......105 A5
Churchfields Academy
  SN3.....................50 F5
Churchfields Ind Est SP2 145 E1
Churchfields Rd SP2.....145 E1
Churchfields, the Village
  School SN12.............92 E8
Church Furlong SP3......129 E2
Church Ground SN3.......36 F4
Church Hatch 1 SP5.....211 B8
Church Hill
  Bromham SN15...........95 F7
  Donhead St Mary SP7...203 A3
  Limpley Stoke BA2.......99 B5
  Nettleton SN14..........53 B3
  Redlynch SP5...........211 D7
  Shaftesbury SP7........202 B2
  West Overton SN8.......173 F7
  Wroughton SN4...........63 F5
Church Hill Rise SN15....96 A7
Churchill Ave
  Broad Blunsdon SN26....21 C2
  Durrington/Bulford SP4.217 D8
  Melksham SN12...........94 D5
Churchill Cl
  Calne SN11..............81 C1
  North Tidworth SP9.....216 B8
  3 Royal Wootton Bassett
  SN4.....................47 F3
  9 Tisbury SP3..........203 E8
Churchill Ct SP2........144 D3
Churchill Est SP3.......203 E8
Churchill Way SN13.......76 F3
Churchill Way E SP1.....146 B1
Churchill Way N SP1.....146 A2
Churchill Way S SP1.....152 B7
Churchill Way W
  Charlton SP10..........193 C1
  Salisbury SP2..........146 A1
Church La
  Amesbury SP4...........217 A3
  Ashbury SN6............164 A7
  Ashton Keynes SN6........6 E1
  Bishopstone SN6........163 E6
  Bishopstone SP5........150 A1
  Box SN13................83 C5
  16 Bratton BA13........186 B7
  Britford SP5...........152 E5
  Brokenborough SN16.....27 D7
  Buttermere SN8.........185 C7
  Codford St Peter BA12..195 B2
  5 Cricklade SN6........19 D8
  Damerham SP6...........209 F2
  Dauntsey SN15...........44 E1
  Downton SP5............159 A5
  Durrington/Bulford SP4.217 D8
  East Kennet SN8........173 D6
  Fovant SP3.............204 D8
  Great Somerton SN15....44 E1
  Hankerton SN16..........15 C2
  Hawkesbury SN14.........38 E5
  32 Hungerford RG17....177 B7
  Kington Langley SN15....70 E6
  Limpley Stoke BA2.......99 A5
  6 Ludgershall SP11....192 A5
  Lyneham SN15...........60 A2
  Marshfield SN14.........74 A8
  Melchet Park & Plaitford
  SO51...................212 E7
  Melksham SN12...........94 C6
  Mildenhall SN8.........175 A8
  Norton SN16.............41 D5
  Ogbourne St Andrew SN8.168 E3
  Pitton & Farley SP5....148 C4
  Rushall SN9............181 E2
  Salisbury SP2..........145 C2
  2 Shaftesbury SP7.....202 C1
  Sherfield English SO51.162 F3
  Sherrington BA12.......194 F2
  Sopworth SN14..........24 D1
  South Cerney GL7........6 F7
  Stanton St Quintin SN14.56 B5
  Stanton St Quintin SN14.56 C6
  Tidworth SP9...........216 D4
  Trowbridge BA14........105 A5
  Vernhams Dean SP11....185 B4
  Westbury BA13..........108 E1
  West Lavington SN10...187 E8

Church La continued
  Wingfield BA14.........104 C6
  Churchlands SP5........105 D2
  Church Leat SP5........211 A8
  Church Mdws 1 SP9.....199 D8
  Church Piece SN15......57 D2
  Church Pk SN15..........59 C3
Church Pl
  Lydiard Millicent SN5...33 C1
  Swindon SN1.............50 A6
Church Rails SP3........141 B1
Church Rd
  Biddestone SN14.........76 E7
  Bratton BA13...........186 B6
  Calne Without SN11......80 A2
  Cheverell Magna SN10..179 B1
  Christian Malford SN15..58 A2
  Derry Hill/Studley SN11.79 F2
  Froxfield SN8..........176 D7
  Ham SN8................177 A1
  Heddington SN13.........89 B1
  Hilmarton SN11.........73 F3
  Idmiston SP4...........133 F8
  Kemble GL7..............4 F7
  Kilmington BA12........123 E5
  Kington Langley SN15....70 E6
  Liddington SN4.........163 A4
  Luckington SN14.........39 E4
  Milston SP4............198 C8
  Norleaze BA13..........108 F8
  Pitton & Farley SP5....154 E7
  Salisbury SP1..........146 E3
  Sherston GL8............25 B5
  Silton SP8.............138 A1
  Stanton St Bernard SN8.173 B1
  Stanton St Quintin SN14.56 B5
  St Paul Malmesbury Without
  SN16....................43 A3
  2 Swindon SN1..........50 D4
  Wanborough SN4.........163 A5
  Woodborough SN9........181 D7
Church Ri SN14...........53 B3
Church Ride SP11........192 A6
Church Rise SN13.........84 E5
Church Row SN14.........163 D6
Church St Cl 15 SP3....203 E8
Church St
  Amesbury SP4...........217 A3
  Atworth SN12............92 D8
  Bath BA1................82 B2
  Berwick St John SP7...203 E1
  Bower Chalke SP5.......205 A2
  Bradford-on-Avon BA15..100 C6
  Calne SN11..............81 B2
  Chiseldown SN4..........65 D4
  Collingbourne Ducis SN8.191 E8
  Corsham SN13............77 A2
  Durrington/Bulford SP4.198 B7
  Great Bedwyn SN8.......176 B2
  Grimstead SP5..........154 C2
  Horningsham BA12.......119 B7
  Hungerford RG17.......177 B7
  Keevil BA14............178 A4
  Lacock SN15............86 D6
  Little Bedwyn SN8......176 D5
  Longbridge Deverill BA12.120 F7
  Maiden Bradley with Yarnfield
  BA12...................118 E2
  Market Lavington SN10..179 C1
  Melksham SN12...........94 A4
  Mere BA12..............139 A5
  Pewsey SN9.............215 D4
  Purton SN5..............33 C4
  Royal Wootton Bassett SN4.47 C2
  Semington BA14.........102 F6
  Sherston SN16...........25 C1
  Southwick BA14.........104 F3
  Swindon SN3.............36 B3
  Tisbury SP3............203 E8
  Trowbridge BA14........101 D1
  Warminster BA12.......116 F7
  Westbury BA13..........109 A3
  West Lavington SN10...187 E7
  Winterbourne Stoke SP3.196 F3
  Wylye BA12.............201 E8
Church Tk SP8...........137 D1
Church View
  Castle Eaton SN6........10 B4
  Chippenham SN14.........70 C2
Churchward Ave SN2.......35 A1
Churchward Dr BA11......110 C7
Churchway SN26...........21 C2
Church Way
  Hungerford RG17.......177 B7
  7 Swindon SN3..........36 B3
Church Wlk
  Ashton Keynes SN6.......6 E1
  Avebury SN8............173 B8
  Bishopstone SN6........163 E6
  Devizes SN10...........214 C3
  Melksham SN12...........94 A4
  Motcombe SP7..........202 A4
  Redlynch SP5...........211 E2
  Swindon SN2.............35 E3
Church Wlk N SN25........34 F3
Church Wlk S SN2.........34 F3
Churn Cl GL7.............6 F7
Chur St SP4.............198 E6
CHUTE CADLEY...........192 E8
Chute Cswy SP11........184 E2
CHUTE STANDEN..........192 F8
Circle The SN2...........35 C2
Cirencester Rd
  Fairford GL7............1 F6
  Latton SN7..............7 E8
Cirencester Way SN2.....50 D8
City Cnr SN4............163 C6
City The SN12............94 A5

Clack La SP6............210 B3
Clanfield Rd SN3.........51 B5
Clanger La BA13.........109 A8
CLANVILLE
  Penton Grafton.........193 A4
  Stanton St Quintin......56 E4
Clapham Cl 6 SN25.......34 E3
Clap La SP5.............207 B4
Clardon La SN5...........33 C6
Clarence Cl 18 SP11....192 A5
Clarence Rd
  Chippenham SN14........77 F7
  Trowbridge BA14........105 F8
Clarence St SN1.........50 C6
Clarendon Acad The
  BA14....................105 C6
Clarendon Ave BA14.....105 E8
Clarendon Cl SP3.......201 F2
Clarendon Ct
  Marlborough SN8.......213 D3
  Tidworth SP9...........216 D7
Clarendon Dr SN4........47 E1
Clarendon Infs Sch SP9.216 D6
Clarendon Pal★ SP5.....147 C1
Clarendon Rd
  Alderbury SP5..........153 D3
  Clarendon Park SP5....152 F6
  Grimstead SP5.........154 A4
  Salisbury SP1..........146 C1
  Trowbridge BA14........105 E8
Clare Wlk SN5............49 B4
Claridge Cl 3 SN8......170 A6
Clark Ave SN11...........81 C5
Clarke Dr SN5............49 B8
Clarke's La SP11........193 A7
Clarkes Leaze SN14......68 F6
Clark's Gdns 25 RG17...177 B7
Clark's Pl 3 BA14......105 E8
Clary Rd SN2.............34 D5
Classics The 16 RG17...165 A1
CLATFORD................174 B7
Clattinger Farm Nature
  Reserve★ SN16..........16 E7
Claudius Cl 15 SP10....193 E2
CLAVERTON................90 B5
Claverton Hill BA2.......90 A4
Claverton Pumping Sta★
  BA1.....................90 C5
Clay Cl BA13............112 C8
Claydon Rd 6 SN25.......34 E7
Clayfurlong Gr GL7.......4 F8
Clayhill Copse SN5.......34 A2
Clays Cl SN2.............35 E3
Clay St
  Little Somerford SN15...44 C6
  Longbridge Deverill BA12.116 E1
  Whiteparish SP5.......161 C2
Clays The SN10..........179 F1
Clay The SN10...........180 A1
Clayton Rd SP4..........217 B3
Clearbury Ring★ SP5....158 C5
Clearbury Vw 7 SP5.....210 F8
CLEARWOOD...............111 F8
Clearwood BA13..........111 F8
Clearwood View BA13....111 D4
Cleasby Cl SN5...........49 C6
Cleavers The 1 SN8....183 D8
Cleaves Ave SN14.........75 A3
Cleevedale Rd SN13.......85 A8
Cleeve Lawns SN3.........50 F3
Cleeves Cl SN5...........49 A6
Cleeves The SP3.........143 B3
Cleeve The
  Corsham SN13............85 A8
  West Knoyle BA12.......140 A6
Clementine Rd 4 SN25...34 B7
Clement's La BA12.......139 B4
CLENCH.................174 E1
CLENCH COMMON.........174 D1
CLEVANCY...............166 C6
Clevedon Cl SN3.........51 A6
Cleveland Gdns BA14....101 E2
Cleveland Rd SN2.........34 C3
Cleveland Way BA13.....108 E2
CLEVERTON................44 D8
Cleverton Ct SN2........35 C5
Cleves Cl SN5............49 A6
Cleyhill Gdns BA13.....111 D5
Cley Hill (Hill Fort)★
  BA12...................116 A6
Cley View 5 BA12........116 E6
Cliffe Dr BA2............99 A6
Cliffords SN6............19 C8
Cliff Rd SN16............40 C8
Clift Ave SN15...........70 E1
Clift Cl SN13............84 A8
Clifton Cl SN14..........78 B8
Clifton Rd SP2..........145 F2
Clifton St SN1...........50 B5
Clifts Bldgs BA11.......110 A4
Clink Farm Ct 6 BA11...110 C6
Clink Rd BA11...........110 E6
Clinton Cl SN5...........48 F4
Clipsham Rise BA14......101 A1
Clive Parade SN2.........35 D3
Clivey BA13.............107 E1
CLOATLEY.................15 E2
Cloatley Cres SN4........61 E8
CLOATLEY END.............16 B1
Cloatley Manor★ SN16...15 D2
Cloatley Mdws Nature
  Reserve★ SN16.........15 E3
Cloatley Rd SN16........15 C2
Cloche Way SN2..........35 E3
Clock Tower Vw SN12.....92 E8
Cloford Cl BA14........101 A1
Cloister Gdn★ SN16.....28 A3
Close End 8 RG17.......165 A1

Close La
Marston SN10 . . . . .179 A3
Rowde SN10 . . . . .96 D2
Close The
Bulkington SN10 . . . . . . .178 E5
Chippenham SN14. . . . . .77 E8
Corsham SN13. . . . . . . .85 C6
Kington St Michael SN14. . .70 A8
Laverstock SP4 . . . . . . 146 D8
Lechlade GL7. . . . . .2 C5
Lydiard Millicent SN5. . . . .48 D8
Melksham SN12. . . . . . . .94 B3
4 Redlynch SP5. . . . . . .211 C6
Salisbury SP1. . . . . . . .152 A8
Tangley SP11. . . . . .193 C5
Warminster BA12 . . . . . .117 A4
Clothier Leaze 2 BA14. . .105 D7
Cloth Yd 1 BA14. . . . . .105 E7
Cloudberry Rd SN25 . . . . .34 E5
Clough La SP5. . . . . . . .149 B7
Clouts Wood SN5. . . . . . .34 A2
Clouts Wood Nature
Reserve* SN4. . . . . . . .63 F4
Clover Cl SN12. . . . . . . .94 C3
Clover Dean SN14 . . . . . .78 A6
Clover Gdns 23 SP11. . . .192 A5
Clover La SP4 . . . . .198 B7
Cloverlands SN25. . . . . . .34 D4
Clover Pk SN2 . . . . .34 D4
Club La SP9. . . . . .216 C4
Club Rd 1 SP4 . . . . . . .198 F7
Clump Way SP4. . . . . . .217 A5
Clydesdale Cl
5 Swindon SN5. . . . . . .49 A4
Trowbridge BA14. . . . . .105 C5
Clydesdale Rd SN13. . . . . .83 D5
CLYFFE PYPARD. 166 A3
Coach Barton BA14 . . . . .178 A3
Coach Hill SP11. . . . . . .192 E6
Coach Ho Mews SP4. . . . .217 B3
Coach Rd
Bradford-on-Avon BA15 . .100 C6
Westbury BA13. . . . . . .109 B5
Coalpit Rd BA1. . . . . . . .82 A4
Coalway La BA11. . . . . . .110 C7
COATE
Bishops Cannings. 180 C8
Chiseldon. 51 C2
Coate La SN10. . . . . . . .214 E5
Coate Rd SN8. . . . . . . .173 B1
Coate Wr Ctry Pk* SN3.. .51 A1
Coate Wr Nature Reserve*
SN3. . . . . .51 B1
Coatside Wy SN3 . . . . . . .51 D1
Cobb Dr 16 SP11. . . . . .193 F2
Cobbett Cl SN25. . . . . . .35 A7
Cobbett Pl BA12. . . . . . .116 F6
Cobden Rd SN2. . . . . . . .50 A8
COBLEY. 208 D7
Cobley Cl SP5. . . . . . . .208 F1
Cob Pl BA13. . . . . .108 F1
Coburg Sq 1 SN12. . . . . .94 B4
Cock-a-Troop La SN8 . . . .175 B8
Cock Hill BA14. . . . . . . .101 A1
Cocklebury La SN15. . . . . .70 F1
Cocklebury Rd SN15. . . . . .78 E8
Cock Rd
Horningsham BA12. . . . .118 F8
Rowde SN10. . . . . .95 F2
Cocks Cl 5 SP4 . . . . . . .197 E7
Codford Circ or Wilsbury
Ring* BA12. . . . . .195 C3
Codford Rd BA12 . . . . . .195 C6
Codford Rising Sun (Hill
Figure)* BA12. . . . . . .195 C2
CODFORD ST MARY. 195 B2
CODFORD ST PETER. 195 A3
Coffin Cl SN6. . . . . .23 A6
Coker's La BA12. . . . . . .123 F7
Colbert Pk SN25 . . . . . . .34 F6
Colborne Cl SN15. . . . . . .79 B5
Colbourne St SN1. . . . . . .50 D7
Colchester Cl SN5 . . . . . .49 D4
COLD HARBOUR
Great Hinton 102 F2
Warminster. 116 F8
Cold Harbour SP4 . . . . . .217 B3
Coldharbour La SP2. . . . .145 F2
Cold Harbour La SN8 . . . .213 E4
Coldharbour Rd RG17. . . .177 B6
Colebrook Inf Acad SN3 . .51 C8
Colebrook Rd SN3. . . . . . .36 B1
Cole Cl
2 Andover SP10. . . . . . .193 E2
Swindon SN3. . . . . .51 D6
Coleridge Cl
Royal Wootton Bassett
SN4. . . . . .47 E3
Warminster BA12 . . . . . .116 D6
Coleridge Rd SN25. . . . . .34 F6
COLERNE. 75 B3
Colerne Airfield SN14. . . . .74 E3
Colerne CE Prim Sch
SN14. . . . . .75 B3
Colerne Industrial Pk
SN14. . . . . .75 A3
Colerne Pk* SN14. . . . . .75 F6
Coles Cres SP7 . . . . . . .202 D1
Cole's La SP7. . . . . .202 A1
Coles's La SP5. . . . . . . .212 A7
Collard Cl SN1. . . . . .50 B2
College Cl SN15 . . . . .78 F8
College Farm La 5 SN6. .164 A8
College Fields SN8. . . . . .213 C2
College Gdns BA14 . . . . .105 D3
College Gr 1 SN4. . . . . .163 A6

College Rd
1 Durrington/Bulford
SP4. . . . . .198 B7
Purton SN5 . . . . .33 C4
Trowbridge BA14. . . . . .105 B6
College St
Salisbury SP1 . . . . .146 B1
Swindon SN1 . . . . .50 C6
College Way 4 RG17. . . .171 E7
Collen Cl 1 SN14. . . . . . .78 A7
Collett Ave SN2. . . . . . . .35 A1
Collett Pl SN6 . . . . .8 C3
Collett Way BA11. . . . . . .110 C7
Collingbourne CE Prim Sch
SN8. . . . . .191 E8
Collingbourne Cl 2
SN8. . . . . .105 D5
COLLINGBOURNE
DUCIS. 191 E8
COLLINGBOURNE
KINGSTON. 183 D2
Collingsmead SN3 . . . . . .51 C5
Collingwood Wlk 4
SP10 . . . . .193 F1
Collins Cl 15 SP10. . . . . .193 D2
Collins Ct SP9 . . . . .216 C8
Collins La SN5. . . . . .33 E5
Colman Pk SN25 . . . . . . .35 A6
Coln Cres SN25 . . . . .35 A4
Coln House Sch GL7 . . . . .1 F6
Colquhoun Rd 2 SP4. . . .198 A6
Colston Cl SN3 . . . . .51 A4
Colston Rd SN10. . . . . . .214 A4
Coltsfoot Cl SP4. . . . . . .217 C3
Column Ride SN8 . . . . . .175 E3
COMBE. 185 F8
Combe La
Bratton BA13. . . . . .186 B3
Hilmarton SN11. . . . . . . .73 F6
Combe View
10 Hungerford RG17. . . .177 B6
Yatton Keynell SN14. . . . .68 F5
Combe Wlk SN10 . . . . . .214 D5
Comet Ave SN9. . . . . . . .182 B2
Comet Cl SN15 . . . . .60 B2
Comfrey Cl
Swindon SN2 . . . . .34 D4
Trowbridge BA14. . . . . .105 E6
Commerce Bsns Ctr
BA13. . . . . .108 E7
Commerce Park BA11 . . . .110 D8
Commercial Rd
Devizes SN10 . . . . .214 A4
Swindon SN1. . . . . .50 B5
Common Dro DT11. . . . . .207 B3
Common Hill
Cricklade SN6. . . . . .19 B7
Great Hinton BA14 . . . . .102 F2
Steeple Ashton BA14 . . . .106 F8
COMMON PLATT. 33 F2
Common Platt SN5 . . . . . .34 A2
Common Rd
Sixpenny Handley SP5. . . .207 F4
St Paul Malmesbury Without
SN16. . . . . .27 D1
Whiteparish SP5 . . . . . . .161 E1
Common Slip SN15 . . . . . .78 E7
COMMON THE
Brinkworth. 46 B7
Broughton Gifford. 93 B5
Winterslow 149 C6
Common The
Bromham SN15. . . . . . . .95 E6
Holt BA14. . . . . .92 F1
Kington Langley SN15. . . . .70 E6
Marlborough SN8 . . . . . .213 D4
Minety SN16. . . . . .17 C1
Shrewton SP3 . . . . .196 E6
The Common SP5 . . . . . .149 D6
Commonweal Rd SN1. . . . .50 B3
Commonweal Sch The
SN1. . . . . .50 B3
Commonwood La SN16. . . .40 D5
COMPTON. 189 F7
COMPTON ABBAS. 206 A5
Compton Abbas Airfield
SP5. . . . . .206 C5
COMPTON BASSETT. 166 B3
COMPTON
CHAMBERLAYNE. 205 A8
Compton Cl
4 Swindon SN3. . . . . . . .51 C4
Trowbridge BA14. . . . . .101 E4
Compton Gdns BA11. . . . .110 C7
Compton Pk* SP3. . . . . .142 C3
Compton Rd
Hilmarton SN11. . . . . . . .73 F3
Tidworth SP9. . . . . .216 D6
Compton's Dr SO51. . . . .212 F1
Conan Doyle Wlk SN3. . . . .51 D4
Concord Wlk SN3. . . . . . .51 A5
Conference Cl 1 BA12. . . .116 F7
Congreve Rd 4 SP4 . . . . .197 E2
Conholt Hill SP11. . . . . . .185 A2
Conholt La SP11. . . . . . .185 B2
Conholt Pk* SP11. . . . . .184 F1
Conifer Crest 5 SN8. . . . .183 D8
Conifers The SN16. . . . . . .17 A2
Coniger the (Tumuli)*
SP3. . . . . .196 F5
Conigre BA14. . . . . .101 C1
Conigre Cl SN12 . . . . . . .94 A3
Conigre Hill BA15. . . . . . .100 C8
Conigre Mead Nature
Reserve* SN12. . . . . . . .94 A4
Conisborough SN5. . . . . . .49 C5
Coniston Cl 5 SP4. . . . . .217 E3

Coniston Rd
Chippenham SN14. . . . . .77 F6
Trowbridge BA14. . . . . .101 E2
CONKWELL. 90 C1
Connaught Rd SP9. . . . . .216 D6
Connelly Cl 4 SN25. . . . . .34 C5
Connemara Cl 2 BA13. . . .108 E2
Connolly Wy SP9 . . . . . .216 D8
CONOCK. 180 E4
Conrad Cl SN3. . . . . .51 D4
Conscience La SN10 . . . . .214 A7
Constable Rd SN2 . . . . . .35 E2
Constable Way SP2. . . . . .151 E2
Constantine Sq 25 SP10 . .193 E2
Convent The* BA10. . . . .123 B2
Conway Cres SN12. . . . . .94 B2
Conway Rd
Chippenham SN14. . . . . .78 A7
Swindon SN3. . . . . .51 C3
Conyers Cl 5 SN5. . . . . . .48 F4
Conyger Rd SP4 . . . . . . .217 C2
Cookham Rd SN5. . . . . . .34 C7
Cook Rd 5 SN8. . . . . . . .170 A7
Cooks Cl
Hullavington SN14. . . . . .56 D6
Salisbury SP2 . . . . .145 B5
Seend SN12. . . . . .178 E8
Cooks La SO51. . . . . . . .162 F7
COOMBE
Donhead St Mary 202 F1
Enford 190 B5
Coombe Barn La BA12 . . .124 D5
COOMBE BISSETT. 150 F1
Coombe Bissett CE Prim Sch
SP5. . . . . .150 F1
Coombe Cl SN4. . . . . . . .64 C5
Coombe La
Atworth SN12 . . . . .92 C7
Enford SN9 . . . . .190 C6
Coombe Rd
Salisbury SP2 . . . . .151 F5
Swindon SN25. . . . . .34 F3
Coombe St BA9. . . . . . . .137 D3
Coombe View BA12. . . . . .194 D3
Cooper Fields SN25. . . . . .35 A5
Coopers Cl
Amesbury SP4. . . . . . . .217 B4
2 Malmesbury SN16. . . . .28 A1
Coopers Mdw SN14 . . . . . .68 F6
Cop Croft SN11. . . . . . . .81 B3
COPED HALL. 47 F4
Copheap La BA12. . . . . . .117 B7
Copheap Rise BA12. . . . . .117 B8
Copper Beech Cl SP3 . . . .196 F6
Copper Beeches SN6 . . . . .22 F5
Coppers Rd SN10. . . . . . .214 C5
Coppice Cl
Chippenham SN14. . . . . .78 B5
Swindon SN2. . . . . .34 D3
Warminster BA12 . . . . . .117 A7
Coppice Hill BA15. . . . . . .100 D7
Coppice La SN16. . . . . . . .15 E8
Coppice St SP7 . . . . .202 C1
Copse Ave SN1 . . . . .50 E8
Copse Dro SN8 . . . . .169 B5
Copse The
Alderbury SP5. . . . . .153 D2
Frome BA11. . . . . .110 B6
Copyhold 2 SN8 . . . . . . .176 B3
Corbin Rd BA14. . . . . . . .101 F1
Corby Ave SN3. . . . . .50 E3
Corfe Cl SN25 . . . . .35 A4
Corfe Cres SN11 . . . . .81 A4
Corfe Rd
Melksham SN12. . . . . . . .94 B3
Swindon SN5. . . . . .49 B4
Coriander Way SN2. . . . . .34 D5
Corinthian Cl 14 SP10. . . .193 E2
Cornbrash BA11. . . . . . . .110 D7
Cornbrash Rise BA14. . . . .102 A1
Corn Cft La SN14. . . . . . .214 F6
Corncockle Cl SN12. . . . . .94 D4
Corner Gd BA12 . . . . . . .117 E5
Corner La SP7. . . . . .202 B5
Cornfield Rd SN10. . . . . . .214 D3
Cornflower Cl SN11. . . . . .81 C5
Cornflower Rd 3 SN25 . . . .34 D5
Cornflower Way
31 Ludgershall SP11. . . . .192 A5
Melksham SN12. . . . . . . .94 B3
Corn Gastons SN16 . . . . . .27 E3
Cornmarket BA12. . . . . . .117 B7
Cornmarsh Way SN3. . . . . .51 E7
Cornpits La SP6 . . . . . . .209 E2
Cornwall Ave SN2. . . . . . .35 A1
Cornwall Cres SN12. . . . . .94 C4
Cornwall Rd SP1. . . . . . .146 A3
Cornwell Cres SN10. . . . . .214 A2
Cornwood Rd 6 SN1. . . . . .50 B1
Coronation Ave BA15 . . . .100 E7
Coronation Cl
Christian Malford SN15. . . .58 A1
Donhead St Mary SP7. . . .203 A1
2 Pewsey SN9. . . . . . . .215 C5
Sutton Benger SN15 . . . . .57 F1
Coronation Dr SP7. . . . . .203 A1
Coronation Rd
Atworth/Whitley SN12 . . . .92 E8
Durrington/Bulford SP4 . . .198 B7
Frome BA11. . . . . .110 B5
3 Ludgershall SP11. . . . .192 B5
Melksham SN12. . . . . . . .94 B3
Salisbury SP2 . . . . .145 D3
Tidworth SP9. . . . . .216 C8
Coronation Sq SP2. . . . . .144 F3
Coronation St
Fairford GL7 . . . . .1 F7

Coronation St continued
4 Trowbridge BA14. . . . .105 D7
Corporation St SN2 . . . . . .50 C7
Corral Cl SN5. . . . . .34 A1
Corry The 1 SP3 . . . . . . .203 E8
CORSHAM. 85 A8
Corsham Ct* SN13. . . . . .77 A2
Corsham Media Pk SN13. . .84 C6
Corsham Pk* SN13. . . . . .77 B2
Corsham Prim Sch SN13. . .77 B1
Corsham Rd
Atworth/Whitley SN12 . . . .85 D1
Lacock SN13. . . . . .85 F8
Swindon SN2. . . . . .35 C5
Corsham Regis Prim Acad
The SN13. . . . . .76 F2
Corsham Sch The SN13. . . .76 F1
Corsham Sports Club
SN13. . . . . .77 A1
CORSLEY. 111 C3
CORSLEY HEATH. 115 B8
CORSTON. 42 F5
CORTON. 194 D3
Corton Cres SN5. . . . . . . .49 B6
Corton (Long Barrow)*
BA12. . . . . .194 D3
Cory Way BA13 . . . . .108 C2
Cosford Cl SN14. . . . . . . .64 D3
Cossington Sq BA13. . . . .108 C2
Cossor Rd SN9. . . . . . . .215 B5
Coster's La SP5. . . . . . . .205 A2
Coster View 5 SN8. . . . . .176 B3
Cote La BA12 . . . . .123 E4
Cotley Pl 4 BA12. . . . . . .194 C5
COTMARSH. 62 B4
Cotswold Cl
Calne SN11. . . . . .81 D2
Melksham SN12. . . . . . . .94 C4
8 Warminster BA12. . . . .117 A8
COTSWOLD COMMUNITY . .6 D4
Cotswold Wr Pk* SN6. . . .6 F4
Cotswold Wr Pk Gateway
Ctr* GL7. . . . . .7 E6
Cottage Mews 13 SP6. . . .210 D1
Cottars Cl SN3 . . . . .36 B3
Cottington Cl SN5. . . . . . .49 A4
Cottle Ave BA15 . . . . . . .100 D8
Cottle Mead SN13. . . . . . .84 E8
Cottles La SN15. . . . . . . .99 F6
Cotton House Gdns
Warminster BA12 . . . . . .117 B7
Warminster BA12 . . . . . .117 B8
Cottrell Cl RG17. . . . . . . .177 C7
Couch La SN10 . . . . .214 A4
COULSTON. 178 E5
Coulston Hollow BA13 . . . .186 F8
Coulston Rd SN13. . . . . . .77 A3
Council Houses The SN15. .44 A4
Countess Rd SP4 . . . . . . .217 A4
County Bsns Pk SN1. . . . . .50 F8
County Rd SN1. . . . . .50 D7
County Way BA14. . . . . . .101 E4
Courtenay Rd SN3 . . . . . .51 A6
Court Farm Cl 8 SP4. . . . .190 A4
Court Farm Rd 1 SP4. . . . .190 A3
Courtfields SN6. . . . . .8 C4
Court Gdns
Bath BA1. . . . . .82 A3
Stanton St Quintin SN14. . .56 B4
Court Hill
Damerham SP6 . . . . . . .209 E8
Potterne SN10. . . . . . . .179 C5
Court La
Bathford BA1. . . . . .82 B1
Bratton BA13. . . . . .186 B7
Corsley BA12. . . . . .111 B1
Edington BA13 . . . . .186 D8
Court St Cl SP3. . . . . . . .203 E8
Courtsknap Ct 6 SN1. . . . .50 A5
Court St
Sherston SN16 . . . . .25 C1
Tisbury SP3. . . . . .203 E8
Trowbridge BA14. . . . . .105 D8
Courtwood Cl 3 SP1. . . . .152 C8
Coventry Cl SN4 . . . . . . .64 B7
COVINGHAM. 51 C7
Covingham Dr SN3. . . . . . .51 C8
Covingham Pk Prim Sch
SN3. . . . . .51 C7
Covingham Sq SN3 . . . . . .51 C7
Cowbridge Cres SN16. . . . .28 C1
Cowdrey Cl SN5 . . . . .49 B4
Cow Dro SP3 . . . . .201 B4
COWESFIELD GREEN 161 F4
Cow La
Kimpton SP11. . . . . . . .192 B2
Laverstock SP1. . . . . . . .146 C1
Cowleaze Cres SN4 . . . . . .63 F6
Cowleaze La BA13. . . . . .186 D8
Cowleaze Wlk SN2. . . . . . .35 F4
Cowley Way SN15. . . . . . .57 D1
Cowley Wlk SN3. . . . . . . .51 B6
Cowslip Bank 8 SN13. . . . .84 E8
Cowslip Gr SN11. . . . . . . .81 B5
Cowslip Way SN14. . . . . . .70 B3
Cowslip Wy SP11. . . . . . .193 F2
Cow St SN5. . . . . .19 B1
Coxhill La SN10. . . . . . . .179 D5
Cox's Hill
Ashton Keynes SN6. . . . . .6 C1
Calne SN11. . . . . .81 B2
Cox's La SN8 . . . . .176 F1
Coxstalls SN4. . . . . .47 D2
Crab La BA12 . . . . .138 A7
Crab Mill La SN16. . . . . . .28 E1
Crab Tree Cl SN16 . . . . . .27 F3
Crabtree Copse SN5. . . . . .34 C2

Crampton Rd SN3. . . . . . .51 A7
Cranborne Chase SN2. . . . .34 C4
Cranborne Dr 1 SP7. . . . .202 C2
Cranbury Cl SP5. . . . . . . .211 A7
Crandon Lea BA14 . . . . . .92 F1
Cranebridge Rd SP2. . . . .152 A8
Crane Furlong SN6 . . . . . .23 A7
Cranesbill Cl SN10. . . . . .214 D5
Cranesbill Rd
Devizes SN10. . . . . .214 D5
Melksham SN12. . . . . . . .94 D4
Crane St SP1 . . . . .152 A8
Cranmore Ave SN3. . . . . . .51 A3
Cranmore Cl BA14 . . . . . .101 A1
Cranwell Cl 6 SN14 . . . . . .78 A6
Cratchcroft La BA14 . . . . .178 A6
Crate La SP7. . . . . .202 C7
Craven Rd RG17. . . . . . . .177 D3
Crawford Cl SN5. . . . . . . .49 A4
Crawlboys La SP11. . . . . .192 B6
Crawley Ave SN3 . . . . . . .36 B1
Crawley Cres BA14 . . . . . .105 A8
Craybourne Rd SN12. . . . . .94 C6
Crays The SN12. . . . . .94 C5
Crench Comm Airfield
SN8. . . . . .174 E4
Crescent Rd
Durrington/Bulford SP4 . . .217 D7
Melksham SN12. . . . . . . .94 C6
Crescent The
Bromham SN15. . . . . . . .96 C7
Calne SN11 . . . . .89 F8
Chiseldown SN4. . . . . . . .65 C3
4 Durrington/Bulford SP4 198 C5
Pewsey SN9 . . . . .215 B4
Swindon SN5. . . . . .33 F2
Westbury BA13. . . . . . . .109 A3
Wilton SP2. . . . . .144 B2
Cresswell Dr BA14 . . . . . .102 B2
Cresswell La SN15. . . . . . .44 B8
Cres The SP2. . . . . .152 B5
Crestmount Dr SP2 . . . . .145 C3
Creswells SN13. . . . . .84 F8
Cricketts La SN15. . . . . . .78 F5
CRICKLADE. 19 E7
Cricklade Leisure Ctr SN6 19 C8
Cricklade Mus* SN6. . . . .19 E8
Cricklade Rd
Highworth SN6 . . . . .22 F5
Purton SN5. . . . . .19 C2
Swindon SN25. . . . . .35 D1
Cricklade St SN1. . . . . . . .50 D5
CRIDDLESTYLE. 210 E1
Crieff Cl SN3. . . . . .51 B6
Crispin Cl 6 SN3 . . . . . . .36 B3
CROCKERTON. 116 E1
Crockerton CE Prim Sch
BA12. . . . . .116 D2
CROCKERTON GREEN. . . .116 F2
Crockford Rd SP5. . . . . . .154 B2
Croft Cl SN6. . . . . .8 C4
Croft Hts SP5. . . . . .161 B3
Croft La SN6. . . . . .8 C4
CROFTON. 176 A1
Crofton Beam Engines*
SN8. . . . . .176 A1
Crofton Rd SN8. . . . . . . .176 A1
Croft Prim Sch The SN1. . .50 D3
Croft Rd
6 Hungerford RG17. . . . .177 B7
Swindon SN1. . . . . .50 C1
Croft Sports Hall SN1. . . . .50 D3
Croft The
Bishopstone SP5 . . . . . .205 E5
Broad Hinton SN4. . . . . .167 D7
Milston SP4. . . . . .198 C8
Newton Tony SP4. . . . . . .199 B3
Trowbridge BA14. . . . . .105 C6
Urchfont SN10. . . . . . . .180 C3
Crombey St SN1. . . . . . . .50 B5
Cromer Cl SN3 . . . . .51 D3
Cromhall La SN14. . . . . . .69 A7
Crompton Rd SN25 . . . . . .35 D6
Cromwell SN5. . . . . .49 B3
Cromwell Rd SN10. . . . . .214 D2
Crooked Cnr SN8. . . . . . .170 A6
CROOKED SOLEY. 170 F3
Crookhays SP7 . . . . .202 C2
Crook Hill SP5. . . . . .204 A1
Crooks La SN10. . . . . . . .180 C4
Crookwood La SN10. . . . . .179 F4
Croome Cl SN25 . . . . .34 B8
Crosbys 3 SN8 . . . . .183 D8
Crosby Wlk SN3 . . . . .51 A3
Croscombe Gdns BA11. . . .110 D6
Cross Hayes La SN16. . . . .28 A3
Crossing La SN15. . . . . . .71 B3
CROSS KEYS. 77 A3
Cross Keys Chequer 5
SP1. . . . . .146 B1
Cross Keys Rd SN13. . . . . .77 A3
Cross La SN8. . . . . .213 D3
Crossling La SN16 . . . . . . .16 E3
Cross St
Swindon SN1. . . . . .50 C5
Trowbridge BA14. . . . . .101 D1
Cross The
Bishopstone SP5 . . . . . .205 E4
Ebbesborne Wake SP5 . . .204 D3
21 Tisbury SP3 . . . . . . .203 E8
Cross Tree Cres GL7 . . . . .10 C7
Crossways Ave SN25 . . . . .35 C3
Crosswood Rd SN3 . . . . . .51 A3
CROUCHESTON. 205 F4

Croucheston Dro SP5 . . . . . .205 E3
Croucheston Hollow SP5 .205 E4
Crowdys Hill Specl Sch
  SN2. . . . . .35 D2
Crowe Hill BA2 . . . . .99 B6
Crowe La BA2 . . . . .99 B5
Crowe Rd 11 RG17 . . . . . . .165 A1
Crown Cl
  Chippenham SN15. . . . . . .79 A5
  Salisbury SP2 . . . . .145 D3
Crown La 4 SP11. . . . . .192 A5
Crown Mews 30 RG17. . . . .177 B7
Crown Way SP10 . . . . .193 F1
Crowood La SN8. . . . . .170 B2
CRUDWELL 14 E6
Crudwell CE Prim Sch
  SN16. . . . . .14 F6
Crudwell La
  Crudwell SN16. . . . . .14 B6
  Long Newnton GL8 . . . . . .13 D6
Crudwell Way SN25 . . . . . . .35 C6
Crusader Pk BA12 . . . . .112 F1
Crusades The 6 SP1. . . . . .146 C5
Cruse Cl SN14 . . . . .77 F8
CUCKOLD'S GREEN 179 C4
Cuckoo La BA11. . . . . .110 A8
Cuckoo Pen Cl SN8 . . . . . . .183 D3
CUCKOO'S CORNER 180 B4
CUCKOO'S KNOB 174 E7
Cuckoo's Mead SN1 . . . . . . .51 E6
Cuckoos Nest La BA12 . . . .116 E7
Cues La SN6. . . . . .163 E7
Cuffs La SP3. . . . . .203 E8
Culborne Rd SN1 . . . . .50 A2
CULKERTON 3 C5
Cullerne Rd SN3 . . . . .36 C1
Cullerns The SN6 . . . . .23 A6
Culpepper Cl 6 SN3 . . . . . .51 A4
Culverhouse Rd SN1 . . . . . . .50 E7
Culvermead Cl SN8 . . . . . . .213 E3
Culver Rd BA15 . . . . .100 E5
CULVERSLADE 66 A2
Culverwell Rd SN14 . . . . . . .78 A7
Cumberland Rd SN3 . . . . . . .50 E6
Cunetio Rd SN8 . . . . .51 C8
Cunnage La BA12. . . . . .139 F1
Cunningham Rd SN2. . . . . . .35 A2
Curie Ave SN1 . . . . .50 A4
Curlcroft Rd SN13 . . . . .84 D7
Curlew Dr SN14. . . . . .70 A2
Curlew Rd 3 SP4. . . . . . . .132 C1
Curnicks The SN4. . . . . .65 C4
Cursus The* SP4 . . . . .197 D6
Cursus The GL7. . . . . .2 C5
Curtis Orch SN12 . . . . .93 B4
Curtis St SN1 . . . . .50 B5
Curzon Cl SN11. . . . . .81 A3
Curzon St SN11. . . . . .81 A3
Cusance Way BA14 . . . . . . .102 A1
Cuthwine Pl GL7. . . . . .2 C5
Cutting Hill RG17 . . . . .177 A2
Cuttle La SN14. . . . . .76 E8
Cutts Cl SN15. . . . . .46 A7
Cvnieto Roman Town*
  SN8. . . . . .175 B8
Cygnet Dr 2 SP4 . . . . .217 C8
Cygnet Pl SN9 . . . . .215 C4
Cygnet Way BA14 . . . . .101 D5
Cygney Way RG17. . . . . . . .177 B8
Cyppa Ct SN15. . . . . .78 E6
Cypress Gr SN2. . . . . .35 A3
Cypress Way 7 BA11 . . . . .110 C7
Cypress Wlk SN14 . . . . .74 F6
Cyprus Terr SN10 . . . . .214 A4

D

Dace Rd SN11 . . . . .81 B4
Dacre Cl 13 SP10 . . . . .193 C2
Dacre Rd SN3 . . . . .51 A6
Dairy Cl 8 SP5 . . . . .211 C7
Dairy Mdw La SP1. . . . . . . .152 D7
Dairy Rd
  Barford St Martin SP3. . . .143 A4
  Chiseldon SN4. . . . . .64 F4
Daisy Cl
  Melksham SN12. . . . . .94 C3
  Swindon SN2. . . . . .34 C3
Dales Cl SN25 . . . . .35 A7
Dales Rd BA13 . . . . .108 E2
Dalewood Rise SP1 . . . . . .146 E2
Dallas Ave SN3 . . . . .51 B7
Dallas Rd SN14 . . . . .78 C8
Dalton Cl SN3 . . . . .50 F7
Dalwood Cl
  Dinton SP3. . . . . .201 E2
  Swindon SN3. . . . . .51 B3
Damask Way BA12. . . . . . . .117 A5
DAMERHAM 209 F2
Dammas Bsns Ctr SN1. . . . .50 D4
Dammas La SN3. . . . . .50 D4
Damson Cres 11 SN25. . . . .34 C5
Damy Gn SN3. . . . . .84 E5
Dando Dr SN8. . . . . .213 B2
Dane Cl BA15. . . . . .99 E7
Danegeld Cl 9 SP10 . . . . . .193 C2
Dane Rise BA15. . . . . .99 E7
Danes Cl SN15. . . . . .78 F5
Danestone Cl SN5 . . . . .48 F7
Daniel Cl 9 SN1. . . . . .49 F4
Daniell Crest BA12. . . . . . . .116 F6
Daniel's Well* SN16. . . . . . .28 A3
Danvers Mead SN15 . . . . . . .79 A4

Danvers Rd SN13 . . . . .76 E1
Danvers Way BA13. . . . . . . .109 B4
Darby Cl SN2. . . . . .34 E1
Darcey Cl SN5 . . . . .48 F6
Darcy Cl SN15 . . . . .78 F8
Darius Way SN25 . . . . .35 A6
Dark La
  Berkley BA11. . . . . .110 E8
  Castle Combe SN14. . . . . .68 B7
  Grafton SN8. . . . . .175 F1
  Kintbury RG17 . . . . .177 D8
  Limpley Stoke BA2. . . . . . .99 B5
  Malmesbury SN16. . . . . . .27 F3
  Mere BA12 . . . . .139 A5
Dark La N BA14 . . . . .178 A3
Dark La S BA14 . . . . .178 A3
Darnley Cl SN3 . . . . .50 F6
Darrell Rd SP4. . . . . .217 C4
Dart Ave SN5. . . . . .35 A3
Dartmoor Cl 7 SN1. . . . . . .49 F4
Dartmoor Rd 2 BA13 . . . . .108 E1
Darwin Cl
  4 Durrington/Bulford
  SP4. . . . . .198 F6
  Swindon SN3. . . . . .51 B8
Dasna Rd SN3 . . . . .216 B5
Daunch Cl SP9. . . . . .216 B7
DAUNTSEY 45 B1
Dauntsey Acad Prim Sch
  SN10. . . . . .187 E8
Dauntsey Dro SP11 . . . . . .192 E1
Dauntsey La SP11. . . . . . . .192 E1
DAUNTSEY LOCK. 59 B5
Dauntsey Pk* SN15 . . . . . . .44 A7
Dauntsey Rd SN15 . . . . . . .187 C2
Dauntsey's Sch SN10 . . . . .187 D8
Davenham Cl SN3. . . . . .51 A3
Davenwood SN2 . . . . .34 F4
Dave Watkins Ct SN2 . . . . . .35 F3
David's Gdn SP5. . . . . .148 C3
David Stoddart Gdns 2 .35 B1
Davies Cl SN8 . . . . .213 A2
Davies Dr SN10 . . . . .214 C6
Davis Pl SN1. . . . . .50 B6
Davis Rd 11 SN10 . . . . .179 F1
Dawbeney Dr SP4 . . . . .217 D3
Dawlish Rd SN3 . . . . .51 B5
Dawneys The SN16 . . . . .14 E6
Day Ho La SN3. . . . . .51 C2
Day's Cl SN3. . . . . .36 A1
Days Ct SN16. . . . . .14 E6
Day's La SN15. . . . . .56 D2
Deacon Rd SP11. . . . . .192 B2
Deacon St SN1 . . . . .50 B5
DEAN 207 E2
Dean Cl
  Frome BA11. . . . . .110 C6
  Melksham SN12. . . . . .94 C6
DEANEND 207 E4
Dean La
  Fovant SP3 . . . . .204 D7
  Sixpenny Handley SP5. . .207 F6
  Whiteparish SP5 . . . . . . .161 D4
Dean La Dro SP5 . . . . .207 F4
DEANLAND 208 A5
Dean Rd SP5 . . . . .155 B3
Deans Cl SP9 . . . . .216 D4
Deansfield SN6 . . . . .19 D7
Dean St SN1 . . . . .49 F5
Dean Sta SP5. . . . . .155 F3
Deansway SN15. . . . . .70 D2
Deben Cres SN25. . . . . .34 F5
Deburgh St SN2 . . . . .49 F6
Deep La BA12. . . . . .111 D2
Deerhurst Way 1 SN5 . . . . .49 D4
Deer Pk* SN8. . . . . .175 E2
De Havilland Pl 4 SN12. .178 B8
Delamere Dr SN3. . . . . .36 A4
Delamere Rd BA14. . . . . . . .101 D2
Delft Cres 1 SN25 . . . . .34 D7
Delius Cl SN25. . . . . .34 E8
Dell The SP11 . . . . .185 B3
Delta Bsns Pk SN5 . . . . .49 D6
Delta Office Pk SN5 . . . . . . .49 D5
De Montfort Gr 8 RG17 . .177 B6
Denbeck Wood SN5. . . . . . . .49 B6
Denbigh Cl SN3. . . . . .50 E3
Denby Rd 4 SN25 . . . . .34 E7
Deneb Dr SN25 . . . . .34 B7
Denes Ave BA12 . . . . .139 A6
Dene The
  Hindon SP3 . . . . .200 B3
  Warminster BA12. . . . . . .117 E6
Denford La RG17 . . . . .177 D8
Denholme Rd SN3 . . . . .51 A3
Denison Rise SP1 . . . . .146 C3
Dennis La SP7. . . . . .203 B1
Denton Dr SP4 . . . . .217 C2
DEPTFORD 195 E1
Derby Cl
  Chippenham SN15. . . . . . .78 F5
  Lambourn RG17. . . . . . . .165 A1
Derby Ct SN3. . . . . .50 E6
Derriads Gn SN14. . . . . .78 A7
Derriads La 3 SN14 . . . . . .77 F6
DERRY FIELDS 17 F8
DERRY HILL 79 F2
Derry Hill CE Prim Sch
  SN11. . . . . .80 A2
Derry Pk SN16. . . . . .17 C2
Derry The SN6. . . . . .17 F8
DERTFORDS 115 B7
Derwent Dr SN2 . . . . .35 F4
Desborough SN5 . . . . .49 A3
Deva Cl SN3 . . . . .51 D8
De Vaux Pl SP1 . . . . .152 A7
Devenish Nature Reserve*
  SP4. . . . . .131 D2

Deverell Cl BA15. . . . . .100 E4
Devereux Cl 8 SN5. . . . . . .48 F5
Devereux Cl SP4 . . . . .217 B3
Deverill Rd
  Sutton Veny BA12 . . . . . .117 E1
  Warminster BA12 . . . . . . .116 F4
Devils Bed & Bolster The*
  BA11. . . . . .107 A8
DEVIZES 214 A3
Devizes Castle* SN10 . . . .214 A3
Devizes Com Hospl SN10 214 B4
Devizes Enterprise Cen
  SN10. . . . . .214 C3
Devizes Leisure Ctr
  SN10. . . . . .214 B3
Devizes Rd
  Box SN13. . . . . .83 E4
  Bromham SN15. . . . . .88 B4
  Calne Without SN11 . . . . .87 F7
  Charlton SN9. . . . . .181 D2
  Derry Hill/Studley SN11 . .79 F1
  Hilperton BA14. . . . . .102 C3
  Potterne SN10. . . . . .179 D6
  Poulshot SN10 . . . . .179 B7
  Rowde SN10 . . . . .96 F2
  Salisbury SP2 . . . . .145 E2
  Swindon SN10. . . . . .50 D4
  Trowbridge BA14. . . . . . .102 B3
  Wroughton SN4. . . . . .64 B6
Devizes Sports Club
  SN10. . . . . .214 C4
Devizes White Horse*
  SN10. . . . . .97 F5
Devon Cl 5 SN14. . . . . .77 F6
Devon Dr BA13 . . . . .109 A5
Devon Rd
  Swindon SN2. . . . . .35 B1
  Upavon Down SN9. . . . . .182 B2
Devonshire Pl SN12. . . . . . .94 C5
Devonshire Rd SP1 . . . . . . .146 A3
Dew Cl SN13. . . . . .85 A8
Dewell Mews SN1 . . . . .50 D3
Dewey Cl SN4 . . . . .65 D4
Deweys La SP11. . . . . .192 A5
Dew's Rd SP2 . . . . .145 F1
Dexter Cl SN5 . . . . .49 B7
Dial Cl SN12. . . . . .178 E8
Dianmer Cl SN4 . . . . .47 F5
Dickens Ave SN13 . . . . .76 F2
Dickens Cl SN3 . . . . .51 D3
Dickenson Rd SN25. . . . . . .34 C5
Dicketts Rd SN13 . . . . .85 A7
Dickson Rd SN15 . . . . .60 A1
Dickson Way 2 SN15 . . . . . .78 F5
Diddledown Rd 8 SP4. . . .217 C2
DIDMARTON 24 C3
Dilton Ct BA13 . . . . .112 B6
DILTON MARSH 112 B8
Dilton Marsh CE Prim Sch
  BA13. . . . . .112 B8
Dilton Marsh Sta BA13. . .108 C1
Dinah's Hollow SP7. . . . . . .206 B7
Dingle The 3 SN4. . . . . . . .163 A6
Dinmore Rd SN25. . . . . .34 F6
Dinnis Wy SP4 . . . . .146 B8
DINTON 201 F2
Dinton CE Prim Sch SP3 201 F2
Dinton Cl 10 SN25 . . . . . . .34 E7
Dinton Rd
  Fovant SP3 . . . . .204 E8
  Wylye BA12 . . . . .201 E8
Dione Cres SN25. . . . . .34 B7
Dior Dr SN4 . . . . .61 E8
Discover Salisbury (Medieval
  Hall)* SP1 . . . . .152 A8
Distillery Mdws Nature
  Reserve* SN16. . . . . . . .31 B7
DITCHAMPTON 144 C4
DITTERIDGE 83 B8
Divinity Cl 2 SN4. . . . . . . .163 B6
Dixon St SN1 . . . . .50 B5
Dixon Way SN11 . . . . .81 B4
Dixon Wy SN5 . . . . .49 C6
Dobbin Cl SN3. . . . . .51 E7
Dobson Cl SN25 . . . . .35 A8
Dockle Way SN2 . . . . .35 F4
Doctors Hill SN13. . . . . .83 B5
Doctors Pl 3 SP3. . . . . . . .203 E8
Dodford La SN15 . . . . .58 D6
Dodgson Cl SP6. . . . . .211 A4
Doggetts La BA13 . . . . .109 A4
Dog Kennel La BA13 . . . . . .109 A1
Dog La SP7. . . . . .203 E1
DOGRIDGE 32 F3
Dogridge SN5 . . . . .33 A3
Dog Trap La SN16. . . . . .16 E1
Dolina Rd SN25. . . . . .34 D6
Dolphin Ind Est SP1 . . . . . .152 D7
Dolphin St SP1 . . . . .152 B8
Donaldson Rd SP1. . . . . . . .146 A2
Doncaster Cl SN14. . . . . . . .77 F5
Don Cl SN25. . . . . .35 A4
Doncombe Hill SN14. . . . . . .74 E7
Doncombe La SN14. . . . . . . .75 A6
Donhead Hollow SP7. . . . . .206 E8
DONHEAD ST ANDREW . . .203 B3
DONHEAD ST MARY 203 A3
Donnington Gr SN3. . . . . . . .50 F4
DORCAN. 51 D5
Dorcan Acad The SN3. . . . . .51 D6
Dorcan Bsns Village SN3. . .51 E6
Dorcan Ind Est SN3. . . . . . . .51 E5
Dorcan Way SN3. . . . . .51 A8
Dorchester Rd SN3 . . . . .50 F3
Dores Cl SN2 . . . . .35 E3
Dores Rd SN2 . . . . .35 D3
Doris Archer Ct SN2 . . . . . . .35 B2
Dormers The SN6. . . . . .23 A6

Dorney Cl BA13 . . . . .108 F1
Dorney Rd SN25 . . . . .34 C8
Dorset Cl SP4 . . . . .217 E8
Dorset Cres SN12. . . . . .94 C3
Dorset Dr BA13 . . . . .109 A5
Dorset Gn SN2. . . . . .34 F2
Dorset Rd SP1. . . . . .146 B3
Doubledays SN6 . . . . .19 D8
Double Hedges SP4. . . . . . .217 E7
Doughty's La SP12 . . . . . . .195 A2
Douglas Brown's Wlk 6
  SP4. . . . . .197 E6
Douglas Haig Rd SP1 . . . . .146 A3
Douglas Rd 5 SN3 . . . . . . .50 F6
Doulting Ct BA11 . . . . .110 D7
Doulton Cl SN25 . . . . .34 D7
Dovecote Cl 3 BA14 . . . . .105 B8
Dovecote Dr SN13 . . . . .76 F2
Dovedale 7 SN25. . . . . .34 F7
Dovers La BA1. . . . . .82 C2
Dovers Pk BA1. . . . . .82 C2
Dover St
  Chippenham SN14. . . . . . .78 C7
  Swindon SN1. . . . . .50 C5
Doves La SP5. . . . . .161 C3
Dovetrees SN3 . . . . .51 D7
Doveys Terr SN15. . . . . .70 E7
Dowding Ave SN13. . . . . . . .84 B8
Dowding Dr 5 SN15. . . . . .166 A1
Dowding Way SN12. . . . . . . .94 C1
Dowlais Cl 2 SN25. . . . . . .34 C6
Dowland Cl SN25 . . . . .34 E8
Dowling St SN1. . . . . .50 C5
DOWN AMPNEY 8 D7
Down Ampney House*
  GL7. . . . . .8 D6
Down Ampney Rd GL7 . . . . .8 B6
Downavon BA15 . . . . .100 D5
Down Barn Cl SP4 . . . . . . .133 B4
Down Barn Rd SP4. . . . . . . .132 F6
Downham Mead SN15. . . . . .78 F8
Downhayes Rd BA14 . . . . .101 D2
Downing St SN14 . . . . .78 C8
Downland Rd
  Calne SN11. . . . . .81 A2
  Swindon SN2. . . . . .34 D4
Downlands 1 RG17. . . . . .171 E7
Downlands Cl SP5 . . . . . . .211 A7
Downlands The BA12 . . . . .117 B7
Downland Way 12 SP4 . . . .198 B7
Downleaze 7 SP4. . . . . . . .198 B7
Down Rd
  Kimpton SP11 . . . . .192 D4
  Marshfield SN14. . . . . . . .66 C7
Downs Cl
  Bradford-on-Avon BA15. .100 B7
  Devizes SN10. . . . . .214 D3
  Lambourn RG17. . . . . . . .171 C8
Downside Cl SN12 . . . . .139 A6
Downside Pk BA14. . . . . . . .101 E2
Downs La SN8 . . . . .185 B8
Downslands Rd SN10 . . . . .214 B1
Downsmead SN8 . . . . .164 B1
Downs Rd SN4. . . . . .65 E4
Downs The SN8. . . . . .170 A5
Downsview BA13 . . . . .186 C7
Downs View
  Bradford-on-Avon BA15 . .100 B7
  Highworth SN6 . . . . .23 A6
  1 Netheravon SP4. . . . . .190 A4
  Royal Wootton Bassett SN4 .47 D1
  Warminster BA12. . . . . . .117 C6
Downsview Rd BA13 . . . . . .109 A4
Downs View Rd SN3 . . . . . . .50 F2
Downsview Way SP11. . . . .191 F3
Downsway SP1 . . . . .146 B4
Downs Wy SN3. . . . . .51 E1
Down The
  Hindon SP3 . . . . .200 B3
  Trowbridge BA14. . . . . . .101 D2
DOWNTON 211 B8
Downton Bus Ctr SP5. . . . .159 A1
Downton CE Prim Sch
  SP5. . . . . .211 A8
Downton Hill SP5 . . . . .211 C8
Downton L Ctr SP5 . . . . . . .210 F8
Downton Meml Gdns*
  SP5. . . . . .211 A8
Downton Rd
  Salisbury SP2 . . . . .152 B5
  Swindon SN2. . . . . .35 B5
Down View SN14 . . . . .78 A7
Downview Rd SP6. . . . . .209 B6
Down View Rd SP1 . . . . . . .146 E2
Downwood Cl 7 SP6. . . . . .210 C1
Dowse Rd SN10. . . . . .214 C4
Doyle Cl 1 SN25. . . . . .34 C5
Dragonfly Rd 3 SN3. . . . . .51 B8
Dragon La SN9 . . . . .181 F6
Drain Hill RG17. . . . . .165 A2
Drake Cl SP1 . . . . .146 C5
Drake Cres SN14. . . . . .77 F6
Drake Ct SP10 . . . . .193 F1
Drakes Ave SN10 . . . . .214 C2
Drakes Mdw SN3. . . . . .50 F7
Drakes Mdw Bsns Pk SN3. 50 F7
Drake's Way SN3 . . . . .50 E6
Drakes Way Bsns Ctr SN3 . 51 A7
Draymans Ct SN4. . . . . .61 D8
Dr Behr Ct SN2. . . . . .35 B2
Drewitts Cl SN10 . . . . .180 E8
Drew's Pond La SN10 . . . . .214 B1
Drew St SN2. . . . . .49 E7

Drifton Hill SN14. . . . . .66 E7
Drive The
  Durnford SP4. . . . . .197 F1
  Melchet Park & Plaitford
  SO51. . . . . .162 C1
  Swindon SN3. . . . . .51 B7
Drove Cl SP5 . . . . .150 F2
Drove La
  Coombe Bissett SP5. . . . .150 F3
  Market Lavington SN10. . .179 F1
  Steeple Ashton BA14 . . . .178 A2
Drove Prim Sch SN1. . . . . . .50 D6
Drove Rd SN1 . . . . .50 D5
Drovers Vw SP11 . . . . .192 A5
Droves The SP5. . . . . .207 E4
Drove The
  Amesbury SP4. . . . . .217 B6
  Hawkeridge BA13. . . . . . .108 D7
  13 Redlynch SP5. . . . . . .211 C2
Dr The SN14. . . . . .61 A7
Druley Hill BA10 . . . . .123 B7
Drummer La SP9 . . . . .216 D5
Drury Cl SN5 . . . . .47 F6
Drury La SN8 . . . . .175 D4
Dryden Cl SP2. . . . . .152 B5
Dryden St SN1. . . . . .50 B5
Dry Hill BA12 . . . . .116 E2
DRYNHAM. 105 D6
Drynham La BA14. . . . . .105 D5
Drynham Pk BA14 . . . . .105 D6
Drynham Rd BA14 . . . . .105 D6
Duchess Way SN2 . . . . .35 D5
Duck La
  Barford St Martin SP3. . . .143 B3
  Laverstock SP1. . . . . .152 E8
  Salisbury SP1 . . . . .146 D2
Duck Pool La BA11. . . . . . . .107 B6
Ducks Meadow SN8. . . . . . .213 D2
Duck's Nest (Long Barrow)*
  SP6. . . . . .209 F7
Duck St
  Berwick St James SP3. . .196 F1
  Ebbesborne Wake SP5 . . .204 C3
  Potterne SN10. . . . . .179 D5
  Steeple Langford SP3 . . .128 D7
  Sutton Veny BA12 . . . . . .194 A4
  Tisbury SP3 . . . . .203 E8
  West Lavington SN10 . . . .187 E8
Dudley Ave SP6. . . . . .210 D2
Dudley Rd SN3 . . . . .50 F6
Dudmore Rd SN3 . . . . .50 D6
Dukes Cl SN2. . . . . .35 E5
Dukes Field GL7. . . . . .8 D7
Duke's La BA12. . . . . .118 A1
Duke St BA14. . . . . .101 D1
Duke's Way SP4 . . . . .217 E8
Dulverton Ave SN3. . . . . . . .51 A5
Dumbarton Terr 2 SN1. . . .50 C5
Dummer La SP11 . . . . .184 E1
Dummer Way SN15 . . . . . . .79 A5
Dunbar Rd SN4 . . . . .64 A7
Dunbeath Ct SN2. . . . . .35 E1
Dunbeath Rd SN2. . . . . .35 E1
Duncan's Cl SP11. . . . . . . .192 D1
Duncan St SN11 . . . . .81 B5
Dunch La SN12 . . . . .93 F7
Dundas Aqueduct* BA2. . .90 B2
Dundas Cl SN10 . . . . .179 C8
DUNFIELD. 10 A8
Dunford Cl
  Amesbury SP4. . . . . .217 D1
  Trowbridge BA14. . . . . . .105 D6
DUNGE. 106 E1
Dunhills La SP11. . . . . .193 F4
DUNKIRK. 179 D8
Dunkirk Bsns Pk BA14. . . .104 D2
Dunkirk Hill
  Devizes SN10 . . . . .179 D8
  Rowde SN10 . . . . .97 A1
Dunley Cl SN25 . . . . .34 D7
Dunley Way SP1. . . . . .146 D6
Dunnet Cl SN11. . . . . .81 B4
Dunnington Rd SN4. . . . . . . .61 D7
Dunns La SN14. . . . . .68 B8
Dunn's La SP8. . . . . .138 A1
Dunraven Cl SN3 . . . . .50 F4
Dunsford Cl SN1. . . . . .49 F4
Dunsley Vale SN1. . . . . .50 A2
Dunspit La DT11. . . . . .207 B1
Dunstable Cnr SP5. . . . . . .148 E7
Dunstan's Dro SP11. . . . . .185 E1
Dunster Cl SN3 . . . . .50 E3
Dunvant Rd SN25 . . . . .34 C7
Dunwich Dr SN5. . . . . .49 D4
Dunworth Rise 6 SP3 . . . .203 E8
Durham St SN1. . . . . .50 C5
Durlett Rd SN10 . . . . .95 F2
DURLEY. 175 D3
Durley Pk SN13 . . . . .84 D6
Durnford Rd SN2 . . . . .35 C5
DURRINGTON. 198 B7
Durrington bAll Saints CE VC
  Infs Sch SP4 . . . . .198 C7
Durrington CE (Controlled)
  Jun Sch SP4. . . . . .198 B6
Durrington Swimming &
  Fitness Ctr SP4. . . . . . . .198 C7
Durrington Walls* SP4 . .217 A8
Durrington Wlk SN2. . . . . . .35 C5
Dursden La SN9 . . . . .215 E6
DURSLEY. 105 D1
Dursley Rd
  Heywood BA13 . . . . .108 F8
  North Bradley BA13 . . . . .105 E1
Dussek Pl 2 SN25. . . . . . . .34 E7
Dutts BA13. . . . . .108 B1
Duxford Cl 11 SN12 . . . . . .178 B8

Dydale Rd
  5 Swindon SN25 . . . . 34 C6
  Swindon SN25 . . . . 34 C6
Dyehouse La SN10 . . . . . 214 A4
Dyer La BA12 . . . . 201 E8
Dyer's Cl SN15 . . . . 79 A6
Dyke Mews SN4 . . . . 65 D4
Dymocks La BA14 . . . . . 121 F8
Dymott Sq BA14 . . . . . . 102 A3
Dyrham Ct 1 SN25 . . . . . 34 F7
Dyson Rd SN25 . . . . 34 E8

E

Eadreds Hyde SN11 . . . . . 89 D8
Eagle Cl SN3 . . . . 51 E7
Eagle Field SP2 . . . . 145 D4
Eagle Pk BA14 . . . . 105 E6
Earl Cl SN5 . . . . 48 F7
Earls Cl SP4 . . . . 217 E2
Earls Cnr SN16 . . . . 15 E8
Earls Ct Rd SP4 . . . . . . 217 B3
Earl's Rise SN3 . . . . 133 A1
Earthpits La SP5 . . . . . . 208 E4
EAST ANTON 193 F2
East Anton Farm Rd 20
  SP11 . . . . 193 F2
Eastbourne Gdns SN4 . . 101 E1
Eastbourne Rd BA14 . . . 101 E1
EASTBURY 171 E8
Eastbury Shute RG17 . . . 171 C5
Eastbury Way SN25 . . . . . 34 E7
EAST CHISENBURY 190 B4
EAST COMPTON 206 A5
EASTCOTT 180 A2
Eastcott Comm SN10 . . . 180 A3
Eastcott Hill 5 SN1 . . . . . 50 C5
Eastcott Rd SN1 . . . . 50 C5
EASTCOURT 15 D6
Eastcourt SN8 . . . . 183 D8
Eastcourt Rd SN8 . . . . . 183 D8
East Dr 6 SN25 . . . . 34 F8
East Dunley Cotts SN14 . . 40 E1
EAST END 74 A8
East End BA12 . . . . 117 B6
East End Ave BA12 . . . . 117 B6
East End La SN15 . . . . . . 44 D5
Eastern Ave
  Chippenham SN15 . . . . . 78 F8
  Swindon SN3 . . . . 50 E6
EASTERTON 180 A2
Easterton La SN9 . . . . . . 215 D4
EASTERTON SANDS 179 F2
EAST EVERLEIGH 191 A8
Eastfield
  Ashton Keynes SN6 . . . . . 6 F1
  2 Littleton Panell SN10 . 187 E8
EAST GARSTON 171 E7
EAST GOMELDON 133 E4
East Gomeldon Rd SP4. . 133 E4
EAST GRAFTON 183 F7
EAST GRIMSTEAD 154 F4
EAST HATCH 203 C7
Easthill BA11 . . . . 110 B4
EAST KENNETT 173 E6
East Kennett (Long
  Barrow)* SN8. . . . . . 173 D5
EAST KNOYLE. 141 E1
Eastlands Wy SN15 . . . . . 70 E1
EASTLEAZE. 49 B6
Eastleaze Rd SN5 . . . . . . 49 C6
Eastleigh Cl 4 BA11 . . . 110 A4
Eastleigh Rd SN10 . . . . 214 D2
Eastman Cl SP5. . . . . . . 211 B7
EAST MARTIN 209 C6
EAST MELBURY 206 B7
Eastmere SN3 . . . . 51 E3
EASTON. 77 D2
Easton Comm Hill SP5 . . 149 E6
EASTON GREY 26 C3
Easton Hollow SP5. . . . . 207 B7
Easton La SN14 . . . . 77 F3
EASTON ROYAL 183 A7
Easton Royal Academy
  SN9 . . . . 183 A7
Easton Sq SN16 . . . . 25 D1
EASTON TOWN 25 D1
Easton Town SN16 . . . . . 25 C1
East Portway SP10 . . . . . 193 C1
EASTRIP 75 D4
Eastrip La SN14 . . . . 75 C3
Eastrop SN6 . . . . 23 B5
Eastrop Inf Sch SN6 . . . . 23 A3
East Sands SN8 . . . . 183 D8
East St
  Bourton SP8 . . . . 137 E1
  Hindon SP3 . . . . 200 A4
  Lacock SN15 . . . . 86 D6
  Salisbury SP2 . . . . . . 145 F1
  10 Swindon SN1 . . . . . . 50 B6
  Warminster BA12 . . . . 117 B6
EAST TOWN 106 E4
East Town Rd BA14 . . . . 106 D3
EAST TYTHERTON 72 B2
Eastview Rd BA14 . . . . . 105 A7
Eastville Rd SN25 . . . . . . 35 C3
Eastwell Rd SN10 . . . . . 179 D5
East Wichel Prim Sch
  SN1 . . . . 50 B2
East Wichel Wy
  Swindon SN1 . . . . 50 A2
  Swindon SN1 . . . . 50 B1
EAST WINTERSLOW . . . 149 C8
Eastwood SO51 . . . . . . 162 E1
Eastwood Ave SN4 . . . . . 47 E1
EAST WOODLANDS 114 B5

East Woodlands Rd
  BA11 . . . . 114 A7
Eastwoods BA11 . . . . 82 B3
East Yewstock Cres SN15 . 70 C1
Eaton Cl 1 SN3 . . . . 51 A4
Eaton Wood SN5. . . . . . . 34 A2
Ebbesborne Hollow SP5 . 204 D2
EBBESBOURNE WAKE. . . 204 C2
Ebble Cl SP9 . . . . 216 D7
Ebble Cres BA12 . . . . . . 117 A5
Ebor Cl SN25 . . . . 34 F7
Ebor Gdns SN11 . . . . 89 C8
Ebor Paddock SN11. . . . . 89 C8
Eccleston Cl SN3 . . . . 51 B3
Echo Lodge Mdws Nature
  Reserve* SN15. . . . . . . 46 E7
Ecklington SN3 . . . . 51 C5
Edale Moor SN3 . . . . 51 E3
EDDINGTON 177 C8
Eddington Hill RG17 . . . . 177 C8
Eddleston Rd 2 SN1. . . . . 50 E7
Edelweiss Cl 29 SP11. . . . 192 A5
Edencroft SN6. . . . . 23 B8
Eden Cl SN12 . . . . 85 D1
Eden Pk Cl BA1. . . . . 82 A4
Eden Pk Dr BA1. . . . . 82 A4
EDEN VALE 108 E3
Eden Vale Rd BA13. . . . . 108 F3
Edgam Pl SP2 . . . . 144 F3
Edgar Cl 6 SP10 . . . . 193 E2
Edgar Row Cl 1 SN4. . . . . 64 A6
Edgecorner La SN14 . . . . . 53 A3
Edgehill SN5 . . . . 49 B3
Edgeware Rd SN1 . . . . . . 50 C6
Edgeworth Cl 4 SN5. . . . . 49 B7
Edinburgh Rd SN11 . . . . . 81 F1
Edinburgh St SN2. . . . . . . 35 D1
Edinburgh Wy SN13. . . . . 84 E7
EDINGTON 186 C8
Edington Cl SN5 . . . . 49 B5
Edington Priory* BA13 . . 186 C8
Edington Rd BA14 . . . . . 178 A3
Edison Bsns Pk SN3 . . . . . 51 D5
Edison Rd
  Salisbury SP2 . . . . . . 151 E8
  Swindon SN3 . . . . 51 D5
Edith New Cl 4 SN25 . . . . 34 E7
Edmonton Wy 3 SP4. . . . 217 F8
Edmund St SN1. . . . . 50 C5
Edrich Sq SP10 . . . . 193 E1
Egerton Cl SN3 . . . . 51 B7
Edric's Gn SP4. . . . . 199 C5
Edridge Cl SN15 . . . . 78 F8
Edridge Pl 1 SN13 . . . . . . 76 E1
Education Cen The SN1. . . 50 F8
Edward Rd SN10 . . . . . . 214 B2
Edward Richardson & Phyllis
  Amey Nature Reserve*
  GL6 . . . . 2 C6
Edwards Hill 12 RG17 . . . 165 A1
Edwards Meadow SN8 . . 213 B3
Edwards Rd SP4 . . . . . . 217 B3
Edward St BA13 . . . . . . 109 A3
Egdon Cl 9 SN25 . . . . 34 D6
Egerton Cl SN3 . . . . 51 B7
Eider Ave SN15 . . . . 60 A1
Elbe Way SP10. . . . . 193 D2
Elborough Rd SN2 . . . . . . 34 D3
ELCOMBE 63 E5
Elcombe Ave 3 SN4. . . . . 64 A6
Elcombe Gdns BA14 . . . . 105 C5
Elcombe Gdns SN10 . . . . 214 A4
Elcombe La SP5 . . . . 204 B2
Elcot Cl SN8 . . . . 213 F3
Elcot La SN8. . . . . 213 F3
Elcot Orch SN8 . . . . 175 A8
ELDENE 51 C5
Eldene Dr SN3. . . . . 51 C5
Eldene Prim Sch SN3. . . . . 51 C5
Elden Rd SP9. . . . . 191 D5
Elder Cl SN2 . . . . 34 C3
Elder Ct 3 SN13. . . . . 84 E8
Eleanor Cl 16 SP11. . . . . . 192 A5
Elgar Cl SN3. . . . . 34 E7
Elgin Dr SN2 . . . . 35 E1
Elgin Ind Est SN2. . . . . . . 35 E1
Eliot Cl SN3. . . . . 51 D3
Elizabeth Cl
  3 Downton SP5 . . . . . . 210 F8
  Melksham Without SN12. . 93 F1
Elizabeth Dr SN10 . . . . . 214 C4
Elizabeth Gdns GL7 . . . . . . 1 A5
Elizabeth Pl SN15 . . . . . . 79 A4
Elizabeth Rd
  16 Durrington/Bulford
  SP4 . . . . 198 B7
  Wilton SP2 . . . . 144 B5
Elizabeth Sq SP9 . . . . . . 216 E7
Elley Gn SN13 . . . . 84 E6
Ellingdon Rd SN4. . . . . . . 63 F7
ELLIOTS GREEN 114 D8
Elliott Cl SN10. . . . . 214 B1
Elliott Gn SP4 . . . . 133 C3
Elliott Pl BA14 . . . . 101 A1
Ellworthy Ct BA11. . . . . . 110 B4
Elm Cl
  Bower Hill SN12 . . . . . . 94 C1
  Calne SN11 . . . . 89 C8
  8 Ludgershall SP11. . . . . 192 B5
  Lyneham SN15. . . . . 60 B2
  Motcombe SP7 . . . . . . 202 A5
  Pitton & Farley SP5. . . . 148 C4
  Rowde SN10. . . . . 96 D1
  Royal Wootton Bassett SN4 . 47 E4
  Salisbury SP1 . . . . 146 D3
  Staverton BA14 . . . . . . 101 D6
  Trowbridge BA14. . . . . . 105 C5
ELM CROSS. 167 D7
Elm Ct SN10 . . . . 214 B1

Elmdale Ct BA14 . . . . . . 105 A7
Elmdale Rd BA14 . . . . . . 105 A7
Elmer Cl SN16 . . . . 28 A5
Elm Farm Cl SN16 . . . . . . 16 D2
Elmfield BA15 . . . . 100 C7
Elmfield 7 SP5 . . . . 211 C7
Elm Gr
  Corsham SN13. . . . . 76 E1
  Salisbury SP1 . . . . 146 C1
  Swindon SN5 . . . . 49 A8
Elm Gr Pl SP1 . . . . 146 B1
Elm Gr Rd SP1 . . . . 146 B1
Elm Hayes SN13 . . . . 85 A7
ELM HILL. 202 A5
Elm Hill BA12 . . . . 113 C1
Elmina Rd SN1 . . . . 50 C7
Elm Leigh BA11. . . . . 110 C6
Elmore SN3 . . . . 51 C5
Elm Pk SN4. . . . . 47 D1
Elm Rd
  Colerne SN14 . . . . 75 A5
  Swindon SN2 . . . . 35 A2
Elms Cl SP6 . . . . 210 B1
Elms Cross Dr BA15. . . . . 100 C5
Elms The
  Bradford-on-Avon BA15 . . 100 B8
  Highworth SN6 . . . . 22 F5
  Holt BA14 . . . . 92 E1
  Swindon SN5 . . . . 48 F8
Elmswood Cl SN2 . . . . . . 35 E5
Elm Tree Cl SN10 . . . . . . 214 D2
Elm Tree Gdns SN10 . . . . 214 D2
Elm View GL7. . . . . 5 F4
Elmwood SN15 . . . . 70 E2
Elmwood Ave 6 SP6. . . . . 210 C1
Elsham Way SN25. . . . . . . 35 A5
ELSTON 196 E7
Elston La SP3. . . . . 196 E7
Elstree Way
  Haydon Wick SN25 . . . . . 34 F6
  Swindon SN25 . . . . 35 A7
Elver Cl 9 SN3 . . . . 51 B8
Ely Cl SN5. . . . . 49 C4
Ely Ct SN4 . . . . 64 A5
Embankment SN1. . . . . . . 50 D3
Embry Cl 3 SN11. . . . . . . 166 A1
Emden Rd 18 SP10 . . . . . 193 D2
Emerson Cl SN25 . . . . 35 A6
Emery Gate SN15 . . . . . . 78 E7
Emery La SN15 . . . . 78 E7
Emlyn Sq SN1 . . . . 50 B6
Emmanuel Cl SN3 . . . . . . 35 A4
Emmaus Sch BA14. . . . . . 101 D5
Emmett Hill Mdws Nature
  Reserve* SN16. . . . . . . 16 D1
Emms La 10 BA13. . . . . . . 186 B7
Empire Rd SP2 . . . . 145 C2
Empress Way SP11 . . . . . 192 A5
Emwell St BA12 . . . . 117 A7
Endeavour Prim Sch
  SP11 . . . . 193 F2
Endeavour Rd 6 SN3. . . . . 51 B8
Endless St SP1 . . . . 146 A1
ENFORD 189 F6
Enford Ave SN2. . . . . 35 C6
Enford Hill SN9. . . . . 189 F6
Engineer Rd BA13 . . . . . 108 C6
ENGLANDS 78 F5
Englefield SN4 . . . . 47 E1
ENHAM ALAMEIN 193 E4
Enham La SP10. . . . . 193 E3
Eningen View SN11 . . . . . 81 B1
ENMORE GREEN 202 B2
Enos Wy SN11 . . . . 110 A6
Ensor Cl SN25 . . . . 35 A8
Enstone Cl 2 SN2 . . . . 34 E2
Epping Cl BA12 . . . . 117 A8
Epping Dr SN15. . . . . 94 C6
Epsom Cl SN14 . . . . 77 F6
Epsom Rd BA14 . . . . 105 E4
Equinox Dr SP4. . . . . 217 E4
Erin Ct 1 SN1 . . . . 50 A5
Eriskay Gdns BA13 . . . . . 108 F2
Eriskay Pl SN5. . . . . 34 B3
Erleigh Dr SN15 . . . . 78 C7
ERLESTOKE 187 A8
Erlestoke Way SN25 . . . . . 35 C6
Ermin Cl SN8. . . . . 170 C8
Ermine St RG17 . . . . 171 A6
Ermin St
  1 Baydon SN8 . . . . 164 C1
  Baydon SN8. . . . . 170 C8
  Blunsdon St Andrew SN26 . 20 F2
  Swindon SN3 . . . . 35 F4
Erneston Cres SN13. . . . . . 76 F1
Ernle Rd SN11 . . . . 81 C4
Erskine Barracks SP2 . . . 144 F4
Escott Cl 4 SN15. . . . . 78 F4
Eshton Wlk SN3. . . . . 51 A3
Esmead SN15 . . . . 78 F8
Espringham Pl SN2 . . . . . . 35 E4
Essex Pl 7 RG17 . . . . 165 A2
Essex Sq SP2 . . . . 151 D6
Essex Wlk SN3 . . . . 50 F6
Estate Yd The SN10 . . . . 172 B3
Estcourt Cres SN10 . . . . 214 B4
Estcourt Rd SP1 . . . . 146 B1
Estcourt St SN10 . . . . . . 214 B3
Estcourt Terr SN10 . . . . . 214 B5
Estella Cl SN25 . . . . 34 D6
Eston Medieval Village of*
  SN14. . . . . 69 D8
ETCHILHAMPTON. 180 C7
Ethelbert Dr 4 SP10. . . . . 193 C2
Ethelred Pl SN13. . . . . 76 E1
Ethendun 11 BA13 . . . . . . 186 B7
Euclid St SN1. . . . . 50 C6

Europa & Brittania Pk
  SN3. . . . . 51 A8
Euro Way SN1 . . . . 48 F3
Evans Cl SN15 . . . . 70 E1
Eveleigh Rd SN4. . . . . 47 E2
Evelyn St SN1. . . . . 50 D3
EVEN SWINDON 49 E6
Even Swindon Prim Sch
  SN2. . . . . 49 F7
Eveque Cl SP2 . . . . 144 F3
Evergreen Ind Pk GL7. . . . . 6 F5
Evergreens Cl SN3. . . . . . . 36 C1
Evergreen Way 10 SP4. . . 217 C2
Everland Rd 18 RG17 . . . . 177 B7
Everland Rd Ind Est
  RG17. . . . . 177 C7
EVERLEIGH 191 A8
Everleigh Barrows* SN9 182 E3
Everleigh Cl BA14 . . . . . . 105 D5
Everleigh Rd
  Collingbourne Ducis SN8. . 191 D8
  Pewsey SN9 . . . . 215 C3
  Swindon SN2 . . . . 35 C3
Ewden Cl SN11 . . . . 50 B2
EWEN 5 C8
Eworth Cl SN5 . . . . 48 F5
Exbury Cl 2 SN25 . . . . 35 A6
Exe Cl SN25 . . . . 34 A4
Exeter Cl SN14. . . . . 77 F5
Exeter House Specl Sch
  SP1 . . . . 146 B3
Exeter St
  Salisbury SP2 . . . . 152 B7
  Swindon SN1 . . . . 50 A6
Exmoor Cl 1 SN2. . . . . 34 C4
Exmoor Rd 6 BA13 . . . . . 108 E1
Exmouth St SN1 . . . . 50 A5
Eyam Rd SN1 . . . . 50 A1
Eyles Rd SN10 . . . . 214 B1
Eyre Cl 1 SN25 . . . . 34 D6
Eyres Dr SP5 . . . . 153 E2
Eyres Way SP1 . . . . 152 B8

F

FABERSTOWN 192 B6
Factory Hill SP8 . . . . 137 F2
Factory La
  Barford St Martin SP3. . . 143 A3
  Warminster BA12 . . . . . 116 F6
Fairbourne Ave BA13 . . . 109 B3
Fairfax Cl
  Amesbury SP4 . . . . 217 A4
  Swindon SN3 . . . . 50 F7
Fairfield
  1 Cricklade SN6 . . . . . . 19 D8
  4 Great Bedwyn SN8. . . 176 B3
  Minety SN16 . . . . 17 B1
  Rode BA11. . . . . 103 F1
  Royal Wootton Bassett SN4 . 47 C3
Fairfield Cl
  Frome BA11. . . . . 110 A7
  Marshfield SN14 . . . . . . 74 A8
Fairfield Meadows BA14 . 104 F3
Fairfield Rd
  Salisbury SP1 . . . . 146 A4
  Warminster BA12 . . . . . 117 B7
Fairfields 22 RG17 . . . . . 177 B7
Fairfoot Cl SN14 . . . . 78 A7
FAIRFORD 1 E1
Fairford Airfield GL7. . . . . . 1 E1
Fairford Cres SN25 . . . . . . 35 C3
Fairground The 2 SP11. . . 192 F1
Fairhaven BA13 . . . . 108 D1
Fairholme Way SN4. . . . . . 35 F4
Fairlane SP7 . . . . 202 C1
Fairlawn SN3 . . . . 51 D3
Fairleigh Rise SN15 . . . . . 70 D3
Fair Mile
  Collingbourne Kingston
  SN8. . . . . 183 F3
  Grafton SN8. . . . . 184 A4
Fairview
  Colerne SN14 . . . . 75 C6
  Swindon SN1 . . . . 50 B5
Fairview Rd
  1 Andover SP11. . . . . . . 192 F1
  Hungerford RG17 . . . . . 177 B7
  Salisbury SP1 . . . . 146 C1
Fair View Rd SP2 . . . . . . 144 E4
Fairwater Ct SN4 . . . . 64 A5
Fairway
  Calne SN11 . . . . 89 C8
  Melksham SN12. . . . . . . 94 C5
Fairway The SN10. . . . . . 214 A1
FAIRWOOD 108 B4
Fairwood Cl BA14. . . . . . 102 A2
Fairwood Rd
  Dilton Marsh BA13 . . . . 108 C5
  North Bradley BA13 . . . . 107 F5
Falcon Dr BA14. . . . . 105 E7
Falconer Mews SN25. . . . . 35 B6
Falcon Rd SN11 . . . . 81 D3
Falconscroft SN3 . . . . 51 C8
Falconsway SP2 . . . . 152 A5
Falcon Way SN12. . . . . . . 94 D1
Falconwood Cl 8 SP6. . . . 210 C1
Falkirk Rd SN4 . . . . 64 A7
Falkner Cl SN8 . . . . 213 B3
Falklands Rd SN4. . . . . . . 64 E3
Fallow Field Cl SN14 . . . . . 70 B2
Falmouth Gr SN3 . . . . 50 E4
Fanshaw Way BA12 . . . . 117 A5
Fanstones Rd SN3 . . . . . . 51 C4

Fantley La SP8. . . . . 138 B1
Faraday Pk SN3 . . . . 51 E5
Faraday Rd
  Salisbury SP2 . . . . 145 E1
  Swindon SN3 . . . . 51 E5
Fareham Cl SN3 . . . . 51 B5
Farfield La SN6 . . . . 19 E4
Fargo Cl SP4 . . . . 198 A6
Fargo Rd SP4 . . . . 217 A2
Faringdon Rd 2 SN1 . . . . . 50 B6
Farleigh Ave
  Melksham SN12. . . . . . . 94 B3
  Trowbridge BA14. . . . . . 105 A7
Farleigh Castle* BA2. . . . 103 E8
Farleigh Cl
  1 Chippenham SN14. . . . 77 F6
  Westbury BA13 . . . . . . 108 F4
Farleigh Cres SN3 . . . . . . 50 E3
FARLEIGH
  HUNGERFORD. 103 E7
Farleigh Pk* BA2 . . . . . . 103 D5
Farleigh Rd BA2. . . . . . . 103 E8
Farleigh Rise BA1. . . . . . . 82 D1
FARLEIGH WICK. 90 F5
FARLEY 154 D8
Farley Cl BA11. . . . . 110 C6
Farley Rd SP1 . . . . 152 C7
Farman Cl SN3 . . . . 51 C4
Farm Ct 3 SN6 . . . . 163 E6
Farmer Cl SN15. . . . . 70 E1
Farmer Cres SN25 . . . . . . 35 C6
Farmer Giles Farmstead*
  SP3 . . . . 201 C3
Farmhouse Cl SN15 . . . . . 78 F4
Farmhouse Dr SN15. . . . . 78 A4
Farm La
  Aldbourne SN8 . . . . 170 A6
  Great Bedwyn SN8 . . . . 176 B3
  Salisbury SP1 . . . . 145 E1
Farnborough Rd SN3 . . . . 51 B3
Farndale Cl 4 SN2 . . . . . . 35 C5
Farne Way SN4 . . . . 48 A2
FARNHAM 207 C2
Farnsby St SN1 . . . . 50 B6
Farrar Dr SN8. . . . . 213 A2
Farrells Field SN14 . . . . . 68 F4
Farrfield SN2. . . . . 35 E4
Farriers Cl SN1 . . . . 50 E8
Farriers Field SN9 . . . . . . 181 F2
Farthing La SN15 . . . . 60 A4
Farthing Row BA11 . . . . . 103 E1
Far View Rd SP3 . . . . 196 F7
Farleader Sq RG17 . . . . . 177 C7
Faverole Way BA14 . . . . 102 A2
Fawley Cl SN25 . . . . 34 C8
Fayre Gdns GL7 . . . . 1 F6
Featherbed La SN6 . . . . . 163 F7
Feather Wood SN5. . . . . . 49 D5
Fell Rd BA13. . . . . 108 E2
Feltham Dr BA11. . . . . . . 110 A3
Feltham La BA11. . . . . . . 110 A2
Fenland Cl
  8 Swindon SN5 . . . . 48 F8
  5 Swindon SN5 . . . . 49 A8
Fenn Cl SN5 . . . . 34 B1
Fennel Cl SN2 . . . . 34 D4
Fennel Rd BA12. . . . . 139 B6
Fenton Ave SN25 . . . . 34 E7
Ferguson Rd SN10 . . . . . 214 D1
Fermoy BA11. . . . . 110 B6
Fernacre Rd SN1 . . . . 50 B2
Ferndale Prim Sch SN2. . . 50 B8
Ferndale Rd SN2. . . . . 49 F8
FERNE 203 D1
Ferne Hollow SP5 . . . . . . 207 A8
Ferne Wall Cnr SP7. . . . . 203 B1
Ferney Way SP5 . . . . 207 C4
Fernham Rd SN25 . . . . . . 34 E3
Ferozeshah Rd SN10 . . . . 214 E6
Ferrers Dr SN5 . . . . 48 F4
Ferris Cl SN10 . . . . 96 E1
Ferris Gr SN12. . . . . 94 C4
Ferris Mead BA12. . . . . . 117 A6
Ferris Way BA14 . . . . 101 F1
Festival Ave SP2 . . . . 145 C3
Feversham Rd SP1. . . . . . 146 B3
Fiddington Clay SN10 . . . 179 F1
Fiddington Hill SN10 . . . . 180 A1
FIDDINGTON SANDS . . . 179 F1
Fiddle The SN6 . . . . 19 C7
Field Barn La SP3. . . . . . 201 F3
Field Cl
  South Cerney GL7 . . . . . . 7 A7
  Westbury BA13 . . . . . . 109 A4
Fieldfare SN3. . . . . 51 D7
Fieldfare Wy 4 SN12 . . . . . 94 D5
Fieldins BA15. . . . . 99 E7
Field La BA9. . . . . 137 B3
Field Rise SN1. . . . . 50 A3
Fieldside SN10 . . . . 187 E8
Fields The
  Mere BA12 . . . . 139 B6
  Swindon SN3 . . . . 36 A1
Field View
  Chippenham SN15 . . . . . 78 D7
  Enford SN9 . . . . 190 A6
Field Way BA14 . . . . 104 F6
FIFIELD 190 A5
FIFIELD BAVANT 204 F4
Figgins La SN8 . . . . 213 D2
FIGHELDEAN 190 B2
Figsbury Cl 5 SN25 . . . . . . 34 C5
Figsbury Rd SP4 . . . . 133 B1
Figsbury Ridge SP4 . . . . . 133 C2
Figsbury Ring* SP4 . . . . . 147 D8

FILANDS 28 A6
Filsham Rd SN25...........34 C7
Finchdale SN3............51 D8
Finches La
2 Baydon SN8.........164 C1
Baydon SN8...........170 C8
Finchley Rd SP2.........145 E2
Finkley Rd SP11.........193 F2
Finnis Ash 1 SP4.......217 C3
Firbank Cres BA12......117 D8
Fire Brigade Mus★ SN10 179 C5
Firecrest View 3 SN3 ...51 E6
Fire Fly Ave SN2.........50 A7
Fir Gn La SN8...........183 D8
Fir Gr SN11.............89 D8
Fir Rd SN14.............74 F6
Firs Cl SP5.............148 C7
FIRSDOWN...............148 C8
Firs Hill Way SN10......179 E5
Firs Rd
Alderbury SP5.........153 C2
Firsdown SP5.........148 B7
First Broad Dr
Barford St Martin SP3....129 A1
Wilton SP2............144 A7
Firs The
Chippenham SN14......78 A6
Inkpen RG17..........177 F3
Limpley Stoke BA2......99 A5
First La SN12...........85 C1
Firth Cl SN25...........35 A3
Fir Tree Cl SN2.........35 A2
Fishers Brook BA11......110 A5
FISHERTON DE LA
MERE...............195 D1
Fisherton Island SP2.....145 F1
Fisherton St SP2........145 F1
Fish Row SP1...........152 A8
Fitkin Cl 1 SN25.......34 E7
Fitwell Rd SN25.........34 C7
FITTLETON..............190 A4
Fitzgerold Ave SN6......22 F7
Fitzmaurice Cl
Bradford-on-Avon BA15 .100 E4
Calne Without SN11 ......79 F2
Swindon SN3..........51 D7
Fitzmaurice Pl BA15....100 D5
Fitzmaurice Prim Sch
BA15................100 D5
Fitzpiers Cl 10 SN25....34 C5
Fitzroy Rd SN1.........50 C2
Fitzwarren Cl SN15......79 A4
Five Ash La BA12........117 C2
Five Lanes Prim Sch
SN10................179 D5
Five Rivers Leisure Ctr
SP1.................145 F3
Five Stiles Rd SN8......213 F2
Five Thorn La SN15......57 D6
Fiveways Cl SN8........164 B1
Fiveways Trading Est
SN13................84 B7
Flamstone St SP5.......205 A4
Flashett The SP5........149 D6
Flaxfields End 13 SP6...210 D1
FLAXLANDS..............47 D6
Flax Mill Pk SN25.......214 C5
Flayburn Rd SN25.......34 E7
Fleece Cotts 2 BA14....105 E7
Fleet Rd SN15..........78 D8
Fleet St SN1...........50 B6
Fleetwood Cl SN13......84 E6
Fleetwood Rise SN12....93 A8
Fleming Cl SP11........192 A5
Fleming Way SN1........50 C6
Flensburg Cl 20 SP10...193 D2
Flers Ct BA12..........117 A6
Fleur De Lys Dr BA14...105 A4
Flint Hill SN5..........49 C4
Flintjack Pl 2 RG17....165 A1
Flint La SP11...........193 A4
Flint Wy SP5...........152 C5
Flisteridge Rd SN16.....16 C3
Flit Croft 4 SP4.......217 C2
FLOOD STREET...........210 E4
Flood The SP5..........149 B7
Florence Ct 21 SP10....193 E2
Florence Mews SP2......144 C3
Florence St SN2........50 C8
Flower La
Amesbury SP4.........217 A3
Melchet Park & Plaitford
SO51...............212 F7
Flowers Mead 6 BA13...186 B7
Flowers Yd SN15........78 E7
Focus School - Wilton
Primary Campus SP2...144 B4
Foghamshire SN15.......78 D7
Folkestone Cl SN14......78 A6
Folkestone Rd
Salisbury SP2.........151 F6
Swindon SN1..........50 B4
Folly Barrow★ DT11....206 B2
Folly Cl
Highworth SN6.........23 A7
Salisbury SP2.........151 F5
Folly Cres SN6.........23 A7
Folly Dr SN6...........23 A7
Follyfield
Bradford-on-Avon BA15 . 100 D4
Hankerton SN16.........15 B2
Folly La
Alderbury SP5.........153 C3
Melksham Without SN12....93 B8

Folly La continued
Salisbury SP2.........145 D3
Warminster BA12.......116 B5
Folly La E SN15.........86 C5
Folly La W SN15.........86 B5
Folly Rd
Inkpen RG17..........177 F3
Lambourn SN8.........164 F1
Roundway SN10........214 C2
Folly The SN15.........44 A2
Folly View SP2.........145 C5
Folly Way SN6..........23 A7
FONTHILL BISHOP........200 D3
FONTHILL GIFFORD.......200 B2
Fonthill Wlk SN3.......50 E5
Fontmell Cl 9 SN25....34 E7
Foot's Hill
Cann SP7............206 A7
Salisbury SP2.........145 A3
Forage La BA12.........117 B7
FORD
Biddestone...........68 A2
Laverstock...........146 D7
Fordbrook Bsns Ctr SN9 .215 C6
Forders Cl 12 SP5.....211 C7
FORDINGBRIDGE..........210 E1
Fordingbridge Hospl
SP6.................210 D1
Fordingbridge Inf Sch
SP6.................210 D2
Fordson Rd SN10........214 D1
Ford St SN1............50 A5
Foreminster Ct BA12....116 F5
Fore St
Ashton Keynes SN6......6 F1
Trowbridge BA14.......101 D1
Warminster BA12.......116 F5
Westbury BA13........109 A4
Wylye BA12...........201 E8
Forest Dale Rd SN8.....175 A8
Forest Dr SP9..........216 E7
Forester Cl 5 SN3.....51 D4
Foresters Pk Rd SN12...94 C4
FOREST HILL............175 B7
Forest Hill SN8........176 B3
Forest La
Chippenham SN15......78 E3
Chute SP11...........192 D8
Melksham Without SN12...86 F2
Forest Park Rd SN5.....34 B1
Forest Rd
Bramshaw SP5.........212 B3
7 Frome BA11........110 B7
Horningsham BA12......118 D8
Melksham SN12........94 B5
Redlynch SP6.........211 D6
Wooton Rivers SN8.....174 F2
Forest Rd Cnr BA12.....118 E2
Forest & Sandridge CE Prim
Sch SN15............94 E5
Forest Wlk BA13.......111 C4
FOREWOODS COMMON......101 C7
Forge Cl
Milton Lilbourne SN9...182 E7
South Newton SP2......130 B1
West Overton SN8.....173 F6
Forge Fields SN5........48 D8
Forge La
West Overton SN8.....173 F7
Zennor BA12..........137 F3
Forge The
Hungerford RG17.......177 C7
Lower Stanton St Quinton
SN14...............56 D6
Forman St SN11.........81 C3
Forres Sandle Manor Sch
SP6.................210 C1
Forrester Gn SN14......75 B3
Forsey Cl 4 SN3.......51 E7
Forsters La OX12.......165 F7
Fortis Hill SP7........203 C3
Fortunes Field SN4.....167 C7
Fortune Way SN15.......78 F5
Forty Acres Rd SN10....214 C3
Forty The
Bishopstone SN6.......163 E7
Cricklade SN6........19 D7
Forum Cl SN3..........51 C8
Fosbury CI SN3.........185 A5
FOSBURY...............185 A5
Foscote Gdns 2 BA11...110 C7
Foscott SN6...........8 C4
FOXCOTE...............193 C2
Foxcotte Cl SP10.......193 C1
Foxcotte La SP11.......193 C2
Foxcotte Rd SP10.......193 C2
Fox Croft Wlk SN15.....78 F4
Foxglove Cl SN12.......94 C3
Foxglove Dr BA14.......101 E4
Foxglove Rd SN25.......34 D5
Foxglove Way SN11......81 B5
Foxgrove SN14.........70 A2
FOXHAM................72 D7
Foxham Wy SN1.........49 F2
Foxhill Cl SN25........34 F3
Foxleaze SN6..........8 D1
FOXLEY................41 F8
Foxley Cl
Swindon SN2..........35 E4
12 Warminster BA12...117 A8
Foxley Cnr SN10........180 D4
Foxley Fields SN10.....180 C4
Foxley Rd
Norton SN16..........41 E8
St Paul Malmesbury Without
SN16...............27 D2
Foxtail Gdns SP11......192 A5
Fox Talbot Mus★ SN15..86 D5
FOX THE...............33 F3
Fox Wood SN5..........49 D5
Foyle Hill SP7.........202 B1
Foyle Rd SP11.........192 C2
Foyle's Mead BA12.....201 E8
Frampton Cl SN5.......49 B6
Frampton Ct BA14......105 A6
Francis Rd 10 SN10....179 F1
Francis St BA14........101 C1
Francis Way SP2.......152 A5
Francomes SN25........34 E4
Francomes Field 17
RG17...............165 A1
Frankel Ave 5 SN25...34 D7
Frankenbury★ SP6......210 F2
Frankland Rd SN1......48 E3
Franklin Rd SN10......214 D6
Frankton Gdns 2 SN3...36 B2
Frank Warman Ct 8 SN3..36 B3
Fraser Cl SN3..........51 B7
Fredericks Ave SN14....77 F7
Fredericks Way SN14....53 D3
Frederick Taylor Ct BA12 116 F4
Freegrove Dr SN15......73 F8
Freegrove Rd SN15......73 F8
Freemans Cl 4 RG17...177 B7
Free's Ave SN8........213 B5
Freesia Cl 2 BA12.....116 E7
Freestone Way 5 SN13...76 D1
Fremantle Rd SP11......191 F4
French Mill La SP7.....202 C1
French Mill Rise 16 SP7.202 C1
Frensham Way SN9......215 D6
Fresden Village★ SN6...23 E4
FRESH BROOK...........49 A4
Freshbrook Way SN5....49 B4
FRESHFORD.............99 B5
Freshford CE Prim Sch
BA2................99 B5
Freshford La BA2.......99 A4
Freshford Sta BA2......99 C5
Friars Cl BA13........112 C8
Friar's Orch 4 SP1....152 B8
Friars The SN12........94 C6
Friary Cl BA15........99 E4
Friary La SP1.........152 B7
Friary The SP1........152 B8
Fricker's La SP3......200 F3
Friday La SN9..........181 D3
Fridays Ham La SN6.....7 B3
Friday St
Christian Malford SN15...58 C3
Swindon SN25.........34 C6
Friesian Cl SN5.......49 A7
Friesland Cl SN5......49 A7
Friggle St BA11.......110 D1
Frilford Dr SN3.......36 A1
FRITHAM...............212 A1
Frith Copse SN5.......34 A2
Fritillary Mews SN1....50 D6
Frobisher Dr SN3......50 F6
Frogden Rd SN1........50 B1
Frog La
Avebury SN8..........173 B8
Chilmark SP3.........201 A3
Great Bedwyn SN8.....176 C3
Great Somerford SN15...44 B3
Hullavington SN14.....41 F1
Longbridge Deverill BA12.121 A6
Motcombe SP7........202 B4
West Overton SN8.....173 F7
FROGMORE.............109 A4
Frogmore Rd BA13......108 F5
Frogwell SN14.........77 F8
Frogwell Pk SN14......78 A8
Frogwell Prim Sch SN14..78 A7
FROME................110 A5
Frome Com Coll SN14....110 A6
Frome Com Hospl BA11..110 A6
FROMEFIELD............110 A7
Frome Leisure Ctr BA11 .110 A7
Frome Rd
Bradford-on-Avon BA15 ..100 C5
Maiden Bradley with Yarnfield
BA12...............118 D5
Southwick BA14.......104 F3
Swindon SN25.........34 F4
Trowbridge BA14.......105 C7

Frome Rd continued
Westwood BA15........100 C3
Wingfield BA14.......104 C6
Frome Sta BA11........110 B4
Frome View BA12.......118 B3
Frome Way BA12........118 E3
Front Horse Hill La SP7 .203 A1
Front La SN26.........21 A4
Front St RG17.........171 E7
Frost Cl 1 SN5........49 D6
FROXFIELD.............176 D7
Fruitfields Cl SN10....214 B1
Fry Cl 2 SN1.........49 F4
Fryern Ct Rd SP6......210 D3
Fry Sq SP10...........193 F1
Fugglestone SP2.......144 F3
FUGGLESTONE ST
PETER..............144 F4
Fulford Rd BA14.......101 E2
Fuller Ave SN13.......84 E8
Fuller Cl SN2.........35 F5
Fullers Ave SN6.......19 D8
Fuller's Cl SN12......94 B5
Fullerton Wlk 6 SN1...49 F4
Fulmar Cl SN12........94 D1
Fulney Cl BA14........101 F2
Furlong BA12..........117 B6
Furlong Cl
Rowde SN10..........96 E1
Swindon SN25.........34 E5
Furlong Cres SP3......196 F7
Furlong Gdns BA14......101 E1
Furlong Way SP3.......196 F7
Furnax La BA12........112 F1
Furrow Wy 11 SN17....193 F2
Furse Cl SN5..........34 A2
Furze Dr SP11.........191 F3
Furzehill SN13........84 F8
Furze Hill La SN10.....179 D7
FURZLEY..............212 F3
Furzley Cl SO51.......212 F3
Furzley Rd SO51.......212 F3
Fussells Lodge (Long
Barrow)★ SP5.......147 D5
FYFIELD..............192 D1
Milton Lilbourne.......215 E5
Fyfield Ave SN2.......35 C5
Fyfield Cl 2 SP1......146 D5
Fyfield Down National Nature
Reserve★ SN8......167 F1
Fyfield La SP11.......192 D1
Fyfield Rd SP11.......192 E1
Fyfield Way SP11......191 F3
Fynamore Com Prim Sch
SN11...............81 A4
Fyne Cl 3 SN5........34 B2

G

Gable Cl SN2..........35 B6
Gables Cl SN10........214 D2
Gabrial Cres SN25......34 C8
Gabriel Cl 4 BA11....110 C6
Gainsborough Ave SN4...47 F3
Gainsborough Cl SP2...145 C3
Gainsborough Ct 1
SP10...............193 D1
Gainsborough Rise BA14 105 A6
Gainsborough Way SN5...49 A3
Gains La SN10.........214 B4
Gairlock Cl SN5.......34 B2
Gaisford Chase SN10...179 B4
Galahad Cl 25 SP10...193 E2
Gales Cl SN15.........78 F8
Gales Gd SN8..........213 E3
Galileo Dr SN15.......70 E1
Gallery at Handel House★
SN10...............214 B3
Galley La SN8.........176 C3
Gallipoli Rd 8 SP4...198 F7
Gallops The SN4.......163 D4
Galloway Cl 13 SN5...49 A7
Galloway Cl SN2.......34 C5
Galsworthy Cl SN3.....51 D4
Galton Way SN2........49 F8
Gambia St SN1.........50 D4
Gamekeepers Cl 9 SN25..34 F7
Gantlettdene SN3......51 E6
Ganton Way SN2........35 E1
Gardeners Gn 2 SP9...199 C8
Gardens The
Heddington SN11......89 B1
Rushall SN9..........181 E3
Swindon SN25.........35 A3
Upavon SN9..........181 F2
Garden The SN2........35 E5
Garden Trading Est
SN10...............214 D6
Gardiner Rd 2 SP4....197 E6
Gardners Dr SN14......55 E8
GARE HILL.............118 A5
Garendon Ct 2 SP6....210 D1
Garfield Cl SN3.......51 C3
Garlings The 6 SN8...170 A6
Garrard Way SN3.......51 A8
Garraways 6 SN4......47 F2
GARSDON..............29 B4
Garsdon Mill SN16.....28 F5
Garsington Dr SN25....34 C7
Garston BA11..........110 A4
Garston La 3 BA11....110 A4
Garston Rd BA11.......110 A4
Garstons The BA1......82 D2
Garth Cl SN14.........70 B1

Garth Rd BA14.........101 F1
Gartons Rd SN5........48 F7
Gascelyn Cl SN14......78 A7
Gascoigne's La SP7....202 C1
Gas La
Cricklade SN6........19 D8
Salisbury SP2.........145 F1
Gason Hill Rd SP9.....216 C8
GASPER...............137 C7
Gasper St BA12........137 C6
Gassons Rd GL7........2 C5
Gassons Way GL7......2 C4
GASTARD..............85 D6
Gaston La SN16........40 C5
Gastons Rd SN16.......27 F3
Gaston's Rd SN14......78 C8
Gaters La SP4.........133 A2
Gauntlet Rd SP4.......217 B4
Gaveller Rd SN25......34 C7
Gawaine Cl 3 SN25...193 E2
Gawthorne Dr SP2......151 F6
Gaynor Cl SN25........35 A6
Gayton Way SN3.......51 B8
Gaza Rd SP4..........198 C2
Geneville Rise 3 SP4..217 C3
Genoa Ct 16 SP10.....193 E2
Gentle St BA12........119 C7
George Cl SN11........81 C3
George Gay Gdns 7 SN3..50 F4
George La SN8.........213 D2
George St Pl BA12.....117 A7
George St (South) 6
SP2................145 F1
George St
Salisbury SP2.........145 F1
Swindon SN1..........50 A6
Trowbridge BA14.......101 D1
Warminster BA12......117 A7
George VI Rd SP9.......216 C8
George Ward Sch The
SN12...............93 F6
Gerard Wlk SN5........49 A6
Germain's La SN14.....76 A8
Geys Hill BA12........115 A7
Giant's Cave (Long Barrow)★
SN14...............39 C2
Giant's Chair The
(Tumulus)★ SP5......158 E2
Gibbs Cl
2 Salisbury SP1.....146 C5
Swindon SN3.........51 E7
Westbury BA13........109 A4
Gibbs Cl SN13.........76 D1
Gibbs La SN14.........55 F8
Gibbs Leaze BA14.....102 A1
GIBB THE.............53 F3
Gibson Cl SN12........94 C1
GIDDEAHALL...........68 D2
Gifford Rd SN3........36 B3
Giffords The BA14.....102 A4
Gigant St
Salisbury SP1.........152 B8
Swallowcliffe SP3.....204 A6
Gilbert's Gn 3 SP9...199 D8
Gilberts Piece SN8....183 E1
Gilbert Way SN1.......146 C4
Giles Ave 1 SN6.....19 D7
Giles La SO51.........212 E4
Giles Rd 8 SN25......34 D6
Gilling Way SN3.......51 B6
Gilman Cl SN25........35 A8
Giotto Cl 11 SN25....34 B7
Gipsy La
Chippenham SN15......78 B5
Frome BA11..........110 B7
Holt BA14............92 F2
Hungerford RG17.......177 D5
Swindon SN2..........50 E8
Warminster BA12......117 B5
Gladstone Rd
Chippenham SN15......78 D7
Trowbridge BA14.......105 B7
Gladstone St SN1......50 C7
Gladys Plumley Gdns SN2 50 C8
Glass's La SP3........204 D7
Glebe Bglws 3 BA12...201 E8
Glebe Cl
7 Aldbourne SN8.....170 A6
Pitton & Farley SP5....148 C4
Glebe Field BA14......117 A6
Glebe Gdns SP7.......202 A4
Glebe La
Kemble GL7..........4 F7
Landford SP5........212 C6
Glebelands 3 BA12...194 C5
Glebe Pl
Chilton Foliat RG17....171 A1
Highworth SN6........23 A6
Glebe Rd
2 Durrington/Bulford
SP4................198 B7
Royal Wootton Bassett SN4 .47 D1
Trowbridge BA14.......105 A7
Glebe The
All Cannings SN10.....180 F8
Calne SN11..........81 C3
Freshford BA2........99 B4
Hinton Charterhouse BA2..98 D2
Glebe Way SN13........76 E1
Glendale Cres SP1.....152 D8
Glendale Rd SP4......198 C2
Gleneagles Cl SN15....78 F7
Glenfield Cl SN3......51 D6
Glenmore Bsns Pk SP2 .151 E8
Glenmore Rd
Haydon Wick SN25....34 C5

Glenmore Rd continued
Salisbury SP1 . . . . 146 C3
Glenside SN12 . . . . 94 C6
Glenville Cl SN4 . . . . 61 E8
Glenwood Cl SN1 . . . . 50 C2
Glevum Cl SN5 . . . . 33 C5
Glevum Rd SN3 . . . . 36 C1
Globe St SN1 . . . . 50 C4
Gloucester Cl 3 SN14 . . . . . 78 A6
Gloucester Rd
  Calne Without SN11 . . . . . . 81 F1
  8 Malmesbury SN16 . . . . . 28 A3
  Trowbridge BA14 . . . . 105 B7
Gloucester Sq SN12 . . . . . . 94 C4
Gloucester St SN1 . . . . 50 B7
Gloucester Wlk BA13 . . . . . 109 A4
Glover Rd SP4 . . . . 197 F7
Glyndebourne Cl SP2 . . . . . 145 C3
Glyn Pl SP7 . . . . 206 B7
GOATACRE 73 F7
Goatacre La SN11 . . . . 73 F7
Goddard Ave SN1 . . . . 50 B4
Goddard Cl 1 SN9 . . . . 215 C5
Goddard Pk Com Prim Sch
  SN3 . . . . 51 B5
Goddard Rd SN9 . . . . 215 C5
Goddards La 11 SN8 . . . . . . 170 A6
Godley La BA14 . . . . 106 A8
Godley Rd SP2 . . . . 152 A6
Godolphin Cl SN5 . . . . 49 A3
Godolphin Prep Sch SP1 146 C1
Godolphin Sch The SP1 . . . . 152 C8
GODSHILL 211 A1
Godwin Ct 9 SN1 . . . . 50 D4
Godwin Rd SN3 . . . . 36 B3
Godwins Cl SN12 . . . . 84 E1
Gogg's La SP5 . . . . 211 D7
Goldcrest Wlk SN5 . . . . 51 E7
Golden Cross SP6 . . . . 211 E4
Golden Rd SN10 . . . . 214 C5
Goldfinch Rd SN12 . . . . 94 E1
Gold Hill 8 SP7 . . . . 202 C1
Golding Ave SN8 . . . . 213 A2
Goldney Ave SN14 . . . . 78 C7
Goldsborough Cl SN5 . . . . . . 49 B6
Gold View SN1 . . . . 49 F4
GOMELDON 133 D4
Gomeldon Medieval Village
  of★ SP4 . . . . 133 C4
Gomeldon Prim Sch SP4 133 C4
Gomeldon Rd SP4 . . . . 133 D5
Gooch La BA11 . . . . 110 D6
Gooch St SN1 . . . . 50 C7
Goodbody Rd 1 SN4 . . . . . 198 A6
Goodes Hill SN13 . . . . 85 D3
Goodings La RG17 . . . . 171 D6
Goodwin Cl BA12 . . . . 117 E8
Goodwood Cl BA14 . . . . 105 E4
Goodwood Way 3 SN14 . . . 77 F5
Goodwyns Cl 5 SP9 . . . . . . 199 C8
Goor La SN8 . . . . 164 B2
Goose Gn RG17 . . . . 165 A2
Gooselands
  Crudwell SN16 . . . . 14 D5
  Westbury BA13 . . . . 108 F2
Goose St
  Marston SN10 . . . . 179 A3
  Southwick BA14 . . . . 105 A2
Gordon Gdns 4 SN1 . . . . . . 50 C6
Gordon Rd 5 SN1 . . . . 50 C6
Gore Cl SN25 . . . . 34 F6
Gore Cross SN10 . . . . 187 E5
Gore La BA13 . . . . 111 B4
Gore Rd SP4 . . . . 197 E7
Gores La SN9 . . . . 181 C5
Gornall Rd SN13 . . . . 84 F6
Gorringe Rd SP2 . . . . 145 D1
GORSE HILL 35 D1
Gorse Hill Prim Sch SN2 . . . 35 D1
Gorse Pl 5 SN13 . . . . 84 E8
Gosditch
  Ashton Keynes SN6 . . . . . . 17 E8
  Latton SN6 . . . . 8 C4
Gosling Cl 15 SN4 . . . . 163 A6
Gosse Ct SN3 . . . . 50 E2
Goughs Way SN4 . . . . 47 E2
Gould Cl 1 SP11 . . . . 192 A5
Goulding Cl 3 SN3 . . . . 36 B2
Gower Cl
  Swindon SN2 . . . . 35 F2
  1 Swindon SN5 . . . . 48 F5
Gower Rd 14 SP7 . . . . 202 D2
Grace Cl SP2 . . . . 145 B5
Grace La SP6 . . . . 211 A4
Graemar La SO51 . . . . 162 E1
Grafton CE Prim Sch
  SN8 . . . . 183 F7
Grafton Pl SN8 . . . . 183 F7
Grafton Rd
  Burbage SN8 . . . . 183 D7
  Swindon SN2 . . . . 35 C5
Graham St SN1 . . . . 50 D7
Grailey Cl SN3 . . . . 51 C4
Grain Wlk 3 SP11 . . . . 193 E2
Gramp's Hill OX12 . . . . 165 F7
Gramshaw Rd 2 SP2 . . . . . 145 D2
Granary Cl
  Corston SN16 . . . . 42 F4
  East Grafton SN8 . . . . 183 F7
  4 Swindon SN5 . . . . 48 F8
Granary Rd 6 SN8 . . . . 176 B3
Grand Ave SN8 . . . . 175 E3
Grandison Cl SN5 . . . . 49 A6
Grand Trunk Rd SP9 . . . . . . 216 B4
Grange Cl
  Atworth/Whitley SN12 . . . . . 85 D1
  Fyfield SP11 . . . . 192 D1
  Highworth SN6 . . . . 23 A5

Grange Cl continued
  14 Wanborough SN4 . . . . . 163 A6
Grange Dr SN3 . . . . 36 B1
Grangefield SN10 . . . . 172 F1
Grange Gdns SP1 . . . . 146 C2
Grange Inf Sch SN3 . . . . 36 B3
Grange Jun Sch SN3 . . . . . . 36 B2
Grange La
  St Paul Malmesbury Without
    SN16 . . . . 43 B5
  Warminster BA12 . . . . 117 E5
GRANGE PARK 48 F5
Grange Pk Way SN5 . . . . 48 F5
Granger Cl SN15 . . . . 78 F4
Grange Rd BA11 . . . . 110 A7
Grange View BA15 . . . . 100 E7
Granham Cl SN8 . . . . 213 D1
Granham Hill SN8 . . . . 213 D1
Granica Cl 5 SN25 . . . . 34 D6
Grans Barrow (Long
  Barrow)★ SP6 . . . . 209 E6
Grantham Cl SN5 . . . . 49 B3
Granthams The 4 RG17 . . . 165 A2
Grantley Cl SN3 . . . . 51 A3
Grants Rd SN9 . . . . 190 A6
Granville Gdns 28 SP7 . . . . 202 C2
Granville Rd SN12 . . . . 94 A6
Granville St SN1 . . . . 50 C6
Grasmere
  Bower Hill SN12 . . . . 94 D1
  Swindon SN3 . . . . 51 E3
  Trowbridge BA14 . . . . 101 E2
Grasmere Cl 1 SP2 . . . . 151 F6
Graspan Rd 12 SP11 . . . . . 192 B5
Grateley Rd SP4 . . . . 199 C5
Gravel Cl SP5 . . . . 211 A8
Gravel The BA14 . . . . 92 E1
Graveney Sq SP10 . . . . 193 E1
Grays Cl SP7 . . . . 202 A4
Grays Leaze BA14 . . . . 105 C2
Graythwaite Cl 3 SN25 . . . . 34 F6
GREAT ASHLEY 91 A1
Great Barn★ SN8 . . . . 167 B1
GREAT BEDWYN 176 B3
Great Bedwyn CE Prim Sch
  SN8 . . . . 176 B4
GREAT CHALFIELD 92 E3
Great Chalfield Manor★
  BA14 . . . . 92 D3
GREAT CHEVERELL 179 C1
Great Croft SP5 . . . . 148 C7
Great Dro SP4 . . . . 132 F1
GREAT DURNFORD 197 F1
Greater La BA13 . . . . 186 C8
GREATFIELD 47 F8
Great Ground 15 SP7 . . . . . . 202 D2
Great Hill BA9 . . . . 137 B3
GREAT HINTON 178 A6
Great La SP7 . . . . 202 C1
Great Lodge Dr SN8 . . . . . . 175 B5
Great Parks BA14 . . . . 92 F1
Great Roc Rd BA13 . . . . 108 E3
GREAT SOMERFORD 44 B2
Great Western Ave SP3 . . . . 200 E8
Great Western Hospl The
  SN3 . . . . 51 D1
Great Western St 7
  BA11 . . . . 110 A4
Great Western Way SN5 . . . . 48 F3
Great Wethers★ SN8 . . . . . . 174 A7
GREAT WISHFORD 129 F3
Great Wishford CE Fst Sch
  SP2 . . . . 130 A4
Greatwoods BA13 . . . . 186 C8
Greenacres
  Dilton Marsh BA13 . . . . . . 112 A8
  2 Downton SP5 . . . . 210 F8
Green Acres 13 SN8 . . . . . . 170 B2
Greenacres Way SN11 . . . . . 80 F4
Greenacre Way 7 SP7 . . . . . 202 D1
Greenaway 4 SN4 . . . . 163 A5
Greenbank Vw BA14 . . . . . . 104 F6
Greenbridge Ind Est SN3 . . . 51 A7
Greenbridge Ret Pk SN3 . . . 51 A8
Green Cl
  East Grafton SN8 . . . . 183 F7
  Holt BA14 . . . . 101 F8
  Whiteparish SP5 . . . . 161 D4
Greencroft St SP1 . . . . 146 B4
Greencroft The 6 SP1 . . . . . 146 B4
Green Dro
  Fovant SP3 . . . . 204 E8
  Grimstead SP5 . . . . 154 B4
  Pewsey SN9 . . . . 215 D3
  Smannell SP11 . . . . 193 E5
Green Farm Rise SN8 . . . . . 176 D7
Greenfield Rd SN10 . . . . 214 C1
Greenfields
  Grimstead SP5 . . . . 154 C2
  Smannell SP11 . . . . 193 F4
  South Marston SN3 . . . . . . 36 E5
Greenfield Vw SN6 . . . . 18 F6
Greenfinch Cl SN12 . . . . 94 D4
Green Gate Rd SN10 . . . . . . 180 D4
Greenham Wlk SN3 . . . . 51 B6
GREEN HILL 32 D1
Greenhill
  Sutton Veny BA12 . . . . 117 F1
  Westwells SN13 . . . . 84 D7
Greenhill Gdns
  Sutton Veny BA12 . . . . 117 F1
  Trowbridge BA14 . . . . 102 A4
Greenhill Pl BA12 . . . . 195 A3
Greenhill Rd SN2 . . . . 34 E2
Greenhills BA13 . . . . 186 C8
Greenhouse Rd SN10 . . . . . 180 F8

Green La
  Ashmore SP5 . . . . 206 E4
  Cheverell Magna SN10 . . . . 179 C1
  Codford BA12 . . . . 195 A3
  Colerne SN14 . . . . 75 A3
  Deanend SP5 . . . . 207 D4
  Devizes SN10 . . . . 214 B1
  Downton SP5 . . . . 211 A8
  Fordingbridge SP6 . . . . 210 D1
  Hinton Charterhouse BA2 . . . 98 E1
  Laverstock SP4 . . . . 146 E8
  Rockbourne SP6 . . . . 210 C3
  Salisbury SP1 . . . . 146 D6
  Sherston SN16 . . . . 25 C1
  Southwick BA14 . . . . 104 D2
  Steeple Ashton BA14 . . . . . 102 C1
  Trowbridge BA14 . . . . 105 E8
  Westbury BA13 . . . . 108 F2
  Winsley BA15 . . . . 99 E6
Green La Hospl SN10 . . . . . . 214 C1
Greenland Cl SN12 . . . . 92 E8
Greenland Mills BA15 . . . . . 100 D6
Greenlands 1 BA12 . . . . 194 C5
Greenlands Cl 20 SP4 . . . . . 198 B7
Greenlands Rd SN2 . . . . 35 C3
Greenland View BA15 . . . . . 100 D6
Greenlane Cl SP4 . . . . 146 D6
Green La Wood Nature
  Reserve★ BA14 . . . . 106 C8
Greenleaze Cl BA14 . . . . . . 105 A4
Green Mdw Ave SN25 . . . . . 34 F4
GREENMEADOW 35 B4
Greenmeadow Prim Sch
  SN25 . . . . 35 A4
Green Pk La BA11 . . . . 107 A6
Green Rd
  Codford BA12 . . . . 195 A3
  Corsham SN13 . . . . 85 B4
  Swindon SN2 . . . . 35 E3
Green Ride BA12 . . . . 123 E5
Greensand Cl 10 SN25 . . . . . 34 F7
Greens Cl SN14 . . . . 41 F1
Green's Ct 3 SP1 . . . . 152 B8
Greensey SP11 . . . . 192 E3
Greens La SN11 . . . . 172 A8
Green's La SN4 . . . . 64 B5
Greens Meade 6 SP5 . . . . . 211 C7
Greenstone Rd SP7 . . . . 202 D1
Green Terr BA14 . . . . 101 C2
GREEN THE 141 A3
Green The
  Alderbury SP5 . . . . 153 C3
  Biddestone SN14 . . . . 76 E8
  Brokenborough SN16 . . . . . 27 D4
  Calne SN11 . . . . 81 B2
  Cheverell Magna SN10 . . . . 179 C2
  Dauntsey SN15 . . . . 59 A8
  Fairford SP5 . . . . 1 F7
  Highworth SN6 . . . . 22 B5
  1 Liddington SN4 . . . . . . 163 A4
  Lyneham & Bradenstoke
    SN15 . . . . 60 A4
  Marlborough SN8 . . . . 213 E3
  Oaksey SN16 . . . . 15 F7
  Pitton & Farley SP5 . . . . . . 148 C3
  Salisbury SP1 . . . . 146 D2
  Upper Woodford SP4 . . . . . 131 D7
  Whiteparish SP5 . . . . 161 D4
Greentrees Prim Sch
  SP1 . . . . 146 C5
Green Valley Ave SN25 . . . . . 34 F4
Greenway SN4 . . . . 60 F2
Greenway Ave SN15 . . . . 70 D1
Greenway Cl SN3 . . . . 51 B7
Greenway Ct SN15 . . . . 70 D2
Greenway Dr SN15 . . . . 73 F8
Greenway Gdns
  Chippenham SN15 . . . . 70 D1
  Trowbridge BA14 . . . . 101 E3
Greenway La SN15 . . . . 70 D2
Greenway Pk SN15 . . . . 70 D1
Greenway Rd SN8 . . . . 169 B1
Greenways RG17 . . . . 165 A1
GREENWICH 200 C5
Greenwich Cl SN25 . . . . 35 A5
Greenwood Ave SN3 . . . . . . 146 D1
Greenwood Gr 4 SN25 . . . . . 34 C6
Greenwood Pl 6 SN25 . . . . . 34 D7
Greenwood Rd SN12 . . . . . . 94 A3
Gregory Cl SN15 . . . . 57 C1
Grenadier Cl 2 BA12 . . . . . . 116 F7
Gresham Cl SN3 . . . . 50 F6
Greyfriars Ct 7 SP1 . . . . 152 B7
Greyhound La 1 SP2 . . . . . . 144 C1
Grey's Cnr BA9 . . . . 136 A5
Greystones SN15 . . . . 96 B8
Greywethers Ave SN3 . . . . . . 50 E3
Grey Wethers or Sarsen
  Stones★ SN8 . . . . 167 F2
Grierson Cl SN11 . . . . 81 B3
Griffin Alley 6 SN16 . . . . 28 A3
Griffins Ct 3 SP2 . . . . 146 A1
Griffiths Cl SN3 . . . . 36 B1
Grimstead Beeches★
  SP5 . . . . 160 D7
Grimstead Rd SP5 . . . . 153 F1
Grindal Dr SN5 . . . . 48 F5
GRITTENHAM 46 C2
GRITTLETON 54 D5
Grittleton House Sch
  SN14 . . . . 54 E4
Grocyn Cl SN14 . . . . 75 B3
Grosmont Dr SN5 . . . . 49 B5
Grosvenor close SP9 . . . . . . 216 E6
Grosvenor Rd
  Shaftesbury SP7 . . . . 202 C2
  Swindon SN1 . . . . 50 A4

Ground Cnr BA14 . . . . 101 D8
Groundwell SN25 . . . . 35 C6
Groundwell Ind Est SN25 . . . 35 D6
Groundwell Rd SN1 . . . . 50 D5
Grouse Rd
  Calne SN11 . . . . 81 B5
  Old Sarum SP4 . . . . 146 B8
Grove Hill SN6 . . . . 23 A7
Grove La
  Kington St Michael SN14 . . . 69 F8
  Redlynch SP5 . . . . 211 D8
  Yatton Keynell SN14 . . . . . . 69 A6
Grovelands Ave SN1 . . . . 50 C3
Grovelands Way BA12 . . . . . 116 E7
Grove Leaze BA15 . . . . 100 B6
Groveley Rd SP3 . . . . 143 B3
Grovely Castle★ SP3 . . . . . . 128 F4
Grovely Cl SN5 . . . . 34 A1
Grovely Rd SP3 . . . . 129 C2
Grovely View SP2 . . . . 144 B1
Grove Orch SN6 . . . . 22 F7
Grove Prim Sch BA14 . . . . . 105 B5
Grove Rd
  Corsham SN13 . . . . 77 A1
  23 Market Lavington SN10 179 F1
  Sherston SN16 . . . . 40 C8
Groves St SN2 . . . . 49 F6
Grove The SN25 . . . . 35 B3
Grove The
  Codford St Peter BA12 . . . . 195 A2
  Crudwell SN16 . . . . 4 C1
  Penton Mewsey SP11 . . . . . 193 A2
  Warminster BA12 . . . . 117 A7
Grundys SN3 . . . . 51 D3
Gryphon Cl BA13 . . . . 108 E3
Guernsey Cl SN25 . . . . 34 D6
Guilder La SP1 . . . . 152 B8
Guildford Ave SN3 . . . . 50 F3
Guildhall Sq 3 SP1 . . . . 152 A8
Gullet The SN13 . . . . 83 F7
Gulliver's La BA14 . . . . 178 A4
Gundry Cl
  Chippenham SN15 . . . . 78 F5
  Devizes SN10 . . . . 214 C4
Gundy Gr BA14 . . . . 106 A8
Gunner St SP4 . . . . 198 E6
Gunsite Rd SN8 . . . . 173 C6
Gunville Hill SP5 . . . . 149 E6
Gunville Rd SP5 . . . . 149 D6
Guppy St SN2 . . . . 49 F7
Gurston Meadow SP5 . . . . . 205 A4
Gurston Rd SP5 . . . . 205 A4
GUSSAGE ST ANDREW . . . 207 E1
Gutherie CE Inf Sch SN11 81 C4
Guthrie Cl SN11 . . . . 81 C4
Guyers La SN13 . . . . 76 D2
Gwyns Piece 14 RG17 . . . . . 165 A4

H

Habrel's Cl SN15 . . . . 78 F6
Hackett Cl SN2 . . . . 35 E4
Hackleton Rise SN3 . . . . 51 B8
Hackney Way BA13 . . . . 108 E3
Hackpen Cl SN4 . . . . 64 B7
HACKTHORN 198 A8
Hackthorne Rd SP4 . . . . 198 B7
Haddon Cl 14 SN5 . . . . 48 F5
Haddons Cl SN3 . . . . 27 E2
Haden Rd 6 BA14 . . . . 105 D7
Hadleigh Cl SN5 . . . . 49 C6
Hadleigh Rise SN2 . . . . 36 A5
Hadrian Rd 20 SP10 . . . . . . 193 E2
Hadrians Cl
  Salisbury SP2 . . . . 145 C1
  Swindon SN3 . . . . 51 C8
Haig Cl SN2 . . . . 35 E4
Haig Rd SP4 . . . . 217 F8
HAILSTONE HILL 8 A1
Haimes La 20 SP7 . . . . 202 C2
HALCOMBE 27 E3
HALE 211 C5
Hale House★ SP6 . . . . 211 A5
Hale La SP6 . . . . 211 B5
Hale Prim Sch SP6 . . . . 211 C6
Hale Rd SP6 . . . . 211 A5
Hales Castle★ BA11 . . . . 114 D5
Hales Cl SN15 . . . . 59 E4
Hales Rd 6 SP4 . . . . 190 A4
Half Hide Down SP5 . . . . . . 207 B3
Half Mile Rd RG17 . . . . 171 A5
Halfpenny La SP5 . . . . 206 E4
Halfpenny Rd SP2 . . . . 151 D7
Halfpenny Row BA11 . . . . . . 103 E1
HALFWAY 113 A4
Halfway Cl BA14 . . . . 101 F2
HALF WAY FIRS 76 C1
Halfway Firs SN13 . . . . 76 C1
Halfway La SN8 . . . . 170 C2
Halifax Cl SN4 . . . . 64 A7
Halifax Rd SN12 . . . . 94 C1
Hallam Moor SN3 . . . . 51 E2
Hall Cl SN4 . . . . 64 A6
Hallsfield SN6 . . . . 8 D1
Hallum Cl SP1 . . . . 146 D4
Halton Cres SN4 . . . . 64 E3
Halton Rd SP11 . . . . 191 F4
Halve The BA14 . . . . 101 D1
HAM. 177 B2
Hambidge La GL7 . . . . 2 C5
Hamble Ct SP10 . . . . 193 F1
Hamble Rd SN25 . . . . 34 F4
Hambleton Ave SN10 . . . . . . 214 E6
Hamblin Meadow RG17 . . . . 177 C8
Hamburg Cl 10 SP10 . . . . . . 193 D2

Ham Cl
  Collingbourne Kingston
    SN8 . . . . 183 D3
  Holt BA14 . . . . 101 D8
  Trowbridge BA14 . . . . 101 B1
HAM GREEN 101 C8
Ham Hill Nature Reserve★
  SN8 . . . . 185 B8
Hamilton Cl
  Amesbury SP4 . . . . 217 E3
  Swindon SN3 . . . . 50 F7
Hamilton Dr
  Chippenham SN14 . . . . 77 F5
  2 Market Lavington SN10 179 F1
Hamilton Pk 3 SP5 . . . . 211 B8
Hamilton Rd SP1 . . . . 146 A2
Ham La
  Biddestone SN14 . . . . 76 C8
  Kempsford GL7 . . . . 10 E6
  South Cerney GL7 . . . . 6 F6
Hamlet Cl SN15 . . . . 70 D1
Hamlet Gdns SP11 . . . . 193 E3
Hamlet The SN15 . . . . 70 E1
Hammer St BA10 . . . . 122 C7
Hammonds SN6 . . . . 19 E8
Hammond Way BA14 . . . . . . 101 D4
Hampshire Cl
  Durrington/Bulford SP4 . . . 217 E8
  7 Swindon SN5 . . . . 49 A7
HAMPSHIRE GATE 185 A1
Hampshire Gdns BA13 . . . . . 109 A4
Hampshire Pl SN12 . . . . 94 B5
Hampsley Rd SN13 . . . . 89 C1
Hampstead Way SN25 . . . . . 34 F7
HAMPTON. 22 D5
Hampton Cl SN12 . . . . 94 C4
Hampton Ct SP2 . . . . 144 F2
Hampton Dr SN5 . . . . 48 F5
HAMPTON HILL 22 E5
Hampton Rd 31 SP11 . . . . . 193 E2
HAMPTWORTH 212 B6
Hamptworth Rd SP5 . . . . . . 211 F6
Ham Rd
  Ham RG17 . . . . 177 A2
  Liddington SN4 . . . . 163 A5
Hamshill Ditches★ SP3 . . . . 143 B7
HAM THE. 108 E5
Ham The
  Durrington/Bulford SP4 . . . 198 C7
  Kington St Michael SN14 . . . 70 A8
  9 Market Lavington SN10 179 F1
  Westbury BA13 . . . . 108 E5
Hamworthy Rd SN3 . . . . 51 C6
Hanbury Rd SN3 . . . . 51 A4
Hancock Cl SN15 . . . . 79 A5
Handel St SN2 . . . . 50 C8
Handley St SP5 . . . . 204 D3
Hanging Bushes La SP11 193 A1
HANGING LANGFORD 128 C7
Hanging Langford Camp★
  BA12 . . . . 201 F6
Hanging Stone★ SN9 . . . . . . 181 B7
Hanging The SP5 . . . . 155 F1
Hangman's Stone★ RG17 164 C4
HANKERTON. 15 C2
Hankerton Priory SN16 . . . . . 15 B4
Hankerton Rd SN16 . . . . 16 C2
Hanks Cl SN16 . . . . 28 A5
HANNINGTON. 22 B7
Hannington Cl SN2 . . . . 35 B6
HANNINGTON WICK 11 A4
Hanover Cl BA14 . . . . 101 E4
Hanover Ct SN3 . . . . 51 D7
Hanwell Cl SN25 . . . . 34 D8
Ha'penny Bridge★ GL7 . . . . . 2 C3
Haragon Dr SP4 . . . . 217 D1
Harbour Cl SN25 . . . . 34 F3
Harcourt Mews 5 BA11 . . . . 110 A4
Harcourt Rd SN2 . . . . 50 A8
Harcourt Terr SP2 . . . . 151 F2
Hardenhuish Ave SN15 . . . . . 70 C1
Hardenhuish La SN14 . . . . . . 70 B1
Hardenhuish Pk★ SN14 . . . . . 70 C1
Hardenhuish Sch SN14 . . . . . 70 C2
Hardens Cl SN15 . . . . 79 A5
Hardens Mead SN15 . . . . . . 79 A6
Hardhams Rise SN13 . . . . . . 84 F8
Hardie Cl SN3 . . . . 36 A1
Harding St 6 SN1 . . . . 50 B6
HARDWAY. 122 A1
Hardwick Cl SN25 . . . . 35 A5
Hardy Cl SN25 . . . . 34 D6
Hardyfair Cl 5 SP11 . . . . . . 192 F1
Harebell Cl SN25 . . . . 34 D5
Harebell Rd 28 SP11 . . . . . 193 E2
Hare Cl SN2 . . . . 35 F5
Harefield Cres SP4 . . . . 190 A2
Hare Knapp BA15 . . . . 100 B6
Harepit Way★ SN11 . . . . 172 F7
Haresdown Hill GL7 . . . . 3 F7
HARESFIELD. 23 B8
Hares Patch SN14 . . . . 70 B5
Hare St
  Bremhill SN15 . . . . 72 C5
  Pewsey SN9 . . . . 182 A7
Hare Warren Cl SP2 . . . . . . 144 C1
Harford Cl 3 SN15 . . . . 78 F5
Harford St 4 BA14 . . . . 105 E8
Hargreaves Rd
  Swindon SN25 . . . . 35 D6
  Trowbridge BA14 . . . . 105 F2
Harlech Cl SN5 . . . . 49 A4
Harlestone Rd SN3 . . . . 51 B8
Harmony Pl 8 BA14 . . . . 105 D7
HARNHAM. 151 E6

Harnham CE Jun Sch
SP2 . . . . .151 F6
Harnham Inf Sch SP2 . . . . .151 F6
Harnham Rd SP2 . . . . .151 F7
Harnham Trad Est SP2 . . . .151 D7
Harnham Trading Est
SP2 . . . . .151 D7
Harnish Way SN14 . . . . .70 B2
Harnwood Rd SP2 . . . . .151 E6
Harper Rd SP2 . . . . .145 D2
Harper's La SN16 . . . . .27 F3
Harptree Cl SN5 . . . . .49 A8
Harriers The SN3 . . . . .51 C7
Harrington Dr **4** SP4 . . . . .198 E6
Harrington Wlk SN3 . . . . . . .51 A7
Harris Cl
Frome BA11 . . . . .110 B4
  5 Lambourn RG17 . . . . . .165 A2
Harris La SN9 . . . . .183 A7
Harris Rd
Ashton Keynes SN6 . . . . .7 A1
Calne SN11 . . . . .81 C5
Swindon SN2 . . . . .35 A2
Harroway La SP11 . . . . .193 B1
Harrow Cl SN3 . . . . .36 A1
Harrow Gr SN15 . . . . .60 B2
Harrow Way SP11 . . . . .193 B1
Harrow Way Com Prim Sch
SP10 . . . . .193 C1
Hart Cl SN4 . . . . .61 E8
Hartfield SN10 . . . . .214 A2
Hartham La SN13 . . . . .76 E5
Harthill Dro SP5 . . . . .211 D7
Hartington Rd
Salisbury SP2 . . . . .145 C2
Swindon SN25 . . . . .34 C7
Hartland Cl SN3 . . . . .51 A5
Hartley Way SP1 . . . . .146 D5
Hartmoor Cl SN10 . . . . .214 A2
Hartmoor Rd SN10 . . . . . . .214 A2
Harts La SN14 . . . . .76 E8
Hartsthorn Cl SN2 . . . . .34 D3
Harvard Cl
  16 Bower Hill SN12 . . . . .178 B8
  1 Salisbury SP2 . . . . .151 F5
Harvester **7** SN5 . . . . .48 F8
Harvest La SP5 . . . . .205 F4
Harvey Gr SN2 . . . . .34 F2
Hastings Ave SN9 . . . . .182 B2
Hastings Cl SN9 . . . . .182 B2
Hastings Dr SN3 . . . . .60 B2
Hastings Rd SN13 . . . . .85 A8
Hatchbury La SP11 . . . . . . .185 C3
Hatcher's Cres SN26 . . . . . .21 B2
Hatches La SP1 . . . . .152 D7
Hatchet Cl SP6 . . . . .211 C6
HATCHET GREEN 211 C6
Hatchet Hill SN4 . . . . .163 D6
Hatchet La SP11 . . . . .193 B5
Hatch La SP3 . . . . .203 C8
Hatch Rd SN3 . . . . .36 B4
Hatfield Cl
  4 Swindon SN25 . . . . .34 E6
Swindon SN25 . . . . .34 E6
Hatfields SN10 . . . . .181 A5
Hathaway Cl SP1 . . . . .145 F4
Hathaway Rd SN2 . . . . .35 E5
Hathaway Ret Pk SN15 . . . .78 E8
HATHERDEN 193 C5
Hatherden CE Prim Sch
SP11 . . . . .193 C5
Hatherell Rd SN15 . . . . .78 F4
Hatherhall Cl SN3 . . . . .36 C2
Hatherleigh Ct SN3 . . . . . . .51 B6
Hatherley Rd SN3 . . . . .51 B7
Hathersage Moor SN3 . . . . .51 E2
Hattem Pl **23** SP10 . . . . . .193 D2
Hatton Gr SN3 . . . . .50 F6
Hatton Way SN13 . . . . .76 E1
Havard Way **2** SP4 . . . . . .217 D2
Havelock Sq SN1 . . . . .50 B6
Havelock St
Swindon SN1 . . . . .50 B5
Trowbridge BA14 . . . . .105 C7
Haven Cl SN3 . . . . .51 B8
Havering La SN9 . . . . .182 E4
Havisham Dr SN25 . . . . .34 D6
Hawcroft BA14 . . . . .92 E1
Hawfinch Cl SN3 . . . . .51 E5
HAWKERIDGE 108 E8
Hawkeridge Pk BA13 . . . . .108 E5
Hawkeridge Rd BA14 . . . . .105 E2
Hawker Rd SN5 . . . . .51 C4
Hawkesdene **17** SP7 . . . . .202 C1
Hawkesdene La SP7 . . . . . .202 C1
Hawkins Cl SN15 . . . . .78 F5
Hawkins Meadow SN8 . . . .213 B2
Hawkins Rd **16** SN8 . . . . . .170 A6
Hawkins St SN2 . . . . .50 A7
Hawksridge **4** SP2 . . . . . .152 A5
Hawkstreet SN15 . . . . .96 B6
Hawkswood SN3 . . . . .51 D8
Hawk's Worth Cl 6
BA11 . . . . .110 C7
Hawksworth Trad Est SN2 .50 A8
Hawksworth Way SN2 . . . . .50 A7
Hawthorn Ave SN2 . . . . .35 C2
Hawthorn Cl
Pewsey SN9 . . . . .215 D5
  1 Salisbury SP2 . . . . . . .145 F1
  2 Shaftesbury SP7 . . . . .202 D2
Hawthorn Gr BA14 . . . . .105 B7
Hawthorn Rd
Bowerhill SN12 . . . . .94 D3
Chippenham SN15 . . . . .70 E1

Hawthorn Rd continued
Frome BA11 . . . . .110 A6
Tidworth SP9 . . . . .216 D7
HAXTON 190 B4
Haydock Cl **4** SN14 . . . . . .77 F5
Haydon Ct SN25 . . . . .34 E5
Haydon Ct Dr SN25 . . . . . . .34 E5
Haydon End La
Haydon Wick SN25 . . . . .34 D6
  3 Swindon SN25 . . . . .34 E5
Haydonleigh Dr SN25 . . . . . .34 E4
Haydonleigh Prim Sch
SN25 . . . . .34 E4
Haydon St SN1 . . . . .50 C7
Haydon View Rd SN25 . . . . .35 C3
HAYDON WICK 34 E5
Haydon Wick Prim Sch
SN25 . . . . .34 E4
Haydown Leas SP11 . . . . . .185 C3
Hayes Cl BA14 . . . . .101 C4
Hayesdown Fst Sch
BA11 . . . . .110 B5
HAYES KNOLL 19 E2
Hayes Knoll Sta SN5 . . . . . .19 F2
Haye's La GL9 . . . . .38 E2
Hayfield SN13 . . . . .74 A8
Hayfield Ct RG17 . . . . .171 C7
Haygrove Cl BA12 . . . . .116 D6
Hay La SN5 . . . . .48 F6
Hayle Rd SN5 . . . . .49 F6
Hayman Cres SN3 . . . . .50 E2
Haynes Cl SN3 . . . . .51 C4
Haynes Rd BA13 . . . . .109 A3
Hay St SN14 . . . . .74 A8
Haywain **6** SP4 . . . . .217 B3
Haywain Cl SN25 . . . . .35 C6
Hayward Cl
Chippenham SN15 . . . . .78 F5
Swindon SN25 . . . . .35 A6
Hayward Pl BA13 . . . . .108 F5
Haywards GL7 . . . . .10 E6
Haywards Pl SN10 . . . . .179 F2
Hazelbury Cres SN3 . . . . . .51 C7
Hazelbury Hill SN13 . . . . . . .83 D6
Hazelbury Manor Gdns***
SN13 . . . . .83 F5
Hazel Cl
Marlborough SN8 . . . . .175 A7
Salisbury SP2 . . . . .145 B3
Hazel Copse **2** SN14 . . . . .77 F6
Hazel End SN4 . . . . .47 E1
Hazel Gr
Calne SN11 . . . . .81 B1
Swindon SN2 . . . . .35 C3
Trowbridge BA14 . . . . .105 B5
Hazel Way SN14 . . . . .75 A5
Hazelwood Academy SN5 49 C4
Hazelwood Rd SN12 . . . . . .94 A3
Hazel Wy **6** SN13 . . . . .76 E1
Hazlemere Cl SN3 . . . . .51 B4
Hazzard's Hill BA12 . . . . . .139 B5
Headington Hts SN11 . . . . . .89 B1
Headlands Gr SN2 . . . . .35 E3
Headley Cl SN4 . . . . .64 D3
Headquarters Rd
  8 Durrington/Bulford
SP4 .198 F6
Westbury BA13 . . . . .108 C6
Heale Gdn* SP4 . . . . .131 D5
Heath Ave SN15 . . . . .57 C2
Heath Cl BA12 . . . . .115 B8
Heathcote Cl SN5 . . . . .49 B8
Heathcote Rd SN12 . . . . . . .94 C5
Heather Ave SN12 . . . . .94 C4
Heather Cl BA13 . . . . .108 F4
Heather Shaw BA14 . . . . . .105 E8
Heather Way SN11 . . . . .81 C1
Heathfield SN15 . . . . .70 E4
Heathfields Way **2** SP7 . .202 C2
Heath La
Buttermere SN8 . . . . .185 C7
Great Somerford SN15 . . . . .43 D2
Heathlands The BA12 . . . . .116 F5
Heath Rd SP2 . . . . .145 D4
Heath Sq **1** SP4 . . . . .197 E6
Heath View Dr SP2 . . . . . . .145 C3
Heathway BA12 . . . . .115 C8
Heath Way SN13 . . . . .51 B8
Heaton Cl SN25 . . . . .35 A6
Heaven's Gate* BA12 . . .115 C1
Hebden Cl **5** SN25 . . . . . . .34 E7
Hebden Rd BA15 . . . . .99 F3
Hector Rd **2** SN25 . . . . . . .34 C7
HEDDINGTON 89 B1
Heddington CE Prim Sch
SN11 . . . . .89 B1
Heddington Cl
Swindon SN2 . . . . .35 B5
Trowbridge BA14 . . . . .105 C5
HEDDINGTON WICK 88 E2
Hedgeditch La GL8 . . . . .26 D7
Hedge Row SN15 . . . . .79 A4
Hedges Cl
  1 Shipton Bellinger SP9 .199 C8
Swindon SN3 . . . . .36 B3
Hedgesparrow La SN13 . . . .83 F8
Hedges The **4** SN4 . . . . . .163 A6
Heights The SN1 . . . . .50 A4
Hei-lin Way **2** SP11 . . . . . .192 A5
Helena Cl SN25 . . . . .34 C8
Helena Terr **7** SP1 . . . . . . .146 B1
Helmdon Rd BA14 . . . . .101 A1
Helmsdale SN25 . . . . .34 F4
Helmsdale Wlk SN3 . . . . . . .51 A4
Helps Well Rd BA14 . . . . . .102 B2
Helston Rd SN3 . . . . .51 A5
Henchard Cres **7** SN2 . . . .34 C5

Henderson Cl BA14 . . . . . .105 B7
Henford Cl BA12 . . . . .117 A5
Henfords Marsh BA12 . . . . .117 B4
Hengest Cl **5** SP10 . . . . . .193 C7
HENLEY
Box 83 C4
Buttermere 185 A6
Henley Dr SN6 . . . . .23 A7
Henley La SN13 . . . . .83 C4
Henley Rd **2** SN3 . . . . .51 A4
Henloke Wy SN16 . . . . .28 C2
Henman Cl
Devizes SN10 . . . . .214 A8
Swindon SN25 . . . . .35 A5
Henn La SN15 . . . . .57 C6
Henry's Garth **7** SN8 . . . .183 D8
Henry St
  1 Swindon SN1 . . . . .50 B6
  9 Swindon SN1 . . . . .50 B6
Henset Village* SN8 . . . .175 E7
Hensler Dr SP4 . . . . .146 C6
Hepworth Rd **5** SN25 . . . . .34 F6
Herbert Ludlow Gdns
SN15 . . . . .59 C3
Herbleaze BA14 . . . . .101 D5
Herbert Rd
  3 Redlynch SP5 . . . . .211 C7
Salisbury SP2 . . . . .145 C7
Herd St SN8 . . . . .213 D4
Herdwick Rd **21** SP11 . . . .193 F2
Hereford Cl SN14 . . . . .78 A5
Hereford Rd SN3 . . . . .50 F3
Hereford Lawns SN3 . . . . . .50 F3
Herepath SN8 . . . . .167 C1
HERITAGE PARK 214 C1
Herman Miller Ind Est
SN14 . . . . .78 B5
Hermitage La SN2 . . . . .35 E3
Hernsham St SP7 . . . . .203 C4
Heronbridge Cl **2** SN5 . . . .49 C5
Heron Cl SN11 . . . . .81 D3
Herongate RG17 . . . . .177 B8
Heronscroft SN3 . . . . .51 D7
Herons Ct **6** SN12 . . . . . . .178 B8
Heronslade BA12 . . . . .117 D5
Heronswood SP2 . . . . .152 A5
Heron Way SN14 . . . . .77 F6
Heron Wlk **12** SP4 . . . . . . .198 C2
Herschell Cl **7** SN25 . . . . . .34 B7
Hertford Cl
  1 Fordingbridge SP6 . . . .210 D2
  4 Swindon SN3 . . . . .50 F6
Hertford Rd SN8 . . . . .213 F1
Hesketh Cres SN1 . . . . .50 D3
Hewers Cl SN4 . . . . .163 A6
Hewitt Cl
Swindon SN3 . . . . .51 C4
Trowbridge BA14 . . . . .105 E7
Hewlett Cl SN15 . . . . .79 A5
Hexham Cl
  4 Chippenham SN14 . . . . .77 F6
Swindon SN5 . . . . .49 B5
Heyford Cl **8** SP4 . . . . .217 E3
HEYTESBURY 194 C5
Heytesbury CE Prim Sch
BA12 . . . . .194 C5
Heytsbury Gdns **4** SN5 . . . .48 F4
HEYWOOD 109 A8
Heywood Cl SN2 . . . . .35 B5
Heywood Prep Sch SN13 . .77 A2
Hicks Cl SN4 . . . . .64 A6
Hidcot Ct SN25 . . . . .34 E7
High Bannerdown BA1 . . . . .82 B4
Highbury Ave SP2 . . . . .145 E2
Highbury Cl **2** SP2 . . . . . .145 E2
Highbury Pk BA12 . . . . .117 C6
Highbury Prim Sch SP2 . . .145 E2
Highbury Rd
Amesbury SP4 . . . . .217 B3
Bradford-on-Avon BA15 . . .100 D7
Salisbury SP2 . . . . .145 E2
Highfield Rise **1** SP3 . . . . .196 F6
Highfold SN4 . . . . .47 F1
Highgate Cottage SN4 . . . . .46 F5
Highgrove Cl SN11 . . . . .81 D2
High La SP5 . . . . .205 B4
Highland Cl
  8 Swindon SN5 . . . . .49 A7
Westbury BA13 . . . . .108 E1
Highlands SN10 . . . . .179 D5
Highlands Cl SN13 . . . . .84 A8
Highlands Rd SP2 . . . . .152 A6
Highlands Way SP5 . . . . . . .161 D4
Highland View SP2 . . . . . . .130 A2
High Lawn SN10 . . . . .179 D8
High Mead SN4 . . . . .47 F2
Highmoor Copse SN5 . . . . . .34 A1
Highnam Cl SN3 . . . . .36 A1
High Post Bsns Pk SP4 . . .132 B5
High Rd
Ashton Keynes SN6 . . . . .6 F1
Bishopstone SP5 . . . . .205 E4
Britford SP5 . . . . .152 D4
Highridge Cl SN5 . . . . .33 A3
High St Brow SN8 . . . . .169 A6

High St
Alderbury SP5 . . . . .153 C3
Amesbury SP4 . . . . .217 A3
Ansty SP3 . . . . .203 F6
Ashbury SN6 . . . . .164 A8
Ashmore SP5 . . . . .206 E4
Avebury SN8 . . . . .173 B8
Badminton GL9 . . . . .38 E2
Bath BA1 . . . . .82 D2
Berwick St James SP3 . . . . .196 F2
Bishopstone SN6 . . . . .163 E6
Box SN13 . . . . .83 C5
Broad Blunsdon SN26 . . . . . .21 B1
Bromham SN15 . . . . .96 A7
Bulford SP4 . . . . .217 D8
Burbage SN8 . . . . .175 C1
Calne SN11 . . . . .81 B3
Chapmanslade BA13 . . . . . .111 B4
Cheverell Magna SN10 . . . .179 C1
Chippenham SN15 . . . . .78 D7
Chiseldown SN4 . . . . .65 D4
Codford BA12 . . . . .195 A2
Colerne SN14 . . . . .75 B3
Collingbourne Ducis SN8 . . .191 E8
Compton Chamberlayne
SP3 .205 A8
Corsham SN13 . . . . .77 A1
Cricklade SN6 . . . . .19 E8
Damerham SP6 . . . . .209 F3
Downton SP5 . . . . .211 B8
Durrington/Bulford SP4 . . .198 B7
Erlestoke SN10 . . . . .187 A8
Figheldean SP4 . . . . .190 B1
  24 Fordingbridge SP6 . . .210 D1
Fovant SP3 . . . . .204 E7
Great Bedwyn SN8 . . . . . . .176 B3
Heytesbury BA12 . . . . .194 C5
Highworth SN6 . . . . .23 A5
Hindon SP3 . . . . .200 A4
Hinton Charterhouse BA2 . . .98 E1
Hungerford RG17 . . . . .177 B7
Idmiston SP4 . . . . .133 D5
Kempsford GL7 . . . . .10 C7
Lacock SN15 . . . . .86 D5
Lambourn RG17 . . . . .164 F3
Lechlade GL7 . . . . .2 C4
Limpley Stoke BA2 . . . . .99 B5
Little Bedwyn SN8 . . . . .176 D4
Littleton Panell SN10 . . . . . .187 D8
  9 Ludgershall SP11 . . . . .192 A5
Maiden Bradley with Yarnfield
BA12 . . . . .118 A3
Malmesbury SN16 . . . . .28 A3
Market Lavington SN10 . . . .179 F1
Marlborough SN8 . . . . .213 A1
Melksham SN12 . . . . .94 A4
Meysey Hampton GL7 . . . . . .1 A5
Netheravon SP4 . . . . .190 A3
Ogbourne St George SN8 . .168 F5
Pewsey SN9 . . . . .215 D5
Pitton & Farley SP5 . . . . . . .148 C3
Porton SP4 . . . . .133 D6
Purton SN5 . . . . .33 B4
Ramsbury SN8 . . . . .170 B2
Rode BA11 . . . . .103 F1
Rowde SN10 . . . . .96 E2
Royal Wootton Bassett SN4 .47 D1
Salisbury SP1 . . . . .152 A8
Seend SN12 . . . . .178 E8
Semington BA14 . . . . .102 F6
  18 Shaftesbury SP7 . . . . .202 C1
Sherston SN16 . . . . .40 C8
Shipton Bellinger SP9 . . . . .199 D8
Shrewton SP3 . . . . .196 E7
Sixpenny Handley SP5 . . . . .208 A4
South Cerney GL7 . . . . .6 F6
Steeple Ashton BA14 . . . . . .178 A3
Stourton with Gasper BA12 .123 F1
Sutton Benger SN15 . . . . . . .57 C2
Sutton Veny BA12 . . . . .117 F1
Swindon SN3 . . . . .50 D4
Swindon SN25 . . . . .34 E4
Tilshead SP3 . . . . .188 B2
Tisbury SP3 . . . . .203 D6
Upavon SN9 . . . . .181 F2
Urchfont SN10 . . . . .180 C4
Wanborough SN4 . . . . .163 B6
Warminster BA12 . . . . .117 A4
Westbury BA13 . . . . .109 A3
West Lavington SN10 . . . . . .179 D1
Winterbourne Stoke SP3 . . .197 A4
Woodgreen SP6 . . . . .211 A4
Worton SN10 . . . . .179 B4
Wroughton SN4 . . . . .64 A5
Wylye BA12 . . . . .201 E8
Zeale SP8 . . . . .137 F3
High View Cl SP3 . . . . .203 E7
HIGHWAY 166 A5
Highway Comm SN11 . . . . .166 B6
Highway The SP5 . . . . .158 F5
Highwood Cl **4** SN2 . . . . . .34 D4
HIGHWORTH 23 B5
Highworth Ind Est SN6 . . . .23 A7
Highworth Rd
Highworth SN6 . . . . .22 D1
Shrivenham SN6 . . . . .23 E1
South Marston SN3 . . . . .36 E6
Highworth Recn Ctr SN6 . .22 F5
HILCOTT 181 D5
Hillary Cl SN25 . . . . .35 C4
Hill Beech Rd SP9 . . . . .216 E7
Hillbourne Cl BA12 . . . . . . .117 B7
Hill Cl **4** SP3 . . . . .203 E8
HILL CORNER 110 E7
Hillcote Hospl SP1 . . . . .146 C1
Hillcrest
Colerne SN14 . . . . .75 C6

Hillcrest continued
Malmesbury SN16 . . . . .28 B2
Hillcroft SN11 . . . . .81 C2
HILL DEVERILL 120 F5
  1 Hill Deverill Manor*****
BA12 . . . . .120 F5
Hill Deverill Medieval Village
of ***** SP3 . . . . .120 F5
Hilldrop Cl **1** SN8 . . . . . . .170 B2
Hilldrop La
Lambourn RG17 . . . . .171 A6
Ramsbury SN8 . . . . .169 F3
Hillfort Mews **1** SP4 . . . . .132 C1
Hill Hayes La SN14 . . . . . . .41 E1
Hillier Rd SN10 . . . . .214 D6
Hilliers Yd SN8 . . . . .213 D3
Hillingdon Rd SN3 . . . . .51 B4
Hillmead Dr SN5 . . . . .34 B1
Hillmead Ent Pk SN5 . . . . . .49 B8
Hillocks The SN4 . . . . .60 B5
Hill Rd
Norton Bavant BA12 . . . . . .194 A4
Salisbury SP1 . . . . .146 E2
Hill Rise SN15 . . . . .70 E2
Hillside
Leigh SN6 . . . . .18 C5
Nettleton SN14 . . . . .53 A4
Hill Side SP3 . . . . .129 E8
Hillside Ave SN1 . . . . .50 A4
Hillside Cl
Heddington SN11 . . . . .89 B1
Mere BA12 . . . . .138 E5
West Tytherley SP5 . . . . . . .155 F2
Hillside Ct SN1 . . . . .50 A4
Hillside Dr
Frome BA11 . . . . .110 B4
Winterbourne SP4 . . . . .133 D3
Hillside Pk BA13 . . . . .109 B3
Hillside Rd
  4 Hungerford RG17 . . . . .177 B6
South Newton SP2 . . . . .130 B2
Hillside Villas SP10 . . . . . .193 D1
Hillside Way SN26 . . . . .21 A1
Hill St BA14 . . . . .101 C1
Hill The
Limpley Stoke BA2 . . . . .99 C5
Little Somerford SN15 . . . . . .44 B6
Hill Top Ave SP9 . . . . .216 C8
Hilltop Cl **2** SP3 . . . . .196 F6
Hill Top Cl SP4 . . . . .190 B2
Hilltop Way SP1 . . . . .146 A5
HILL VIEW 215 B3
Hillview SP5 . . . . .204 C3
Hill View SN8 . . . . .181 B8
Hillview Cl SP4 . . . . .217 B4
Hill View Rd
  6 Salisbury SP1 . . . . .152 B8
Swindon SN3 . . . . .36 C1
Hill Vw La SN15 . . . . .59 D3
Hillwell SN16 . . . . .15 B2
Hillwood Cl BA12 . . . . .116 F5
Hillwood La BA12 . . . . .116 F5
Hillwood Rd **15** SN8 . . . . . .170 A6
Hillworth Rd SN10 . . . . .214 A2
Hillyard Cl **3** SN5 . . . . .48 F4
Hilly Fields SN13 . . . . .84 E8
HILMARTON 166 A6
Hilmarton Ave **1** SN2 . . . . .35 C5
Hilmarton Prim Sch
SN11 . . . . .166 A6
HILPERTON 102 A3
Hilperton CE Prim Sch
BA14 . . . . .102 A3
Hilperton Dr BA14 . . . . .102 A2
HILPERTON MARSH 101 F5
Hilperton Rd BA14 . . . . .101 E1
Hilton Cl SN1 . . . . .50 D6
Hinde's Meadow SP3 . . . . .196 F7
HINDON 200 B3
Hindon La SP3 . . . . .200 B3
Hindon Rd
Chilmark SP3 . . . . .201 B3
East Knoyle SP3 . . . . .141 C2
Kingston Deverill BA12 . . . .126 D7
Hinkson Cl SN25 . . . . .34 F8
HINTON CHARTERHOUSE .98 E1
Hinton Hill
Bishopstone SN4 . . . . .163 D6
Hinton Charterhouse BA2 . . .98 A1
Hinton Ho* BA2 . . . . .98 E1
Hinton La BA14 . . . . .178 A5
HINTON PARVA 163 D6
Hinton Priory* BA2 . . . . . .98 F3
Hinton Springs SN6 . . . . . .163 D6
Hinton St SN2 . . . . .50 D8
HISOMLEY 112 C7
Hitchings Skilling SN14 . . . .75 B3
Hither Cl SN14 . . . . .78 A8
Hither Spring SN13 . . . . . . .84 F8
Hither Way SN15 . . . . .86 D5
Hoadley Gn SP1 . . . . .146 D4
Hobbes Cl SN16 . . . . .27 F4
Hobbs Hill BA14 . . . . .178 B5
Hobbs Wlk SN13 . . . . .77 A1
Hobhouse Cl BA15 . . . . . . .100 E4
Hobley Dr SN3 . . . . .36 A3
Hocketts Cl SN15 . . . . .60 A3
Hodds Hill SN5 . . . . .34 B2
Hodge La SN16 . . . . .27 F6
Hodges Barn Gdns* GL8. . .26 F8
HODSON 65 A5
Hodson Rd SN4 . . . . .65 A4
HOGGINGTON 104 D4
Hoggington La BA14 . . . . . .104 D4
Hoggs La SN5 . . . . .33 A4
Holbein Cl **6** SN5 . . . . .49 A5
Holbein Ct SN5 . . . . .49 A5
Holbein Field **12** SN5. . . . . .49 A4

Holbein Mews **5** SN5.....49 A5
Holbein Pl SN5.........49 A5
Holbein Sq **10** SN5.....49 A4
Holbein Wlk **11** SN5....49 A4
Holborn Hill OX12....165 E8
Holbrook La BA14....105 D6
Holbrook Prim Sch
BA14...............105 D6
Holbrook Vale SN12....93 F1
Holbrook Way SN1....50 B6
Holcombe La BA2....82 A1
Holdcroft Cl SN26....21 C2
Holden Cres SN25....35 A6
Holden Garson Rd SN25...35 B6
Holders Rd SP4.....217 C4
Holford Cres GL7....10 E6
Holinshead Pl **4** SN5....49 A5
Holinshed Mews **3** SN5...49 A5
Holland Cl SN15....79 A4
Holland Dr **11** SP10....193 D2
Holliday Cl SN25....35 A6
Hollies La BA1.......82 A6
Hollins Moor SN3....51 D2
Hollis Gdns SN14....39 E4
Hollis Way BA14....104 F3
HOLLOWAY..........141 A1
Holloway SN16......28 A3
Holloway Cl SP4....217 D1
Holloway Hill SN14...66 E8
Holloway La SP3....141 B1
Hollow La SN8......184 A7
Hollows Cl SP2.....151 F6
Hollow St SN15......43 F2
Hollows The SP2....144 B4
Hollow Way
  Bratton BA13.....186 A7
  Chirton SN10.....180 F4
  Corsley BA12......111 B1
  Dilton Marsh BA13...112 C8
  Shrewton SP3.....196 E2
  Sixpenny Handley SP5...208 A4
  Steeple Langford SP3...128 C5
Hollow Way SN15....59 D3
Hollybush Cl
  Acton Turville GL9...53 A6
  Chippenham Without SN14...70 A2
  Winsley BA15......99 E7
Hollybush La SN9...215 D6
Hollybush Rd BA12...117 A8
Holly Cl
  Bower Chalke SP5...204 F2
  Calne SN11.......81 C1
  Pewsey SN9.......215 D6
  Swindon SN2......35 A2
Holly Cres **6** SN13...84 E8
Holly Ct BA11......110 B7
Holly Dr SN14......74 F6
Holmbury Cl BA11...110 C6
Holme La **7** BA13...186 B7
Holmeleaze BA14...178 A4
Holmes Cl SN15....78 F4
Holmes Rd SP1....146 D5
Holmfield **1** SN10...187 E8
Holmleigh SN25.....34 E4
Holmoak Ct **5** SN3...50 D4
Holne Rd SN1......50 A1
Holst Rd SN25.....34 E8
HOLT.............92 E1
Holt La
  Tangley SP11......193 B8
  Teffont SP3.......201 C2
Holt Rd
  Bradford-on-Avon BA15...100 E6
  Witham Friary BA11...123 C8
Holt VC Prim Sch BA14...92 F1
HOLWELL..........139 B5
Holy Cross Catholic Prim Sch
  SN3...............50 D5
Holy Family Cath Prim Sch
  SN3...............51 B6
Holy Rd Church* SN3...50 E4
Holy Rood Cath Inf Sch
  SN1..............50 C5
Holyrood Cl BA14...105 B5
Holy Trinity CE Acad
  SN11.............81 C1
Holy Trinity CE Prim Acad
  The SN10..........187 B8
Home Cl
  Chiseldown SN4...65 C4
  Fovant SP3.......204 D8
  Trowbridge BA14...105 D7
Homefarm SN6.....22 F6
Home Farm Cl
  Heddington SN11...89 B1
  Mildenhall SN8...175 B8
  Steeple Ashton BA14...178 A3
Home Farm Gdns **10**
  SP10.............193 C2
Home Farm Rd SP2...144 C1
Homefield
  Mere BA12........138 F5
  Motcombe SP7....202 C2
  Royal Wootton Bassett SN4...47 E2
Homefields
  Longbridge Deverill BA12...120 F6
  Marlborough SN8...213 F2
Home Fields SN14...68 F5
Homefield Way RG17...177 B7
Home Gd
  Cricklade SN6.....19 C8
  Royal Wootton Bassett SN4...48 A2
Homelands The **1** BA12...116 E5
Home Mead **5** SN13...76 E1
Home Mill Bldgs BA14...105 D8
Homes Mead **7** SN13...76 D1
HOMINGTON.......151 D1

Homington Rd
  Britford SP5......151 D3
  Coombe Bissett SP5...157 B8
Honeybone Wlk SN3...51 E4
Honeybrook Cl SN14...78 B8
Honeybunch Cnr SN8...164 C6
Honeyfields **10** RG17...177 B7
Honey Garston SN11...81 C3
Honey Hill **2** RG17...165 A2
Honey Knob Hill SN14...55 F1
Honey La
  Norton SN16......41 E6
  Westbury BA13....112 D8
Honeylight View **3** SN25...35 A6
Honeymans **2** BA14...105 F8
Honeymead SN11....81 C3
Honeysuckle Cl
  Calne Without SN11...80 F4
  Chippenham Without SN14...78 B3
  Melksham SN12....94 D4
  1 Swindon SN25...34 D5
  4 Trowbridge BA14...105 C7
Honiton Rd SN3....51 B5
HOOK.............47 F6
Hook Cl SN5.......34 A1
Hooks Hill SN5.....33 C4
Hooks La SN10.....179 A7
Hook St
  Hook SN4.........47 F6
  Swindon SN5......48 F4
HOOK STREET......48 B6
Hookwood La SP11...192 E8
Hoopers Pl SN1....50 D4
Hop Gdns The SP5...161 C3
Hopgood Cl SN10...214 F6
Hopkinson Way SP10...193 B1
Hops Cl SP3.......201 A3
Hopton Cl SN5.....49 B3
Hopton Pk Ind Est SN10...214 C6
Hopton Rd SN10...214 D6
Horace St SN2.....49 F7
Horcott Rd
  Fairford GL7......1 F6
  Peatmoor SN5....34 B2
Horder Mews SN3...50 D4
Horham Cres SN3...51 A4
Hornbeam Cl **1** BA11...110 C6
Hornbeam Cres SN12...94 A3
Hornbeam Ct SN2...35 B2
Hornbeam Rd BA14...105 C5
Hornbury Cl SN16...17 A2
Hornbury Hill SN16...17 A2
Hornchurch Rd **20** SN12...178 B8
Horne Rd SP4.....198 E6
HORNINGSHAM.....119 A7
Horningsham Prim Sch
  BA12.............119 B7
Hornsey Gdns SN2...36 A5
Horn's La SN4.....167 B8
HORPIT...........163 B7
Horse Barrow* SP4...133 D3
Horsebrook Pk SN11...81 B3
Horsebrook The SN11...81 C2
Horsefair La SN15...59 C3
Horse Leaze SN10...214 F6
Horsell Cl **2** SN4...47 C2
Horseponds **8** SP7...202 B2
Horse Rd BA14....101 F4
Horseshoe Cres SN5...34 A1
Horseshoe La SP11...193 F8
Horse Shoe La SP3...142 C3
Horsley Cl SN25....34 D8
HORTON..........172 C2
Horton Ave SN10...214 E6
Horton Cl BA15....100 E4
Horton Rd
  Bishops Cannings SN10...172 B2
  Devizes SN10.....214 F7
  Swindon SN2......35 E6
Hospital Rd BA13...109 A2
Hossil La SN6.....22 B1
Houldsworth Ave BA12...117 D8
Howard Cl SN3....50 F6
Howard-Vyse Rd SP4...197 F7
Howgare Rd SP5...205 B2
Howse Gdn SN2....50 A8
Hread Parkway Sch SN2...34 E3
Hubble View SN25...34 B6
Hubert Hamilton Rd SP4...198 E6
Huddleston Cl SN2...50 D8
Hudson Rd
  Amesbury SP4....217 C4
  Malmesbury SN16...27 F4
  Salisbury SP1.....145 F3
Hudson Way SN25...35 A5
HUDSWELL........84 C8
Hudswell La SN13...84 C8
Hughes Cl SN8....213 A2
Hughes St SN2.....49 F7
Hugo Dr SN25.....35 A6
HUISH...........174 A2
Hulbert Cl SN13....76 E1
HULLAVINGTON....41 E6
Hullavington Airfield
  SN14.............56 A7
Hullavington CE Prim Sch
  SN14.............41 F1
Hull Rd **4** SN2....34 E2
Hulse Rd SP1.....146 A2
Humber La SP9...216 B4
Hummingbird Gdns
  BA14.............105 E6
Humphrey's La **3** RG17...171 E7
Hungerdown La SN14...78 A6
HUNGERFORD......177 A6
Hungerford Ave BA14...105 A7

Hungerford Hill
  Great Shefford RG17...171 F4
  Lambourn RG17....165 A1
Hungerford La
  Andover SP10.....193 E3
  Chute SP11.......185 A1
  Kintbury RG17....177 F6
  Tangley SP11.....193 A8
Hungerford Leisure Ctr
  RG17.............177 B6
HUNGERFORD
  NEWTOWN........171 D2
Hungerford Prim Sch
  RG17.............177 B7
Hungerford Rd
  Buttermere SN8...185 B7
  Calne SN11.......81 B4
  Chippenham SN15...70 D1
  Grafton SN8......184 A7
  Hungerford RG17...177 D6
  Kintbury RG17....177 F5
Hungerford Sta RG17...177 C7
Hunsdon Cl SN3...51 A6
Hunt Cl The BA14...102 F5
HUNTENHULL GREEN...111 C3
Huntenhull La BA13...111 D4
Hunters Chase BA13...108 F2
Huntersfield SN16...25 D1
Hunter's Gr SN2...35 B1
Hunters Mead SP7...202 A5
Hunters Meadow SN14...68 F5
Huntingdon Pl BA15...100 C5
Huntingdon Rise BA15...100 C7
Huntingdon BA15...100 C8
Huntingdon Way SN14...78 A6
Huntley Cl SN3....50 F7
Hunts Hill SN26....21 B2
Huntsland SN4....47 F2
Hunts Mead SN15...96 A4
Hunts Mill Rd SN4...61 A8
Hunts Rise SN3....36 C7
Hunt St SN1.......50 C5
HURDCOTT........146 E8
Hurdcott La SP4...146 E8
Hurley Cl **5** SN2...217 D3
Hurricane Rd SN12...94 C1
Hurst Cres SN2....35 C3
Hurst's La SN9....181 C7
Huxley Ct GL7......7 A7
Hyam Cotts SN16...27 C4
HYDE............35 D7
Hyde La
  Marlborough SN8...213 C3
  Purton SN5......33 C4
Hyde Rd
  Royal Wootton Bassett
  SN4..............47 F1
  Swindon SN25....35 D6
  Trowbridge BA14...101 C2
Hyde The SN5.....33 D4
Hylder Cl SN2.....34 D4
Hyson Cres **6** SP11...192 B5
Hysopp Cl SN2.....34 C4
Hythe Rd SN1.....50 B5

IBTHORPE........193 F8
Icknield Sch SP10...193 F1
Icknield Way
  Andover SP10.....193 E2
  Bishopstone SN6...163 E6
Icomb Cl SN5.....49 C4
Idlebush Barrow* SN7...164 E7
IDMISTON........133 F8
Idmiston Rd SP4...133 E6
Idovers Dr SN5...49 C4
IDSTONE.........163 F7
Idstone Hill SN6...163 F7
Idstone Rd SN6...164 A7
Iffley Rd SN2......49 F8
Iford Fields BA15...99 E3
Iford Hill BA15....99 E2
Iford La BA15.....99 D3
Iford Manor* BA15...99 E3
Iles Cl SN11.......73 F7
Ilkeston Rd SN25...34 C7
Ilynton Ave SP5...148 C7
IMBER..........187 A3
Imber Ave
  Amesbury SP4....217 D2
  Warminster BA12...117 C7
Imber Pl SP3.....188 B3
Imber Rd
  Bratton BA13.....186 C6
  10 Shaftesbury SP7...202 D2
  Warminster BA12...117 D8
Imber Wlk SN2....35 B6
Imberwood Cl BA12...117 C7
Imby Cl SP1.......117 F1
Imperial Wy BA11...110 D7
India Ave SP2.....145 E2
Indigo Gdns BA13...108 F3
Indigo La BA13....108 F3
Ingles Edge RG17...177 E2
INGLESHAM.......2 B1
Inglesham Cl **3** BA14...105 D5
Inglesham Rd SN2...35 C4
Inglesham Village* SN6...2 B1
Inglewood Rd RG17...177 E5
Ingram Pl BA13....108 F4
Ingram Rd SN12...94 D5
Ingram St SN16...28 A3
INKPEN..........177 E3
Inkpen Prim Sch RG17...177 E3
Inkpen Rd RG17...177 C5
Inlands SN9......215 C5

Inmarsh La SN12...178 E7
Inmead BA13.....186 C8
Innox Mill Cl BA14...101 B1
Innox Rd BA14....101 B1
Intercity Trad Est SN2...49 A5
Interface Distribution Pk
  SN4..............47 F1
Inverary Rd SN4...64 A7
Ipswich St SN2....50 C8
IRELAND.........105 B2
Ironstone Cl SN25...34 E7
Irston Way **4** SN5...49 B4
Irving Way SN8...213 D4
Isambard Com Sch SN25...34 D7
Isambard Wy SN25...34 D7
Isbury Rd SN8....213 E2
Isis Cl
  Calne SN11.......81 A4
  Swindon SN25....35 A3
Islandsmead SN3...51 C6
Island The SN10...214 B3
Islay Cres SN6....22 F6
Isles Rd **6** SN8...170 B2
Islington BA14....101 D1
Islington St SN1...50 C6
Itchen Cl **2** S051...212 F6
Ivies The SN9.....181 F5
IVY CROSS........202 C2
Ivy Fields SN5....35 A3
Ivy La
  Broad Blunsdon SN26...21 B2
  Chippenham SN15...78 D7
  South Wraxall BA15...91 E5
Ivy La SN15......78 D8
Ivy Mead BA12....139 B5
Ivy Rd SN15......78 D7
Ivy Rd Ind Est SN15...78 D7
Ivy St SP1.......152 B8
Ivy Terr BA15.....100 C5
Ixworth Cl **10** SN5...49 A7

Jackaments Barn GL7...4 B6
Jacklins Cl BA14...101 F5
Jack Paul Cl BA12...139 A6
Jack's Hedge Cnr BH21...208 F2
Jacksom's La SN15...70 D5
Jackson Cl
  3 Corsham SN13...84 F8
  Devizes SN10.....214 C2
Jack Thorne Cl SN5...34 A2
Jacob Cl **22** SP11...193 F3
Jacob's Barrow* SP5...211 E4
Jacobs Piece GL7...1 E6
Jacobs Wlk SN3...51 D4
Jacob Wy BA12....116 D7
Jagdalik Rd SP9...216 C4
Jaggards La SN13...84 D5
Jaggard View SP4...217 C3
Jagoda Ct **7** SN25...34 D6
James Cl SN15.....79 A4
James Rd SP4.....217 C4
James's Hill BA10...122 A7
James St
  Salisbury SP2.....145 F1
  Trowbridge BA14...101 D2
James Watt Cl SN2...50 A7
Jamrud Rd SP9...216 B5
Jarvis St SN9.....181 F2
Jasmine Cl
  Calne SN11.......81 B1
  Chippenham SN14...70 A1
  Swindon SN2......34 D4
Jasmine Way BA14...105 E7
Jason Cl SN25.....34 A7
Javelin Cl **6** SP4...217 D3
Jay Cl BA11.......110 B6
Jay Dr SP4........132 C1
Jeanneau Cl **24** SP7...202 C2
Jefferies Ave SN2...35 D2
Jefferies Cl SN8...213 D2
Jellicoe Ct SP10...193 F1
Jenkins St BA14...101 C1
Jenner Cl SN4....163 A6
Jenni Manners Ct **2** SN5...49 D6
Jennings St SN2...49 F6
Jenson Ave BA11...110 D8
Jerram Gall The* SP1...152 B8
Jersey Rd SN5.....49 B8
Jervis Cl **1** SP10...193 F1
Jewel Cl **2** SN5...48 F5
Jewell Cl SP1.....146 D4
Joanna Cl **4** SP5...210 F4
Jobbers La SP3...203 E7
Jockey La SN15...96 A7
John Alder Cl SN4...65 C3
John Aubrey Cl SN14...68 F6
John Bentley Sch SN11...89 B8
John Bentley Sch The
  SN11.............81 B1
John Betjeman Cl **1**
  SN16.............28 A5
John French Way SP4...217 E8
John Gay Rd **5** SP4...217 B3
John Herring Cres SN3...36 A1
John Ivie Ctr Pru SP1...152 B8
John of Gaunt Rd GL7...10 D6
John of Gaunt Sch The
  BA14.............105 B8
John O'Gaunt Sch RG17...177 B6
John Rennie Cl
  Bradford-on-Avon BA15...100 E4
  Devizes SN10.....214 A2
John Rumble Cl SN10...214 C3
Johnson Way **35** SP11...192 A5
John St SN1.......50 B6

Joiner La SN1.....50 D4
Jole Cl SN2.......35 E5
Joles La BA11.....110 F1
Jolliffe St **7** SN1...50 A5
Jones Hill BA15...100 C5
Jones La SP9.....216 D8
Jone's Mill Nature Reserve*
  SN9.............215 D6
Jopp Cl **9** SN25...34 C5
Jordan Cl SN15...78 F5
Joseph St **4** SN1...50 A5
Joule Rd **3** SP10...193 B1
Joyce Cl SN25.....35 A6
Jubb's La SN8....169 A5
Jubilee Cl
  Bermerton Heath SP2...145 C3
  3 Sandleheath SP6...210 C1
  Westbury BA13....109 A3
Jubilee Ct
  North Tidworth SP9...216 D7
  3 Salisbury SP2...145 F2
Jubilee Gdns GL7...6 F7
Jubilee Hill SP4...197 F1
Jubilee Rd
  Chippenham SN15...70 E1
  Devizes SN10.....214 D3
  Sandleheath SP6...210 C1
  Swindon SN2......34 D3
Juggler's La SN11...166 C2
Juliana Cl **2** SN5...49 A7
Jump Farm SN10...214 C6
Jump Farm Rd SN10...214 C6
Junction Rd
  Alderbury SP5....153 E3
  Bradford-on-Avon BA15...100 D6
Juniper Cl SN3....51 B8
Juniper Dr SP1....146 A5
Juniper Rd SP5...148 C7
Juno Way SN1....49 F4
Jutland Cres **3** SP10...193 D2

Kandahar SN8....170 A7
Kandy Rd **3** SP4...198 E6
Karachi SP9.......216 C7
Karslake Cl **6** SN3...51 C4
Kashmir Rd **1** SP4...198 E6
Katherine House Gall*
  SN8.............213 C2
Katherine's Wlk GL7...2 D4
Katifer La SN16...28 A3
Kavanagh Cl **10** SP7...202 D1
Keates Cl BA14...101 D1
Keats Cl
  3 Melksham SN12...94 B4
  Royal Wootton Bassett SN4...47 F3
Keats Cres SN2...35 E4
Keats Mdw SP5...208 B4
Keble Cl
  Lechlade GL7......2 D5
  Swindon SN3......51 C7
Keel Cl SP4.......217 C2
Keels SN6.........8 C1
Keepers Rd SN10...214 C5
KEEVIL..........178 C5
Keevil Airfield BA14...178 C4
Keevil Ave SN11...81 A3
Keevil CE Prim Sch BA14...178 B5
Kelham Cl **8** SN3...50 F4
Kelham Gdns SN8...213 E3
KELLAWAYS.......71 E4
Kellsborough Rd SN4...63 F7
Kelly Gdns SN25...34 F6
Kelmscot Rd SN25...35 C3
Kelsey Rd SP1....146 B1
Kelso Ct **3** SN14...78 A5
Kelston Rd SN8...176 C4
Kelvin Rd SN3....51 A7
KEMBLE..........4 E7
Kemble Bsns Pk GL7...4 A3
Kemble Dr SN2....50 A7
Kemble Enterprise Pk GL7...4 A6
Kembles Cl SN16...28 C2
Kemble Sta GL7....4 F8
KEMBLE WICK.....4 E4
Kembrey Bsns Pk SN2...35 E2
Kembrey St SN2...35 D2
Kemerton Wlk SN3...51 A3
Kemmel Rd SP11...191 F4
Kemp Cl SN10....214 C6
Kempsfield SN10...214 C1
KEMPSFORD.......10 E6
Kempsford CE Prim Sch
  GL7..............10 C7
Kemp's La BA11...110 F7
Kempton Pk Ct **10** SN14...77 F6
Kencot Ct **5** SN2...35 C6
Kendal SN5.......49 B4
Kendrick Ind Est SN2...49 E8
Kenilworth Gdns SN12...94 B3
Kenilworth Lawns SN3...50 F3
Kenley Cl SN12...94 E1
Kennedy Ave SN12...85 D1
Kennedy Dr SN3...51 D4
Kennedy Meadow RG17...177 B6
Kennel Dr GL9....38 E2
Kennet Ave SN25...35 B3
Kennet & Avon Canal Mus
  The* SN10........214 B4
Kennet Cl
  Melksham SN12...94 A6
  Warminster BA12...117 A5

Kennet Gdns BA15 . . . .**100** D5
Kennet Mews SN8 . . . .**213** D3
Kennet Pl SN8 . . . .**213** E3
Kennet Rd
  Devizes SN10 . . . .**214** C2
  South Tedworth SP9 . . . .**216** E6
  Wroughton SN4 . . . .**64** A7
Kennett Valley CE Prim Sch
  SN8 . . . .**173** D8
Kennet Valley Mews
  SN8 . . . .**169** D1
Kennet Way
  Hungerford RG17 . . . .**177** B8
  Trowbridge BA14 . . . .**101** D3
Kennet Wy RG17 . . . .**177** C8
Ken Savage Cl SN3 . . . .**51** A6
Kensington Cl BA14 . . . .**101** D2
Kensington Fields BA14 . . .**104** F7
Kensington Rd [1] SP2 . . . . .**145** F2
Kensington Way SN4 . . . . . .**77** F7
Kent Cl SN14 . . . .**78** A6
Kent End SN6 . . . .**7** A1
Kent End Cl SN6 . . . .**7** A1
Kenton Cl SN3 . . . .**51** B6
Kenton Dr BA14 . . . .**101** F1
Kent Rd
  Salisbury SP2 . . . .**151** E6
  Swindon SN1 . . . .**50** B4
Kents Hill SP3 . . . .**201** A3
Kenwin Cl SN3 . . . .**36** B2
Kenwood Cl BA14 . . . .**105** F8
KEPNAL **215** E5
Kerby Ave SP4 . . . .**190** B3
Kerrs Way SN4 . . . .**64** A6
Kerry Cl
  Derry Hill/Studley SN11 . . .**79** F2
  Swindon SN5 . . . .**49** A7
Kershaw Rd SN3 . . . .**51** C4
Kestrel Dr
  Swindon SN3 . . . .**51** E6
  [4] Winterbourne SP4 . . . . .**132** C1
Keswick Rd SN3 . . . .**51** B3
Kettle La BA14 . . . .**106** A2
Ketton Cl BA14 . . . .**101** A1
Kew Dr [4] BA14 . . . .**105** A7
Kewlake La SO51 . . . .**212** F1
Keynes Ctry Pk ★ GL7 . . . . . .**6** B5
Keyneston Rd
  Swindon SN3 . . . .**50** F5
  Swindon SN3 . . . .**51** C6
Keynsham Wlk SN3 . . . .**51** A4
Kibblewhite Cl SN5 . . . .**33** B3
Kickdom Cl SP4 . . . .**217** D2
Kidston Way SN13 . . . .**84** A8
Kiel Dr SP10 . . . .**193** D2
Kilben Cl SN5 . . . .**48** F7
Kilda Rd SN6 . . . .**22** E7
Kilford Cl SP4 . . . .**217** C1
Kill Barrow (Long Barrow) ★
  BA12 . . . .**187** D3
KILMINGTON **123** E5
KILMINGTON COMMON . . .**123** D4
Kiln Cl
  Alderbury SP5 . . . .**153** F1
  Devizes SN10 . . . .**214** D3
Kiln La
  Redlynch SP5 . . . .**211** D8
  Swindon SN2 . . . .**34** F1
Kilns The SN11 . . . .**81** C4
Kilsby Dr SN3 . . . .**51** B8
Kilsyth Cl SN5 . . . .**49** B5
Kilve Cl SN3 . . . .**51** B6
Kilverts Cl SN14 . . . .**78** A6
Kimber Cl SP9 . . . .**216** C7
Kimberley Rd SN3 . . . .**51** A4
Kimbers Field [16] SN4 . . . . .**163** A6
Kimbolton Cl [6] SN5 . . . .**49** A4
Kimmeridge Cl SN3 . . . .**51** C6
KIMPTON **192** C1
Kimpton Thruxton & Fyfield
  CE Prim Sch SP11 . . . . . .**192** C1
King Alfred Cl SN9 . . . .**215** D5
King Alfreds Cl BA12 . . . . . .**126** B7
King Alfred St SN15 . . . .**78** C8
King Alfred Way SN15 . . . . . .**99** D2
King Alfred's Way SP7 . . . . .**202** C2
King Arthur's Way SP10 . . .**193** D2
King Barrow ★
  Bishopstrow BA12 . . . .**117** F5
  Winterbourne Stoke SP4 . . .**197** C4
King Charles Rd SN5 . . . .**49** A4
Kingdom Ave BA13 . . . .**108** D5
Kingdom Cres SN25 . . . .**34** D8
Kingdown Sch BA12 . . . . . .**117** D6
Kingfisher Cl
  Salisbury SP2 . . . .**152** A5
  Trowbridge BA14 . . . .**105** E6
Kingfisher Dr
  Bower Hill SN12 . . . .**94** D1
  Devizes SN10 . . . .**214** E5
  [7] Durrington/Bulford
    SP4 . . . .**198** C7
  Swindon SN3 . . . .**51** D7
  Westbury BA13 . . . .**109** A4
Kingfisher Pl GL7 . . . .**7** B7
Kingfishers [2] SP9 . . . .**199** D8
Kingham Cl SN14 . . . .**78** C7
KINGHAY **202** F8
King Henry Dr
  Chippenham SN15 . . . .**79** A4
  Swindon SN5 . . . .**48** F4
King John's House ★ SP5 **207** B4
King John St [3] SN1 . . . .**50** D4
King La BA12 . . . .**116** E5
King Oak ★ SN8 . . . .**175** C4

Kings Ave
  Chippenham Without SN14 . .**77** F6
  Corsham SN13 . . . .**76** F2
  Highworth SN6 . . . .**23** A5
Kingsbere La [5] SP7 . . . . . .**202** D2
Kingsbourne Cl SP4 . . . .**133** B1
Kingsbury Cl SN12 . . . .**94** B3
Kingsbury Sq [3] SP2 . . . . . .**144** D3
Kingsbury St
  Calne SN11 . . . .**81** B2
  Marlborough SN8 . . . .**213** D3
Kings Cl [3] SN5 . . . .**164** A8
Kingscote Cl [1] SN5 . . . .**48** F8
Kings Ct [5] BA12 . . . .**116** E5
KINGSDOWN
  Box **82** F3
  Stratton St Margaret **35** F5
Kingsdown Gr BA1 . . . .**82** F2
Kingsdown Ind Est SN2 . . . . .**36** A6
Kingsdown Rd
  Stratton St Margaret SN2 . . .**36** A6
  Swindon SN2 . . . .**35** F5
  [3] Trowbridge BA14 . . . . . .**105** C5
Kingsdown Sch SN2 . . . .**35** F5
Kings Dr SN8 . . . .**175** C8
Kingsettle Hill BA10 . . . .**122** C2
Kingsfield Cl BA15 . . . .**100** D7
Kingsfield Grange Rd
  BA15 . . . .**100** E7
Kingsford Cl [9] SP5 . . . .**211** C7
Kings Gate SN12 . . . .**144** E4
Kings Gdns BA14 . . . .**101** E5
KINGSHILL **50** B5
Kings Hill [18] SP7 . . . .**202** C2
Kingshill Rd SN1 . . . .**50** A4
King's House ★ SP1 . . . .**152** A7
King's La SP3 . . . .**203** F5
Kingsland Rd SP2 . . . .**145** F2
Kingsley Ave SN4 . . . .**47** E3
Kingsley Gdns SN10 . . . . . .**214** C3
Kingsley Pl BA14 . . . .**100** F1
Kingsley Rd
  Chippenham SN14 . . . .**78** B6
  Devizes SN10 . . . .**214** C3
Kingsley Way SN2 . . . .**35** D5
Kings Lodge Prim Sch
  SN15 . . . .**79** A5
Kingsman La [13] SP7 . . . . .**202** C1
Kingsmanor Wharf SN10 . . .**214** D5
Kingsmead
  Lechlade GL7 . . . .**2** C5
  Stoford SP2 . . . .**130** A3
Kingsmead House SN15 . . . . .**44** A5
Kingsmead Mill ★ SN15 . . . . .**43** F6
Kings Meadow SN16 . . . .**14** D5
Kings Orch BA12 . . . .**116** E5
Kings Paddock SP5 . . . .**149** A5
Kings Rd
  Easterton SN10 . . . .**180** A4
  Enham Alamein SP11 . . . . .**193** E4
  Market Lavington SN10 . . . .**179** F2
King's Rd SP1 . . . .**146** A2
Kings Rise BA12 . . . .**116** E5
King St
  Melksham SN12 . . . .**94** A3
  [3] Swindon SN1 . . . .**50** B4
  Warminster BA12 . . . .**116** E5
  Wilton SP2 . . . .**144** D4
Kings Terr GL9 . . . .**24** B3
Kingsthorpe Gr SN3 . . . .**51** C8
Kingston SN16 . . . .**43** F8
Kingston Ave BA15 . . . .**100** E5
KINGSTON DEVERILL **126** B6
KINGSTONE WINSLOW . . .**164** A8
Kingston La BA12 . . . .**118** F2
Kingston Pk SO51 . . . .**212** F4
Kingston Rd
  [4] Bradford-on-Avon
    BA15 . . . .**100** D6
  Shalbourne SN8 . . . .**176** F1
  Swindon SN3 . . . .**51** A4
King's Wall SN16 . . . .**28** A3
Kingsway
  Preshute SN8 . . . .**168** B1
  Wilton SP2 . . . .**144** D4
Kingsway Bsns Ctr SP2 . . . .**144** D4
Kingsway Cl [1] SN3 . . . .**50** F4
Kingswood
  Trowbridge BA14 . . . .**104** F6
  Wroughton SN4 . . . .**64** A6
Kingswood Ave SN3 . . . .**51** A5
Kington La SN14 . . . .**56** B4
KINGTON LANGLEY **70** E7
KINGTON ST MICHAEL **70** A8
Kington St Michael CE Prim
  Sch SN14 . . . .**70** A8
Kingway View SN16 . . . .**42** E4
King William St CE Prim Sch
  SN1 . . . .**50** C4
King William St SN1 . . . .**50** C4
Kinneir Cl SN13 . . . .**85** A8
Kintbury Rd RG17 . . . .**177** F3
Kipling Gdns SN2 . . . .**35** E4
Kirby Cl SN3 . . . .**50** F4
Kirby Rd SN13 . . . .**76** E1
Kirkee Rd SP9 . . . .**216** C5
Kirkstall Cl SN5 . . . .**49** C4
Kirktonhill Rd SN5 . . . .**49** D6
Kishorn Cl [5] SN5 . . . .**34** B2
Kitchen Barrow ★ SN10 . . .**172** E3
Kitchener Rd SP4 . . . .**217** B3
Kitchener St SN1 . . . .**50** C8
Kitefield [2] SN6 . . . .**19** D8
Kite Hill SN4 . . . .**163** A5
Kite's Nest La SP8 . . . .**137** E2
Kivel Ct SP2 . . . .**146** A2
Kiwi Prim Sch SP4 . . . .**198** E6

Kiwi Rd [6] SP4 . . . .**198** F7
Kiwi The ★ SP4 . . . .**198** F6
Knap Barrow (Long
  Barrow) ★ SP6 . . . .**209** D6
Knap Hill (Causewayed
  Enclosure) ★ SN8 . . . . . .**173** E2
KNAPP **205** A4
Knapp Cl SN2 . . . .**35** A2
KNAPP HILL **202** A5
Knapp Hill SP5 . . . .**205** A4
Knapps The BA14 . . . .**102** F5
Knapp The
  Calne SN11 . . . .**81** C3
  Great Bedwyn SN8 . . . .**176** B3
  [7] Shaftesbury SP7 . . . . . .**202** B2
Knap The BA14 . . . .**102** A3
KNIGHTON **170** D2
Knighton Barrow (Long
  Barrow) ★ SP4 . . . .**197** E8
Knighton Rd SP5 . . . .**205** C4
Knightsbridge Rd SP11 . . . .**193** F4
Knights Cl
  [1] Chippenham SN15 . . . . . .**78** F4
  West Overton SN8 . . . .**173** F6
KNIGHTS ENHAM **193** E3
Knights Enham Prim Sch
  SP10 . . . .**193** E2
Knights Maltings BA11 . . . .**110** A3
KNOCKDOWN **24** F5
Knockdown Rd SN16 . . . .**25** C1
Knole Cl [4] SN25 . . . .**34** F7
Knoll Cl OX12 . . . .**165** F8
Knoll The
  [12] Aldbourne SN8 . . . . . .**170** A6
  Kempsford GL7 . . . .**10** D7
  Malmesbury SN16 . . . .**28** B2
  Westbury BA13 . . . .**109** A4
Knolton Wlk SN3 . . . .**51** A4
KNOOK **194** D4
Knook Barrow (Long
  Barrow) ★ BA12 . . . .**194** F7
Knook Castle ★ BA12 . . . . .**195** A7
Knook Manor ★ BA12 . . . . .**194** D4
Knowlands SN6 . . . .**23** A7
KNOWLE **215** C6
Knowledge Hill [2] SN8 . . . .**170** B2
Knowle The [1] SN13 . . . .**84** F8
Knowsley Rd SN3 . . . .**51** A4
Kohat Ct SP9 . . . .**216** B7
Komat Rd SP9 . . . .**216** C5
Kopernik Rd SN25 . . . .**34** D6
Kyneton Way SN14 . . . .**70** A8

L

Labour-in-Vain Hill
  SN11 . . . .**172** A8
Labrador Gdns [7] SP4 . . . .**217** H8
Laburnam Dr SN4 . . . .**47** E3
Laburnum Cl [3] BA11 . . . . . .**110** B7
Laburnum Dr SN12 . . . .**94** A3
Laburnum Gr BA14 . . . .**105** B6
Laburnum Rd SN2 . . . .**35** C3
Lacemakers Rd SN16 . . . .**28** A5
Lackham Cir SN14 . . . .**78** B6
Lackham Ctry Pk ★ SN15 . . .**78** F1
Lackham Mus SN15 . . . .**78** F1
LACOCK **86** D5
Lacock Abbey ★ SN15 . . . . . .**86** D5
Lacock CE Prim Sch SN15 **86** D5
Lacock Gdns BA14 . . . .**102** B2
Lacock Pottery ★ SN15 . . . .**86** D6
Lacock Rd
  Corsham SN13 . . . .**85** D8
  Swindon SN2 . . . .**35** C4
Ladbrook La SN13 . . . .**77** C1
Ladds La SN15 . . . .**78** E7
Lady Coventry Rd SN15 . . . . .**78** F7
Lady Diana Ct [15] SP11 . . . .**192** A5
Ladydown SN1 . . . .**81** B4
Lady Down View [5] SP3 . . .**203** E8
Ladyfield Rd SN14 . . . .**78** B7
Lady Godley Cl SP9 . . . .**216** C5
Lady Jane Wlk [22] SP11 . . .**192** A5
Lady La SN5 . . . .**21** B1
Lady Margaret Hungerford
  Almshouse ★ SN13 . . . . . .**77** A1
Lady Mead SN6 . . . .**19** D8
Ladysmith SP4 . . . .**133** D3
Ladysmith Rd
  Chiseldon SN4 . . . .**65** D1
  Salisbury SP2 . . . .**145** D3
Ladywood [8] SN10 . . . .**179** F1
Lafranc Cl SP4 . . . .**146** B7
Laggar The SN13 . . . .**77** A2
Lagos St [3] SN1 . . . .**50** C7
Lagpond La SP3 . . . .**204** B7
Lahore Cl SP9 . . . .**216** C7
Lahore Rd SP9 . . . .**216** C5
Laines Head SN14 . . . .**70** C2
Lainesmead Prim Sch
  SN3 . . . .**50** B5
Lainey's Cl SN8 . . . .**213** D4
LAKE **197** F2
Lake Group (Tumuli) ★
  SP4 . . . .**197** D3
Lake House ★ SP4 . . . .**197** F1
Lake Louise SN6 . . . .**8** C3
Lakeside
  Fairford GL7 . . . .**1** F6
  South Cerney GL7 . . . .**7** B7
  Swindon SN3 . . . .**50** F2
Lakeside Cl SP10 . . . .**193** C1
Lake View SN11 . . . .**89** D8
Lake Vw SN4 . . . .**61** A7
Lamb Ale Gn BA14 . . . .**105** D6

Lambdown App SP11 . . . . . .**191** F3
Lambdown Terr
  North Tidworth SP11 . . . . .**216** F6
  Perham Down SP11 . . . . . .**191** F4
Lambe Cl GL7 . . . .**1** E6
Lambert Cl SN5 . . . .**49** B3
Lamberts SN14 . . . .**78** A8
LAMBOURN **165** B2
Lambourn Ave SN3 . . . .**50** E3
Lambourn CE Prim Sch
  RG17 . . . .**165** A1
Lambourne Cr [4] SN12 . . . . .**94** B4
Lambourne Cres SN12 . . . . . .**94** B4
Lambourn La BA13 . . . .**186** C8
Lambourn Pl [10] RG17 . . . .**165** A2
LAMBOURN
  WOODLANDS **171** A6
Lambrok Cl BA14 . . . .**104** F6
Lambrok Rd BA14 . . . .**104** F6
Lammas SN11 . . . .**166** A6
Lamora Cl [12] SN5 . . . .**48** F8
Lampeter Rd SN3 . . . .**36** C6
Lamplighters Wlk BA14 . . . .**105** C7
Lanac Rd SN3 . . . .**36** A1
Lancaster Cl [6] RG17 . . . . .**177** B6
Lancaster Mews SN3 . . . .**36** C6
Lancaster Pl SN3 . . . .**36** C6
Lancaster Rd
  Bower Hill SN12 . . . .**94** B1
  Kempsford GL7 . . . .**10** E6
  Wroughton SN4 . . . .**64** A6
Lancaster Sq
  Hungerford RG17 . . . .**177** B6
  Lyneham SN15 . . . .**60** B3
Landale Cl [3] SP11 . . . .**193** E4
LANDFORD **212** C6
LANDFORDWOOD **212** D8
Landor Rd SN25 . . . .**34** F8
LANE END **115** A8
Lane's Cl SP4 . . . .**217** C4
Lanes End SN13 . . . .**85** D5
Lanes End Hill BA12 . . . . . .**115** A8
Lane-side [9] SP7 . . . .**202** C2
Lane The
  [4] Ashbury SN6 . . . .**164** A8
  Bishopstone SN4 . . . .**163** C7
Lanfear Cl SP4 . . . .**217** C4
Langdale Dr SN5 . . . .**49** B3
Langdean Rd [5] SN1 . . . .**50** B1
Langet GL7 . . . .**6** E6
Langfields SN8 . . . .**170** A2
Langford Gr SN3 . . . .**50** E6
Langford La SP5 . . . .**160** A3
Langford Rd
  Great Wishford SP2 . . . . . .**129** F4
  Trowbridge BA14 . . . .**101** C2
Langfords La [3] SP7 . . . . . .**202** B1
Langham Pl BA11 . . . .**103** F1
Langholm Ave BA12 . . . .**116** D6
Langholm Cl BA12 . . . .**116** D6
LANGLEY BURRELL **71** A3
Langley Fitzurse CE Prim Sch
  SN15 . . . .**70** E6
Langley Gdn SP6 . . . .**210** E2
Langley Pk SN15 . . . .**70** E1
Langley Pk SN15 . . . .**70** F1
Langley Rd
  Chippenham SN15 . . . .**70** E1
  Swindon SN5 . . . .**34** B1
  Trowbridge BA14 . . . .**105** C5
Langley Wood National
  Nature Reserve ★ SP5 . . .**211** F7
Langport Cl [1] SN5 . . . .**49** B4
Langstone Way SN5 . . . .**49** C6
Lanham's Cl BA13 . . . .**109** A4
Lanhill (Long Barrow) ★
  SN14 . . . .**69** B2
Lanhill View SN14 . . . .**70** B2
Lanhydrock Cl [9] SN5 . . . . . .**49** A4
Lansbury Dr SN2 . . . .**35** F4
Lansdown Cl
  Melksham SN12 . . . .**94** C6
  Trowbridge BA14 . . . .**105** B7
Lansdowne Cl SN11 . . . .**81** A4
Lansdowne Cres SN11 . . . . . .**79** F2
Lansdown Gr SN15 . . . .**70** D1
Lansdowne Terr SN10 . . . . .**214** A3
Lansdown Gr SN1 . . . .**50** B4
Lansdown Rd SN1 . . . .**50** B4
Lapwing Cl [1] SN5 . . . .**51** E6
Lapwing Cres SN14 . . . .**70** B3
Lapwing Dr SP4 . . . .**132** C1
Lapwing Rd SN12 . . . .**94** D5
Larch Cl SN12 . . . .**94** A3
Larchfield Cl BA11 . . . .**110** B7
Larch Gr BA14 . . . .**105** B6
Larchmore Cl SN25 . . . .**35** A3
Larch Rd SN14 . . . .**74** F6
Larch Row SP6 . . . .**210** F1
Lark Cl SP9 . . . .**216** D7
Lark Down BA14 . . . .**101** E1
Larkham Rise SN15 . . . .**78** F6
LARKHILL **197** F6
Larkhill Prim Sch SP4 . . . . .**197** E7
Larkhill Rd SP4 . . . .**198** B7
Lark La [5] SP4 . . . .**132** C1
Larkrise Sch BA14 . . . .**101** E1
Larksfield SN3 . . . .**51** C8
Larkspur SN4 . . . .**47** D2
Larmer Tree Gdns ★ SP5 . .**207** B3
Late Broads BA15 . . . .**99** D7
Latimer Gdns SN14 . . . .**41** E1
LATTON **8** C4
Latton Cl SN2 . . . .**35** B6
Laughton Way SN25 . . . .**35** A6
Launcelot Cl [22] SP10 . . . .**193** C2
Laundry La [5] SP7 . . . .**202** B1
Laura Pl SN13 . . . .**83** F7
Laurel Cl BA11 . . . .**110** B7

Laurel Dr
  Colerne SN14 . . . .**74** F6
  Marlborough SN8 . . . .**213** F2
Laurel Gr BA14 . . . .**105** C6
Laurels The
  Hungerford RG17 . . . .**177** C8
  Melksham Without SN12 . . . .**86** A1
  Westwood BA15 . . . .**99** F3
Laurence Ct [10] SP11 . . . . .**192** A5
Lavender Cl
  Melksham SN12 . . . .**94** C3
  [5] Trowbridge BA14 . . . . . .**105** E7
Lavender Ct BA11 . . . .**110** B7
Lavender Dr SN11 . . . .**81** B1
LAVERSTOCK **146** E2
Laverstock Pk SP1 . . . .**146** D1
Laverstock Pk W SP1 . . . . . .**146** D2
Laverstock Rd SP1 . . . .**146** C1
Laverton Ct [1] BA13 . . . . . .**109** A3
Laverton Gn [3] BA13 . . . . . .**108** F1
Laverton Rd BA13 . . . .**108** F1
Lavington Cl [10] SN8 . . . . . .**183** D8
Lavington Comp Sch
  SN10 . . . .**179** E1
Lavington Hill SN10 . . . .**187** B8
Lavington La SN10 . . . .**187** E8
LAVINGTON SANDS **179** E2
LAWN **50** F3
Lawn Farm SN9 . . . .**182** E7
Lawn Prim Sch SN3 . . . .**50** F2
Lawns The SN4 . . . .**47** D2
Lawrence Cl
  [4] Amesbury SP4 . . . .**217** C3
  Devizes SN10 . . . .**214** C1
  Swindon SN3 . . . .**51** C4
Lawrence Mead [3] SN8 . . . .**170** B2
Lawrence Rd SP4 . . . .**197** F7
Lawson Rd [3] SP4 . . . .**198** A6
Lawton Cl SN3 . . . .**51** A3
Layton La SP7 . . . .**202** C1
LEA **28** F1
Lea Cl SN25 . . . .**35** A7
Leaden Hall Sch SP1 . . . . . .**152** A7
LEAFIELD **84** E7
Leafield Ind Est SN13 . . . . . .**84** E6
Leafield Pl BA14 . . . .**100** F1
Leafield Rd SN13 . . . .**84** E6
Leafield Way SN13 . . . .**84** E6
Leafy La SN13 . . . .**76** A1
Lea & Garsdon CE Prim Sch
  SN16 . . . .**28** F2
Lea House SN16 . . . .**28** D1
Leamington Gr SN3 . . . .**50** F2
Leap Gate
  Hilperton BA14 . . . .**102** A1
  Trowbridge BA14 . . . .**106** A8
Leatler Cl SP3 . . . .**204** D8
Leaze Rd
  Marlborough SN8 . . . .**213** C4
  Melksham SN12 . . . .**94** C6
Leaze St SN1 . . . .**50** A2
Leaze The
  Ashton Keynes SN6 . . . .**6** F1
  Durrington/Bulford SP4 . . .**217** E8
  South Cerney GL7 . . . .**6** F6
LECHLADE-ON-THAMES **2** D4
Lechlade Rd
  Buscot SN7 . . . .**2** E2
  Highworth SN6 . . . .**23** A7
  Inglesham SN6 . . . .**12** A6
Ledge Hill SN10 . . . .**179** E2
Ledger Hill Cl SP4 . . . .**217** D8
Lee Cres SN15 . . . .**57** C1
Leehurst Swan SP1 . . . .**146** B2
Lees Ct SP2 . . . .**145** F2
Legate Cl SN15 . . . .**79** B5
Legg Rd [12] SP7 . . . .**202** D1
Leicester St SN1 . . . .**50** D6
LEIGH **18** C5
Leigh Cl BA13 . . . .**108** E1
LEIGH DELAMERE **55** C3
Leighfield Cl [8] SN1 . . . .**50** C5
Leigh La SP3 . . . .**202** E8
Leigh Pk Rd BA15 . . . .**100** D8
Leigh Rd
  Bradford-on-Avon BA15 . . . .**91** E1
  Holt BA14 . . . .**92** C1
  Swindon SN2 . . . .**35** C4
  Westbury BA13 . . . .**108** F1
Leighton Ave SN3 . . . .**50** F4
Leighton Gn BA13 . . . .**109** A2
Leighton La BA13 . . . .**109** A1
Leighton Pk N [4] BA13 . . . .**108** F1
Leighton Pk Rd [5] BA13 . . .**108** F1
Leighton Pk W [2] BA13 . . . .**108** F1
Leigh Woods La SN10 . . . . .**214** F6
Leisler Gdns BA14 . . . .**106** A8
Leland Cl [5] SN16 . . . .**28** A5
Le Marchant St [2] SN10 . . .**214** D5
Lena Cl [26] SP11 . . . .**192** A5
Lennards The GL7 . . . .**7** A7
Lennox Dr SN3 . . . .**50** E6
Lenta Bsns Ctr SN1 . . . .**50** B6
Lenton Cl SN14 . . . .**77** F7
Leonard Cheshire Cl [4]
  SP4 . . . .**217** D2
Lesley Anne Skeete Ct
  SN3 . . . .**51** B4
Leslie Cl SN5 . . . .**49** A4
Leslie Rise BA15 . . . .**99** F3
LETCOMBE BASSETT **165** F8
Lethbridge Prim Sch SN1 **50** C3
Lethbridge Rd SN1 . . . .**50** C3
Letteridge Rd SN5 . . . .**34** C2
Levell Ct [12] SP11 . . . .**192** A5
Leven SN5 . . . .**49** A3
Leventon Pl BA14 . . . .**102** B2
Leversedge Rd [2] BA11 . . .**110** A7

LEVERTON 171 B1
Leverton Gate SN3. . . . . . . .50 F1
Leverton La RG17. . . . . . . .171 B1
Lewington Cl SN12. . . . . . . .94 A3
Lewington Mews [14]
RG17. . . . . .177 B6
Lewis Cl
Corsham SN13. . . . . .84 D8
Swindon SN25. . . . . .34 F6
Lewisham Castle★ SN8 .169 E4
Leylands SN13. . . . . .76 B1
Leys Hill BA11. . . . . .110 A6
Leys La BA11. . . . . .110 A6
Leystone Cl BA11. . . . . . . .110 A6
Ley The SN13. . . . . .83 D5
Lichen Cl [3] SN2. . . . . .34 D4
Lickhill Rd SN11. . . . . .81 A4
Lidbury Camp★ SN9 . .190 C8
Liddiards Gn SN8. . . . . . . .168 F5
LIDDINGTON. 163 B4
Liddington Castle (Fort)★
SN4. . . . . .163 A2
Liddington St SN1. . . . . .35 C3
Liddington Way BA14. . . . .105 D5
LIDEN. 51 D3
Lidenbrook [2] SN4. . . . . . .163 A4
Liden Dr SN3. . . . . .51 D4
Liden Prim Sch SN3. . . . . . .51 D3
Light Cl SN13. . . . . .77 C6
Lightfoot Rd SN4. . . . . . . .197 F7
Lightning Rd [1] SP4. . . . . .217 D2
Light's La SP5. . . . . .153 C2
Light The SN16. . . . . .27 F3
Liguiel Ct [9] RG17. . . . . . .177 B6
Lilac Ct SN2. . . . . .35 F2
Lilac Gr BA14. . . . . .105 B5
Lilac Way SN11. . . . . .81 B1
Lilian Cl [8] SN25. . . . . .34 C6
Lilian Lock Gdns SN2. . . . . .35 C5
Lillywhite Cres [1] SP10 . .193 E2
Lilypad St [5] SN3. . . . . .51 B8
Lily Wlk [11] SP4. . . . . .198 C7
Lime Ave
Badminton GL9. . . . . .38 C1
Melksham SN12. . . . . .94 A3
Lime Cl
Colerne SN14. . . . . .75 A5
Frome BA11. . . . . .110 B7
Lyneham & Bradenstoke
SN15. . . . . .60 C2
Pewsey SN9 . . . . .215 D6
Lime Kiln SN4. . . . . .47 D3
Lime Kiln Cl BA12. . . . . . . .113 A1
Limekiln Rd SP11. . . . . . . .192 E6
Lime Kiln Sports Ctr SN4 .47 D3
Lime Kiln Way SP2. . . . . . .152 A6
Limes Ave SN2. . . . . .35 B3
Limes Pl SN6. . . . . .8 C4
Limes Rd GL7. . . . . .4 F7
Limes The
Badminton GL9. . . . . .38 E2
Motcombe SP7. . . . . .202 A4
Porton SP4. . . . . .133 E6
Shrewton SP3. . . . . .196 E7
South Cerney GL7. . . . . .7 A6
Limestone Dr
[6] Corsham SN13. . . . . . . .76 D1
Corsham SN13. . . . . .84 D8
Lime Tree Cl SN11. . . . . . . .81 A3
Lime Trees SN15. . . . . .58 A2
LIMPERS HILL. 139 D4
LIMPLEY STOKE. 99 A6
Limpley Stoke Rd BA15 . .99 D6
Lincoln Gn SN12. . . . . .94 C7
Lincoln Gr SN12. . . . . .94 C1
Lincoln St SN1. . . . . .50 C6
Linden Ave SN2. . . . . .35 C3
Linden Cl
Calne SN11. . . . . .81 B2
Colerne SN14. . . . . .74 F6
Ludgershall SP11. . . . . . . .192 B5
Royal Wootton Bassett SN4 .47 E3
Salisbury SP1. . . . . .146 D1
Linden Cres BA15. . . . . . . .100 A3
Linden Gr [2] SN12. . . . . . . .94 A2
Linden Lea GL7. . . . . .8 E8
Linden Pk SP7. . . . . .202 D1
Linden Pl BA14. . . . . .101 B1
Linden Way SN5. . . . . .34 C2
Lindford Rd SP1. . . . . .146 D5
Lindisfarne [1] SN4. . . . . . . .48 A3
Lindisfarne Cl BA15. . . . . . .99 E7
Lindlar Cl [13] SP7. . . . . . . .202 C2
Lindley Cl SP9. . . . . .216 D6
Lineacre Cl SN5. . . . . .48 F4
Lingen Cl [12] SP10. . . . . . .193 D2
Lingfield Cl [6] SN14. . . . . . .77 F5
Link Ave SN5. . . . . .49 B5
LINKENHOLT. 185 E5
Link La BA15. . . . . .83 A1
Link Rd BA13. . . . . .108 E2
Links The
Corsham SN13. . . . . .84 B7
Pewsey SN9 . . . . .215 B4
Link Way SP1. . . . . .146 C3
Linley Cl SN1. . . . . .50 C2
Linley Rd SN26. . . . . .21 C2
LINLEYS THE 85 B6
Linnet La SN12. . . . . .94 C5
Linnet Rd SN11. . . . . .81 C5
Linnetsdene
[6] Salisbury SP2. . . . . . . .152 A5
Swindon SN3. . . . . .51 C8
Linnet Way BA11. . . . . . . .110 B6
Linslade SN2. . . . . .50 A7
Linslade St SN2. . . . . .49 F6

Linsvale Cl BA11. . . . . . . .110 C5
Linsvale Dr BA11. . . . . . . .110 C5
Lipgate SN10 . . . . .180 F8
Lipman Wy SN16. . . . . .28 C2
Liskeard Way SN5. . . . . . . .49 B4
Lisle Cl SN5. . . . . .49 A5
Lismore Rd SN6. . . . . .22 E6
Lister Gr BA15. . . . . .99 F3
Lister Rd SN4. . . . . .64 B7
Litchfield Cl [11] SP10. . . . .193 C2
Litherland Cl SN14. . . . . . . .78 B6
Little Ave SN2. . . . . .35 A1
LITTLE ASHLEY 91 A2
LITTLE BADMINTON. 38 E5
Little Badminton La SN16 . .28 F2
LITTLE BEDWYN. 176 D5
Little Brittox SN10 . . . . . .214 A3
LITTLE CHALFIELD 92 C3
Little Challows SN14. . . . . . .76 D7
LITTLE CHEVERELL 187 D8
Little Clarendon★ SP3 . .201 F7
Little Comm BA14. . . . . . . .105 D3
Little Content La [17] SP7. .202 C2
Littlecote Cl [3] SN5. . . . . . .49 D5
Littlecote Rd
Chippenham SN14. . . . . . . .78 A6
Froxfield SN8. . . . . .176 D7
Littlecote Roman Villa★
RG17. . . . . .170 D1
LITTLECOTT
Enford 190 A6
Hilmarton 166 A7
Little Ct La BA13. . . . . .186 E8
LITTLEDOWN 185 D4
Littledown SP7. . . . . .202 C2
Little Down SN14. . . . . .78 B7
Little Dro SP6. . . . . .211 A4
LITTLE DURNFORD. 131 D1
Little Englands SN15. . . . . . .78 E6
LITTLE FARINGDON. 2 E8
Littlefield La SP5. . . . . .208 A4
Little Hill BA12. . . . . .116 E2
LITTLE HORTON. 172 C1
Little Ingleburn SN16. . . . . .28 A2
Little Island
Pewsey SN9 . . . . .215 B5
Pewsey SN9 . . . . .215 B5
Littlejohn Ave SN12. . . . . . .94 C6
LITTLE LANGFORD. 129 A6
LITTLE LONDON. 166 E2
Little London
Heytesbury BA12. . . . . . .194 C5
[1] Swindon SN1. . . . . .50 D4
LITTLE MARSH. 102 F4
Little Mead SN8. . . . . .176 F1
Littlemill La SP6. . . . . .209 F3
Little Parks BA14. . . . . .92 F1
Little Pk Cl SN15. . . . . .59 F1
Little Rose La SN26 . . . . . . .20 F5
LITTLE SALISBURY. 182 E7
Little Sands SN14. . . . . .68 F5
LITTLE SOMERFORD. 44 B5
LITTLETON. 178 B7
LITTLETON DREW. 53 E5
Littleton Drew La GL9. . . . . .53 A6
LITTLETON PANELL. 179 D1
Little Woodbury★ SP5 . .152 B4
Little Woodfalls Dr SP5 . .211 C6
LITTLEWORTH 182 E8
Littleworth La SN12. . . . . . .85 C2
Livery Rd
West Dean SP5. . . . . .155 B7
Winterslow SP5. . . . . .149 B4
Livia Cl [13] SP10. . . . . . . .193 E2
Lockem Rd SN10. . . . . .214 E6
LOCKERIDGE 174 A6
Lockeridge Cl BA14. . . . . . .105 D5
Lockeridge La SN8. . . . . . . .174 B7
Locke's Dro SP11. . . . . . . .193 E8
Locking Cl SN12. . . . . .178 B8
Locks Cross SN13. . . . . .84 E5
Locksgreen Cres [1] SN2 . .34 E3
Lock's Hill BA11. . . . . .110 A3
Lockside [1] SN15. . . . . .78 F5
Locks La SN5. . . . . .33 B5
Locks The SN10. . . . . .179 D8
Lockswell Cl SN15. . . . . . . .79 A4
Loddon Way BA15. . . . . . . .100 E5
Lode Hill SP5. . . . . .211 B8
Lodersfield GL7. . . . . .2 C4
Loder's La SP3. . . . . .204 A5
Lodge Cl SN11. . . . . .81 A3
Lodge Ct BA14. . . . . .105 F8
Lodge Dr [6] SP11. . . . . . . .192 F1
Lodge Dro SP5. . . . . .211 C6
Lodge Hill BA11. . . . . .110 F5
Lodge La SP11. . . . . .192 E6
Lodge Rd
Chippenham SN15. . . . . . . .79 A5
Horningsham BA12. . . . . . .119 A8
Lodge Vw SP3. . . . . .188 A2
Lodowicks SN13. . . . . .80 D7
Logan Cl [1] SN3. . . . . .50 E6
Loiret Cres SN16. . . . . .28 A6
Lomond Cl SN3. . . . . .34 B2
Londonderry Gdns SP4. . .198 A5
London La SN5. . . . . .17 C1
London Rd
Amesbury SP4. . . . . .217 B4
Bishops Cannings SN10 . .214 A6
Box SN13. . . . . .83 D7
Calne SN11. . . . . .81 B2
Chippenham SN15. . . . . . . .78 F6
Marlborough SN8. . . . . . . .213 E2
Salisbury SP1. . . . . .146 C3

London Rd *continued*
Shrewton SP3. . . . . .196 F7
London Rd E BA1. . . . . .82 A3
London Ride SN8. . . . . . . .176 A5
London St SN1. . . . . .50 B6
Long Acre SN5. . . . . .33 B4
Long Barn Rd [18] SP11. . . .193 F2
Longbarrow Cross Roads
SP4. . . . . .197 C4
Long Barrow Rd SN11. . . . . .81 A3
Long Bottom SP11. . . . . . . .192 D6
LONGBRIDGE DEVERILL. .120 F6
Long Cl
Chippenham SN15. . . . . . . .78 F6
Downton SP5. . . . . .211 A8
Long Cl Ave SN13. . . . . .76 B1
Long Cl W SP5. . . . . .211 A8
Longcombe Dr BA12. . . . . .115 E3
Longcot Cl SN3. . . . . .36 A1
Longcroft Ave SN10. . . . . .214 C3
Longcroft Cres SN10. . . . . .214 C3
Longcroft Rd SN10. . . . . . .214 C3
LONG CROSS 138 B5
Long Cross
Bramshaw SO43. . . . . . . .212 C2
Shaftesbury SP7. . . . . . . .202 B2
LONG DEAN. 68 C4
Long Dro
Burbage SN8. . . . . .183 D8
Grimstead SP5. . . . . .154 B4
Longfellow Cl SN25. . . . . . . .35 A8
Longfellow Cres SN4. . . . . . .47 F3
LONGFIELD. 105 E8
Longfield Cl [11] SP4. . . . . .198 B7
Longfield Rd BA14. . . . . . . .105 D7
Longfields SN8. . . . . .173 B8
Longfields Wlk SN10. . . . . .214 C2
Longford Castle★ SP5 . .153 A2
Longford CE (VC) Prim Sch
SP5. . . . . .152 D5
Longford Pk★ SP5. . . . . .152 D2
Longford Rd SN12. . . . . .94 A2
Long Ground
[4] Corsham SN13. . . . . . . .76 D1
Corsham SN13. . . . . .84 D8
Long Harry SN8. . . . . .213 F1
LONGHEDGE. 115 D5
Long Hedge RG17. . . . . . . .165 B1
Long Hill BA12. . . . . .138 F5
Longhill Dr [1] SP2. . . . . . .152 B5
Long Hollow BA13. . . . . . . .186 D7
Long La
Bourton SP8. . . . . .137 B1
Cann SP7. . . . . .206 A8
Longland SP2. . . . . .145 E1
Longlands Cl BA13. . . . . . . .186 C7
Longleat Gdns SN2. . . . . . . .35 C4
Longleat House★ BA12 . .114 F3
Longleat Safari Pk★
BA12. . . . . .115 B4
Longleaze SN4. . . . . .47 E3
Long Leaze La SN12. . . . . . .94 C3
Longleaze Prim Sch SN4. . .47 E3
Longleys Cl SN10. . . . . . . .214 E2
Longmead SP7. . . . . .202 C2
Longmeadow Prim Sch
BA14. . . . . .105 E7
LONG NEWNTON. 13 C5
Long Ridings SN14. . . . . . . .70 C3
Long River Rd BA13. . . . . .109 D2
Long Row SN6. . . . . .10 B4
Longsplatt SN13. . . . . .83 D3
Long St SN10 . . . . .214 B3
Long Steeple La SP6. . . . . .210 C6
Longstock Ct SN5. . . . . .49 B6
Longstone Rd [1] SN14. . . . .70 A1
Long Stones★ SN8 . . . .173 A8
LONGSTREET. 190 A6
Longthorpe Cl SN5. . . . . . . .49 D4
Longworth Dr SN5. . . . . .34 B7
Lonsdale Cl SN26. . . . . .21 C2
Lonsdale Gdns
Bowerhill SN12. . . . . .94 E1
Melksham SN12. . . . . .94 A2
Loop Rd SN8 . . . . .175 A7
Lopcombe Cnr SP4 . . . . . .135 D3
LOPCOMBE CORNER. 135 D3
Lopes Way BA13. . . . . .108 F4
Lords Cl SN4. . . . . .64 E3
Lords Croft SP4. . . . . .217 B4
Lord's La SN15. . . . . .78 E7
Lord's Mead SN14. . . . . .78 A8
Lordsmead Rd BA12. . . . . .139 B4
Lorne St SN1. . . . . .50 A5
Lotmead [1] BA14. . . . . . . .101 D5
Lottage Rd SN8. . . . . .170 A7
Lottage Way [2] SN8 . . . . .170 A7
Lotts The SN6. . . . . .17 F8
Loughborough Cl [1] SN5. .48 F4
Lourdes Cres [15] RG17. . . .177 B6
Louviers Way SN1 . . . . .50 C2
Lovage Way BA12. . . . . . . .139 B6
Loveage Cl [5] SN2. . . . . . . .34 D4
Love La
Box SN13. . . . . .83 F7
Salisbury SP1. . . . . .152 B8
[4] Shaftesbury SP7. . . . . .202 B1
Woodgreen SP6. . . . . .211 A4
Lovell Cl SN3. . . . . .51 D7
Lovel Rd BA12. . . . . .194 E3
LOVER. 211 D6
Loveridge Cl
[5] Andover SP10 . . . . . . .193 E2
Swindon SN2. . . . . .35 E6
Lover's La SN16. . . . . .28 A4
Loves La BA14. . . . . .104 C7
Love's La SN8 . . . . .170 B3
Lovett Gn SP1. . . . . .146 C4

Lowa Cl SP9. . . . . .216 C6
Lowa Rd SP9. . . . . .216 B6
Lowbourne SN12. . . . . .94 B4
Lowden SN15. . . . . .78 C7
Lowden Ave SN14. . . . . . . .78 C8
Lowden Hill SN15. . . . . .78 C7
Lower Alma St BA14. . . . . .105 E8
Lower Backway [7] SP3. . . .196 E6
Lower Bartons [30] SP6. . . .210 D1
Lower Blandford Rd
Cann SP7. . . . . .206 A7
[5] Shaftesbury SP7. . . . . .202 C1
LOWER BLUNSDON. 21 B3
LOWER BURGATE. 210 D2
LOWER CHICKSGROVE. . .201 B1
Lower Churchfields SN8 . .213 D2
LOWER CHUTE 192 F8
Lower BA14. . . . . .101 C1
Lower Densome Wood
SP6. . . . . .211 A4
LOWER EVERLEIGH. 182 E1
Lower Folly SP2. . . . . .144 B3
Lower Goatacre SN11. . . . .166 A7
Lower Gr SP6. . . . . .210 B5
LOWER GREEN. 177 D3
Lower Ho SN16. . . . . .15 B8
Lower Kingsdown Rd
SN13. . . . . .83 A4
Lower Marsh Rd BA12. . . . .117 A5
LOWER MOOR 17 A4
Lower N Rd SP5. . . . . .207 C5
Lower Prospect SN8. . . . . .213 E3
Lower Rd
Bratton BA13. . . . . .186 A6
Britford SP5. . . . . .152 C5
Coombe Bissett SP5. . . . .151 C1
Downton SP5. . . . . .159 B4
Edington BA13. . . . . .186 C8
Erlestoke BA13. . . . . .178 F2
Netheravon SP4. . . . . . . .190 A3
Odstock SP5. . . . . .152 D4
Salisbury SP2. . . . . .144 F2
LOWER RUDGE. 107 D4
LOWER SEAGRY. 57 F7
Lower S Rd SP5. . . . . .207 C4
Lower St
Donhead St Andrew SP7. .203 B3
Netheravon SP4. . . . . . . .190 A4
Rode BA11. . . . . .103 E1
Salisbury SP2. . . . . .151 E7
LOWER STANTON ST
QUINTIN. 56 D6
Lower Stoke
Limpley Stoke BA2. . . . . . . .99 A5
Monkton Combe BA2. . . . . .90 A1
LOWER STRATTON 36 B2
LOWER STUDLEY. 105 E6
LOWER WANBOROUGH . . .163 B6
Lower Westbury Rd
BA13. . . . . .109 E5
LOWER WOODFORD. 131 C2
LOWER WOODROW SN12 . .86 F1
LOWER WRAXALL. 91 B5
LOWER ZEALS. 138 D5
Lowes Cl [2] SN5. . . . . .34 B2
Low La SN11. . . . . .81 D2
Lowmead BA14. . . . . .101 E1
Low Rd SN10 . . . . .179 C1
Loxley Cl SN12. . . . . .94 B6
Loxley Wlk SN3. . . . . .51 B3
Loyalty St SN14. . . . . .78 C7
Lubeck Dr [22] SP10. . . . . .193 D2
Lucerne Cl
Royal Wootton Bassett
SN4. . . . . .47 D4
[10] Swindon SN5. . . . . . . .48 F8
Lucetta Rise [6] SN25. . . . . .34 D5
Lucewood La SP5. . . . . . . .154 C7
Luckett Way SN11 . . . . .81 C4
LUCKINGTON. 39 E4
Luckington Com Sch
SN14. . . . . .39 E5
Luckington Ct★ SN14. . . . .39 F5
Lucknam Pk★ SN14. . . . . .75 B6
Luddesdown Rd SN5. . . . . .49 C4
LUDGERSHALL. 192 A5
Ludgershall Castle★
SP11. . . . . .192 A6
Ludgershall Rd
Collingbourne Ducis SN8. .191 E8
[4] Swindon SN1. . . . . .49 F4
Tidworth SP9. . . . . .216 D7
Ludgershall Sports Club
SP11. . . . . .192 A5
Ludlow Cl
Chippenham SN15. . . . . . . .79 A5
[10] Frome BA11. . . . . . . .110 C6
Swindon SN3. . . . . .50 F4
Warminster BA12. . . . . . . .116 F4
Westbury BA13. . . . . .108 F4
Ludmead Rd SN13. . . . . . . .85 A8
LUDWELL. 203 A1
Ludwell Com Prim Sch
SP7. . . . . .203 A1
Ludwell Hill SP7. . . . . .203 A1
Lugbury (Long Barrow)★
SN14. . . . . .53 E2
Lukas Cl SN25. . . . . .34 F7
Luke St SP7. . . . . .203 E1
Lulworth Rd SN25. . . . . .34 E3
Lumley Cl
[2] Swindon SN5. . . . . .49 A4
Westwood SP2. . . . . .145 B5
Lumley Wlk [3] SP4. . . . . . .217 D3
Luxfield Rd BA12. . . . . .116 A5
Lyall Cl SN25. . . . . .34 F8
Lyburn Rd SP5. . . . . .212 A5

Lev–Mai 233

Lyddon Way SN25. . . . . .34 F4
Lydford Cl [4] SN5. . . . . .49 A8
Lydiard Fields Bsns Pk
SN5. . . . . .48 E3
Lydiard Gn SN5. . . . . .33 A1
LYDIARD GREEN. 48 B8
LYDIARD MILLICENT. 33 D1
Lydiard Millicent CE Prim
Sch SN5. . . . . .48 B8
Lydiard Pk★ SN5. . . . . . . .48 E6
Lydiard Pk Academy SN5 . .48 F5
LYDIARD PLAIN. 32 B1
Lydiard Rd SN14. . . . . .78 A6
LYDIARD TREGOZE. 48 E6
Lydiard Way BA14. . . . . . . .105 D5
LYE GREEN. 100 A4
Lyes Gr BA13. . . . . .112 B8
LYE'S GREEN. 111 B1
Lye The SN7. . . . . .178 E8
Lyme Ave BA12. . . . . .116 F6
Lymers The SN11. . . . . . . .166 E2
Lyme Way SN25. . . . . .35 A5
Lynch Cl BA12. . . . . .139 B5
Lynchet Cl [7] SN10. . . . . . .179 F1
Lynchets Rd SP4. . . . . .217 B3
Lynchfield Rd [7] SP4. . . . . .217 B3
Lynch Field The [5] SN4 . .163 A5
Lynch La RG17. . . . . .165 A2
Lynch The SN8. . . . . .176 F1
Lynden Cl SN8. . . . . .184 A7
Lyndhurst Cres SN3. . . . . . .51 A6
Lyndhurst Rd
Amesbury SP4. . . . . .217 C3
Landford SP5. . . . . .212 C6
LYNEHAM 60 B2
Lyneham Cl SN2. . . . . .35 B6
Lyneham Prim Sch SN15. . .60 B2
Lyneham Way BA14. . . . . . .105 D5
Lynmouth Rd SN5. . . . . .49 F6
Lynt Farm Cotts SN6. . . . . .12 B6
Lynton Rd SN2. . . . . .34 E1
Lynt Rd SN6. . . . . .12 A5
Lynwood Gr SN2. . . . . .34 D3
Lynwood Rd BA14. . . . . . . .101 A1
Lyons Wlk [1] SP7. . . . . . . .202 C1
Lypiatt Cl SN13. . . . . .84 F6
Lypiatt Mead SN13. . . . . . . .85 A8
Lypiatt Prim Sch SN13. . . . .84 F6
Lypiatt Rd SN13. . . . . .85 A7
Lysander Rd
Bower Hill SN12. . . . . .94 B1
Laverstock SP4. . . . . .146 C8
Melksham Without SN12. .178 B8
Lysley Cl SN15. . . . . .79 A5
Lyster Rd SP6. . . . . .210 E1
Lytchett Way SN3. . . . . .51 C6
Lytham Cl SN15. . . . . .78 F7

M

MacAdam Way SP10 . . . . .193 B1
McArthur Glen Designer
Outlet Village SN2. . . . . . .50 A6
MacCullum Rd SP11. . . . . .193 E4
Macie Dr SN13. . . . . .84 E3
MacKenzie Cl [1] SN3 . . . . .51 D4
McKie Rd [3] SP4. . . . . .217 D2
Mackintosh Davidson Wood
Nature Reserve★ BA12 .140 D3
MacKlin Cl [21] RG17. . . . . .177 B7
MacKlin Rd SP2. . . . . .145 E2
MacNeice Dr SN8. . . . . . . .213 A2
McNeill Rd SP4. . . . . .198 A7
MADDINGTON. 196 F6
Maddington [2] SP3. . . . . . .196 E6
Maddington St SP3. . . . . . .196 E7
Maddle Rd RG17. . . . . .164 E4
Maddock's Hill BA14. . . . . .116 E5
Maddocks Rd SN14. . . . . . .101 A4
Magdalene La [7] SP7. . . . .202 C1
Magdalen La BA14. . . . . . .104 B7
Magdalen Rd SN4. . . . . . . .163 A6
Magic Rdbt SN1. . . . . .50 E6
Magister Rd SN12. . . . . .94 D1
Magnolia Cl [1] BA11. . . . . .110 C2
Magnolia Ct SN2. . . . . .35 B2
Magnolia Rise
Calne SN11. . . . . .81 B1
Trowbridge BA14. . . . . . . .105 E7
Magnon Rd BA15. . . . . .100 B7
Magpie La SN3. . . . . .51 E6
Magpie Mews SN16. . . . . . .214 B3
Maidavale [3] SN25. . . . . . . .34 D6
MAIDEN BRADLEY. 118 C2
Maidencroft Cotts GL7. . . . .10 E6
Maiden La SN11. . . . . .166 B1
Maidstone Rd SN1. . . . . . . .50 B4
Main Dr
[5] Swindon SN25. . . . . . . .34 F8
Westonbirt GL8. . . . . .25 C8
Main Rd
Amesbury SP4. . . . . .217 D2
Cherhill SN11. . . . . .166 B1
Christian Malford SN15. . . .58 E5
Ogbourne St Andrew SN8. .213 D8
St Paul Malmesbury Without
SN16. . . . . .42 E4
Sutton Benger SN15. . . . . .57 F2
Main St E BA13. . . . . .108 C6
Main St
Great Hinton BA14. . . . . . .178 A6
Westbury BA13. . . . . .108 C6
Maitland Cl SN15. . . . . .79 A4
Maitland Rd SN3. . . . . .51 A7

Maize Cl 6 SP11 . . . .**193** F2
Majestic Cl 4 SN5 . . . .**49** A7
Maldwyn Cl 9 SN5 . . . . . .**48** F8
Mallard Ave SN15 . . . .**60** B1
Mallard Cl
  7 Bower Hill SN12 . . . . .**178** B8
  Calne SN11 . . . .**81** D2
  Salisbury SP2 . . . .**151** F7
  Swindon SN3 . . . .**51** E6
  Trowbridge BA14 . . . . . .**105** E7
  Westbury BA13 . . . .**109** B4
Mallards The
  South Cerney GL7 . . . .**7** A5
  20 West Tisbury SP3 . . . .**203** B8
Mallory Pl SN12 . . . .**94** C2
Mallow Cl
  2 Swindon SN2 . . . .**34** D4
  4 Trowbridge BA14 . . . .**105** D6
Mall The
  South Tedworth SP9 . . . .**216** A4
  Swindon SN1 . . . .**50** B3
MALMESBURY **28** B3
Malmesbury Abbey★
  SN16 . . . .**28** A3
Malmesbury CE Prim Sch
  SN16 . . . .**28** A4
Malmesbury Com Hospl
  SN16 . . . .**28** B1
Malmesbury Gdns SN3 . .**51** A5
Malmesbury House★
  SP1 . . . .**152** A8
Malmesbury Ind Est SN16 **28** A4
Malmesbury Rd
  Chippenham SN15 . . . . . .**70** D1
  Leigh SN5 . . . .**17** E3
Malmesbury Sch SN16 . . .**27** E3
Malmesbury Swimming Pool
  SN16 . . . .**27** E4
Malmpit Hill BA12 . . . . . .**195** B2
Malthouse Cl
  Ashbury SN6 . . . .**164** A8
  Broad Blunsdon SN26 . . . .**21** C2
Malthouse La
  Chute SP11 . . . .**192** E8
  4 Salisbury SP2 . . . . . .**146** A1
Malt House La SP11 . . . . .**193** F4
Maltings The
  Malmesbury SN16 . . . .**28** A3
  Royal Wootton Bassett SN4 .**47** D1
  Salisbury SP2 . . . .**146** A1
  8 Wanborough SN4 . . . .**163** B6
  Warminster BA12 . . . . . .**116** F6
  Yatton Keynell SN14 . . . . .**68** F6
Malt Shovel La RG17 . . . .**164** F2
Malvern Cl
  Melksham SN12 . . . .**94** D4
  7 Warminster BA12 . . . .**117** A8
Malvern Rd SN2 . . . .**35** C1
Malvern Way SP4 . . . .**133** D6
Mampitts La SP7 . . . .**202** D1
Manchester Rd SN1 . . . . . .**50** C7
Mand Wood BA14 . . . .**101** F8
Manley Cl BA14 . . . .**101** C1
Manning Cl 8 SP1 . . . . . .**146** C5
MANNINGFORD
  ABBOTS **182** A5
MANNINGFORD
  BOHUNE **181** F4
MANNINGFORD BRUCE . . .**181** F5
Mannington La SN5 . . . . . .**49** D5
Mannington Pk SN2 . . . . . .**49** E4
Mannington Ret Pk SN1 . .**49** E4
Manor Ave GL7 . . . .**2** E3
Manor Bridge Ct SP9 . . . .**216** D7
Manor CE VC Prim Sch The
  SN12 . . . .**94** B4
Manor Cl
  Broad Blunsdon SN26 . . . . .**21** C2
  28 Fordingbridge SP6 . . .**210** D1
  Semington BA14 . . . .**102** F5
  Sherston SN16 . . . .**25** C1
  4 Shipton Bellinger SP9 .**199** D8
  Trowbridge BA14 . . . . . .**105** A6
  Wroughton SN4 . . . .**64** B5
Manor Copse SP11 . . . . . .**193** C6
Manor Cotts SN14 . . . .**24** D1
Manor Cres SN2 . . . .**34** F2
Manor Ct SN9 . . . .**215** C4
Manor Dr BA1 . . . .**82** B2
Manor Farm Cl SP5 . . . . .**205** C4
Manor Farm SN14 . . . . . .**173** D6
Manor Farm Dr SN15 . . . .**57** C2
Manor Farm La
  Great Wishford SP2 . . . . .**129** F4
  Patney SN10 . . . .**180** F5
Manor Farm Rd
  Salisbury SP1 . . . .**146** C1
  1 Sandleheath SP6 . . . .**210** C1
Manor Fields 5 BA13 . . . .**186** B7
Manor Fields Prim Sch
  SP2 . . . .**145** E2
Manor Gdns
  Bradford-on-Avon BA15 . .**100** D8
  Burbage SN8 . . . .**175** D6
  Swindon SN2 . . . .**34** F1
  Warminster BA12 . . . . . .**117** A4
Manor Ho SN14 . . . .**68** E5
Manor House Cl SN4 . . . . .**47** D3
Manor House The★ SN9 .**182** F7
Manor La
  Baydon SN8 . . . .**170** C8
  Broad Hinton SN4 . . . . . .**167** C2
Manor Orch SN6 . . . .**19** E8
Manor Pk
  Froxfield SN8 . . . .**176** D6

Manor Pk *continued*
  Great Somerford SN15 . . . .**44** A2
  South Marston SN3 . . . . . .**36** E4
Manor Rd
  Chippenham SN14 . . . . . .**78** A8
  Corsham SN13 . . . .**76** F2
  7 Great Bedwyn SN8 . . .**176** B3
  Mere BA12 . . . .**138** F7
  Salisbury SP1 . . . .**146** C1
  Swindon SN1 . . . .**49** F5
  Trowbridge BA14 . . . . . .**105** A6
  Upton Lovell BA12 . . . . .**194** E3
Manor The★
  Keevil BA14 . . . .**178** A4
  Longbridge Deverill BA12 .**120** F5
Manor View SN16 . . . .**28** F2
Manor Vw SN4 . . . .**163** A4
Mansion House Mews
  SN13 . . . .**77** A1
Mantles La BA12 . . . .**194** C5
MANTON **213** A1
Manton Cl
  Marlborough SN8 . . . . . .**213** A1
  Trowbridge BA14 . . . . . .**105** C6
Manton Dro SN8 . . . .**174** C6
Manton Hollow SN8 . . . . .**213** A2
Manton Rd SN8 . . . .**174** C7
Manton St SN2 . . . .**49** F7
Maple Cl
  Calne SN11 . . . .**81** B1
  Melksham SN12 . . . .**94** D5
  Pewsey SN9 . . . .**215** D6
  5 Shaftesbury SP7 . . . .**202** C2
Maple Cres
  7 Ludgershall SP11 . . . .**192** B5
  Wilton SP2 . . . .**144** F3
Maplecroft 3 SP2 . . . . . .**152** A5
Maple Ct 8 BA11 . . . .**110** A4
Maple Dr
  Firsdown SP5 . . . .**148** C7
  Royal Wootton Bassett SN4 .**47** E4
Maple Gr
  Swindon SN2 . . . .**35** C2
  Trowbridge BA14 . . . . . .**105** C6
Maple Way
  Chippenham SN15 . . . . . .**70** D2
  3 Durrington/Bulford SP4 **198** B7
  Maple Wy SP4 . . . .**217** D4
Mapperton Hill SP8 . . . . .**138** E1
Marabout Rd 13 SP7 . . . .**202** D1
Maranatha Christian Sch
  SN6 . . . .**22** E1
Marbeck Cl SN25 . . . .**34** E7
Marbrean Cl 4 SP6 . . . . .**210** C1
March Cl SN25 . . . .**35** A6
Marchment Cl SP2 . . . . . .**144** F4
MARDEN **181** A4
Marden Henge★ SN9 . . . .**181** B5
Marden Way SN11 . . . .**81** A2
Marden Wlk 2 BA14 . . . . .**105** D6
Margaret Leckie Ct 5
  SN3 . . . .**50** F6
Margarets Cl SP4 . . . .**217** D2
Margaret Stancomb Infants'
  Sch BA14 . . . .**101** C1
Margery Holroyd Rise
  SN16 . . . .**27** F3
Margha Rd SP9 . . . .**216** C6
Marie Ave 5 SP5 . . . .**210** F8
Marigold Cl
  Melksham SN12 . . . .**94** C3
  Swindon SN2 . . . .**34** D4
Marina Dr BA14 . . . .**101** C4
Marina Rd
  23 Durrington/Bulford
  SP4 . . . .**198** B7
  Salisbury SP1 . . . .**152** C7
Mariner Rd SN25 . . . .**34** B7
Maristow St BA13 . . . . . .**109** A3
Marjoram Cl 4 SN2 . . . . . .**34** D5
Markan Rd SP4 . . . .**133** F7
Markenfield 2 SN5 . . . . . .**49** D4
Market Hill SN11 . . . .**81** B3
MARKET LAVINGTON **179** E1
Market Lavington Mus★
  SN10 . . . .**179** F1
Market Pl
  Box SN13 . . . .**83** D6
  Chippenham SN15 . . . . . .**78** E7
  Colerne SN14 . . . .**75** B3
  Lechlade GL7 . . . .**2** C4
  18 Market Lavington SN10 **179** F1
  Marshfield SN14 . . . .**74** A8
  Pewsey SN9 . . . .**215** C5
  Warminster BA12 . . . . . .**117** A7
  4 Westbury BA13 . . . . .**109** A4
Market Pl The SN10 . . . . .**214** A4
Market Sq The 4 SN3 . . . .**50** D4
Market St
  Bradford-on-Avon BA15 . .**100** D7
  4 Malmesbury SN16 . . . .**28** A3
  Swindon SN1 . . . .**50** B6
  Trowbridge BA14 . . . . . .**105** D8
Markham Cl SN3 . . . .**50** F7
Markham Rd SN4 . . . .**64** A5
Markova Gr 9 SN25 . . . . . .**34** C6
Markton Cl 3 SN25 . . . . . .**34** C6
MARLBOROUGH **213** F3
Marlborough Bsns Pk
  SN8 . . . .**213** E1
Marlborough Cl SN10 . . . .**214** F7
Marlborough Coll SN8 . . .**213** C2
Marlborough Craft Ctr★
  SN8 . . . .**213** E3
Marlborough Ct SN14 . . . .**78** C7
Marlborough La SN1 . . . . .**50** D3

Marlborough Leisure Ctr
  SN8 . . . .**213** C3
Marlborough Rd
  5 Aldbourne SN8 . . . . .**170** A6
  Bulford SP4 . . . .**198** E6
  Burbage SN8 . . . .**175** C1
  Chiseldon SN3 . . . .**51** C2
  Collingbourne Ducis SN8. .**183** E1
  Everleigh SN8 . . . .**183** A1
  Liddington SN4 . . . .**51** E1
  Pewsey SN9 . . . .**215** B6
  Royal Wootton Bassett SN4 .**61** E7
  Salisbury SP1 . . . .**146** A2
  Swindon SN3 . . . .**50** D3
  Wroughton SN4 . . . .**64** B6
Marlborough St 5 SN1 . . .**50** A5
Marlborough White Horse★
  SN8 . . . .**213** C1
Marl La SP6 . . . .**210** D1
Marlowe Ave SN3 . . . .**50** F7
Marlowe Way SN4 . . . .**47** F3
Marlstones The SN1 . . . . . .**50** B4
Marne Rd 3 SP4 . . . .**198** F6
Marney Rd SN5 . . . .**49** A5
MARR GREEN **183** D7
Marshall Rd
  Roundway SN10 . . . .**214** D1
  Swindon SN5 . . . .**49** B8
Marshall St SN14 . . . .**78** C7
Marshall Wy BA11 . . . .**110** D8
Marsh Farm La SN1 . . . . . .**50** E7
MARSHFIELD **74** A8
Marshfield CE VC Prim Sch
  SN14 . . . .**74** B8
Marshfield Rd SN15 . . . . . .**78** C8
Marshfield Way SN3 . . . . . .**36** A2
Marshgate SN1 . . . .**50** F8
Marsh La
  Breamore SP6 . . . .**210** A5
  Cherhill SN11 . . . .**166** A1
  Coombe Bissett SP5 . . . . .**150** F2
  Hungerford RG17 . . . . . .**177** A7
  Nettleton SN14 . . . .**53** C4
  Pen Selwood BA9 . . . . . .**137** A4
  Rowde SN10 . . . .**96** D2
  Salisbury SP2 . . . .**145** F2
Marshmead BA14 . . . .**101** F4
Marshmead Cl SP5 . . . . . .**152** F6
Marsh Rd
  Berkley BA11 . . . .**107** C1
  Rode BA11 . . . .**103** F1
  Trowbridge BA14 . . . . . .**101** E5
Marsh St BA12 . . . .**117** A5
Marsh The SN4 . . . .**51** F3
Marshwood SP3 . . . .**201** E3
Marsland Rd SN2 . . . .**35** D2
MARSTON **179** A3
Marston Ave SN2 . . . .**35** D4
MARSTON HILL **1** C4
Marston Rd BA14 . . . .**105** B4
Marsum Cl 1 SP10 . . . . . .**193** D2
MARTEN **184** C7
Martha's La SP3 . . . .**140** F4
Marti Cl SN12 . . . .**94** C4
Martigny Rd SN12 . . . .**94** B3
MARTIN **209** B6
Martinbushes Rd SP4 . . . .**198** A7
Martin Cl SN4 . . . .**216** E6
Martin Crest BA12 . . . . . .**116** E5
Martin Dro End SP6 . . . . .**209** A7
MARTIN DROVE END **209** A8
Martinfield SN3 . . . .**51** D7
Martingale Rd SN8 . . . . . .**183** D7
Martingate SN13 . . . .**77** A1
Martins Cl
  Chippenham SN15 . . . . . .**79** A8
  2 Salisbury SP2 . . . . . .**152** A5
  Steeple Ashton BA14 . . . .**178** C4
Martin's Cl SN9 . . . .**181** C6
Martins Croft SN14 . . . . . .**75** B3
Martinsell La SN9 . . . .**215** D5
Martinsell Hill (Fort)★
  SN8 . . . .**174** D2
Martins La BA14 . . . .**178** C4
MARTINSLADE **178** E8
Martins Rd BA14 . . . .**178** C5
Martins Rise SP5 . . . .**161** C4
Martin's St 4 SP7 . . . . . .**202** C1
Martin Way SN11 . . . .**81** D3
Martlesham Rd SP4 . . . . . .**217** D2
Martlet Cl SN12 . . . .**94** D1
Martor Ind Est SN14 . . . . .**66** A2
Marvins Cl SP3 . . . .**188** B2
Mary Barters La SP3 . . . .**204** E8
Maryland Cl SP2 . . . .**145** B5
Mascroft Rd BA14 . . . . . .**106** A8
Masefield SN4 . . . .**47** F3
Masefield Ave SN2 . . . .**35** E3
Masefield Rd BA12 . . . . . .**116** E6
Maskeleyne Way SN4 . . . .**63** F6
Mason Rd SN25 . . . .**35** B6
Masons La BA15 . . . .**100** D7
Masons The SN5 . . . .**33** A3
Masons Way SN13 . . . .**76** D1
Massey Cl SN15 . . . .**78** E5
Massey Rd 4 SN10 . . . . .**214** D1
Massinger Wlk SN3 . . . . . .**50** F6
Matford Hill SN15 . . . .**79** A8
Matilda Way SN10 . . . . . .**214** D4
Matley Moor SN3 . . . .**51** E2
Matravers Cl BA13 . . . . . .**108** F3
Matravers Sch BA13 . . . . .**108** F8
Matrons Cotts SP5 . . . . . .**153** F1
Matthews Cl SN10 . . . . . .**172** F1
Mattocks Path 2 SN1. . . . .**50** B1
Matty Hull Cl 19 SP7 . . . .**202** D1
Maud Cl SN10 . . . .**214** D4

Maud Heath Ct SN15 . . . . .**78** E8
Maud Heath's Cswy
  Chippenham SN15 . . . . . .**70** E1
  Langley Burrell Without
  SN15 . . . .**71** B3
Maud Heath's Mon★
  SN11 . . . .**80** C8
Maud Heath's Stone★
  SN11 . . . .**80** C8
Maulton Cl BA14 . . . .**101** D8
Maunders Dr BA14 . . . . . .**101** D4
Maundrell Cl SN10 . . . .**96** D2
Maundrell Rd SN11 . . . .**81** C5
Maunsell Way SN4 . . . .**63** F7
Maur Cl SN15 . . . .**78** C7
Maurice Wy SN8 . . . .**175** A4
Maurys SL SO51 . . . .**212** F6
Maxcroft La BA14 . . . .**101** E5
Maxey Cl SN5 . . . .**49** B8
Maxwell St SN1 . . . .**50** A6
Maybold Cres 8 SN2 . . . . .**34** D5
May Cl SN2 . . . .**35** C1
Mayenne Pl SN10 . . . .**179** C8
Mayfair Rd SP1 . . . .**146** D1
Mayfield 1 SN4 . . . .**163** A5
Mayfield Ave Ind Pk
  SP11 . . . .**192** E1
Mayfield Cl
  4 Shipton Bellinger SP9 .**199** C8
  Swindon SN3 . . . .**51** B7
Mayfield Rd 2 SP6 . . . . . .**210** C1
Mayflower Rd 1 SN3 . . . . .**51** B8
Mayfly Cl 4 SP6 . . . .**210** D1
Mayfly Rd SN25 . . . .**34** A7
May La SP5 . . . .**204** D3
Mayo Cl SN13 . . . .**76** E2
Mays Firs SP6 . . . .**211** D5
May's La SN4 . . . .**65** D4
Maytree Cl 6 BA11 . . . . . .**110** B7
May Tree Rd 9 SP10. . . . .**193** C1
Mazurek Wy SN25 . . . .**34** E6
Mead Com Prim Sch The
  BA14. . . . .**102** B1
Meadens La SP5 . . . .**151** A1
Meade Rd 2 SP11 . . . .**192** B5
Meadland SN13 . . . .**76** E1
Meadow Ave 10 SP6 . . . .**210** D1
Meadow Cl
  Chippenham SN14 . . . . . .**78** A7
  8 Fordingbridge SP6. . . .**210** D1
  Yatton Keynell SN14 . . . . .**68** F6
Meadowcroft SN2 . . . .**35** F3
Meadow Ct
  11 Fordingbridge SP6. . .**210** D1
  Trowbridge BA14 . . . . . .**101** D4
  Whiteparish SP5 . . . .**161** E4
Meadow Dr SN10 . . . .**214** C3
Meadowfield BA15. . . . . . .**100** B6
Meadow La
  Little Somerford SN15 . . . .**44** A5
  Warminster BA12 . . . . . .**116** D6
  Westbury BA13 . . . .**109** A4
Meadow Pk BA1 . . . .**82** B3
Meadow Pk Sch SN6. . . . . .**19** E7
Meadow Rd
  Durrington/Bulford SP4 . .**217** E8
  Melksham SN12 . . . .**94** C7
  3 Salisbury SP2 . . . . . .**145** F1
  Swindon SN2 . . . .**49** E7
Meadow Rd (South) 6
  SP2 . . . .**145** F1
Meadow Rise SN8 . . . .**174** A6
Meadow Springs SN5 . . . . .**48** E8
Meadows The
  Bourton SP8 . . . .**137** F2
  Lydiard Tregoze SN5 . . . . .**47** F5
  Salisbury SP1 . . . .**152** D8
Meadowsweet Cl 2 SN25 . .**34** E5
Meadowsweet Dr SN11 . . .**80** F3
Meadow View
  5 Fittleton SP4 . . . .**190** A4
  Kempsford GL7 . . . .**10** C7
Meadow Way
  Chiseldon SN4 . . . .**65** E7
  South Cerney SN6 . . . .**6** F7
Meadow Well SN8 . . . .**183** C8
Mead Pk SN12 . . . .**84** F1
Meads Rd SP4 . . . .**198** B2
Meads The SN14 . . . .**53** B3
Mead The
  Ashton Keynes SN6. . . . . .**17** F8
  Warminster BA12 . . . . . .**117** A7
  Westbury BA13 . . . .**109** A5
  Winsley BA15 . . . .**99** E7
Meadway
  4 Shrewton SP3 . . . . . .**196** F6
  Wingfield BA14 . . . .**105** A8
Mead Way SN5 . . . .**34** B2
Mead Wy 11 SP7 . . . .**202** D1
Meares Dr SN5 . . . .**49** B8
Mears Rd 4 SP4 . . . .**198** A6
Medbourne Rd SN4 . . . . . .**163** A4
Medbourne Rd SN4 . . . . . .**163** A4
Medgbury Pl SN1 . . . .**50** D6
Medgbury Rd SN1 . . . .**50** C6
Medieval Hall★ SP1 . . . . .**152** C8
Medina Way SN2 . . . .**35** F4
Medlar Ct SN2 . . . .**35** B2
Medway Cl SN25 . . . .**34** F4
Medway Rd SN25 . . . .**34** F4
Meerut Rd SP9 . . . .**216** C6
Melbourne Cl SN3 . . . .**50** F7
Melbourne Gdns 5 SP4. . .**198** F6
Melbourne St BA13 . . . . . .**186** B7
MELBURY ABBAS **206** B7
Melbury Abbas Mill★
  SP7 . . . .**206** A7
Melbury Down★ SP5 . . . .**206** C6

Melbury St SP7 . . . .**206** A6
Melbury Way 12 SP7 . . . .**202** D2
Melchet Cl SO51 . . . .**162** D1
Melchet Vw SO51 . . . .**162** D2
Melford Wlk SN3 . . . .**51** C7
Melfort Cl SN5. . . . .**34** B2
Meliot Rise 12 SP10 . . . . .**193** E2
MELKSHAM **94** A5
Melksham Blue Pool
  SN12 . . . .**94** A4
Melksham Cl SN2 . . . .**35** B6
Melksham Com Hospl
  SN12 . . . .**94** B3
MELKSHAM FOREST **94** D6
Melksham La SN12 . . . .**93** C4
Melksham Oak Com Sch
  SN12 . . . .**94** D1
Melksham Rd
  Chippenham SN15 . . . . . .**78** B5
  Holt SN12 . . . .**93** A2
  Lacock SN15 . . . .**86** D5
Melksham Sta SN12 . . . . . .**94** A6
Mellow Gd SN25 . . . .**34** E5
Melrose Ave BA12 . . . .**116** A6
Melrose Cl
  Easterton SN10 . . . .**180** A1
  1 Swindon SN5 . . . .**49** C6
  4 Warminster BA12 . . . .**116** E6
Melsome Rd SN15 . . . .**59** F1
Melstock Rd SN25 . . . .**34** C6
Melton Rd BA14 . . . .**101** C2
Melusine Rd 4 SN3. . . . . . .**51** B8
Melville Cl 3 SN3 . . . .**50** F6
Melvin Cl SP1 . . . .**146** D1
Mendip Cl
  1 Frome BA11. . . . .**110** A4
  8 Melksham SN12 . . . . . .**94** C4
  Swindon SN25 . . . .**35** C3
  6 Warminster BA12 . . . .**117** A8
Mendip Dr BA11 . . . .**110** A7
Menham Cl SN2 . . . .**35** D2
Merchants House The★
  SN8. . . . .**213** C3
Mercia Ave SP10 . . . .**193** C2
MERE **139** B5
Mere Ave SN14 . . . .**41** F1
Mere Castle★ BA12 . . . . .**138** F6
Mere Mus★ BA12. . . . . . .**139** A3
Mere Sch BA12. . . . .**139** B5
Meriden Wlk SN3 . . . .**51** B4
Meridian Wlk BA14 . . . . . .**105** A8
Meriton Ave SN13 . . . .**77** A1
Merlin Cl 23 SP10 . . . . . .**193** E2
Merlin Rd 1 SN11 . . . .**81** B5
Merlin Theatre BA11. . . . .**110** A7
Merlin Way
  Bower Hill SN12. . . . .**94** B1
  Stratton St Margaret SN3. .**51** D8
  Swindon SN3 . . . .**36** D1
Merrifield Rd SP4. . . . .**146** C6
Merrivale Gr SN3 . . . .**50** E5
Mersey Cl SP10 . . . .**193** F1
Merton Ave SN2 . . . .**35** D4
Merton Cl 6 SP6 . . . .**210** D2
Merton St 2 SN1. . . . .**50** C6
Mervyn Webb Pl SN2 . . . . .**50** D8
Mesh Pond SP5. . . . .**210** F8
Methuen Ave SN12. . . . . . .**94** B6
Methuen Cl BA15 . . . .**100** E4
Methuen Dr 1 SP1 . . . . . .**152** C8
Methuen Pk 5 SN14 . . . . . .**77** F5
Methuen Way SN13 . . . . . .**76** F2
Metis Cl SN25 . . . .**34** B8
Mews The
  Highworth SN6 . . . .**23** A6
  Lydiard Millicent SN5 . . . .**48** D8
  Warminster BA12 . . . . . .**117** A7
Meynell Cl SN25 . . . .**34** F8
Meyrick Ave SP2 . . . .**152** A5
Meysey Cl GL7. . . . .**1** A5
MEYSEY HAMPTON. **1** A5
Michaelmas Dro SP11. . . .**192** E1
Michael Pym's Rd SN16 . . .**28** A5
Middle Farm Cl SN15 . . . . .**45** B1
Middle Farm Ct GL7 . . . . . .**10** D7
Middle Field SN10. . . . . . .**214** C3
Middle Gd
  Cricklade SN6 . . . .**19** C8
  Fovant SP3 . . . .**204** E7
  Royal Wootton Bassett SN4 .**48** A2
Middle Green La SN15 . . . .**45** B1
MIDDLEHILL **83** A6
Middle La
  Atworth/Whitley SN12 . . . .**85** D1
  Cherhill SN11 . . . .**166** B1
  Martin SP6. . . . .**209** A7
  Trowbridge BA14 . . . . . .**101** F2
Middleleaze Dr SN5. . . . . . .**48** F8
Middlemass Gn SN9 . . . . .**215** D5
Middlemead La
  Hannington SN6 . . . .**22** B8
  Hannington Wick SN6 . . . .**11** A1
Middle St SP2 . . . .**151** E7
Middle Stoke BA2. . . . .**99** A6
Middleton SP5. . . . .**149** B7
Middleton Cl
  Swindon SN3 . . . .**50** F6
  4 Warminster BA12 . . . .**116** E6
Middleton Medieval Village
  of★ BA12 . . . .**194** A7
Middleton Rd
  Salisbury SP2 . . . .**145** F2
  The Common SP5 . . . . . .**149** B7
Middletons Cl RG17. . . . . .**177** C8
MIDDLEWICK **76** D3
Middlewick La SN13 . . . . . .**76** D3
MIDDLE WINTERSLOW **149** B7
MIDDLE WOODFORD **131** B4

MIDFORD 98 C6
Midford Hill BA2. . . . . .98 C4
Midford La BA2. . . . . . .98 E7
Midford Rd BA2 . . . . . .98 B7
Midhurst Ave SN3 . . . . .51 B5
Midlands Ind Est The
  BA14. . . . . .92 E1
Midlands The BA14 . . . .92 E1
Mid Summer Pl SP4 . . .217 E5
Midwinter Cl SN5. . . . . .34 B2
Midwinter Gdns SN3. . . .36 A2
MILBOURNE 28 C4
Milbourne La SN16. . . . .28 C4
Milbourne Pk SN16. . . . .28 C4
MILDENHALL 175 A8
Mildenhall Way SN2 . . . .35 B6
Mildmay Cl 12 SN5. . . . .48 F5
Mile Dr SN15. . . . . . . .44 E1
MILE ELM 89 A7
MILE END 165 A3
Miles's La SP5. . . . . . .161 E5
Milestone Way SN15 . . . .70 C2
MILFORD. 152 A8
Milford Hill SP1. . . . . .152 B8
Milford Hollow 6 SP1. . .152 C8
Milford Ind Est SP1. . . .152 C8
Milford Manor Gdns SP1 152 D8
Milford Mill Rd SP1. . . .152 D8
Milford Pk SP1 . . . . . .152 D8
Milford St
  Salisbury SP1. . . . . .152 B8
  Swindon SN1. . . . . . .50 C6
Milford Way SN15 . . . . .78 F4
MILKHOUSE WATER. . .215 D6
MILKWELL. 203 B2
Milland Cl SN25 . . . . . .35 B6
Millard Cl 2 SN15. . . . .78 F4
Millards Cl BA14 . . . . .101 F4
Millards Wy BA11. . . . .107 B1
Millbourn Cl BA15 . . . . .99 D7
Millbrook 2 SP1. . . . . .146 B2
Millbrook La SP3 . . . . .141 C1
Millbrook Prim Sch SN5 . .49 A3
Millbuck Cl SN2 . . . . . .35 E1
Mill Cl
  Devizes SN10 . . . . . .214 C1
  Great Bedwyn SN8. . . .176 B2
  Longbridge Deverill BA12. 120 F6
  South Cerney GL7 . . . . . .7 A7
  Winterbourne SP4. . . .133 B4
  Wroughton SN4. . . . . .64 B6
Mill Ct 18 SP6 . . . . . .210 D1
Milldtich 15 BA13 . . . . .186 B7
Mill Dro SN8 . . . . . . .183 C1
Mill End SP6. . . . . . . .209 F2
Millennium Cl 2 SP2 . . .152 B5
Millennium Visitor Ctr*
  GL7. . . . . .6 B4
Miller Cl
  Chirton SN10. . . . . . .180 F4
  Salisbury SP1. . . . . .145 E5
  Swindon SN5. . . . . . .48 F8
Miller's La DT11. . . . . .207 D1
Millfield 5 RG17. . . . . .165 A1
Millgreen Rd 1 SP4 . . .217 E2
Millgrove St SN25. . . . . .34 D7
Millhand Villas BA14. . .105 E7
Mill Head SN10 . . . . . .179 A4
Mill Hill Ave SP9. . . . . .216 C8
Mill Hollow La SP7. . . .206 A7
Millington Dr 3 BA14. . .105 A7
Mill La
  Bishopstone SN6 . . . .150 A1
  Bourton SP8 . . . . . . .137 E2
  Box SN13. . . . . .83 C7
  Bradford-on-Avon BA15 . 100 D6
  Broughton Gifford SN12. .93 C3
  Bulkington SN10. . . . .178 E5
  Cherhill SN11 . . . . . .166 B1
  Chilmark SP3. . . . . . .200 F2
  Fairford GL7. . . . . .1 F7
  Fovant SP3 . . . . .204 D8
  Heytesbury BA12. . . . .194 C5
  Lambourn RG17. . . . . .165 B1
  Lechlade GL7 . . . . .2 F4
  Little Somerford SN15. . .43 F5
  Malmesbury SN16. . . . .28 A3
  Melbury Abbas SP7. . . .206 A7
  Mere BA12 . . . . .139 B5
  Monkton Combe BA2. . . .98 E8
  Poulshot SN10. . . . . .179 A5
  Ramsbury SN8. . . . . .170 B2
  Salisbury SP1. . . . . . .145 C5
  Selwood BA11. . . . . .114 F8
  Shalbourne SN8. . . . . .176 F2
  Stanton Fitzwarren SN6 . .22 A2
  St Paul Malmesbury Without
    SN16. . . . . .42 E5
  Swindon SN1. . . . . . . .50 A3
  The Common SP5 . . . .149 E6
  Westbury BA13 . . . . .112 D8
  West Lavington SN10 . .187 E8
  Winterbourne Monkton
    SN4. . . . . .167 C3
  Winterslow SP5. . . . . .149 D7
  Zeale SP8 . . . . .137 F2
Mill Rd
  Devizes SN10 . . . . . .214 C1
  Netheravon SP4 . . . . .190 A4
  Potterne SN10. . . . . .179 D5
  Salisbury SP2 . . . . . .145 F1
  Worton SN10. . . . . . .179 A4
Mill Rise SP8 . . . . . . .137 E2
Mill Sch The SN10 . . . .179 C6
Mills Rd SN12 . . . . . . .94 C4
Mill St
  Calne SN11. . . . . .81 B2
  Fontmell Magna SP7. . .206 A3

Mill St continued
  Heytesbury BA12. . . . .194 C5
  Trowbridge BA14. . . . .105 D8
Millstone Cl SN4. . . . . .47 F1
Mill Stream App SP2. . .146 A1
Mills Way SP4 . . . . . . .217 D4
Milne Cres 3 SP4 . . . . .197 E6
Milne Rd SP4. . . . . . . .198 E6
MILSTON. 198 B8
Milston Ave SN2. . . . . . .35 C5
Milston Down (Long
  Barrows)* SP4. . . . . .198 E8
Milston Dro SP4 . . . . . .190 D7
Milston Rd
  Bulford SP4. . . . . . . .198 C7
  Durrington/Bulford SP4 . 217 D8
Milston View 2 SP4 . . .198 C7
MILTON 141 B3
Milton Ave
  6 Andover SP10 . . . . .193 C1
  Melksham SN12. . . . . .94 B4
MILTON LILBOURNE. . .182 F7
Milton Rd
  Amesbury SP4. . . . . .217 E2
  Pewsey SN9 . . . . . . .215 E5
  Salisbury SP2 . . . . . .152 B6
  Swindon SN1. . . . . . . .50 B6
Milton St GL7 . . . . .1 F6
Milton's Way SN4. . . . . .47 C1
Milverton Ct SN3 . . . . . .51 A5
MINCHINGTON 207 D1
Minden Cl 13 SP10 . . . .193 D2
MINETY. 17 B2
Minety CE Prim Sch SN16 17 B2
MINETY COMMON 31 C8
Minety La SN16. . . . . . .16 A7
Minety Rd SN2. . . . . . . .35 B5
Minnow Cl
  3 Calne SN11 . . . . . . .81 B5
  Swindon SN25. . . . . . .34 A7
Minories Rd SP9. . . . . .216 E6
Minot Cl SN16 . . . . . . .28 A5
Minster CE Prim Sch The
  BA12. . . . . .116 F7
Minster Cl SN25 . . . . . .34 F7
Minster St
  7 Salisbury SP1. . . . .146 A1
  Wilton SP2. . . . . . . .144 D3
Minster View BA12. . . .116 F7
Minster Way SN14 . . . . .78 A5
Mint Cl SN2 . . . . .34 D4
Minton Distribution Pk
  SP4. . . . . .217 C4
Minty's Top SN15 . . . . . .96 A3
Mir Cres 3 SN25 . . . . . .34 B7
MISSELFORE 204 F1
Mitchell Cl
  3 Andover SP10 . . . . .193 C1
  Royal Wootton Bassett SN4 .47 D1
Mitchell Dr SN12 . . . . .178 B8
Mitchell Rd SP2. . . . . .151 D8
Mitchells Cl 6 SP5 . . . .211 C7
Mizmaze* SP6 . . . . . . .210 D7
Moat Rd BA13 . . . . . . .108 D6
Moberly Rd SP1 . . . . . .146 B3
Model Farm La SP5. . . .148 C3
Moffat Rise SN16 . . . . . .28 A5
Moggs La SN11. . . . . . .172 A8
Moldens The BA14. . . . .105 B6
Mompesson Ho* SP2. . .152 A8
Monastery Rd BA13 . . .186 C8
Monet Cl SN25. . . . . . . .34 F6
Moneyer Rd 5 SP10 . . .193 D2
Monkley La BA14 . . . . .104 C1
Monks Cl SP9. . . . . . . .216 C5
Monk's La SN13. . . . . . .85 B6
MONK'S PARK 85 A6
Monks Pk SN16 . . . . . . .28 D4
Monks Pk Gdns SN13 . . .85 B5
Monks Way SN15 . . . . . .79 A4
Monks Wlk GL7. . . . . . . .2 E3
Monkton Cl SN3 . . . . . . .51 B4
MONKTON COMBE 98 E8
MONKTON DEVERILL . .126 D7
Monkton Dro BH21 . . . .208 D1
MONKTON FARLEIGH . . .90 F7
Monkton Hill SN15. . . . .78 D7
Monkton House* SN12 . . .93 C1
Monkton Pk SN15. . . . . .78 F7
Monkton Pk Prim Sch
  SN15. . . . . .78 E7
Monmouth Cl 4 SN3 . . . .50 F4
Monmouth Dr BA11. . . .110 B5
Monmouth Rd SP3. . . . .203 D8
Mons Ave SP4 . . . . . . .198 E6
Mons La SN15 . . . . .86 D8
Montague Cl SN15. . . . . .79 A7
Montague Ct BA14 . . . .102 A1
Montague Pl SN12. . . . . .94 C5
Montague Rd SP2 . . . . .151 D7
Montagu St SN2 . . . . . . .49 F7
Monteagle Cl SN5 . . . . . .49 A4
Montgomery Ave SN2. . . .35 E2
Montgomery Gdns SP2. .145 E2
Montgomery Rd SP11 . .193 E3
Montreal Wy 8 SP4 . . .217 E5
Montrose Cl SN2 . . . . . .34 E2
Monument Hill SN10. . .214 E1
Monxton Cl 3 SP1. . . . .146 D5
Moody's Hill SP5. . . . . .155 E2
Moon Cl SN14 . . . . .75 B3
Moonrakers SN10. . . . .214 D5
Moor Barton SN13. . . . . .84 D6
Moore Cl SN4 . . . . .64 C8
Moore's Pl 12 RG17 . . .177 B7
Moores Yd BA14 . . . . .104 C6
Moorgate GL7. . . . . .2 B4

MOOR GREEN. 84 D6
Moorhen Cl
  Swindon SN3. . . . . . . .51 E5
  Trowbridge BA14. . . . .101 D4
Moor Hill SP3 . . . . . . .204 D8
Moorings The SN1. . . . . .50 A5
Moor Cl
  7 Andover SP10 . . . . .193 E2
  Downton SP5. . . . . . .211 B7
Moot Gdns SP5. . . . . . .211 A7
Moot La SP5. . . . . .211 A7
Moot (Motte & Bailey) The*
  SP5. . . . . .211 B8
Mopes La SN3 . . . . .33 C7
Moray Rd SN2 . . . . .35 E1
MOREDON. 34 E3
Moredon Jun Sch SN2. . .34 E2
Moredon Pk SN2 . . . . . .34 D3
Moredon Prim Sch SN2. . .34 E3
Moredon Rd SN25 . . . . . .34 F3
Moresby Cl SN5 . . . . . . .49 C6
Morgan's La
  Pentridge SP5. . . . . .208 E5
  Winterbourne SP4. . . .133 A2
Morgans Rise Rd 3 SP4 .211 C8
Morgans Vale Rd SP5. . .211 C7
Morgan's Vale & Woodfalls
  CE Prim Sch SP5. . . . .211 C8
Morgan Wlk BA13. . . . .108 E2
Morie Cl SN5 . . . . .34 B1
Morley Field BA12. . . . .117 C7
Morley Pl 23 RG17. . . . .177 B7
Morley St SN1. . . . . . . .50 C5
Morris Cl BA1 . . . . .82 B3
Morris La
  Bath BA1. . . . . .82 B3
  Devizes SN10 . . . . . .214 B3
Morrison St SN2. . . . . . .49 F7
Morris Rd SN8 . . . . . . .213 B2
Morris St SN2 . . . . .49 E6
Morse Cl
  Chippenham SN15. . . . .78 E4
  Malmesbury SN16. . . . .28 A4
Morse St SN1. . . . . .50 B5
Morstone Rd SN4 . . . . . .61 D8
Mortimer Cl 5 SN5. . . . .49 B7
Mortimer St BA14 . . . . .105 C7
Mortimores SN14 . . . . . .75 B2
Moss Mead SN14 . . . . . .77 F8
MOTCOMBE 202 A4
MOTCOMBE CE VA Prim Sch
  SP7. . . . . .202 A4
Motcombe Rd SP7. . . . .202 B3
Moulton Dr BA15 . . . . .100 D4
MOUNTAIN BOWER. 66 F4
Mountain Wood BA1. . . . .82 B2
Mount Carmel Rd SP11 .199 F3
Mountford Manor Prim Sch
  SN3. . . . . .50 F6
Mount Hts SP4 . . . . . . .135 E3
Mount Nile SP4 . . . . . . .101 D2
Mountings The SN4. . . . .64 B8
Mount La
  Barford St Martin SP3. .143 B4
  Warminster BA12. . . . .117 A5
Mountpleasant SP3. . . .203 D8
Mount Pleasant
  Atworth SP4. . . . . .85 A1
  Atworth/Whitley SN12. . .93 A8
  4 Bishopstone SN6 . . .163 E6
  Bradford-on-Avon BA15 . 100 D7
  Chippenham SN14. . . . .70 A1
  Kilmington BA12. . . . .123 F4
  Lechlade GL7. . . . . . . .2 C4
  South Newton SP2 . . . .130 A4
Mountsfield BA11. . . . .110 A2
MOUNT SORREL 205 B3
Mount The BA14. . . . . .101 D2
Mowlems The BA14. . . .104 F4
Moxhams 21 SP6 . . . . .210 D1
Moyle Pk BA14 . . . . . . .102 A1
Moyne Cl SN10 . . . . . . .179 D8
Moyne Gdns 7 SP4. . . .217 D3
Muddyford Rd SP5. . . . .211 C8
Mud La SN5 . . . . .32 F2
Muirfield SN25 . . . . .34 D7
Mulberry Cl SN14 . . . . . .70 B1
Mulberry Ct
  Frome BA11. . . . . . . .110 B7
  Sixpenny Handley SP5. .208 B4
Mulberry Gr SN2. . . . . . .35 A2
Mulcaster Ave SN5 . . . . .48 F5
Mulling Cl SN14 . . . . . . .75 A3
Mundy Ave SN3. . . . . . .51 C4
Munks Cl 3 SP2. . . . . .151 E7
Munnings Ct 2 SP10 . . .193 D1
Munro Cl SN3 . . . . .50 E6
MURCOTT. 14 F4
Murdock Rd SN3. . . . . . .51 B6
Murrayfield SN15. . . . . . .70 E1
Murray Rd BA14 . . . . . .101 D2
Murray Wlk SN12 . . . . . .94 B5
Muscott Cl 3 SP9 . . . . .199 C8
Muscovey Cl SN14 . . . . .60 A2
Mustang Cl 1 BA13. . . .108 E2
Mustang Wy SN5. . . . . . .34 C2
Mustard Wy 7 SP11 . . .193 F2
Mustons La SP3 . . . . . .202 C2
Mycroft Rd 2 SN25. . . . .34 D6
Myrrfield Rd 7 SP1. . . .146 D5
Myrtle Ave BA12 . . . . . .116 F6

Myrtle Gdns SN2. . . . . . .35 C2
Mythern Meadow BA15 . .100 E5

N

Nadder Cl 13 SP3 . . . . .203 E8
Nadder La SP2. . . . . . . .144 F2
Nadder Rd SP9. . . . . . .216 D6
Nadder Terr SP2. . . . . .144 C2
Nahalsen Cl SP4 . . . . . .133 D6
Naini Tal Rd SP9. . . . . .216 C6
Nantwich SN5 . . . . .49 A3
Napier Cl SN2 . . . . .50 A7
Napier Cres SP1. . . . . .146 B1
Napiers 1 SN8. . . . . . .176 B3
Napier Wlk SP3 . . . . . .193 F1
Narrow Wine St BA14. . .105 D8
Nash Cl SN25 . . . . .35 A8
Nash Rd SN8 . . . . .173 A8
National Monuments Records
  Ctr* SN2 . . . . .50 A7
Naughton Ave SN10 . . .214 E6
Naunton Rd SN3. . . . . . .51 A6
Navigator Cl BA14 . . . .101 E4
Neal Cl 1 SN5. . . . . . . .146 C5
Neale's Barrow* SP2. . .150 A6
Neeld Cl SN14 . . . . .68 F6
Neeld Cres SN14 . . . . . .78 B8
Neigh Bridge Ctry Pk* GL7 .5 F2
Nell Hill SN6. . . . . .22 A7
Nelson Cl 1 SN5 . . . . . .198 F6
Nelson Rd SP2. . . . . . .146 A2
Nelson St SN1 . . . . .49 F5
Nelson Wlk SP10 . . . . .193 F1
Nepaul Rd SP9 . . . . . . .216 C7
Neptune Cres 2 SN3 . . . .51 B8
Ness Cl SN5 . . . . .34 B2
Nestings The BA14. . . . .105 A5
NESTON. 84 E6
Neston Cres SN13. . . . . .84 E6
Neston Pk* SN13 . . . . . .84 E3
Neston Prim Sch SN13. . .84 E5
NETHERAVON. 190 A3
Netheravon Cl SP1. . . .146 B2
Netheravon Rd
  Durrington SP4 . . . . . .198 B7
  Figheldean SP4 . . . . . .190 B1
  Salisbury SP1 . . . . . .146 B2
Nethercote Cl SN15 . . . . .86 D6
NETHERHAMPTON 151 A8
Netherhampton Bsns Ctr
  SP2. . . . . .151 A8
Netherhampton Rd
  Netherhampton SP2 . . .150 F8
  Quidhampton SP2 . . . .144 F1
Nethermore SN13. . . . . .84 D6
Netherstreet SN15. . . . . .96 D6
NETHERTON 185 F4
Netherton Cl SN3 . . . . . .51 B4
Netherton House* SP11 .185 F4
Nettlebed Nursery 14
  SP7. . . . . .202 C2
Nettlecombe 6 SP7 . . . .202 D2
Nettlemead La BA12 . . .201 E8
NETTLETON 53 C1
Nettleton Green SN14 . . .53 B3
Nettleton Rd SN14 . . . . .53 B3
NETTLETON SHRUB 67 C7
NETTON. 131 E6
Netton St SP5 . . . . .205 E4
Nett Rd SP3 . . . . .196 F6
Nevil Cl 4 SP5 . . . . . . .217 D1
Neville Cl SP1. . . . . . . .146 C4
Neville Terr SN15. . . . . . .57 D1
Nevis Cl SN5. . . . . .34 B2
Newall Tuck Rd SN15. . . .78 F7
Newark Cl SN5 . . . . .49 B3
New Bottom Rd SP4. . . .145 E7
Newbourne Gdns SN14. . .56 D6
New Bridge Cl 4 SN1. . . .50 C7
New Bridge Rd SP1. . . .152 A7
New Bridge Sq 5 SN1. . . .50 C7
New Broughton Rd SN12. .94 A5
New Brunswick Cl 4
  SP4 . . . . .217 F8
Newburgh Pl SN6. . . . . .22 F6
Newburn Cres SN1. . . . . .49 F5
NEWBURY. 119 C8
Newbury Ave SN11. . . . .80 F4
Newbury Dr
  Chippenham SN14. . . . .77 F5
  Swindon SN5. . . . . . . .49 B3
Newbury Rd
  Andover SP10 . . . . . .193 E2
  Lambourn RG17. . . . . .165 B1
Newbury St RG17. . . . . .165 A1
Newby Acre SN8. . . . . .213 D4
Newby Cl 4 SN10. . . . . .187 E8
New Canal SP1. . . . . . .152 A7
Newcastle St SN1. . . . . .50 D6
New Cl
  Bourton SP8 . . . . . . .137 E2
  West Knoyle BA12. . . .140 E7
New Close Com Sch
  BA12. . . . . .117 B6
New Coll SN3 . . . . .50 F5
New Coll Wlk SN3 . . . . .50 F5
Newcombe Dr SN2. . . . .50 A7
Newcombe Trad Est SN2. .50 B7
New Cres SP11 . . . . . . .192 A5
New Dro SP11. . . . . . . .192 A5
Newfield Cl BA13. . . . . .108 F4
New Forest CE (VA) Prim Sch
  The SP5. . . . . .212 B4

NEWGROUNDS. 211 B1
New Haig Rd 7 SP4 . . . .198 E6
New Hall Hospl SP5 . . . .158 F8
Newhall St SN1 . . . . .50 B5
New Harnham Rd SP2. . .152 A6
New Hayward Bottom
  RG17. . . . . .171 C2
New House La SP11. . . .192 E4
Newhurst Pk BA14 . . . .102 A2
New King Barrows* SP4 197 F5
New La
  Cann SP7. . . . . .202 D1
  Seend SN12. . . . . . . .178 D7
Newland Rd SN25. . . . . .35 A3
Newlands Cl SN15 . . . . .70 E7
Newlands Rd SN13. . . . . .77 A1
New Lawns SN12 . . . . . .94 B4
Newleaze
  Steeple Ashton BA14 . .178 A4
  Trowbridge BA14. . . . .101 F4
Newleaze Pk SN12 . . . . .93 B4
Newman Rd SN10. . . . . .214 C1
Newmans Wy SP4 . . . . .217 E5
Newmarket Ave BA14 . . .105 C4
Newmarket Cl 9 SN14. . .77 F6
Newmeadow Copse SN5 . .34 A1
Newopaul Way BA12. . . .116 E5
Newopaul Wy BA12 . . . .112 F1
New Pk Rd SN10. . . . . .214 B4
New Pk St SN10 . . . . . .214 A4
Newport BA12. . . . . . . .117 A2
Newport St SN1. . . . . . .50 D3
New Rd
  Bath BA1. . . . . .82 C2
  Bradford-on-Avon BA15 .100 C7
  Bromham SN15. . . . . . .96 A5
  Calne SN11 . . . . .81 B2
  Calne Without SN11 . . .79 F3
  Chippenham SN15. . . . .78 D7
  Chiseldon SN4 . . . . . . .65 D3
  Codford BA12 . . . . . . .195 A4
  Donhead St Andrew SP7. .203 B4
  22 Durrington/Bulford SP4 198 B7
  East Knoyle SP3 . . . . . .141 B3
  Erlestoke BA13 . . . . . .179 A2
  Kilmington BA12 . . . . .123 D6
  Landford SP5. . . . . . . .212 D5
  Limpley Stoke BA2. . . . .99 B5
  Maiden Bradley with Yarnfield
    BA11. . . . . .123 A4
  Marlborough SN8 . . . . .213 D3
  Melksham Without SN12. .94 E7
  Purton SN5 . . . . .33 C5
  Rockbourne SP6 . . . . .210 A5
  Royal Wootton Bassett SN4 .47 D1
  2 Shaftesbury SP7 . . . .202 B2
  1 Trowbridge BA14. . . .105 D7
  Zeale SP8 . . . . .138 A3
New Severalls The SN9 . .182 E7
Newson Rd
  5 Swindon SN25. . . . . .34 C5
  8 Swindon SN25. . . . . .34 D5
New St
  16 Market Lavington
    SN10. . . . . .179 F1
  Salisbury SP1 . . . . . .152 A7
  Winterbourne Stoke SP3. .196 F3
Newstead Cl 1 SN25 . . . .34 F6
New Terr BA14 . . . . . . .101 C4
Newth's La SN5. . . . . . . .19 D2
NEWTON. 161 B2
Newton Abbot Cl 6 SN4. .77 F6
Newton Barrow* SP2 . . .130 E3
Newton Cl SP5 . . . . . . .161 C3
NEWTON GROVE 27 E4
Newton La SP5 . . . . . . .161 B3
Newton Rd SP2. . . . . . .145 D1
Newtons Wlk SN8. . . . . .170 B8
NEWTON TONY 199 B3
Newton Tony CE Prim Sch
  SP4. . . . . .199 B3
Newton Way SN2 . . . . . .35 C4
NEWTOWN
  Shalbourne 176 E2
  West Tisbury 203 B7
NEW TOWN
  Alton 173 D3
  Farnham 207 C2
  Ramsbury 170 C2
  Sixpenny Handley 207 F2
  Swindon. 50 D6
Newtown
  Bradford-on-Avon BA15 .100 C8
  Heytesbury BA12. . . . .194 C5
  Hullavington SN14. . . . .41 F1
  Trowbridge BA14. . . . .105 C8
  Westbury BA13 . . . . . .109 C3
Newtown Com Prim Sch
  BA14. . . . . .105 C8
New Town La SN6 . . . . .163 E6
Newtown Rd BA14 . . . . .170 C2
New Ward Rd SP4 . . . . .198 E7
New Zealand Ave SP2. . .145 D2
Nicholas Ct SN1 . . . . . . .50 C2
Nicolson Cl 6 SP4. . . . .217 E3
Niebull Cl SN16. . . . . . . .28 A5
Nightingale Ave BA11. . .110 B6
Nightingale Cl
  Melksham SN12. . . . . . .94 D4
  8 West Wellow SO51. . .212 F6
Nightingale Dr BA13 . . .109 B4
Nightingale La
  South Marston SN3. . . . .36 F4
  Tisbury SP3 . . . . .203 C6
Nightingale Rd BA14. . . .105 A8

Nightingale Wlk SP2.....145 E2
Nightingale Wy GL7.......7 A6
Nightjar Cl SN12........94 D4
Nightwood Copse [3] SN5. 34 A1
Nindum Rd SN3..........36 C1
Nine Acre Dr SN13.......76 D1
NINE ELMS..............49 A8
Nive Rd SN4............168 E8
Noade St SP5...........206 E4
Noble St SN16..........40 C8
Nocton Rd SN4..........64 E3
Nolan Cl [1] SN25.......34 F8
Nolands Rd SN11........166 D2
NOMANSLAND............212 C4
Norcliffe Rd SN3.......51 B4
Noredown Way SN4.......47 E1
Noremarsh Com Jun Sch
　SN4..................47 E1
Nore Marsh Rd SN4......47 E1
Norfolk Cl [1] SN3.....50 F6
Norfolk Rd SP2.........151 E7
NORLEAZE...............108 F8
Norley La SN11.........80 C3
Norman Cl SN15.........79 A4
Norman Dr
　Old Sarum SP4........146 C8
　[7] Winterbourne SP4..132 C1
　Winterbourne SP4.....132 C1
Normandy Rd SN4........64 E3
Normandy Way [14] SP6..210 D1
Norman Rd SN2..........35 C1
NORMANTON.............197 F3
Norney Rd BA13........179 A4
Norridge View [4] BA12.116 E7
NORRINGTON COMMON.....93 C6
Norrington La SN11....93 C6
Norrington Manor* SP5 204 A2
Norris Cl SN4.........65 C3
Norris Rd BA14........102 B3
Northacre Ind Est BA13. 108 D5
Northampton St SN1....50 D6
North Bank Rise SN4...47 F2
Northbourne Rd SN25...35 A7
NORTH BRADLEY.........105 D4
North Bradley CE Prim Sch
　BA14................105 D2
NORTH BREWHAM.........122 A6
Northbrook SN3........179 E1
Northbrook La SN10....179 F1
Northbrook Cl [1] SN10.179 F1
Northbrook Rd SN12....93 F7
North Cft SP3.........188 B3
NORTH CHARFORD........211 C6
North Charford Crossing
　SP6................210 C6
North Charford Dro SP6. 210 C8
North Comm La SP5.....212 B7
North Cote SN11.......81 A4
Northcote Cres [7] BA11.110 A7
Northcroft Rd SN13....76 D1
North Dr [4] SN25.....34 F8
Northen Cl GL7........10 E6
NORTHEND..............82 A5
NORTH END.............6 E2
North End SN11........81 A4
North End Gdns SN16...25 C1
Northen Terr
　Durrington SP4......197 F7
　Larkhill SP4........198 A4
Northern Rd SN2.......35 A1
North Farm Cl RG17....165 B2
Northfield BA15.......99 F7
Northfield La SN14....66 A2
Northfields
　Bulkington SN10.....178 E5
　Calne SN11..........81 A4
　[1] Lambourn RG17...165 A2
Northfield Way SN3....51 B7
Northgate Gdns SN10...214 A4
Northgate St SN10.....214 A4
North La SP5..........212 C4
Northlands Ind Est BA12. 117 B7
Northleaze SN13.......76 D1
North Lease Cl SN2....34 F3
Northleigh BA15.......91 E1
Northleigh Terr SP2...144 D3
North Mdw National Nature
　Reseve* SN6.........8 C1
North Mdw Rd SN6......8 C1
Northmoor La GL7......6 F8
NORTH NEWNTON........181 E4
North Rd
　Amesbury SP4........217 E2
　Ashmore SP5.........206 E5
　Mere BA12...........139 A4
North Row BA12........117 A7
Northside SP4.........146 D8
North St
　Broad Chalke SP5....205 B4
　Calne SN11..........81 A4
　Mere BA12...........139 A5
　Pewsey SN9..........215 C5
　Salisbury SP2.......145 F1
　Swindon SN1.........50 C5
　Wilton SP2..........144 D3
North Standen Rd RG17. 177 A6
North Star Ave SN2....50 B8
North Star Ind Est SN2. 50 B7
NORTH STREET.........210 E5
NORTH TIDWORTH.......216 D8
Northview [20] RG17....177 C7
North View
　Berwick St James SP3. 196 F2
　Highworth SN6.......22 F5
North View Hts RG17...177 C7

North View Pl SN8......213 D4
North Wall SN6.........19 D8
Northway SP4...........134 B7
North Way
　Calne SN11..........81 A4
　Trowbridge BA14.....105 A4
North Wlk SP1.........152 A8
North Wlk SN15........70 E2
NORTH WRAXALL........67 B3
NORTH WROUGHTON......64 B8
NORTON...............41 D5
NORTON BAVANT.......194 A6
Norton Dr SP4........146 D6
NORTON FERRIS.......124 C6
Norton Gr SN3........50 D5
Norton Rd BA12.......117 F1
Norwood Castle (site of)*
　SN16...............4 F2
Norwood Cl [3] SN3...51 D4
NOTTON...............86 B8
Notton House Sch SN15. 86 B8
Nova Hroed Acad SN2...34 D2
Noyes Cl
　Chippenham SN14....77 F8
　Haydon Wick SN4....34 C5
Nuffield Cl SN5......49 B8
Nunns Pk SP5.........161 D4
NUNTON..............152 D1
Nunton Dro SP5.......152 D1
Nunwick Wy [4] SN1...50 A2
Nurseries The
　Christian Malford SN15.58 A2
　Swindon SN1........50 B4
Nursery Cl
　[4] Amesbury SP4...217 B3
　Atworth/Whitley SN12.92 E8
　Trowbridge BA14....102 A3
　Wroughton SN4......64 A5
Nursery Gdns
　Corsham SN13.......85 A8
　Mere BA12..........139 A5
Nursery Rd
　Colerne SN14.......75 A3
　Salisbury SP2......145 E1
Nursery The SN16.....27 F6
NURSTEED.............214 E1
Nursteed Cl SN10.....214 D2
Nursteed Com Prim Sch
　SN10...............214 E3
Nursteed Pk SN10.....214 C2
Nursteed Rd SN10.....214 C2
Nursteed Rd Ind Est
　SN10...............214 C1
NUTBANE.............193 A4
Nutbane La SP11......193 A4
Nuthatch Cl [4] SN3..51 E6
Nuthatch Rd SN11.....81 B5
Nutley Ct [8] SN8....183 D8
Nutmeg Cl [7] SN2....34 D4
Nyland Cl SN3........51 C7
Nyland Sch SN3.......51 B7
NYTHE...............51 C7
Nythe Rd SN3.........36 B1

O

Oakapple Cl [4] SN4...163 B6
Oak Ash Gn SP2........144 C2
Oak Ave GL8...........24 F7
Oakbournes The [5] SP1.146 C5
Oak Cl
　Bishops Cannings SN10.172 B2
　Pitton & Farley SP5..154 E7
　South Newton SP2....130 B2
　Tidworth SP9........216 E7
Oak Dr
　Alderbury SP5.......153 D2
　Highworth SN6.......22 F5
　Trowbridge BA14.....105 C3
Oakes Ct [9] SP7......177 B7
Oakes La GL9..........52 B5
Oakford La SN14.......74 B2
Oakford Wlk SN3.......51 A6
Oak Gdns SN3..........36 A4
Oakham Cl SN5.........49 C5
Oak Hill SN8..........176 E6
Oakhurst Com Prim Sch
　SN25...............34 B7
Oakhurst Way SN25.....34 C7
Oakie Cl SN25.........35 A5
Oak La
　Easterton SN10......179 F2
　Figheldean SP4......190 B2
　Mere BA12...........139 B4
Oaklands SN15.........70 D2
Oaklands Cl [12] SP6..210 D1
Oaklea La SP5.........153 E2
Oakleaze SN16.........17 B2
Oakleigh Dr SP5.......212 C5
Oakley Bsns Pk SP3....201 E5
Oakley Flats GL7......10 D6
Oakley La
　Farnham DT11........207 D2
　Sixpenny Handley SP5.208 B4
Oak Lodge Cl SN14.....78 C8
Oak Pk BA14...........104 F5
Oak Pl SP4............217 C4
Oak Rd
　Chippenham Without SN14.77 F6
　Colerne SN14........74 F5
　Down Ampney GL7.....8 E6
OAKSEY...............15 F7
Oaksey Rd
　Minety SN16.........16 C4
　Swindon SN2.........35 C4
Oak St GL7............2 C4

Oaks The
　Chippenham SN15.....70 D2
　Coate SN1...........51 A2
　Kemble GL7..........4 F7
　Warminster BA12.....117 A8
Oak Tree Ave SN2......35 D3
Oak Tree Bsns Pk SN3..36 C7
Oak Tree Cl BA14......101 B1
Oak Tree Prim Sch SN3. 51 A4
Oak Way GL7...........6 F6
Oakwood Dr SN12.......94 B4
Oakwood Gr SP5........153 D3
Oakwood Rd SN5........49 C7
Oamaru Way SN10.......214 D3
OARE................174 B2
Oare Hill SN8.........174 C2
Oare Prim Sch SN8.....174 B2
Oasis Leisure Ctr SN2. 50 B7
Oasthouse Cl [3] SN5..49 A8
Oate Hill SN15........78 F6
Oatfields BA14........101 D4
Oathill La GL7........3 B8
Oathills SN13.........84 F8
Oatmeal Row SN1.......152 A8
Oat Rd [13] SP11......193 F2
Oatway Rd SP9.........216 D8
Obelisk Terr [6] BA12. 116 F7
Oberon Way SN5........35 A5
Ocotal Way SN1........50 D8
Odcroft Cl SN15.......79 A7
Oddford Vale [17] SP3. 203 E8
O'Donnell Cl SN15.....70 E1
ODSTOCK.............152 A1
Odstock Prim Sch SP5..152 B1
Odstock Rd
　Britford SP2........152 B4
　Swindon SN2.........35 C6
Offerton Rd [3] SN1...50 A2
Ogbourne SN14.........75 B3
OGBOURNE MAIZEY.....213 C7
OGBOURNE ST
　ANDREW............168 F3
OGBOURNE ST GEORGE..169 A5
Ogbourne St George & St
　Andrew CE (Controlled)
　Prim Sch SN8.......168 F5
Ogbury Camp* SP4......198 A1
Ogilvie Sq SN11.......81 C3
Okebourne Pk SN3......51 C3
Okeford Cl SN3........51 C7
OKUS................50 A4
Okus Gr SN3...........35 D4
Okus Rd SN1...........49 F3
Okus Trad Est SN3.....50 A4
Olaf Cl [10] SN2......193 E2
Old Alexander Rd SN16. 27 F4
Old Bakery Cl SN16....28 F2
Old Barn GL8..........3 C5
Old Batch The BA15....100 B8
Old Beasants SN8......174 A6
Old Blandford Rd SP2.. 151 F6
Old Boundary Rd SP7...202 C2
Old Brickyard Rd SN2.. 210 B1
Old Broughton Rd SN12. 94 A5
Oldbury Castle (Hill Fort)*
　SN11...............172 C8
OLDBURY ON THE HILL.. 24 B5
Oldbury Prior SN11....81 C1
Oldbury Way SN11......81 A3
Old Castle Rd SP1.....146 A5
Old Chapel Cl SP5.....153 D3
Old Chase Rd SN8......169 A4
Old Coach Rd
　Durrington/Bulford.. 217 D8
　North Wraxall SN14.. 67 D2
　Shipton Bellinger SP11.191 F1
Old Coach Works [19]
　RG17...............165 A1
Old Comm Way [13] SP11.192 A5
Old Ct SN4............47 D1
Old Dairy Cl
　Bermerton Heath SP2.145 C3
　Swindon SN2........35 E3
Old Dairy Ct SN12.....94 C5
Old Dairy Dr The SN14. 68 B7
Old Dairy The
　Amesbury SP4.......217 A2
　Nunton SP5.........152 D1
Old Derry Hill SN15...79 D2
Old Dilton Rd BA13....112 F2
Old Down Rd GL9.......52 C8
Olde Fairfield SP8....138 A2
Oldenburg Cl SN5......34 C2
Oldenburgh Rd [3] BA13. 108 E1
Old English Dr [2] SP10.193 D2
Old Estate Yd The GL7. 8 D7
Old Farm Cl SN16......15 C2
Old Farmhouse The
　SN10...............214 C1
Old Farm Rd BA14......105 F7
Oldfield Pk BA13......108 E3
Oldfield Rd
　Salisbury SP1.......146 C5
　Westbury BA13.......108 E4
Oldford Hill BA11.....110 A8
Old Forge Cl
　Brinkworth SN15.....45 E6
　Heytesbury BA12.....194 C5
Old Granary La SP4....217 B3
Old Hardenhuish La SN14. 70 B1
Old Hayward La RG17...171 B1
Old Hollow BA12.......139 B6
Old Hospl Rd SN9......215 B6
Old King Barrows* SP4. 197 F5
Oldlands Wlk SN3......51 A3
Old Malmesbury Rd SN4. 47 E4

Old Malthouse La SP4...147 B7
Old Manor House*
　BA12...............194 A4
Old Mdws Wlk SP2......151 E7
Old Midford Rd BA2....98 A7
Old Mill La SN3.......50 D3
Old Oak Cl [5] SP11...193 F2
Old Orch The SN16.....28 A6
Old Post Office La [5]
　SP4................190 A3
Old Pound Ct SP8......137 D1
Old Rd
　Alderbury SP5.......153 C4
　Chippenham SN15.....78 D8
　Derry Hill/Studley SN11.80 B2
Old Rly Cl [1] SN16...28 A4
Old Ropeworks The*
　SN8................213 D1
Old Sarum* SP1........145 F6
Old Sarum Barracks SP4. 146 C8
Old Sarum Bsns Pk SP4. 146 C8
Old Sarum Pk SP4......146 C8
Old Sarum Prim Sch
　SP4................146 C8
Old Sawmills The RG17. 177 F3
Old Sawmill The BA12.. 123 F5
Old Sch Ct SN3........96 C7
Old Sch Ct SN3........51 B6
Old School Cl SN4.....190 A3
Old School Ct SN14....74 A8
Old School Dr [33] SP11.192 A5
Old Sch Yd SN13.......85 A8
Old Severalls The SN9. 182 E7
Old Shaftesbury Dro
　SP2................150 A6
Old Shaftesbury Dro SP2.151 D5
Old Shaw La SN5.......48 F8
Old Sodom La SN15.....59 B8
Old Sta Yd The SN5....152 A6
Old Sta Yd The [14] RG17.165 A1
Old Surgery Cl SN5....33 C4
OLD TOWN.............50 D3
Old Track BA2.........98 F7
Old Vicarage La GL7...4 F7
Old Vineries The [16] SP6.210 C1
Old Wardour Castle*
　SP3................203 D5
Old Ward Rd [5] SP4...198 E6
Old Were Ct [3] BA12.. 117 A7
Olive Gr SN2..........35 B3
Olivemead La SN15.....45 C1
Oliver Ave SN13.......76 F2
Oliver Cl SN5.........48 F6
Oliver's Castle (Fort)*
　SN10...............97 C6
Olivers Cl SN11.......166 B1
Olivers Hill SN11.....166 B1
Oliver's La [5] SN16..28 A3
Oliver Tomkins CE Inf Sch
　SN5................49 B5
Olivier Cl SP2........145 C5
Olivier Rd
　Swindon SN25.......35 B6
　Wilton SP2.........144 B5
Olympiad L Ctr* SN15.. 78 E8
Olympian Rd SN9.......215 B5
Olympia The SN8.......168 B3
Olympic Pk Rd [30] SP11.193 E2
Omar Rd SN13..........84 F6
Omdurman St SN2.......35 B1
Ontario Wy [6] SP4....217 F8
Orange Cl SN6.........23 A4
Orbital Sh Pk SN25....34 E6
Orchard Cl
　Calne SN11.........81 C2
　Devizes SN10.......214 B1
　[34] Fordingbridge SP6.210 D1
　Kemble GL7.........4 F7
　Lechlade GL7.......2 B4
　[5] Ramsbury SN8...170 B2
　[2] Wanborough SN4.163 A6
　Warminster BA12....117 B8
　West Ashton BA14...106 B4
　Westbury BA13......112 C8
　Westwood BA15......99 F3
Orchard Cres SN14.....78 B7
Orchard Ct
　[17] Bratton BA13..186 A7
　St Paul Malmesbury Without
　　SN16.............28 A2
Orchard Dr BA14.......104 E2
Orchard End SP4.......217 D8
Orchard Gdns
　Melksham SN12......94 A3
　Purton SN5.........33 A3
Orchard Gr
　Bromham SN15.......96 D7
　Swindon SN2........35 D5
Orchard Mead [3] SN4..48 A2
Orchard Pk Cl [3] RG17.177 B7
Orchard Pl SN10.......187 E8
Orchard Rd
　Chippenham SN14....78 B7
　Corsham SN13.......77 A2
　Marlborough SN8....213 D3
　Redlynch SN5.......211 C8
　Salisbury SP2......145 D2
　Trowbridge BA14....105 D7
　Westbury BA13......109 A3
Orchard The
　Chirton SN10.......180 F4
　Chiseldown SN4.....65 E4
　Kington St Michael SN14.70 A8
　Limpley Stoke BA2..99 C5
　Salisbury SP1......146 C2
　Semington BA14....102 A6
　Sixpenny Handley SP5.208 B4
　Upton Scudamore BA12.112 F4

Orchard Way
　Amesbury SP4.......217 C3
　Longbridge Deverill BA12.116 E1
　Trowbridge BA14....105 C3
ORCHESTON...........196 D8
Orchid Cl SN25........35 C3
Orchid Dr [30] SP11...192 A5
Orchids The SN15......70 E2
Orchid Vale Prim Sch
　SN25...............34 D6
Orchid Vw [17] SP7....202 D1
Ordnance La SP11......192 E1
Ordnance Rd SP9......216 D6
Orford Rd SP4.........217 D2
Orkney Cl SN5.........49 B7
Orlando Cl [4] SN5....48 F5
Orpen Cl SN3..........50 E2
Orpington Way BA14....102 B1
Orrin Cl SN5..........34 B1
Orwell Cl
　Malmesbury SN16....28 A5
　Swindon SN25.......35 A5
Osborne Rd BA14.......101 E3
Osborne St SN2........50 B8
Oslings La BA1........82 B2
Osmund Cl SN10........214 D3
Osmund Rd SN10........214 D2
Osprey Cl
　Bower Hill SN12....94 D1
　Swindon SN3........51 E6
Osterley Rd SN25......34 E6
Otter Row [7] SN8.....51 B8
Otter Way SN4.........47 F2
OUTMARSH............102 F7
OUTWICK.............210 D4
Overbrook SN5.........51 C3
Overhouse Dr [12] SP3. 203 E8
Overton Gdns SN3......36 B2
OVERTOWN............64 D4
Overtown Hill SN4.....64 C5
Overway La SP7........203 B2
Owen Cl SN10..........214 D3
Owl Cl SN3............51 E6
Owlets The SN3........51 E6
Owlswood [9] SP2......152 A5
Ox Dro
　Berwick St John SP5. 207 B7
　Bishopstone SP5....205 F2
　Bower Chalke SP5...208 A8
　Kimpton SP11.......192 A1
　Teffont SP3........201 C5
Oxencroft [8] SP7.....202 C2
OXENWOOD............184 E6
Oxford Gdns BA14......101 F1
Oxford Pl
　Calne SN11.........81 B3
　Swindon SN3........36 A1
　Upavon Down SN9....182 B2
Oxford St
　Aldbourne SN8......170 A6
　Hungerford RG17....177 C8
　Lambourn RG17......165 A1
　Malmesbury SN16....28 A3
　Marlborough SN8....213 D3
　Ramsbury SN8.......170 B2
　Swindon SN1........50 B6
Oxon Pl SN6...........163 E6
Ox Path The SN8.......174 B2
Ox Row [4] SP1........152 A8
Oxyard SP4............195 B2
Ox Yd GL7.............3 C8

P

Pack Hill SN4.........51 F2
Packhorse Bridge* SN15. 86 E5
Packhorse La SN5......33 E8
Pack Horse La BA2.....98 A7
Packington Cl SN5.....49 B7
Packway The
　Durrington SP4.....197 D7
　Shrewton SP3.......197 A7
Paddington Dr SN5.....49 E5
Paddock Cl
　Enford SN9.........190 A6
　Great Somerford SN15.44 A2
　[4] Shaftesbury SP7. 202 D1
　Sixpenny Handley SP5.208 A3
　Swindon SN25.......34 E5
　Winterbourne SP4...133 B2
Paddock End SN14......70 A7
Paddock La
　Chilmark SP3.......200 F2
　Corsham SN13.......84 D8
Paddocks The
　[10] Aldbourne SN8. 170 A6
　Chippenham SN15....78 E6
　Mere BA12..........139 A5
　[14] Ramsbury SN8..170 B2
　[5] Swindon SN3....36 A2
　Westbury BA13......109 A4
Paddock The
　[5] Bradford-on-Avon
　　BA15.............100 D6
　Highworth SN6......23 A5
　Market Lavington SN10.180 A1
　[8] Tisbury SP3....203 E8
Paddock Way SP1.......146 E2
Paddock Wood [13] SP4. 198 B7
Padfield Gdns SN11....93 F1
Padstow Rd SN5........49 F5
Page Cl
　Calne SN11.........81 C3
　Chippenham SN14....78 A7
Paget Cl SP9..........216 B8
Pagnell La SN10.......179 D1
Pagoda Pk SN5.........49 D7

Pains Way [3] SP4........217 C2
Painters Mead BA14......102 A2
Pakenham Rd SN3........51 B4
Palairet Cl BA15........100 D4
Palestine Rd SP11......199 F3
Palmer Dr BA15........100 D8
Palmer Gr BA14........102 F6
Palmer Rd
  Devizes SN10..........214 C5
  Salisbury SP2........145 E2
  Trowbridge BA14......101 D2
Palmer St SN14........78 C7
Palmerston Meadow
  SN9................190 A6
Palmers Way [11] SN4....163 A6
Palm Rd SN14........75 A5
Palomino Pl SN5........34 B2
Pampas Ct [1] BA12....116 E6
Pans La SN10..........214 B2
Panters Rd SP3........204 C8
Pantiles The [12] SP6....210 C1
Parade The
  Marlborough SN8......213 D3
  Swindon SN1........50 C6
Paradise La BA12........116 E1
Parham La SN10........179 E2
Parhams Ct SN4........47 E1
Parham Hill SP3........203 B1
Parham Wlk [7] SN5....48 F5
Park Ave
  Chippenham SN14......78 B8
  Corsham SN13........84 A8
  Highworth SN6........23 A5
Park Cl
  Calne SN11..........81 C2
  Malmesbury SN16......27 F4
  Salisbury SP1........146 A4
  Trowbridge BA14......105 D3
PARK CORNER..........99 A4
Park Dr SP3..........201 B3
Park End SN6..........17 F8
Parkers La SN15........70 D6
Park Field SN10........214 C5
Park Fields SN15........78 C8
Parkhouse Cnr SN4......199 D6
Parkhouse Rd SP9......199 C8
Park La
  Castle Combe SN14......68 A7
  Cherhill SN11........166 C1
  Chippenham SN15......78 D8
  Corsham SN13........76 D1
  Great Somerford SN15....44 A2
  Heytesbury BA12......194 D5
  Heywood BA13........109 C7
  Lea & Cleverton SN16....29 D3
  Lydiard Millicent SN5....48 D7
  Malmesbury SN16......27 E5
  North Wraxall SN14....68 A2
  Odstock SP5..........152 D4
  Salisbury SP1........146 A3
  Sutton Benger SN15....57 D2
  Swindon SN1........50 A6
  West Dean SP5........149 F1
Parklands
  Malmesbury SN16......27 E4
  Trowbridge BA14......101 D2
Parklands Cl SN16......27 E4
Parklands Rd SN3......50 D5
Parklands The SN14....55 E8
Parkland Way SP4......133 D6
Park Mead SN16........27 F4
PARK NORTH..........51 A5
Park Pl SN6..........6 F1
Park Rd
  Fordingbridge SP6......210 D1
  Malmesbury SN16......27 F4
  Market Lavington SN10....179 E1
  Rushall SN9..........181 F3
  Salisbury SP1........146 D2
  Tidworth SP9........216 D5
  Tisbury SP3..........203 E8
  Trowbridge BA14......105 D8
  Westbury BA13........112 B8
Parkside
  Chippenham SN15......78 D8
  Swindon SN3........36 A3
PARK SOUTH..........51 A4
Park Springs SN5......49 C5
Park St
  Charlton SN16........29 A6
  Heytesbury BA12......194 C5
  Hungerford RG17......177 B7
  Salisbury SP1........146 B2
  Swindon SN3........36 C2
  Trowbridge BA14......105 C7
Parkstone Wlk SN3......51 B3
Park Terr SN15........78 C8
Park The
  Erlestoke SN10........179 A1
  [8] Lambourn RG17......165 A2
Park View
  Chirton SN10........180 F4
  Devizes SN10........179 D8
Park View Dr
  Lydiard Millicent SN5....48 D8
  [1] Westbury BA13......108 F1
Park Vw Point DT11......207 A3
Parkwater Rd SP5......161 E1
Park Way RG17........177 B6
Parliament Row SN16....28 C4
Parliament St SN14......78 B7
Parr Cl SN5..........49 A6
Parsley Cl SN2........34 D5
Parsloes Cl SN4........64 E3
Parsonage Cl
  [31] Fordingbridge SP6....210 D1
  Salisbury SP1........145 E5

Parsonage Down National
  Nature Reserve* SP3....196 D5
Parsonage Gn SP2......151 E6
Parsonage Hill SP5......154 D7
Parsonage La
  Charlton Musgrove BA9....136 C2
  Hungerford RG17......177 B7
  [9] Lambourn RG17......165 A1
  [20] Market Lavington SN10..179 F1
Parsonage Pk Dr [3] SP6..210 D1
Parsonage Pl [9] RG17....165 A2
Parsonage Rd
  Amesbury SP4........217 B3
  Swindon SN3........36 A3
  Trowbridge BA14......102 A1
Parsonage The SP5......208 B4
Parsonage Vale SN8......183 D2
Parsonage Way SN15....70 F1
Parsons Cl SP4........133 D5
Parsons Gn [4] SP3......196 E6
Parsons La BA12........116 E2
Parsons Pool [19] SP7....202 C2
Parsons Way SN4......47 E1
Partridge Cl
  Chippenham SN14......70 B2
  [4] Corsham SN13......76 E1
  Swindon SN3........51 E6
Partridge Hill SP5......212 E6
Partridge Way SP4......146 C8
Passmore Cl SN3........51 E7
Pasteur Dr SN1........50 A3
Pasture Cl SN2........49 E7
Pastures The BA15......99 E3
Pasture Wlk [19] SP11....193 F2
Patchway SN14........78 B8
Patchway The SN10....214 D3
Pathfinder Way
  Bowerhill SN12........94 C2
  [5] Swindon SN25......34 B7
PATNEY............180 F5
Patney Rd SN10........180 F5
Pat-yat GL7..........4 B5
Paulet Ct [3] SN4......49 A4
Pauls Croft SN6........19 D7
Paul's Dene Cres SP1....146 A5
Paul's Dene Rd SP1....146 A5
Paul St SN13..........76 F1
Pavely Cl SN5..........78 C6
Pavely Gdns BA14......102 A1
Paven Cl SN5..........33 A4
Pavenhill SN5..........33 A4
PAXCROFT............102 C3
Paxcroft Way BA14......105 F8
Paxmans Rd BA13......108 E5
Payne Cl SN15........78 E4
Payne's Hill [2] SP1....152 B8
Peacock Cl SN3........51 E7
Peaks Down SN5........34 B2
Peak The SN5..........33 B3
Pealsham Gdns [6] SP6..210 D1
PEAR ASH............137 C4
Pear Ash La BA9......137 C4
Pearce Cl SN2........35 E6
Pearce Way SP1........146 D5
Pearl Rd SN5..........49 A7
Peartree Cl
  Atworth/Whitley SN12....85 C1
  Purton SN5..........33 C5
  [7] West Wellow SO51....212 F6
Pear Tree Dr SP5......212 C5
Pear Tree La SN10......187 B8
Pear Tree Orch [2] BA13..186 B7
PEATMOOR..........34 B1
Peatmoor Com Prim Sch
  SN5..............34 A2
Peatmoor Way SN5......34 A1
PECKINGELL..........71 B2
Peel Cir SN13........84 D8
Peel Ct SN12........94 A3
Pegasus Way SN12......94 C1
Peglars Way SN1......49 F3
Pelch La SN12........178 D8
Pelham Ct SN8........213 E3
Pembridge Rd SP6......210 E1
Pembroke Cl [1] BA14....105 D6
Pembroke Ctr SN2......34 E1
Pembroke Gdns SN25....34 E3
Pembroke Gn SN16......28 F1
Pembroke Park Prim Sch
  SP2..............145 D4
Pembroke Rd
  Chippenham SN15......79 A4
  Melksham SN12......94 B4
  Salisbury SP2........145 C2
  Upavon Down SN9......182 D3
Pembroke St SN1......50 B4
Pen Cl SN25..........35 A4
Pendennis Rd SN5......49 A3
Penfold Gdns SN1......50 C4
PENHILL............35 C5
Pen Hill BA10........122 F1
Penhill Dr SN2........35 C4
PENKNAP............112 E8
Penleigh Cl SN13......84 F8
Penleigh Rd BA13......108 D2
Pen Mill Hill BA9......137 C3
Penneys Piece [2] BA11..110 C6
Penn Hill Rd SN11......81 C3
Pennine Cl SN12......94 D4
Pennine Way SN25......34 F7
Penning Rd SP2........145 B4
Pennings Dro SP5......157 A8
Pennings Rd
  North Tidworth SP9......191 D5
  Tidworth SP9........216 C8
Pennycress Cl SN25....34 E4
Pennycress Dr SN12....94 C3

Penny Farthing Cl RG17..177 A7
Pennyfarthing St SP1....146 B1
Penny Hill SN8........191 E8
Penny La
  Amesbury SP4........217 D1
  Chippenham SN15......78 F4
  Swindon SN3........50 F7
Penny Royal Cl SN11....80 F3
Penny's Cl [3] SP6......210 D2
Penny's Cres [4] SP6....210 D2
Pennys La SP6........210 D2
Penny's La
  Pitton & Farley SP5....154 E7
  [2] Wilton SP2........144 D3
Penrose Wlk SN3......51 A4
Penruddock Cl SP2......145 C3
PENSELWOOD..........137 B4
Pensford Way BA11....110 D6
PENTON CORNER......193 A1
PENTON GRAFTON......193 A2
Penton La SP11........193 A3
PENTON MEWSEY......193 B2
PENTRIDGE..........208 E4
Pentridge St SN3......51 C7
Pentylands Cl SN6......22 F7
Penzance Dr SN5......49 F5
Pepperacre La BA14....101 F1
Pepperbox Hill SN5....34 B2
Pepperbox Rise SP5....153 E2
Pepperbox The* SP5....160 C6
Peppercombe Cl [6]
  SN10..............180 B4
Peppercombe Wood Nature
  Reserve* SN10........180 B4
Peppercorn Orch BA14....178 A6
Pepper Pl BA12........117 D7
Percheron Cl [11] SN5....49 A7
Percheron Rd BA13......108 D2
Percy St SN2..........49 F7
Peregrine Dr SN3......51 D8
Peregrine Ct [2] SN11....81 B5
Perham Cres [1] SP11....192 B5
PERHAM DOWN........191 F4
Periwinkle Cl SN2......34 C3
Perrinsfield GL7......2 D6
Perriwinkle Cl BA12....116 D6
PERRY GREEN........29 B7
Perry's La
  Seend SN12..........178 D8
  Wroughton SN4........64 A6
Perth Rd SP11........191 F4
Peshawar St SP9......216 B7
Peter Furkins Ct SN1....50 A5
Petersfield Rd SN3......51 B4
PETERSFINGER........152 E7
Peters Finger Rd SP5....152 E7
Peto Gdn The* BA15....99 E2
Petter Cl SN4........64 B7
Petticoat La
  Redlynch SP5........211 D8
  Westbury BA13........112 C8
Pettridge La BA12......139 A5
PETTY FRANCE........38 B8
Petty La SN11........79 F3
Pevensey Way SN5......49 C5
Pew Hill SN15........70 E2
PEWSEY............215 D4
Pewsey Downs National
  Nature Reserve* SN8..173 C2
Pewsey Prim Sch SN9....215 B5
Pewsey Rd
  Marlborough SN8......213 D2
  Rushall SN9..........181 E2
Pewsey Sports Ctr &
  Swimming Pool SN9....215 B5
Pewsey Sta SN9......215 B5
Pewsey Vale Sch SN9....215 B5
PEWSEY WHARF......215 B7
Pewsey White Horse*
  SN9..............215 E1
Pewsham Lock SN15....78 E4
Pewsham Rd SN2......35 D5
Pewsham Way SN15....78 E4
Pheasant Bsns Pk SN14..78 B5
Pheasant Cl
  [8] Chippenham Without
    SN14............77 F6
  Swindon SN3........51 E5
Pheasant Dr SP4......146 B8
Pheasantry The GL7....8 E7
Philip Cl SN12........94 C6
Philip Ct SP2........145 D3
Philipps House & Dinton Pk*
  SP3..............201 E2
Philip Rd
  [21] Durrington/Bulford
    SP4............198 B7
  Wilton SP2..........144 B5
Phillip Cl SN10........214 C4
Phillips Cl SN14......77 F7
Phillips La
  Salisbury SP4........145 E6
  Swindon SN1........50 D4
Phillips Way BA14......105 E2
Phipps Cl BA13........108 F4
Phoebe Way SN25......34 B7
Phoenix Rise BA13......108 E3
Phoenix Sq SN9......215 C4
Picked Mead [1] SN13....84 E8
Picket Cl SP6........210 D1
Picket Cnr SP6........211 F3
Picketlease SN14......78 A7
Picket Post Gate BA12....116 A4
Pickford Way SN25......35 B6
PICKWICK..........76 E2
Pickwick SN13........76 D2
Pickwick Cl SN2........35 E5
Pickwick Rd SN13......76 F2

Picquet The [12] BA13....186 B7
Picton Rd SN5........49 A7
Pictor Cl SN13........76 D1
Piernik Cl SN25........34 E6
Pigeon House La SN3....36 A3
Pig La
  Bishops Cannings SN10..172 C1
  Hullavington SN16......41 A3
Pigott Cl [4] SP4......190 A4
Pigtrough La SP7......203 B4
Pike Cnr SN16........17 D7
Pikefield Cres SN16....29 A6
Pike House La SN6......19 C8
Pilgrim Cl SN5........49 A7
Pilgrims Ct SP1........146 E2
Pilgrims Mead SP1......146 C5
Pilgrims Wy SP1......146 E2
Pill Hill SP5..........161 C4
Pilots View SP4........217 D3
Pilton Cl SN5..........49 A8
Pimperleaze Rd BA12....139 C1
PINCKNEY GREEN......90 E5
Pinckneys Way [13] SP4..198 B7
Pine Cl
  Corsham SN13........76 A1
  Landford SP5........212 C5
  Melksham SN12......94 A3
Pine Ct [2] BA11......110 B7
Pine Gr BA14........105 C6
Pine La SN4..........35 E2
PINEHURST..........35 D3
Pinehurst Rd SN2......35 C2
Pinehurst Sports Ctr SN2..35 B3
Pines Rd SN10........214 C2
Pines The SP6........211 A1
Pinetree Rise SN2......35 B3
Pinetum Cl SN10......214 A2
Pineview SP5........211 C6
Pine Wlk
  Amesbury SP4........217 D3
  Trowbridge BA14......105 C3
Pinewoods Cl SP2......145 B4
Pinewood Way
  Colerne SN14........74 F7
  Salisbury SP4........145 B4
Pinfield La SN15......78 F4
Pinhills SN11........81 A2
Pink La SN16........29 E5
Pinkney Pk* SN16......25 F1
Pinnegar Way SN3......51 E6
Pinnocks Pl SN2......35 F4
Pintail Cl SN5........60 B1
Pintail Way BA13......109 B4
Pinto Cl SN2..........34 C3
Pioneer Cl [3] SN5......49 A7
Pipehouse La BA2......98 F4
Pipers Cl SN4........61 D8
Pipers Way SN1........50 C1
Pipistrelle Cres BA14....106 A8
Pipitdene SN3........51 D7
Piplar Gd BA15........100 D4
Pippins The [3] BA12....116 F7
Pippin The SN11......81 B3
Pippit Pl [5] SN12....94 D5
Pipsmore Rd
  [5] Chippenham SN14....70 A1
  Chippenham SN14......78 A8
Pitchens End SN4......167 C7
Pitchens The SN4......64 B5
Pitman Ave BA14......105 B7
Pitman Ct BA14......105 B6
Pit Mead La BA12......117 E4
Pitt Cl [3] SN1........50 E7
PITTON............148 C3
Pitton CE Prim Sch SP5..148 B3
Pitton Rd SP5........154 D8
Pitts Croft SN13......84 E5
Pittsfield SN6........19 D7
Pitts La
  Bishopstone SP5......205 F4
  Chitterne BA12......195 D7
  Sedgehill & Semley SP7..202 B7
PITTS THE..........205 F5
Pit Wlk SP4..........199 C4
Pix Mead Gdns [1] SP7..202 D1
Place Rd SN12........94 A4
PLAITFORD..........212 E6
PLAITFORD GREEN......212 F8
Plane Tree Cl SN12....85 C1
Planks The SN3........50 D4
Plantation Rd
  Chippenham SN14......78 C8
  Tidworth SN9........216 D5
  Wellow SO51........212 F4
Plantation The SP5......149 A5
Plants Gn BA12........117 B6
Plassey Rd SP9........216 C2
Platford St SN11......81 B2
Platt Cl RG17........177 D6
Plattes Cl SN5........49 B8
Platt La RG17........170 E7
Play Cl SN5..........33 C4
Player Ct [8] SP6......210 D2
Playhouse Salisbury*
  SP2..............146 A1
Pleydell Rd SN1......50 C2
Pleydells SN5........19 D8
Plough La
  Kington Langley SN15....70 C5
  Marston SN10........179 A3
Plough Wy [9] SP11....193 F2
Plume of Feathers La
  SN8..............213 D1
Plum Cl SN10........180 E4
Plummer Cl SN4......64 A6
Plumpton Cl SN14......77 F6
Plymouth St SN1......50 D6

Poachers Way SN25......34 F7
Pockeredge Dr SN13....84 C7
Pockeridge Rd SN13....84 E7
Pointers Way SP4......217 D3
Polaris Way SN2........50 B7
Polden Rd SP1........152 C7
Polebarn Rd BA14......105 C8
Pollen Cl SP4........190 B2
Pollen La SP4........190 B2
Polonez Ct SN25......34 D6
Poltondale SN3........51 D7
Pomeroy La BA14......104 B6
Pond La SN5..........19 B1
Pond St SN5..........34 F5
Ponting's Cl SN26......21 C2
Ponting St SN1........50 C7
POOLE KEYNES......5 C4
Poole Keynes House GL7..5 B4
Poole Rd SN25........34 E3
Pool Gastons Rd SN16....27 F3
Pool Gn SN13........84 E6
Poores Rd [17] SP4......198 B7
Pope Cl SN25..........34 F5
Popham Ct SN15......78 E6
Poplar Ave SN2........35 C2
Poplars The
  Chippenham SN14......70 A1
  Fovant SP3..........204 D8
  Trowbridge BA14......105 A5
Poplar Tree La BA14....104 B3
Poplar Way
  Colerne SN14........75 A5
  Salisbury SP1........146 C5
Popplechurch Dr [5] SN3..51 E7
Poppy Cl SN11........80 F4
Porchester Cl [8] SP10..193 C2
Portal Ave SN13......84 B8
Portal Cl SN15........70 C1
Portal Pl SN15........60 A1
Portal Rd SN2........35 A2
PORTASH..........201 B2
Port Down RG17......177 C7
Porte Marsh Ind Est SN11..81 C5
Porte Marsh Rd SN11....81 C5
Portfield Rd SP5......150 A4
Porth Cl [3] SN25......34 C7
Port Hill SN8........213 D5
Portland Ave
  Britford SP5........151 F5
  Swindon SN1........50 A4
Portland Way SN11....81 C2
Portman Rd SN12......94 A6
Portmore Cl SN5......34 C2
Portnell's La BA12....137 F4
PORTON............133 D6
Porton Rd SP4........217 D3
Port Regis Prep Sch SP7..202 A3
Portsmouth St SN1....50 D6
Portway
  Chippenham SN14......78 B6
  Frome BA11........110 A4
  Laverstock SP4......146 B7
  Warminster BA12......117 A7
  Winterbourne SP4......133 A3
Port Way BA13........186 A6
Portway Gdns [10] BA11..110 A4
Portway Ind Est SP10....193 B1
Portway La BA12......117 A8
Portway The SP1......145 F4
Portwell [3] SN6......19 D7
Poseidon Cl SN25......34 B6
Postmill Dr SN4......47 F1
Post Office La
  Atworth/Whitley SN12....92 F8
  Broad Hinton SN4......167 C3
  Corsham SN13........77 A1
Post Office Rd RG17....177 F3
Poston St SN4........99 D7
Pot La BA11........110 F8
Potley La SN13........84 E5
Potterdown Rd [3] SN2..35 C5
POTTERNE..........179 D5
Potterne Rd SN10......214 A1
POTTERNE WICK......179 E4
Potters Way SP1......152 D8
Pottery La RG17......177 E3
Pottle St BA12........119 A6
Pottows Field SN11....166 B1
Poulsen Cl BA12......117 A5
POULSHOT..........179 B6
Poulshot Rd SN10......179 A5
Poulton BA15........100 D5
Poulton Hill SN8......213 E4
Poulton La BA15......100 E5
Poulton St SN2........50 C8
Pouncette Cl SP4......217 D1
Pound Cl
  Lyneham SN15........60 A3
  Semington BA14......102 F6
Pound Farm Cl BA14....101 E4
Pound Hill
  Melchet Park & Plaitford
    SO51............212 F7
  St Paul Malmesbury Without
    SN16............43 A3
Pound La
  Bradford-on-Avon BA15..100 C5
  Damerham SP6........209 E3
  Melchet Park & Plaitford
    SO51............212 F7
  Semington BA14......102 E6
  Shaftesbury SP7......202 D2
  Swindon SN2........35 B2
  Wilcot SN8..........174 B2
Pound Mead SN13......84 F8

Pound Piece
Ashbury SN6 . . . . .164 A8
5 Hungerford RG17 . . . . . .177 B7
Pound Pill SN13 . . . . .77 A1
Pound Rd SN6 . . . . .22 F7
Pound Row BA12 . . . . .116 F6
Pound St
Ebbesborne Wake SP5 . . . .204 D3
Warminster BA12 . . . . .116 F6
Pound The
Bromham SN15 . . . . .96 B7
Mere BA12 . . . . .139 B5
Poveys Pl 1 SN6 . . . . .163 E6
Powell Pl 3 SN2 . . . . .34 E2
Powell Rise SN16 . . . . .28 B5
Power Rd SP4 . . . . .197 E7
Pownall Rd SP4 . . . . .198 A6
Poynder Pl SN11 . . . . .166 A6
Poynder Rd SN13 . . . . .76 E1
Poynings Way SN5 . . . . .48 F4
Prescombe Down National
  Nature Reserve★ SP5 . . .204 C4
Preshute CE Prim Sch
  SN8 . . . . .213 A1
Preshute La SN8 . . . . .213 B2
Prestbury Dr BA12 . . . . .117 C5
Prestly Wood 3 SN13 . . . . .76 B1
PRESTON
Aldbourne 170 B4
Lyneham and Bradenstoke . . .60 D1
Preston La SN15 . . . . .60 D1
Pretoria Rd 18 SP11 . . . . . .192 B5
Priddy Cl BA11 . . . . .110 C7
Prideaux Dr SP7 . . . . .202 A5
Priestley Gr SN11 . . . . .81 C2
Priestley Prim Sch SN11 . . . .81 C2
Priestly Wood Rd 6 SN13 .76 B1
Primmers Pl BA13 . . . . .108 F5
Primrose Cl
Calne SN11 . . . . .81 B5
Swindon SN2 . . . . .34 D5
Primrose Cnr BA14 . . . . . . .101 D4
Primrose Dr SN12 . . . . .94 C4
Primrose Hill
Tockenham SN4 . . . . .60 D6
Wilton SN1 . . . . .144 D4
Primrose La
Manningford SN9 . . . . .181 F6
Redlynch SP5 . . . . .211 C7
Primrose Pl 26 SP4 . . . . . .198 B7
Primrose Rd
24 Ludgershall SP11 . . . . . .192 A5
Salisbury SP2 . . . . .145 C4
Primrose Way SN14 . . . . . . .70 B2
Primrose Wlk 1 BA12 . . . . .116 E7
Prince Charles Cl 14
  SP11 . . . . .192 A5
Prince Charles Dr SN11 . . .81 C3
Princecroft La 3 BA12 . . . .116 E6
Princecroft Prim Sch
  BA12 . . . . .116 E6
Princes Cl SP5 . . . . .211 D8
Princes Hill SP5 . . . . .211 D8
Princess Anne Rd 9
  BA11 . . . . .110 A7
Princess Gdns
Trowbridge BA14 . . . . .101 C4
Warminster BA12 . . . . .117 D6
Princess Margaret Hospl
  SN3 .51 D1
Princess Mary Gdns 19
  SP11 . . . . .192 A5
Princes St 4 SN1 . . . . .50 C5
Prior Pk Prep Sch SN6 . . . . .19 E7
Priorsfield SN8 . . . . .213 E2
Prior's Hill SN4 . . . . .64 B5
Priors Wlk GL7 . . . . .2 E3
Priory Ave RG17 . . . . .177 B6
Priory Cl
Alderbury SP5 . . . . .153 F2
Bradford-on-Avon BA15 . . .100 C7
5 Hungerford RG17 . . . . . .177 B6
5 Shrewton SP3 . . . . .196 E6
Wilton SN1 . . . . .144 C2
Wilton SP2 . . . . .144 D2
Priory Coll SN1 . . . . .50 C4
Priory Gn SN6 . . . . .23 A6
Priory La SN16 . . . . .28 B2
Priory New Rd SN13 . . . . . . .76 F2
Priory Pk BA15 . . . . .100 D7
Priory Pl 1 RG17 . . . . .177 B6
Priory Rd
Hungerford RG17 . . . . .177 B6
Swindon SN3 . . . . .51 A4
Priory Sq 5 SP2 . . . . .146 A1
Priory St SN13 . . . . .76 F2
PRIORY VALE 34 C8
Pritchard Cl SN2 . . . . .35 F5
Private Rd BA11 . . . . .123 C8
Privet La SP11 . . . . .192 D2
Privet Wy 2 SN13 . . . . .84 E8
Proby Pl BA14 . . . . .102 A1
Professions Cnr SP5 . . . . . .206 D6
Pro Logis Pk SN3 . . . . .36 C6
Prospect
Box SN13 . . . . .83 B4
Corsham SN13 . . . . .85 A7
Prospect Fields SN12 . . . . .92 F8
Prospect Hill SN1 . . . . .50 C5
Prospect Pl
Bathford BA1 . . . . .82 D2
Mere BA12 . . . . .138 F5
Swindon SN1 . . . . .50 C4
Trowbridge BA14 . . . . .101 D1
Prospect Rd RG17 . . . . .177 B7

Prospect Sq 3 BA13 . . . . .109 A3
Prospero Wy
7 Swindon SN25 . . . . .34 C6
Swindon SN25 . . . . .34 D6
Proud Cl SN5 . . . . .33 B3
Providence La SN13 . . . . . . .76 F1
Providence Terr SN15 . . . . . .78 D7
Provis Mead SN5 . . . . .79 A4
Provost St 23 SP6 . . . . .210 D1
Pub La SN10 . . . . .180 F8
Pucklands SN10 . . . . .180 E5
Puck Well Nature Reserve★
  BA12 . . . . .140 C4
Puddlesloh La SP6 . . . . . . .210 C2
Pullman Dr SP2 . . . . .145 B3
Pulsar Rd 14 SN25 . . . . .34 B7
Pump La
Bathford BA1 . . . . .82 B1
Long Newnton GL8 . . . . .13 C4
Purbeck Cl SN3 . . . . .51 C7
Purbeck Pl SN11 . . . . .81 D2
Purcell Rd SN25 . . . . .34 E8
Purleigh Rd SN13 . . . . .76 E1
Purley Ave SN3 . . . . .51 B3
Purley Rd SN4 . . . . .51 F1
Purley Way S051 . . . . .212 E6
PURLPIT 93 A8
Purlpit SN12 . . . . .85 A1
Purlyn Acre SN8 . . . . .213 D4
PURTON 33 B4
PURTON COMMON 33 A5
Purton Mus★ SN5 . . . . .33 C4
Purton Rd SN2 . . . . .34 C3
PURTON STOKE 19 C1
Purvis Cl 4 SP4 . . . . .217 C3
Pyatts Cnr BA14 . . . . .178 C4
Pye La SN4 . . . . .167 A8

Q

Quadrangle The SN15 . . . . .78 C6
Quakers Rd SN10 . . . . .214 C5
Quakers Wlk SN11 . . . . .73 F7
Quantock Cl
Melksham Without SN12 . . . .94 C4
5 Warminster BA12 . . . . . .117 A8
Quarr Barton SN11 . . . . .81 B3
Quarries The SN1 . . . . .50 C3
Quarry Cl
Corston SN16 . . . . .42 E5
Winsley BA2 . . . . .99 D6
Quarry Cres SN6 . . . . .22 F6
Quarrydale Cl SN11 . . . . .81 B2
Quarry Fields Ind Est
  BA12 . . . . .138 E5
Quarry Hill SN13 . . . . .83 E6
Quarry La
Colerne SN14 . . . . .75 B3
Melbury Abbas SP7 . . . . . . .206 A7
Quarry Mews SN1 . . . . .50 C3
Quarry Rd SN1 . . . . .50 C4
Quartermaster Rd BA13 . . .108 C2
Quarterway La BA14 . . . . . .101 C1
Quavey Rd SP5 . . . . .211 D7
Quebec Rd
Bulford SP4 . . . . .217 B8
Chiseldon SN4 . . . . .168 E8
Queen Alexandra Rd
  SP2 . . . . .145 D3
Queenborough SN5 . . . . .49 C4
Queen Elizabeth Dr SN2 . . .34 C4
Queen Manor Rd
Clarendon Park SP5 . . . . . . .147 B3
Laverstock SP5 . . . . .152 E8
Queen Mary Rd SP2 . . . . . .145 D3
QUEEN OAK 138 A3
Queen Oak★ SN8 . . . . .175 C4
Queens Ave
Corsham SN13 . . . . .76 F3
Highworth SN6 . . . . .23 A6
Queen's Barrow★ BA12 . . .201 A7
Queensberry Rd
Amesbury SP4 . . . . .217 C4
Salisbury SP1 . . . . .146 A3
Queens Chase BA12 . . . . . .117 C4
Queens Cl
27 Ludgershall SP11 . . . . . .192 A5
Sutton Benger SN15 . . . . . . .57 D2
Queens Club Gdns BA14 . .105 A8
Queens Cres SN14 . . . . .78 A6
Queen's Crescent Prim Sch
  SN14 . . . . .78 A6
Queens Dr SN3 . . . . .51 B2
Queen's Dr SN3 . . . . .50 E6
Queensfield SN2 . . . . .35 D5
Queens Gdns
32 Fordingbridge SP6 . . . . .210 D1
Trowbridge BA14 . . . . .101 E4
Queens Gr BA9 . . . . .137 C3
Queens Rd
Hannington SN6 . . . . .21 F8
Mere BA12 . . . . .139 B6
Salisbury SP1 . . . . .146 B2
7 Tisbury SP3 . . . . .203 E8
Trowbridge BA14 . . . . .101 C2
Queen's Rd
Devizes SN10 . . . . .214 A2
Royal Wootton Bassett SN4 . .47 E2
Westbury BA13 . . . . .108 E3
Queens Sq
Box SN13 . . . . .83 D5
Chippenham SN15 . . . . .78 F6
Queen St
Hale SP6 . . . . .211 B5
Salisbury SP1 . . . . .146 A1

Queen St continued
Swindon SN1 . . . . .50 B6
Swindon SP2 . . . . .144 D2
QUEEN STREET 31 B3
Queensway
Andover SP10 . . . . .193 F1
Melksham SN12 . . . . .94 C4
2 Netheravon SP4 . . . . . . .190 A3
Warminster BA12 . . . . .117 D6
Queens Way SN8 . . . . .213 F2
Queintin Rd SN1 . . . . .50 D3
QUEMERFORD 89 D8
Quemerford
Calne SN11 . . . . .81 C1
Calne Without SN11 . . . . .89 D8
QUIDHAMPTON 145 A2
Quidham St SP5 . . . . .204 F2
Quilling Cl BA14 . . . . .105 E7
Quinton Pl BA12 . . . . .195 A3

R

Rabley Wood View SN8 . . .213 E4
Radcliffe Rd SP2 . . . . .152 A6
Radcot Cl SN4 . . . . .34 A1
Radley Bottom
Hungerford Newton
  RG17 . . . . .171 D2
Kintbury RG17 . . . . .177 F7
Radley Cl SN3 . . . . .51 C7
Radnor Cl SN10 . . . . .214 C2
Radnor Pk SN16 . . . . .42 E4
Radnor Pl 3 SN12 . . . . .94 A2
Radnor Rd SN3 . . . . .146 A3
Radnor St SN1 . . . . .50 A5
Radstock Ave SN3 . . . . .51 B6
Radway Rd SN3 . . . . .35 F3
Raffin La SN9 . . . . .215 C4
Raggett St SN1 . . . . .50 C5
Ragleth Gr BA14 . . . . .101 E2
Railway Cl BA13 . . . . .108 F3
Railway Village Mus★
  SN1 .50 B6
Railway Wlk 9 BA11 . . . . . .110 A4
Rainer Cl SN3 . . . . .36 B3
Rainham Rd 2 SN25 . . . . . . .34 F7
Rake Wy 10 SP11 . . . . .193 F2
Raleigh Ave SN3 . . . . .50 F6
Raleigh Cres SP4 . . . . .217 E3
RAM ALLEY 175 B2
Rambler Cl BA14 . . . . .105 A8
Rambridge Cres SP2 . . . . . .145 B5
Ramleaze Dr
Salisbury SP2 . . . . .145 C5
Swindon SN5 . . . . .49 A7
Rampart Rd SP1 . . . . .146 B1
RAMSBURY 170 A2
Ramsbury Ave SN2 . . . . .35 B6
Ramsbury Dr
Hungerford RG17 . . . . .177 C7
Old Sarum SP4 . . . . .146 B2
Ramsbury Manor★ SN8 . . .169 F1
Ramsbury Prim Sch SN8 . .170 B2
Ramsbury Terr RG17 . . . . . .177 C7
Ramsbury Wlk BA14 . . . . . .105 D6
Ramscliff SN10 . . . . .187 F7
Ramscombe La BA1 . . . . .82 A6
Ramsden Rd SN1 . . . . .48 F3
Ramsthorn Cl SN2 . . . . .34 D4
Randall Cres SN5 . . . . .49 A8
Randall's Croft SP2 . . . . . . .144 B2
Randolph Cl SN3 . . . . .50 F5
Rank The BA14 . . . . .105 C3
Rannoch Cl 4 SN5 . . . . .34 B2
Ransome Cl SN5 . . . . .49 B8
Raspberry La 8 SP7 . . . . . .202 B1
Ratcliff's Gdn 15 SP7 . . . .202 C1
Ratcoombe Rd SN5 . . . . .34 A2
RATFORD 80 E5
RATFYN 217 C5
Ratfyn Barrow★ SP4 . . . . . .217 B4
Ratfyn Rd SP4 . . . . .217 B4
Raven Cl SP9 . . . . .216 D6
Ravenglass Rd SN5 . . . . .49 C6
Ravenhurst SN16 . . . . .14 E6
Ravenscroft
7 Salisbury SP2 . . . . .152 A5
Swindon SN3 . . . . .51 C8
Ravenscroft Gdns BA14 . . .101 F1
Ravensdale 7 SN1 . . . . .50 A5
Ravensroost Wood & Mdws
  Nature Reserve★ SN16 . . .31 A5
Ravens Wlk SN4 . . . . .48 A2
Rawlence Rd
Salisbury SP2 . . . . .145 B3
Wilton SP2 . . . . .144 C2
Rawlings Cl SN3 . . . . .36 E4
Rawlings Ct SP11 . . . . .192 A5
Rawlingswell La SN8 . . . . . .213 E3
Rawlinson Rd SP4 . . . . .198 E6
Rawlins Rd SN9 . . . . .215 C5
Rawston Cl SN3 . . . . .51 C6
Raybrook Cres SN2 . . . . .49 E6
Ray Cl
Chippenham SN15 . . . . .78 F5
Swindon SN25 . . . . .35 A4
Rayfield Gr SN2 . . . . .50 B8
Reading St 4 SN1 . . . . .50 B6
Read St SN1 . . . . .50 A5
Rea Rd SN13 . . . . .84 F6
Recreation Rd
10 Durrington/Bulford
  SP4 . . . . .198 B7
Ludgershall SP11 . . . . .192 A6

Rectory Cl
Alton SN8 . . . . .181 C8
Overtown SN4 . . . . .64 E3
Stanton St Quintin SN14 . . . .56 B4
11 Warminster BA12 . . . . . .117 A8
Rectory Hill SP5 . . . . .155 F3
Rectory La
Alderbury SP5 . . . . .153 E2
Breamore SP6 . . . . .210 E5
Charlton Musgrove BA9 . . . .136 B1
Cricklade SN6 . . . . .19 E8
Letcombe Bassett OX12 . . . .165 F8
Rectory Pl 4 SP11 . . . . .192 F1
Rectory Rd
Alderbury SP5 . . . . .153 E2
Salisbury SP2 . . . . .151 F8
Sutton Mandeville SP3 . . . . .204 C7
Rectory Wood 1 SN8 . . . . .170 A6
Reculver Way 6 SP10 . . . .193 C2
Redbridge Cl 1 SN1 . . . . . .49 F4
Redcap Gdns SN5 . . . . .49 A7
Redcliffe St SN2 . . . . .49 F6
Red Cross House★ SN10 . .214 B4
REDENHAM 192 D4
Redenham Dro SP11 . . . . . .192 E4
Redford Cl SP11 . . . . .146 D3
Red Gables Cl SN5 . . . . .33 A3
Redgrave Cl BA14 . . . . .105 D6
Redhill Cl SN11 . . . . .79 F2
Redhills SN4 . . . . .62 B1
Redhorn Gdns SN10 . . . . . .214 B2
Red House Cl SP7 . . . . .202 A5
Redhouse Gdns 2 SN25 . . .34 D7
Redhouse Way SN25 . . . . . . .34 D7
Redhouse Wy SN25 . . . . .34 D7
Red La
Mildenhall SN8 . . . . .169 B2
Sixpenny Handley SP5 . . . . .208 A3
Redland SN14 . . . . .78 B8
Redland La BA13 . . . . .108 F2
Redland Prim Sch SN14 . . .78 B8
REDLANDS 22 F3
Redlands 3 BA13 . . . . .186 B7
Redlands Cl SN6 . . . . .23 A4
Red Lion La SN6 . . . . .19 E8
Red Lion Mews SN6 . . . . . . .23 A6
Red Lodge Cl SN4 . . . . .61 E8
REDLYNCH 211 D8
Redlynch Cl SN2 . . . . .35 C5
Redman Rd SN11 . . . . .81 C6
Redmans La SP7 . . . . .206 A7
Redposts Dr SN1 . . . . .49 E4
Redruth Cl SN3 . . . . .51 B5
REDSTOCKS 95 A2
Redstocks La SN12 . . . . .95 A2
Red Way The BA12 . . . . .115 F3
Redwing Ave SN14 . . . . .70 B2
Redwing Rd SN12 . . . . .94 D5
Redwood Way SN14 . . . . .75 A8
Redworth Dr SP4 . . . . .217 C2
Redworth Wlk SP4 . . . . .217 C2
Reed Ct SN3 . . . . .36 C1
Reeds SN6 . . . . .19 C8
Reeds Farm Rd SN16 . . . . . .28 A4
Reeds Gd SN8 . . . . .213 F3
Reed Wlk 10 SP4 . . . . .198 C7
Reeves Cl 2 SN3 . . . . .51 C4
Reeves Piece 14 BA13 . . . .186 B7
Reeves Rd SN10 . . . . .214 D1
Regent Circus 6 SN1 . . . . .50 C5
Regent Cl
15 Hungerford RG17 . . . . . .177 B7
Swindon SN1 . . . . .50 C6
Regents Pl
Bradford-on-Avon BA15 . . .100 D5
Studley Green BA14 . . . . . . .104 F6
Reid's Piece SN5 . . . . .33 B3
Reith Way 2 SP10 . . . . . . .193 B1
Rendall's Barn GL7 . . . . .4 E5
Rendells Ct SN10 . . . . .214 B3
Renoir Cl SN25 . . . . .35 A8
RESTROP 33 A2
Restrop Rd SN5 . . . . .33 A3
Restrop View SN5 . . . . .33 A4
Retingham Way SN2 . . . . . . .36 A5
Reto Gr BA15 . . . . .99 F3
Retreat The
Frome BA11 . . . . .110 B4
Highworth SN6 . . . . .22 F4
Revell Cl SN2 . . . . .35 E4
REYBRIDGE 86 D7
Reynolds Ct 4 SP10 . . . . . .193 D1
Reynolds Rise 18 SP7 . . . .202 D1
Reynolds Way SN25 . . . . . . .35 A8
Rhine Cl SN1 . . . . .49 F4
Rhuddlan SN5 . . . . .49 B6
Ricardo Rd SN15 . . . . .78 D8
Richard Jefferies Mus★
  SN3 .51 B2
Richards Cl SN4 . . . . .47 D1
Richards Dr SN4 . . . . .66 E1
Richards Way SP2 . . . . .151 E7
Richard Webb Mews SN1 . .50 B3
Richborough Dr 3 SP10 . .193 C2
Richmond Cl 2 BA14 . . . . .105 A7
Richmond Cres SP9 . . . . . . .216 E6
Richmond Ct SN6 . . . . .6 F1
Richmond Rd
Calne Without SN11 . . . . .81 A4
2 Salisbury SP2 . . . . .145 D3
Rickbarton 2 SN10 . . . . . . .187 E7
Rickfield SN15 . . . . .100 B6
Rickworth Pl BA12 . . . . .195 A3
Rickyard The 9 SP7 . . . . . .202 D1
RIDGE 200 F2

Ridge Gn SN5 . . . . .49 B7
Ridgemead SN11 . . . . .81 B4
Ridge Nether Moor SN3 . . . .51 D2
RIDGE THE 85 B5
Ridge The
Broad Blunsdon SN26 . . . . . .21 B2
Redlynch SP5 . . . . .211 C7
Ridgeway SP3 . . . . .201 A3
Ridge Way SP7 . . . . .202 C3
Ridgeway Cl SN2 . . . . .34 F2
Ridgeway Ct BA12 . . . . .117 B6
Ridgeway La SN5 . . . . .44 E1
Ridgeway Rd
Salisbury SP1 . . . . .146 B2
Swindon SN2 . . . . .35 E5
Ridgeway Sch The SN4 . . . .64 B7
Ridgeway The
Chiseldon SN4 . . . . .65 D2
Crudwell SN16 . . . . .14 E6
Liddington SN4 . . . . .163 A2
Warminster BA12 . . . . .117 B6
Ridgmount 6 SP4 . . . . .198 B7
Ridings Mead SN14 . . . . .70 C2
Ridings The SN14 . . . . .70 A8
Rifles La SP7 . . . . .202 D1
Rigel Cl SN25 . . . . .34 C7
Rigsby's La SN16 . . . . .16 F5
Ringsbury Camp★ SN5 . . . .32 E2
Ringsbury Cl SN5 . . . . .32 F3
Ringwood Ave 5 SP4 . . . . .217 C3
Ringwood Cl SN3 . . . . .51 B6
Ringwood Rd 27 SP6 . . . . .210 D1
Rinsdale Cl SN5 . . . . .34 B1
Ripley Rd SN1 . . . . .50 C4
Ripon Cl SN14 . . . . .78 A5
Ripon Way SN3 . . . . .51 A3
Ripple Field SN5 . . . . .49 B4
Rise The SN11 . . . . .89 C8
Risingham Mead SN5 . . . . . .49 C5
RIVAR 184 F8
Rivar Rd SN8 . . . . .176 F1
Rivenhall Rd SN5 . . . . .49 C5
Riverbourne Rd
Laverstock SP1 . . . . .146 D1
Salisbury SP1 . . . . .152 D8
Riverdale Cl
9 Fordingbridge SP6 . . . . .210 D1
Swindon SN1 . . . . .50 C2
Riverdale Wlk SN1 . . . . .50 C2
Rivergate SN5 . . . . .49 C8
Rivermead SP4 . . . . .133 F8
Rivermead Dr SN5 . . . . .49 C7
Rivermead Ind Est SN5 . . . .49 C7
River Mead Sch SN12 . . . . .94 B5
River Par SN5 . . . . .78 D7
River Pk SN8 . . . . .213 D2
River Ray Ind Est SN2 . . . . .49 E7
Riverside
Calne SN11 . . . . .89 D8
Wilton SP2 . . . . .144 D3
Riverside Cl
Salisbury SP1 . . . . .146 D2
South Newton SP2 . . . . .130 A4
Riverside Dr
Chippenham SN15 . . . . .79 A8
Melksham SN12 . . . . .94 A6
Riverside Pk SN15 . . . . .44 A2
Riverside Pl SP6 . . . . .210 E1
Riverside Rd SP1 . . . . .146 D2
Riverside Terr SP3 . . . . .129 E7
Rivers Reach 6 BA11 . . . . .110 A4
River St
Chippenham SN15 . . . . .78 E7
Pewsey SN9 . . . . .215 C5
Rivers Way SN6 . . . . .22 F6
River Way
5 Durrington/Bulford
  SP4 . . . . .198 C7
South Cerney GL7 . . . . .6 F7
Trowbridge BA14 . . . . .101 C1
Roach's La GL9 . . . . .38 C1
Road Hill
Box SN13 . . . . .82 E8
Colerne SN14 . . . . .74 D1
Robbers' Stone★ SN10 . . .187 E6
Robbins Ridge SP4 . . . . . . .217 C3
Robert Franklin Way 7 GL7 . .7 A7
Robert Le Kyng Prim Sch
  SN1 .50 A5
Roberts Cl SN4 . . . . .64 B5
Roberts of Kandahar Rd
  BA12 . . . . .113 F1
Roberts Rd
North Tidworth SP11 . . . . . .192 A5
Salisbury SP2 . . . . .145 D3
Robin Cl BA12 . . . . .117 C6
Robin Hill La SP4 . . . . .217 C6
Robin Hood's Ball★ SP4 . .189 C1
Robin Hood's Bower★
  BA12 . . . . .117 B1
Robinia Cl SN9 . . . . .215 D5
Robin Rd SP4 . . . . .132 C4
Robins Cl
Chippenham SN14 . . . . .70 B4
Royal Wootton Bassett SN4 . .48 A2
Swindon SN3 . . . . .51 D7
Robinsgreen SN3 . . . . .51 D7
Robins Hill RG17 . . . . .177 F3
Robinson Cl SN3 . . . . .51 D6
Rochdale Ave SN11 . . . . .81 B4
Roche Cl SN3 . . . . .51 D4
Rochelle Ct 19 SN10 . . . . . .179 F1
Rocher Cl BA13 . . . . .108 F3
Rochester Cl 5 SN5 . . . . . . .49 B4
Rochford Cl SN5 . . . . .49 B6
ROCKBOURNE 210 A5
Rockbourne La SP6 . . . . . . .209 F3
Rockbourne Mus★ SP6 . . .210 A3

Rockbourne Roman Villa★
SP6 .210 A4
Rockdown Ct SN2 . . . . .35 D4
Rocker Bench SN6 . . . . . .163 E6
Rockfel Rd RG17 . . . . . . .165 A1
Rockfield SN14 . . . . .75 B3
Rock La BA12 . . . . .117 D6
ROCKLEY 168 C2
Rockley Rd SN8 . . . . .213 C7
Rockmoor La SP11 . . . . . .185 C5
Rock Rd BA14 . . . . .105 B7
RODBOURNE
  St Paul Malmesbury
  Without 43 A3
  Swindon 35 A1
RODBOURNE BOTTOM 43 A2
RODBOURNE CHENEY 35 B2
Rodbourne Cheney Prim Sch
  SN25 . . . . .35 A5
Rodbourne House SN16 . . .43 B4
Rodbourne Rd
  St Paul Malmesbury Without
  SN16 . . . . .42 F4
  Swindon SN2 . . . . .49 F7
Roddenbury Cl BA11 . . . . .110 B5
Roddenbury View BA12 . . .115 A8
Rodden Manor★ BA11 . . . 110 D4
Rodden Rd BA11 . . . . .110 A5
Rode Bridge★ BA11 . . . . .103 E1
RODE HILL 103 F1
Rode Hill BA11 . . . . .103 F1
Rode Tropical Bird Gdns★
  BA11 . . . . .103 D2
RODMARTON 3 C8
Rodney Ct SP10 . . . . .193 F1
Rodsleigh BA14 . . . . .104 F6
Rodway 13 SN4 . . . . .163 A6
Rodway Cl BA14 . . . . .101 E2
Rodwell Cl 3 SN3 . . . . . . .51 A4
Rodwell Pk BA14 . . . . . . .101 E2
Roebuck Cl SN4 . . . . .47 F2
Roger Penny Way SP6 . . .211 C3
Rogers Cl
  Quidhampton SP2 . . . . . .145 A3
  Swindon SN3 . . . . .51 A4
Rogers Meadow SN8 . . . . .213 D5
Rogers's La RG17 . . . . . . .171 D7
Roger Wy
  Old Sarum SP4 . . . . .146 C8
  8 Winterbourne SP4 . . . .132 C1
ROLLESTONE 196 F6
ROLLESTONE CAMP 197 B7
Rollestone Rd SP3 . . . . . .196 E6
Rollestone St 1 SP1 . . . . .146 B1
Rolleston St 1 SN1 . . . . . .50 C5
Roman Cres SN1 . . . . .50 B3
Roman Meadow SP5 . . . . .211 A8
Roman Rd SP2 . . . . .145 D2
Roman Way
  Andover SP10 . . . . .193 E2
  Chippenham SN15 . . . . . . .79 B5
  Highworth SN6 . . . . .22 F5
  Lechlade GL7 . . . . .2 D5
  15 Market Lavington SN10 179 F1
Roman Way Prim Sch
  SP10 . . . . .193 E2
Roman Wy
  Warminster BA12 . . . . . . .112 F1
  Warminster BA12 . . . . . . .116 F8
Romer Rd SP2 . . . . .152 A6
Romney Cl BA12 . . . . .116 D7
Romney Rd 23 SP11 . . . . .193 F2
Romney Way SN5 . . . . .49 A6
Romsey Rd
  Amesbury SP11 . . . . .217 D2
  Whiteparish SP5 . . . . . . .162 B3
Romsey St SN2 . . . . .49 F7
Ron Golding Cl SN16 . . . . .28 A5
ROOD ASHTON 106 D4
Rookery Cottages SP5 . . .155 F4
Rookery La
  Ansty SP3 . . . . .203 F6
  Breamore SP6 . . . . .210 D5
  Swallowcliffe SP3 . . . . . .204 A6
Rookery Meadow SN8 . . . .174 A6
Rookery Pk SN11 . . . . .89 C7
Rookes La SN10 . . . . .179 D5
Rooks La BA11 . . . . .110 E6
Rooks Nest SN15 . . . . .78 F4
Rook St BA12 . . . . .139 A4
ROOK STREET 139 A4
Rookwood Gdns 9 SP6 . . .210 C1
Ropewind SN8 . . . . .176 F1
Rope Wlk SN12 . . . . .94 B3
Rope Yd SN4 . . . . .47 D1
Rosary The SN4 . . . . .47 E2
Rosebery St SN1 . . . . .50 D7
Rosebrock Gdns SN12 . . . .94 C3
Rosedale Gdns BA14 . . . . .101 A1
Rosedale Rd SN3 . . . . .51 B4
Rosefield Way BA13 . . . . .108 F4
Rosehill Cl SN15 . . . . .59 D3
Roseland Ave SN10 . . . . . .214 C3
Rosemary Cl
  Calne SN11 . . . . .80 F4
  Great Bedwyn SN8 . . . . .176 B3
  Laverstock SP1 . . . . .146 D1
  Swindon SN2 . . . . .34 D5
Rosemary La
  Freshford BA2 . . . . .99 B4
  2 Salisbury SP1 . . . . . . .152 A8
Rosemary Wy SN2 . . . . .34 D5
Rosenheim Rise 1 BA13 .186 B7
Rose St SN2 . . . . .49 F7
Rosetta Ct 6 SN25 . . . . . . .34 B7
Rosewood Ct SN3 . . . . .51 D3
Rossett Gdns BA14 . . . . . .105 A8
Ross Gdns SN2 . . . . .36 A4

Ross Rd SP4 . . . . .197 E7
Rother Cl SN25 . . . . .34 F5
Rothe Rise SN10 . . . . .108 F1
Rotherstone SN10 . . . . . . .214 A4
Rotten Row SN4 . . . . .163 A6
Rougemont Cl SP1 . . . . . .146 B1
Roughmoor Way SN5 . . . . .34 A1
Rough St SN13 . . . . .84 F5
Roundaway La SP11 . . . . .193 A5
Round Barrow SN14 . . . . . .75 B3
Round Hill 25 SP6 . . . . . .210 D1
Round Hill★ SN14 . . . . . . .67 A7
Roundhills Mead SN6 . . . . .23 B6
Round House SN11 . . . . . . .81 D1
Roundpond SN12 . . . . .93 F6
Roundponds SN12 . . . . . . .93 F6
Roundstone St BA14 . . . . .101 D1
ROUNDWAY 214 D7
Roundway Cl SN11 . . . . . . .89 B1
Roundway Down SN5 . . . . .49 B3
Roundway Gdns SN10 . . . .214 B6
Roundway Ind Est SN10 . .214 C5
Roundway Pk SN10 . . . . . .214 C6
Roundwood View SN5 . . . . .58 A3
Rovers Farm & Visitor Ctr★
  SN6 . . . . .37 B6
Roves La SN6 . . . . .23 B1
Rowan Cl
  Colerne SN14 . . . . .75 A5
  5 Durrington/Bulford SP4 198 B1
  Salisbury SP2 . . . . .145 B4
Rowan Ct
  Frome BA11 . . . . .110 B7
  Melksham SN12 . . . . .94 A3
Rowan Dr
  Bishops Cannings SN10 . . .214 F6
  Royal Wootton Bassett SN4 .47 E1
Rowan Rd SN2 . . . . .35 A3
Rowans The SN16 . . . . .27 F4
Rowbarrow SP2 . . . . .152 B5
Rowbarrow Cl 3 SP2 . . . . .152 B5
Rowbarrow La 4 SP2 . . . .152 B5
ROWDE 96 D2
Rowde CE Prim Acad
  SN10 . . . . .96 E2
Rowde Ct Rd SN10 . . . . . . .96 D1
Rowdeford Sch SN10 . . . . .96 D3
Rowden Hill SN15 . . . . .78 C6
Rowden La
  Bradford-on-Avon BA15 . . 100 D4
  Chippenham SN15 . . . . . . .78 C5
Rowden Rd SN15 . . . . .78 C6
Rowe Mead SN15 . . . . .78 E5
Rowe's Hill BA12 . . . . .119 C8
Row La SN12 . . . . .178 C7
Rowland Hill Cl SN3 . . . . . .51 E4
Rowlands Cl BA1 . . . . .82 B2
Rowley Medieval Village of★
  BA15 . . . . .99 F1
Rowley Pl SN12 . . . . .94 B4
Row The SP5 . . . . .211 C8
Rowton Heath Way SN5 . . .49 A4
Royal Cescent The SP9 . . .216 C7
Royal Cres SP9 . . . . .216 D7
Royal Field Cl SN14 . . . . . .55 E8
Royal Oak Cl SN15 . . . . . . .78 F6
ROYAL WOOTTON
  BASSETT 47 C2
Royal Wootton Bassett Acad
  SN4 . . . . .47 D3
Royal Wootton Bassett Inf
  Sch SN4 . . . . .47 C1
Royal Wootton Bassett Mus★
  SN4 . . . . .47 D1
Royce Cl 5 SP10 . . . . .193 B1
Royston Rd SN3 . . . . .51 A4
Rubens Cl 2 SN25 . . . . . . .34 F8
Ruckley Gdns SN3 . . . . . . .36 B2
RUDGE 107 D5
Rudge Hill BA11 . . . . .107 C5
Rudge La
  Beckington BA11 . . . . . . .107 B6
  Wilcot SN8 . . . . .174 B1
Rudge Rd BA11 . . . . .107 B2
RUDLOE 76 B1
Rumble Dene SN15 . . . . . . .78 C5
Rune Dr 4 SP10 . . . . .193 D2
RUSHALL 181 E2
Rushall CE Prim Sch
  SN9 . . . . .181 E3
Rushall Cl SN2 . . . . .35 B5
Rushall Dro SN9 . . . . .181 D1
Rushall Rd SN9 . . . . .181 F3
Rushcroft Cl SN16 . . . . . . .28 F1
Rushey La BA15 . . . . .91 F3
Rushmead La SN14 . . . . . . .66 A3
Rushmere Path SN25 . . . . .34 E5
Rushmore Pk★ SP5 . . . . . .207 C5
Rushton Rd SN3 . . . . .51 A3
Rushworth Row SP4 . . . . .217 C4
Rushy Platt Ind Est SN5 . .49 E4
Rushy Platt Nature Reserve★
  SN1 . . . . .49 F4
Ruskin Ave
  Melksham SN12 . . . . .94 A4
  Swindon SN2 . . . . .35 F3
Ruskin Dr
  Royal Wootton Bassett
  SN4 . . . . .47 F3
  Warminster BA12 . . . . . . .116 D6
Ruskin Jun Sch SN2 . . . . . .35 F4
Russel Cl GL9 . . . . .24 B4
Russell Mill La SN10 . . . . .179 D1
Russell Rd SP2 . . . . .145 E2
Russell St SP2 . . . . .144 D3
Russell Wlk SN3 . . . . .50 E6
Russet Ave GL7 . . . . .2 E3

Russet Ct BA12 . . . . .116 F7
Russley Cl SN5 . . . . .33 F1
Russley Gn 3 SN8 . . . . . . .164 C1
Russley Pk★ SN8 . . . . . . .164 A3
Rusty La SN12 . . . . .178 E8
Rutland Cl SN12 . . . . .94 C3
Rutland Cres BA14 . . . . . .105 C6
Rutland Rd 1 SN3 . . . . .50 F5
Rutter Cl 16 SP7 . . . . .202 D1
Rutts La 3 SN10 . . . . .187 E7
Ruxley Cl SN4 . . . . .47 D1
Ryan Ave SN14 . . . . .78 A7
Ryan Cl SN5 . . . . .34 B2
Rybury Camp (Hill Fort)★
  SN10 . . . . .173 A2
Rycote Cl SN5 . . . . .49 A6
Rydal Cl SN25 . . . . .34 F5
Rye Cl SN5 . . . . .49 A7
Ryeland Way BA14 . . . . . .105 E7
Ryeland Wy 26 SP11 . . . . .193 D2
Ryeleaze SN10 . . . . .179 D5
Rye Wy 14 SP11 . . . . .193 F2
Rylands Way SN4 . . . . .47 E2
Rylane SN1 . . . . .50 B1
Ryles La SN8 . . . . .174 B6
Ryon Cl 11 SP10 . . . . .193 E2
Rysy Ct 3 SN25 . . . . .34 E6

S

Sabis International Sch UK
  SN14 . . . . .74 C4
Sack Hill BA12 . . . . .113 F1
Sackville St 6 SN3 . . . . . . .50 F7
Saddleback Cl SN11 . . . . . .81 C2
Saddleback La SN10 . . . . .179 E5
Saddleback Rd SN5 . . . . . . .49 A7
Saddlers Mead SP2 . . . . . .144 C3
Saddlers Mews SP11 . . . . .192 D1
Saddlers Way SN8 . . . . . . .183 D7
Sadlers Mead SN15 . . . . . .78 E8
Sadlers Rd RG17 . . . . .177 C3
Sadler Wlk SN3 . . . . .50 F3
Saffron Cl
  Royal Wootton Bassett
  SN4 . . . . .47 E4
  2 Swindon SN2 . . . . .34 E1
Saffron Meadows SN11 . . . .80 F3
Sage Cl SN3 . . . . .34 D5
St Albans Cl
  Salisbury SP1 . . . . .146 D5
  Swindon SN2 . . . . .49 E7
St Aldhelm Rd BA15 . . . . .100 E5
St Aldhelms Cl SN16 . . . . . .27 F4
St Aldhelms Rd SN16 . . . . .27 F4
St Alphege Gdns 7
  SP10 . . . . .193 D1
St Ambrose Cl SN3 . . . . . . .51 E6
ST ANDREW RIDGE 35 A8
St Andrews St 1 . . . . .146 D2
St Andrew's CE VA Prim Sch
  SP1 . . . . .146 E3
St Andrews Cl SN4 . . . . . . .64 B7
St Andrew's Cl
  Wilton SN3 . . . . .144 B2
  Wooton Rivers SN8 . . . . .174 F1
St Andrews Rd
  Tidworth SP9 . . . . .216 C6
  Warminster BA12 . . . . . .116 D6
St Andrew's Rd
  Melksham SN12 . . . . .94 C5
  Salisbury SP2 . . . . .145 C2
  South Newton SP2 . . . . .130 B2
St Annes Cl SP4 . . . . .217 C4
St Ann Pl SP1 . . . . .152 B8
St Ann St SP1 . . . . .152 B8
St Arild's Rd GL9 . . . . .24 B4
St Athan Cl BA14 . . . . .178 B4
St Augustines Cath Coll
  BA14 . . . . .105 B8
St Augustine's Rd 5
  BA14 . . . . .105 B8
St Austell Way SN5 . . . . . . .49 F6
St Barnabas CE Sch
  SN10 . . . . .179 F1
St Bartholomew's CE Prim
  Sch SN4 . . . . .47 E2
St Bartholomew's St SP7 203 B4
St Bedes Cl SP1 . . . . .146 D5
St Birinus Gdns SP10 . . . .193 D2
St Birinus Rd 4 SP5 . . . . .211 C7
St Birstan Gdns 9 SP10 . .193 D1
St Brendans Cl SP1 . . . . . .146 C5
St Catherines Cl SN11 . . . .81 C4
St Catherines RC Prim Sch
  SN2 . . . . .35 F5
St Christophers Cl 4
  SP1 . . . . .146 D5
St Clair Rd SP2 . . . . .152 B6
St Clements Ct SN3 . . . . . .51 A4
St Clements Way SP1 . . . .146 C5
St Davids Cl SP1 . . . . .146 D5
St David's Way SN8 . . . . . .213 D3
St Dennis Rd 7 SN16 . . . . .28 A3
St Dunstan CE Prim Sch
  SN11 . . . . .81 C4
St Dunstan Cl SN11 . . . . . .81 B5
ST EDITH'S 96 D5
St Edith's Cl SP2 . . . . .144 C1
St Edith's Marsh SN15 . . . .96 D5
St Edmund's Church St 2
  SP1 . . . . .146 B1
St Edmund's Girls' Sch
  SP1 . . . . .146 E3
St Edmund's RC Prim Sch
  SN11 . . . . .81 C5

St Edwards 12 SP7 . . . . . .202 C2
St Edwards Meadow SP4 133 B2
St Edwards Sch SO51 . . . .162 B2
Saintes Cl SP1 . . . . .146 D5
St Francis Ave SN15 . . . . . .78 C6
St Francis CE VA Prim Sch
  SN25 . . . . .34 C5
St Francis Rd SP1 . . . . . . .146 A4
St Francis Sch SN9 . . . . . .215 B6
St George's CE Prim Schl
  BA14 . . . . .102 E6
St Georges CE Sch SP8 . .137 E1
St George's Cl
  Ogbourne St George SN8 .169 A5
  Warminster BA12 . . . . . .117 E5
St Georges Pl BA14 . . . . . .102 E5
St Georges RC Prim Sch
  BA12 . . . . .117 D5
St Georges Rd
  35 Fordingbridge SP6 . . .210 D1
  Tidworth SP9 . . . . .216 C6
St George's Rd
  Salisbury SP2 . . . . 151 D7
  Semington BA14 . . . . . . .102 E5
  11 Shaftesbury SP7 . . . .202 C1
St Giles Cl SN16 . . . . .29 A2
St Gregory's Ave SP2 . . . .145 D2
St Helens Gdns SN4 . . . . . .64 B5
St Helens View SN1 . . . . . .49 F4
St Ives Cl SN3 . . . . .51 B7
ST JAMES 202 C1
St James Cl SN15 . . . . .59 A7
St James Cl SN2 . . . . .35 D5
St James Gdns SN10 . . . . .214 B4
St James's Cl SP1 . . . . . . .146 D5
St James's St SP7 . . . . . . .202 B1
St John Rd SN4 . . . . .64 A6
St Johns Alley SN10 . . . . .214 A3
St John's Catholic Prim Sch
  BA14 . . . . .105 B8
St John's CE Prim Sch
  SP3 . . . . .203 D8
St John's CE Sch BA12 . .117 C6
St Johns Churchyard
  SN10 . . . . .214 A3
St Johns Cl
  Pewsey SN9 . . . . .215 D5
  19 Tisbury SP3 . . . . .203 E8
St John's Cl
  Donhead St Mary SP7 . . .203 A1
  Marlborough SN8 . . . . . .213 D4
  2 Salisbury SP1 . . . . . . .152 D8
St John's Cres BA14 . . . . .104 F6
St Johns Ct SN10 . . . . . . .214 A3
St John's Ct SP2 . . . . .144 C3
St John's Hill 7 SP7 . . . . .202 B1
St John's Marlborough
  SN8 . . . . .213 D1
St John's Priory Pk GL7 . . .2 E3
St John's Rd
  Frome BA11 . . . . .110 B5
  Warminster BA12 . . . . . .117 C5
St John's St
  Devizes SN10 . . . . .214 A3
  Lechlade GL7 . . . . .2 C4
  Malmesbury SN16 . . . . . . .28 B2
  Salisbury SP1 . . . . .152 B8
St John's Wy SN16 . . . . . . .29 A6
St Joseph's Catholic College
  SN3 . . . . .50 E7
St Joseph's Catholic Prim
  Sch SN10 . . . . .179 D8
St Joseph's Catholic Sch
  SP1 . . . . .146 E3
St Josephs Cl SP1 . . . . . . .146 C4
St Joseph's Dr SN15 . . . . . .78 C6
St Josephs RC Prim Sch
  SN16 . . . . .28 B3
St Josephs Wy SN15 . . . . . .60 B2
St Judes Cl SP1 . . . . .146 D4
St Julians Cl SN3 . . . . .36 E4
St Just Cl SP4 . . . . .199 B3
ST KATHARINES 175 F4
St Katharine's CE (VC) Prim
  Sch SN8 . . . . .175 E3
St Katherine Gn 2 SN3 . . . .51 E7
St Katherines SN4 . . . . . . .167 C6
St Katherine's Pl 17 SN4 .163 A6
St Laurence CE Prim Sch
  GL7 . . . . .2 D3
St Laurence Rd BA15 . . . .100 E5
St Laurence Sch BA15 . . .100 C7
St Lawrence Cl SP15 . . . . .145 E5
St Lawrence Cres 6
  SP7 . . . . .202 C2
St Lawrence Rd GL7 . . . . . .2 C4
St Lawrence Sq
  31 Hungerford RG17 . . . .177 B7
  8 Hungerford RG17 . . . . .177 B7
St Leonard's Cl SN16 . . . . .16 D3
St Leonard's CE Prim Acad
  SN26 . . . . .21 C1
St Leonard's Church★
  BA12 . . . . .194 A4
St Leonards Cl SN16 . . . . . .16 D3
St Leonard's Cl SP4 . . . . .217 D8
St Lukes Cl 8 SP1 . . . . . . .146 D5
St Lukes Dr SN15 . . . . .78 C6
St Luke's Sch SN2 . . . . .35 D5
St Margarets Cl SN11 . . . . .81 A4
St Margaret's Cl 2 SP1 . . .152 C8
St Margarets Gdns SN15 . .78 C6
St Margaret's Gdns SN12 . .94 C5
St Margaret's Grn 1 SN3 . .36 B2
St Margaret's Hill 1

St Margaret's Mead SN8 .213 F2
St Margaret's Pl 2 BA15 100 D6
St Margarets Ret Pk SN4 .36 D2
St Margaret's Rd SN1 . . . . .50 D3
St Margaret's St 100 D6
St Margaret's Villas 3
  BA15 . . . . .100 C6
St Mark's Ave SP1 . . . . . . .146 B3
St Marks CE Jun Sch
  SP1 . . . . .146 B3
St Mark's Rd SP1 . . . . .146 B2
St Martins SN8 . . . . .213 E3
St Martin's CE VA Prim Sch
  SP1 . . . . .152 C8
St Martin's Chapel★
  SN8 . . . . .176 C4
St Martin's Church St 5
  SP1 . . . . .152 B8
St Martins Cl SP3 . . . . . . .143 A4
St Martin's Cl SP3 . . . . . . .143 A4
St Mary's Ave SN8 . . . . . . .213 E3
St Marys Cath Prim Sch
  SN2 . . . . .35 A1
St Mary's CE Inf Sch SN8 213 E2
St Marys CE Prim Sch
  Broughton Gifford SN12 . . .93 B3
  Purton SN5 . . . . .33 C4
  Steeple Ashton BA14 . . . .178 A3
St Mary's Church (remains
  of)★ SP2 . . . . .206 A5
St Mary's Cl
  Chitterne BA12 . . . . .195 D6
  Dinton SP3 . . . . .201 E2
  Kempsford GL7 . . . . .10 E6
  Lyneham SN15 . . . . .59 C3
  Potterne SN10 . . . . .179 D5
  Redlynch SP5 . . . . .211 D7
  Sixpenny Handley SP5 . .208 A4
  Trowbridge BA14 . . . . . .101 E4
  Wilton SP2 . . . . .144 C1
  1 Wylye BA12 . . . . .201 E8
St Mary's Ct BA12 . . . . . . .112 C4
St Marys Field GL7 . . . . . . .1 A5
St Marys Gdns SN10 . . . . .214 B4
St Marys Gdns BA14 . . . . .101 E4
St Marys Gr SN2 . . . . .35 B1
St Marys La
  Dilton Marsh BA13 . . . . .108 B1
  Westbury BA13 . . . . .112 C8
St Mary's La 2 SN16 . . . . . .28 A3
St Mary's Pl SN15 . . . . .78 D8
St Mary's RC Prim Sch
  SN15 . . . . .78 C6
St Mary's Rd
  Dinton SP3 . . . . .201 E2
  Frome BA11 . . . . .110 B5
  12 Market Lavington SN10 179 F1
  Salisbury SP2 . . . . .151 F7
St Mary's Sch
  Calne SN11 . . . . .81 B3
  Coombe SP7 . . . . .202 B1
St Mary's St 1 SN16 . . . . . .28 A3
St Mary St SN15 . . . . .78 E7
St Matthews Cl
  Rowde SN10 . . . . .96 D2
  6 Salisbury SP1 . . . . . . .146 D5
St Mellion Cl SN15 . . . . . . .78 F7
St Michael's Ave SN6 . . . . .22 E6
St Michael's CE Aided Prim
  Sch SN8 . . . . .170 A6
St Michael's CE Prim Sch
  SP4 . . . . .190 B2
St Michaels Cl
  Lyneham & Bradenstoke
  SN15 . . . . .59 F4
  Tidworth SP9 . . . . .216 C5
St Michael's Cl
  8 Aldbourne SN8 . . . . . .170 A6
  Brinkworth SN15 . . . . . . .45 E6
  3 Lambourn RG17 . . . . .165 A1
  Trowbridge BA14 . . . . . .102 A3
  Wilton SP2 . . . . .144 B1
St Michael's Rd
  Melksham SN12 . . . . .94 C4
  Salisbury SP2 . . . . .145 C4
St Michaels Vw BA12 . . . .138 F5
St Michael's Way SP9 . . . .216 E7
St Nicholas CE Prim Sch
  SP4 . . . . .133 E6
St Nicholas CE VC Prim Sch
  SN15 . . . . .96 A7
St Nicholas Cl
  Calne SN11 . . . . .81 C4
  11 Ludgershall SP11 . . . .192 B5
  Trowbridge BA14 . . . . . .105 D3
  Wilton SP2 . . . . .144 B1
  Winsley BA15 . . . . .99 D7
St Nicholas' Rd SP1 . . . . . .152 A7
St Nicholas Sch SN14 . . . . .70 C2
St Osmund's Catholic Prim
  Sch SP1 . . . . .152 A7
St Osmund's Cl SP1 . . . . . .146 A5
St Patricks Ave SP9 . . . . . .216 B5
St Patrick's Catholic Prim
  Sch SN13 . . . . .77 A1
St Paul's Dr SN3 . . . . .51 E6
St Paul's Rd SP2 . . . . .145 F1
St Paul's St SN12 . . . . .35 C1
St Paul St SN15 . . . . .78 D8
St Peter's CE Prim Sch
  Appleshaw SP11 . . . . . . .192 E4
  Chippenham SN14 . . . . . . .78 A8
St Peter's CE VA Prim Sch
  SN8 . . . . .213 E3

St Peter's Church★ SP3 127 D4
St Peters Cl
  Chippenham SN15..........78 C6
  5 Shipton Bellinger SP9 . 199 D8
St Peter's Cl
  Wilton SP2..............144 B2
  Winterbourne Stoke SP3...196 F3
St Peter's Pump★ BA12..123 C3
St Peters Rd SP1.........146 C5
St Philip's Rd SN2........35 E3
St Rumbold's Rd 9 SP7..202 C1
St Sampson's CE Prim Sch
  SN6......................19 D8
St Sampsons Inf Sch SN6.19 D8
St Stephen's Pl SP4.......105 D8
St Swithin Way 8 SP10.193 D1
St Teresas Cl 7 SP1......146 C5
St Teresa's Dr SN15......78 C7
St Thomas à Becket C of E
  (Aided) Prim Sch SP3...188 B3
St Thomas Cl 14 SP10....193 D2
St Thomas' Rd BA14......101 D1
St Thomas's Sq SP1......146 A1
St Thomas's Way SP1.....146 C5
St Ursula's Cl 9 SP1.....146 D5
Salamander Ct SP9.......216 D7
SALISBURY..............152 C7
Salisbury Arts Ctr★ SP1 .146 B1
Salisbury Bsns Pk SP1....152 D7
Salisbury Cath★ SP1......152 A8
Salisbury Cath Sch SP1..152 A7
Salisbury Cl 1 SN14......78 A6
Salisbury District Hospl
  SP5.....................152 B3
Salisbury Hill SN8........213 E1
Salisbury Hollow BA13...186 D8
Salisbury Mus & Stonehenge
  Gallery★ SP1............152 A7
Salisbury Racecourse
  SP2.....................150 E5
Salisbury Rd
  Amesbury SP4...........217 B3
  Breamore SP6...........210 F5
  Chilmark SP3............201 A4
  Downton SP5............211 A8
  Fordingbridge SP6.......210 E1
  Hungerford RG17........177 B6
  Marlborough SN8........213 E2
  Netheravon SP4.........190 A3
  Pewsey SN9.............215 C3
  Plaitford/Landford S051..212 E6
  14 Shaftesbury SP7.....202 C1
  Shipton Bellinger SP9...199 D7
  9 Shrewton SP3........196 E6
  South Tedworth SP9.....216 C3
  Steeple Langford SP3...128 C8
  Wilton SP2..............144 E3
Salisbury Rd Ind Est SN9 215 B3
Salisbury Sch of English
  SP1.....................152 B8
Salisbury Sixth Form Coll
  SP1.....................152 B8
Salisbury St
  Amesbury SP4...........217 A3
  Devizes SN10...........179 D8
  26 Fordingbridge SP6...210 D1
  Mere BA12..............139 A5
  3 Shaftesbury SP7......202 C1
  Swindon SN1.............50 D7
Salisbury Sta SP2........145 F1
Salisbury & S Wiltshire Mus
  & Stonehenge Gall★
  SP1.....................152 A7
Salisbury Swimming Baths
  SP1.....................146 B1
Sally In the Wood BA11..90 C6
Sally Kings La 5 SP7....202 B2
Salmons Leap SN11.......81 A5
Saltash Rd SN5...........49 F5
Salter Cl BA14...........105 E7
Saltersford La SN14......78 A6
SALTERTON..............131 D4
Salt La
  Salisbury SP1...........146 B1
  Winterbourne SP4.......133 C3
Saltram Cl SN3...........51 C6
Salt Spring Dr SN4.......47 C1
Salzgitter Dr SN25.......35 A8
SAMBOURNE.............116 F5
Sambourne CE Prim Sch
  BA12...................116 F6
Sambourne Chase BA12..117 A7
Sambourne Gdns BA12...117 A6
Sambourne Rd
  Minety SN5..............17 D2
  Warminster BA12.......117 A6
Sambre Rd SN4...........65 D1
Sams La SN26............21 C1
Sanctuary The★ SN8....173 D6
Sandacre Rd
  1 Swindon SN5.........34 A1
  3 Swindon SN5.........48 F8
Sandalwood Rd 1 BA13 108 E1
Sandbourne Rd 7 SN25..34 D5
Sanden Cl RG17..........177 B7
Sanders Cl SN2...........35 F4
Sanders Rd SN14.........101 C2
Sandes Cl SN15..........78 C7
Sandfield
  Littleton Panell SN10....187 E8
  Sutton Veny BA12.......194 A5
Sandford Pk BA14........104 F7
Sandgate SN3............36 B1
Sandhills Rd SP3.........142 A4

6 Westbury BA13.......108 F1
  Westbury BA13..........112 E8
Sandlea Cl SN14..........68 F5
Sandleaze SN10..........179 C4
Sandle Copse SP6........210 B1
SANDLEHEATH...........210 B2
Sandleheath Rd SP6......210 A1
Sandown Ave SN3.........50 E3
Sandown Ctr BA14.......105 E4
Sandown Dr SN14........77 F6
Sandown Pl 7 SP2.......145 F1
Sandpiper Bridge SN3....51 E7
Sandpiper Gdns SN14....70 A2
Sandpit Hill SP3..........141 A2
Sandpit Rd SN11.........81 D4
Sandpits La
  Sherston SN16...........25 C1
  Steeple Ashton BA14...106 E6
Sandridge Comm SN12...94 C5
Sandridge Hill SN12......95 A6
Sandridge La SN15........95 C7
Sandridge Pk★ SN12.....95 B6
Sandridge Rd SN12........94 B5
Sandringham Rd
  Swindon SN3..............50 F3
  Trowbridge BA14........105 B5
Sandringhams The SP5...153 E1
Sandroyd Sch SP5........207 C5
Sands Cl SN10............96 D1
Sands' La SP7............203 C3
Sand's La SN10...........96 D2
Sand St BA12............121 A6
Sands The SN9...........181 C7
Sandstone Rd SN25.......34 F7
Sandwood Cl SN5.........34 B2
Sandy La
  Edington BA13..........186 C7
  Redlynch SP5...........211 D8
  Swindon SN1.............50 B4
SANDY LANE.............88 B4
Sandy Lea Ave 5 SN13..76 B1
Sandy Leaze BA15.......100 C6
Sandy Ridge SN11........81 C1
Sanford St 3 SN1.........50 C6
Sangster Ave SN12.......94 B4
SANHAM GREEN.........177 B5
Sarsen Cl SN1............49 F4
Sarson La SP11..........192 E1
Sarum Ave SN12.........94 B2
Sarum Cl
  Salisbury SP2...........145 E3
  Shipton Bellinger SP9..199 C8
Sarum Dr SN10..........214 C2
Sarum Gdns BA13.......109 A4
Sarum Rd SN14..........78 A6
Sarum St Paul's CE Prim Sch
  SP2.....................145 F2
Sarum Way
  Calne SN11..............81 A3
  2 Hungerford RG17....177 B6
Sasson Cl SP2............145 C3
Sassoon Cl BA12........116 D6
Saunders Ave SN14......146 C6
Saunders Gr SN13........76 D1
Saunders Meadow SN8..183 E1
Savernake Ave SN12......94 C6
Savernake Cl 4 BA12....117 A8
Savernake Cres SN8.....213 F2
Savernake Ct SN8........213 E2
Savernake Hospl SN8....175 A7
Savernake Rd
  Burbage SN8............175 D1
  Corsham SN13...........84 D8
Savernake St SN1.........50 B5
Savill Cres SN4...........63 F7
Sawpit Dr SN8...........175 C5
Sawpit Hill BA12.........140 B4
Sawyer Cl SN25...........35 B6
Sawyers Cl SN16..........17 A2
Sawyers Cres 3 SN13....76 D1
SAWYERS HILL...........17 A2
Sawyers Hill SN16.........17 A2
Saxby Rd SN15...........70 E1
Saxifrage Bank SN12......94 C3
Saxon Cl
  Cricklade SN6............19 D7
  14 Market Lavington SN10 179 F1
  Sherston SN16...........25 C1
  Westbury BA13.........109 A4
Saxon Ct
  North Tidworth SP9.....216 D7
  8 Swindon SN3.........50 D4
Saxon Dr BA14..........101 E4
Saxonhurst 4 SP5.......211 B8
Saxon Leas SP5..........149 C6
Saxon Meadow SP5......211 A8
Saxon Mill SN4............65 D5
Saxon Rd SP2...........151 F6
Saxon Rise SN8..........183 E1
Saxons Acre BA12.......116 D6
Saxon Spur 10 SP7......202 C2
Saxon St SN14............78 B4
Saxon Way
  Andover SP10...........193 D2
  Winsley BA15............99 F7
Saxton Wlk SN5...........49 B8
Scallows La S051.........212 F7
Scamblers Mead SP11...193 A2
Scamell's Rd SN12.......146 A2
Scarborough Rd SN2......49 F8
Scarlet Cl 8 SN25........34 F7
Scholard's La 16 SN8....170 B2
Scholars Cl 34 SP11.....192 A5
School Cl
  Chiseldown SN4..........65 E4
  Keevil BA14.............178 B5

School Cl continued
St Paul Malmesbury Without
  SN16....................28 A1
  Vernhams Dean SP11...185 C3
School Dr 25 SP4........198 B7
School Hill
  Alderbury SP5...........153 C2
  Brinkworth SN15.........45 E5
School La
  All Cannings SN10.......180 F8
  1 Amesbury SP4.......217 B3
  Badminton GL9...........38 E2
  Bromham SN15...........96 A7
  Castle Combe SN14......68 A7
  Castle Eaton SN6........10 B4
  East Garston RG17......171 E8
  Grittleton SN14..........54 E5
  Hindon SP3..............200 B3
  Lea SN16.................29 A2
  Little Bedwyn SN8......176 C5
  Marlborough SN8........213 A6
  Melbury Abbas SP7.....206 B7
  Melksham Without SN12..93 D8
  Meysey Hampton GL7.....1 A4
  South Cerney GL7........6 F7
  Staverton BA14.........101 D5
  Westbury BA13.........108 E1
  Wroughton SN4...........64 A6
School Rd
  Calne SN11..............81 A4
  1 Durrington/Bulford
  SP4....................198 C7
  Kemble GL7...............4 F7
  Nomansland SP5........212 C4
  Redlynch SP5...........211 E6
  Seend SN12.............178 D8
School Wlk SN14..........78 A7
Scorhill La SN1...........50 A2
Scotby Ave SN3...........50 E2
Scotchel Gn SN9.........215 D5
Scotland Hill SN15........57 A5
Scotland La
  Beckington BA11.......107 C4
  Landford SP5...........212 B8
Scotland Rd SN12.........94 A6
Scotney Cres 2 SN25....34 F6
Scots La SP1.............146 A1
Scott Cl SN8.............183 C8
Scott's Cl SP5...........211 A8
Scott's Hill SP7..........203 C4
Scott Way SN1............49 E3
Scratchbury Camp★
  BA12...................194 B7
Scrubbity Barrows★ SP5 207 E4
Scythe Cl 12 SP11.......193 F2
Seacole Cres SN1..........50 A3
Seaford Cl SN5...........49 A6
Seagram Rd SP2.........144 C2
Seagry CE Prim Sch SN15 57 D2
Seagry Ct SN2.............35 B5
Seagry Hill SN15..........57 D3
Seagry Rd
  Hullavington SN14........56 D6
  Sutton Benger SN15.....57 D2
Seaton Cl SN25...........34 F5
Second Broad Dr SP3...128 C2
Secret Gdn The GL7.......6 F7
Sedgebrook SN3...........51 D2
Sedgefield Gdns SN10...214 B4
Sedgefield Way SN14.....77 F6
SEDGEHILL..............202 C7
Sedge Rd 29 SP11.......193 F2
SEEND..................178 E7
Seend CE Prim Sch
  SN12...................178 D8
SEEND CLEEVE..........178 C7
Seend Hill SN12.........178 F8
Sefton Way SN25.........34 C7
Selby Cres SN5...........49 B4
Seldon Cl 4 SN3..........50 E6
Selions Cl SN14...........70 B2
SELLS GREEN............95 E1
Selwood Acad BA11.....110 B6
Selwood Cl 1 SN1........50 E7
Selwood Cres 1 BA11...110 A7
SEM HILL...............202 E5
SEMINGTON.............102 E5
Semington Rd
  Berryfield SN12..........94 A1
  Melksham Without BA14..178 A8
Semington Turnpike
  BA14...................102 F5
SEMLEY................202 F5
Semley Ceva Prim Sch
  SP7....................202 F5
Semley Wlk SN2...........35 C4
Senior Dr SP2...........152 A5
Sergeant Rogers Way
  SN10...................214 E7
SERRINGTON............129 D7
Seth Ward Dr SP1.......146 D4
Seven Barrows★
  Lambourn RG17.........165 A5
  South Tedworth SP9...191 B3
Sevenfields SN6...........23 A7
Seven Fields Nature
  Reserve★ SN5...........35 B5
Seven Fields Prim Sch
  SN2.....................35 B4
SEVENHAMPTON.........23 B2
Severn Ave SN25.........35 A4
Severn Cl SN11...........81 A5
Severn Rd SN12...........94 A6
SEVINGTON..............55 A2
Seymour Ct BA14........101 C1
Seymour Gdns SP4......217 A3

Seymour Rd
  Chippenham SN15........78 F8
  Trowbridge SN3..........50 F6
  Trowbridge BA14.......101 C2
Seymours Ct★ BA11.....107 A6
Shackleton Cl SN12.......94 D1
Shackleton Rd SN10.....214 D2
Shackleton Sq SP10.....193 F2
Shady Bower SP1........152 C8
Shady Bower Cl SP1.....152 C8
SHAFTESBURY...........202 A1
Shaftesbury Ave SN3.....51 B4
Shaftesbury CE Prim Sch
  SP7....................202 D2
Shaftesbury Ct BA14....105 A6
Shaftesbury Dro SP2....151 E5
Shaftesbury Leisure Ctr
  SP7....................202 C1
Shaftesbury Mus★ SP7 .202 C1
Shaftesbury Rd
  Barford St Martin SP3..143 B3
  Mere BA12..............139 B4
  Motcombe SP7..........202 A3
  Wilton SP2..............144 B3
Shaftesbury Sch SP7....202 C1
Shaftesbury St 19 SP6...210 D1
Shaftsbury Cl SN5.........33 C5
Shails La
  Melksham Without SN12..178 A8
  Trowbridge BA14.......101 C1
Shakespeare Ave SP10..193 C1
Shakespeare Dr SN8.....213 C2
Shakespeare Path SN3...35 F3
Shakespeare Rd
  Royal Wootton Bassett
  SN4.....................47 F3
  Salisbury SP1...........145 F4
SHALBOURNE............176 F2
Shalbourne CE Prim Sch
  SN8....................176 F2
Shalbourne Cl
  Hungerford RG17.......177 A7
  Swindon SN3.............35 B5
Shalford La BA9.........136 A3
Shallowbrooks La
  Sherston SN14...........39 F8
  Sherston SN14...........40 A6
Shallows The SP6........210 F4
Shallow Wagon La BA13 108 F6
Shambles The BA15......100 D7
Shanklin Rd SN2..........34 E4
Shaplands 4 SN3.........36 A2
Shapwick Cl SN3..........51 C7
SHARCOTT...............182 A6
Sharcott Dro SN9........215 A4
Share La SP3............203 C6
Sharp Cl SN5.............49 B7
Sharplands SN15..........57 D2
Sharpley SP6............210 D2
SHARPSTONE.............99 A4
Sharratt Ave 4 SP1.....146 C5
Shave La BA12...........122 A4
SHAW
  Melksham Without........93 D7
  Swindon.................49 B7
Shaw CE Prim Sch SN12..93 D8
Shawgrove SN8..........176 B3
Shaw Hill
  Collingbourne Ducis SN8..191 E7
  Melksham Without SN12..93 D7
Shaw Rd SN5.............49 B7
Shaw Ridge Leisure Pk★
  SN5.....................49 B6
Shaw Ridge Prim Sch
  SN5.....................49 B7
Shaw Village★ SN8.....173 F4
Shear Cross BA12.......116 E1
Shearings The SN1........50 C4
Shearman St BA14......105 D7
Shears Dr
  Amesbury SP4...........217 C1
  Amesbury SP4...........217 C1
Shearwater Way SN13...84 D7
Shearwood Rd SN5.......34 A1
Sheasby Cl SP5..........208 A3
Sheen Cl
  Salisbury SP2...........145 B5
  4 Swindon SN5.........49 A4
Sheepbridge Rd SP4....198 E7
Sheepcote Barton 3
  BA14...................105 E7
SHEEPDROVE............165 B2
Sheepdrove Rd RG17....165 B2
Sheep Fair Way 13 RG17 165 A1
Sheepridge SN8.........168 E3
Sheepscroft SN14.........70 B2
Sheep St
  Devizes SN10...........214 B3
  Highworth SN6...........23 A6
Sheepwash La 2 BA12..201 E8
Sheerwold Cl SN3.........36 B3
Sheffield La SN13.........76 D1
SHEFFORD
  WOODLANDS............171 E4
Shelburne Rd SN11.......81 C1
Shelburne Way SN11.....79 F2
Sheld Dr SN15............60 A1
Sheldon Bsns Pk SN14...77 D8
Sheldon Manor & Gdns★
  SN14....................69 D1
Sheldon Rd SN14.........78 B7
Sheldon Sch SN14........70 B1
Shelfinch SN5............49 B7
Shelley Ave 2 SN4.......47 F3
Shelley Gdns SN12.......94 B4
Shelley St SN1............50 B5
Shelley Way BA12.......116 D6

Shelly's Wlk GL7...........2 D4
Shenton Cl SN3...........36 B3
Shepherds SN3............38 D6
Shepherds Breach 1 SN4 47 E2
Shepherds Cl
  Coombe Bissett SP5....151 A1
  Odstock SP5............152 A1
Shepherds Dro BA14....106 C3
Shepherd's La
  Donhead St Andrew SP7..203 B2
  Selwood BA11...........114 D6
Shepherds Mead BA13..112 A8
Shepherd Spring Jun & Inf
  Sch 33 SP10...........193 E2
Shepherds Rise SP11....185 C3
Sheppard Cl SN15........78 F5
Sheppard's Acre SN16...29 A6
Sheppards Rise SN15.....46 B7
Sheppard St SN1.........50 B7
Shepperton Way SN25...34 F6
Sherborne Pl SN3........51 B7
Sherborne Rd BA14.....100 F1
Sherborne St GL7.........2 C4
Sherbourne Dr
  Old Sarum SN4.........146 B8
  Winterbourne SP4......132 C1
Sherfield SP4............133 A2
Sherfield English La
  S051...................212 F7
Sherfield English Rd
  SP5....................212 E6
Sherfields SN4............47 E1
Sherford Rd SN25.........34 E4
Sheridan Dr SN4..........47 F3
Sheringham Ct SN3.......51 D3
Sherington Mead SN15...79 B4
SHERRINGTON..........194 F1
Sherrington La BA12.....195 A2
Sherrington Mead SN15..79 B4
SHERSTON...............25 B1
Sherston Ave SN2.........35 C5
SHERSTON PARVA OR
  PINKNEY................25 E2
Sherston Rd
  Brokenborough SN16....27 E4
  Luckington SN14........39 E5
Sherwood Ave SN12......94 C6
Sherwood Cl 3 BA12....117 A8
Sherwood Rd SN3........51 B4
Shetland Cl
  Swindon SN5.............49 B7
  Westbury BA13.........108 D2
Shetland Gdns SN5.......49 A7
Shipley Dr SN25...........34 F6
SHIPTON BELLINGER....199 D8
Shipton Bellinger Prim Sch
  SP9....................199 C8
Shipton Gr SN3...........50 E5
SHIPTON MOYNE.........26 E8
Shiptons La SN15.........43 F2
Shire Cl SN5.............49 A7
Shire Ct 2 SN1...........50 A5
Shire Hill SN14...........66 A7
Shires Sh Ctr The BA14..105 C8
Shire Way BA13.........108 F2
Shirley Cl SN3............50 F7
SHOCKERWICK............82 E5
Shockerwick La BA1......82 D4
Shoddesden La SP11....192 B4
Shoemaker La SN15......45 F6
SHOE THE...............66 F1
Shop La
  Badminton GL9...........38 E2
  Wingfield BA14.........104 C6
Shoreland Cl BA13.......108 F3
Shore Pl BA14...........100 F1
SHORNCOTE...............6 A6
Short Dro SN4...........163 C6
Short La
  Andover SP11...........193 B1
  Barford St Martin SP3..143 A4
Shortlands SP2..........144 B3
Short River Rd BA13....109 D2
Shorts Gn La SP7.......202 B2
Short St
  Ludgershall SP11.......192 A5
  Melksham SN12..........94 C6
Shoscombe Gdns 3
  BA11...................110 C2
Shoscombe Gn SN3.......51 B6
Showfield SN4............47 D3
Shrapnel Rd 1 SP4......197 E7
Shrewsbury Rd SN3......50 F6
SHREWTON..............196 E6
Shrewton CE Prim Sch
  SP3....................196 E7
Shrewton Cl BA14.......105 D6
Shrewton Rd BA12......195 E6
Shrewton Wlk SN25......35 C5
Shrivenham Rd
  Highworth SN6...........23 B4
  Swindon SN1.............50 E7
  Swindon SN3.............36 B4
Shropshire Cl
  Salisbury SP2...........145 C5
  1 Swindon SN5.........49 B7
Shurnhold SN12..........93 F5
Shute End Rd SP5.......153 B4
Shutts La SP5...........151 A1
Sidbury Circular Rd SP9 .216 B7
Sidbury Hill Ave SP9....216 C8
Sidings The 2 SP5......211 B8
Sidmouth Par SN10.....214 B3
Sidney Cl
  3 Swindon SN3.........50 E6
  Swindon SN5.............48 F4
Sidney St SP2...........145 F1
Sidney Wood Ct SN14...78 C7

Sigerson Rd 2 SN25 . . . . . . 34 C5
Signal St SP4 . . . . 198 E6
Signal Way SN1 . . . . 50 D3
Silbury Cl
  Chippenham SN14 . . . . 78 A6
  Westbury BA13 . . . . 108 F4
Silbury Hill ★ SN8 . . . . 173 C7
Silbury Mews SN25 . . . . 34 E3
Silbury Rd SN11 . . . . 81 A3
Silchester Way SN5 . . . . 49 C6
Sillen La SP6 . . . . 209 B6
Sillington La SN10 . . . . 179 B7
Silman Cl SN13 . . . . 76 D1
Silton Rd SP8 . . . . 137 F2
Silver Barrow ★ SP3 . . . . . . 188 D2
Silver Birch Rd BA14 . . . . . . 105 B5
Silver Cl SN16 . . . . 17 B2
Silver La BA11 . . . . 114 C6
Silverless St SN8 . . . . 213 D3
Silver Meadows BA14 . . . . . 105 A5
Silver Rd SN9 . . . . 215 B5
Silver St La
  Bromham SN15 . . . . 87 D1
  Trowbridge BA14 . . . . 105 B5
Silver St
  Alderbury SP5 . . . . 153 B2
  Bradford-on-Avon BA15 . . . 100 D6
  Calne SN11 . . . . 81 B1
  Calne Without SN11 . . . . . . 89 B8
  Colerne SN14 . . . . 75 B3
  Corsham SN13 . . . . 85 C6
  Kington Langley SN15 . . . . . 70 F1
  Malmesbury SN16 . . . . 28 A3
  Minety SN16 . . . . 17 B2
  Potterne SN10 . . . . 179 D5
  Salisbury SP1 . . . . 152 A8
  Sherston SN16 . . . . 40 C8
  South Cerney GL7 . . . . 6 F7
  Steeple Ashton BA14 . . . . . 178 A3
  Trowbridge BA14 . . . . 105 D8
  Warminster BA12 . . . . 117 A4
  Westbury BA13 . . . . 112 C8
  Wilton SP2 . . . . 144 D3
Silverton Rd SN3 . . . . 51 B6
Silver Wood SP5 . . . . 153 C3
Silverwood Dr SP1 . . . . 146 E2
Simmance Way SP4 . . . . . . 217 C3
Simnel Cl SN5 . . . . 48 F5
Simonds Rd 17 SP11 . . . . . . 192 A5
Sir Bernard Lovell Rd
  SN16 . . . . 28 C1
Siren Cl 8 SN3 . . . . 51 B8
Six Acre La
  Shalbourne RG17 . . . . 176 F3
  West Knoyle BA12 . . . . . . 140 A4
SIXPENNY HANDLEY 208 A4
Sixpenny Handley Fst Sch
  SP5 . . . . 208 A4
Skew Bridge Cl SN4 . . . . 47 C1
Skew Bridge Rd SP2 . . . . . . 145 D2
Skew Rd SP2 . . . . 145 B2
Skinner's Cl SN6 . . . . 22 B7
Skye Cl SN6 . . . . 22 F7
Skylark Rd 6 SN12 . . . . 94 D5
Slab La SP5 . . . . 211 C7
Slade Dr SN3 . . . . 36 B1
Sladesbrook BA15 . . . . 100 E8
Sladesbrook Cl BA15 . . . . . . 100 D8
Slade St SN2 . . . . 34 E2
Slades The SN11 . . . . 81 C3
Slag La BA13 . . . . 108 F5
Slater Rd SN9 . . . . 215 C5
Slate Way SP5 . . . . 148 B3
SLAUGHTERFORD 76 A8
Slaughterford Rd SN14 . . . . . 68 C1
Slay Barrow ★ SP4 . . . . . . 189 A6
Sleightholme Ct 2 BA14 . . . 105 C7
Sleight La SN10 . . . . 179 F6
Sleight Rd SN10 . . . . 214 E1
Slessor Rd
  Lyneham & Bradenstoke
    SN15 . . . . 166 A8
  Lyneham SN15 . . . . 60 A1
Sling Orch SP3 . . . . 204 E7
Sling Rd SP4 . . . . 198 E7
Slipper La SN4 . . . . 65 D4
Slipway The BA14 . . . . 101 D4
Slodbrook La SP8 . . . . 138 D1
Slowgrove Cl BA14 . . . . 105 F8
Smallbrook Gdns 3
  BA14 . . . . 101 D5
Smallbrook La BA12 . . . . . . 117 D5
Smallbrook Mdws Nature
  Reserve ★ BA12 . . . . . . 117 C5
Smallbrook Rd BA12 . . . . . . 117 B5
Small St SN10 . . . . 180 F4
Smannell Rd SP11 . . . . 193 F2
Smart Cl SN25 . . . . 34 E8
Smay Down La SN8 . . . . . . 184 E6
Smeaton Rd
  1 Andover SP10 . . . . 193 B1
  Salisbury SP2 . . . . 145 E1
Smitan Brook SN3 . . . . 51 D6
Smitham Bridge Rd
  RG17 . . . . 177 B7
Smithfield St 2 SP4 . . . . . . 217 B3
Smiths Cl SN9 . . . . 215 B5
Smith's Ct SN5 . . . . 33 C5
Smith's Hill OX12 . . . . 165 F7
Smith St SN14 . . . . 67 A6
Smiths Yd SN13 . . . . 77 A2
Smithy La SN8 . . . . 181 C6
Smithys La SN8 . . . . 183 C8
Smithywell Cl BA14 . . . . . . 105 F8
Snail-Creep Hanging ★
  SP3 . . . . 200 E7
Snails' La SN10 . . . . 214 A3
Snappersnipes BA13 . . . . . . 109 A3

Snapps Cl SN4 . . . . 64 B5
Snap Village ★ SN8 . . . . . . 169 C7
Snarlton La SN12 . . . . 94 D5
Snoddington Rd
  Fyfield SP11 . . . . 192 D1
  Shipton Bellinger SP9 . . . . 199 E7
Snowberry La SN12 . . . . 94 C3
Snowdon Pl SN2 . . . . 35 E4
Snowdrop Cl 2 SN25 . . . . . . 34 D5
Snow Hill
  Dinton SP3 . . . . 201 F2
  Hilmarton SN11 . . . . 73 F5
Snowshill Cl SN25 . . . . 34 F5
Snowswick La SN7 . . . . 12 E7
Snuff St SN10 . . . . 214 A4
Sobers Sq SP11 . . . . 193 B2
Sock's La BA10 . . . . 122 A7
SODOM 59 C7
Sodom La SN15 . . . . 59 C7
Solar Wy SP4 . . . . 217 F4
Soldier's Ring ★ SP6 . . . . . 209 D4
Solstice Pk Ave SP4 . . . . . . 217 D4
Solstice Pk Bsns Park
  SP4 . . . . 217 D4
Solstice Rise SP4 . . . . 217 B3
Somerdale Cl SN5 . . . . 49 C6
Somerford Cl SN2 . . . . 35 C4
SOMERFORD KEYNES 5 F3
Somerford Lakes Reserve ★
  GL7 . . . . 5 D2
Somerfords Walter Powell
  VA CE Prim Sch SN15 . . . . 44 B2
Somerleyton Cl SN10 . . . . . 187 D8
Somerset Cl 1 RG17 . . . . . . 177 B7
Somerset Cres SN12 . . . . . . 94 B3
Somerset Ct 11 SN4 . . . . . . 163 B6
Somerset Dr BA13 . . . . 109 A5
Somerset Rd
  Salisbury SP1 . . . . 146 B3
  Swindon SN2 . . . . 34 F1
Somerset Way BA14 . . . . . . 102 F6
Somerton Gdns BA11 . . . . . 110 C7
Somerville Ct 2 SP10 . . . . . 193 F1
Somerville Rd SN3 . . . . 50 F6
Somme Rd SP11 . . . . 191 F4
Sopwith Pk 7 SP10 . . . . . . 193 C1
Sorley Cl SN8 . . . . 213 B3
Sorrel Cl
  Melksham SN12 . . . . 94 B3
  Royal Wootton Bassett SN4 . 47 E4
  Trowbridge BA14 . . . . 105 D5
Sorrel Dr SN14 . . . . 70 B3
Sound Copse SN5 . . . . 34 B2
South Alley 3 BA12 . . . . . . 116 E5
Southampton Rd
  Alderbury SP5 . . . . 153 D3
  Fordingbridge SP6 . . . . . . 210 E1
  Salisbury SP1 . . . . 152 C7
Southampton St SN1 . . . . . . 50 D6
Southay BA13 . . . . 186 B7
South Bank SN8 . . . . 174 F2
Southbank Gdns RG17 . . . . 165 B1
Southbank Glen SN4 . . . . . . 47 F2
Southbourne Way SP4 . . . . 133 D6
SOUTH BREWHAM 122 A4
SOUTHBROOK 139 B4
Southbrook Rd 139 B4
Southbrook Gdns BA12 . . . . 139 B4
Southbrook La BA13 . . . . . . 178 B1
Southbrook Rd SN10 . . . . . . 93 F6
Southbrook St SN2 . . . . 35 B1
Southbroom Infs Sch
  SN10 . . . . 214 C2
Southbroom Rd SN10 . . . . . 214 B3
Southbroom St James
  Church Academy SN10 . . . 214 C2
SOUTH CERNEY 7 A6
South Charford Dro SP6 . . . 210 D6
South Cliffe Rd 6 SN10 . . . 179 F1
SOUTHCOTT 215 D3
Southcott Rd SN9 . . . . 215 D4
Southcroft Dr BA13 . . . . . . 111 D4
Southcroft Rd 2 SN13 . . . . . 76 B1
South Cross La SN10 . . . . . 179 C3
Southdown 3 SN4 . . . . 163 A5
South Down Wy BA12 . . . . 116 D7
South Dr
  South Tedworth SP9 . . . . . 216 C4
  Swindon SN25 . . . . 34 F8
SOUTHEND 168 F4
Southernwood Dr SN2 . . . . . 34 C4
Southerwicks SN13 . . . . 84 F8
Southey Cl 3 SN25 . . . . 34 F8
Southfield
  2 Aldbourne SN8 . . . . . . 170 A6
  Southwick BA14 . . . . 104 F7
  West Overton SN8 . . . . . . 173 F6
Southfield Jun Sch SN6 . . . . 23 A3
Southfields BA11 . . . . 110 A3
Southfield Wy BA11 . . . . . . 110 A3
Southgate
  Devizes SN10 . . . . 214 B2
  Stonebridge BA11 . . . . . . 110 D7
Southgate Cl SN10 . . . . 214 B2
South Hills Sch SP2 . . . . . . 150 D8
South La
  Downton SP5 . . . . 211 A8
  Nomansland SP5 . . . . . . 212 C4
Southleigh BA15 . . . . 100 C5
Southleigh View BA12 . . . . . 117 C5
SOUTH MARSTON 36 F5
South Marston CE Prim Sch
  SN3 . . . . 36 E4
South Marston Park SN3 . . . 36 C7
South Mdw La SN5 . . . . 19 F3

Southmead SN14 . . . . 78 B6
South Mill Cl SP4 . . . . 217 B2
Southmill Hill SP4 . . . . 217 B1
South Mill Rd SP4 . . . . 217 B2
SOUTH NEWTON 130 B2
South Pk ★ SP11 . . . . 192 B4
South Pl
  Calne SN11 . . . . 81 B2
  Corsham SN13 . . . . 77 A1
Southside
  Laverstock SP4 . . . . 146 D8
  Shipton Moyne GL8 . . . . . . 26 E7
South St
  Aldbourne SN8 . . . . 170 A6
  Avebury SN8 . . . . 173 B8
  Broad Chalke SP5 . . . . . . 205 B4
  Corsham SN13 . . . . 77 A1
  Great Wishford SP2 . . . . . 130 A3
  8 Salisbury SP2 . . . . . . 145 F1
  Swindon SN1 . . . . 50 C4
  Warminster BA12 . . . . . . 116 E5
  Wilton SP2 . . . . 144 C1
SOUTH TIDWORTH 216 D4
South Ugford Medieval
  Village of ★ SP2 . . . . . . 144 A2
South View RG17 . . . . 177 B7
South View Ave SN3 . . . . . . 50 E5
South View Pl SN8 . . . . 213 E3
Southview Rd BA14 . . . . . . 105 D6
Southville Rd BA15 . . . . . . 100 E5
Southward La SN8 . . . . 170 A6
Southwark Cl SP9 . . . . 216 E6
Southway SP4 . . . . 134 D7
South Way
  Alderbury SP5 . . . . 153 E2
  Trowbridge BA14 . . . . 105 D7
Southway Rd BA15 . . . . . . 100 D4
Southwell Cl 2 SN14 . . . . . . 78 A5
South Western Rd SP2 . . . . 145 F1
SOUTHWICK 104 F3
Southwick Ave SN2 . . . . 35 B5
Southwick CE Prim Sch
  BA14 . . . . 104 F3
Southwick Ctry Pk ★
  BA14 . . . . 104 F5
Southwick Rd BA14 . . . . . . 105 C2
South Wilts Grammar School
  for Girls SP1 . . . . 146 A3
Southwold Cl SN25 . . . . 34 B6
Southwood Rd BA14 . . . . . . 105 F8
SOUTH WRAXALL 91 D6
Sovereign Cl SP2 . . . . 145 F1
Soyuz Cres 12 SN25 . . . . . . 34 B7
Spackman La SN13 . . . . 84 E8
Spa Cl SN6 . . . . 23 B6
Spa Ct SN12 . . . . 94 B3
Spanbourn Ave SN14 . . . . . . 78 D7
Sparcells Dr SN5 . . . . 34 B2
Spa Rd SN12 . . . . 94 B3
Sparrow St BA14 . . . . 105 E6
SPA THE 94 C2
Spa The BA14 . . . . 92 E1
Speedwell Cl
  Melksham SN12 . . . . 94 C2
  1 Swindon SN25 . . . . 34 E5
  3 Trowbridge BA14 . . . . . 105 D6
Spencer Cl
  Melksham SN12 . . . . 94 A6
  Swindon SN5 . . . . 48 F7
Spencers Orch
  Bradford-on-Avon BA15 . . . 100 D5
  Wroughton SN4 . . . . 64 B6
Spenser Cl SN3 . . . . 51 A7
Spereholt SN5 . . . . 49 D4
Spey Ct SN14 . . . . 193 F1
Spiders Island SP5 . . . . 153 F2
Spiers Piece BA14 . . . . 178 B3
Spindle Tree Ct SN2 . . . . . . 35 B2
Spine Rd (East) GL7 . . . . 7 C4
Spine Rd W GL7 . . . . 6 A2
Spingfield Rd BA12 . . . . . . 139 B5
Spin Hill SN10 . . . . 179 E1
Spinners Croft 5 BA14 . . . . 105 D7
Spinners Way BA12 . . . . . . 139 B6
Spinney Cl
  Chippenham SN14 . . . . 78 A6
  3 Liddington SN4 . . . . . . 163 A4
Spinney Rd SP11 . . . . 192 A5
Spinney The
  Lechlade GL7 . . . . 2 C4
  3 Littleton Panell SN10 . . 187 E8
  Trowbridge BA14 . . . . 105 E8
SPIRTHILL 73 B4
Spitalcroft Rd SN10 . . . . . . 214 C4
Spital La SN6 . . . . 19 E7
Spitfire Rd SP4 . . . . 146 D8
Spitfire Way SN3 . . . . 36 C7
Spode Cl SN25 . . . . 34 D7
Spout La SN12 . . . . 178 E4
Spouts La SO51 . . . . 212 F7
Spracklands SP3 . . . . 201 F2
Sprats Barn Cres SN4 . . . . . 47 D3
Spratsgate La GL7 . . . . 6 B4
Spray Leaze 10 SP11 . . . . . 192 B5
Spray Rd RG17 . . . . 177 C2
Sprays 9 SN8 . . . . 183 D8
Spread Eagle Hill SP7 . . . . . 206 B6
Spreckley Rd 1 SN11 . . . . . 166 A1
Spring Cl SN1 . . . . 50 C6
Springers Cl SN10 . . . . 214 D4
Springfield BA15 . . . . 100 E6
Springfield Bldgs SN15 . . . . 78 D8
Springfield Cl
  Corsham SN13 . . . . 84 A8
  7 Shaftesbury SP7 . . . . . 202 C2
  Trowbridge BA14 . . . . 101 E2
Springfield Cres
  11 Redlynch SP5 . . . . . . 211 C7

Springfield Cres continued
  Royal Wootton Bassett SN4 . 47 D2
Springfield Dr SN11 . . . . 81 A3
Springfield Gdns SN12 . . . . . 85 C1
Springfield Pk
  18 Tisbury SP3 . . . . 203 E8
  Trowbridge BA14 . . . . 101 E1
Springfield Rd
  Rowde SN10 . . . . 96 D1
  Swindon SN1 . . . . 50 C3
  Westbury BA13 . . . . 108 F2
Springfield Sports Ctr
  SN13 . . . . 76 F1
Springfields Sch SN11 . . . . . 81 A3
Spring Gdns
  Lechlade GL7 . . . . 2 C4
  Swindon SN1 . . . . 50 C6
Springhead BA12 . . . . 194 A4
Springhill Cl 3 SN5 . . . . 49 C5
Spring La SN13 . . . . 84 C7
Springlines 10 SN4 . . . . . . 163 B6
Spring Meadow SN8 . . . . . . 191 D8
Spring Meadows BA14 . . . . 105 A5
Spring Rd BA11 . . . . 110 A6
Spring The 5 SN10 . . . . . . 187 E8
Spring Tining SN13 . . . . 76 F1
Spur The BA13 . . . . 112 D8
Spur Way SN2 . . . . 35 E3
Squalls La SP3 . . . . 203 F6
Square The
  Calne SN11 . . . . 81 B3
  Mere BA12 . . . . 139 A4
  Pewsey SN9 . . . . 215 C5
  7 Swindon SN3 . . . . 50 D4
Squarey Cl SP5 . . . . 211 A7
Squires Copse SN5 . . . . 34 A1
Squires Hill Cl
  4 Royal Wootton Bassett
    SN4 . . . . 47 F2
  7 Royal Wootton Bassett
    SN4 . . . . 48 A2
Squirrel Cres 1 SN4 . . . . . . 47 F2
Squirrel's Cnr BH21 . . . . . . 208 D1
Stable Cl SP11 . . . . 192 A5
Stables Rd SP9 . . . . 216 C4
Stacey's La SN4 . . . . 163 B5
Stackpole Cres SN25 . . . . . . 34 C8
Stafford St SN1 . . . . 50 B5
Stag Hill RG17 . . . . 171 A1
Stainers Mead SP7 . . . . 202 A5
Staldon Rd SN1 . . . . 50 B2
Stallard St BA14 . . . . 105 C8
Stalls The BA12 . . . . 114 F5
Stambrook Pk BA1 . . . . 82 A5
Stamford Cl SN5 . . . . 49 B5
Stanbridge Pk 9 SN5 . . . . . 49 A7
Stanbury Rd SN15 . . . . 192 C1
Stancomb Ave BA14 . . . . . . 101 E1
Stancombe Pk 1 SN5 . . . . . 49 D5
Standen Way SN25 . . . . 34 A7
STANDERWICK 107 B2
Standings Cl 6 SN5 . . . . . . 49 A8
Stanford Rd SN25 . . . . 34 C7
Stanier Cl BA11 . . . . 110 C6
Stanier Rd SN11 . . . . 81 C6
Stanier St SN1 . . . . 50 B5
STANLEY 80 A6
Stanley Cl 9 SN4 . . . . 163 B6
Stanley Ct SN2 . . . . 151 E8
Stanley Honey Ct 7 SN3 . . . 50 F6
Stanley La SN15 . . . . 79 D6
Stanley Little Rd SP2 . . . . . 145 B3
Stanley St SN1 . . . . 50 C5
Stanley Terr SN10 . . . . 214 B2
Stanmore St SN1 . . . . 50 A5
Stannon La SN1 . . . . 50 B2
Stansfield Cl 5 SN5 . . . . . . 49 D4
Stanton Cl BA14 . . . . 105 D5
Stanton Cty Pk ★ SN6 . . . . 36 B8
STANTON FITZWARREN 22 B1
Stanton La SN14 . . . . 56 A1
Stanton Pk Farm ★ SN6 . . . 36 B8
Stanton Pk Nature Reserve ★
  SN6 . . . . 36 B8
STANTON ST BERNARD 173 A1
STANTON ST QUINTIN 56 B4
Stanton St Quintin Prim Sch
  SN14 . . . . 56 B4
Stanway Cl 5 SN3 . . . . 51 A4
STAPLEFORD 129 C7
Stapleford Castle Ring &
  Bailey ★ SP3 . . . . 129 D8
Stapleford Cl SN15 . . . . 78 E4
Stapleford Way SN2 . . . . 35 B6
Staples Hill BA2 . . . . 99 C3
Stapleton Cl SN6 . . . . 22 F5
Stardust Cres 13 SN25 . . . . 34 B7
Star Ground BA14 . . . . 101 E8
Staring Cl 6 SN5 . . . . 48 F8
Star La SN14 . . . . 74 D8
Star The BA14 . . . . 101 E7
STARTLEY 43 D1
Station App
  4 Frome BA11 . . . . 110 A4
  32 Ludgershall SP11 . . . . 192 A5
  Melksham SN12 . . . . 94 A6
  Minety SN16 . . . . 17 C1
  Swindon SN1 . . . . 50 D3
  Westbury BA13 . . . . 108 E4
Station Hill SN15 . . . . 78 D8
Station Ind Est SN1 . . . . 50 B6
Station Rd
  Ashbury SN6 . . . . 164 A8
  Badminton GL9 . . . . 38 F1
  Calne SN11 . . . . 81 B2
  Chiseldown SN4 . . . . 65 D4
  Christian Malford SN15 . . . 58 A2
  Codford BA12 . . . . 194 F3

Station Rd continued
  Corsham SN13 . . . . 77 A1
  Devizes SN10 . . . . 214 A3
  East Garston RG17 . . . . . 171 E7
  Great Wishford SP2 . . . . . 129 F3
  Highworth SN6 . . . . 22 F6
  Holt BA14 . . . . 92 E1
  19 Hungerford RG17 . . . . 177 B7
  Kemble GL7 . . . . 4 F7
  10 Lambourn RG17 . . . . . 165 A1
  Lechlade GL7 . . . . 2 D5
  Limpley Stoke BA2 . . . . . . 99 C5
  Minety SN16 . . . . 17 C1
  Purton SN5 . . . . 33 C5
  Royal Wootton Bassett SN4 . 47 D1
  Sandleheath SP6 . . . . 210 C1
  Sedgehill & Semley SP7 . . . 202 D5
  South Cerney GL7 . . . . 7 B7
  Swindon SN1 . . . . 50 B7
  Tidworth SP9 . . . . 216 D5
  Warminster BA12 . . . . . . 117 B7
  Westbury BA13 . . . . 108 E5
Station Terr 4 SP2 . . . . . . 145 F1
Station Way BA14 . . . . 105 C8
STAVERTON 101 C6
Staverton Way 2 SN3 . . . . . 35 C6
Stavordale Priory ★ BA9 . . . 136 D5
Steadings The
  Royal Wootton Bassett
    SN4 . . . . 47 F1
  Salisbury SP4 . . . . 146 D6
Steam Mus of the Great
  Western Rly ★ SN2 . . . . . 50 A6
Stedham Wlk SN3 . . . . 51 B4
Steele Cl SN10 . . . . 214 D4
Steels Dro SP6 . . . . 211 A4
Steels La SP6 . . . . 209 F2
Steel's La BA9 . . . . 137 A3
Steepe Way SN8 . . . . 175 C1
Steep Hollow SP3 . . . . 201 E3
STEEPLE ASHTON 178 B3
STEEPLE LANGFORD 128 D8
Steeple Vw SN1 . . . . 50 D4
Steep St BA12 . . . . 139 A6
Steiner Academy Frome
  BA12 . . . . 111 D2
Stenbury Cl SN25 . . . . 35 A7
Stenness Cl SN5 . . . . 34 C2
Stephen Martin Gdns 7
  SP6 . . . . 210 D1
Stephens Cl 1 SP2 . . . . 151 E7
Stephenson Dr BA11 . . . . . . 110 C6
Stephenson Rd
  Salisbury SP2 . . . . 145 E1
  Swindon SN25 . . . . 35 C7
  The Ham BA13 . . . . 108 D5
Stephens Rd SN3 . . . . 36 A1
Stephens Way BA12 . . . . . . 116 F8
Steplake La SO51 . . . . 212 F8
Steplake Rd SO51 . . . . 212 F8
Stepping Stones Pre Prep
  Sch SN8 . . . . 176 E6
Sterling Pk 1 SP10 . . . . . . 193 C1
STERT 180 B6
Stert Valley La SN10 . . . . . 180 A6
Stevenson Rd SN2 . . . . 34 C5
Stewart Cl
  Chippenham SN15 . . . . 78 F4
  Swindon SN25 . . . . 35 B6
Steway La BA1 . . . . 82 B6
STIBB GREEN 175 D1
Stibb Hill SN10 . . . . 187 F7
Stickleback Rd SN11 . . . . . . 81 B6
Still Man Cl BA14 . . . . 101 E8
Stirling Cl
  3 Bower Hill SN12 . . . . . 178 B8
  Wroughton SN4 . . . . 64 A7
Stirling Rd
  Market Lavington SN10 . . . 180 A1
  South Marston Park SN3 . . . 36 C6
Stirling Way BA11 . . . . 110 C6
STITCHCOMBE 175 D8
Stitching's La SN9 . . . . 181 D5
Stobberts Pl 4 SN10 . . . . . 179 F1
Stobberts Rd 3 SN10 . . . . . 179 F1
Stockbridge Copse SN5 . . . . 34 A2
Stockham Cl SN6 . . . . 19 E8
Stockham Gdns SN6 . . . . . . 19 F8
Stock La
  Aldbourne SN8 . . . . 169 D4
  Landford SP5 . . . . 212 C7
STOCKLEY 89 C4
Stockley Hollow SN11 . . . . . . 89 C4
Stockley La SN11 . . . . 89 C6
Stockley Rd SN11 . . . . 89 C2
Stockport Rd SP4 . . . . 217 D1
Stocks Bridge La SP5 . . . . . 151 A1
Stock's Cross SO43 . . . . . . 212 D2
STOCKS THE 178 C7
STOCKTON 195 B1
Stockton Earthworks ★
  BA12 . . . . 201 A6
Stockton House ★ BA12 . . . 195 B1
Stockton Rd SN2 . . . . 35 C4
Stockwell Rd SN10 . . . . . . 214 C4
Stockwood Cl SP1 . . . . 146 C3
Stockwood Rd SN14 . . . . . . 78 B6
STOFORD 130 A3
Stoke Comm La SN5 . . . . . . 19 A2
Stoke Common Mdws Nature
  Reserve ★ SN6 . . . . 18 E1
STOKE FARTHING 205 D4
Stokehill BA14 . . . . 106 A8
Stoke Mead BA2 . . . . 98 F7
Stokesay Dr SN5 . . . . 49 C4

Stokes' Croft SN11 . . . . . .81 B4
Stokes Rd SN13 . . . . .85 A8
Stonar Sch SN12 . . . . .92 B8
Stone Ave★ SN8 . . . . . . .173 C8
STONEBRIDGE 110 C7
Stonebridge Cl SN8 . . . . .213 F3
Stonebridge Dr BA11 . . .110 B7
Stone Cl
  Half Way Firs SN13 . . . .76 C1
  The Common SP5 . . . . .149 C6
Stonecrop Way SN25 . . . .34 E5
Stonefield Cl SN5 . . . . . . .49 C7
Stonefield Dr SN6 . . . . . . .23 A5
Stonehenge★ SP4 . . . . .197 E5
Stonehenge Cursus★
  SP4 . . . . .197 C6
Stonehenge Rd
  Amesbury SP4 . . . . . . .198 A4
  Swindon SN1 . . . . .50 A2
Stonehenge Sch The
  SP4 . . . . .217 B4
Stonehenge Visitor Ctr★
  SP4 . . . . .197 C5
Stonehill Barn GL8 . . . . . . .3 C6
Stonehill Gn SN5 . . . . .49 D6
Stonehill La GL8 . . . . .3 C6
Stone La
  Lydiard Millicent SN5 . . .33 E1
  Ramsbury SN8 . . . . . . .175 D8
Stonelea Cl SN14 . . . . . . .78 B7
Stoneleigh Rise BA11 . . .110 A6
Stoneover La
  Lydiard Tregoze SN4 . . .48 A3
  Royal Wootton Bassett SN4 .47 F2
Stone (site of King's Elm)★
  SP3 . . . . .142 B1
Stones La SN6 . . . . .8 B1
Stonewall Terr BA11 . . . .110 A3
Stoneworks The SN13 . . .84 C6
Stoney Bridge BA12 . . . .140 D5
Stoney Cross 20 SP11 . .192 A5
Stonybeck Cl SN5 . . . . . . .49 D6
Stony Gutter BA14 . . . . .102 D1
Stony La
  Damerham SP6 . . . . . . .209 E2
  Lambourn RG17 . . . . . .171 B6
Stoppers Hill SN15 . . . . . .46 B7
Stops Hill SP3 . . . . .200 B3
Stop St SP3 . . . . .200 C2
Stork House Dr 18 RG17 .165 A1
STORMORE 112 A8
Stormore BA13 . . . . .111 F8
Storridge Rd BA13 . . . . .108 C6
Stour Cl 5 SO51 . . . . . . .212 F6
Stourhead House & Gdns★
  BA12 . . . . .123 F1
STOURTON 123 F1
Stourton House Flower Gdn★
  BA12 . . . . .123 F1
Stourton La BA12 . . . . . .123 E3
Stourton Pk BA14 . . . . . .102 B3
Stour Wlk SN25 . . . . .35 B4
Stowell Pk★ SN8 . . . . . .182 A8
Stradbrook BA13 . . . . . . .186 B7
Straight La
  Dean SP5 . . . . .207 E3
  Lambourn RG17 . . . . . .171 C6
STRAIGHT SOLEY 171 A3
STRAND THE 178 B6
Strand The
  Calne SN11 . . . . .81 B3
  Steeple Ashton BA14 . .178 A3
STRANGWAYS 198 A6
Stranks Cl SN6 . . . . .23 A4
Stratford Cl SN5 . . . . .49 D5
Stratford Rd SP1 . . . . . . .146 A3
STRATFORD SUB
  CASTLE 145 F5
Stratford Sub Castle CE Prim
  Sch SP1 . . . . .145 D5
STRATFORD TONY 150 C2
Stratford Tony Rd SP5 . . .150 E2
Stratton Orch 1 SN3 . . . .36 A2
Stratton Rd
  Pewsey SN9 . . . . .215 C4
  Swindon SN1 . . . . .50 F8
Stratton Rd & Marshgate Ind
  Est SN1 . . . . .50 F8
STRATTON ST
  MARGARET 36 A3
Strattons Wlk SN12 . . . . .94 B4
Strawberry Hill SN10 . . .187 E7
Strawberry La GL7 . . . . . . .1 A4
Street La
  Brewham BA10 . . . . . . .122 F4
  Sedgehill & Semley SP7 .202 C6
Street The
  All Cannings SN10 . . . .172 F1
  Alvediston SP5 . . . . . . .204 B4
  Bishops Cannings SN10 .172 B3
  Brinkworth SN15 . . . . . .45 F6
  Broughton Gifford SN12 .93 B4
  Castle Combe SN14 . . . .68 A7
  Castle Eaton SN6 . . . . . .10 B4
  Charlton SN16 . . . . .29 B6
  Cherhill SN11 . . . . .166 B1
  Chilmark SP3 . . . . .201 A3
  Chirton SN10 . . . . .180 F4
  Crudwell SN16 . . . . .14 E5
  Didmarton GL9 . . . . .24 C3
  East Knoyle SP3 . . . . . .141 C1
  Holt BA14 . . . . .101 D8
  Hullavington SN14 . . . . .41 F1
  Kilmington BA12 . . . . . .123 F4
  Latton SN6 . . . . .8 C4

Street The continued
  Lea SN16 . . . . .28 F1
  Liddington SN4 . . . . . . .163 A4
  Little Somerford SN15 . . .44 C5
  Luckington SN14 . . . . . .39 E4
  Lydiard Millicent SN5 . . .48 D8
  Marden SN10 . . . . .181 A4
  Marston Maisey SN6 . . . .9 D6
  Milton Lilbourne SN9 . .182 E7
  Motcombe SP7 . . . . . . .202 A5
  Nettleton SN14 . . . . . . .53 B4
  Oaksey SN16 . . . . .15 F8
  Pitton & Farley SP5 . . . .154 E7
  Shipton Moyne GL8 . . . .26 E8
  Swindon SN25 . . . . .34 E3
  West Knoyle BA12 . . . .140 D5
  Winterslow SP5 . . . . . .149 A5
  Yatton Keynell SN14 . . . .68 F6
Stroma Way SN6 . . . . .22 E7
Strongrove Hill RG17 . . .177 A7
Strongs Cl BA14 . . . . . . .178 C4
Stroud La SN10 . . . . .179 F5
Stroud's Hill SN4 . . . . . . .65 D4
Stuart Cl
  2 Swindon SN3 . . . . . .50 F6
  Trowbridge BA14 . . . . .101 E4
Stuart Gn BA12 . . . . .117 A6
Stubbs Ct 3 SP10 . . . . . .193 D1
Stubbs La SN14 . . . . .70 A7
Stubhampton Bottom
  DT11 . . . . .206 C3
Stubsmead SN3 . . . . .51 C5
Stuckton Rd SP6 . . . . . . .210 E1
Studland SN3 . . . . .51 B3
Studland Pk BA13 . . . . . .109 B2
STUDLEY 80 B3
Studley Castle★ SN6 . . .211 F3
Studley Gn Prim Sch
  BA14 . . . . .105 A6
STUDLEY GREEN 104 F7
Studley Hill SN11 . . . . . . .80 A4
Studley La SN11 . . . . .80 A3
Studley Rise BA14 . . . . . .105 D6
STURFORD 115 E6
Sturford La BA12 . . . . . . .115 D6
Styles Ave BA11 . . . . . . .110 C4
Styles Cl BA11 . . . . .110 B4
Styles Hill BA11 . . . . .110 B4
Styles Pk BA11 . . . . .110 B4
Styles The SP5 . . . . .205 F4
Sudeley Dr GL7 . . . . .4 F6
Sudeley Way SN5 . . . . . . .49 A5
Sudley Way SN5 . . . . .48 F5
Suffolk Cl SN16 . . . . .29 A7
Suffolk Pl GL7 . . . . .8 D7
Suffolk Rd
  Salisbury SP2 . . . . .151 E6
  Westbury BA13 . . . . . . .112 D8
  5 Westbury Leigh BA13 .108 E1
Suffolk St SN2 . . . . .50 C8
Sully BA15 . . . . .100 A6
Summerdown Ct BA13 . .109 A4
Summer Down Wlk
  BA14 . . . . .105 C5
Summerhouse Rd SN4 . . .63 F7
Summer La
  Castle Combe SN14 . . . .53 F3
  Monkton Combe BA2 . . .98 D8
Summerleaze
  2 Corsham SN13 . . . . . .76 D1
  Trowbridge BA14 . . . . .105 A4
Summerlock App 2 SP2 .146 A1
Summer Oaks SP7 . . . . .202 A5
Summer Rd BA13 . . . . . .108 F4
Summers La SN4 . . . . . . .167 C2
Summers St SN2 . . . . .49 F7
Sumsions Dr 8 SN13 . . . .76 D1
Sunderland Cl 14 SN12 . .178 B8
Sunflower Wy 1 SP11 . . .193 F2
Sun La SN3 . . . . .108 E1
Sunningdale Cl SN15 . . . .78 F7
Sunningdale Rd SN25 . . . .35 C4
Sunnyhill SN8 . . . . .191 D8
Sunnyhill La SN8 . . . . . . .174 C1
Sunnyhill Rd SP1 . . . . . . .146 A4
Sunnyside SN10 . . . . . . .187 E8
Sunnyside Ave SN1 . . . . . .50 A4
Sunnyside Cl SP10 . . . . . .193 C1
Sunrise Wy SP4 . . . . .217 D4
SUNTON 183 E1
Surrendell Cottage SN14 . .55 B8
Surrey Pl
  Trowbridge BA14 . . . . .105 B7
  1 Trowbridge BA14 . . .105 B7
Surrey Rd SN2 . . . . .35 A1
Sussex Rd SP2 . . . . .151 E6
Sussex Sq SN3 . . . . .50 E6
Sutherland Crescent SN14 .70 B3
Sutherland Ct 5 SP10 . . .193 D1
Suthmere Dr SN8 . . . . . .183 D8
SUTTON BENGER 57 C2
Sutton Benger CE Prim Sch
  SN15 . . . . .57 D2
Sutton Bottom SP3 . . . . .141 D5
Sutton Hill
  Sherrington BA12 . . . . .195 A2
  Sutton Mandeville SP3 .204 C7
Sutton La
  Langley Burrell Without
    SN15 . . . . .71 C5
  Sutton Benger SN15 . . .57 D1
SUTTON MANDEVILLE . .204 C8
Sutton Pk SN26 . . . . .21 C1
Sutton Rd
  Fovant SP3 . . . . .204 D7
  Kington Langley SN15 . . .70 F2
  Swindon SN3 . . . . .51 C4

SUTTON ROW 204 B7
SUTTON VENY 117 F1
Sutton Veny CE Prim Sch
  BA12 . . . . .194 A4
Suvla La 6 SP4 . . . . .198 E6
Swaddon St SN11 . . . . . . .81 B4
Swaledale Rd BA12 . . . . .116 D6
Swallet House SN15 . . . . .58 D5
SWALLETT GATE 59 A6
Swallow Cl
  Tidworth SP9 . . . . .216 D6
  2 Warminster BA12 . . .116 E5
SWALLOWCLIFFE 204 A6
Swallowdale SN3 . . . . . . .51 D7
Swallow Dr
  Frome BA11 . . . . .110 B6
  4 Trowbridge BA14 . . .105 B8
Swallowfield Ave SN3 . . . .50 F5
Swallowmead 1 SP2 . . . .152 A5
Swallows Mead 9 SN4 . . .48 A2
Swanage Wlk SN25 . . . . . .34 E3
Swan Barton SN16 . . . . . .40 C8
SWANBOROUGH 22 C4
Swanborough Cl 6 SN15 .78 F4
Swanborough Tump★
  SN9 . . . . .181 F6
Swanbrook SN3 . . . . .51 D8
Swan Cl
  9 Durrington/Bulford
    SP4 . . . . .198 C7
  Lechlade GL7 . . . . .2 C4
  Salisbury SP2 . . . . .152 A4
  South Cerney GL7 . . . . . .7 A6
  1 Swindon SN3 . . . . . . .51 C8
Swan Ct BA14 . . . . .104 F3
Swan Dr BA14 . . . . .101 D5
Swangate RG17 . . . . .177 B8
Swan La SN6 . . . . .17 F5
Swan Meadow SN9 . . . . .215 D3
Swan Rd
  Corsham SN13 . . . . .76 E1
  Pewsey SN9 . . . . .215 C4
Swan's Bottom 7 SN8 . .170 B2
Swan's Cl 9 SN8 . . . . . . .170 B2
Swansfield GL7 . . . . .2 D6
Swans Mdw GL7 . . . . .2 E3
Swattons Cl SP4 . . . . . . .217 E8
Swayne Cl 6 SN15 . . . . . .78 F5
Swayne Rd SP2 . . . . .144 C2
Swaynes Cl 1 SP1 . . . . . .146 B2
Sweet Briar Rd SN12 . . . .94 C3
Sweetmans Rd SP7 . . . . .202 C2
Swift Ave SN25 . . . . .35 A7
Swiftdown 5 SP2 . . . . . .152 A5
Swift Dr BA14 . . . . .105 E6
Swift Link GL7 . . . . .7 A6
Swift Mead BA12 . . . . . . .116 E5
Swillbrook Lakes Nature
  Reserve★ SN16 . . . . . .16 F8
Swinburne Pl SN4 . . . . . . .47 E3
SWINDON 50 E4
Swindon Academy SN2 . . .35 B2
Swindon Arts Ctr★ SN1 . .50 C4
Swindon Coll
  Marlborough SN8 . . . . .213 D3
  Swindon SN2 . . . . .50 B8
Swindon & Cricklade Rly★
  SN25 . . . . .33 F8
Swindon Mus & Art Gall★
  SN1 . . . . .50 D4
Swindon Rd
  Cricklade SN6 . . . . .19 F7
  Highworth SN6 . . . . .22 F3
  Hilmarton SN11 . . . . . . .73 F3
  Kington Langley SN15 . . .70 F5
  Lydiard Tregoze SN4 . . . .48 C2
  Royal Wootton Bassett SN4 .47 F3
  Swindon SN1 . . . . .36 A1
  Wroughton SN4 . . . . . . .64 C7
Swindon St SN6 . . . . .23 A5
Swindon Sta SN2 . . . . . . .50 B7
Swindon Town Football Club
  SN1 . . . . .50 D7
Swinford Paddocks SN16 .27 E2
Swinley Dr SN5 . . . . .34 A1
Sword Gdns 5 SN1 . . . . . .49 F4
Swynford Cl GL7 . . . . .10 D6
Sycamore Cl
  Long Newnton GL8 . . . .13 B4
  Lyneham & Bradenstoke
    SN15 . . . . .60 C2
  North Tidworth SP9 . . .216 E6
  Sixpenny Handley SP5 . .208 A4
Sycamore Dr
  8 Frome BA11 . . . . . . .110 B7
  Salisbury SP1 . . . . .146 C4
Sycamore Gr
  Swindon SN2 . . . . .35 C2
  Trowbridge BA14 . . . . .105 C5
  Westbury BA13 . . . . . . .108 F3
Sydnalls La BA12 . . . . . . .115 D6
Symonds SN5 . . . . .49 B3
Syon Cl
  Corsham SN13 . . . . .84 E8
  4 Swindon SN25 . . . . . .34 F6
Syringa Ct SP2 . . . . .145 D1
Sywell Rd SN3 . . . . .51 C8

T

Tadpole Farm CE Prim Acad
  SN25 . . . . .34 B8
Tadpole La
  Blunsdon St Andrew SN25 .34 D8
  Purton SN5 . . . . .33 F8
Talavera Rd SN4 . . . . . . .168 E8
Talbot Cl
  Melksham SN12 . . . . . . .94 D5
  Salisbury SP1 . . . . .146 C4
Talbot Rd BA14 . . . . .105 A7
Talboys (Medieval Hall
  House)★ BA14 . . . . . . .178 B4
Tallis Wlk SN5 . . . . .49 A5
Tallow La 5 SN4 . . . . . . .163 A6
Tamar Cl SN25 . . . . .35 A4
Tamar Rd SN12 . . . . .94 A6
Tamesis Dr GL7 . . . . .4 F7
Tame Wy GL7 . . . . .1 E6
Tamworth Dr SN5 . . . . . . .49 A7
Tanarisk Cl SN11 . . . . .81 C1
Tangier Cl BA12 . . . . .117 A8
TANGLEY 193 A4
Tangmere Cl 13 SN12 . . .178 B8
TANIS 96 F2
Tankard La 15 SN8 . . . . .170 B2
Tankey's Cl 5 BA11 . . . . .110 A7
Tank La SP5 . . . . .205 B4
Tan La SP8 . . . . .138 A2
Tanner Cl SN15 . . . . .78 F5
Tanners Cl
  Royal Wootton Bassett
    SN4 . . . . .47 D2
  Winterbourne SN4 . . . .133 A1
Tanners Field SP4 . . . . . .217 D3
Tanners Hill SN16 . . . . . . .40 C8
Tanners La
  Sandleheath SP6 . . . . .210 A1
  Shrewton SP3 . . . . .196 E7
  Winterbourne SP4 . . . .133 A1
Tansley Moor SN3 . . . . . . .51 E3
Tanyard La 6 SP7 . . . . . .202 B1
Taplow Wlk SN3 . . . . .51 A4
Taramah Gdns 10 SP3 . .203 E8
Targetts Mead SP3 . . . . .203 E8
Tarka Cl SN25 . . . . .34 F7
Tarragon Cl SN2 . . . . .34 C4
Tarrant's Hill 24 RG17 . .177 B7
Tarters The SN4 . . . . .40 D8
Tascroft BA12 . . . . .116 B5
Tasker Cl SN13 . . . . .84 E8
Taskers La SN8 . . . . .183 D8
Tattershall SN5 . . . . .49 C3
Taunton Cl 2 SN14 . . . . . .77 F5
Taunton St SN1 . . . . .50 A6
Tavinor Dr SN15 . . . . .78 E4
Tavistock Rd SN3 . . . . . . .51 B5
Tawney Cl SN13 . . . . .84 C6
Tawny Owl Cl SN3 . . . . . . .51 C8
Taylor Cres SN3 . . . . .36 A4
Taylors Cl SN16 . . . . .17 B1
Taylors Gn SN8 . . . . .174 A7
Taylors La SN8 . . . . .168 B1
Taylors View BA14 . . . . . .101 D1
Teal Ave SN15 . . . . .60 A1
Teal Cl BA13 . . . . .109 B4
Tealgate RG17 . . . . .177 B8
Tealsbrook SN3 . . . . .51 D7
Teal Wy GL7 . . . . .7 A6
Teapot St BA12 . . . . .201 E8
Teasel Cl
  Devizes SN10 . . . . .214 E2
  28 Ludgershall SP11 . .192 A5
Teasels The BA12 . . . . . .116 F6
Techno Ind Est SN2 . . . . . .35 E1
Tedder Ave SN13 . . . . .84 A8
Tedder Cl SN2 . . . . .35 B2
Tees Cl SN25 . . . . .35 A4
Teeswater Cl SN5 . . . . . . .49 A6
TEFFONT EVIAS 201 C2
Teffont Field Bldgs★
  SP3 . . . . .201 D4
TEFFONT MAGNA 201 C5
Teffont Manor★ SP3 . . . .201 D2
Telford Pool SN2 . . . . .49 F8
Telford Rd SP2 . . . . .151 E4
Telford Way SN1 . . . . .49 E4
Tellcroft Cl SN13 . . . . .84 F8
Tellings Orch SN16 . . . . . .16 D3
TELLISFORD 103 E4
Tempest Rd 9 SP4 . . . . .217 D3
Templar's Firs SN4 . . . . . .61 E8
Templars Way Ind Est
  SN4 . . . . .61 D7
TEMPLE 115 C6
Temple St SN1 . . . . .50 C5
TEMPLETON 177 D5
Ten Acres SP7 . . . . .202 C2
Tenby Cl SN3 . . . . .50 F3
Tench Rd SN11 . . . . .81 B5
Tennis Cnr Dro BA11 . . . .107 D2
Tennyson Cl BA12 . . . . . .116 E6
Tennyson St SN4 . . . . .47 F3
Tennyson St SN1 . . . . .50 B5
Tenzing Gdns SN25 . . . . . .35 C3
Tern Cl SN11 . . . . .81 D2
Terncliff SN3 . . . . .51 D7
Tetbury Hill SN16 . . . . . . .27 F6
Tetbury La SN16 . . . . .14 D6
Tetbury Rd BA13 . . . . . . .186 C2
Tethering Dro SP6 . . . . . .211 C6
Tewkesbury Way
  Lydiard Millicent SN5 . . .48 E7
  Swindon SN25 . . . . .49 A6
Thackeray Cl SN3 . . . . . . .51 D4
Thackeray Cres SN12 . . . .94 B4
Thames Ave SN25 . . . . . . .34 E5
Thames Cl BA12 . . . . .117 C5
Thames Cres SN12 . . . . . .94 A6
Thamesdown Dr
  Haydon Wick SN25 . . . .34 C7
  Swindon SN25 . . . . .35 A7
Thames La SN6 . . . . .19 C4
Thames St GL7 . . . . .2 C3

Thames View
  Ashton Keynes SN6 . . . .17 F8
  Ewen GL7 . . . . .5 C8
Thatcham Cl SN11 . . . . . . .81 A4
Thatchers The SN25 . . . . .35 C7
Theatre Sq SN1 . . . . .50 C6
THEOBALD'S GREEN . . .172 A8
Theobald St SN1 . . . . .50 B6
Thestfield Dr BA14 . . . . .101 C4
Thetford Way SN15 . . . . . .34 C5
Thicketts Rd SN8 . . . . . . .169 C1
THICKWOOD 75 D6
Thickwood La SN14 . . . . . .75 C6
THINGLEY 77 F1
Thirsk Cl SN14 . . . . .78 A5
Thistlebarrow Rd SP1 . . .146 A4
Thistledown 6 SN4 . . . . .163 A6
THISTLETON 75 C6
Thomas Bunn Cl BA11 . . .110 A7
Thomas Byron Rd SN10 . .214 C1
Thomas Hardy Dr 8
  SP7 . . . . .202 D2
Thomas Mead SN15 . . . . .78 E5
Thomas St SN2 . . . . .49 F7
Thomas Wyatt Rd SN10 . .214 B1
Thompson Cl SP2 . . . . . . .151 F5
Thompson Ct SN5 . . . . . . .33 A3
Thompsons Hill SN16 . . . .40 C7
Thomson Way SN8 . . . . . .213 B2
Thorley Cl SN25 . . . . .35 A6
Thornbank SN2 . . . . .94 A3
Thornbridge Ave SN3 . . . .51 A4
Thornbury Rd BA13 . . . . .108 F4
Thorne Cl SP5 . . . . .150 F1
THORNEND 58 C1
Thorne Rd
  2 Netheravon SP4 . . . .190 A4
  Swindon SN5 . . . . .51 C4
Thorneydown Rd SP4 . . .133 C1
Thorney Pk SN3 . . . . .64 B3
Thornford Dr SN5 . . . . . . .49 C5
THORNHILL 61 F1
Thornhill Dr SN25 . . . . . . .35 A8
Thornhill Ind Est SN2 . . . .35 E1
Thornhill Mews SN16 . . . .27 E2
Thornhill Rd BA12 . . . . . .116 D5
Thorns The SN8 . . . . .213 D5
Thornton Cres SN2 . . . . .144 F4
Threadgill Way 6 SP9 . . .199 C8
Three Barrows★ SN8 . . .164 B3
Three Cuppes La 4 SP1 .146 B1
Three Horseshoes Wlk
  BA12 . . . . .117 A7
Three Oak Hill Dr SN8 . . .175 D4
Three Post La 15 RG17 . .165 A2
Three Shire Stones★
  SN14 . . . . .74 D1
Three Sisters Rd 1 SN4 .163 B6
Thresher Dr SN25 . . . . . . .35 C6
Thrushel Cl SN25 . . . . . . .34 E4
Thruxton Motor Racing
  Circuit★ SP11 . . . . . . .192 C1
Thurlestone Rd SN3 . . . . .50 E5
Thurlow Cl 10 SP4 . . . . . .217 E3
Thursday St SN25 . . . . . . .34 D6
Thyme Cl SN2 . . . . .34 C3
Thyme Rd SN12 . . . . .94 D3
Tibb's Meadow SP11 . . . .192 D8
Tiberius Rd 24 SP10 . . . .193 E2
TIDCOMBE 184 C5
Tidcombe (Long Barrow)★
  SN8 . . . . .184 D4
TIDDLEYWINK 68 F4
Tidford Cts GL7 . . . . .2 C3
Tidling Cnr SN16 . . . . .16 C5
TIDPIT 209 C6
TIDWORTH 216 E7
Tidworth Cl 3 SN1 . . . . . .49 F4
Tidworth Coll SP9 . . . . . .216 D6
Tidworth Leisure Ctr
  SP9 . . . . .216 D6
Tidworth Oval★ SP9 . . . .216 C5
Tidworth Rd
  Bulford SP4 . . . . .199 A7
  Collingbourne Ducis SN8 .191 D7
  Ludgershall SP11 . . . . .191 C5
  Milston SP4 . . . . .191 B1
  Porton SP4 . . . . .133 E7
Tile Hill BA10 . . . . .122 A5
Till Cl 15 SP11 . . . . .193 E2
Tilley's La SN3 . . . . .36 A2
TILSHEAD 188 B3
Tilshead Wlk SN2 . . . . . . .35 B5
Timandra Cl SN25 . . . . . . .35 A6
Timberley La SP5 . . . . . . .211 E2
Timber St SN15 . . . . .78 E2
Timbrell St BA14 . . . . . . .101 D1
Timbrells The GL7 . . . . .5 C8
Timoney Pl 3 SN1 . . . . . . .50 B1
Timor Rd BA13 . . . . .108 E2
Tinhead Rd BA13 . . . . . . .186 C8
Tinings The SN15 . . . . . . .79 A8
Tinkers Field SN4 . . . . . . .47 D2
Tinkers Mead SN9 . . . . . .215 D4
Tinneys Cl SP5 . . . . .211 C6
Tin Pit SN8 . . . . .213 E4
Tintagel Cl
  18 Andover SP10 . . . . .193 E2
  Swindon SN5 . . . . .49 B4
Tintern Rd SN10 . . . . .214 B1
Tippett Ave 3 SN25 . . . . .34 E4
TISBURY 203 D8
Tisbury & District Sports Ctr
  SP3 . . . . .203 D8
Tisbury Rd SP3 . . . . .204 D3
Tisbury Row SP3 . . . . . . .203 F8
Tisbury Sta SP3 . . . . .203 E7

Tismeads Cres SN1 ....50 C2
Titan Barrow BA1 ....82 C2
Titchfield Cl 5 SN5 ...48 F5
Tithe Barn Cres SN1 ...49 F3
Tittymouse La SP11 ...192 F1
Tiverton Rd SN2 ....35 C1
Tobruk Cl 5 SP11 ...193 E4
Tobruk Rd SP11 ....191 F3
Tobys Ct 25 SP7 ...202 C2
TOCKENHAM 60 E3
Tockenham Cnr SN4 ...60 D6
Tockenham Way SN2 ...35 D4
TOCKENHAM WICK 60 D7
Toghill Cres SN13 ....76 B1
Tokes La SP7 ....202 E6
Tollard Cl SN3 ...51 C6
TOLLARD FARNHAM 207 B2
TOLLARD ROYAL 207 B4
Toll Down Way SN14 ...53 A4
Tollgate Cl SP4 ....217 A5
Tollgate Pk SP7 ...202 C3
Tollgate Rd
  Andover SP10 ....193 C1
  Salisbury SP1 ....152 B8
Tombs Rd SP4 ....198 A6
TOOTHILL 49 C4
Top La
  Atworth/Whitley SN12 .....85 C1
  Stourton with Gasper BA12 ....137 D7
Toppers Cl SN25 ....35 A3
Top Rd GL7 ....10 C7
Top St SN15 ....44 A2
Tormarton Rd
  Acton Turville GL9 ...52 E6
  Marshfield SN14 ....66 A2
Tornio Cl SN10 ....214 D4
Toronto Rd SP4 ....217 F8
Torr Cl SN14 ....70 B2
Torridge Cl SN25 ...34 F4
Torrington Ct SN3 ....51 A5
Torun Way SN25 ....34 D6
Tottenham Ho* SN8 ...175 F2
Tottenham Pk* SN8 ...175 F3
Totterdown Cl 3 SN1 ...51 E7
Totterdown La GL7 ...1 F3
Totts La SN14 ....75 B3
Totworth Rd SN25 ...34 C8
Toucan St BA14 ....105 E6
Touchorne La SP3 ....141 A4
Tournament Rd SP2 ...145 C3
Tout Hill SP7 ....202 B2
Tovey Ct 3 SP10 ...193 D1
Tovey Rd SN2 ....35 B2
Tow Barrow (Long Barrow)* SN8 ....184 B4
Towcester La SN14 ...77 F5
Towcester Pl 1 SN14 ...77 F5
Towcester Rd
  North Bradley BA14 ...105 E4
  Swindon SN3 ....51 C8
Towell Rd 5 SP4 ....198 A6
Tower Cl
  Andover SP10 ....193 C2
  Trowbridge BA14 ....105 A7
Tower Hill
  Dilton Marsh BA13 ......112 D7
  Iwerne Minster DT11 ...206 A1
Tower Mews SP1 ....146 B2
Tower Rd
  Melksham SN12 ....94 C5
  Stourton with Gasper BA10 122 D4
  Swindon SN5 ....34 B2
Tower View SN10 ....96 D2
Town Bridge Bradford-on-Avon* BA15 ....100 C6
Town Cl SN14 ....69 F8
Town Farm Pl SP5 ....208 B4
Townfield 10 SN8 ....170 B2
Town Gdns* SN1 ....50 C4
Town Mill SN8 ....213 D2
Town Path SP2 ....151 E7
TOWNSEND
  Poulshot 179 A6
  Urchfont 180 C3
Townsend
  Chitterne BA12 ....195 D7
  Pitton & Farley SP5 ....148 A5
Town's End BA12 ....138 F5
Townsend Cl BA12 ....138 F5
Townsend La SP6 ....209 A6
Townsend Pl SN14 ....77 F8
Towpath Rd BA14 ....101 D4
Tracy Cl SN25 ....35 A6
Trafalgar Ho* SP5 ....159 D1
Trafalgar Sch at Downton The SP5 ....211 A8
Trajan Rd SN3 ....36 C1
Transfer Bridges Ind Est SN1 ....50 D8
Travellers Rest SN13 ...76 C1
Trecastle Rd 1 SN1 ...50 A2
Treforest Cl 1 SN25 ...34 C7
Tregantle Wlk SN3 ...51 C6
Tregoze Prim Sch SN5 ...49 A6
Tregoze Way SN5 ...48 F6
Trenchard Ave
  Box SN13 ....84 A8
  Calne Without SN11 ...81 F1
  4 Corsham SN13 ...76 B1
  Winterbourne SP4 ....133 C2
Trenchard Cl 5 SN14 ...78 A6
Trenchard Rd
  Lyneham SN15 ....60 A1
  Stanton Fitzwarren SN6 ...22 B2
Trent Cres SN12 ....94 A6
Trentham Cl SN3 ....51 A4
Trent Rd SN25 ....35 A4

Trevello Rd SN1 ....50 B2
Trevithick Cl 5 BA11 ...110 C6
Trimm's Dro SP6 ....211 A4
Trimnells SN14 ....75 B3
Trinity CE Prim Sch SN10 ....214 C5
Trinity Cl SN3 ....51 A3
Trinity Rise SN11 ....81 C1
Trinity St SP1 ....152 B8
Tropenell Cl 2 SN13 ...76 E1
Trout La SN13 ....84 B7
TROWBRIDGE 101 E3
Trowbridge Com Hospl BA14 ....101 D2
Trowbridge Lodge Pk BA14 ....105 F8
Trowbridge Mus* BA14. 105 D8
Trowbridge Rd
  Bradford-on-Avon BA15 ...100 E5
  Bratton BA13 ....186 A4
  Seend SN12 ....178 C7
  Trowbridge BA14 ....102 A2
  Westbury BA13 ....109 B5
Trowbridge Sports Ctr BA14 ....105 B6
Trowbridge Sta BA14 ...105 C8
Trow La
  Brinkworth SN15 ....59 F8
  Maiden Bradley with Yarnfield BA12 ....118 C4
Trowle BA14 ....101 A2
TROWLE COMMON 100 F2
Truman Cl SN3 ....51 C4
Truro Wlk SN14 ....77 F6
Truscott Ave SN25 ....34 E8
Trusloe SN8 ....173 B8
Tryhorn Dr SP1 ....146 C5
Tryon Cl SN3 ....51 D2
Tubbs Farm Cl 6 RG17 ...165 A1
Tucker Cl 6 SP4 ....217 C2
Tuckers La SN4 ....163 D6
TUCKINGHAM 203 D8
Tuckwell Rd GL7 ....10 E6
Tudor Cl SN15 ....79 A4
Tudor Cres SN3 ....36 B1
Tudor Dr BA14 ....101 E4
Tudor Wlk SN3 ....50 F6
Tugela Rd SN15 ....70 E1
Tuggy's La BA2 ....98 E1
Tulip Tree Cl SN2 ....35 C2
Tulse Hill
  Zeale BA12 ....138 A4
  Zennor BA12 ....137 F3
Tumlins SN10 ....180 F8
Tunball La SN8 ....184 F4
Tunnel Hill SP5 ....153 C2
Tunnicliffe Cl SN3 ...50 E2
Tupman Rd SN13 ....76 E2
Turf Ho La SN11 ....72 D1
Turin Cl 17 SP10 ....193 E2
TURLEIGH 99 F6
Turl St SN1 ....50 C6
Turnball SN4 ....65 D4
Turnberry Cl SN15 ....78 F7
Turner Cl 2 SP2 ....151 E7
Turner Cl SP10 ....193 D1
Turner St SN1 ....50 A5
Turnham Gn SN5 ....49 A4
Turnpike 4 SN8 ....170 A6
Turnpike La BA14 ....102 F5
Turnpike Rd
  Blunsdon St Andrew SN26 ...35 C8
  Highworth SN6 ....23 A6
Turnpike The
  Chippenham SN15 ...79 B5
  East Knoyle SP3 ....202 D8
Turnstile Wlk 3 BA14 ...105 F7
Turntable Pl BA13 ....108 F5
Turpin Way SN14 ....77 F7
Tuscan Rd SN25 ....34 D7
Tutton Hill SN14 ....75 B3
Twatley Cotts SN16 ....27 C4
Tweed Cl SN25 ....34 F4
Twickenham Cl SN3 ...51 B8
Twickenham Way SN15 ...70 E1
Twineham Gdns SP5 ...153 F2
Twineham Rd SN25 ...34 C8
Twyford Cl SN3 ....51 A4
Twynham Cl SP5 ....211 A7
Twynnoy Cl SN16 ....28 A5
Tyburn Cl SN5 ....49 B5
Tydeman St SN1 ....35 D1
Tye Gdns SN5 ....48 F5
Tylees Ct SN10 ....214 B3
Tylers Cl SP2 ....151 D7
Tyndale Gdns SN3 ....51 C6
Tyndales Meadow SP3 ...201 F2
Tyneham Rd SN3 ....51 B6
Tyning Cl 1 BA14 ....105 A7
Tyning La 8 BA13 ....186 B7
Tyning Pk SN11 ....81 C1
Tyning Rd
  Bathampton BA2 ....82 A2
  Winsley BA15 ....99 E7
Tynings The
  Biddestone SN14 ....76 D7
  Westbury BA13 ....108 F2
Tynings Way BA15 ....99 F3
Tyning The BA2 ....99 B4
Tyrone Ave SP4 ....198 E7

Tythe Cl 17 SP11 ....193 F2
TYTHERINGTON 194 B4
Tytherington Rd BA12 ...194 C5
Tytherley Rd SP5 ....149 E6
TYTHERTON LUCAS 71 D1

U

Uddens Rd SP5 ....207 C4
UFFCOTT 167 E8
UGFORD 144 A3
Ullswater Cl SN3 ....51 E3
Ulysses Rd 2 SN25 ....34 B7
Umbers Hill 2 SP7 ....202 B1
Underacre Cl BA14 ....106 B8
Underdown Cl 12 SN4 ...163 A6
UNDERHILL 140 F2
Underhill
  Mere BA12 ....138 F5
  Pen Selwood BA9 ....137 B2
Underwood Dr SP4 ....217 D2
Union Rd
  Chippenham SN15 ....78 D8
  Tisbury SP3 ....203 D7
Union Row SN1 ....50 D4
Union St
  Melksham SN12 ....94 A4
  Ramsbury SN8 ....170 B2
  Swindon SN1 ....50 C5
  Trowbridge BA14 ....101 D1
Unity St SN14 ....78 C7
UPAVON 181 F2
Upavon Airfield SN9 ....182 B1
Upavon Ct SN2 ....35 C5
Upavon Prim Sch SN9 ...182 A1
Upcott SN6 ....8 C4
Upfield SN3 ....51 D3
Upham Rd SN3 ....50 E5
Upham Village* SN8 ...169 C8
Upland Rise BA13 ....109 B2
Uplands 28 RG17 ....177 B2
Uplands Cl BA2 ....98 F7
Uplands The
  Warminster BA12 ....117 C7
  Warminster BA12 ....117 C7
Upnor Cl SP11 ....191 F4
Upper Backway SP3 ...196 F7
Upper Broad St BA14 ...101 C1
UPPER BURGATE 210 E3
UPPER CASTLE COMBE ...68 B8
UPPER CHICKSGROVE ...201 A1
Upper Church Fields SN8 ....213 E1
UPPER CHUTE 192 D8
Upper Dro SP10 ....193 C1
UPPER EDDINGTON RG17 ...177 C8
UPPER ENHAM 193 F4
Upper Folly SP2 ....144 B1
Upper Garston La 8 BA13 ....186 B7
UPPER GREEN 177 E2
UPPER INGLESHAM 12 B5
Upper Isbury SN8 ....213 E2
Upper La SN13 ....84 D7
UPPER LAMBOURN 164 F3
Upper Lambourn Rd RG17 ....165 A2
Upper Ley SN13 ....83 D5
Upper Marsh La BA12 ...117 A5
Upper Marsh Rd BA12 ...117 A6
UPPER MINETY 16 D3
Upper Noremarsh SN4 ...47 F1
Upper North Rd SP5 ...207 C5
Upper Pavenhill SN5 ...32 F4
UPPER PICKWICK 76 C3
Upper Potley SN13 ....84 E7
Upper Regents Pk BA15 ...100 D6
UPPER SEAGRY 57 D6
Upper St SP1 ....151 D7
UPPER STRATTON 35 E4
UPPER STREET 210 D5
UPPER STUDLEY 105 A5
UPPER TOWN 58 D4
UPPER UP 6 E6
UPPER UPHAM 169 C8
Upper Waterhay Nature Reserve* SN6 ....18 D7
UPPER WOODFORD 131 C7
UPPER WRAXALL 66 E2
Upper Wr St BA12 ....139 B5
Uppington La SP3 ....129 E8
Up St BA12 ....194 E4
UPTON
  East Knoyle 141 A5
  Vernhams Dean 185 D2
Upton Cl
  Swindon SN25 ....34 C8
  5 Warminster BA12 ....116 E7
Upton Great Barrow* BA12 ....194 F5
UPTON LOVELL 194 E3
UPTON SCUDAMORE 112 E5
URCHFONT 180 C4
Urchfont CE Prim Sch SN10 ....180 B4
Urchfont Way SN2 ....35 C4
Ursa Wy 16 SN25 ....34 B7
Utah Cl SN1 ....49 F4
UTC Swindon SN1 ....50 A6
Utterson View SN15 ....78 C7
Uxbridge Rd SN5 ....49 A3

V

Vale Leaze SN15 ....44 C5
Valens Terr SN13 ....83 C6
Valentia Ct 19 SN12 ....178 B8
Vale Rd
  Pewsey SN9 ....215 B5
  Redlynch SP5 ....211 C7
Vale View SN4 ....47 C1
Vale View Rd SP2 ....130 B2
Valiant Cl 9 SN12 ....178 B8
Valletta Gdns SN14 ....56 B5
Valley Cl SP5 ....211 C7
Valley Rd SN13 ....76 E1
Valleyside SN1 ....50 A4
Valley The SP2 ....145 C5
Valley View SN11 ....81 A2
Valley Vw 18 SN8 ....170 A6
Valley Way SN14 ....75 C6
Vanbrugh Gate SN3 ...50 E3
Vancouver Dr 9 SP4 ...217 F8
Van Diemen's Cl SN8 ...213 C1
Vanessa Ave SP1 ....146 D1
VASTERN 60 F8
Vasterne Cl SN5 ....33 B5
Vastern Wharf SN4 ....61 A7
Vaughan Williams Wy SN25 ....34 D7
Vega Cl 10 SN25 ....34 B7
Velley Hill SN13 ....85 C5
Venice Ct 30 SP11 ....193 F2
Venn The 11 SP7 ....202 C2
Ventnor Cl SN2 ....34 E4
Ventry Cl 3 SP1 ....146 B2
Ventry The 4 SP1 ....146 B2
Verden Way 19 SP10 ....193 D2
Verney Cl SN3 ....51 D6
Vernham Bank 185 B3
VERNHAM DEAN 185 C3
Vernham Dean Gullum's Prim Sch SP11 ....185 C3
VERNHAM ROW 185 B4
VERNHAM STREET 185 C3
Vernon Cl 2 SP4 ....217 E3
Verona Rd SP1 ....145 F4
Verulam Cl SN3 ....51 D8
Verwood Cl SN3 ....51 B4
Vespasian Cl SN3 ....51 C6
Vespasian Rd
  19 Andover SP10 ....193 E2
  Forest Hill SN8 ....175 A7
Vetch Wy 27 SP11 ....193 F2
Vicarage Cl
  Calne SN11 ....81 B3
  Marlborough SN8 ....213 B3
Vicarage Cotts SN15 ...57 F6
Vicarage Gdns
  Malmesbury SN16 ....28 B2
  3 Netheravon SP4 ....190 A3
Vicarage La
  Charlton SN16 ....29 B7
  Colerne SN14 ....75 C3
  Easterton SN10 ....179 F2
  Hankerton SN16 ....15 B1
  Highworth SN6 ....23 A6
  Steeple Ashton BA14 ...178 A3
  Upavon SN9 ....181 F2
Vicarage Mews BA14 ...116 F7
Vicarage Pk 1 SP5 ....211 C7
Vicarage Rd
  Redlynch SP5 ....211 E7
  Swindon SN2 ....34 F1
  Tisbury SP3 ....203 E8
Vicarage St BA12 ....116 F7
Vice Cl SO51 ....212 E2
Victoria Cl
  Lyneham SN11 ....73 E8
  Wilton SP2 ....144 C3
Victoria Cross Rd SN4 ...63 F7
Victoria Ct SP1 ....146 A3
Victoria Dr
  10 Bulford SP4 ....217 B8
  Lyneham SN15 ....60 B1
Victoria Gdns
  14 Sandleheath SP6 ...210 C1
  Trowbridge BA14 ....101 E2
Victoria Pk SN10 ....187 B8
Victoria Rd
  Devizes SN10 ....214 A4
  Frome BA11 ....110 A4
  Salisbury SP1 ....146 A2
  Sandleheath SP6 ....210 C1
  Swindon SN1 ....50 C5
  Trowbridge BA14 ....101 C3
  Warminster BA12 ....116 C6
  Wilton SP2 ....144 C3
Victoria St 21 SP7 ....202 C2
Victoria Terr SN11 ....81 B3
Victory Rd BA13 ....108 C6
Viking Cl SN25 ....34 F7
Viking Way
  Andover SP10 ....193 E2
  Salisbury SP2 ....152 B5
Vilett St SN1 ....50 B6
Village Mus the Castle Combe* SN14 ....68 A7
Village St SN8 ....173 D1
Villiers Cl
  Chippenham SN15 ...78 F7
  Lydiard Tregoze SN5 ...48 F7
Vimoutiers Ct 16 SP6 ...210 D1
Vimy Cres
  Bulford SP4 ....217 F8
  8 Durrington/Bulford SP4 198 E6
Vincent Cl SN12 ....94 C4
Vincients Rd SN14 ....69 F1

Vincients Wood Nature Reserve* SN14 ....77 F7
Viner's La GL9 ....53 B5
Vinescroft 4 BA14 ....101 D5
Vines Ct SN12 ....94 D5
Virginia Cl 1 SP4 ....217 E3
Virginia Dr BA12 ....116 E7
Viscount Way SN3 ....36 C6
Vista Ct 4 BA13 ....109 A3
Vistula Cres 2 SN25 ....34 E6
Vockins Cl SP9 ....216 C5
Volpe Cl SN5 ....48 F4
Volta Rd SN1 ....50 C6
Vorda Rd SN6 ....23 A7
Vowley View SN4 ....47 F1
Voyager Dr SN25 ....34 B7

W

Wade Hill SN6 ....22 F5
Wade Mews SN15 ....70 E1
Wade Rd 3 SN25 ....34 D7
WADSWICK 84 B4
Wadswick La SN13 ....84 B3
Wadworth Rd SN10 ....214 C4
Waggoner Cl SN25 ....35 B6
Wagtail Cl SN3 ....51 C8
Waiblingen Way SN10 ...214 A4
Wain-a-Long Rd SP1 ...146 C1
Wainwright Cl 4 SN3 ...51 D4
Wainwright Dr 5 BA11 ...110 C6
Wainwright Mews SN4 ...64 B6
Waite Meads Cl SN5 ...33 C4
Wakefield Cl
  Kempsford GL7 ....10 E6
  Swindon SN5 ....49 A4
Walbury Hill (Fort)* RG17 ....185 F8
WALCOT EAST 50 F6
Walcot Rd SN3 ....50 F6
WALCOT WEST 50 E5
Walden Lodge Cl SN10 ...214 B2
Waldron Cl 3 SN3 ....51 C4
Waleran Cl SP5 ....153 E2
Walker Rd BA11 ....110 A3
Walker's La 3 RG17 ....165 A2
Walkinshaw Rd 5 SN2 ...34 E2
Wallbridge BA11 ....110 B4
Wallbridge Ave 2 BA11 ...110 A4
Wallbridge Gdns 1 BA11 ....110 A4
Wallbridge Mills BA11 ...110 B4
Waller Rd SN10 ....214 E7
Wallingford Cl SN5 ....49 C3
Wallingtons Rd RG17 ...177 F4
Wallis Dr SN25 ....35 A8
Wallsworth Rd 4 SN3 ...51 A4
Walmesley Chase BA14 ...102 A1
Walnut Cl
  3 Netheravon SP4 ....190 A4
  Pewsey SN9 ....215 D5
  Rowde SN10 ....96 D1
  Sutton Veny BA12 ....121 F8
Walnut Dr SN14 ....74 F6
Walnut Gr BA14 ....105 B6
Walnut Rd BA12 ....139 B4
Walnut Tree Cl SN3 ....36 B2
Walnut Tree Gdns SN5 ...48 D8
Walnut Trees Hill SN6 ...164 A8
Walnut Wlk 1 BA11 ....110 B7
Walronds Ct SN8 ....170 C6
Walsingham Rd SN3 ....50 F6
Walter Cl SN5 ....49 A6
Walter Sutton Cl SN11 ...80 F3
Walter Wy 2 SP4 ....132 C1
Walton Cl 5 SN3 ....50 F4
Walwayne Ct Prim Sch BA14 ....105 B8
Walwayne Field SN2 ....36 A5
Walworth Rd SP10 ....193 F1
WANBOROUGH 163 A5
Wanborough Prim Sch SN4 ....163 A6
Wanborough Rd
  Swindon SN3 ....36 C1
  Wanborough SN4 ....51 F6
Wansdyke* SN11 ....172 C5
Wansdyke Com Sch SN10 ....214 B1
Wansdyke Dr SN11 ....81 B3
Wansdyke Rd SN8 ....176 B4
Wantage Rd RG17 ....165 B2
Waram Cl RG17 ....177 C8
Warbeck Gate 11 SN5 ...48 F5
Warbler Cl 1 BA14 ....105 B8
Warburton Cl BA14 ....105 A6
Wardley Cl SN3 ....51 A4
WARDOUR 203 D6
Wardour Cl SN3 ....50 E3
Wardour Pl 4 SN12 ....94 A2
Wardour RC Prim Sch SP3 ....203 C6
Wardour Rd 13 SN14 ....78 A6
Wardrobe Mus* SP1 ...152 A8
Wareham Cl SN5 ....49 B5
WARLEIGH 90 D5
Warleigh Dr BA1 ....82 A3
Warleigh La BA1 ....82 B1
War Meml Ave 13 RG17 ...177 B6
Warmer's Inn La SN16 ...27 D8
WARMINSTER 116 E7
Warminster Ave 2 SN2 ...35 C5
Warminster Coll BA12 ...117 A7

Warminster Com Hospl
  BA12....................117 A7
WARMINSTER
  COMMON..............116 E5
Warminster Dewey
  Musuem★ BA12......117 B7
Warminster Rd
  Claverton BA2..........90 B4
  Frome BA11..........110 B4
  Westbury BA13.......108 F1
  Wilton SP2...........144 D5
Warminster Sch BA12...116 F7
Warminster Sports Ctr
  BA12................117 D6
Warminster Sta BA12....117 B7
Warneage Gn **2** SN4..163 A5
Warneford Cl **4** SN3...49 D4
Warner Cl **2** SN3......36 B3
Warren Bsns Pk SN11....24 F5
Warren Cres SN11........81 C4
Warrener Cl SN25........35 B7
Warren Rd BA14.........101 D5
Warrens La SP5.........159 A4
Warwick Cl
  Chippenham SN14......77 F5
  Salisbury SP1........145 F3
Warwick Cres SN12......94 B3
Warwick Rd SN1.........50 C5
Washbourne Rd SN4......47 E1
Washern Cl SP2........144 C1
Washers Pit★ DT11....206 D3
Washington Rd BA13....108 C6
Washmeres SN2...........75 B2
Washpool La GL7.........10 E8
Wason Rd **5** SP4....197 E6
Waste Dr GL8............25 A8
Wastfield SN13..........84 F8
Watercrook Mews **2** SN5..49 D5
Waterdown Cl **2** SN2...34 C4
Water Ditchampton SP2..144 C4
Water Field SN5.........33 A3
Waterford Beck BA14...104 F6
Water Furlongs **2** SN6..19 D7
Watergate La SP4......217 C7
Watergates SN14.........75 C3
WATERHAY................18 C7
Waterhouse La BA2......98 F8
Water La
  Castle Combe SN14.....68 A7
  Enford SN9...........190 B6
  Horningsham BA12....119 A8
  Salisbury SP1........152 A8
Water Lily Cl BA14....101 D4
Waterloo Rd SP1.......152 C7
Watermead SN3..........36 C2
Watermeadow La **2** SN5..195 C1
Water Meadows SN16.....28 A2
Watermint Way SN11.....80 F4
Waters Bank Rd SN13....84 B8
Waters Edge SN15.......78 E5
Waterside Pk Ind Est SN2..49 E8
Waterside Way SN3......51 A1
Watersmeet Rd SP2.....152 A6
Waters Rd SP1.........146 A4
Water St
  Berwick St John SP7..203 E1
  Durrington/Bulford SP4..217 D8
  Mere BA12...........139 B5
  Upton Lovell BA12...194 E3
Waterworks Rd BA14....105 B7
Watery La
  Donhead St Mary SP7..203 A3
  Shaftesbury SP7......202 C1
  Sutton Veny BA12....117 F4
Watling Cl SN2.........49 E6
Watson Rd SP4.........197 E4
Watson's Ct **2** SN12..94 B4
Watt Cl **4** SP10....193 C1
Watt Rd SP2...........151 D8
Watts La SN14..........41 F1
Watt's Way **22** SN10..179 F1
Wavell Rd
  Salisbury SP2........152 A6
  Swindon SN2..........35 B2
  Tidworth SP9........216 B8
Waverley Cl
  7 Fordingbridge SP6..210 D2
  Frome BA11..........110 C6
Waverley Cl SN13.......85 A8
Waverley Gdns SN12.....94 A3
Waverley Rd
  Fordingbridge SP6....210 D2
  Swindon SN3..........36 C1
Waylands
  Cricklade SN6.........19 E7
  Devizes SN10........214 D3
Wayne Cl SN25..........35 A5
Wayside Cl
  Frome BA11..........110 C6
  Kington Langley SN15..70 E2
  Swindon SN2..........49 E7
Wayte St **5** SN25....34 E3
Weavealand Rd **2** SP3..203 E8
Weavern Ct SN14........78 A7
Weavern La SN13........76 A5
Weavers Cl
  Chippenham SN14......77 F7
  3 Malmesbury SN16..28 A5
Weavers Crofts SN12....94 A5
Weavers Dr BA14.......105 D7
Weavers La RG17.......177 E3
Weavers Mead SN10....179 C1
Weavers The SN3........50 D4
Webb Cl SN15...........78 E5
Webbers Ct BA14......105 A6

Webbington Rd SN15.....78 E5
Webbs Ct SN15..........60 A3
Webb's La SN10........179 D8
Webbs Way
  Burbage SN8.........183 D8
  Malmesbury SN16......28 A5
Webbs Wood SN5........34 A2
Wedgewood Cl SN2......50 A7
WEDHAMPTON...........180 E4
Wedmore Ave SN15......70 C1
Wedmore Cl BA11......110 C7
Weedon Rd SN3.........51 B8
Weeke Cl **1** SP5....210 F8
Weir Heyes Ave **7** SN13..76 B1
Weir La SN14...........74 A8
Weirside Ave SN4.......64 B6
Weir The BA13.........186 C8
Welbeck Cl SN3.........50 F5
Welcombe Ave SN3.......51 A5
Welford Cl SN3.........51 C8
WELL BOTTOM...........206 E3
Well Cl SN4............65 D4
Weller Rd SN13.........76 F2
Welle Sley Cl **18** SN12..178 B8
Wellhead Dro BA13.....109 A1
Wellhead La BA13......109 A1
Well House Cl SP6.....210 B6
Well La
  Godshill SP6.........211 A1
  Hawkesbury GL9.......38 E5
  4 Shaftesbury SP7..202 B2
Wellow Dr BA11.......110 C7
Wellow La BA2..........98 D1
Wellow Wood Rd SO51...212 F8
Wells Cl
  Chippenham SN14......78 A5
  Durrington SP4......198 A6
Wells Rd SP4..........198 A6
Wells St SN1...........50 C6
Wellworthy Dr SP4....151 D7
Welsh Way GL7...........1 D8
Welton Rd SN5..........49 D6
Wembley St SN2.........49 F8
Wenhill Hts SN11.......81 B2
Wenhill La SN11........81 A1
Wensleydale Cl SN5.....49 B6
Wentworth Cl SN15......78 F7
Wentworth Pk **1** SN5..49 A4
Were Cl **3** BA12....116 E7
Werg SN8.............175 B8
Wesley Cl BA14.......104 E2
Wesley La BA14.......104 E2
Wesley Rd BA14.......105 C7
Wesley St SN1..........50 C4
Wessex Cl
  Calne SN11............81 C3
  Melksham SN12.........94 B3
  Semington BA14......102 E5
Wessex Coll BA12......117 C6
Wessex Pl **20** RG17..177 B7
Wessex Rd
  Chippenham SN14......78 B8
  Salisbury SP1........146 C1
  Wilton SP2..........144 C1
Wessex Way SN6........23 B7
Wessex Wlk BA13......109 A4
Wessington Ave SN11....81 C1
Wessington Ct SN11.....81 C1
Wessington Pk SN11.....81 C1
West Allcourt GL7.......2 C4
WEST AMESBURY........198 A4
WEST ASHTON..........106 B3
West Ashton CE Prim Sch
  BA14...............106 B4
West Ashton Rd BA14...105 E8
Westbourne Cl SP1.....152 C8
Westbourne Gdns **6**
  BA14...............105 B8
Westbourne Rd
  Trowbridge BA14.....105 B8
  Westbury BA13.......109 A3
West Bourton Rd SP8...137 D1
WESTBROOK.............95 E8
Westbrook Cl
  Chippenham SN14......78 A7
  14 Hungerford RG17..177 B7
Westbrook Gn SN15.....95 E8
Westbrook Rd
  Bromham SN15.........88 A1
  Swindon SN2..........35 A1
WESTBURY.............109 B2
Westbury Ind Est BA13..108 E5
Westbury Infants' Sch
  BA13...............108 F3
WESTBURY LEIGH........108 E1
Westbury Leigh BA13...108 E1
Westbury Leigh CE Prim Sch
  BA13...............108 E1
Westbury Pk SN4.......47 D1
Westbury Rd
  Bratton BA13........186 A4
  Cheverell Magna SN10..179 C1
  Heywood BA13.......109 A8
  North Bradley BA14..105 E3

Westbury Rd continued
  Swindon SN2..........35 B5
  Warminster BA12.....113 A2
Westbury Sta BA13....108 E5
Westbury View SN12.....94 C4
Westbury Visitor Ctr★
  BA13...............109 A3
Westbury White Horse★
  BA13...............109 F3
West Cepen Way
  Chippenham SN14......70 B3
  Chippenham Without SN14..77 F5
WEST CHISENBURY......189 F7
Westcombe La BA12....195 E1
Westcott Cl **9** BA11..110 C6
Westcott Pl SN1........50 A5
Westcott St SN1........50 A5
Westcroft SN14.........78 A5
Westcroft St BA14....101 C1
WEST CRUDWELL.........14 D7
WEST DEAN...........155 F3
West Ditch La BA14...106 E4
West End
  Bishops Cannings SN10..172 B3
  Melksham SN12.........94 A3
  Westbury BA13.......109 A3
West End La
  Bishopstone SN6.....163 E6
  Donhead St Andrew SP7..203 B3
West End Rd
  Salisbury SP2........145 E2
  Swindon SN3..........36 A1
West Ennox La SN13.....84 A6
Westerham Wlk SN11.....81 C2
Westerleigh Cl SN14....78 B6
Western Downland CE Aided
  Prim Sch SP6........210 D1
Western St SN1.........50 C5
Western Way
  Melksham SN12.........93 F3
  Salisbury SP2........145 B3
Westfield BA15........100 B7
Westfield Chase **13** SN8..170 A6
Westfield Cl
  15 Durrington/Bulford
    SP4................198 B7
  Laverstock SP1......146 D2
  Trowbridge BA14.....105 A6
Westfield Est BA12....137 F4
Westfield Rd BA14.....105 A7
Westfield Way SN2......34 D4
WEST GRAFTON.........183 E7
WEST GRIMSTEAD.......154 C2
Westgrove **17** SP6...210 D1
WEST HATCH..........203 C7
West Hay Gr GL7........4 F7
West Highland Rd SN25..34 F7
WEST HILL.............85 B1
West Hill
  Broad Blunsdon SN26...21 B2
  Melksham Without SN12..85 B1
Westhill Cl SN6........22 F5
WEST KENNETT........173 D7
West Kennett Long Barrow★
  SN8................173 C6
WEST KINGTON..........66 F7
WEST KINGTON WICK.....67 B6
WEST KNOYLE.........140 E6
West La
  Kemble GL7............4 F7
  Melbury Abbas SP7...206 A7
Westlake Pl SN15.......57 D1
Westland Cl **3** SP4..217 D3
Westlands **2** BA14..194 C5
Westlands La SN12......85 F2
WEST LAVINGTON......187 E8
WESTLEA..............49 D5
Westlea Campus SN5....49 C7
Westlea Dr SN5.........49 C5
Westlea Prim Sch SN5...49 C6
Westlecot Rd SN1.......50 B3
Westleigh BA12.......116 E6
West Manton SN8......174 C7
Westmead Cres BA14...105 B4
Westmead Dr SN5......49 D6
Westmead Ind Est SN5...49 D6
Westmead Terr SN15....78 E6
West Mill La SN6........8 C1
Westminster Cl
  Dunkirk SN10........179 D8
  1 Shaftesbury SP7..202 D2
Westminster Gdns SN14..78 B7
Westminster Meml Hospl
  SP7................202 B1
Westminster Rd
  Salisbury SP2........145 F2
  Swindon SN5..........49 B4
Westmorland Rd SN1.....50 D5
WESTONBIRT...........25 D8
Westonbirt Arboretum★
  GL8................25 B8
Westonbirt Sch GL8.....25 E8
Weston Ct **1** SP11..193 E4
Weston La SP5........149 B5
WEST OVERTON........173 F6
West Par BA12........116 F6
West Pk SP11.........192 E3
West Pk★ SP6.........210 A3
West Pk Dr SP6.......209 F3
West Pk La SP6.......209 F3
West Pk Rd SN13.......76 E1
Westpoint Bsns Pk SN14..70 A1
West Portway SP10....193 C1
WESTROP...............77 C1
Westrop SN6...........23 A6
Westrop Prim Sch SN6...22 F6
West St Pl BA12......116 E6

Westside SP4.........199 A2
Westside Cl SP4......146 C8
West St
  Aldbourne SN8.......170 A6
  Barford St Martin SP3..143 A4
  Castle Combe SN14....68 A7
  22 Fordingbridge SP6..210 D1
  Great Somerford SN15..43 F7
  Great Wishford SP2..129 F4
  Lacock SN15..........86 D5
  4 Malmesbury SN16..28 A4
  Salisbury SP2........145 F1
  Trowbridge BA14.....105 C8
  Warminster BA12.....116 E6
  Wilton SP2..........144 C3
WEST STOWELL........173 F1
West Swindon Sh Ctr SN5 49 B5
West View SN3.........51 B7
West View Cres SN10...214 A3
Westview Orch BA2......99 B5
West View Rd BA12......82 A3
West Vw Rd SN8.......191 A8
West Way GL7...........2 C5
WESTWELLS.............84 C6
Westwells SN13........84 C6
Westwells Rd SN13......84 B7
West Wick **6** SP5...210 F8
West Wiltshire Craft Ctr★
  BA13...............108 D7
West Wilts Trading Est
  BA13...............108 D7
WEST WINTERSLOW.....148 F5
West Wlk SP1.........152 A7
WESTWOOD
  Salisbury............145 B5
  Westwood............99 F2
Westwood Manor House★
  BA15...............100 A3
Westwood Rd
  Corsham SN13.........84 B8
  Salisbury SP2........145 B4
  Swindon SN2..........35 C6
  Wingfield BA14......100 D2
Westwoods BA1.........82 B3
Westwood St Thomas Sch
  SP2................145 A4
Westwood-with-Iford Prim
  Sch BA15.............99 F3
WEST YATTON..........68 D3
Wetherby Cl **1** SN14..78 A5
Wetherby Gdns **24** SP10..193 D2
Wet La BA12..........139 D2
Wet Pits La SN8......168 E3
Wexcombe.............184 B6
Wexland Ave SP4......189 F3
Wey Cl SN25...........35 A4
WEYHILL.............192 F1
Weyhill Cl SN3.........51 B5
Weyhill Gdns **7** SP11..192 F1
Weyhill Rd SP11......193 A1
Weymouth St BA12.....117 A6
WHADDON
  Alderbury...........153 E1
  Hilperton...........102 C7
Whaddon La
  Hilperton BA14......102 B5
  Trowbridge BA14.....102 A3
Whalley Cres SN4......63 F6
Wharf Ct SN12.........94 B3
Wharf Ctr The★ SN10...214 A4
Wharfings The GL7......10 D6
Wharf La
  Kempsford GL7........10 D6
  Lechlade GL7..........2 D3
Wharf Rd SN4..........49 C1
Wharf St SN10........214 A4
Wharf The SN13........83 D6
Wharf Theatre & Ctr The
  SN10...............214 A4
Wharncliffe St SN25....34 D8
Whatcombe Brow SP3...196 D8
Whatley Dr SN9.......215 C5
Whatleys Cl SN10.....179 A4
Whatleys Orch SN6....163 E6
Wheat Cl BA14........105 F7
Wheatcroft Wy SN1.....50 E7
Wheatlands SN25.......34 E4
Wheatsheaf La SN16....16 A8
Wheatstone Rd SN3.....51 E4
Wheeler Ave SN2.......35 D2
Wheeler Cl SN9.......215 B5
Wheeler Pl SN11.......96 E1
Wheelwright's Cl SP5..208 A4
Whelford Rd GL7.......10 D7
Whilestone Way SN3....36 C1
Whinyates Rd **2** SP4..197 E2
Whistley Rd SN10.....179 C8
Whitbourne Ave SN3....50 F5
WHITBOURNE MOOR.....115 C7
WHITBOURNE SPRINGS..115 E5
Whitbred Cl **2** SN5...49 B7
Whitbred Rd SP2......145 C5
Whitby Gr SN2.........34 F1
Whitchers Meadow SP5..153 D4
Whitcombe Cl SN15.....73 F8
White Barrow (Long
  Barrow)★ SP3.......188 B1
White Beam Ct SN2.....35 B2
Whitebridge Rd SP1...146 D1
White Castle SN5......49 C3
White Cliff★ BA13...186 B6
Whitecroft BA13......112 C8
WHITE CROSS..........137 E5
White Eagle Rd SN25...34 D5
White Edge Moor SN3...51 D2
White Ennox La SN13...83 F7
White Farm La SN8....185 C7
Whitefield Cl BA1.....82 B4

Whitefield Cres SN5....34 A1
Whitefriars La SN6......6 E3
Whitefriars Rd **1** SP1..152 B7
Whitegates BA8........A8
White Hart La **12** SP7..202 C1
Whiteheads La BA15....100 D7
Whitehead St SN1.......50 B5
WHITE HILL...........139 C2
Whitehill BA15.......100 D7
White Hill
  Bishopstone SN4.....163 D5
  Pitton & Farley SP5..148 C3
Whitehill Cl **11** SN8..170 B2
Whitehill Ind Pk SN4...47 B1
Whitehill La SN4.......47 B2
Whitehill Way SN5......48 F3
Whitehorn Cl SN4......47 E4
Whitehorn Dr SP5.....212 C5
White Horse Bsns Pk
  BA14...............105 D4
White Horse La BA14...105 D6
White Horse Dr **8** BA11..110 C6
White Horse Rd
  Cricklade SN6.........19 D8
  Forest Hill SN8.....175 A7
  Winsley BA15.........99 E7
White Horse Sports Ctr
  SN11...............81 C1
White Horse Way
  Calne SN11............81 B1
  Westbury BA13.......109 A4
White Horse Wy
  Devizes SN10........214 C5
  Devizes SN10........214 D6
Whitehouse La GL8......26 B8
Whitehouse Rd SN2......50 B8
Whiteland Rise BA13...109 B2
Whitelands Rd SN3......36 A1
Whitelawn La BA14....106 F4
White Lion Pk SN16.....27 E4
Whitelocks Piece RG17..171 A1
Whiteman St SN2........50 C8
Whitemarsh BA12......139 B4
WHITEPARISH..........161 B4
Whiteparish All Saints CE
  Prim Sch SP5.......161 D3
White Pit La SP7.....206 B6
WHITEPITS...........126 A7
White Rd
  Mere BA12...........139 B6
  Savernake SN8.......175 A6
White Row Hill BA14...105 A5
Whiterow Pk BA14.....105 A6
Whitesbury Rd SP5....152 B1
Whites Cnr SN12.......85 D1
White Sheet Castle★
  BA12...............124 E1
Whitesheet CE Prim Acad
  BA12...............138 C4
White Sheet Hill Nature
  Reserve★ BA12......124 E2
White Sheet La BA12...124 C5
White's Hill SN6......169 F2
Whiteshoot SP5.......211 D6
Whiteshoot Hill SP5..211 D6
White Shute RG17.....171 A8
White St
  Easterton SN10......180 A1
  Horningsham BA12...119 B8
  21 Market Lavington SN10 179 F1
Whitestone Rd BA11...110 B6
Whites Wy SN15........57 C2
White Way
  Broad Town SN4.....167 A8
  Pitton & Farley SP5..148 C3
Whitfield Cl
  Warminster BA12....117 C7
  Warminster BA12....117 C7
Whitgift Cl SN5.......48 F6
WHITLEY.............85 C1
Whitley Rd **14** SN8..170 A6
Whitlock Rise SP5....205 F5
Whitmarsh Rd **7** SP4..190 A4
Whitmore Cl SN5......48 F6
Whitney St SN1........50 C5
WHITSBURY..........210 B5
Whitsbury Rd SP6.....210 D2
Whittingham Dr SN4....64 E3
Whittington Rd SN5....49 C6
Whittle Ave SN11.....166 A1
Whittle Cl SN14.......78 A7
Whittle Rd
  4 Andover SP10...193 B1
  Salisbury SP2........145 D1
WHITTONDITCH........170 D3
Whittonditch Rd SN8..170 C2
Whitworth Rd SN25.....35 A3
Wichelstok Cl SN1.....50 C3
WICK................210 F8
Wick Ball Camp★ SP3..201 D3
Wickdown Ave SN25.....34 F3
Wicker Hill BA14.....101 C1
Wickfield SN10.......214 B2
Wick La
  Devizes SN10........214 B1
  Downton SP5........210 E8
  Lacock SN15..........85 E4
  Manningford SN9....181 F5
  Wanborough SN4......51 F6
Wick Rd SN16..........16 A8
Wicks Cl SN25.........34 E5
Wicks Dr SN5..........78 F5
Wickwater La GL7.......7 C4
WIDBROOK...........100 E4
Widbrook Meadow BA14..105 A8
Widbrook View BA15....100 E5
WIDHAM..............33 C5
Widham SN5............33 C6

Widhill La SN26 . . . . .21 A1
Wigmore Ave SN3 . . . . . . .50 F3
WILCOT 182 A1
Wilcot Ave SN2 . . . . .35 D5
Wilcot Cl
  Amesbury SP4 . . . . .217 D2
  Trowbridge BA14 . . . . .105 C6
Wilcot Rd SN9 . . . . .215 B5
Wilcox Cl SN2 . . . . .35 C2
Wild Acre 9 SN4 . . . . . . .163 A6
Wilderness The BA15 . . . .100 C7
Wildern Sq SN3 . . . . .36 A4
WILDHERN 193 D5
Wildmoorway La GL7 . . . . . .7 B7
Wiley Terr SP2 . . . . .144 D4
Wilkins Cl SN2 . . . . .35 F5
Wilkinson Cl SN12 . . . . . .94 C5
WILLESLEY 25 C6
Willesley Dr GL8 . . . . .25 B7
William Cl SP1 . . . . .146 D1
William Rd SN10 . . . . . . .214 D2
William Robbins Ct SN25 . .34 F3
Williams Cl 6 SN12 . . . . .94 B4
Williams Gr SN13 . . . . .85 A8
Williamson Cl 3 SP11 . . .192 A5
William St
  Calne SN11 . . . . .81 C4
  Swindon SN1 . . . . .50 A5
William Stumpes Cl 7
  SN16 . . . . .28 A5
Willington Rd SN25 . . . . .34 E7
Willis Cl
  5 Chippenham SN15 . . . . .78 F4
  Great Bedwyn SN8 . . . . . .176 C3
Willis Way SN5 . . . . .33 B3
Willoughby BA13 . . . . . . .108 E2
Willoughby Rd SP4 . . . . .197 E6
Willow Ave 5 SP6 . . . . . .210 D1
Willowbank SN5 . . . . .70 A2
Willowbrook SN5 . . . . .33 C4
Willowbrook End SN15 . .57 D2
Willow Cl
  Laverstock SP1 . . . . 146 D2
  Melksham SN12 . . . . .94 A3
Willow Cres
  Broughton Gifford SN12 . . .93 A5
  Warminster BA12 . . . . . . .117 C5
Willow Dr
  Devizes SN10 . . . . .214 E5
  4 Durrington SP4 . . . . . .198 B7
Willow Gr
  Chippenham SN15 . . . . . . .70 E2
  South Cerney GL7 . . . . .7 A6
  Trowbridge BA14 . . . . .105 B5
  Westbury BA13 . . . . .108 E3
Willowherb Cl SN25 . . . . .34 E5
Willows Ave SN2 . . . . .35 C3
Willows The
  Calne SN11 . . . . .89 E8
  Highworth SN6 . . . . .23 A4
  Swindon SN5 . . . . .34 A2
Willow View BA14 . . . . . .105 C3
Willow View Cl SN16 . . . .27 F4
Willow Way SP7 . . . . .202 A4
Willow Wlk SN4 . . . . .64 B6
Wills Ave SN1 . . . . .50 E8
Wilman Way SP2 . . . . . . .151 F5
Wilmot Cl SN5 . . . . .48 F6
WILSFORD
  Wilsford 181 B4
  Wilsford cum Lake 197 F2
  SP4 . . . . .197 D2
Wilsford Rd SN9 . . . . .181 C5
Wilson Rd
  Larkhill SP4 . . . . .197 E6
  Swindon SN25 . . . . .34 F6
Wilson Sq BA12 . . . . .117 C7
WILTON
  Grafton 184 A8
  Wilton 144 C3
Wilton and Barford CE Prim
  Sch SP2 . . . . .144 B2
Wilton Carpet Factory ★
  SP2 . . . . .144 D4
Wilton Dr BA14 . . . . .105 D6
Wilton Ho ★ SP2 . . . . . . .144 D2
Wilton Pk ★ SP2 . . . . . . .144 D1
Wilton Rd
  Barford St Martin SP3 . . . .143 C3
  East Grafton SN8 . . . . . . .184 A7
  Quidhampton SP2 . . . . . . .144 F3
  Wylye BA12 . . . . .201 F8
Wilton Sh Village SP2 . . .144 E3
Wilton Windmill ★ SN8 . .184 B8
Wilton Wlk SN2 . . . . .35 C6
Wiltshire Ave SN2 . . . . . . .50 A8
Wiltshire Cl
  Bulford SP4 . . . . .217 F8
  3 Hungerford RG17 . . . . .177 B7
Wiltshire Coll
  Chippenham SN15 . . . . . . .78 E1
  Chippenham SN15 . . . . . . .78 E8
  Devizes SN10 . . . . .214 B3
  Melksham SN12 . . . . .94 A5
  Trowbridge BA14 . . . . .105 B6
  Trowbridge BA14 . . . . .105 C8
  Westbury BA13 . . . . .109 A3
Wiltshire Cres
  Melksham SN12 . . . . .94 C3
  Royal Wootton Bassett SN4 .61 A7
Wiltshire Dr SN10 . . . . . .105 D5
Wiltshire Gall The ★ SP1 .145 F1
Wiltshire Heritage Mus ★
  SN10 . . . . .214 A3
Wiltshire Music Ctr
  BA15 . . . . .100 B8
Wiltshire Rd SP2 . . . . . . .151 E6

Wiltshire Way BA13 . . . . .109 A4
Wimpole Cl SN3 . . . . .51 B4
Winchcombe Gdns GL7 . . . .6 F6
Winchester Cl
  Amesbury SP4 . . . . .217 D2
  2 Chippenham SN14 . . . . .78 A6
  North Bradley BA14 . . . . . .105 C2
  Swindon SN3 . . . . .36 B1
Winchester St SP1 . . . . . .146 B1
Wincombe Bsns Pk SP7 . .202 C3
Wincombe La SP7 . . . . . .202 C2
Wincombe Pk ★ SP7 . . . .202 D3
Windbrook Meadow SN2 . .36 A4
Windermere SN3 . . . . .51 D3
Windermere Rd BA14 . . .101 E2
Windflower Rd SN25 . . . . .34 E5
Winding Way SP2 . . . . . . .145 B3
Windlass Way SN15 . . . . . .78 E5
Windlesham Rd SP1 . . . . .146 B4
Windmill Cl
  3 Aldbourne SN8 . . . . . .170 A7
  Alderbury SP5 . . . . .153 E2
  4 Shaftesbury SP7 . . . . .202 C1
Windmill Hill Bsns Pk SN5 48 F3
Windmill Hill (Causewayed
  Enclosure) ★ SN4 . . . . . .167 A2
Windmill Hill Prim Sch
  SN5 . . . . .49 A3
Windmill La
  Hurstbourne Tarrant
  SP11 . . . . .193 F8
  Winterbourne SP4 . . . . . .133 B4
Windmill Piece SN4 . . . . . .65 D4
Windmill Rd
  Kemble GL7 . . . . .4 F8
  Royal Wootton Bassett SN4 .47 F1
Windmill Tump (Long
  Barrow) ★ GL7 . . . . .3 A7
Windrush SN6 . . . . .22 E5
Windrush Rd SN25 . . . . . .35 A3
Windsor Ave SN12 . . . . . .94 B3
Windsor Cl
  Chippenham SN14 . . . . . . .78 A6
  Lydiard Tregoze SN4 . . . . . .47 F6
Windsor Cres BA11 . . . . .110 A5
Windsor Dr
  Devizes SN10 . . . . .214 D3
  1 Trowbridge BA14 . . . . .105 B5
  Westbury BA13 . . . . .109 B4
Windsor Mews 8 SP4 . . .198 B7
Windsor Rd
  Calne Without SN11 . . . . . .81 F1
  9 Durrington/Bulford SP4 198 B7
  North Bradley BA14 . . . . . .105 E4
  9 Salisbury SP2 . . . . . . .145 F1
  Swindon SN3 . . . . .50 F2
Windsor St 10 SP2 . . . . . .145 F1
Windwhistle Cnr SP7 . . . .202 E2
Windwhistle La
  Alderbury SP5 . . . . .160 B7
  Grimstead SP5 . . . . .154 B1
Windwhistle Way SP5 . . . .153 F2
Wine St
  Bradford-on-Avon BA15 . . .100 C6
  Devizes SN10 . . . . .214 B3
Wingate Par SN2 . . . . .35 A2
WINGFIELD 104 C6
Wingfield SN2 . . . . .36 A5
Wingfield Ave SN2 . . . . . . .35 C6
Wingfield CE Prim Sch
  BA14 . . . . .104 C6
Wingfield Rd BA14 . . . . . .105 A4
Win Gn View 7 SP7 . . . . .202 D2
Wing Rd SP4 . . . . .198 E6
Winifred St SN1 . . . . .50 D3
Winkelbury Hill (Hill Fort) ★
  SP7 . . . . .207 C8
Winkins La SN15 . . . . .44 A2
Winkworth Cottage SN16 . .29 C2
Winlaw Cl SN5 . . . . .49 C7
Winnipeg Rd 1 SP4 . . . . .217 F8
Winscombe Ct BA11 . . . . .110 B5
WINSLEY 99 E7
Winsley CE Prim Sch
  BA15 . . . . .99 E7
Winsley Cl SN3 . . . . .35 C4
Winsley Hill BA2 . . . . .99 B6
Winsley Rd BA15 . . . . . . .100 B7
Winstanley Cl 8 SN5 . . . . .49 A4
Winston Rd SN12 . . . . .93 F1
WINTERBOURNE
  BASSETT 167 B5
WINTERBOURNE
  DAUNTSEY 133 B2
WINTERBOURNE EARLS . .133 A1
Winterbourne Earls CE Prim
  Sch SP4 . . . . .133 A1
WINTERBOURNE
  GUNNER 133 D3
WINTERBOURNE
  MONKTON 167 B3
WINTERBOURNE STOKE . .196 F6
Winterbourne Stoke Group
  (Tumuli) ★ SP4 . . . . .197 C4
Winter Gn SN11 . . . . .80 F3
Winterslow CE Prim Sch
  SP5 . . . . .149 B6
Winterslow Rd
  Idmiston SP4 . . . . .198 C1
  Porton SP4 . . . . .133 D6
  Swindon SN2 . . . . .35 B5
  2 Trowbridge BA14 . . . . .105 B5
Winton Cl SP9 . . . . .216 D4
Winton Rd SN3 . . . . .36 B4
Winwick Rd SN5 . . . . .49 B4
Wirral Way SN25 . . . . .34 F7
Wirr The SP3 . . . . .128 D7

Wise Cl SN2 . . . . .35 E3
Wise La SP3 . . . . .141 A2
Wiseman Cl 2 SN3 . . . . . . .51 E6
Wishart Way SN15 . . . . . . .78 F5
Wishford Rd SP2 . . . . . . .144 B5
Witan Cl 8 SP10 . . . . .193 E2
Witchcombe Cl 1 SN10 . .187 B6
Witchcombe La SN10 . . . .179 B1
Witchell La SN10 . . . . .180 B3
Witfield Cl SN5 . . . . .33 B5
Witham Way SN2 . . . . .35 F4
Withering Rd SN1 . . . . .50 A3
Witherington Rd
  Alderbury SP5 . . . . .153 C2
  Downton SP5 . . . . .159 C5
Witherington Ring (Field
  System) ★ SP5 . . . . .159 D7
Witheys The 10 SN4 . . . . .163 A6
Withies The SN8 . . . . .175 D1
Withy Bed SN4 . . . . .61 C1
Withybed La RG17 . . . . . .177 F5
Withy Cl
  Royal Wootton Bassett
  SN4 . . . . .47 D3
  Trowbridge BA14 . . . . .101 E3
Withymead Rd SN14 . . . . .74 A8
Wittenham View SP4 . . . .217 C2
Wittensford La SO51 . . . .212 F1
Witt Rd SP5 . . . . .149 D5
Witts La SN5 . . . . .33 B5
Wivenhoe Ct 7 BA11 . . . .110 C6
Wizard Education SN1 . . . .50 C5
Woburn Cl
  Swindon SN25 . . . . .34 F6
  Trowbridge BA14 . . . . .105 A8
Wolferstan Dr SP1 . . . . . .146 D5
Wolfhall Rd SN8 . . . . .183 D8
Wolsely Ave SN3 . . . . .51 A4
WOLVERTON 138 B4
Wolverton Cl SN14 . . . . . . .77 F6
WOODBOROUGH 181 D6
Woodborough CE Aided Prim
  Sch SN9 . . . . .181 C6
Woodborough Cl BA14 . . .105 D5
Woodborough Rd
  Beechingstoke SN9 . . . . . .181 B6
  Corsham SN13 . . . . .85 B7
  Pewsey SN9 . . . . .215 A5
Woodbury RG17 . . . . .165 B1
Woodbury Cl 2 SN5 . . . . .49 A8
Woodbury Gdns SP2 . . . . .152 A5
Woodbury La SP2 . . . . . . .152 B5
Woodbury Rise SP2 . . . . . .152 B5
Woodbury Yd 5 SP2 . . . . .152 B5
Woodchester SN5 . . . . .49 C5
WOODCOCK 117 C6
Woodcock Cl SP9 . . . . . . .216 D6
Woodcock Gdns BA12 . . . .117 C6
Woodcock Ind Est BA12. 117 D7
Woodcock La BA12 . . . . . .117 B7
Woodcock Pk BA12 . . . . . .117 C6
Woodcock Rd BA12 . . . . . .117 C6
Woodcombe SN12 . . . . . . .94 C6
Woodcote Rd SN8 . . . . . . .185 B8
Woodcutters Mews
  SN25 . . . . .35 C6
WOODCUTTS 207 D7
WOODFALLS 211 D7
Woodfern SP6 . . . . .210 F1
Woodfolds SN16 . . . . .15 F7
Woodford Cl
  Devizes SN10 . . . . .214 C1
  3 Swindon SN3 . . . . .35 C6
Woodford Valley CE
  Prim Sch SP4 . . . . .131 C5
WOODGREEN 211 A4
Woodhayes Rd BA11 . . . . .110 C6
Wood H Dr SN2 . . . . .34 D3
Woodhenge ★ SP4 . . . . . .217 A7
Woodhill Ave SN11 . . . . . . .81 C3
Woodhill Pk ★ SN4 . . . . . .166 E7
Woodhill Rise SN11 . . . . . .81 C4
Woodhill Village ★ SN4 . .166 D8
WOODHOUSE 193 F3
Woodhouse Castle
  (rems of) ★ BA12 . . . . . .114 E1
Woodhouse Gdns BA14 . .102 B2
Woodhouse Rd 3 SN3 . . .50 F5
Wood La
  Brinkworth SN15 . . . . .46 D7
  Chapmanslade BA13 . . . . .111 D4
  Chippenham SN15 . . . . . . .78 E6
  Fonthill Gifford SP3 . . . . . .200 C2
  Lydiard Millicent SN5 . . . . .32 A1
  Nettleton SN14 . . . . .67 B8
  Purton SN5 . . . . .31 E1
  Sherston GL8 . . . . .25 B5
Woodland Dr SP5 . . . . . . .149 B6
Woodland Heritage Ctr
  The ★ BA13 . . . . .107 F5
Woodland Ind Est BA13 . .108 F2
Woodland Pk SN11 . . . . . .81 B2
Woodland Rd
  Patney SN10 . . . . .180 F5
  2 Warminster BA12 . . . . .116 E6
Woodlands SN13 . . . . .76 E2
Woodlands Bglws SN14 . . .78 B7
Woodlands Cl SN15 . . . . . .58 A3
Woodlands La SP7 . . . . . .203 E1
Woodlands Manor ★
  BA12 . . . . .139 A3
Woodlands Prim Sch
  SP2 . . . . .145 B4
Woodlands Rd
  Chippenham SN14 . . . . . . .78 C6
  Mere BA12 . . . . .139 B2
  Mildenhall SN8 . . . . .169 A1
  Pewsey SN9 . . . . .215 D4

Woodlands Rd Ind Est
  BA12 . . . . .139 B4
WOODLANDS ST MARY . . .171 B6
Woodlands The BA13 . . . .113 A1
Woodland View
  Westbury BA13 . . . . .112 B8
  Wroughton SN4 . . . . .50 B1
Woodland Way
  Devizes SN10 . . . . .214 A1
  Salisbury SP1 . . . . .146 E2
Woodland Wy BA11 . . . . . .110 D7
Woodlea SN14 . . . . .75 C6
Woodlea Grange SP5 . . . .153 E2
Wood Leaze SN10 . . . . . . .214 F6
Woodling Cres SP6 . . . . . .210 F1
Woodman Mead 5 BA12 116 F7
Woodmarsh BA14 . . . . . . .105 D4
Woodman Rd SN25 . . . . . .35 B6
Woods's La SP3 . . . . .200 F2
Wood St
  Calne SN11 . . . . .81 B3
  Clyffe Pypard SN4 . . . . . . .61 D1
  Royal Wootton Bassett SN4 .47 D4
  Swindon SN1 . . . . .50 D4
Woodstock Ct SN8 . . . . . .213 F2
Woodstock Gdns SN12 . . .94 B3
Woodstock Rd SP1 . . . . . .146 B2
Woodvill Rd SP1 . . . . .146 D4
Woodway Cotts GL9 . . . . .24 E5
WOODYATES 208 D6
Woolands La 11 SP7 . . . . .202 B2
Woolcott La SP8 . . . . .137 C1
Woolford Grange 2 SN4 . .48 A2
Wool House Gdns BA12 . . .195 A2
Woollaton Cl SN5 . . . . .49 A5
WOOLLEY 100 E7
Woolley Cl BA15 . . . . .100 E7
Woolley Dr BA15 . . . . .100 E7
WOOLLEY GREEN 100 F8
Woolley St BA15 . . . . .100 E6
Woolley Terr BA15 . . . . . . .100 E6
Woolmer Dro SN8 . . . . . . .168 F6
Woolpack Meadows
  BA14 . . . . .105 E7
WOOLVERTON 103 C1
Wootton Bassett Rd SN5 . .49 E5
WOOTTON RIVERS 174 F2
Wor Barrow (Long
  Barrow) ★ SP5 . . . . .208 C4
Worcester Lodge ★ GL9 . . .24 A3
Wordsworth Cl 1 SN4 . . . .47 F3
Wordsworth Dr SN2 . . . . . .35 F4
Wordsworth Rd SP1 . . . . .146 B2
Worlidge Dr SN5 . . . . .49 B8
Wormcliff La SN13 . . . . . . .83 A4
Worsley Rd SN5 . . . . .49 A4
Worsted Cl BA14 . . . . .105 E7
Wortheys Cl SN16 . . . . . . .28 A5
Worthington Cl 2 SN3 . . . .51 B7
WORTON 179 B4
Worton & Marston
  Prim Sch SN10 . . . . .179 B4
Worton Rd SN10 . . . . .179 C4
Wouldham Cl SP11 . . . . . .191 F4
Wren Cl
  Frome BA11 . . . . .110 B7
  3 Warminster BA12 . . . . .116 E5
Wren Ct
  Calne SN11 . . . . .89 E8
  Trowbridge BA14 . . . . .105 B8
Wrenscroft 8 SP2 . . . . . .152 A5
Wrenswood SN3 . . . . .51 D8
WROUGHTON 64 A5
Wroughton Airfield SN4 . . .63 F2
Wroughton Inf Sch SN4 . . .64 A7
Wroughton Jun Sch SN4 . .64 A7
Wroughton Science
  Museum ★ SN3 . . . . .64 B1
Wych Elm Rd BA11 . . . . . .110 C6
Wychurch Rd 4 SN16 . . . .28 A5
Wyck Village ★ SP3 . . . . .203 E7
Wycombe Cl SN11 . . . . . . .79 F2
Wycombe La SN10 . . . . . .172 F1
Wyke Rd BA14 . . . . .101 E4
Wyld Ct SN25 . . . . .34 E8
Wyle Down National
  Nature Reserve ★ BA12 .201 E7
WYLYE 201 F8
Wylye Cl
  Swindon SN25 . . . . .34 A4
  Warminster BA12 . . . . . . .116 C6
Wylye Rd
  Steeple Langford SP3 . . . . .128 B7
  Tidworth SP9 . . . . .216 D2
  Warminster BA12 . . . . . . .117 A5
  Wylye BA12 . . . . .201 F8
Wylye Valley CE VA Prim Sch
  BA12 . . . . .195 B3
Wymans Field SN8 . . . . . .173 F6

Wyncies The 2 SN6 . . . . .163 E6
Wyndham Cl SN15 . . . . . . .79 A8
Wyndham La SP4 . . . . . . .199 A2
Wyndham Pk SP1 . . . . . . .146 B2
Wyndham Pk Inf Sch
  SP1 . . . . .146 B3
Wyndham Rd
  Salisbury SP1 . . . . .146 A2
  Swindon SN2 . . . . .50 A7
Wyndham Terr SP1 . . . . . .146 B2
Wynd The SN11 . . . . .81 B4
Wynford Rd BA11 . . . . . . .110 B6
Wynndale Cl SN3 . . . . .36 A4
Wynsome St BA14 . . . . . .104 F3
Wynwards Rd SN25 . . . . . .35 A5
Wythburn Rd BA11 . . . . . .110 C5
Wyver Coll SN8 . . . . .213 C1
Wyvern Ave SN11 . . . . .81 C3
Wyvern Cl SN1 . . . . .50 C2
Wyvern Coll SP1 . . . . .146 E3
Wyvern Rd
  Bowerhill SN12 . . . . .94 D1
  Durrington/Bulford SP4 . . .198 E6
Wyvern Theatre & Arts Ctr ★
  SN1 . . . . .50 C6
Wyvern Wlk BA13 . . . . . . .108 E3
Wyville Rd BA11 . . . . .110 C6

Y

Yard Ct BA12 . . . . .117 B6
Yard La SN15 . . . . .96 D7
Yardlee Wlk 2 SN1 . . . . . .50 A2
Yardley Cl SN2 . . . . .34 F2
Yard's La SN9 . . . . .181 C5
Yarmley La SP5 . . . . .149 B6
Yarmouth Cl SN5 . . . . .49 B4
YARNBROOK 105 F3
Yarnbrook Rd
  Steeple Ashton BA14 . . . . .102 E1
  West Ashton BA14 . . . . . . .105 F2
Yarnbury Castle (Fort) ★
  BA12 . . . . .196 B3
Yarnton Cl SN5 . . . . .49 A8
Yarrow Cl
  East Anton SP11 . . . . .193 F2
  Swindon SN2 . . . . .34 C3
YATESBURY 166 E2
YATTON KEYNELL 68 E6
Yatton Rd SN14 . . . . .68 E1
Yeates Field Vw BA12 . . . .117 D5
Yeatmans Cl 6 SP7 . . . . .202 B2
Yeatmans La 3 SP7 . . . . .202 B2
Yeats Cl SN25 . . . . .35 A8
Yelland Wlk 4 SN1 . . . . . . .50 B1
Yellowhammer Cl 2 SN3 .51 C8
Yellow Way Rd BA11 . . . . .118 A5
Yeoman Cl
  5 Market Lavington
  SN10 . . . . .179 F1
  Swindon SN5 . . . . .49 A7
Yeoman Way BA14 . . . . . .105 C2
Yeovil Ct SN3 . . . . .51 B5
Yerbury St 1 BA14 . . . . . .105 E8
Yews The BA12 . . . . .139 A6
Yewstock Cres W SN15 . . .70 C1
Yewtree Cl 8 SP4 . . . . . . .198 C7
Yew Tree Cl
  Calne SN11 . . . . .81 A3
  Chirton SN10 . . . . .180 F4
  The Common SP5 . . . . . . .149 B6
Yew Tree Gdns SN3 . . . . . .36 E4
Yew Tree La SN4 . . . . .167 C2
Yew Wy SN13 . . . . .84 E8
Yiewsley Cres SN3 . . . . . . .36 B2
Yockney Cl SN13 . . . . .76 E1
Yonder Way 7 SN4 . . . . . .163 A6
York Bldgs BA14 . . . . .101 C3
York Cl
  Chippenham SN14 . . . . . . .78 A6
  Corsham SN13 . . . . .76 F2
York Dro SP5 . . . . .212 C4
York La SN15 . . . . .46 A7
York Rd
  7 Hungerford RG17 . . . . .177 B6
  Lyneham SN15 . . . . .60 B2
  Salisbury SP2 . . . . .145 F1
  Stapleford SP3 . . . . .197 B1
  Swindon SN1 . . . . .50 D6
  Upavon Down SN9 . . . . . . .182 B1
Youngs Paddock SP5 . . . .149 C6
Yule Hill SP3 . . . . .203 F6

Z

Zakopane Rd 4 SN25 . . . .34 D6
Zander Rd SN11 . . . . .81 B5
ZEALS 137 C4
Zeals Gn Dr BA12 . . . . . . .138 A4
Zeals Rise BA12 . . . . .137 F4
Zig Zag Hill SP7 . . . . .206 C7
Zion St SP11 . . . . .199 F3
Zoar Cl SN4 . . . . .64 A6
Zouch Ave SP9 . . . . .216 C7
Zouch Cl SP9 . . . . .216 C7
Zouch Farm Rd SP9 . . . . .216 C7
Zouch Prim Sch SP9 . . . . .216 B8